HISTORY OF GERMANY IN THE
NINETEENTH CENTURY

TREITSCHKE'S HISTORY OF GERMANY IN THE NINETEENTH CENTURY

TRANSLATED BY EDEN & CEDAR PAUL

WITH AN INTRODUCTION BY
WILLIAM HARBUTT DAWSON

VOLUME TWO

NEW YORK
McBRIDE, NAST & COMPANY
1916

INTRODUCTION.

IN the first volume of his History, Treitschke traces the later stages in the decay of the Holy Roman Empire of the German Nation down to its final dissolution in 1806 at the bidding of Napoleon, with the eclipse of Prussia which coincided with it, and follows the fortunes of the War of Liberation to its victorious close in 1814, culminating in Napoleon's downfall, his abdication, Elba, and the first Peace of Paris.

The second volume, after the interlude of a hundred days has been left behind, is mainly occupied with the beginnings of the Germanic Federation, which rose upon the ruins of the old Empire, and the efforts of the German peoples to find themselves again when the period of chaos and demoralisation was succeeded by one of order and reconstruction. All Europe, Princes and people alike, breathed again freely after 1814, and most relieved of all were those German Sovereigns who had bartered themselves into Napoleon's service, had taken their orders from him, marched under his banners, fought his battles against their own countrymen, and had been proud to receive their crowns and electors' hats at his hand.

Now the German nation hoped to see its regained independence confirmed and assured by political unity. In the darkest hours of humiliation it had been cheered, and its heaviest sacrifices had been sweetened, by the thought that it was fighting not only to liberate Germany from foreign oppression, but to win for it unity, by ties stronger and more intimate than those which held together the old empire. Now that danger was over, it was to learn by bitter experience that it had been cherishing an illusion. Germany was not yet ready to become either an empire or a federal State, and even if it had been ready the rulers were not willing to forego any substantial part of their independence. Austria, above all, was bent on maintaining the old divisions under new sanctions, as the surest guarantee of its continued domination.

By the Final Act of the Congress of Vienna (June 8, 1815) the forty-one sovereign States were formed into a loose association—it could not properly be called a union—with the name *Deutscher Bund* or Germanic Federation. With this arrangement the rulers were on the whole well contented ; but the nation at large received it with disappointment and disgust. But what else could have been expected ? The Congress of Vienna was exclusively an affair of the Princes and Governments. They only decreed, appointed and composed it, and only their interests and wishes had voice or hearing in its deliberations. It was a typical creation and expression of the old diplomacy, which yet continues to be the diplomacy of Europe to-day, more than a century later. In this august areopagus, in which the elect of the diplomatic world of Europe was assembled,—Blucher, fresh from the battle-field, where niceties of language are impossible, called it a " council of thrice-accursed constables and lazy-bones "—the German nation had no part or lot whatever, though its political destinies were being determined for generations to come ; it had no share in its deliberations ; its opinion was not once given, because it was never sought ; nowhere was the nation as such mentioned in the Act under which the new Federation was constituted.

In a sense the Federation was not even the work of the Princes themselves ; they accepted it, but the idea was that of Metternich, the powerful Austrian Chancellor, who presided over the Congress and bent it to his will, concerned only to divide the States, so that Austria might rule them, so maintaining in the new Germany the same paramount influence which it had held in the old. Austria was made the head of the Federation, but its position was now merely presidential, and conferred upon it no special powers or prerogatives. The time for a new German Emperor had not yet come, much as the ardent friends of national unity wished for the restoration of the ancient office and title. " Poor, faithful German nation," wrote Arndt in bitterness of soul, " thou art to have no Emperor ! Thy Princes wish themselves to play the Emperor. Instead of one lord, thou art to have two dozen (in point of fact, there were over three dozen) who will never be able to agree upon German questions." But that was just what Austria wanted.

The Federal Act of June 8, 1815, defined the purpose of the Bund as " the maintenance of the external and internal security of Germany and the independence and inviolability of the several German States." Such a purpose was all-important, yet it did not require a wide range of functions, and the jurisdiction assigned to the Bund was, indeed, very restricted. Its executive organ was the Federal Diet, which met and acted in two capacities, first as an inner council, forming which body its members exercised altogether seventeen votes, eleven States having one each, and the remaining States voting in six groups, one vote for each group ; and then—chiefly for the determination of questions relating to organic changes in the composition of the Bund, its jurisdiction, the declaration of war and the conclusion of peace—as a plenary body (*plenum*), in which sixty-nine votes were disposable, one for each State as a minimum and the rest allotted in rough proportion to population, all the six kingdoms having four votes each. The Bund began its career handicapped by distrust and odium, and it lived up to its first reputation. For just fifty years it maintained a more or less impotent and futile existence, its Diet chiefly useful as a coward's castle from which the liberties of the people could be safely assailed, and as affording an arena in which Austria and Prussia were able to contend for the hegemony of Germany.

By the Federal Act the allied Sovereigns reciprocally guaranteed each other's territories against attack from without or within. It was, perhaps, the most important provision in the Treaty, since the Congress of Vienna had introduced many and momentous changes in the map of Germany ; some States had lost and some had gained territory. Here Prussia was specially affected. The readjustment of its frontiers did not increase its area (though it increased its population) beyond that of 1805, before Napoleon, by the Peace of Tilsit, robbed Prussia of one-third of its territory; for while it gained largely in the west, by additions on the Rhine, by the absorption of part of Saxony—Prussia wanted the whole, and would have got it but for the opposition of Austria, France, and England—and the greater part of Westphalia, it had to surrender a large slice of Poland. On the whole, therefore, Prussia became more German, while still remaining a mixed and somewhat incongruous State, made up of divers races and civilisations, a basket of fragments gathered from all sides, out of which a unity could be made only after long time and effort.

Prussia had suffered more than any other part of Germany in the long-drawn-out struggle from 1805 to 1815. Hence its pressing need was internal reorganisation, for the purpose not merely of righting the evils done by the war, but, as far as practicable, of assimilating the life and institutions of the diverse territories and populations which made up the rehabilitated kingdom. Here great results were achieved in a marvellously short time. During the second decade of the century, something was done to develop and extend local government and to unify law and justice ; national taxation was systematised ; a customs system was introduced which gave a frank recognition, unique in those days, to the principle of free trade,—in 1818 Huskisson in the English House of Commons spoke of the Prussian customs tariff as the most enlightened in Europe—and which, by means of successive treaties, was gradually to be extended to all Germany. A free course was given to the intellectual influences set loose by the searching ordeal through which the nation had passed ; new universities were established and existing ones reorganised—the University of Berlin dates from 1810, that of Bonn from 1811, and that of Breslau in its present form from the same year, all three being founded when Prussia was still in the worst throes of the war—and with the more stringent application of the principle of compulsory education the foundations were laid of the modern system of primary and secondary schools. Simultaneously the military system was placed upon a basis which, in its main features, was to continue for a century, and to serve as the model for the rest of Germany.

In one thing the Prussian nation was doomed to bitter disappointment. It looked for political liberty, for a constitution and a beginning in parliamentary life, but in vain. The nation imagined that after the war constitutional rights would fall into its lap like ripe fruit. Its devotion and sacrifice had been fed and fanned by the promise of them. The German Princes in the Manifesto of Kalisch in February, 1813, in appealing to their peoples to make a supreme effort to crush the despot, held out the prospect of constitutions as the prize and the reward. On May 22, 1815, the Prussian King, yielding to pressure from his Chancellor Hardenberg, then still favourably disposed towards the constitutional movement, issued an ordinance in which he promised a national assembly developed from the provincial estates. The following month the whole of the German Princes signed their names to the Federal Act, Article 13 of which provided that " In all the federal States there shall be a constitutional representation of the Estates of the Realm." It was not said what sort of a representation this was to be, or when it was to be given, but those were days of great hopes and of an inexhaustible confidence, and

---

it occurred to few people to suspect that a pledge so solemnly made would not be honourably fulfilled. A rude awakening soon came. Metternich lost no time in letting it be understood that Austria had no idea of giving effect to Article 13 in any form whatever, and he used all his influence and all his wiles to prevent the rest of the States from doing so.

It was left to Karl August of Weimar to set an example to the greater rulers of Germany of fidelity to plighted word, for he granted a constitution before a year had passed. Treitschke, in belittling this act, which was one of wisdom as much as of honour, scoffs, not generously, at the petty Court of Weimar and its large conceit of itself. Yet Weimar and the corner of Germany to which it belonged were a centre of culture, of sweetness and light, at a time when large parts of Prussia intellectually were still little more than a waste, howling wilderness, producing only crops of soldiers, serfs, and cabbage squires. Bavaria followed the example of Weimar a little later, and then after an interval came Würtemberg. Treitschke holds that the South German constitutions proved a strength and support of particularism. It is certain that the States of the South in which constitutions were first given gained thereby a superiority in political education and capacity which they have held ever since ; their peoples are to-day the freest in Germany ; and nowhere else in the empire are the relationships between rulers and ruled on the whole so intimate and harmonious.

Prussia, governed by a King who never knew his own mind and a Minister who had not the courage to shake off Austrian influence, lagged behind while the smaller States went forward. By the ordinance of May 22, 1815, Frederick William III promised at once a national representation, to be chosen by the provincial estates, which were to be restored where efficient. Treitschke regrets that in issuing this ordinance he signed away his liberty to choose the right moment for action. But what did it matter, seeing that the promise was never to be fulfilled ? In the following month a commission, consisting of twenty-two members of the Council of State, was appointed to make a grand inquest of the nation. Instead of calling witnesses to Berlin, however, the King resolved that three Ministers should act as travelling commissioners, visiting the provinces, and collecting evidence on the spot, just as the Elector Joachim I had himself done in 1525, when he was bent on reforming the system of local government. Their inquiries were confined almost exclusively to the landed nobility,—in other words, to the representatives of existing conditions, and for the most part these men wanted no change ; the existing provincial diets were for them both satisfactory and sufficient. Only the Polish aristocracy recognised the need of a higher form of representation, capable of reflecting the mind of the nation at large. All the work of the commissioners was wasted. No sooner had their reports been submitted than the King hardened his heart and decided not to grant a constitution at all.

Later, in 1819, Hardenberg himself drew up the outlines of a constitution based on the representation of the existing estates, and Treitschke says that he did it with " a serious and honest purpose." It is true that the document ended with the excellent sentiment " *Salus publica suprema lex esto !* " yet for all that, Stein's reproach, that Hardenberg offered " liberal phrases and despotic realities," was well founded. All the scheme proposed was that a " general " Diet should be elected by the provincial assemblies out of the privileged classes of which they were composed ; it was to be allowed to consider and report on legislative proposals put before it by the ministry, but the King reserved an unconditional veto, as well as undivided executive power. With all its deficiences, however, the scheme was too liberal for the King, and he refused to proceed with it.

Treitschke deals with this episode in the political history of Prussia fully, but not sympathetically, and in consequence he does far less than justice to the single-minded men—many of them among the foremost figures of their day, Stein, Humboldt, Schön, Vincke, Gneisenau, not to speak of men like Niebuhr, Arndt, and Dahlmann—who dared, at great risk to their reputations, to identify themselves with the political aspirations of the Prussian nation. He tries to show that the nation did not look for a reward, and speaks of the " wonderful story," the " party legend," that came into currency at the end of the war, to the effect that the federal Princes, and the King of Prussia with them, had by the promise of constitutions " filled the German people with illusory hopes." He scorns the idea, as Bismarck did, that patriotism could be requited in any such way, like a debt paid over a counter. Nevertheless, the fact remains that, whether as reward or not, the promise of a constitution was deliberately made and deliberately broken by Frederick William III, not once but several times, and that more than a generation had to pass before the pledge was

Introduction

made good, and then it was redeemed grudgingly by another Sovereign.

Treitschke has not a word of reproach or disapproval for this act of perfidy. On the contrary, he speaks of the King's promises as unfortunate and his disregard of them as laudable. He says in his justification that the country needed "several years more of political dictatorship." As if Prussia had ever had anything else! In point of fact, the dictatorship was to last unaltered not for several but for over thirty years more, and it has not altogether disappeared even to-day. Again, he urges that the medley of races, German and French, Saxon, Swedish and Polish, made it dangerous to give a constitution. But it was from just the opposite standpoint that the far-seeing Bismarck proceeded when, in the hope of creating unity out of a still greater diversity, he promised in 1866 and established in 1867 the North German Diet and made it eligible by a franchise which is still as democratic as any in Europe. Worst of all, says Treitschke, the Prussian nation was unripe and unfit for political emancipation. This is the plea that has been advanced by the advocates of oligarchy in that country ever since, and it is the stock argument of the reactionary parties to-day. All such transparent pretexts suggest that Treitschke himself was conscious that he had a bad case to defend. The pity is that he should have tried to defend it at all.

This, however, was the last time Frederick William III gave a thought to constitution-making. Reaction set in all over Germany, and in repressing political movements and aspirations the Princes who had broken the pledge of 1815 found a congenial occupation. Then came the forcible dissolution of the *Burschenschaften*, an act of stupid intolerance which inspired perhaps the most moving elegy in the German language—" Wir hatten gebauet ein stattliches Haus "; the persecution of the demagogues, most of whom were no demagogues at all, but moderate, sober-minded citizens whose only sin was that they took their rulers at their word ; the strangling of free thought in every form in which it dared to show itself ; the shackling of the printing press ; the suppression, so far as force could do it, of every popular effort and aspiration after political emancipation. In telling the story of that pitiful war against the spirit of a nation, the true *Kulturkampf* of the nineteenth century, Treitschke has no indignation for the unspeakable infamies which were perpetrated in the name of *raison d'état*, and no enthusiasm for the men who were fighting for the right to serve their country and generation with free minds and unfettered wills.

The reaction seemed to triumph, to triumph completely, yet the popular movements of that day, though checked and apparently extinguished, powerfully influenced the course of domestic history during the succeeding half century, as the cause of political liberty became identified more and more closely with that of national unity.

WILLIAM HARBUTT DAWSON.

TABLE OF CONTENTS.

VOL. II.   BOOK TWO.

THE BEGINNINGS OF THE GERMANIC FEDERATION,
1814–1819.

xiii

BOOK II.

THE BEGINNINGS OF THE GERMANIC
FEDERATION,

1814-1819

B

CHAPTER I.

THE CONGRESS OF VIENNA.

§ I. CHARACTER OF THE CONGRESS. PERSONALITY OF ITS PARTICIPANTS.

WHEN Frederick William set out for Vienna in the autumn, he expected to make a stay of about three weeks. Fully nine months were to elapse from the first conference of the plenipotentiaries of the four allied powers on September 18, 1814, to the final signing of the last act of the congress on June 19, 1815. Who could have found energy and satisfaction for the speedy despatch of the business ? The five senses claimed their rights after the convulsive anxieties and unrests of these two wild decades. Just as Paris after the fall of the Terror had plunged into a vortex of enjoyment, so did the old princely and noble Europe now draw a deep breath, rejoicing at its regained security. The great plebeian had fallen, he who had once taught the highly born what the untamed energy of a single man is capable of effecting in an old world ; the heroes of the sword disappeared from the scene, and with them disappeared the great passion, the pitiless veracity of war. Like worms after rain, the petty talents of the boudoir and the antechamber crawled out of their hiding-places and stretched themselves luxuriously. The distinguished world was once more at ease, in full possession of itself. Who could have imagined that the veteran Prince de Ligne who had been the lion of the salons in France under the kings, and was now on the edge of the grave, was once more to enjoy all the glory and all the splendour of highly noble society, and was to construct witty and mischievous epigrams about the distinguished congress, which danced indeed but made no progress ?

Yet it failed to return, that ingenuous nonchalance of the good old times when it was so clearly understood that humanity really began with the baron, when never a word of the mockery and of the free-thought of the great lords could make its way

3

through to trouble the happy simplicity of the mob. By the new generation, the fear of the revolution was still felt in every limb. Amid the intoxicating pleasures of the congress there came sinister news of the Italian secret league of the carbonari and of the dull ferment in France, of the angry speeches of the disillusioned Prussian patriots, of the conspiracies of the Greeks, and of the heroic struggle of the Serbs against their Turkish tyrants. However carefully the doors were closed, however sedulously the loud knocking of the new democratic epoch was ignored, people no longer felt perfectly at ease. As of old mockery had been the mode, so now was belief ; even the man of the world must have at his disposal a few unctuous words about Christianity and the divine right of kings. Although pigtails and powder were not revived, the effeminate love of adornment of the eighteenth century was still manifest in the beardless faces, the snuff-boxes, the shoes and the silk stockings, in the deliberate elegance of masculine clothing ; and yet the tone of intercourse had already become much freer and less formal. No longer was anything heard of the old disputes about rank and title, or of the pedantic quarrels regarding the shape and the colour of chairs ; the ministers met to deliberate now here, now there, where any one of the plenipotentiaries might be housed, and signed the documents in alphabetical order, or just as they happened to be sitting at table. Most strikingly were the changed customs manifested upon the great ceremonial days of the congress. The Middle Ages celebrated ecclesiastical festivals, and the century of Louis XIV celebrated courtly festivals ; the new age exhibited a distinctively militarist character. Parades and inspection of troops were invariable whenever the modern state wished to shine in all its glory. Even Austria, at that time the least warlike among the great states of the continent, dared not wholly ignore the colossal force of the new great armies. Fifty years before, the military aspect of the Prussian court had aroused mockery ; but now Prussian customs had everywhere taken root, and even Francis, the weapon-shy, had sometimes to appear in uniform.

A congress of diplomats can never work creatively ; all it can do is to effect a tolerable arrangement of the results of the war, and to give these a secure foundation. How could this assembly at Vienna have done anything more ? An indescribable exhaustion burdened the spirits of all, as had happened long before at the congress of Utrecht, at the close of the bloody age of Louis XIV. Just as the crown prince Frederick had then

deplored the general decadence of European statecraft, so now
the exhausted and harassed diplomatic world timorously ignored
all the inchoate new ideas of the time, and found itself once more
at home amid the comfortable political views of the old century,
when the state was regarded as a mere agglomeration of so many
square miles and so many inhabitants. The atmosphere of Vienna
contributed its effect. Here, in the centre of the huge family
property which was termed Austria, in this confusion of forcibly
married lands and peoples, there had never been any inkling of
the moral energies which hold together a national state-structure ;
and it was quite in keeping with the spirit of the old Hapsburg
policy that Austria and Bavaria should now dispute with one
another whether the subjects of the mediatised, who brought in
very little to their suzerain lord, were to be counted as half a unit
of population or only as a third. It was with disgust that the
liberated nations learned that they were again to be treated as
nothing more than a great herd, of value only in respect of number.
In the *Rheinische Merkur*, Görres stormed against "the heartless
statistical methods" of the Viennese diplomats ; and Blucher
wrote fiercely to his old friend Rüchel, "The worthy congress of
Vienna is like the annual market of a little town to which everyone
drives his beast to sell or to exchange." To prevent a revival of
the French power by an arbitrary distribution of lands and people—
now, as formerly at Utrecht, this one idea monopolised the entire
wisdom of the cabinets. Just as in those days Catel de St. Pierre
had imagined that by a new and completely arbitrary reconstitution of the map, an unalterable state of peace might be brought
into being, so now there reawakened the unmanly dream of
perpetual peace, this most certain characteristic of politically
exhausted and mentally impoverished epochs. Many excellent
men of every class and every nation seriously cherished the hope
that world-history was at length to desist from its eternal movement, that its progress was to be arrested in obedience to the
decisions of the Viennese Areopagus.

Prussian diplomacy had not attained to the same level as
Prussian military strategy ; not one Prussian statesman possessed
the bold, free, and secure vision of Gneisenau. But the incomplete and inefficient outcome of the Vienna negotiations was
determined by the very nature of things, and could not be attributed to the mistakes of individual men. The War of Liberation
had failed to cure the most serious disease of the old system
of states, to which in the latest volume of his *Geist der Zeit*

Arndt had warningly referred, namely, the state of disintegration of Germany and of Italy. Since in both these countries
public opinion was still completely immature, the main result
of the congress was for both peoples to bring about a restoration :
for the Italians, the territorial distribution of 1795 ; for the
Germans, the re-establishment of that loose association of minor
monarchies which had formerly arisen out of the princes' revolution of 1803. On both sides of the Alps, Austria had acquired a
mediate, cleverly veiled suzerainty, which was incomparably firmer
than the Napoleonic world-empire, and which deprived Germans
and Italians alike of all possibility of peaceful national development. A Germanic Federation including Austria and the still
unconverted satraps of Bonaparte, would mean nothing else than
eternalised anarchy ; an Italy subjected to Austria, to Pope,
Bourbons, and archdukes, would perforce remain in a condition of pitiable weakness. A long schooling of sorrows was still
requisite until the two nations whose destinies were so closely
akin could gain a knowledge of the ultimate causes of their
misfortune ; until that illusion of a peaceful dualism which still,
and not by chance, continued to dominate the leading intelligences,
had been recognised as completely vain ; and until the ancient
and proud Frederician traditions had once more been restored to
honour. The establishment of a well-secured North German
power, such as was needed by the nation, was from the first
impossible to secure in Vienna, since Prussia's destiny was here
largely dependent upon the will of her enemies and rivals. It is
possible that a bold and talented statesman at the head of
Prussia would have given a much simpler course to the involved
interplay of the Viennese negotiations, would have brought about
a quicker crisis and a quicker decision ; yet so unfavourable were
the circumstances that it would have been difficult for anyone
to effect more than was actually effected.

In view of the weakness, for the time still incurable, of
Central Europe, the new system of the European balance of
power which was founded in Vienna could be nothing more than a
makeshift, a weakly structure which owed its endurance not to its
own solidity but merely to the general exhaustion and the general
desire for peace. Many of the most difficult and dangerous
problems of international law were left unsettled, the members
of the congress contenting themselves with the opportunist phrase
which soon became the mode, *c'est une question vide*. Nevertheless, from the bitter lessons of these terrible years of war, at

least one great and new idea emerged and became a common possession of the political world. Even the average frivolous diplomat began to understand that the state is not, as the last century had dreamed, merely power, that its life does not consist wholly in keeping a watchful eye upon neighbouring states and in craftily overreaching them. The prospect of the triumph which the dissensions of the old powers had prepared for the revolution and for its crowned hero, had at length awakened a living European sense of community. The liberated world had earnestly determined to live as a peaceful society of states ; it felt that the nations, notwithstanding all their divergent interests, had numerous great civilising tasks to fulfil, and that these could be fulfilled only through friendly understanding. Even though the old mechanical view of the state still predominated, the conscienceless *raison d'état* of the old cabinet policy was already passing into discredit, and it remained a permanent historical service of the congress of Vienna that it furnished new forms and new rules for the neighbourly intercourse of the society of states. It was a definite advance that an agreement should at length be secured concerning the rules of international etiquette, concerning the precedence of diplomatic agents, and concerning other inconspicuous but indispensable preliminaries to an orderly intercourse between the nations. Upon the sea, indeed, everything remained as of old. Here there was no international law, but only the power of England ; the pride of the queen of the seas would not even consent to an understanding about salutes to the flag.

Still more important were the consequences of the agreements regarding navigation upon the rivers which by convention were common to several neighbouring states, a laborious piece of work, in which Humboldt's diligence and perspicuity were invaluable. The commercial policy of the eighteenth century had on principle sought the advantage of any particular state in the injury it could inflict upon its neighbours ; now for the first time did a European treaty appeal to the doctrine of political economy, in the sense of a recognition that the facilitation of intercourse was a joint interest to all the nations. In addition, a great common work of Christian compassion was already contemplated : the powers agreed upon the abolition of the slave trade. At first, indeed, this agreement touched only the principle of the matter, for Spain and Portugal would not give binding pledges. None the less, the way was broken for a long series of treaties by which there was woven ever more closely the fabric of international intercourse, and which provided an ever securer basis for the legal rights of the foreigner. The newly awakened national pride had by no means destroyed the healthy nucleus of the old German cosmopolitan sense. Hardly had the Imperator been overthrown, when Sethe, the Prussian jurist, laid before Stein a memorial, in which he showed how severe and hostile to foreigners were the provisions of the *code Napoleon*;[1] men of learning and men of business combined to demand from German diplomacy the safeguarding of the rights of the foreigner. With the Vienna congress there began a new epoch of international law, a more humane age, which gradually made the great name of the society of nations an actual reality, and which, in especial, at length gave a positive content to the idea of international civil law.

Unquestionably in this advance of international law the increase of world-trade played a greater part than did the conscious insight of the members of the congress. How would it have been possible for a serious and profound political sense to develop in this brilliant assembly, the most distinguished and most numerous which the world had seen since the great days of the Council of Constance? All the powers of Europe, with the single exception of the Porte, were represented. In the Graben and upon the bastions of old Vienna, in the Prater and at the great bourse of the diplomatists, the Hotel of the Empress of Austria, there thronged a motley concourse of princes and pretenders, statesmen and officers, priests and professors, adventurers, sharpers and suppliants, most humbly admired and most humbly plundered by the good-natured Viennese, who could never see enough of the high dignitaries. The original sin of the everyday work of diplomatists, the intermingling of serious business of state with trifling, the intrigues and the chatter of the drawing-rooms, flourished luxuriantly. Even more hateful than the unavoidable immorality of this great bacchanal of princes, appeared the ludicrous mendacity which here became a fine art ; anyone who wished to shine in this field, must learn how in the morning to conclude a great war-alliance against his daily table companion, and in the afternoon to greet this same friend with undisturbed affection.

Over the whole glittering and dazzling activity lay the atmosphere of that trivial thoughtlessness which the rule of the Hapsburgs had established upon the soil of Vienna. The time

[1] Sethe to Stein, Düsseldorf, May 13, 1814.

had long passed since the valiant burghers of the faithful German town of Vienna had constructed the magnificent churches of the place. What was there of beauty which had been built during these three long centuries since the town on the Danube had become the centre of the great empire? Absolutely nothing— at most the cupola of the Karlskirche and the Belvedere Castle might be said to display a certain individuality. Everywhere else, in the hideous houses of the city, and in the palaces of the wealthy nobility, was manifest the same lack of taste. There were a few art-collections in the town, but nobody went to see them. The treasures of the Ambras collection were forgotten; Charles Augustus of Weimar was the first to rediscover them, for the talented prince took no pleasure in the insipid nullity of these social pleasures, and ranged the town on the look-out for more refined enjoyments. It was still the same old Vienna which had been mocked by Schiller, the town of the Phæacians with their eternal Sunday and the ever-turning spit. There was no trace of scientific activity: who had ever heard anything of the venerable university, except that it possessed a well-ordered hospital with a few able physicians? Over the town lay the heavy hand of the secret police, and there prevailed in the political world a general atmosphere of dullness. Not a soul in this pleasure-seeking nation troubled himself about the political activities of the congress; during nine months Austrian observers produced one single article discussing the affairs of the illustrious assembly, and no one was astonished at this dearth of literary activity. The theatre alone still served to show that a highly talented branch of the human race lived in Vienna, and that the decayed intellectual life might once again awaken. In the circles of the Austrian magnates, culture was still entirely French; it was only with the Prussian visitors that people spoke German in order to show a kindly feeling for the northern Teutonism. The wit of the old Bourbon aristocracy was indeed altogether lacking; even the leading Jewish financiers, who now, thanks to the financial need of the House of Austria, for the first time attained to power and made their way into the distinguished world, the members of the firms of Arnstein, Eskeles, and Herz, were by no means richly endowed with this quality.

It was inevitable that the spiritual poverty of the environ- ment should react upon the tone of the congress. Deliberate pleasure-seeking offered here the only protection against tedium. Masks and drives in the Prater, dances and gaming parties, banquets and tableaux, followed one another in monotonous succession, so that the work of the diplomats could hardly be begun. A caustic observation of Prince de Ligne, a scandalous story about Metternich, who never honoured less than two ladies at once with his favour, or a witty remark about the newly discovered hobby-horse of Baron Drais, whose limping progress so strongly resembled that of the congress itself, or some judgment uttered by that high court of refined taste which at the table of Talleyrand ceremoniously declared the cheese of Brie to be the king of cheeses. Such were the only reliefs amid this colossal insipidity. It seemed as if the re-established old princely society of the nations of Europe now desired to display to the world for what useless purposes it flourished. " We have learned much from Napoleon," Charles Augustus said bitterly, " and among other things we have learned effrontery."

Emperor Francis, the host of the assembly, played, not without ability, his part of honourable patriarch among the high nobility, although he was as yet barely forty-seven years of age. He did not grudge the daily expenditure of fifty thousand gulden for the imperial table, and for the congress as a whole the expenditure of sixteen million gulden, whilst his unpaid veterans were begging in the streets ; the crafty reckoner knew well the advantages he gained by the position of host. How touching, to the serene highnesses who were his guests, seemed this unpretending figure in a shabby blue coat, with his good-natured petty bourgeois manners. Born in Florence, Francis had not come to the Danube until he was already a young man ; but the mask of the frank, true-hearted, blunt Austrian, which he had then assumed, now fitted him like a glove, because it was suited to his phlegmatic disposition and to his vulgar inclinations. No one could ever induce him to feel any sentiment of cordial benevolence ; the changes of destiny of this gigantic time passed over his dull egoism without leaving a trace. He never commuted a death-sentence unless the offender himself begged for death ; he himself supervised the maltreatment of political prisoners, himself determined the weight of the chains, and the number of the days of fasting, and knew no more enjoyable recreation than the reading of intercepted letters ; he had already lost two wives, and was soon to bury the third, in order with invincible equanimity to marry the fourth : on principle he surrounded himself with people of a dubious past, whom he could at any time dismiss at will. Notwithstanding all this, and notwithstanding the evil expression in his cold, hard eyes, notwithstanding his close resemblance to Philip II of Spain to whom he was akin not in blood only but in spirit, all the world believed in the child-like innocence of the heartless and suspicious despot. His political system was the simplest possible. After all the troubles and distresses of these desolate years, he wished at length to secure his own peace, wished at length to function as a diligent privy councillor, covering the margins of official documents with unmeaning observations, to play the fiddle in his leisure hours, cut out paper images, varnish bird-cages, and engage in other imperial dissipations. Stupid and dull-witted like the majority of his forefathers, completely incapable of even beginning to understand a new political thought, he regarded all the revolutionary and national ideas which were animating the new century as nothing more than wickedness and stupidity, as merely a punishable rebellion against the pious archducal house. With this poverty of spirit there was, however, associated a thorough-going peasant cunning, a certain rude instinct for the politically attainable. The emperor felt very truly that his house had already gained almost everything which was desirable, and that it must necessarily regard any change in the society of states as a danger. Consequently, from inclination, on principle, and by calculation, he was the sworn enemy of all innovations, the suspicious opponent of the two ambitious neighbour powers, Russia and, above all, Prussia.

Whilst to the good emperor it was a difficult matter to emerge from his unostentatious daily habits and to take part in the brilliant society of the congress, the adroit Metternich could swim like a fish in this sparkling whirlpool. He had never had such an enjoyable time since the dissipated days of his youth, during his education in the easy-going spiritual courts of his Rhenish home. No one knew so well as he how to carry through a political intrigue between dinner and a masked ball, how before going to keep an assignation to send off a quickly drafted official despatch, or while looking affectionately into the beautiful blue eyes of one of his intimates to lie from the bottom of his soul. Nor was he at all displeased when his Prussian friends regarded him as far more frivolous than he actually was, and when they took for forgetfulness and neglect what had been done from deliberate intention. For just as in his own household, notwithstanding all his display, he remained ever a careful host, frugal to the point of avarice, so amid the distractions of social intercourse he held tenaciously to his political plans. In this great conference upon Austrian soil, he saw a brilliant triumph of the Hapsburg-Lorraine statecraft, regarded the decisions of the illustrious assembly as his own work, and imagined that by these means bounds would be set once for all to the movements of national life. Like the emperor, he saw that his Austria could follow no policy but one of conservatism, and like the emperor he wished to control the revolutionary ideas of the nations by a strict police supervision, and to bridle the ambition of the two aspiring young eastern powers whilst displaying towards them in appearance the most tender friendship. It was owing to these considerations that he formed a firm alliance with the English-Hanoverian tories, whose sentiments resembled his own, and it was for these reasons that he remained on excellent terms with the Bourbon court. Prussia's national policy had already imposed a barrier in the way of the treaties with the Rhenish Confederate states ; the first thing to do now was, by rescuing Saxony, to bind the petty thrones more firmly to the House of Austria, and thus to safeguard Turkey against Russian attack. It was in a fight with the Turks that Austria had first come to the front, and through this in reality that she had first become a state ; to the thoughtless love of power of this new political wisdom it now seemed, on the other hand, a sacred duty to preserve the last fragments of the Turkish dominion. The sorrows of the Serbian and Greek rayahs, sorrows which cried to heaven, aroused in the Hofburg no more than a frivolous smile. A sentiment of inner kinship bound to the Sublime Porte this new Austria, who in her Italian provinces could maintain herself only by the power of the sword. Since the beginning of 1813, Gentz had been engaged in regular confidential correspondence with Janko Karadja, the Wallachian hospodar, who in the Divan was to keep " our most faithful allies " precisely informed concerning the situation of the world and the intentions of the court of Vienna. In vain, since the autumn, had Metternich been working for the same end, endeavouring to persuade the czar that the sultan must be accepted into the European family of princes, and that his possessions must be solemnly guaranteed by all the powers in common.

The gap in the great system of the policy of stability was now to be filled in. Could this be effected, and could Alexander's Polish plans be also frustrated, in Metternich's view the work of the congress would be safeguarded for an indefinite period. Such was his view of the world. Pleasure and repose were to him the highest aims of political life, and nothing but the dread of a disturbance of the peace could spur him to a valiant resolution. A persistent state of disintegration in Germany, so that the sovereign petty kings should voluntarily turn to Austria for protection against Prussia and against " the dangerous idea of German unity " ; the eternal powerlessness of Italy, which, as Lord Castlereagh dryly answered to complaints of the Piedmontese, must ever remain partitioned for the peace of Europe, and which in the eyes of the Hofburg was no more than a geographical expression ; France watched by a number of peaceful states of secondary importance surrounding their dangerous neighbour from the Texel to the Ligurian Sea, and cutting her off from all contact with the great powers ; Russia held in check by a united Europe which was to take Turkey under her protection ; the revolution crushed by the united resistance of the courts wherever and whenever it might show itself—such were the forms of the new Europe, led by Austria, as they presented themselves to the mind of Metternich. It was a system of pusillanimity, the off-spring of a mind devoid of ideas ; one which had no inkling of the motive forces of history : but this policy corresponded to the momentary needs of the Austrian monarchy ; it harmonised with the general desire for repose felt by the exhausted world ; it set to work with calculated cunning, with profound knowledge of all the mean impulses of human nature and it was based, in masterly fashion, upon those petty arts of good-natured and smiling mendacity wherein from ancient days had lain the strength of the Hapsburg statecraft.

Among the foreign guests it was the English who attracted most attention. It was long since the polished continentals had seen such a toilette as that of the gigantic Lady Castlereagh, one so old-fashioned, hideous, and tasteless. The islanders, who for years had been shut off from the Continent, seemed like figures from another world ; everywhere they aroused mockery by the extraordinary crotchetiness of their disposition, and everywhere hostility by their preposterous arrogance. The whole of the polite world laughed with malicious delight when the Viennese cab-drivers once actually inscribed upon the back of General Sir Charles Stewart the universal opinion regarding British humility. It was not until towards the end of the congress that Wellington put in an appearance, this time at length a worthy representative of the great naval power ; but he also understood no more of German affairs than did his poor-spirited colleagues Castlereagh and Cathcart, and like both of these the duke was guided by the counsels of the Austrians and the Hanoverians. How differently did the czar know how to make his influence felt. He still was glad to play the part of the handsome young man, and was sometimes to be seen walking arm-in-arm with the illustrious young cavaliers of the Bohemian or the Hungarian nobles' guard. At the same time he continued to maintain the sacred character of saviour and liberator of the world ; never before had he spoken so eloquently and softly regarding the promotion of the happiness of the human race. In a memorandum despatched from Vienna to all of his ambassadors he assumed a tone which reminds us of the language of the *Rheinische Merkur*. The fall of Napoleon, he said in so many words, had been effected through the victory of public opinion over the views of most of the cabinets ; in future every nation must be empowered to defend its own independence ; consequently there must be no further partition of countries, and a representative system must everywhere be introduced ! Now, too, Alexander was in the fortunate situation of finding that his ideas of world-liberation coincided precisely with his personal interests. On the way to Vienna, he had stayed for a few days at Pulawy, Czartoryski's beautiful castle, enjoying here the intoxicating homage of the charming Polish ladies ; now he had brought his Sarmatian friend with him to Vienna, and displayed himself openly as the constitutional king of the new Polish realm.

Nesselrode, Metternich's friend, almost fell into disfavour ; his word counted for little as compared with the views of Czartoryski and Capodistrias. This talented Corfiote hardly cared to conceal that he regarded the Russian service as no more than a step by which he hoped to become the hero and liberator of his Greek fatherland ; all enslaved peoples were to him objects for help and, above all, unhappy Italy, which was dear to him as sister in destiny to his own Hellas. The newly founded Hetairia (Society of Friends) of Odessa, and the Philomuse League of Athens, found in him a protector. Soon some Russian lords were to be seen wearing the golden and iron rings of the two Hellenic leagues, and the young prince Ypsilanti was active on behalf of the Greek cause. German princes, statesmen, and men of learning, also became numbered among the Philhellenes ; Haxthausen's fine collection of modern Greek ballads was passed from hand to hand, simultaneously awakening ancient classical memories and ¦Christo-Romantic enthusiasm. However conservative the times might be, the German idealists could not agree to regard as a legitimate prince this Grand Turk, who at the very time was flaying, impaling, and roasting the Serbs in masses. Metternich saw with regret that the desired freedom of the European city for his Turkish protégé was still remote, and he observed with increasing mistrust the revolutionary sentiments of the czar, who had now resumed friendly relations with Stein, and who desired for the Germans a really viable federal constitution. It was unfortunate that Stein held no office, so that whilst he could express his opinions freely to all, at the critical moment of the negotiations he could not utter a decisive voice.

To the unpretentious mind of Frederick William the eternal pomp soon became unendurable ; he yearned to be at home once more, engaged in orderly work in his quiet castle, and was utterly bored by all the festivals, although to some small extent he was shyly paying court to the beautiful countess Julie Zichy. He remained firmly convinced that the Russian alliance was indispensable, yet he did not venture at present to oppose a decisive negative to the different views of Hardenberg and Humboldt, and even took pleasure in daily intercourse with Knesebeck, the declared enemy of Russia, who, always a zealous adherent of Austria, was now, like Metternich, an enthusiast for the sultan. The easy-going chancellor was quite at home amid these multifarious activities ; it pleased him when the palm for grace and amiability was allotted to himself among the older men of the congress, as it was to Metternich among the younger ; but it was manifest that his declining energies suffered from the unending distractions. Humboldt was better able to endure the fatigues of a life of enjoyment, and amid the hurly-burly of social pleasures to maintain his tenacious industry. In intelligence and culture, in alertness and uprightness of feeling, the Prussian statesmen were not lacking. Next to Gentz, Humboldt and the privy councillors of Hardenberg's chancellery, Staegemann, Jordan, and Hoffmann, were the best workers at the congress ; it was they almost alone who carried out the difficult statistical calculations which served as the basis for the reconstitution of the map of Europe, and their pitiless enumeration of figures was often wearisome to those of other nations, and especially to the French, to whom geography had always seemed a tedious subject. Of the learned statistician Hoffmann, Talleyrand said once, in a rage : " Who on earth is that little man who counts all the heads and loses his own ? " But the buoyant resolution which might have found a secure way out of the labyrinth of diplomatic intrigues was lacking to these loyal workers. On the whole, the king's small following, not excepting the men of pleasure, Prince Augustus and Hardenberg, proved straightforward and honourable ; the pretty, pleasure-loving women of Vienna simply could not understand why the king's brother, the handsome and much-courted Prince William, who had displayed his lion-like courage in the face of the enemy, should be so shy and girlish in women's society, and why he could never forget his much-loved wife.

The most numerous and variegated portion of the distinguished assembly was naturally constituted by the German petty princes. There was not one of them, from the Bavarian Max Joseph down to Henry LXIV of Reuss, who did not diligently court the favour of the foreign rulers ; the Russians related with unconcealed contempt what piles of begging letters from German serene highnesses had accumulated in the czar's cabinet. There was not one who did not regard his arrogated sovereignty as an unapproachable holy of holies ; since the agreements of the previous autumn, they felt once more so secure in the possession of this Napoleonic gift, that one of the smallest said openly to Stein : " I know very well that my sovereignty is an abuse, but it suits me very well." With the sovereigns were associated the crowd of the mediatised, who still continued to hope for the recognition of their formally incontestable rights, although their fate had already been decided at Ried and Fulda. Their leader was the dowager princess of Fürstenberg, a brave and sagacious woman ; unweariedly she advocated the interests of her partners in misfortune, in association with privy councillor Gärtner, the much-derided *surchargé d'affaires*, who was maintained by the discrowned at their own charges.

In addition there were representatives from various German territories which demanded the restoration of their old dynasties : Baron von Summerau and Doctor Schlaar representing the Austrian party in Breisgau, a deputation from Düsseldorf, which town desired reunion with the Bavarian Palatinate, and so on. Not less zealously did Wamboldt, Helfferich, and Schies, the three orators of the Catholic Church in Germany, demand the re-establishment of the spiritual states which had been destroyed by the principal decision of the Diet of Deputation, or at least the surrender of the stolen ecclesiastical property. They were under the protection of the papal nuncio, the able and witty Cardinal Consalvi ; with them were associated Friedrich Schlegel

the convert, Goethe's nephew, Councillor Schlosser, from Frankfort, and a large circle of clericals containing many men of conspicuous ability. Yet even in the ecclesiastical sphere there was
manifest the hopeless disintegration of German life. For beside
these representatives of the Roman Church, there appeared the
vicar-general of Constance, Baron von Wessenberg, one of the
gentle, enlightened, highly noble princes of the church characteristic of the century that had passed away—*famosus ille Wessen-
bergius*, he had been named in a papal bull. His hope was for a
German national Church, and it was his endeavour to secure the
primacy of Germany for his principal Dalberg, the dethroned
grand-duke of Frankfort. In addition there were a number of
honourable republican statesmen from the Hansa towns, led by
Smidt of Bremen, who had played a valiant part on the great
headquarters-staff during the winter campaign, and who had
won general respect by his prudence and trustworthiness ; there
was also Jacob Baruch of Frankfort, as representative of German
Jewry ; the able bookseller Cotta of Stuttgart, whose sagacity
already led him to recognise that the decisive voice in German
affairs was Austria's, and who therefore placed his *Allgemeine
Zeitung* at the disposal of the Hofburg ; and an unending series,
in addition, of place-hunters, eavesdroppers, and toadies.

It was the chiefs of the middle-sized states who appeared as
the genuine representatives of what the French termed " la
troisième Allemagne." The hearts of all these creatures of Napoleon were filled with envy for victorious Prussia. It was unendurable that the state of Frederick should have restored to the
Germans a fatherland, should have given them once more the
right to feel joyful self-satisfaction. Down with the powerful
eagle into the general mire of German powerlessness, quarrelsome-
ness, and poverty of spirit—here was the thought in which the
satraps of Bonapartism were all happily united. To weaken the
state which alone could defend the fatherland seemed to them all
to be a self-evident precondition of German freedom. Even that
most bourgeois of all the kings, Max Joseph, who day after day
wandered about the streets of Vienna, joking and chatting with
everyone, the good-natured lord with whom all were acquainted,
who with his rough and merry manner reminded people now of a
French colonel of the old days and now of a Bavarian brewer,
even he carried on the anti-Prussian campaign in deadly earnest,
commanding his plenipotentiary that when in presence of the
monarchs he should agree to nothing at all so long as the king of

Saxony was not restored to his rights. Similar were the views of his son, the eccentric crown prince Louis, although, to his father's great annoyance, the prince adhered to the party of the Teutonising enthusiasts, and was fond of using high-sounding language about the Teuton spirit and the preservation of Teutonism.

Far more provocative was the attitude of the despot of Würtemberg. As doyen among the crowned heads he had everywhere precedence, and consequently, with the naive arrogance of the German estate of petty princes, he determined that he would now really be the most distinguished of them all. He always gave the largest tips, in order to display the magnificence of the new Swabian crown ; he endeavoured in word and gesture to imitate the fallen Imperator, as far as his colossal girth of body rendered this possible ; unabashed, and in rough and angry speeches, he announced his anger at the disappearance of the glories of the Confederation of the Rhine. His heir, like the heir to the Bavarian throne, was an opponent of the Bonapartist sentiments of the father. The soul of the crown prince William was fired by a restless ambition ; having in the last winter campaign shown himself a brave and able officer, he hoped to become commander-in-chief of the army of the Germanic Federation. His beloved Princess Catharine strengthened him in such dreams; the youthful couple understood how to diffuse around them such a nimbus of spiritual grandeur that even sober-minded men believed that the court of Stuttgart would inaugurate a new age for Germany. The prince was widely over-estimated, and many already saw in him the future German emperor ; German particularism would not hear a word about the infinitely greater performances of the Prussian generals.

Among the statesmen of the minor courts three were especially conspicuous, Wrede, Münster, and Gagern, each after his own manner a typical representative of the impotent megalomania characteristic of the diplomatists of the petty states, a mania which had already brought so much ignominy upon Germany, and which for half a century yet to come was to play a leading part in the councils of the fatherland. Wrede had always shown himself a courageous swordsman, from those days when he led the Landsturm of the peasants of Odenwald against the sansculottes down to the time of the " decisive battle " of Arcis, as it was named by the servile Bavarian press. Of genuine military talent he had as little as he had of noble sentiments or real culture ; the unhappy Tyrolese insurgents had had sufficient experi-

ence of his brutal roughness.[1]   The far-seeing Bavarian officers did
not themselves believe in this manufactured greatness ; they knew
that his comrade Deroy, the reformer of the Bavarian infantry,
who had remained in Russia, had been an incomparably greater
soldier ; they knew that the glories of Bavarian arms were to be
sought, not in the campaign of the previous winter, but in the
wars of the Confederation of the Rhine.   However, the lucky man
had abandoned France at the right moment, and had concluded
the treaty of Ried which was of so much advantage to Austria.
Since that time he had enjoyed the special favour of the court of
Vienna ; the coarse blusterer was easier to get on with than was
Montgelas with his tenacious cunning.   Moreover, the Austrian
army was itself so poorly provided with men of talent, that many
of the Austrian diplomats seriously believed Wrede to be a commander.   When he came to Vienna, he was still intoxicated by
the praises which the allies had showered upon him after the
defeat of Hanau ; he boasted that he would chastise Prussian
greed by force of arms, whilst he demanded for Bavaria altogether immoderate compensation, even Mainz, Frankfort, and
Hanau.   He was now prince and field-marshal, for Bavaria, too,
must have her Blucher, and he endeavoured to secure honour for
his title by loud abuse of the quill-drivers, exclaiming, " a marshal
Wrede signs only with the sword ! "

A remarkable contrast to this sabre-rattling boaster was
furnished by the rigid, worthy, and dignified Münster, one of those
enviable men who believe in themselves so profoundly that the
uninitiated are inclined to share the delusion.   To the servile natures
of ducal and grand-ducal diplomacy, this gigantic man with a long
face, reminding everyone of the well-known hereditary beauty
of the House of Hapsburg, seemed magnificent when with unrestrained frankness he sang his own praises.   The count did in
fact possess a many-sided, although superficial, culture.   Married
to a princess of Bückeburg, and for so many years an associate
of the proudest nobility of the world, he was glad to play the part
of the great lord.   Moreover, he had good reason to look down
upon the small fry of the Rhenish Confederate states, for he had
had rich experience in the service of the English crown.

[1] In the first two editions of this work there followed here in the text an
observation regarding the act of pillage which Wrede is said to have perpetrated
in the year 1807 in the castle of Oels (related by Arndt, *Wanderungen mit Stein*,
p. 218).   The passage has now been omitted because, as the outcome of
enquiries made in Oels, I have come to the conclusion that the story is inaccurate.
See Appendix.

and had displayed great endurance in the struggle with Bonapartism. Yet he was rather courtier than statesman, rather
junker than aristocrat. Having made himself indispensable to
the Guelphs by petty complacencies in the wearisome domestic
negotiations of the royal house—chamberlain's services, to which
neither the pride of Stein nor the suppleness of Hardenberg would
ever have stooped—his conception of the great struggles of the
century did not rise above the level of the simple prejudices of
caste. "The principal struggle of our time," he was accustomed to say, "is that the ante-chamber wants to find its way
into the drawing-room." As a correct official representative of
electoral Brunswick, he demanded the restoration of the imperial
dignity, whose abolition had indeed never been recognised by the
Guelphs ; but the glories of the illustrious House of Guelph
must not be diminished by this. His open contempt for the
"kinglets" of the Confederation of the Rhine did not prevent
him at the congress from immediately demanding (without the
knowledge of the prince regent) a Hanoverian kingletship for
his Guelphs—a pretentious kingly crown, whose untenable claims
were in days to come to press as a heavy burden upon the little
country.

It was the curse of this world of petty states that an
honourable national pride was here impossible. However
often Münster might talk at large of the greatness of Germany,
it was his pride that his children were English. And however
loudly he was accustomed to speak of the free spirit of the true
aristocracy, he was himself utterly enmeshed in the servile ideas
which the professional falsifications of particularist history had
caused to flourish in the German minor states. This Guelph
house, which since the days of Henry the Lion had done almost
nothing for the German nation, was to him the most glorious in
the world. Just as uncritically as the servile Göttingen professors did he describe the brilliancy of English parliamentarism
(which had, however, developed solely through the congenital
incapacity of the Guelph Georges, and to the detriment of their
authority), ascribing these glories to the wisdom of the House of
Brunswick, and rediscovering the much-loved "Guelph freedom"
in the petrified junker rule of the Hanoverian territories. This
great moment, when Germany at length once more belonged to
herself, was one which he hoped to utilise in order to reverse the
justified punishment which Henry the Lion had received for his
misdeeds more than six hundred years before ; on the other hand

he found it preposterous that Prussia, on her side, should desire to secure atonement for the maltreatment suffered only seven years before.

The Guelph statesman, although he had never made any attempt to acquire even a superficial understanding of Prussian affairs, was inspired by an ardent hatred for the Prussian neighbour. Among the political sins which for this unhappy nation barred the road to power and freedom, there was nothing so disastrous as the general failure to understand the true significance of the new history of the fatherland—a failure almost miraculous in a cultured nation. Of all the remarkable transformations which had been first rendered possible by the creation of the Prussian national army and the consequent liberation of Germany, hardly anything was known in the petty states. Whilst the Rhenish Confederates related extraordinary fables about the stupidity of the servile Brandenburg peasants and the tyranny of the Prussian junkers, the Hanoverians spoke disdainfully of the polyarchy of the Berlin bureaucracy. Even the wisest in Hanover were not free from such conceits. It was during the years in which the Hanoverian state was no longer in existence that Rehberg, the most notable man among those bourgeois councillors to whom the work of the noble Hanoverian ministers was entrusted, wrote his book upon administrative work under a monarchy, a glorification of the Guelph nobles' rule in opposition to the Prussian regime of slavery ; the apt rejoinder of Friedrich von Bülow, based upon a thorough knowledge of both states, attracted no attention. Thus Münster also had formed his ideas of the Prussian state solely out of current talk, perhaps with the aid of Wilhelmina's memoirs ; with unbounded contempt he expressed his feelings about the miseries of the corporal's administration of Berlin. Just as in the year 1804, from petty-minded mistrust, he had frustrated the Prussian occupation, which perhaps might still have saved his homeland, so upon the outbreak of the War of Liberation he believed that Prussia lived only as a memory ; and when this fine dream had been dispersed, he wrote, greatly troubled, to Gagern, that now Austria had been rounded off in the east and half excluded from Germany, the aggrandisement of Prussia was the greatest danger. Fear and jealousy were the motive forces in the German policy of these *ministeriunculi*, as Stein contemptuously termed them. In Vienna, Münster was at first cautious ; it was his wish, so he wrote to the prince regent, not to anger the Prussian statesmen, and not to impose difficulties in the way of the fluctuating negotiations concerning the rounding-off of the Guelph realm. His was an easy-going and dilettantist nature, that of "the painter," as his friends were accustomed to call him. He was in any case disinclined to persistent activity, and he was long kept to his room by an illness; but wherever he had opportunity he worked zealously against Prussia, and he was unfortunately only too precisely informed concerning the ideas of the chancellor by that evil-minded talebearer, the Hanoverian Hardenberg.

In Hans von Gagern, the constitutional federalist, was incorporated yet another variety of the particularist pro-foreign spirit. Who did not know this busybody, the restlessly moving little man with the brightly flashing eyes and the winning smile? He must always be there wherever there was amusement and feasting, and wherever there was any negotiation concerning a territory and a people; completely uninvited, he thrust himself into all the affairs of the congress, with an unceasing flow of great words regarding the European balance of power and the protection of the lesser states. The celebrated wine-cellar of the House of Nassau and the friendship of Talleyrand, afforded him the means of making a nest for himself among the ambassadors of the great powers. Years before, the much-occupied imperial knight had been an enthusiast on behalf of the Holy Empire; subsequently, always with the same zeal for the fatherland, he had served the Confederation of the Rhine, and had philanthropically saved from destruction a good dozen of condemned petty princes. Now he recommended a federation of perfectly equal kings, grand-dukes, and dukes, under the protection of the Austrian imperial crown, but he also recommended a considerable number of fundamental rights for the German people, for this wonderful man, ever young in spirit, remained a faithful liberal and a child of the French enlightenment.

Gagern sought in Holland, just as Münster sought in England, the centre of gravity of Central European policy. Quite recently thrown by chance into the Dutch service, he had in his inconstant imagination conceived an ideal image of the European destiny of the House of Orange; and just as Münster spoke of "Guelph freedom," so did Gagern speak of the "Orange policy of the golden mean." What did it matter to him that the old, heroic race of Orange had long passed away, and that the new line of Nassau-Diez had not inherited the least trace of the great sentiments of its ancestors? Generally speaking, the enthusiast

was untroubled even by the insatiable land-hunger of the new king
of the Netherlands, although he was occasionally alarmed by this
excess of avarice. For Germany, especially, he anticipated wonderfully happy results from the wise policy of the princely house whose
motto was *je maintiendray!* In his intoxication, he was no longer
able to distinguish between Dutch and German interests. He
sent his favourite and most talented son into the Dutch army,
without for a moment feeling that he was sending him into
foreign service ; just as recklessly did he endeavour to secure
for his master one fragment after another detached from the
German left bank of the Rhine. His king would hear nothing
of the Germanic Federation ; and the ambassador himself regarded
it as a doubtful policy to attach to the German state, in accordance
with Hardenberg's desire, the whole of the Netherlands as a
member of the Germanic Federation ; and he therefore put forward the preposterous proposal that the Netherlands, like Austria,
Prussia, and Denmark, should adhere to the Germanic Federation only with a portion of the Netherlands territory, that of
Luxemburg. This half-measure was by no means regarded by
Gagern as a last resource, but rather as a triumph of genuinely
Germanic statecraft ; for the more intricate, absurd, and nebulous
the frame of German constitutional law, the more, to his mind,
did this seem to correspond to the ancient spirit of German freedom. In the old empire there was nothing he had admired so
greatly as the extraordinary legal relationships of Silesia and
Old Prussia, of which no one had been able to say with certainty
whether they belonged to Germany or not. It was in such bastard
structures that he foresaw the true essence of the *corpus nomenque
Germaniæ ;* how delighted he was with the hope of adorning the
western frontier of Germany with a similar master-work of Teutonic
state-construction.

At first the grown-up children of particularism trotted along
joyfully upon their hobby-horses, delicately patching and polish-
ing at the state structure of their fatherland, until the German
constitution became as meaningless, mendacious, and senseless
as had formerly been that of the old empire. Towards Prussia,
Gagern cherished a strange sentiment of mingled terror and
respect ; in this good-natured soul there was no place for hatred,
for he ever looked upon all that came in his way, animate or in-
animate, from the most friendly side. In his historical fantasies,
when he went back as far as the days of William III, he even
at times regarded Brandenburg and Holland as natural allies,

and ardently assured his Prussian friends that the existing system of states was largely dependent upon the good understanding between Berlin and The Hague. But the contentious neighbour state must not draw too near to his beloved Holland ; moreover the Saxon claims of Prussia seemed monstrous to the old advocate of the petty princedoms. With fiery zeal he constituted himself the defender of the " most sacred rights " of the German high nobility, and wrote to the Prussian statesmen expressive letters in that ludicrously didactic tone which this pigmy was always glad to employ towards the long-suffering great ones of the earth. On one occasion, when he sent the chancellor one of his well-meaning, confusedly-learned pamphlets, he permitted himself to express the censure : " There is so much that is noble in your disposition that I return ever to the best hopes, even though things have happened which I find myself unable to approve." Thereupon Hardenberg, playing gently upon the protean nature of the particularist patriot, replied : " Regarding your annotation, however much value I place upon your approval, I do not feel it necessary to recognise in you the censor of my public actions, just as little as I venture to compare your excellency's own political behaviour in different epochs of your life, or to decide which of us two has done the most for Germany's peace and harmony, and for the establishment of her internal confidence." Notwithstanding such sarcasms, Hardenberg's good nature made it impossible for him to become seriously annoyed with this wonderful saint. His friends regarded the indefatigable man with a touch of humour. Alopeus wrote aptly : " This restless statesmen, to whom it is a matter of indifference what subject occupies his talents as long as he can appear thoroughly busy, has now become a Dutchman."[1]

Among statesmen of such a calibre, it was inevitable that the influence of Talleyrand should soon make itself felt, for of all the diplomats at the congress he was the ablest and the most determined opponent of Prussia. Upon the slippery floor of the salon, an imperturbable firmness of tread has always been more conducive to victory than a courteous amiability. Whilst Metternich and Hardenberg obtained great successes in the distinguished society by means of agreeable and winning methods Talleyrand's cynical audacity proved even more irresistible. What an impression was produced when the ungainly figure of this

Gagern to Hardenberg, November 12 and 18 ; Hardenberg to Gagern, November 16 ; Alopeus to Humboldt, October 11, 1814.

limping club-footed man, dressed in an old-fashioned style dating from the Directory, pushed into the brilliant circle of the court : above the high stock was an enormous mouth with black teeth ; the small, deeply-set grey eyes were utterly devoid of expression ; the features were repulsively common, the countenance was impassive ; he was incapable of blushing or of betraying the inner movement of his thoughts. A thoroughly mephistophelian figure was his. In Hardenberg's diary he is always spoken of as "Talleyrand with the goat's foot." The ladies were intoxicated with delight when, with a fawning smile, he threw to them some double-meaning observation or ill-natured jest ; to the questions of the diplomats he gave unctuous answers with imperturbable and cold-blooded phlegm. Unclean habits, which in another would have been termed plebeian, were in him regarded as original ; the distinguished lord from the ancient house of the princes of Perigord, the oracle of all the epicures of Europe, the habitué of courts, dictated the laws of good society. He had seen them all come and go, the ephemeral heroes of a time of confusion ; he had been acquainted with the *marquis* of the *ancien régime*, with the orators of the revolution, and with the minions of the empire. He had seen into the innermost soul of the petty German sovereigns during the days when he had been in charge of the territorial exchanges of the Rhenish Confederate policy, always ready to take money from anyone's hand, but good-natured as well, obliging to devoted friends, profoundly impressed with the truth that one hand must wash the other. Consequently he, almost alone among the contemporaries of the old regime, had always remained the successful favourite of fortune, and was glad to boast that the limping tortoise had after all come sooner to the goal than the Napoleonic hare. None knew better than he how to spread the opinion that he had been a party to all Napoleon's successes and had counselled against every one of the emperor's mistakes. He possessed that dignified demeanour and secure knowledge of men which were peculiar to the noble princes of the Church in the eighteenth century, and was further regarded as deeply initiated in all personal secrets of the distinguished world He had been of service to every party ; in the celebrated *Dictionary of Political Weathercocks*, his name indisputably occupied the first place. As indifferently as in his episcopal days he had prayed for the salvation of enfranchised France, so now did he stand as lord high chamberlain behind the throne of the legitimate king, waving the oriflamme at the coronation festival of the Bourbons. " It has been my invariable experience," he said with dignity, "that every system from which I detached myself collapsed shortly afterwards." In the depths of his soul he had, however, always remained a thorough-going aristocrat. For this reason he had ever desired an alliance between the old powers of Austria and England, for he could get on with the proud nobles of these two countries ; whereas the rule of the Russian upstarts, and still more the bourgeois-military straightforwardness of the Prussian state, were to him contemptible.

Thus in Vienna he could, with inward satisfaction, play the part which was imposed upon him by the interests of his court ; he appeared as the representative of the most legitimate of all the dynasties, describing boastfully, only a few months before the Hundred Days, how firmly established was the power of the French royal house, how every threatened right would find protection in the Bourbons, and he delighted the empty-headed protagonists of the dynastic policy with the cleverly coined catch-word "legitimacy." With an unctuous formality he at once announced the three principal aims of Bourbon statecraft, which had already been declared in his memorandum. These were : the deposition "of the man who rules in Naples " (the name of Murat was never allowed to pass the chaste lips of Talleyrand) ; the warding-off of the Russian attack upon Poland ; finally, and above all, the reinstatement of the king of Saxony. It was in the Saxon negotiations that the Frenchman's keen insight recognised the wedge which was to drive the coalition asunder. Pathetically he spoke of the cause of Frederick Augustus as "the cause of all kings " ; and expressed his sorrow for unhappy Europe, whose public law was so seriously threatened by the violent deeds of Prussia and Russia.

§ 2. THE TERRITORIAL NEGOTIATIONS.

The mere formal leadership of this many-headed and variegated assembly offered the greatest difficulties, more especially since the leading men could for the most part appear only as modest assistants of the monarchs. Since Russia and Austria had deliberately postponed the decision of all contested matters until the congress, the great powers were for the moment united upon nothing, not even upon the question as to who was entitled to take part in the deliberations. Consequently the formal opening of the congress was at first impossible, nor could there take place a common sitting of all its members, nor even an examination of credentials ; it was only when a separate understanding had been signed that the negotiators exchanged their credentials.

In order to bring a certain amount of order into this chaos, the ministers of the four allied great powers met for preliminary deliberations as early as the middle of September, before the arrival of the French. The Prussian statesmen jealously maintained the newly acquired position of their state as a great power ; anti-French from the foundation, not only did they resist the Napoleonides, but they also demanded the enforcement of that secret article by which the Bourbon court was excluded from all negotiations regarding distribution of territory. For both these reasons they endeavoured to exclude the petty states from the more important deliberations, for the participation of these would inevitably strengthen the influence of France. It was in this sense that Humboldt drew up a plan for the conduct of the business,[1] which he handed to the "Committee of Four." The congress, according to this document, was not a peace congress, for the peace had long been concluded ; and it was not in any way a deliberative assembly of Europe, since Europe did not exist as a constituted whole. The purpose of the congress was to deal with a number of different affairs, which must be treated in different ways ; questions of territorial distribution, special concerns, and institutions which were important for the whole of Europe. In the case of the territorial questions, the Polish problem was, according to treaty, reserved for the decision of the three partitioning powers, but England could play the part of mediator in a manner welcome to the other three powers. The general principle regarding the distribution of German territory was, in accordance with the peace of Paris, the concern of the four powers alone ; France, Holland, Denmark, and Switzerland must be kept aloof, because they did not look at the matter from the European standpoint ; and Bavaria and Würtemberg could not be admitted to participation until after the conclusion of the deliberations. The distribution of Italian territory was a matter for deliberation between Austria, Piedmont, the pope, the Bourbons of Sicily, and their protector, England ; Murat was excluded. Among the "special concerns," the most important was the German constitutional question : this was to

[1] Humboldt's *Proposals for the Management of the Congress*, drawn up on September 18th and following days.

be decided by the German states alone, with the addition of Denmark (on account of Holstein) ; the Netherlands, which must have a say in the matter ; and Switzerland, for a perpetual alliance between the Germanic Federation and the Swiss Confederacy would be "extremely desirable." There thus remained for the common deliberations of all the powers, only a few common concerns. The chief of these was the constitution of Switzerland, since a civil war was imminent in that country. Next came the Neapolitan affair ; the ruler of Naples, who was not recognised by all the powers, must be deposed. There was the removal of Napoleon from Elba, for this fire-brand must not remain in such threatening proximity to Europe. Finally, there were the abolition of the slave-trade, the regulation of the international navigation of rivers, and the precedence of the diplomats. These affairs of general European import should be discussed by a committee and then laid before the whole congress.

The Prussian proposals immediately encountered vigorous resistance, although they were strictly based upon the incontestable legal foundation of the treaty of Paris. Talleyrand had long before taken care that his secret memorandum should reach the hands of the Hofburg, and the Austrians gratefully recognised the praiseworthy designs of the court of the Tuileries regarding the Saxon and Polish questions. They now found it most improper that France should be excluded from any important part of the negotiations. Castlereagh agreed with the Austrians, for the relations between the courts of Paris and London had been continually improving, and Castlereagh on his way to Vienna had once more paid a visit to the Tuileries. King Louis esteemed the Guelphs even more highly than the Lorrainers, for the latter had committed an unpardonable sin against legitimacy by the marriage alliance with the Corsican. Russia alone supported Prussia. Thus there was a dead-lock, two against two ; and at length on September 23rd harmony was reached by the adoption of an unfortunate middle course. It was determined that the German constitutional questions should be elaborated by a committee of the five German royal courts ; that all European affairs should be dealt with by the four allied great powers and the two Bourbon powers (France and Spain). But the designs for the territorial distribution, in accordance with the understanding of Paris, was in the first place reserved for the four powers ; these were subsequently to communicate their decisions to France and Spain, and finally were to inform also the smaller courts.

Obviously this compromise enabled the French to overthrow all that had been previously resolved, and Talleyrand, who had now appeared upon the scene, was not slow to take advantage of the error. On September 30th, when the French minister and his devoted friend Don Labrador, the ambassador of the Spanish Bourbons, were invited to the Committee of Four in order to learn the decision of the four powers, Talleyrand's impassive face lighted up with triumph. With incomparable audacity, as if the secret article of the Peace of Paris had had no existence, the Frenchman demanded that all the states should take part in the negotiations of the congress, and by resounding phrases regarding the sacredness of public law he so greatly confused the ministers of the four powers that the sitting was suspended without any decision having been arrived at. Not one of the other ambassadors possessed sufficient presence of mind to make a quiet appeal to the peace of Paris, and thus to nip in the bud the Frenchman's presumption, which was contrary to the treaty. Hardenberg, owing to his unfortunate deafness, could not readily find the right thing to say in face of such surprises. Humboldt, however, and the Russian plenipotentiary were plainly altogether unprepared for so audacious an infringement of the treaty that had so recently been signed. Finally, Castlereagh and Metternich, through their secret negotiations with the Tuileries, had themselves already broken the Peace of Paris. In a theatrically coloured report, which was calculated word by word to effect the conspicuous display of the superiority of the writer, Talleyrand informed Louis XVIII of the victory he had secured. To his Rhenish Confederate friends he said proudly : " J'ai su m'asseoir."

The Frenchman did not at first secure a decisive success. In the following sittings he proposed that all sovereigns who had not formally declined, including, therefore, Frederick Augustus of Saxony, should be admitted to the congress, and that then a number of committees should be appointed by the states as a whole. Both these proposals were rejected, for they manifested too plainly the intention to secure for the French court, as the well-wisher of the petty states, the leadership of the congress. Finally it was resolved to appoint an executive committee from among the eight powers which had subscribed the peace of Paris. This committee of eight was the official congress, but it was rarely summoned and then only *pro forma*, for three of the signatory powers still counted for very little in the society of states. So far Talleyrand had simply secured that everything should be shapeless and involved.

Without asking the committee of eight, the four allied great powers began among themselves confidential negotiations concerning the Polish question.

How notably had Talleyrand's prestige increased within a few days! When he first arrived he had been anxiously avoided in the drawing-rooms, and so had his colleague the duke of Dalberg, who, as a turn-coat, was in bad repute among the Germans; it was only the good-natured Gagern who would speak to the neglected man. Now the diplomats eagerly sought favour with the clever Frenchman, and most eagerly of all the harassed Saxons. It is extremely probable that Talleyrand, like Metternich, had received large sums of money from the Saxon court. In these circles this was regarded as a perfectly harmless proceeding; Gentz in his diary recorded with a good conscience the sums which had been paid to him by the French ambassador. Talleyrand's secret intercourse with the imprisoned king was well known to the Prussian statesmen,[1] and he was not accustomed to give his friendly services for nothing. Documentary proof of his corruption will probably never be attainable, for the accounts of the Saxon privy purse were subsequently burned by order of the king of Saxony, who doubtless had his reasons. Moreover, the whole question is of importance only to the scandal-monger or to the minor moralist, and not to the serious historian. Talleyrand's venality is universally known, and is not denied even by his panegyrist Hans von Gagern; it is therefore indifferent how often and from whom he received bribes. To the Saxon court, however, the disgrace attaches of this continuance of the ancient policy of treason; and whether money was or was not paid on this account is of no importance. These tainted negotiations remained altogether without influence upon the course of the congress; it was not the money of the Albertines but the well understood interest of their own states which determined the attitude of the Austrian and of the Bourbon statesmen. The French ambassador in Berlin declared openly to everyone that Frederick Augustus of Saxony had been the most faithful ally of France, and that France could not desert him.

At the same time, Talleyrand played the part of the magnanimous protector of the German sovereigns. The petty princes were all in an evil humour; in Vienna there was no prospect of territorial enlargements, and the natural predominance of the great powers made itself strongly felt. With masterly skill

---

[1] Humboldt to Hardenberg, January 27, 1815.

Talleyrand availed himself of this ill-humour of the middle-sized states ; he alleged that the whole fabric of public law was put in question if the rulers of Bavaria and Würtemberg could not have the same voice in the reordering of Europe as had Prussia or Russia. Consequently within a brief period he restored his humiliated country to its traditional position as leader of the German petty states. It was with good reason that the French esteemed their adroit negotiator. King Louis overwhelmed him with praise, and felt himself entirely satisfied when the minister wrote pathetically that it seemed to him very unseemly that here in Vienna three or four kings and a number of princes could be found at a dance in the house of a private individual, adding, " One must go to France in order to see kingship in that glory and dignity which make it appear at once sublime and lovable in the eyes of the people ! " Alexander, however, said : " Talleyrand is playing here the role of minister of Louis XIV ! " This was an apt mot which has since then been frequently applicable to the neo-French policy.

In barely a fortnight after that stormy sitting Gentz had completely reconciled himself with the audacious Frenchman. The czar, too, summoned this dangerous opponent on several occasions to secret conversations regarding Poland, and thus gave him the right to intrude into the Polish negotiations. Above all, the German petty states thronged zealously around the magnanimous man who so expressly advocated the equal rights of Russia and of Schwarzburg-Sondershausen. Victorious Germany had now to endure the disgrace that her high nobility should once more seek the favour of a French subordinate official, as they had sought it in the days of German defeat. Just as the petty lords had in the year 1803 gone to Matthieu, and three years later to old Pfeffel, as place-hunters, so now they abased themselves in the modest room before Talleyrand's confidential adviser, the same La Besnardière who, seven years before, had in Poland practised the art of establishing German fatherlands. The most clamorous were the Bavarians ; on the journey to Vienna, Talleyrand had had a conversation with Montgelas in Baden. Even Charles Augustus of Weimar could not lift himself above the sentiment of cousinly participation, and did not until a late date draw back from the Albertines, when he saw through the unclean *arrières pensées* of the Saxon party. Busily did the French negotiators retail all kinds of arrogant utterances which were supposed to have been heard in the Prussian camp. The newspapers of

Paris reported that "the insolent behaviour of the Prussian generals in Vienna" had repelled even the warmest friends of the land-hungry state, whereas of all the notable Prussian generals the only one present in Vienna was the dignified and cautious Knesebeck.

The objections to Prussia's Saxon plans raised by historians at a later date, had occurred to no one in the year 1814. To us to-day it appears a weak idea that the imprisoned king should not be simply dethroned, and that he should be compensated elsewhere with land and people; but the allotting of such compensation seemed a matter of course to the sentiments of those days, and if it had not been proposed to give it, the Prussian plan would have appeared to the other courts far more ruthless. The learned man of to-day may well think that Frederick Augustus was hardly more blameworthy than the king of Bavaria, upon whom favours were now heaped; but neither Max Joseph nor Talleyrand advanced such reasons in excuse of their Saxon protégé. Nor did the sober-minded statesmen in Vienna ever think about the reputed services of the Wettins on behalf of German civilisation. The party contrast which manifested itself in the Austrian capital was far simpler. On one side was the desire of the young German great power to provide for its lacerated and threatened territory a tenable southern frontier, and at the same time to give the treasonable sentiments of the Rhenish Confederate courts a wholesome warning; on the other side was the traditional enmity of Austria and France for the state wherein they obscurely perceived the culture-ground of German unity, and there was the dynastic envy of the petty courts. The House of Wettin was a "house" like that of Wittelsbach and that of Würtemberg, and all the thoughts of the petty princes were centred in the preservation of the power of their houses. Talleyrand speedily recognised how to gather round himself all the forces of resistance, and he did not conceal his view that the fate of Frederick Augustus was far nearer to his heart than the destiny of Poland. The *Rheinische Merkur* wrote warningly that the Napoleonic bees and wasps were still hidden among the Bourbon lilies. That great European alliance which assembled under the banner of France, gave the Saxon negotiations a historical significance far greater than the value of the country that was in dispute. The Prussian state now learned, as at the time of the Silesian war, that the whole world was united in fighting Prussia.

Meanwhile the prisoner of Friedrichsfelde played with considerable ability, and certainly in good faith, the part of profoundly injured innocence. All his life he had conscientiously taken his stand upon the ground of positive law, and as long as the Holy Empire had persisted he had precisely fulfilled his duties as an imperial prince. But the idea that the sovereign king of Saxony could possibly sin against Germany, remained altogether incomprehensible to his intelligence. In the summer of 1814 he sent a memorial to the czar, setting out in absolute seriousness the compensations which Saxony had a right to demand from Prussia ! The landless king magnanimously demanded from the conqueror no more than the Beeskow-Storkow circle, a few Prussian enclaves, and favourable assistance for the Saxon negotiations ; in addition, compensation for Warsaw. However preposterous this bungling piece of work may appear, it constituted a suitable prelude to a second memorial which was printed at Nuremberg in July, with the approval of the Bavarian government. In this it was stated that the king had heard with the utmost astonishment a report that the allies were proposing to deprive him of his hereditary dominions ; he feared that he would do wrong to the exalted powers if he were to place any credence in such a calumny. Next the conduct of the Saxon court was justified, all errors having been due to *force prépondérante* (such was the phrase now used by the great ally) ; and with all the self-satisfied frankness of the German petty prince, the apt truth found expression that " great states alone can remain faithful to their ideals." Frederick Augustus then declared to all the courts that he would never agree to abdicate, and in an autograph letter of September 19th appealed for help to Louis XVIII. His envoy in Vienna, Count Schulenburg, was not indeed admitted to the negotiations of the congress, and in the deliberations of the committee on the German constitution the king of Saxony was regarded as non-existent. But Wrede serviceably reported to the Saxon all that was worth knowing. At the same time Prince Antony treated secretly with his brother-in-law, Emperor Francis : the Saxon Langenau was the most intimate confidant of Gentz. The cause of the Albertines gained ground day by day.

Among the Saxon people, too, the condition was very different from what the chancellor imagined. A number of far-sighted Saxon nobles had sided with the general government of Prince Repnin. Among these were Carlowitz, Miltitz, Oppell, Vieth, and some of the higher officials, such as Schiller's friend, the father of Theodor Körner. With their aid, the Russian administration had done excellent work; within a brief time it had uprooted a number of obsolete abuses. Among the bourgeoisie there existed a small Prussian party, for the merchants of Leipzig had long been out of humour with the rule of the nobles. It was from the existence of these friendly circles that Stein and Hardenberg derived their hopeful view of the mood of the country. In reality the mass of the people was in a condition of profound languor, exhausted by the tribulations of the war. Under the rule of the nobles, the population had been disaccustomed to political thought; like all Germans, in all ages, they regarded a tribal princely house as an indispensable jewel of the fatherland in the narrower sense, but at first they remained passive and equable. There were only two notable Saxons who took part in the lively paper warfare which accompanied the diplomatic struggle concerning the future of Saxony : Carl Müller, who wrote from the Prussian point of view; while Kohlschütter was representative of the servile officialdom. One party alone displayed lively activity, that of the oligarchs of the high nobility. They had ruled the land for centuries, and the strong hand of the Prussian kingship threatened to reduce them to the rank of ordinary subjects. As long as the war continued, the court nobility and the higher officials had remained on terms of intimate friendship with the numerous French prisoners in Dresden ; their emissaries exercised an influence over the Saxon troops in Rhineland ; they kept up a lively correspondence with the friendly diplomats in Vienna ; accustomed to dominate, they knew how to browbeat the docile populace to such an extent that the great majority soon united in the cry, " Let us have our king back again ! " People began to stigmatise as renegades the excellent men who were at the head of the provisional administration. A few years ago there was still living in the poorhouse at Wahren an old man who was popularly spoken of as " the traitor " ; during the bloody battle at Möckern, he had guided a Prussian battalion along a hidden pathway.

In the memory of the people the image of recent events gradually became distorted ; the king's sins were forgotten, and the change in side of the troops during the battle of Leipzig was soon regarded as simply a shameful desertion of the flag. A partition of the country seemed, indeed, even less desirable than incorporation in the Prussian state. Appeals were made to the czar, who to Saxon deputations had repeatedly guaranteed " the integrity of their country." Such was the lack of political perception among the masses that they failed to recognise that this integrity was possible only if the former king did not return. The favourable news from Vienna increased the immeasurable self-esteem which lies in the very nature of particularism ; the Saxons cheerfully expected that the whole of Europe would take up arms in order to restore to the imprisoned Albertine the last of his villages. It is true that the leaders of the particularist party had more insight than this, but they would rather continue the ancient supremacy of the nobles in a diminished Saxony than subject themselves to the common law of the Prussian state. Prince Repnin, the governor-general, wrote after the catastrophe sharply and aptly to his assistant, the able councillor Merian : " My complaint against the higher officials is that, just like myself, they were convinced that the return of the king could not be effected without the dismemberment of their country. These egoists preferred a disaster to the fatherland to the loss of their personal advantages. The Saxons wanted their prince back again, and by their behaviour gave moral support to the aim of that power which regarded the partition of Saxony as advantageous." [1]

Such was the position of affairs when the four powers began their indefinite negotiations concerning Poland. Hardenberg was still unable to see that his Saxon hopes must inevitably be ruined if in the Polish negotiations he worked hand in hand with Austria and England. Either the czar would yield to the resistance of the three united courts, and in that case the Prussian crown would be once more encumbered by her faithful ally with those Polish possessions which Prussia herself regarded as dangerous, and Prussia would at the same time lose all claim to compensation in Saxony ; or else both parties would agree upon a compromise, and this issue seemed the more probable, since at this moment neither Austria nor England desired war. For it could be anticipated with certainty that Alexander, if embittered by Prussia's opposition, would no longer support the Saxon claims of the Prussian court. Abandoned on all sides, our state, if it were unwilling to venture a struggle against the whole of Europe, would be forced to content itself with a strip of land along the Warthe and with a few fragments of Lusatia. So simple was the calculation. Metternich's first task was to delude the chancellor about the inseparable connection between the Polish question and the Saxon ; to postpone the solution of the Saxon problem ; and for the moment, in unison with Prussia and England, to resist Alexander's

[1] Repnin to Merian, Vienna, February 15-25, 1815.

designs. In this way the alliance between Russia and Prussia would be broken, and the humiliation of the North German power would be assured. The snare was astonishingly clumsy. As early as September, Gentz wrote hopefully to Karadja that if it were but possible to restrict Russia's enlargement in what had formerly been Prussian Poland, the sole ground for the annexation of Saxony would be removed !

In actual fact the attention of the Prussian statesmen was almost completely engaged in Polish affairs. The generals were unanimous in demanding an eastern frontier that should be tenable from the military point of view. Humboldt's wish was that Prussia should act on behalf of the threatened European balance of power. With the certainty of genius Stein declared to the czar that the construction of a Polish kingdom under the Russian sceptre would lead, either to the detachment of Poland from Russia, or else to the complete subjection of the Poles. In Hardenberg's entourage could be found certain eloquent friends of the Poles ; among these were the amiable prince Anton Radziwill, and the privy councillor Zerboni, a talented liberal and an enthusiastic admirer of Sarmatian freedom. To the chancellor himself, the advance of Russia westward seemed far less dangerous than the re-establishment of the kingdom of Poland and the threatening Polish propaganda. All these tendencies, however fundamentally divergent, coincided in the idea that Alexander's plans must be resisted, and the question was not even seriously mooted how in that case Prussia's own claims could be secured.

The czar was, however, somewhat alarmed by the unanimous opposition of the court of St. Petersburg, and he began to doubt whether he could expect the Russians to accept the union of Lithuania with Poland ; nevertheless he held obstinately to his idea of the re-establishment of the Polish kingdom. In Vienna, he immediately and openly proposed that the whole of Warsaw as far as the Prosna, including Thorn and Cracow, should be handed over to the Russian imperial house as an independent kingdom. At the same time he warmly supported Prussia's claims upon Saxony, and on September 28th he gave a formal pledge to hand over the administration of the country to Prussia without delay. In the German constitutional question, too, he expressly advocated the Prussian plans ; he did not conceal how profoundly he despised the self-seeking of the Rhenish Confederate courts, but he prudently avoided all intrusive intervention. Capodistrias also ardently desired the consolidation of the Germanic Federation, and the younger Alopeus, Alexander's ambassador in Berlin, was a fervent admirer of Prussian military renown. In a word, Russia's attitude towards Prussia remained thoroughly friendly, although Prussia had not as yet pledged herself in any way to support the Polish plans of the czar. It seemed indisputable that, by an open advance to the side of the czar, Hardenberg could secure an understanding also about Thorn and Kulmerland, and could secure the unqualified adhesion of the two powers. But the chancellor remained upon the side of Metternich, hoping that England and Austria would, like Russia, agree to the provisional occupation of Saxony by Prussia.

The king regarded the chancellor's policy with some anxiety, and considered that the immediate occupation of Saxony would be a premature step, for he himself, less sanguine than Hardenberg, drew the right conclusion from the behaviour of Emperor Francis, that Austria would with difficulty be induced to countenance the expulsion of the Albertines. Had it been possible to effect the occupation a year earlier, immediately after the battle of Leipzig, this would have been an effective means of paving the way for complete annexation. In the existing posture of affairs, immediately before the decision of the congress, the occupation no longer offered any advantage, but exposed Prussia to the danger of humiliation in case she should not prove to be in a position to retain the whole of the occupied territory. For this reason, the king opposed the step. Yet he had too little confidence in his own judgment, especially where diplomatic questions were concerned ; he unwillingly let the chancellor follow his own counsel, and subsequently, when Hardenberg's plans came to nought, the king said angrily, after his manner : " I told you so, but you all wanted to be wiser." But when Hardenberg proposed to nominate Prince William as viceroy of Saxony, Frederick William immediately refused, for he would not expose any of the personalities of the royal house to humiliating defeat.

The reasonable anxieties of his royal master did not disturb the chancellor's self-satisfaction. In alliance with Metternich he opened his diplomatic campaign against the czar. Upon the invitation of the three partitioning powers, England undertook to mediate, and hardly ever in the whole history of modern diplomacy was any negotiator so stupid and clumsy as the noble lord, of whom his political associates were accustomed to say : " For all good things we must thank God and Castlereagh." He was to mediate, and he conducted himself as a partisan, immediately putting forward demands which went far beyond the wishes of Austria and Prussia. The simplest consideration of propriety demanded that he should display moderation, for in accordance with the wording of the treaties England had no right to intervene in the Polish negotiations ; and yet from the first he assumed an aggressive tone which no crowned head, and least of all the excessive conceit of Alexander, could possibly tolerate. In his very first memorandum of October 4th he hurled at the czar the accusation that Russia's procedure was in absolute opposition to the letter and to the spirit of the treaties—a plainly false assertion, for Alexander had wisely guarded himself against giving any binding pledges whatever. Castlereagh was even audacious enough to falsify the intentions of his principals, and declared that Austria and Prussia would gladly greet the re-establishment of a completely independent Polish realm, a view in absolute conflict with the opinions of the courts both of Vienna and of Berlin.

The only excuse for this unprecedented conduct was to be found in Castlereagh's profound ignorance ; it was quite obvious that he had no idea as to what the independence of Poland really signified. With ingenuous self-satisfaction, he wrote to Wellington in Paris saying that the vigorous language of his memorandum could not fail to make an impression upon the czar.[1] Still more plainly was manifested the incapacity of this remarkable mediator in his second memorandum of October 14th. Here he demanded that Austria, if possible in unison with Prussia, should submit the following proposals to the czar : Either the re-establishment of the free realm of Poland under an independent prince, as it had existed before 1772 ; or, if this were unattainable, the re-establishment of the *status quo* of 1791 ; or, in the last resort, a partition of the duchy of Warsaw in such a way that Prussia should receive all the country as far as the Vistula, whilst Russia should retain merely the narrow strip to the east of this river. Whilst Hardenberg had never asked more for Prussia than the line of the Warthe, this Englishman, who was supposed to be speaking in Prussia's name, wished to burden our state once more with almost the whole of its ancient Polish dominion, and he even declared that Prussia was prepared " to make all necessary sacrifices " for the re-establishment of the Poland of 1771— that is to say, to hand over once again to the Sarmatians the Marienburg and the Vistular territories of the Teutonic Knights !

[1] Goltz's Report, Paris, October 21, 1814.

Nay more, Castlereagh demanded that all the documents exchanged in the Polish negotiations should be laid before the congress, and that all the European states should be asked to oppose the designs of Russia. In his blind zeal he thus adopted the guileless Talleyrand's proposals, and desired, in opposition to the treaties, to draw all the petty states into the Polish negotiations, which would have involved making France the arbiter of Europe! In a third memorandum, dated November 4th, he permitted himself the use of language which at other times could only have been heard just before the outbreak of war. He declared that the intentions of the czar "threw to the ground all the accepted principles of international loyalty and faith," and he asserted once more that a Russian emperor who ruled as far as the Prosna could at his will hurl his armies against the Danube and the Oder, and hold Austria and Prussia completely in check.

It seemed as if Castlereagh desired to stimulate the czar to the extremity of resistance. Alexander was in fact profoundly affronted; and in two memorials, dated October 30th and November 21st, he bluntly rejected the proposal. In high-sounding words he developed the views which have since then remained dominant in semi-official Russian histories. In the spring of 1813, he said, Russia could readily have concluded a glorious peace, and had continued the struggle only on behalf of Europe. The enlargement Russia demanded was not a menace for Russia's neighbours but was essential to content the Russians as well as the Poles. Therewith came a well-deserved snub for Castlereagh: "A mediator is useful only when he brings people nearer together!" If matters should be carried further on such lines, the world, which was yearning for peace, would soon be driven into a new war.

Meanwhile the Prussian chancellor was far from comfortable in the society of his strange allies. He saw the British mediator making demands which had no longer anything in common with Prussia's own views, and yet he himself was still far from certain whether his faithful friends would support him in his Saxon plans. Hardenberg therefore resolved to obtain certainty, and on October 9th sent a cordial letter to Metternich to the following effect: Prussia desired to remain faithful to the system "d'une Europe intermédiaire" (that is to say, to the system of a closer alliance of the three " German " great powers), but in her present insecure situation she must think first of her own interests, and therefore desired a plain answer to three questions. Would Austria agree to the Prussian annexation of the whole of Saxony ? Did the Austrian imperial government approve of the transference of Frederick Augustus to the Legations ? Did Austria renounce the idea of handing Mainz over to Bavaria ? (Concerning this intention, which two months before had been still unknown to Humboldt, Hardenberg had at length arrived at a clear understanding.) If the Austrian imperial government would answer these three questions in the affirmative, and would at the same time promise to give a firm support to Prussia's intentions in respect of Mainz and Saxony, then, said Hardenberg, " I shall be able to act in the fullest understanding with you in respect of the Polish question." Last of all Metternich was asked to agree at once to the provisional occupation of Saxony. The same request was made to Castlereagh. Hardenberg still hoped that his Austrian friend would magnanimously give to him Saxony, and in addition the Polish territory for which Saxony was to serve as a compensation !

Castlereagh answered on October 11th, approved the provisional occupation, and declared that his court would also agree to the complete annexation of Saxony. England desired the entire re-establishment of the Prussian power, and the chastisement of the political immorality of Frederick Augustus. He continued, in exceedingly bad French : " If this annexation should be effected as a means to compensate the Prussian state for the losses which it might suffer through the disquieting and dangerous enterprise of Russia, and as a means to place Prussia with undefended frontiers in manifest dependence upon Russia," then he could not hold out any prospect of the assent of England. What was the meaning of this rigmarole ? Prussia declared : First give us a guarantee for the possession of Saxony, only then can we venture to break the alliance with Russia and to support your Polish plans. Castlereagh replied : " First bring it about that Russia will not advance her western frontier too far, and then we will agree to your annexation of Saxony." Thus Castlereagh simply turned the Prussian demand upside down and attached an impossible condition to his assent. Since at this moment none of the three powers desired war with Russia, it was plainly not within the power of Prussia alone to effect a moderation of the Russian demands ; and yet the Prussian enlargement was to be made dependent upon this senseless condition, whereas the gains of Austria in Italy had secured the unconditional assent of England ! This extraordinary contradictoriness makes so ambiguous an impression, that the involuntary suspicion arises that Metternich or Münster must have guided the noble lord's pen. Nevertheless the clumsy English statesman was beyond question acting in good faith, and was by no means hostile towards Prussia ; just as little as Hardenberg did he understand that, in the existing situation, Prussia was forced to choose between Warsaw and Saxony, and could not possibly demand both at the same time.

Hardenberg's plain enquiries put the Austrian statesmen in a position of painful embarrassment. Gentz wished straightway to break with Prussia and Russia ; more passionately than ever did he rage against the greed of the Prussian revolutionaries, and against Alexander's tutor, Laharpe, who so audaciously displayed his liberal principles ; more confidential than ever became his intercourse with Talleyrand and Langenau. Metternich saw further. He realised that it was not yet time to drop the mask, and wished to keep his credulous Prussian friend a prey to the latter's fine illusion until Prussia had herself broken with Russia and stood completely alone ; for this reason he was inclined to agree to the provisional occupation of Saxony. A few days later, on October 14th, Gentz himself was brought over by Castlereagh's persuasion to the views of his calmer friend. Austria agreed that Prussian troops should enter Saxony—*sans reconnaître le principe*, as Gentz added with satisfaction. This indication of good feeling strengthened the Prussian chancellor in his artless confidence, and yet Metternich was left free for the ultimate decision.

All the more difficult became the answer to Hardenberg's three questions, and Metternich was not ready to reply until October 22nd. The second of the Prussian questions, that relating to the transference of Frederick Augustus to the Legations, was ignored in the Austrian reply, and this, in accordance with ancient diplomatic custom, was tantamount to an unconditional refusal. The third question, that regarding Mainz, was answered with a definite negative. This place, which in the year 1797 Emperor Francis had himself sacrificed to the French in exchange for Venice, was now declared by Metternich to be the only fortress which hindered a march upon the Danube, and to be the only commercial centre which gave Austria access to the northern seas—an astonishing claim which was explicable only in view of the still more astonishing geographical and economic ideas of the imperial statesman. " Never," he said, " will the emperor renounce Mainz." If the Germanic Federation were to be subjected to the equally balanced influence of Austria and Prussia, and if the legitimate claims of South Germany were to be satisfied, Prussia must not advance beyond the left bank of the Moselle. Thus even Coblenz was now refused to the Prussian friend, and the most untenable of all the German river frontiers was offered! To Hardenberg's first question, finally, Metternich replied, that it was only with pain that the emperor could witness the dethronement of one of the oldest royal races ; the annexation was opposed to Austrian interests, and among the German princes could not fail to arouse mistrust of Prussia and to give rise to complaints against Austria ; the emperor hoped that Prussia would leave the imprisoned king at least a portion of land on the Bohemian frontier. " If, however, the force of circumstances should render the annexation of Saxony unavoidable," then Austria would reserve for herself the right of discretion regarding the fortresses and frontier places, regarding commerce and navigation. The emperor counted on " an unconditional agreement upon procedure " between the two courts in respect of Polish affairs, and on an understanding regarding the common carrying out of the " luminous " memorial of Castlereagh. Metternich, in addition, permitted himself the unbecoming observation that the personal feelings of King Frederick William ought not to be allowed to stand in the way of a sound policy.

On receipt of this reply a resolute Prussian statesman should immediately have recognised that there was no dependence to be placed upon the two allies, and that a firm adhesion to the side of Russia was essential. Of the three Prussian conditions, Metternich had flatly refused two ; and anyone who knew how little even a decisive assent signified in this mouth, might easily reckon what the unwilling, confused, and half-hearted assent to the third condition was really worth. Was it not obvious that " the force of circumstances would no longer render the annexation of Saxony unavoidable," if Prussia were to retain the greater part of Warsaw ? Metternich, however, counted upon the credulous confidence of his Prussian friend, and was delighted with the adroitness with which he had concealed his thoughts. Gentz, also, was in agreement with his friend's documentary achievement, and prophesied at Wiede's table that within a fortnight the system of European alliances would have been disarranged—meaning that a rapprochement between Austria and France would have been effected.

It was Gentz who had persuaded Metternich to give so distinct a negative in the matter of Mainz : his angry feeling was that Mainz must be saved from Prussian greed even though it should entail an alliance with France. This view found support in the undying tendency of our petty princes to do anything other than that which was plainly expedient, and always to entrust the threatened parts of the fatherland to the weakest hands. The Ernestine courts, Nassau and Hesse, declared on October 25th that this important fortress should not be handed over to any of the greater states, neither to Bavaria nor to Prussia ; it belonged to Germany as a whole. It was resolved to establish a new Teutonic Order for the protection of the fortress on the Rhine. So general was the opposition to the establishment of Prussian power upon the Middle Rhine, that Baron von Stein at length conceived the artificial plan of installing the crown-prince of Würtemberg in Mainz, as German field-marshal. Anyone who chose to open his eyes could perceive from other indications that Austria was antagonistic to Prussia. The map, shown to Metternich in absolute confidence, displaying that " isthmus " of southern Hanoverian territory which Prussia demanded to connect the eastern with the western provinces, had been, as Münster himself related, betrayed to the Guelph diplomats by the Austrian statesman.

Simultaneously with the reply to Hardenberg (October 22nd) Metternich declared, in a despatch to Castlereagh, that it was only with extreme unwillingness that Austria could allow the destruction of a buffer state which had so often proved useful to the balance of power in Germany and in Europe ; but if the annexation of Saxony was regarded by the allies as unavoidable, then Austria would accept this severe sacrifice upon the twofold condition, that the balance of power in Germany should not be disturbed by the advance of Prussia southward of the Moselle, and that the annexation " should not constitute a precedent for demanding assent to further enlargements of territory." The almost verbal coincidence of this obscure sentence with Castlereagh's note of October 11th suggests the idea that the noble lord had in this confused intrigue been no more than an innocent tool in the hands of Metternich. The Austrian statesman regarded the game as already won, and was so sure of the blind assent of the Prussian chancellor that, in a new note of November 2nd, he even demanded that Prussia should, in unison with Austria, support the preposterous Polish programme of Lord Castlereagh. Prussia was to demand, either the restoration of the Polish realm of 1771, or the *status quo* of 1791, or at least the partition of Poland by the line of the Vistula ! This "at least" was obviously the true aim of the Hofburg. Prussia's statesmen must indeed be stricken with blindness if they did not even yet observe that Austria was everywhere, in Saxony, in Poland, and on the Rhine, pursuing aims which absolutely conflicted with those of Prussia.

Yet it was still some time before the eyes of the chancellor and of Humboldt were opened. It is astonishing to note how the two able men turned hither and thither in order to avoid seeing what lay obviously before them, the disloyal game played by the Hofburg. Immediately after the receipt of the Austrian note of October 22nd, lively discussions began in the Prussian cabinet. On October 23rd Humboldt put together the leading ideas for an answer to the Austrian note.[1] In this he still speaks quite without mistrust, reiterates all the grounds that favour the annexation of Saxony ; Prussia's claim to compensation based upon the treaties, and the need that " a political demonstration should be given that a prince cannot escape punishment if he act against the interests of the nation to which his people belongs." The treaty of Kalisz and the enlargement of Russia in Poland were undesirable but unavoidable consequences of the situation—" of the false system by which the excessive power of the west was fought by the east. Precisely in order that this might not recur, the powers of Central Europe, and especially Prussia, must be strengthened." Scattered domains in Poland, Germany, or Belgium, did not suffice to effect this strengthening ; the great powers must not be treated as mere numerical values. Consequently the annexation of Saxony was a sacrifice to be made by Austria, not to the Prussian alliance, but on behalf of the European balance of power ; a partition of the country seemed altogether unacceptable. Next Humboldt discussed the Mainz question and declared : " Since we regard the place as necessary for the defence of Germany against France, we have only to demand that Bavaria shall gain no influence over Mainz, unless this state should openly and honourably adhere to the Germanic Federation, and should renounce the right of independent warmaking." This inalienable right of Bavaria as a European power had, during the last few days, been boastingly advocated by Wrede in the committee on the German constitution. Humboldt, however, continued, with imperturbable moderation, that if Bavaria

---

[1] Humboldt's Memorandum regarding Prince Metternich's letter, October 23, 1814.

should exhibit a better sentiment towards the Germanic Federation, " we must endeavour to win over this court instead of regarding it with suspicion." Finally, the question of the Moselle frontier was purely a statistical one ; it could easily be dealt with if Austria should agree to accept the results of Prussian territorial negotiations with the minor German states.

Thus Humboldt continued to see in the Hofburg the loyal but unfortunately somewhat weak friend who must be furnished with reasonable arguments in support of his praiseworthy resolves ; he himself hoped to convert the Bavarians, who were already without concealment preaching war against Prussia ; finally, in order to keep Austria in a good humour, he wished to give up Mainz and to abandon the right bank of the Moselle. The town of Coblenz itself was, indeed, not included in this concession.

Two days later the mood of the Prussian cabinet was already less friendly. It is obvious that in the meanwhile the English and Austrian despatches had been examined more closely, and no doubt something had been learned of the secret intercourse between Gentz and Talleyrand. Perhaps the king himself may have remarked to his diplomats that the agreement of the Hofburg to the annexation of Saxony was a very indefinite one, and that Lord Castlereagh's Polish plans went far beyond Prussia's own wishes. However this may be, a second memorial from Humboldt to Hardenberg[1] displays lively anxiety ; it gives a very striking picture of the brilliant mind of its author, furnishes a broad exposition of the wealth of his ideas, which come to light in mutual opposition, and yet in the end does not effect a plain, clear, and unambiguous utterance. Humboldt has examined Castlereagh's proposals, and now at length propounds the obvious idea that the frontier question and the constitutional question must be kept distinct. It is undesirable to oppose the Polish constitutional plans of the czar ; for " Alexander certainly finds himself in a position of great embarrassment if he wishes to carry out what he appears to have promised to the Poles, and the powers will increase this embarrassment if they fail to offer to his views an opposition which must not be too decisively expressed. Regarded from this point of view, the proposed Polish constitution is perhaps an antidote to the disadvantages which arise from the successful enlargement of Russia." Regarding the frontier question he remarks that hitherto Prussia has

---

[1] Humboldt's Memorial *sur le mémoire de Lord Castlereagh*, October 25, 1814.

never asked more than the line of the Warthe with Thorn and Cracow, and that the occasionally voiced demand for the Vistular frontier has never been seriously made. A prudent moderation is requisite to avoid the danger of " bringing about a breach, and of leading to an appeal to Europe—that is to say, above all, to France against Europe. France will always take advantage of disputes, especially with the aim of rendering perpetual the dissensions between the cabinets, in order to derive a casual profit therefrom, and subsequently to sacrifice us and to come to an understanding with Russia, as soon as the private interests of the French nation have been gratified."

He then turns to consider Prussia's peculiar position. In addition to what Russia offered, Prussia demanded only Thorn and some half-German areas ; Austria, on the other hand, demanded the important Cracow, which the Poles would never surrender. Thus the gain for Austria was incomparably greater, whereas we, on account of more trifling advantages, ran the danger of breaking with Russia, and of finding ourselves in an extremely embarrassing situation. Deserving of very serious consideration, too, was " the manner in which Austria has agreed to the annexation of Saxony. Instead of saying loudly and boldly that the imperial government will defend Prussia's cause against all, she agrees only with reluctance, as if out of complaisance, and wishes us to buy this favour by other and most grievous sacrifices. It must be plainly conceded to be as very doubtful whether we shall not sacrifice the true and permanent interests of Prussia to a purely temporary advantage, if in the Polish affair we go hand in hand with Austria. It must rather be admitted that Prussia would in that case sacrifice her personal interests in the cause of Europe. But Prussia must always act in accordance with principles and must never seek simple convenience." Prussia's demand, he went on, was that, in the establishment of the frontiers claimed by Russia, the allied powers should take into account Prussia's difficult situation ; in such a way that they " should defend the cause of Prussia and of her new acquisitions, openly and vigorously against all other powers ; that they themselves should undertake the task of conscientiously carrying out the treaties which secured for Prussia complete re-establishment and even moderate enlargement of territory ; that, finally, they should agree formally to our occupation of the strip of land without which we should remain dependent upon Russia." If the powers should refuse to give these pledges then, indeed,

Prussia would not follow a policy she herself condemns, but would to her great regret feel compelled "to think first of her own self-preservation." Once more, in conclusion, Prussia must yield in the constitutional question, and must demand only the Warthe line ; should Alexander refuse, the three powers could not conclude any treaty with him, but must leave the question open, and must definitely declare themselves unable to change their views ; but in this case also they must hold as far aloof as possible from France.

It is astonishing to note how this able man again and again rides his horse up to the edge of the ditch, and yet cannot pluck up heart to leap over it. He sees that the alleged allies are following designs altogether different from those of Prussia, that Prussia can in this diplomatic field win nothing of importance for herself ; he perceives the valuelessness of the Austrian promises ; he sees that a struggle between Prussia and Russia would bring advantage to France alone. We imagine, as we read, that the only possible conclusion is on the brink of utterance by the far-sighted thinker. Then an extraordinarily artificial thought-process leads him to the preposterous view that the first and self-evident duty of every Prussian statesman, the duty to safeguard the power of his own country, is a base pre-occupation for "the personal interest of Prussia"! Even this cool head is intoxicated by the hypocritical English phrase of "the cause of Europe"! It is the same superhuman magnanimity, and same over-intellectualised weakness of will, which in our history, with a sinister regularity, invariably follows the great times of bold and incisive activity. The learned Hoffmann, too, contents himself with fruitless complaints regarding the hostility displayed towards Prussia by almost all the other powers.[1] Just as little as Humboldt does he draw the simple conclusion that the oppressive mass of opponents must be shattered, and that an agreement must be come to with at least one of the foreign powers.

Only to good-natured weakness could there still be any doubt as to what was to be expected from Austria. At this very moment, upon the emperor's orders, Metternich, Stadion, and Schwarzenberg assembled in council and determined that in any case Prussia must advance as far as the line of the Vistula. At the same time Metternich informed the czar in confidence that Austria was prepared to yield in the Polish question if Russia would no longer support Prussia's Saxon claims. Alexander

---

[1] Hoffmann's Notes upon his statistical survey, October 30, 1814.

gave Frederick William his definite personal assurance that this offer had been made. Metternich, after his custom, denied everything. Since, however, this offer harmonises precisely with the policy which was subsequently carried out by Austria, we may be certain that on this occasion it was not the czar who was lying.

An unprecedented humiliation was now imminent for the Prussian state, but Frederick William came to the rescue. It was perhaps the most valuable diplomatic resolve of his life. On November 6th he had a prolonged private interview with the czar.[1] The two friends came to an understanding, and the king at length ventured to recommend to his diplomats the policy which he had himself for months regarded as the only safe one. He ordered the chancellor to refrain in future from any hostile steps against Russia. Frederick William had never wished to reacquire the millions of disloyal Poles, and could therefore learn only with hostility how obstinately England and Austria were demanding the Vistular frontier. He knew better than did Hardenberg what obstacles there were to the annexation of Saxony; from confidential personal association he had justly perceived that the czar had at least more upright good feeling towards Prussia than had the good emperor Francis. His straightforward understanding could not conceive why Prussia should run the risks of losing her best ally simply in order to resist at all hazards the fantastic idea of the Russo-Polish kingdom, which would be far more dangerous to Russia herself than to Germany. Now, when he saw his own statesmen vacillating in hopeless confusion, he determined upon personal intervention, and exhibited once more the clear and far-seeing soldier's vision which he had displayed on the day of Kulm, and so often upon the battle-fields of the last winter campaign. It is possible that personal inclination may have played some part, but sober political calculation was here in harmony with his emotional impulses.

Hardenberg was profoundly hurt by the decisive appearance of his royal master upon the scene, and seriously thought of demanding his dismissal; Metternich and Castlereagh endeavoured to strengthen him in this resolve. The king's change of position was immediately taken advantage of by the adroit opponents. The French circulated an effective fable relating that Alexander had talked his friend and himself into an emotional state, and

---

[1] It is possible that this interview took place on November 5th, as Hardenberg reports in his diary, which, however, is often extremely inaccurate.

had then secured the momentous promise from the unsuspecting king. This story found the readier credence among the ill-natured foreign diplomats inasmuch as the king's determination completely disordered all their calculations; since the well-known appearance at the grave of Frederick the Great, everyone knew how much the czar was able to effect in artificially stage-managed emotional scenes. As early as November 7th, Talleyrand triumphantly informed Gentz of the great act of treason of the Prussians, and then gave the word, which was soon repeated by Metternich and Castlereagh, that Prussia had abandoned " the cause of Europe," and that therefore she could not retain Saxony! But this falling away of false friends was not the fault of the king; there can be no doubt that it would have occurred within a few weeks whatever Frederick William had done; and had events been different it would have occurred with the co-operation of the czar himself. It remains the king's service that in face of the inevitable conflict with Austria and the western powers, he secured for Prussia the co-operation of Russia, and thus at least rendered certain a tolerable compensation.

Unfortunately the king did not carry his good work to a conclusion. It sufficed him to have put an end to the breach with Prussia's only ally; after his retiring manner he left the rest to the chancellor. In the conversation above recorded, the monarchs had come to an agreement upon two points alone : since the czar guaranteed the king in the possession of Saxony, Frederick William wished no longer to oppose Alexander's assumption of the crown of Poland, and he rejected the demand for the Vistular frontier made by Austria and England as extreme, and as being disadvantageous to Prussia herself. But opinions diverged widely regarding the future of the territory between the Warthe and the Prosna, and it was certainly Hardenberg's duty to get rid of this boundary question immediately by means of confidential negotiations, to settle all the contested points that still existed between Russia and Prussia, so that these two powers, safeguarded doubtless by binding mutual pledges, might encounter the western powers and the Hofburg with a common programme. The king's definite command had completely changed the situation. The chancellor could no longer play the part of mediator, and must now become a partisan. In view of the disloyal subterfuges of Metternich, the senseless phrases of Castlereagh, and the manifest hostility of Talleyrand and all the minor courts, it was Prussia's duty to think of nothing but her own safety.

The hypocritical charge of "treason to the cause of Europe" had now to be faced.

In addition, however, to the Prosna line already offered by Russia, it was only Thorn and the neighbouring domains of the ancient Ordensland which were indispensable to Prussia. These important positions on the Vistula and their German hinterland must be restored to the great fatherland ; this was an indispensable task of national policy. At the first indefinite news of the proposed reunion, the local governments of Engelsburg and Rheden immediately expressed to the chancellor their cordial delight, relating in moving terms with what indescribable sensations during seven long years they had watched close to their frontier the happiness of the Prussians, and had themselves been forced to bear the yoke of foreign tyranny.[1] The re-acquirement of these loyal German territories was, as the result showed, by no means impossible, although Alexander regarded the fortress of Thorn as one of great value. All that was necessary was to adopt a definite resolve, to renounce the purely Polish areas round Kalisz and Czenstochowa, and, above all, no longer to give any support to Austria's claims upon Cracow. Cracow, if Prussia could acquire the town, would be of inestimable value as a frontier fortress, and also as a market for the Upper Silesian trade ; under the Prussian rule it might be anticipated that this old nursery of German citizenship would soon re-acquire a German stamp. But as things were, it was only Austria and Russia which were disputing for possession of the place ; and why should Prussia prefer the neighbourliness of Austria to that of Russia, or indeed support the claims of the Hofburg to Zamosc and to the flats of the Nida ? As soon as the king had come to a decision, it was essential to secure an immediate understanding with Russia regarding the frontier question.

Hardenberg, however, had already been too greatly influenced by the English and Austrian views, and could not overcome his mistrust of Russia. All his honourable hopes for Germany's future were based upon the "league of the three German great powers." For this reason he even now desired to steer a middle course between the two parties, and the day after the above conversation (November 7th) he wrote confidentially to Castlereagh. He guarded himself, indeed, against saying anything about the king's command, and merely narrated how in the course of the conversation he had gained the conviction that Alexander's Polish

[1] Petition to Hardenberg, November 5, 1814.

crown must be recognised. For Prussia he once again demanded the Warthe line and Thorn ; for Austria, the territory as far as the Nida, Cracow, and Zamosc, although Metternich himself regarded the last-named place as of little value. It was hardly possible to act more maladroitly. The chancellor was trying to sit between two stools. By recognising the kingdom of Poland he gave the Hofburg the desired excuse for complaining of Prussia's treachery ; and at the same time he ran counter to the czar's wishes by demanding a frontier which Russia would not accept.

Nor did Humboldt obey the king's command without remonstrance. In a third memorial, dated November 9th, he drew attention to the danger that by our alliance with Russia Austria would be rendered hostile to Prussia in all German questions :[1] " Since these matters remain the nearest and most important for Prussia, Russia cannot give us any compensation. Repose, balance, and security are no longer conceivable should Prussia, without the most just and important motives, detach herself from her natural political system, an alliance between Austria, Germany, England, and Holland." Again and again the fine dream of German dualism diffused its atmosphere through the minds of the Prussian statesmen. Moreover, a very remarkable reason was discovered by Humboldt's over-acute spirit in favour of Hardenberg's policy ; namely, the circumstance that the two worst enemies of Prussia and of the peace of Europe, France and Bavaria, were also in conflict with Russia ; from this it was deduced, not as ordinary persons would imagine, that Prussia, should she unite with these enemies, would most probably be shamefully betrayed, but conversely that " France and Bavaria would at once lose all interest in the matter as soon as Prussia should adopt the same side as their own in respect of Polish affairs ! "

From such artificial premises were drawn the conclusion that Prussia ought to side openly with England and Austria ; but she must demand that the two powers should in a definite understanding immediately recognise Prussia's just demands, and should in especial guarantee the annexation of Saxony. If it should happen that, contrary to expectation, the powers should refuse to agree to these conditions, " they would then show that they had not the interest of Europe truly at heart, and that they were unwilling to concede to Prussia the energies which the latter requires to preserve her independence ; consequently Prussia would then be justified in detaching herself from them in the face

[1] Humboldt's Memorial upon the Polish question, November 9, 1814.

of Europe, and in carving out a way of her own in unison with Russia."

In truth, a blind devotion to Russia is the very last reproach that can be made to the diplomats of the Prussian chancellery; until the twelfth hour they continued to build upon Austria's friendship. Within a few days it became apparent that neither Austria nor England would give any definite pledges for the re-establishment of Prussia. For some weeks thereafter Hardenberg continued to exhaust himself in fruitless attempts at mediation ; Prussia secured, first of all, on account of her " desertion," nothing more than the hatred which usually accrues in consequence of any change of diplomatic front. But when subsequently the dispute became embittered, it resulted from the nature of things, almost in opposition to the will of the Prussian statesmen, that that grouping of parties which the clear insight of the king had from the first recognised as inevitable, came into existence. On one side were Prussia and Russia ; upon the other Austria, England, all the petty enviers of the growing German state, and as leader of the great conspiracy, France. The Prussian state, bleeding from a thousand wounds, had its king alone to thank for its ability to emerge from such a struggle without complete humiliation.

On November 8th Prince Repnin handed over the Saxon administration to the Prussian plenipotentiaries, General von Gaudy and Minister von Reck. The Leipzig burgomaster Siegmann and the commercial delegates immediately expressed in the name of the town and of the mercantile class their complete confidence, thanking the chancellor for his admirable choice of the higher officials.[1] There was no lack of unedifying disputes, for the northern state with its strict supervision made a sudden entry amid the cobwebs and the dusty traditional institutions of this decayed old feudal administration. Councillor Friese was appointed at the head of financial affairs ; he was one of the finest intelligences of the Prussian officialdom, the same man who in Königsberg had played so effective a part in connection with Stein's reforms. He could not find terms sufficiently strong for the description of the sins of the national economy, which indeed was not more seriously indebted than were the exhausted finances of Prussia, but which had gone to wreck through a lazy,

---

[1] Petition from the commercial delegates of Leipzig to the Chancellor, November 15, Siegmann to Hardenberg, November 16, 1814.

cumbrous, and venial administration ; and Friese came into serious conflict with the members of the Saxon financial college.[1] The Saxon nobles, who had hitherto presided over the department of the general government, had now associated with them bourgeois officials, such as the privy councillor Krüger, a true son of the efficient, relentlessly severe Old Prussian official school, and the Saxon councillor Ferber, an old opponent of the feudal dominion and long abused by the nobles as a demagogue. Consequently great wrath was displayed. The offended nobles regarded the sacred rights of " the Saxon nation " as endangered, for the confusion of personal interests with general interests remains the original sin of the particularist mind. They even brought their troubles before the congress. Stein, whose attitude in quarrels between nobles and " officials " was seldom impartial, found fault with the roughness of the Prussians. The chancellor, however, rejected the complaints with some severity saying : " You cannot make these purely personal differences an affair of the Saxon people, for you can by no means be regarded as representatives of that people."

In Leipzig, reasonable business men soon conceived a confidence in the new strict and just regime ; the value of the treasury bills and of the Saxon bank-notes immediately rose. Gruner, the commercial counsel, thanked the chancellor warmly ·for opposing the regime of the nobles, for in this, said Gruner, is to be found the true reason " of the cumbrousness characteristic of our administration." The head of the great banking house of Reichenbach expressed himself in still more decisive terms.[2] Certainly some of the ancient abuses were dear even to the valiant citizens of Leipzig. The town had hitherto formed almost a state within the state ; it maintained its own town soldiers ; no sovereign troops might appear within its walls ; the town council enjoyed the convenient right of having to account to no one concerning the administration of communal property. Requests were immediately made for the preservation of these privileges. The chancellor, however, dear to him as the town was, could agree merely to the preservation of the old fair-privileges and of a free communal constitution ; he also promised that the necessary new taxes should be imposed only " with the assent of an

[1] Upon this matter we have an express report from Finance Minister von Bülow to the chancellor, dated Berlin, December 8, 1814.

[2] Gruner to Stägemann, November 27, Reichenbach to Hardenberg, November 28, 1814.

assembly of the estates to be elected from the nation," and undertook not to impose a garrison upon the town in time of peace.[1] He went no further. It was impossible that the common law of the monarchical administration should allow oligarchical privileges to persist undisturbed.

There is no doubt that a few mistakes were made in Saxony; in none of our new provinces could the emergence from the narrows of particularism be effected without a certain harshness of touch. The mass of the people, however, notwithstanding their unquestionably particularist sentiments, had no thought of resistance. Von Zeschau, commissary of the government in Wittenberg and subsequently Saxon minister of finance, who possessed a profound knowledge of the situation, declared frankly that it could not be expected "that the Saxon people should completely forget a prince under whose rule they had, until the year 1806, lived very happily"; yet the moderation of the government was finding recognition; certainly no disturbances were to be feared, and the people would soon accustom themselves to the new order.[2] Everyone knows how precisely this prophecy was subsequently fulfilled in the northern half of Saxony. But just because it was so, because it was unquestionable that the country would readily become fused with the Prussian state, the nobles' club in Dresden, the old meeting-place of the high nobility and of the bureaucracy, passionately resisted the threatened loss of their old supremacy. The forest-rangers—almost the only men in the country to whom the old king had displayed his human side, free from the oppression of etiquette—eagerly forwarded the letters of the prisoner and of his agent Marcolini. The uncertainty of the future gave continually fresh nourishment to the intrigues of the junkers. People anxiously looked for every item of news from Vienna, for every hint from Freidrichsfelde. In November, when the Duke of Brunswick passed through Dresden, he regarded it as his duty as a Guelph to speak to everyone about the approaching return of the tribal sovereign. Privy Councillor Krüger immediately noticed how the excitement in the palace increased, and he wrote to the chancellor: " My own office is quaking at the prospect ! "[3]

[1] Hardenberg to Miltitz, December 12, 1814 ; Hardenberg to Bülow, January 25, 1815.

[2] Despatch of Zeschau to von Bülow, provisional chief of the Saxon police, November 18, 1814.

[3] Krüger's Report to Hardenberg, November 29, 1814.

Meanwhile, throughout the camp of the Rhenish Confederates, and loudest of all in Bavaria, there raged a furious paper war, so hopelessly mean in character that the Saxon Carl von Nostitz aptly described it as " pamphleteering incendiarism." These pamphlets, mostly issued by the cabinets themselves or at their instigation, served only to excite the passions of the day and to aggravate the conflict. Here was assembled the entire armoury of poisoned weapons which from that date onwards for a whole generation were directed against Prussia ; there was already manifest the design, which subsequently in the days of the persecution of the demagogues was crowned with so much success, of inspiring the crown of Prussia with suspicion regarding the War of Liberation and its heroes. The Guelph Sartorius here rivalled Adam Müller, the friend of Gentz, the editor of the ultramontane *Tiroler Boten*. The learned historian of Göttingen, when, in the ante-rooms of the diplomats at Vienna he was engaged in confidential intercourse with Gentz, composed under the name of " A Prussian Patriot " the pamphlet *Upon the Union of Saxony with Prussia*. With all the sorrow and shame of a loyal Prussian, he recorded the rumour that blind counsellors wished to besmirch the hands of the king with stolen goods. Corruption was on the watch ; the state stood at the parting of the ways. Was the *suum cuique rapit* once again, as formerly in Silesia, West Prussia, and Hanover, to be the motto of our eagle ? At this juncture, as in every great crisis of our recent history, the *Augsburger Allgemeine Zeitung* was among the enemies of Prussia.

Still more vigorous was the language of Aretin and Hörmann, the two tried catchpoles of Bonapartism, in the *Münchener Alemannia*. Aretin's writing *Saxony and Prussia* exposes the idea which has since then been a favourite notion of our federalists : The inflated Prussian frog must remain a power of the second rank ; should it attain to the first rank, the quiet and the balance of Europe will be destroyed. This is followed by the usual assurance that the Prussian land-hunger aspires also towards Hamburg, Bohemia, and Moravia. Simultaneously from the circles of Montgelas and of the Bavarian government was issued a pamphlet *Prussia and Germany* which after a flood of invective made a solemn appeal to " the Saxons, Rhinelanders, and Mainzers " to defend their freedom against the talons of the Prussian eagle. The climax of this literature was found in the *Sächsische Aktenstücke aus der Dresdener umgeschrieben Zeitung*, secretly printed in Bavaria— this was a falsification of so preposterous a character that we find it difficult to understand to-day how it could ever have found any credulous readers. Here Duke Ernest of Coburg intercedes on behalf of his imprisoned relative in a touching epistle which had plainly been composed by La Besnardière upon Talleyrand's orders. The Prussian generals (York, Bülow, Kleist, Gneisenau, and Massenbach) write a threatening address to the chancellor, demanding, with rattling of sabres, the immediate annexation of Saxony ; and saying " where would the Prussian monarchy be if we had blindly obeyed the pusillanimous cabinet ? " In a memorial Hardenberg warns the king of the unbridled spirit that prevails in the army, and of the dangerous intrigues of those secret societies which had been so useful in the struggle against Napoleon. Wilhelm Humboldt writes triumphantly to Niebuhr pointing out that the Prussians have well understood how to follow the example of the robber nation of the Romans, so magnificently depicted by the great historian himself : " Nothing now stands in our way but Bavaria with its iron ministry ! " In face of such feats of Bavarian Bonapartism, the trifling manifestations in Saxony itself seemed tame and harmless. From Saxony came a pitiful " appeal to all the German nations," an anonymous pamphlet issued at the publishing house of " St. Land-Hunger," a few letters by officials and barristers, with repeated assurances that the writers took up their pens only out of " inward conviction "— that is all. Even the few pamphlets favourable to annexation that appeared in Saxony, displayed the same character of political decadence. Nowhere is there a great national outlook ; nothing but petty bourgeois complaints of the misdeeds of the noble nepotists and of the bigotry of the Catholic court—how different was it in Prussia, where princesses and burghers' wives alike wore the order of Louise, and where all the religious parties enjoyed the royal justice !

Even foreign newspapers began to intervene in the party quarrel, and all of them against Prussia. Since the tory cabinet at first appeared favourable to the Prussian claims, the whigs, in accordance with the old rule of English party tactics, eagerly took the side of the imprisoned king, alike in parliament and the press, and they were supported by public opinion. During the last two generations the English nation has been just as hostile as the French to the strengthening of the German North, although the English have not made so much noise about the matter. At that time it was the English view that her dearest commercial interests were threatened by Prussia ; Leipzig, a leading centre of British trade, must not be allowed to enter into a customs-union with a great state. In holy anger, the whig orators denounced the cunning attacks of the despots against " the Saxon nation," and with the same sublime enthusiasm the union of Genoa with Piedmont was stigmatised as the death-blow to Italian freedom. The French press adhered like one man to Napoleon's faithful ally. On November 7th, before Paris had received news of Frederick William's decisive step, the semi-official *Quotidienne* openly announced the programme of the Bourbon Confederation of the Rhine. The government of the most Christian king was perhaps the only one in Europe which could count upon the support of a unanimous popular vote. " The justified greatness of France, the legitimate and inalienable strength of the country, is found in its adoption of the fine role of defender of the oppressed and protector of the weak, or armed guarantor of the sacredness of treaties " ; for this reason there must be demanded the complete independence of Poland, which as a state already in existence required merely to be established on a firmer foundation, there must be unrestricted sovereignty for the German states, respect for the national individuality of the Saxons, of the Bavarians, and of the other German peoples ; " then a free and strong Confederation will for ever separate the French arms from the arms of Austria and Prussia."

The *Rheinische Merkur* valiantly resisted the full-voiced chorus of the Rhenish Confederates, and was for this reason spoken of by the journalists of Montgelas as the Thersites of the German newspapers. Görres in his figurative language issued warnings against the basilisk eggs of the Gallic cock. But not even in these circles was there any assured understanding of the great problem of power. The *Merkur* opened its columns not to friends alone, but also to the moderate opponents of the Prussian claims. Among these must be reckoned Jacob Grimm, who, delighted at the return of his Hessian electoral prince, desired the like joy for the Saxons. An impassioned article begged the sons of Germania to spare Saxony, " the more spiritual brother, who has studied alone "—as if this brother could not have continued his studies undisturbed under Prussian tutelage ! The literary defence of Prussian policy was, on the whole, conducted only by men who stood near to the government. At the request of the chancellor, Varnhagen published a pamphlet, as superficial as everything else which this political dilettantist wrote about affairs of state, full of empty phrases concerning " the spirit of liberalism which animated Prussia's endeavours." Arndt, Eichhorn, and J. G. Hoffmann wrote more seriously and more worthily. The statistician's *Prussia and Saxony*, written with a quiet modesty, gives an eloquent answer to the fashionable complaints concerning Prussian arrogance. Never, says Hoffmann frankly, had Prussia been so unanimously abused by the German world as in the days of the laws of Stein and Hardenberg ; yet good must preponderate in the Prussian state, for the nation had made such memorable sacrifices for the re-establishment of this abused community. This cool-headed and documented demonstration of the faults of the imprisoned king, aroused such bitterness in Friedrichsfelde, that the Saxon minister, Count Einsiedel, was audacious enough to demand that the Prussian government should suppress Hoffmann's work ; naturally the note was returned to him.

By far the most important work produced during this paper war was Barthold Niebuhr's pamphlet *Prussia's Right against the Saxon Court*. In general, it may be said to be the most notable production of the German publicists at this epoch, combining as it does, Arndt's noble passion and rhetorical fire with the wealth of ideas and the wide political knowledge of Friedrich Gentz. How freely and boldly does the great historian expound the two central ideas of our national policy, never before expressed with the same clarity, but which since then have become part of the very tissue of all noble-minded Germans. He shows that a great nation, conscious of its own unity, must punish as felony a desertion of the national cause, even when the traitor has not infringed any written law. "The community of nationality is higher than the relationships of state which unite or separate the different peoples belonging to a single stock." Then, with the certainty of the seer, he prophesies that the days of German particularism are numbered : weak communities, those which are unable to maintain themselves by their own energies, "cease to be states." Such are the views forced upon this conservative thinker, who, within a year of the battle of Leipzig, sees the German petty princes once more following the banner of France. In the confidential exchange of letters among the Prussian diplomats, their disquiet concerning the revival of particularism finds even sharper expression. Alopeus wrote to Humboldt : "The very men who after the battle of Leipzig were crying out 'serves him right,' are now expressing their compassion for the pious king; and the Bourbons, who in June had their work cut out to keep their own heads above water, have now energy to spare for the preservation of others. One is almost carried away by one's anger to see that the very German emperor who was so scandalously abandoned by his vassals, now receives in the imperial town, with all the honours due to sovereigns, this crowd of vassals besmirched with the crime of treason-felony. We ask ourselves what can be the hidden aim of a condescension which there is no need to display ? "

Naturally neither the wrathful words of Niebuhr, nor the reasoned considerations of Hoffmann exercised any influence upon the course of the congress. It had been the hope of Austria, in conjunction with England and Prussia, to drive the czar into a corner, and then to come to an understanding with Russia over Prussia's head. This plan had now been frustrated by the king's intervention, and Metternich immediately altered his tactics. To him, as to the French, the Saxon question was far more important than the future of Poland. As early as November 11th, in conversation with Castlereagh and Hardenberg, he took back the word he had given to the chancellor, and declared that the general resistance to the annexation of Saxony was invincible, and that at least Dresden and the southern portion of the country must be restored to the imprisoned prince. In this way the idea of the partition of Saxony, which in the summer had already been mooted by Stadion to the negotiators of Frederick Augustus, was at length openly declared to be the aim of Austrian policy. The Hofburg was quite unconcerned at the contemplation of this arbitrary disruption of the old Saxon community, at the disturbance of its customary channels of intercourse by the institution of new customs-barriers. The intention of Austria was simply to re-establish the faithful House of the Albertines in a position where it would be a nuisance to Prussia, and at the same time to keep a sore open in the body of the Prussian friend. Since the Lorrainers themselves had never attempted to awaken an Austrian national sentiment among the immediate subjects of their house, they naturally had no understanding whatever of the nation-building energy of the Prussian monarchy ; it was their hope that partitioned Saxony would become for Prussia a second Poland. Emperor Francis said confidentially to the duke of Weimar : " Now, now, what are you worrying about ? If the country is partitioned, it will soon come together again."

Hardenberg decisively rejected Metternich's proposal, and himself suggested that the Albertines should be compensated, not by the Legations, but by a portion of Catholic Westphalia. In Vienna he had at length noticed that Austria desired to retain for herself the northern portion of the Pontifical State, and hoped that this offer would render the Hofburg more compliant. No one in all Germany had at that time drawn the attention of the Prussian statesmen to what was signified by handing over the two fortresses of Romanism in the German north, Münster and Paderborn, as an independent state, into the hands of a bigoted Catholic princely house. By all the free spirits of that generation, the Holy See was lightly esteemed and was regarded as utterly powerless, whilst by the romanticists it was admired as an enemy of the revolution. On the other hand, the patriots recognised very justly that, in accordance with Hardenberg's latest proposal, which was unquestionably rendered inevitable by the course of the diplomatic discussions, the Saxon negotiations lost much of their national significance. If the most faithful of Napoleon's vassals was to be re-established upon German soil, the question was whether he should receive the passes of the Erzgebirge, or a portion of Lower Saxony. No doubt this question was still one of considerable importance in relation to Prussia's military power, but it could no longer count upon awakening the warm interest of the general public. Even Arndt admitted that, henceforward, the Saxon problem was to him a matter of indifference. Metternich declared that this plan also was extremely unsatisfactory, and repeated with increasing definiteness that nothing but the restoration to the prisoner of a portion of his territory could appease the profound discontent of the German princes.

England, also, withdrew from her pledged word. Castlereagh now reaped the fruits of his arrogant presumption. He had offered the greatest affronts to the czar ; and since Prussia refused to take part any longer in the diplomatic campaign against Russia, the logic of facts threw the English statesmen upon the side of that power which was most decisively attacking Prussia and Russia. As early as November 15th, the fairly honourable Charles Stewart came to Stein and complained, full of distress and shame, that the English were forced to throw themselves into the arms of France ! The dread of the British cabinet before the angry speeches of the parliamentary opposition, and the sympathy of the prince regent for the imprisoned king, accelerated the change of front. Castlereagh received orders from home that he should completely abandon the Prussian cause, and such was his thickheadedness that he never clearly perceived the treacherous character of this abandonment. Even in parliament, the noble lord, when excusing his change of sentiment, could only say that public opinion in Germany was definitely unfavourable to the annexation of Saxony—surely a remarkable opinion to find expression in the mouth of this high tory, who in all other respects displayed the utmost contempt for the wishes of the people.

Nothing but Castlereagh's stupidity and Metternich's cunning can explain how it was that England and Austria should now suddenly declare all that to be black which they had previously proclaimed to be white. The Polish crown of Alexander, which they had so long contested, now appeared to them to be a " snare " which the czar had set for his own hurt ; the annexation of Saxony, which both of them had accepted in dubious words, was now regarded by them as a grave infringement of international law. It had been recognised that Russia could not be diverted from her Polish plans without a war ; " the Polish affair," wrote Gagern on December 1st, " is nearly finished from lack of fighters." All the more securely did Metternich reckon upon the frustration of the Prussian claims, which were far less strongly supported. He was now fully in unison with Talleyrand, and in conjunction with the Frenchman he examined and approved the formulation of new securities for justice on behalf of the imprisoned king.

Delighted at such success, Talleyrand's demands became daily more exacting. He made Dalberg and La Besnardière compose an apology for the Albertine. He assured the faithful Gagern that France would never again tolerate the Prussians on the left bank of the Rhine, nor yet in Saxony. A " Memorial concerning Saxony from the French Point of View " enumerated Prussia's sins against the German fatherland : the peace of Basle, the principal resolution of the Diet of Deputation, the neutrality of 1805, all sins from the French point of view ! The *Moniteur* solemnly announced : " The only prince who might perhaps have the right of condemning Frederick Augustus, the king of France, discharges the accused." The article went on to speak enthusiastically of eternal dismemberment as the glorious characteristic of the German nation : " In the German character we find a strong adhesion to sacred customs ; the most sacred of these is obedience to particular princes."

These *princes particuliers* were in full accord with the *Moniteur's* philosophy of history. Upon Talleyrand's demand they were ready to sign a common protest against the annexation of Saxony, and nothing prevented the undertaking but a warning from the czar. For every one of the petty princes, Talleyrand had alluring promises ready, and each one of them hoped to gain at least a thousand souls at the great territorial market of Vienna. The sentiment of German particularism found faithful expression in the numerous memorials of the Landgrave of Hesse-Homburg, which expounded the luminous thesis that " since all the neighbouring powers had been enlarged," so also must Homburg be enlarged in order not to decline from her historical position of power, and it was absolutely necessary that she should annex the villages of Ober-Ursel and Ober-Rossbach ! Von Türkheim, the envoy of Darmstadt, even ventured, amid this high legitimist society, to base the claims of his serene master for compensation upon a formal appeal to the inalienable *droits de l'homme*.[1] If Talleyrand's plans should prove successful, if Prussia should receive compensation neither upon the Rhine nor in Saxony, there would remain more land available to satisfy the desires of the petty princes ; for this reason, all, without exception, were upon the side of France, and the conquered enemy once more appeared to them as the powerful protector of Germany.

The wretched dispute about Saxony brought all the other labours of the congress to a stand-still. The committee upon the German constitution had already broken up some time before, with nothing accomplished. In the interim, pitiful personal disputes were rife. Metternich, endeavouring to arouse suspicion of the Prussian chancellor in the mind of Alexander, laid before the czar the anti-Russian note which Hardenberg had written at the opening of the congress—and in general made all the mischief he could. Notwithstanding these proofs of Austrian friendship, the chancellor allowed himself to be persuaded by Metternich to intermediate once more between Russia on the one hand and England and Austria on the other. On November 23rd, he made the old demands : the line of the Warthe for Prussia, Cracow and Zamosc for Austria—although by the king's command he was pledged not to separate himself from Russia. Fortunately Stein came to his assistance. This great man had perceived in the meanwhile that he had taken too one-sided a course in opposing the Polish plans of the czar. In accordance with his frank and admirable manner, he immediately determined to atone for the previous error, and at once devoted all his energies to saving Saxony

---

[1] Memorial of the hereditary prince of Homburg to Humboldt ; of Türkheim to Hardenberg (January and February, 1814).

for Prussia. It was through his good offices that Alexander's answer was comparatively favourable. On November 27th, the czar declared that he would never abandon his Prussian ally, who had supported him "so energetically, nobly, and enduringly." He demanded the whole of Saxony for Prussia, Mainz for the Germanic Federation ; of his Polish claims he abandoned Thorn and Cracow, which were both to be recognised as neutral free towns.

This declaration solved the Mainz problem. Metternich renounced the design of handing over the fortress to Bavaria, for in opposition to this plan Russia and Prussia were in unison with the particularist envy of the petty princes. Hardenberg would not entrust the key of Rhineland to faithless hands ; the petty princes, on their side, were afraid, as the Würtemberg plenipotentiaries expressed it, that a strong state in possession[1] of Mainz " would subordinate the destiny of all the other German states to its own." Thus an expedient was adopted which, however unnatural and absurd it might be, was nevertheless in a sense a necessary outcome of the chaotic conditions of the Germanic Federation. The golden Mainz, once the seat of the most distinguished of German princes, was subjected to the supremacy of the grand-duke of Darmstadt, because this potentate could never be a danger to his neighbours ; the fortress was occupied by the Germanic Federation with an Austro-Prussian garrison. Here, at any rate, Prussia was to keep a foot in the stirrup. No one foresaw the unending dispute which was to result from the joint occupation with Austria ; people still cherished the dream of a peaceful dualism. Just as artificial was the Russian proposal to make Thorn and Cracow free towns ; it was inevitable that a republic of Cracow would be the focus of an extremely dangerous Polish propaganda, dangerous especially to Austria. For the moment, however, the only thought of the Hofburg was to secure that the dominant position on the Upper Vistula should not serve as a frontier fortress for the Russians. Metternich raised little objection to the plan.

The Polish negotiations now offered little further difficulty, especially since Alexander dropped the idea of uniting Lithuania and Poland, and demanded merely the Warsaw territory for the new Polish kingdom. To the complaints of Czartoryski he replied indeed, with the secret consolation that this mutilated kingdom was merely *une pierre d'attente*. Nevertheless, the Saxon

[1] Wintzingerode and Linden to Hardenberg, December 8, 1814.

question remained henceforward the only serious point in dispute among the powers. More and more violent became the general opposition to the Prussian plans. In his perplexity, the chancellor determined upon one of the greatest diplomatic mistakes of his life. Upon December 3rd he wrote to Metternich an incredible letter, which was to touch the good heart of his Austrian friend through its moving expressions. " Dear Prince, save Prussia from her present difficulties," and he added some turgid verses from the *Rheinische Merkur*, inviting the double eagle to be good enough to build its eyrie side by side with the black eagle of Prussia upon the same giant oak !

In a confidential note of December 10th, Metternich replied with scarcely concealed disdain. He now officially withdrew his formal consent, and offered his Prussian friend no more than a fifth of Saxon territory, a portion of Lusatia with somewhat over 400,000 inhabitants : if the Albertine were not to receive his crown back, the Germanic Federation could not come into existence, and France would regain the protectorate of the petty states. Whilst he himself thus warned Prussia of the French intrigues, on December 16th, upon the command of Emperor Francis, he showed this confidential note to Talleyrand, in order that King Louis might learn " how complete was the harmony of views " between Austria and France in the Saxon question ! The faithlessness of the Hofburg was manifested so unashamedly as to lead the honourable Görres to write angrily that Prussia need merely print the two Austrian notes of October 22nd and December 10th side by side for all right-minded people to see that she was in the right. Hardenberg had fallen as if from the clouds. " Non fidem servavit," he wrote despairingly in his diary when recording the receipt of this " totally unexpected answer." [1] He saw very well that the opinion of right-minded people amounted to nothing in this struggle for power. To the Austrians, in a joint note with Alexander dated December 16th, he expressed his profound astonishment at the change of sentiment of the Hofburg, and since his Westphalian plan of compensation did not find acceptance, he now proposed that a portion of territory on the left bank of the Rhine, with Treves and Bonn, should be provided for Frederick Augustus. To-day, no one can fail to recognise the preposterous nature of this proposal, which was the outcome merely of the most painful embarrassment : to establish the Albertine close to the French frontier would simply open for the

---

[1] Hardenberg's Diary, December 10 and 12, 1814.

French a convenient gate of attack upon Germany. But when Metternich immediately detected the weak side of the Prussian proposal and unctuously rejoined that the left bank of the Rhine must never again be thus exposed to the French, he was only playing with words, being himself already in cordial understanding with this dreaded land of France. In order to divide his opponents, Hardenberg simultaneously demanded that Bavaria should restore the Franconian margravates. This was an unfortunate move, although the blustering ill-nature of the Bavarian statesmen merited chastisement. It is true that the chancellor had not yet ceded Ansbach-Bayreuth in a formal treaty, but he had on several occasions verbally declared that he was prepared to accept the duchy of Berg as compensation. By now reopening the old dispute, without the remotest prospect of success, he gave a welcome excuse to Metternich, Wrede, and Talleyrand to complain of " Prussian trickery." He closed his note with the assurance that Prussia still counted above all upon the support of Russia and Austria.

In reality both parties were already weighing the possibility of a war. Among the Prussian people embitterment was manifestly increasing. An address from Berlin placed the forces of the country at the king's disposal for the justified struggle. Stägemann sang wrathfully :

> "The flag of Brandenberg, my song,
>   Streams on the breeze once more,
> And once again our wrath is stirred,
>   Seize steel like those of yore ! . . .
> The dogs of France, from our last chase,
>   Their wounds still gape amain—
> On, Lightning-blast, on, Lance and Mace,
>   Fierce hounds with leash astrain ! "

It was learned from Goltz[1] that the French army was being quietly strengthened, upon Talleyrand's advice. It was reported that there was a plan that the Saxon troops which were to the north of the Moselle, under Prussian command, should at the chosen moment be united with the Bavarian and Austrian forces upon the right bank of the Moselle. Among the Austrian generals, Schwarzenberg displayed the most cheerful confidence of victory, for in the last war he had learned enough to despise the mean intelligence of Blucher and Gneisenau. On December 16th,

[1] Goltz's Reports from Paris, November 24 and December 19, 1814.

Metternich disclosed to Count Münster his intention to form a Germanic Federation without Prussia, unless Prussia should abandon her Saxon claims ; of course Austria was to demand merely the modest position of first among equals. The Guelph statesman immediately recognised that this would mean war and the dissolution of the congress ; he was ready for anything, although the Austrian greed of power and the unfavourable geographical situation of Hanover caused him some anxiety, and he demanded from England the prolongation of the subsidies-treaty in order that the Guelph army might be equipped.

The Prussian Minister of War at once took measures for resistance. On December 26th Grolman sent the chancellor the plan of campaign he had drawn up in conjunction with Boyen, Gneisenau, and Schöler.[1] In accordance with the good old Frederician manner, two great armies were to open the campaign simultaneously by a bold offensive in Saxony and on the Rhine, whilst an observation corps protected Silesia. The situation was so threatening that all ordinary considerations of military precedence were disregarded, and Blucher and Gneisenau were recommended as commanders of the respective armies ; after these two Bülow was the only general to be considered, since York, Kleist, and Tauentzien were no more than excellent leaders of army corps. Colonel Krauseneck, who commanded the Prussian garrison in Mainz under the Austrian governor Frimont, received orders that, at the first sign, he should seize the fortifications on the right bank ; they would be sufficient to hold the place in check, but his modest force would not suffice for the occupation of the whole fortress. Boyen also had the other fortresses secretly equipped. The Saxon troops on the Rhine were quietly moved northward, into the vicinity of Prussian regiments. Boyen assumed that the smaller North German contingents, with the exception of the Hanoverians, must all follow the Prussian flag. The monarchy was determined to make its appearance immediately as master of North Germany ; who, in such a struggle for existence, could pay any attention to the outcries and the claims for sovereignty of the petty princes ?

Amid this general confusion, Talleyrand saw his harvest ripening. After Metternich had officially communicated to him the last Austrian note concerning Saxony, the Frenchman considered himself justified in intervening officially in the Saxon negotia-

[1] Grolman to Hardenberg, December 29, 1814, with a memorial upon the plan of operations.

tions, and answered his Austrian friend on December 19th. Since, he said, the Polish problem had become a mere question of frontier, the Saxon affair was now the matter of greatest importance to Europe from the point of view of principle. Here the principles of legitimacy and of the balance of power were both at stake. To-day the detestable doctrine was diffused that kings could be sentenced, that the punishment of confiscation could be reintroduced, that the nations could be divided like the herds of a dairy farm, that there was no such thing as public law, " that everything was just for the stronger." But Europe execrated these doctrines ; " they arouse the like detestation in Vienna, St. Petersburg, London, Madrid, and Lisbon " (not, that is to say, in Berlin). The annexation of Saxony would also destroy the balance of power in Europe, introducing into the Germanic Federation " an offensive power of incomparable strength." For this reason the legitimate king must be restored ; if certain cessions of territory were unavoidable for the compensation of Prussia, France would advise the legitimate ruler in this sense.

By this note, Talleyrand tore up the secret article of the treaty of Paris, and threw the fragments at the feet of the four powers. Whilst for a long time he had worked counter to the treaty in obscurity, he now entered into the territorial negotiations with an official memorial, into those negotiations from which by treaty France had been excluded, and he supported the Austrian proposal for the partition of Saxony—although this did not prevent him in the same breath from expressing the execration of Europe for the policy of partition. A second note from the Frenchman to Castlereagh (December 26th) assumed the tone of legitimist unction which was irresistible to the high tory. The aim of the congress was " to close the revolution " ; formerly republic and monarchy were fighting one another, to-day it was a struggle between the revolutionary and the legitimist dynasties; the revolutionary dynasties had disappeared with one exception, that which ruled in Naples, and the legitimist dynasties had been all re-established with one exception, that of the unfortunate king of Saxony; " consequently the revolution was not yet concluded " ; France expected that the congress would fulfil its duty. The proceedings of the next few days showed that France's breach of the treaty was extremely welcome alike to the Austrian and to the English statesmen. The three powers were at one. As early as December 14th, Metternich regarded the coming triple alliance as so sure, that he told the Saxon agent Schulenburg to write to his royal master that Saxony was rescued !

Since these formless negotiations led to nothing, it was finally determined that the Committee of Four should be summoned once more, and that the territorial questions should be ceremonially laid before the forum of the four allied great powers. On December 29th the committee reassembled. As was to be expected, the course of the proceedings was as follows. Everyone was agreed about Mainz ; everyone was agreed about the principal point in the Polish affair ; it was only the Saxon problem regarding which nothing had been settled. A new note from Hardenberg to Metternich (December 29th) asked of the opponents : " Is Prussia to have the necessity forced upon her of striving in the future for enlargement ? " This aroused a storm of indignation, for the justice of the reproach was perceived. A memorial from Stein (December 20th) served only to strengthen the Austrian minister in his views. Stein declared that a re-established Saxony would be as great a source of dissension in the north as was Bavaria in the south ; he did not realise that the Hofburg desired nothing more ardently than this North German Bavaria.

The secret aims of Austria were displayed already in the first sitting of the Committee of Four, when Metternich demanded that Talleyrand should be admitted to the committee ; at the same time he declared that the Saxon question could not be decided without the approval of Frederick Augustus. This meant that the Albertine was to be made master of the situation. Castlereagh would not go so far as this, but he also advocated the admission of the French minister. According to the Englishman's wonderful logic, the admission of France was necessary " because, in accordance with the secret article of the treaty of Paris, the treaties of Kalisz and Reichenbach are legally binding upon France as well "—and yet this very article expressly excluded France from all co-operation in the territorial negotiations. These demands were repeatedly and strongly opposed by Russia and Prussia ; they did not desire to admit Frederick Augustus in any circumstances, and they were willing to admit Talleyrand to the committee only after the four powers had come to an agreement. Bitter expressions, and even serious threats, were exchanged. It was under the influence of this passionate scene that Castlereagh first hit upon the unhappy idea for which the way had been paved for months by Talleyrand through agitation and incitement. He secretly proposed a war alliance between England, Austria, France, and their smaller well-wishers. It is essentially futile to demand the motives that actuated such a mind as his. The noble lord was what his countrymen speak of as *stubborn ;* with a blind ardour the English bull charged upon the red cloth of the Saxon question which Metternich and Talleyrand, the adroit matadors, waved before his eyes. Moreover, Castlereagh had just received news that in Ghent England had concluded peace with the United States, and that the English armies were therefore free. There was not indeed a single interest in the world which could lead the English state into war with Prussia ; but for many weeks the diplomats had been working up their indignation against the country which was supposed to have betrayed the cause of Europe, and once again the fire laid by "the dogs of France" was about to burst out into bright flames. Even Gagern, seeking excuse for the British frenzy, could find nothing more to say than : " The pot boiled over."

Whilst Metternich was discussing with the western powers an attack upon the Prussians, the social intercourse of the diplomatic world was pursued with undisturbed serenity. The good emperor Francis played the host with the accustomed loyal good-nature to those princely guests whom he hoped to stab in the back. As late as January 2nd, Metternich wrote " to his dear prince " Hardenberg a friendly note, inviting him on the ground of urgent business to postpone that day's sitting until the morrow.[1] A few hours later, he came personally to visit the chancellor for a consultation regarding the article about Thorn and Cracow. The reports of the sitting of January 3rd record only that Austria, in general agreement with the Russian proposals, demanded an increase in the Austrian share of Poland. On the same day on which the course of affairs was so decisive, Metternich signed with Castlereagh and Talleyrand a war-alliance against Prussia and Russia. The wording of this remarkable treaty was no less obscure than were the intentions of its originators ; there was good reason for shunning the light. " In consequence of recently published claims," the three powers pledged themselves mutually to support one another with at least 150,000 men, in case any one of them should be attacked or threatened on account of the just and proper proposals they had brought forward in common ; an attack upon Hanover or the Netherlands was to be regarded as tantamount to an attack upon England. At the same time it was

---

[1] Metternich to Hardenberg, January 2, 1815.

the purpose of the three powers " to complete the proposals of the treaty of Paris in the manner which would express as fully as possible its true purpose and spirit." Other powers, especially the Netherlands and Hanover, were to be invited to co-operate. Thus, in order to carry into effect the treaty of Paris, which refused France any right to intervene in the territorial questions, Austria and England concluded an alliance with France! The treaty spoke only of a defensive alliance; its real object was offensive. For should any opposition be offered to the " recently published claims," the status of Prussia in Saxony must first be attacked. In addition, a secret article contained the definite threat that if Bavaria, Hanover, or the Netherlands would not accept the invitation, they would " lose every right to the advantages which they might claim in virtue of the present treaty."

In the view of its prime originator, Talleyrand, the unquestionable intention of the alliance was to attack exhausted Prussia with an overwhelming force, and to overthrow her newly acquired position as a great power. The Frenchman stood at the goal of his desires. He said with perfect justice, " I have gained for France a position which could hardly have been secured by fifty years of fortunate negotiations "; and he sent for General Ricard from Paris, to discuss with Schwarzenberg and Wrede the plan of campaign for the ensuing spring. Troops were already assembled in Bohemia, Wrede boasted of certain victory, but Münster displayed the spirit of this incomparably disloyal policy by the frivolous exclamation, "We are playing a game *en trois ;* if the enemy is beaten we shall then quarrel with one another." Henceforward, Stein was never willing to repose any confidence in the Guelphs. In Friedrichsfelde a breath of relief was drawn. The imprisoned king gave his brother Antony full power to assume the regency in Saxony as soon as the army of the triple alliance should enter the kingdom, and received from the prince the joyful message : " My brother-in-law Francis will not treat our neighbours very graciously ! " Count Schulenburg looked for the speedy approach of the happy days when Prussia's power should have fallen, and Hanover should assume the leadership of the north—a prophecy in which may be readily recognised the echo of Guelph boasts.

The compact of January 3rd had long-enduring indirect consequences. It reintroduced France into the society of states, and founded between the western powers that widely celebrated *entente cordiale* which has since then, broken only by brief intervals, persisted down to our own days. At the court of Vienna, it led to the revival of Choiseul's idea of an alliance between the Catholic great powers, a policy which henceforward never failed to find powerful friends at the Hofburg. At the same time it foreshadowed a natural grouping of the powers, a grouping that was sure of a great future: on the one side, the western powers, Austria and the Porte; on the other, the young states, Prussia, Russia, and the United States of America. Finally, Prussia learned what was to be expected from Austria, even under the ægis of peaceful dualism. Hardenberg, indeed, magnanimously and all too soon, forgot the " unhappy precipitation " of his Austrian friends; but among the younger and more vigorous men of governmental circles, the memory of this breach of faith long remained active. The ancient and glorious Frederician traditions once more secured courageous recognition; and Eichhorn, the statesman who in the subsequent long and quiet years of peace was to pursue with caution the policy of the great king, Eichhorn the principal founder of the customs-union, took part in the Saxon negotiations with his incisive pen, and formed his judgment upon Austria from his experience of the congress of Vienna.

There exists, however, an ultimate stage of folly, which in an orderly society of states cannot permanently be surpassed. Hardly had the treaty been signed when Castlereagh came to ask himself how he could face parliament with so utterly un-English a policy. Had England been fighting against the French power for a quarter of a century, in order that now 150,000 of Napoleon's veterans should once more cross the Rhine under the banner of the lilies? In Vienna, notwithstanding Talleyrand's denials, the Bonapartist sentiments of the French army were well known. Was the peace which had only been attained at the cost of bloody struggles to be disturbed once more—for the sake of one of Napoleon's satraps? The criminal folly of such an undertaking began to enter the Englishman's understanding; and even Metternich was concerned at the loud jubilation of the French and of the Rhenish Confederates. During the following weeks, Sardinia, Bavaria, Hanover, and Darmstadt joined the alliance of January 3rd, and the inertia of the Orange government was so great as to lead to the tragi-comic result that the Netherlands did not formally join the war alliance against Prussia until April —at a moment when the world had for some time been metamorphosed once more by Napoleon's return, and when Prussia's army was already on the way to defend the Netherlands against France. But in truth the alliance was still-born, and a real danger of war existed for six days only.

Already in the sitting of January 9th, Austria and England, upon Castlereagh's instigation, took the first step towards reconciliation. They gave a formal declaration that the negotiations about Saxony had as their sole purpose to provide for the Prussian state the compensation promised by treaty, and that, for this reason, the decision was in no way dependent upon the assent of Frederick Augustus. It was upon this condition alone that Prussia and Russia agreed to the now unavoidable participation of the French minister in the negotiations. On January 12th, Talleyrand took his place in the council of the great powers. The Committee of Four became enlarged to a Committee of Five, and these five constituted the real congress.[1] The illustrious assembly had taken four months to constitute itself! The overwhelming strength of the five great powers was manifested in face of all opposition. Now even Talleyrand did not find the hegemony of the great powers incompatible with " public law " ; not a word did he now utter of the fine-sounding reasons with which, at the beginning of the congress, he had defended the equal rights of all the states of Europe.

The Prussian statesmen, too, began to recognise that some concessions were necessary. They did not, indeed, know anything at all about the compact of January 3rd. When the frontier negotiations made no advance, the Prussian plenipotentiaries, on one occasion, threatened the Netherlands minister, Nagell, that if Holland continued to prove intractable, Prussia would join herself to France. The Dutchman, triumphing over the unsuspecting ignorance of the Prussians, immediately reported this threat to his English friends—so little was Hardenberg's chancellery aware that the war-alliance of the opponents had already been concluded. But the Prussians had long recognised that war was possible ; among numerous other threatening signs, there now came the definite news that England and Austria, upon Talleyrand's instigation, were endeavouring to induce the Porte to make an attack upon Russia. It could no longer be ignored that the annexation of Saxony could probably be secured only at the cost of a European war. Was the question whether the Albertine was to establish himself in Münster, Treves, or Dresden,

---

[1] Thus writes Humboldt in his manuscript *Systematic Description of the Proceedings of the Congress of Vienna*, June 15, 1815.

of sufficient importance, for it to be necessary on that account to summon the exhausted nation once more to arms ? The well-meaning men of the Prussian chancellery could not fail to be overcome at times by sentiments of patriotic shame when they looked back upon the lamentable course of the congress ; four months of unceasing disputes, and yet not a single positive gain for Germany ! So high did this discontent rise in the disillusioned nation, that even Goethe on one occasion descended wrathfully from his Olympian repose. On January 2nd, one of the Jena papers published a poem by the old master in which he declared that the congress had wasted its time in junketing, but had done nothing to establish the fatherland on a secure foundation—and, having delivered himself of this censure, the old man went imperturbably to the jubilee festival to wish happiness to the "worthy and upright" Frankenberg, the minister of Gotha. Varnhagen assures us that the distinguished contempt expressed by the poet made a profound impression upon the best of the German diplomats : they realised even more painfully than before that as yet nothing whatever had been effected. Was the congress, which had been summoned in order to secure a permanent ordering for this distracted corner of the world, to end with a new European war ?

Hardenberg speedily recognised that he could not accept such a responsibility. On January 12th, in the sitting of the Five, he still, indeed, demanded the whole of Saxony ; but secretly he had for several days been discussing with the faithful Hoffmann whether it was not desirable to renounce a portion of Saxony, and on January 13th he drew up a *Plan très-confidentiel*, wherein he admitted the possibility that 840,000 of the inhabitants of Saxony should be restored to Frederick Augustus. In return for this concession, he demanded Bayreuth, " the cradle of our ancestors. Political and military considerations urge us, and the other powers as well, not to allow France, Bavaria, and Saxony to enter into the possession of an unbroken line cutting across Germany from the French frontier to Bohemia and Prussia." The dread of a new Confederation of the Rhine was now, as before, determinative of Prussia's policy.

As soon as this resolution had been made known to the Five, the ground was levelled for an understanding. The Saxon affair ceased to be a matter of principle, and there began an unedifying dispute for the individual fragments of Saxon territory. But the task of the Prussian negotiators still remained extremely difficult. They demanded, above all, the defiles of the Saale as well as the fortresses of Wittenberg and Torgau ; the importance of these positions for the warfare of the day had been sufficiently proved in the wars of 1806 and 1813, and Hardenberg and Humboldt did not attempt to conceal their view that for many years to come it would be impossible to hope for a friendly and neighbourly relationship with the Albertines. They also demanded the greater part of Lusatia, with the wealthy Görlitz, and, finally, Leipzig. The place was not only of much importance as the centre of the spiritual and economic life of Upper Saxony ; the great fair-town, if it were to remain a Saxon frontier town, was likely to be extremely dangerous for the Prussian customs-system, as the seat of a vigorous smuggling traffic. Almost every one of these demands was vigorously opposed by the allies of January 3rd. Talleyrand trembled for the German balance of power : if Torgau were to be allotted to Prussia, Austria would be compelled to maintain an invincible and costly army. Metternich desired to limit the Prussian share to Lower Lusatia, and even offered the chancellor Tarnopol, which had already been specified for Austria herself, if he would only moderate his Saxon claims. Castlereagh, finally, wished to save Leipzig, in especial, for the Albertines, that is to say, to save it for the English smuggling traffic.

It is extremely probable that Prussia, in face of so general a resistance, would, in this last stage of the Saxon question, still have chosen the shorter course, however reluctant to use the sword. But now there became manifest the advantageous consequences of the king's greatly criticised change of front. The czar firmly and openly supported all his friend's claims ; and since the opponents, with the solitary exception of France, did not really desire war, they ultimately conceded most of the Prusso-Russian demands. Talleyrand's muse revelled once more in the discovery of devices by which the firm understanding of the two powers might be broken. Alexander was supposed to have angrily exclaimed : " Oh ! if only I had not committed myself so far ! If only I had not given my word ! " and numerous similar anecdotes were circulated. It is quite possible that Czartoryski advised his imperial friend to sacrifice Prussia : Talleyrand himself described the Pole as his most useful go-between. But the interests whereby Russian policy was bound to Prussian were stronger than Alexander's caprices, and stronger than the anti-German spirit of his Sarmatian adviser. Unless Prussia were to be adequately compensated, Russia could not acquire the desired Prosna frontier. For this reason the czar remained true to his friend ; and, as Gentz angrily wrote to Karadja, he advocated the Prussian claims as zealously as his own. In the whole course of these final negotiations, Russia did not once separate herself from Prussia. If ultimately the czar derived greater advantage from the dispute than his ally, this was not owing to any breach of faith on the part of the Russians, but because it was only the Prussian claims, and not the Russian, which were any longer disputed by Austria and the western powers. It was the king's judicious policy which Prussia had to thank for the fact that, after arduous disputes, the defiles of the Saale and the North Thuringian land of Luther, the fortresses of the Elbe and Görlitz, were acquired. It was only Leipzig which was obstinately defended by the English commercial policy. When all attempts at an understanding came to nought, Alexander finally resolved, upon the urgent representation of Castlereagh, to make a " sacrifice " which went very much against the grain. On February 8th he offered as a substitute the fortress of Thorn and its neighbourhood.

This was a poor exchange, and yet it was a proof of Alexander's goodwill. His Russians had long before made themselves thoroughly at home in the fortress on the Vistula, and it was long before they could forgive the czar for yielding in this respect. Taking everything into consideration, the only possible solution, in view of the approximate equality in strength of the two parties, and in view of the reluctance of both to enter upon a war, was the partition of the land in dispute, however painful this compromise might be to the Saxon nation ; and it was due solely to Russia's assistance that the partition was conducted in a way so favourable to Prussia and that the Albertine had to surrender the greater half of his domain.

The next thing to do was to seek elsewhere in Germany for the territory still necessary for Prussia's complete compensation. The chancellor soon abandoned the unhappy idea of re-opening the Bayreuth question. On the other hand, Metternich relinquished the Moselle frontier to which he had so long and so obstinately adhered ; Prussia received Coblenz and the mountain country between the Saar and the Nahe. The Prussians did not conceal their feeling that the king took over the territory on the left bank of the Rhine for the sake of Germany, " only on behalf of the general welfare " ; in this way Prussia entered into a threatened position just as much as Austria had formerly done so by the acquirement of Belgium. It was precisely this endangerment, forced upon his rival, which was in Metternich's eyes the only consolation for the unwelcome advance of Prussia towards South Germany. " What a good thing it is," he said to his confidants, " that Prussia is now directly 'compromised' with France ! " For the rest, he grudged a sufficient rounding-off of territory for Prussia even upon the left bank of the Rhine. A portion of the old department of Saar was retained, in order that here, immediately upon the endangered frontier, the claims of Oldenburg, Coburg, Homberg, Strelitz, and Pappenheim, should be satisfied. In Austria's view, it was a wise policy to involve as many petty states as possible in the defence of the Rhine frontier. It seemed as if the Hofburg desired to convince the neighbouring Alsace-Lorraine of the blessings of French national unity by offering a daily spectacle of the miseries of German particularism. Castlereagh, too, agreed that the demands of territory put forward by Hanover and the Netherlands ought to be somewhat modified for Prussia's advantage.

During the last weeks an understanding was arrived at also in the Polish negotiations. By the convention of May 3, 1815, the neutral republic of Cracow was founded. A commission of the three partitioning powers (on which Jordan and Stägemann represented Prussia) went to Cracow, to draw up the new constitution But it was felt from the first how nonviable was this most ludicrous of all the artificial creations of the congress ; the very instructions to the commissaries threatened the intervention of the three powers if the young Free State should become a centre of disturbance.

The English plenipotentiary could not refrain from assuming once more that role which was so agreeable to British virtue, and at the same time so inexpensive, of protector of Sarmatian freedom ; he hoped in this way to pacify the whigs regarding the sacrifice of Poland. In a verbose circular note of January 12th, he demanded that, since an independent Poland under a Polish ruling house was unfortunately impossible, the three partitioning powers should at least pledge themselves " to treat the Poles as Poles." To the frank ignorance of the noble lord, it seemed possible to treat the three partitioning powers alike in this respect ; who could have hammered into his head the idea that Prussia was in quite another position towards the small territory of Posen, which was already partially Germanised, from that occupied by Austria in relation to the Polish-Ruthenian Galicia, or by Russia in relation to the main part of the old nobles' republic ? If the eastern powers had wished to deal with this new and uncalled-for encroachment of England according to its deserts, they should have urgently exhorted the cabinet of St. James's to begin by treating the Irish as Irish. But they wisely refrained from provoking a vain struggle, and answered in polite, unmeaning letters. Hardenberg replied (January 30th) : Prussia was prepared to give to the Posen territory a constitution suitable to the customs and spirit of the inhabitants, and to show that national existence could continue undisturbed under any government. He would not agree to any limitation of Prussian sovereignty. For Austria as for Prussia, it was an urgent duty that the hands should not be tied, for no one could foresee the course of Alexander's Polish experiments ; and the czar himself did not desire to be supervised in his plans for the promotion of national happiness. Consequently neither the closing act of the congress, nor the convention entered into by the three partitioning powers on May 3rd, contains a word to the effect that the Poles had any claim to political independence. All that the three powers said was : " Their Polish subjects are to retain institutions which shall secure the maintenance of Polish nationality in accordance with the governmental forms which the three participating governments respectively think proper to impose." There was also an agreement concerning freedom of trade, subject at most to a duty of ten per cent., in the spontaneous produce of all the regions which had formerly been Polish ; and concerning free transit, subject to moderate duties, and free shipping (not subject to any prohibitions) upon the Polish rivers down to the seaports. The partitioning powers were pledged only to respect the language and the customs of the people, and · to favour commerce to a moderate extent ; in all other respects they retained a free hand.

Towards the middle of February, the territorial negotiations among the great powers were nearly completed. Talleyrand's desire for war had encountered an insuperable obstacle in the general longing for peace ; he gained no decisive influence in the Committee of Five, and the yelping pack of his Rhenish Confederate associates was simply ignored by the great powers. It is true that the German constitution still remained in profound obscurity ; but since the Hofburg regarded the speedy solution of this question as of trifling importance, Gentz drew up a pompous manifesto to announce to a wondering world, " the great work of the congress is now concluded." At this moment Napoleon returned from Elba, and before the breath of the Imperator the card-house of the Bourbon glories, which had been so boastfully described by Talleyrand, was dispersed to all the winds of heaven. The French minister, who had just given a pathetic assurance that millions of French arms would be raised against the Corsican, became in a single night an impotent man. On January 4th, Talleyrand had written in triumph to the king : " The coalition is dissolved for ever ! " Now the common danger once more drew the four allied powers together, and the remaining territorial questions were speedily settled. Vainly did Napoleon endeavour to break the new coalition by sending to the czar the original copy of the compact of January 3rd which he had found in the Tuileries, in Louis XVIII's writing-table. Alexander, in Stein's presence, burned the unclean document before Metternich's unashamed eyes. It was no longer a time to think of past disloyalties.

The Imperator's return brought to a final conclusion the long drawn out negotiations concerning the future of Italy. Here in the south, as elsewhere, England proved the most trusted ally of the Hofburg. With Russia's aid, however, the Piedmontese statesmen, D'Aglié and Brusasco, frustrated the secret aim of Metternich to constitute an Italian league of princes under Austrian leadership. Austria's desire to exclude the Savoy-Carignan line from the succession to the throne of Piedmont also proved impossible of attainment owing to the decisive opposition of Russia and France. All the more tenaciously did the Hofburg maintain its old claims upon the Legations ; Austria had occupied the entire Pontifical State with her troops, and hoped with good reason to retain at least the land to the north of the Apennines. Metternich rejected the proposal of the Bourbon court to constitute an Italian committee at the congress, after the example of the German committee, for the decision of this question ; he feared to be outvoted, especially since the Bourbons also had put in a claim for Tuscany. Meanwhile disturbances began in the peninsula ; the premature rejoicings of the Lombards on account of the entry of the *Tedeschi* soon gave place to profound discontent ; the populace of Romagna intrigued against the Austrian troops ; a few patriotic conspirators carried on secret intercourse with the prisoner of Elba. When now the greatest of the Italians opened his adventurous campaign, and when Murat in Naples armed for war, in Vienna incalculable complications were feared. A prudent change of policy was effected, and an understanding was speedily arrived at with the so-called legitimist powers of the peninsula. Tuscany was rescued for the archdukes, the Bourbons were temporarily put off with Lucca, and the whole of the old Pontifical State was restored to the pope. It was only Polesine, the rich lowlands in the delta of the Po, which remained in Austrian hands. Prussia took little part in these negotiations; but the king, out of consideration for his new Catholic subjects, regarded it as his loyal duty to intervene repeatedly and expressly on behalf of the re-establishment of the Pontifical State; in the general view of those romantic days the existence of the Roman Church was inseparably associated with the temporal power of the papacy. The Roman See entered a formal protest against the reduction in size of the Pontifical State. No one paid any attention. Modern Europe was already accustomed to find that all its great peace-determinations were accompanied by the execrations of the curia. The nuncio, however, conveyed to Piquot, the Prussian chargé d'affaires, the pope's cordial thanks for the good feeling that the chancellor had displayed towards the Catholic Church.[1]

No understanding was reached upon the eastern question; nowhere else was so crudely displayed as here that internal decay from which, despite all external glitter, the Austrian monarchy was unmistakably suffering. The state which in former days when the Turks were a great power had been the defender of the Christian world against Islam, now, when the Porte had been overthrown, blind to the signs of the times, pusillanimously left to Russian policy the completion of its own work. In February, the czar laid before the powers a comprehensive proposal in accordance with which they were all to pledge themselves to intervene on behalf of the rights of the rayahs, Russia in especial playing the part of protector of the Orthodox Christians, and Austria and France that of protectors of the Latin Christians. "There is," said the Russian note, "an unwritten law-book of international rights, whose powers are in full operation, and which guarantees equal rights to all nations." Metternich rejected this revolutionary proposal with great indignation. The czar, however, was far from inclined to give the guarantee desired by the Hofburg for the existence of Turkey; nor was England willing to burden herself with such incalculably onerous responsibilities. The result was that in Vienna absolutely no resolution was arrived at regarding Turkey, and the eastern

[1] Piquot's Report, Vienna, September 29, 1814.

question was tacitly shelved among the numerous other unsolved duties of the congress.

Whilst the great powers were carrying on their deliberations, Hardenberg completed another difficult diplomatic task, the settlement with Hanover, Sweden, and Denmark. These three-fold negotiations, which were protracted over several months, displayed, in their extraordinarily complicated interconnections, how wide a horizon must be embraced by the vision of Prussian statesmen, and how closely our state, thanks to its central position, was affected even by the most remote affairs of Europe. They secured for the fatherland one permanent gain, the liberation of Pomerania from the last vestiges of foreign dominion. Notwithstanding the peace of Kiel, which handed over to Denmark the territory to the north of the Peene, the chancellor held firmly to his plan to secure Hither Pomerania and Rügen for Prussia ; the hard struggle in which, with pen and with sword, the Hohenzollerns had for nearly two hundred years been engaged on behalf of their ancient hereditary dominion, was to be terminated once for all. But how was the legal possessor, Denmark, to be compelled to cede the country, since Prussia had nothing whatever to demand from the Danish crown ? Hardenberg rendered this important acquisition possible by a clever utilisation of the confused disputes which were agitating the Scandinavian world.

In order to influence the Danes to an amicable cession of Hither Pomerania, it was first of all necessary to resume friendly relations with this thorny little neighbour. It was characteristic of Hardenberg's finesse that, on August 25, 1814, he unhesitatingly signed peace with Denmark. The wits mocked Hardenberg's family peace ; the chancellor signed for Prussia, and his son, Count Hardenberg-Reventlow (who was completely estranged from his father), signed for Denmark. Since the two powers could hardly be said to have fought seriously against one another, the treaty involved no more than the simple confirmation of the peace of Kiel, and the repetition of the assurance given in that peace that Denmark should receive compensation for Norway in addition to Swedish Pomerania. But Prussia reserved the right to demand compensation for the losses which her flag had suffered from the Danish privateers. Regarding Heligoland, which by the peace of Kiel had been definitely ceded to England, not a word was said either in these Berlin negotiations or subsequently at the congress of Vienna. There was no legal right to demand the

island for Germany, since it had never belonged to the old empire;
such was the inland limitation of German policy that there
was no general understanding of the value of this place, whose
importance in relation to German trade had so recently been displayed in the days of the Continental System. The widespread
enthusiasm for generous-hearted Albion found no objection in
England's quiet foundation of a little North German Gibraltar.

Confiding in this treaty, the king of Denmark came to
Vienna, hoping there to acquire, in addition to Hither Pomerania,
Lübeck and Hamburg, or at least the princedom of Lübeck. He
was the boon companion of the illustrious society, arousing much
amusement by his droll sailor's jests, but his policy found no supporters; Napoleon's faithful ally stood quite alone among the
statesmen of legitimacy. Lord Castlereagh did not consider it
his duty even to keep the pledge given to the little state upon
which England had twice made a predatory attack. All that the
king of Denmark could secure was the continuance of the Sound
dues, which was, indeed, a valuable concession to the Danish
finances. When Metternich, taking leave, said to the king, " Sire,
vous emportez tous les cœurs ! " the betrayed man answered,
with a sigh, " Mais pas une seule âme." Meanwhile, even Hither
Pomerania had been lost to the Danes. The Norwegians, led by
the Danish stadtholder, Prince Christian, had disregarded the
peace of Kiel, had given their land an independent constitution,
and had chosen their stadtholder as king ; thereupon Bernadotte
had invaded the country with his Swedes, and, after a campaign
lasting a fortnight, in the treaty of Moss (August 14, 1814)
Prince Christian abandoned his claims. Subsequently, by negotiations between the crown of Sweden and the Storthing of Norway,
the union of the two kingdoms of the Scandinavian peninsula
was effected. Even to this day it remains obscure to what
extent the famous Danish loyalty co-operated in this uprising of
the Norwegians. Naturally, however, the cunning Frenchman who
now guided the destinies of Sweden had no doubt regarding the
complicity of the court of Copenhagen ; he declared that the
peace of Kiel had been broken by Denmark, and that for this
reason Hither Pomerania could not be handed over.

Naturally, it was not for Prussia to play the part of unprejudiced judge in these unedifying negotiations among the northern
powers. National policy demanded that the dispute for German
territory among the foreigners should be turned to German
advantage, in order to restore the lost Mark to the fatherland.

The task was one specially created for Hardenberg's supple adroitness. Fortunately, on this occasion, Austria and France, in former days the most obstinate enemies of the Pomeranian policy of the Hohenzollerns, remained altogether indifferent. The chancellor first came to an understanding with Sweden. Bernadotte was prepared to cede to Prussia his claims upon Hither Pomerania in return for a sum of money; on May 13, 1815, Münster reported it to the prince regent as indubitable that Prussia and Sweden had long before come to terms. Thus protected on the side of Sweden, Hardenberg produced his claims against the Danish privateers, endeavouring to induce the Danes to renounce Hither Pomerania. This could be effected only by the offer of some compensation in land and people, for Denmark had unquestionably the better legal right to Hither Pomerania. In the whole wide world there was, however, only one territory which might perhaps be offered to the Danes in compensation. This was the duchy of Lauenburg, on the right bank of the Elbe. But what a proposal! For the seventy-five square miles [German] of wealthy Hither Pomerania, were to be offered nineteen square miles in Lauenburg; for the naval fortress of Rügen, for the beautiful Stralsund, and for the University of Greifswald—no more than the tomb of Till Eulenspiegel, and two-thirds of the good town of Ratzeburg (for the cathedral square belonged to Strelitz)! Nothing but the difficulties by which the Copenhagen cabinet was threatened from all sides made it seem possible that Denmark would agree to so unequal an exchange, which offered but one advantage, the rounding-off of the Holstein territory.

Legally, however, Lauenburg belonged to the House of Hanover, and for this reason the acquirement of Hither Pomerania was dependent upon an understanding with the Guelphs, to whom, in addition, Prussia was indebted to the extent of 250,000 to 300,000 souls on account of the enlargement stipulated for at Reichenbach. It was already determined that Hildesheim was to be utilised for this compensation; on the other hand, the king had steadfastly rejected the cession of East Frisia, and since then the loyal little people had become even dearer to his heart. Nevertheless disquieting rumours ran through the country, where it was believed that cession to the Guelphs was still likely to be effected. Greatly concerned, Vincke, the lord-lieutenant, wrote to the chancellor; on no account must this essentially German people be sacrificed, for an East Frisian was worth more than twenty semi-French Rhenish Confederates; moreover, the possession of the Ems afforded the only free access to the north, and was the sole means of escaping the Rhine dues of the Dutch.

Thus the dispute for Hither Pomerania gave the Guelph diplomats a convenient excuse for renewing the attempt which had failed at Reichenbach. The chancellor now demanded Lauenburg from the Guelphs, and since in addition he had in accordance with the treaty to provide further enlargement for Hanover, Münster speedily saw his advantage, and in compensation asked for East Frisia and that " isthmus " of Göttingen territory which, according to Hardenberg's plans, was to connect the eastern province of Prussia with the western. This last demand could not be rejected, but it was long remembered in Berlin as a plain proof of the ill-will of the Guelphs, for if Hanoverian sentiments had been honourable, if there had been a genuine desire to keep on good terms with Prussia, to be surrounded by Prussia could not have been regarded by the Guelph court as a threatening situation. Still more profoundly hurt was the king by the proposal regarding East Frisia ; no other of the many disillusionments of this unhappy period touched him so profoundly. For many months, on into March, he obstinately refused ; how often did he send Knesebeck to the chancellor on this account, and this was always an unmistakable sign of depression. The Guelphs, however, stood fast upon their documentary rights. It was not as if the mouth of the Ems had any real significance to them from the point of view of commercial policy ; in the eyes of the nobles' government of the Guelphs, the magnificent rivers of Lower Saxony existed simply in order to be burdened with lucrative customs dues. But East Frisia bordered on Holland ; and alike in London, in Hanover, and in The Hague, an uninterruptedly continuous north-western Guelph-Orange power was regarded as essential to maintain a balance against the Prussian neighbour. For this reason Münster persisted in his demand, and Frederick William was ultimately forced to decide whether Hither Pomerania or East Frisia was the more important for Prussia. Hardenberg's opinion was absolutely in favour of retaining Hither Pomerania ; for, since the land frontier in the east had been rendered so unfavourable by the loss of Warsaw, it was indispensable to Prussia that upon the coast at least she should be able to protect herself, and should retain the control of the mouths of the Oder entirely in her own hands ; East Frisia, important as it was, was after all no more than an outpost.

A still more serious consideration in Hardenberg's eyes was

that of national policy. The long struggle for the liberation of Pomerania must not come to an end by the instalment of the Danes, who were already in the bay of Kiel, upon the Strela Sound. On the other hand, Hanover, even during her union with England, had always counted as a German land ; and at that time, when Princess Charlotte was still alive, its complete separation from Great Britain seemed near at hand, for this might be expected to follow upon the death of the prince regent. Ceded to Hanover, East Frisia would not be lost to Germany. It was not in criminal levity that Hardenberg sacrificed East Frisia, although such was the accusation brought against him by embittered patriots ; he weighed the pros and cons of the complicated question conscientiously, and then, with his sound political sense, chose the lesser of two evils. As early as February 15th, he had an article for the Berlin newspapers composed in the chancellery, intended to prepare readers for the cession of East Frisia, and at the same time to indicate that this painful sacrifice was the only means for the acquirement of the incomparably more valuable Hither Pomerania. This article, however, was unnoticed alike by contemporaries and by subsequent historians. Finally, in March, the king gave a reluctant assent. Thereupon there appeared an ultimate and unexpected obstacle. According to the absurd family tradition of the Guelphs, East Frisia was an ancient hereditary dominion of the Guelph House, which had accrued to Prussia only through force and cunning. Consequently the prince regent learned with extreme indignation that for the return of this primitively Guelph territory he was to hand over Lauenburg. He resisted to the utmost ; this most unloving of all sons suddenly experienced sentiments of filial tenderness, declaring that it was impossible for his " delicacy " to allow him to cede a province while his mentally disordered father was still alive. Münster had to use all his eloquence ; he explained to the enraged prince that Lauenburg was in fact absolutely essential for Prussia's Pomeranian plans. Should difficulties be raised, it was likely that the king of Prussia, already greatly embittered, would throw up the entire negotiation ; finally, too, there was the delightful prospect that in the new war with Napoleon Prussia would once more have need of the good English gold, and then Lauenburg could be again detached from the ally ! This reasoning had its due effect, and the tender conscience of the Guelph was appeased.

Thus on May 29th the treaty of exchange between Prussia and Hanover came into effect : Lauenburg was exchanged for

Hildesheim, Goslar, East Frisia, and part of County Lingen; in addition, there were to be two Prussian military roads through Hanover as a substitute for the desired "isthmus." In this way, the demands the Guelphs had formerly made at Reichenbach were by the Saxon negotiations reduced by about 50,000 souls. On June 4th Denmark ceded her rights in Swedish Pomerania to Prussia, receiving in exchange Lauenburg with two million thalers; but the state-treasury was so utterly depleted that it had to be made a condition that this trifling sum should be paid in four half-yearly instalments, beginning with the new year of 1816! Finally, on June 7th, Sweden, in return for three and a half million thalers, abandoned her last claims to German soil, and simultaneously restored to the new suzerain the Hither Pomeranian domains which had been alienated during recent years. Thus Prussia exchanged East Frisia and more than five million thalers for a land which at that time (it is true under very lax administration) produced a yearly surplus of no more than 224,000 thalers. From the purely mercantile outlook, this was certainly a bad stroke of business, and it was only Sweden which stood to gain by the complicated transaction; but the German nation had good reason to thank the chancellor for the fulfilment of this difficult task.

It was full time to separate Hither Pomerania from the life of Scandinavia. For nearly two centuries the country had been wholly attached to the three crowns of the north; how late in life had even Arndt, when nearly forty years of age, regained consciousness of his German nationality! How many hundred times had the people of Rügen opened their festivals to the strains of the ancient Swedish song: *Gustafs skål!* In the beginning of the century, upon solemn occasions, the merchants of Stralsund sang the national song:

> "Themselves let politicians please!
> Should France or England win the day,
> No ship of ours can either seize.
> What matters then to us the fray?"

Subsequently, when the blue and yellow flag could no longer adorn the vessels of the Stralsund shippers, this comfortable sentiment began indeed to give place to a more manly feeling; but the landed gentry and the patriciates of the towns, loaded by the Swedish crown with valuable privileges, regarded the equal justice of Prussian administration with extremely mixed sentiments. Then the feeling of the country became transformed with remarkable speed. The crown of Sweden itself recognised that the natural order of things was re-established by the entry of the Prussians. King Charles XIII, taking leave of his loyal Pomeranians, said that Sweden had gained " an insular situation " by the acquirement of Norway, and was therefore less than ever in a position to defend the remote German province. And within a few years this valiant German land was to confirm the promise uttered by Count Bohlen, the spokesman of the knighthood, at the swearing in, when he said : " We shall show that under a foreign government we have not forgotten how to be Germans."

In East Frisia, on the other hand, profound distress prevailed. For a long time no one would believe the bearers of evil tidings ; the royal authorities gave repeated assurances that they had no official news of the cession. The brave Landwehr regiment of the province continued to fight under the Prussian flag at Ligny and Waterloo ; as late as July, 1815, a deputation of the estates was despatched to Paris, whose members, in unison with the men of the Landwehr, implored the king not to hand over the province. Hostility to the noble land of Hanover was so general in this country of commerce and of peasant freedom, that the authorities did not venture to complete the cession until the end of 1815. Even then the old loyalty persisted. For how long a date did the East Frisian students in Göttingen continue to wear the black-and-white cockade in their caps, and when, singing the Landesvater, they raised the strains, *Friedrich Wilhelm lebe hoch,* it was with tears in their eyes. Until the king's death, East Frisia continued to celebrate its " ancient and glorious festival " ; as late as August 3, 1830, the visitors at the marine spa of Norderney saw with astonishment that at every fisherman's cottage on the island the Prussian flag was waving.

Whilst in these transactions the chancellor was able cleverly to maintain the interests of the state, in the negotiations with the Netherlands he had to pay the consequences for his early precipitation. None of the extravagant concessions which, during the winter campaign, had been made to the pet child of English policy, could now be recalled ; nor did Hardenberg himself, while in Vienna, succeed in learning that this House of Orange, which had been re-established by the force of Prussian arms, cherished decidedly hostile sentiments towards Germany. He continued to regard the Netherlands as a firm outwork of Germany, and was delighted that Luxemburg, at least, should join the Germanic

Federation. Although this little country was still animated by a warlike spirit and by decidedly anti-French sentiments, the memory of the Austrian Latour-dragoons and of the yagers of Le Loup, still remained fresh in the minds of the people. The Prussian diplomats did not resent the legitimist zeal exhibited by the Orange representative in the Saxon negotiations, for, to Gagern's astonishment, they manifested an " unusually yielding disposition."

There was, indeed, no longer any question of Jülich and other promises made in Paris ; but Prussia declared herself to be prepared to cede a portion of Guelderland and the vicinity of the fortress of Venloo, and here once again learned the hostile sentiments of the English statesmen. Gagern demanded *la lisière de la Meuse ;* Prussian Guelderland was to be cut off from its natural water-course, the Meuse ; the frontier was to be withdrawn everywhere at least two and a half miles to the east of the river. He appealed to the duke of Wellington, who, still completely under the dominion of the doctrine of the balance of power traditional in the eighteenth century, and inspired by a profound mistrust of restless Prussian ambition, had expressed as a military expert the extraordinary view that without this *lisière* the Netherlands would be threatened by Prussia. In the good-natured hope of securing the House of Orange for all future time as a grateful ally, Hardenberg was weak enough to give way to this preposterous claim ; and it was in this way that Germany acquired that northwest frontier whose like cannot be found upon the map of Europe.

Within the next few months, Prussia was to learn the gratitude of the Dutch traders. Among all Prussia's neighbours, the House of Orange displayed itself as the most hostile and the most grasping. In opposition to the spirit and the wording of the treaties of Vienna, the Netherlands immediately reimposed those scandalous Rhine dues whereby the Dutch Republic had formerly misused the German hinterland. Since the statistical resources of that day were extremely defective, and Hasselt's *Handbook of Geography* served the diplomats as the last source of wisdom, into all the territorial agreements of the congress there entered a few minor errors, which by a little good feeling on the part of the states concerned could subsequently have easily been rectified. It was through such an oversight that the two Prussian roads from Aix-la-Chapelle to Eupen and Geilenkirchen passed, for two short stretches, across Dutch territory ; here the Dutch temporarily erected customs houses, and subjected the Prussian internal traffic to their tolls. When at length a mixed commission met to effect a definite determination of the frontier, the Dutch contested every soul, every tree, and every inch of land.[1] Concerning the zinc-mines of Altenburg it was absolutely impossible to come to an understanding ; this celebrated " neutral territory " on the Belgo-Prussian frontier still reminds us to-day of the friendly and neigh-bourly sentiments of the Dutch. Such accumulated proofs of Orange gratitude, and in especial the increasing hindrance offered to the Rhine shipping, soon had as their result the cooling of the friendly feelings of the Berlin cabinet for the court of The Hague.

Another of Prussia's smaller opponents, Bavaria, had occa-sion bitterly to repent her foolish hostility. If any one of the German princely houses was dependent upon the friendship of Prussia by dynastic interests, this was unquestionably the House of Wittelsbach, which had so often been saved by the Hohen-zollerns. Even in the year 1814, Prussian statesmen, despite their well-grounded mistrust of Montgelas, had no hostile feelings towards the Bavarian state. It is true that they did not wish to confide the fortress of Mainz to these untrustworthy hands ; but in Paris Hardenberg was inclined to give the Palatinates of Baden and of the left bank of the Rhine to Bavaria ; and even in Vienna Humboldt advised that the Bavarians should be won over by concessions if they should exhibit any kind of goodwill for the Germanic Federation. The shamelessly un-German sentiment openly displayed by the associates of Montgelas, the boastful hostility of Wrede, and the filthy attacks of the " literary incendiaries " of the court of Munich, compelled the chancellery to adopt a different attitude. By old inclination and by custom Montgelas was bound to France, and was personally hostile to the leaders of the North German patriots, especially to Stein and Görres. Wrede hoped by his noisy zeal on behalf of Frederick Augustus to secure the gratitude of Austria, England, and France, and with their help to gain valuable compensation for Salzburg and the Lower Inn region. This was a grave political error even when regarded from the outlook of purely dynastic policy. England never concerned herself much about the South German territorial questions; towards the close of the congress France lost all influence, and Austria soon manifested herself to be a faithless friend.

The great powers came to terms over the Saxon question, and the only result of Wrede's presumptuous importunity was that he incurred general dislike ; even in the circles of the Rhenish

[1] *Cf.* Sack's General Report, March 31, 1816.

Confederate diplomats, the Bavarians were spoken of as " les Prussiens du Midi." Above all, the czar was profoundly embittered, and gladly listened to the reiterated assurances of Baron von Stein that it would be extremely dangerous to permit the aggrandisement of the central state of the Confederation of the Rhine. Frederick William was astonished to learn from Küster, the Prussian envoy, that in patriotic circles in Munich there was general talk concerning a war against Prussia " as one of the most natural and easiest things in the world." [1] Was this state to be permitted to hem in the whole of South Germany? But the chancellor could not now regard in any other light the union of the Badenese Palatinate with Bavaria, since the desired settlement of Austria on the Upper Rhine had not been effected. Was Prussia bound in any way by those ready promises which Metternich had, on his own initiative and secretly, given to the Bavarians? If Prussia had been unable to secure the formally promised uninterrupted continuity of her domains, why should not Bavaria have to make a like renunciation? Why should Baden and the two Hesses, which could never be a serious danger to Germany, suffer severe robbery in order to effect a quite inequitable aggrandisement for the most powerful state of the Confederation of the Rhine?

These simple political and legal considerations gradually led the king and the chancellor to determine that the court of Munich should be allowed no more than full compensation for the provinces ceded to Austria. It is true that the Bavarian negotiators, after they had chaffered throughout the winter with a commission of the great powers, succeeded, on April 23rd, 1815, in concluding a provisional treaty with the powers of the coalition, in accordance with which, for Salzburg and the Lower Inn region, Bavaria was to receive disproportionate compensation, namely, the greater part of the Palatinate on the left bank of the Rhine, Hanau, and a large portion of the eastern Odenwald ; in addition, it was promised that the Wittelsbachs should receive " the reversion of the Badenese Palatinate," as soon as the ruling line of the House of Baden should become extinct. Since that time the *réversibilité du Palatinat* has run like a red thread through all the transformations of recent Bavarian policy. Above all the crown prince Louis was under the dominion of this idea ; he had now to hand over his beautiful and beloved Salzburg, where during recent years he had established his court, and he desired to regain in return, at

[1] Küster's Report of May 17, 1815. Similarly in several other despatches.

least the " cradle of his race," although there was absolutely no legal ground for the claim. Years before, Bavaria had ceded the Palatinate on the right bank of the Rhine, in return for excessive compensation, and without reserve ; there was no obvious reason why the territory should revert to the Wittelsbachs as soon as the succession in Baden passed to the counts of Hochberg. It was only the disapproval of the great powers for the neglectful regime of the grand-duke Charles of Baden, which favoured for a time these presumptuous Bavarian claims. But the April treaty was still-born for it was expressly subject to the " assent of the sovereigns concerned," and Würtemberg, Baden, and the two Hesses immediately raised loud objections. Prior to this, Marschall, the Badenese plenipotentiary, had written to the chancellor: " Through all the sanguinary wars which disturbed Europe during his reign, Louis XIV did not gain one million inhabitants for the French monarchy, and now Bavaria, by a *coup de main*, by a simple negotiation, is to enrich herself by 400,000 subjects." [1] He now renewed his protest. Frederick William, too, found it extremely unjust that Hanau should be detached from Electoral Hesse without any legal ground. The consequence was that the April treaty was not ratified, and the final act of the congress left the dispute unsettled.

It was amid such struggles that the re-establishment of the Prussian monarchy was effected. The outcome of the Viennese negotiations was a partial defeat for Prussian policy, for neither upon the Rhine, nor in Saxony, nor yet upon the Polish frontier, had Prussia completely gained her ends. As compared with the *status quo* of 1805, the country was at least six hundred square miles [German] smaller, and had been increased by barely half a million inhabitants ; the promised rounding-off had not been effected, for Prussia was still separated into two widely detached areas. In addition, a royal house hostile to the Hohenzollern had been reinstated, a nonviable middle-sized state, which could never reacquire healthy political conditions. The four petty kings ruled nearly one-fourth of the domain of the Germanic Federation ; Napoleon's pet creation, the new power of the middle-sized states, had weathered all the storms of the time. Profound dissatisfaction was felt throughout the Prussian nation at the issue of the diplomatic struggle. Blucher aptly voiced public opinion when he wrote : " We drove a fine bull to Vienna and brought

[1] Marschall to Hardenberg, March 5, 1815.

away in exchange a mangy old ox." Prussia's enemies made no concealment of their malicious joy. Not satisfied with the results they had actually attained, they spread abroad the fable that the Prussian state had unwillingly been compelled to burden herself with Rhineland in place of the southern half of Saxony, whereas Hardenberg's desire had from the first been to acquire Rhineland as well as Saxony. All, however, were agreed in hoping that so artificial a political structure could not possibly endure.

Yet Prussia's enemies exulted too soon. The artificiality of this state-structure was not found in the fact that it simultaneously ruled the furthest boundaries of the east and of the west, but simply in this, that it was not yet complete, that the territories which constituted the natural connecting links between these two provinces, had not yet been acquired. Notwithstanding all failures in matters of detail, Prussia had gained through the Viennese negotiations the possibility of healthy and vigorous further development. The danger of a new Confederation of the Rhine, which in Vienna seemed so threatening, was abolished for a long time by Napoleon's return and subsequent defeat. The weakness of the Bourbons was plain to all ; the influence of France upon the small courts, an influence which Prussia had so obstinately resisted, remained in fact during subsequent decades extremely trifling. How different now, too, was the position of Germany in relation to the restless neighbour nation, now that the North German great power had undertaken to guard the Rhine in place of those miserable spiritual princes who were in the pay of the court of Versailles. Free from her burdensome Polish possessions, Prussia became more closely entwined than ever with the life of Germany ; to the young trans-Elbian colonies there were added the old lands of Rhenish civilisation with their mighty towns and their developed manufacturing industry. Henceforward there were no German interests which were not intimately associated with the Prussian state. As Frederick William said, Prussia possessed not a single village except with the assent of the whole of Europe, and thereby acquired the needed security for the permeation of the variegated new domains with the Prussian spirit and the Prussian system. If this unspeakably difficult task should be fulfilled, if the truth should be proved of the fine phrase used at this time by the king, " Germany has gained what Prussia has gained," then the half success of the Viennese negotiations might readily become as full of blessing as had in former days been the diplomatic defeat of the Great Elector at the Westphalian peace congress. It was not, in truth, in arrogance that Hardenberg had asked his opponents whether they really wished to force Prussia to strive for fresh enlargements. Only to the stupidity of the Hofburg and of the petty states was the delusion possible that the new structure of Prussia was one devoid of capacity for endurance, that a great power could not persist in so unnatural a situation. Half of Germany was under the Prussian sceptre. If here the unified state of Germany should first be firmly and securely grounded, sooner or later the hour must come when the sword of Frederick would again be drawn from the scabbard in order to restore to the fatherland the other half which still manifested in all its members the after-effects of two hundred years of foreign dominion.

§ 3. THE GERMANIC FEDERATION.

A generation later, when the representatives of the nation, without the co-operation of the princes, were discussing the reconstitution of the German unified state, they wasted the fortunate hour in deliberations concerning the fundamental rights of the people. The same obscure impulse towards self-seeking dominated the diplomats who, without the co-operation of the nation, were negotiating in Vienna concerning Germany's future; at a very early stage, the work of constructing the German constitution became arrested, the dispute concerning the dynastic interests of the House of Wettin continued for months to occupy all the energies of the congress, and it was not until towards the end of the great diet of princes, when affairs had already assumed an altogether hopeless aspect, that in excessive haste the German federal act was drafted. Certainly prospects had never been extremely favourable. It was *per se* an impossible task to give a firm political form to a country whose boundaries could be defined by no one, to give such a form to the indefinite idea " Germany." The pitiless pressure of necessity, which had formerly compelled the individual states of North America unwillingly to renounce their sovereignty, was not operative at this moment when all the world hoped for a period of prolonged peace. Consequently the political natural law which drives every state to defend its own ego, its independence, to the utmost, was displayed in all its harshness and nakedness. Veneration for the great fatherland, gratitude towards its liberators, shame for their own criminality, were not to be expected from the slaves of Napoleon.

Moreover a cultured public opinion, a passionate national will, strong enough to carry onward the reluctant, were not anywhere to be found. All that this generation possessed in the way of creative political capacity had been wholly exhausted in the colossal struggle for the liberation of the fatherland. The hopes of the patriots were indeed high-pitched, and Arndt said that they were expecting new glories such as had not been seen for centuries. The constitutional ideas of the Revolution had everywhere, though quietly, struck roots upon German soil ; " constitution " and " representative system " were now regarded as synonymous terms. At the same time, amongst men of very different degrees of culture, the confident prophecy became audible that, just as the ecclesiastical reformation had in the sixteenth century spread from Germany throughout the world, so now would it be with the political reformation in the nineteenth century. Romantic memories from Germany's earliest history became associated with these modern ideas ; it seemed as if the never-to-beforgotten disgrace of the days of Ratisbon had been wiped out, as if with the re-establishment of emperor and empire, the power of the Othos would return to the Germans. Never has a highly-gifted and highly-cultured generation been a prey to such childishly obscure political ideas ; everything which this epoch thought about the state, came from the emotions, from an inward and extravagant yearning which sought for its ideals as individual preferences might dictate, now in the past and now in the future. Unrestrainedly the primevally old was welded together with the fire-new. Whilst the *Rheinische Merkur* recommended Scharnhorst's military system and the abolition of all internal customs-dues in Germany, the paper at the same time disinterred Dante's *De Monarchia* from the dust, and expected to heal the afflictions of the new emperorless time with the ideas of the thirteenth century. For the majority of these publicists it was still an unknown idea that the politician should stick to his point and consistently advocate his views; innocently and diffidently everyone expressed his opinions and plans in newspapers and pamphlets, ready to adopt simultaneously the most opposing outlooks. Arndt declared apropos : " Such is the nature of our time that an intelligent man may endeavour to disseminate ideas simply from the love of dissemination, and because he has grasped the necessity for shaking up the Germanic spirits, for in many respects we are still far too inert." But how rightly had Fichte judged his contemporaries when he said that the German could never desire one thing alone, but must always simultaneously desire its opposite !

What a morbid excess of self-confidence was displayed, too, amid this unsteadiness of public opinion ! The newspapers gave unceasing assurances that, apart from matters of detail, the entire nation was at one, well aware what would be advantageous to it and what it was justified in demanding ; they spoke with unending contempt of the game of hazard played by the politicians and of the sham fights of diplomatists. This generation could with good reason pride itself upon a heroic struggle fought to a successful issue, and now that the constitutional upbuilding of the new Germany lagged so lamentably far behind the expectations of the War of Liberation, there arose in the nation an error weighty with consequences, which for two generations was a curse in German life. This was the illusion that the disintegration of the fatherland was the fault of the courts alone, and that it was not also the fault of conflicting aims and defective will, of the vacillation of the nation between patriotic aspirations and particularist traditions. The language of publicist literature displayed a peculiar mixture of unction and bitterness. Nowhere was this more plainly manifest than in the columns of the *Rheinische Merkur*, whose circulation, as early as the summer of 1814, was prohibited in the Rhenish Confederate states of the south. Let the princes seriously reflect, said Görres threateningly, how their peoples are likely to receive them if they return home bringing with them a disintegrated fatherland, for then we shall have no choice open between humiliation and revolt ! The image of the German constitution present to the minds of the majority of the patriots, corresponded in no small degree to that proposal for the armorial bearings of the future empire which was published by the *Rheinische Merkur :* " The double eagle tenderly embracing the black eagle, and the Bavarian lion standing peacefully beside them both ! " Unquestionably it was not the outcome of mere despondency when Goethe said : " The slumber has been too profound ; this one shaking-up will not suffice."

So far as it is possible to recognise a clearly conceivable political idea in this medley of good proposals and fantastical desires, the plan for the re-establishment of the Hapsburg emperordom outside the old Prussian provinces continued to receive most support. What was known in the petty states about the tragical role which the House of Austria had continued to play

even in the very latest war? Many a fine fellow could see no
important difference between Schwarzenberg and Gneisenau,
between Gyulay and Bülow. The *Rheinische Merkur* admired
the genuine and touching character of Emperor Francis. In
him there was no guile, no touch of the tyrant. Even though
Metternich was sometimes blamed for his weakly good-nature,
there was no doubt about his German sentiments. What
seemed more natural than a return to the consecrated forms of a
history dating back for a thousand years : only an emperor could
awaken the German sleeping beauty. The ancient imperial dream
found new expression in prose and in verse :

> "Loudly now the yearning's spoken :
> 'Emperor, will ye choose us never?
> Home comes no knight proudly bringing
> Germany, the deserted bride?'"

The question whether the hopeless conjunction of German
and foreign interests was to recommence was evaded with a
few fervent patriotic exhortations. Görres bluntly declared :
"German princes upon foreign thrones must never entangle their
German territory in foreign affairs!" Still more movingly did
Rückert recall the thought of the Hapsburg eagle :

> "Not the foreign Seville Orange
> Is it which to thee belongs :
> Thine the Apple imperial
> On German Oaks flourishing!
> Wilt not dwell on our oaks
> Beside the Apple, Staff, and Crown?"

Oken, the naturalist, a warm-hearted patriot, inspired by a
vigorous but restricted radicalism, declared in the Jena *Nemesis*
that, with the re-establishment of the imperial crown, all the other
demands of the nation would be spontaneously fulfilled, and that
thereby Germany would reacquire the first rank in Europe. The
talented philologian, F. G. Welcker, writing two years later in
the *Kieler Blätter*, referred all the distresses of the fatherland to
the fact that "no emperor could be found for fallen Germany."
Thus vividly was the thought of the emperordom cherished, but
who could endow that thought with any practical form? The
patriots troubled themselves little about the hard fact of
German dualism. If the Lorrainers, as the *Rheinische Merkur*

suggested, were to conclude a mutual agreement of succession with the Hohenzollerns, genuine unity would be spontaneously established for an indefinite period. Till then, indeed, Prussia must continue to exist in a state of dependency beside and beneath the Austrian imperial crown. An essay in the *Merkur* wished to establish Emperor Francis at the head of a bipartite Reichstag, of which Prussia was to lead the North German and Protestant electoral body, and Austria the Rhenish and Catholic. In this duplex empire, the Prussian state was to supply the creative and driving energy ; for since Frederick's state had regained its ancient powers, elsewhere in the empire, as in the eighteenth century, the comfortable view had been cherished, that Prussia was predestined by a kindly fate serviceably to relieve the other Germans from the burden and labour of high policy. To the Austrians, Görres assigned the more agreeable task of constituting " the inner warming and nourishing element " in the German empire, since this corresponded to the Austrian " tribal character." Similar views were advocated by Schmidt, the well-meaning privy-councillor of Hildburghausen, in his book *The Renascence of Germany*. He regarded the Prussian crown as the vicegerent of the empire of the north, and at the same time as a hortatory counsellor and tribune of the people vis-à-vis the Austrian hereditary emperor.

Even what Arndt wrote, upon Stein's instigation, "concerning the future representative constitution," shows that the excellent man had as yet given no serious consideration to the leading notions of constitutional law. He demanded an emperor, and a Reichstag constituted from the deputies of the provinces, without giving a thought to the rights of the princes ; he demanded the restoration of the provincial diets, though he did not do this quite so unconditionally as the romanticist of Coblenz, who proclaimed the trinity of the estates of teaching, arms, and nourishment. Arndt's ideas were couched in more modern terminology. The ministers were to be responsible to these ancient feudal corporations. The few political propositions found in the writing are isolated, like shells upon the sea-shore, in the thick sand of moral, historical, and ethnographical considerations. The entire culture of the period still remained utterly unpolitical. Among all the German publicists of the day, methodical political thought and the art of logical exposition were possessed by two only : Niebuhr, who never expressed any opinion upon the German constitutional question ; and Gentz, the writing-implement of the Hofburg. How remote even from the best Germans of those days was the calm and sustained national pride of a great people. On the one hand there was a fanatical hatred of the French, a hatred which even after the war Arndt glorified as the sacred fantasy, the religion of our people ; on the other hand there was an equally blind admiration for England, the only free country, which alone among all the contemporary nations glittered with many distinguished names—and this in the mouth of the fellow-countrymen of Goethe, Stein, Blucher, and Gneisenau. When the Guelph plans were disclosed at the congress, it is true that the faithful Arndt's eyes were opened, and in one of his finest writings, the *Outlook from the Present into the Future*, he utters cordial truths about English pettiness and Hanoverian arrogance.

Everywhere, even in the writings of the most well-informed publicists, it was preached as an irrefutable truth that particularism was the glory of Germany, the vigorous culture-ground of our freedom and of our civilisation ; the old, unhappy confusion between liberty and polyarchy recurred in the most manifold forms. But since it was desired to mix the water of particularism with the fire of national power, the door was opened for all kinds of political jugglery. The manifest reality of the German individual states enforced a sober restraint upon the publicists ; with regard to the rights of the diets, there already existed a certain harmony of views ; everyone demanded the right of petition and of the presentation of grievances, and also the right of granting supply ; most, too, demanded participation in legislation. On the other hand, the measureless greatness of the German united state offered a convenient field of experiment for dilettantist crotchets and sportive arbitrariness ; there was no folly which appeared too absurd for the great fatherland. Thus, Professor Lips of Erlangen recommended an emperorship which should pass in rotation every five years from one German prince to another. A Hanoverian statesman sent to the congress the draft for a German federal constitution whose seventh article attained to the following brilliant proposition : " The great question upon which everything else depends is this—what is to happen in the future in Germany, and what constitution is to be provided ? Hic nodus Gordius."

Side by side with the involved fantasies of the patriots, there became manifest once more the greedy desires of particularism. The talented and laboriously learned Carl Salomo Zachariä, a worthy representative of that subservient old professordom which was now becoming rarer, had when summoned to Heidelberg immediately undergone transformation from a servile electoral Saxon to a servile Badenese, and now, altogether in the spirit of the Rhenish Confederate sentiment of Carlsruhe, wrote : *A Proposal for the Fundamental Treaty of the German Federation of States.* We no longer find a word here of the thousand years' history of the German nation ; the sovereign princes of Germany can combine solely in order to secure internal peace and to provide for defence against the foreigner ; in all other affairs there prevails the *liberum veto*, in such a way that the resolves of the Federation are binding only upon those who assent to them. This chaos is to be presided over by a Bundestag in Vienna, led by Austria as protector, and by Prussia as arch-chancellor. Still more plainly did Sartorius, Münster's assistant, express himself in a pamphlet recommending a separate federation of all the middle-sized and small states. The limit was attained by a pamphlet secretly circulated throughout the diplomatic world, entitled, *To the Vienna Congress*, probably composed with the aid of La Besnardière. Here the restoration of the Confederation of the Rhine for the south and for the west, was openly advocated ; the north could hold fast to Prussia. But even in a well-meaning patriotic book, *Ideas Concerning the Formation of a Free German Federation of States*, we find a proposal for the constitution of a federation of the petty states, under the leadership of Bavaria. This was probably written by the Leipzig bookseller, Baumgärtner, the consul-general of the king of Prussia. The incredible confusion of ideas that was to characterise the two succeeding decades was already manifested in the significant fact that, immediately after the War of Liberation, a brave and intelligent German could, in all innocence, treat the Prussian state as a semi-foreign power !

In this paper war, the Old Prussian provinces took no part. After the convulsive tension of the unequal struggle, nature demanded her rights. Moreover, many far-seeing persons recognised that the dream of Prussian emperordom, which had so often been discussed in the circles of the volunteers, remained for the present quite out of the question. Only in the *Deutsche Blätter* of the Leipzig bookseller F. A. Brockhaus, was the opinion voiced, that the claims of Prussia were to a certain extent justified. An article entitled *Tantæ molis erit Germanam condere gentem* put forward, with a sobriety at that time unexampled, the following considerations. The right moment has not yet arrived for the unified state which must remain our aim ; from a renewal of the old, so-called free, federative constitution, nothing can be expected except the return of those lamentable times when Germany was " the general tavern, recruiting ground, and brothel " of the rest of Europe. At the moment, the only task before Germany must be to ensure the development of internal freedom, and from this point of view there was but one state in which hope could be placed, namely, Prussia. But the writer hardly ventured to make it plain, even between the lines, that he expected Prussia one day to effect the completion of the national unity.

Young Thorn, aide-de-camp to Charles Augustus, set to work much more valiantly upon the question of the future of Germany. This man was subsequently to play a part in the history of the customs-union, as head of the finances of Weimar. He had fought with Lützow's yagers, and even during the congress he had faithfully maintained the proud, patriotic sentiments of the wartime. When now he contemplated the utter failure of the Viennese negotiations, he wrote a brief and incisive essay, *What has the Future in Store for Us?* " [1] He showed that as yet nothing more could be effected than a loose alliance without a head ; the old empire was for ever dead, and henceforward all the hopes of the nation must repose upon the internal development of Prussia. If this state should gain internal energy, it would become strong enough at some future date to drive out of the country the non-German powers of Austria and England, to destroy the middle-sized states, structures manufactured by Napoleon, and to unite the entire nation under its own crown. Such were the ideas of a German soldier in May, 1815. To his contemporaries they remained unknown, as did Fichte's writing of the summer of 1813 ; it is possible that Charles Augustus may have glanced at the essay of his young aide-de-camp, and may have seen there some echo of his own youthful dreams of a league of princes. But how sinister appears the cumbrous slowness of national development when contrasted with the rapid thought-flow of the short-lived individual human being ! A hundred and fifty years earlier, Puffendorf had prophesied the constitution of the Germanic Federation ; now at length had the seer's words become true. Yet how many more decades, full of sorrow, shame, and toil, were still to pass before the fulfilment of the prophecy of this new and nameless prophet, the only one among all his contemporaries to

---

[1] First printed in Weimar in 1867, under the title, *Aus den Papieren einer Verstorbenen.*

foresee the detachment from Austria and the unification of Germany under the Prussian crown !

So confused a public opinion could not give the cabinets any direction towards definite goals ; the one thing it could effect was that a German federal constitution should come into existence. Even in Teplitz it had been the intention of the Austrian statesmen to unite the German sovereigns, like the Italian, with the Hofburg, simply for the purpose of a defensive alliance. During the war, however, Metternich had come to the conclusion that, in view of the tense expectations of the German nation, it would be necessary to agree to a more firmly established form of federal constitution. For this reason, out of dread of the revolution, in Chaumont he yielded to Hardenberg's persuasion, and approved the concession of " a federative bond " for the German states. Herein also was manifested the strengthening of the new Germany, that none of the foreign powers in Vienna put forward a claim to intervene directly in the German constitutional negotiations. To this work, which seemed to him the most sacred of earthly opportunities, Stein applied all the energy of his heroic will. It was with horror that the petty princes and ministers saw this untamable man on one occasion, his great eyes sparkling and his nose pale with wrath, shaking his fist in the face of the Bavarian crown prince. But what could passion, what could tenacity, effect in the prosecution of a task which had already been rendered altogether insoluble by the dualism of the great powers, by the ill-will of the Rhenish Confederate courts, and, above all, by the general obscurity of the political vision of the time—an obscurity shared by Stein himself ?

As soon as the imperial knight had become convinced that Austria obstinately rejected the assumption of the imperial dignity, he relinquished his Teplitz plans, and while still in Chaumont elaborated, on March 10, 1814, a new proposal for a federation which entrusted the executive authority to the four greatest German states. His aim was now principally to limit " the sultanism " of the petty despots ; for this reason, fundamental rights, the " rights of Germanism " were guaranteed to every German by the electoral authority, and there was to be established a mixed Bundestag composed of delegates from the princes and from the Landtags. Next summer this proposal was redrafted, and in July was thoroughly discussed in Frankfort at a meeting between Stein, the chancellor, and Count Solms-Laubach. Reluctantly did the baron now agree to exclude the delegates of the Landtag from the Bundestag, for he bitterly contended that if the Bundestag was to consist of princes alone, the protection of representative institutions would be entrusted precisely to those hands whose interest it was to overthrow them! But the impossibility of bringing a German parliament into existence in face of the opposition of Austria and the Rhenish Confederate courts, was plainly manifest; and no less obvious was it that an unduly numerous Confederate assembly without a head, would be hopelessly cumbrous; moreover in view of the power which the sovereign princes possessed, it would in fact be unseemly to have their representatives swamped by a majority of popular representatives. The obvious idea of constituting a house of states for the princes and a popular assembly for the representatives of the people, had as yet occurred to no one; no serious attention had hitherto been paid in Germany to the constitution of the United States of North America.

The proposal thus metamorphosed was on September 2nd at the instigation of Hardenberg, laid by Count Solms before the Austrian minister. How strangely had these well-meaning North German patriots turned about and about, in order to discover how to square the circle, and how to bring Austria, which was hardly half-German, into the same fold with the true Germany. They recognised justly that Austria could not dispose of any effective federal authority; but since they started from the idea of the complete equality of Austria and Prussia, as if it had been an inviolable article of religious faith, not only did they demand for the House of Lorraine the restoration of that privileged and peculiar position which for centuries the hereditary dominions of the emperor had assumed in the ancient empire, but they also proposed that Austria should enter the federation in the narrower sense with no more than the land to the west of the Inn, and Prussia with no more than the provinces leftward of the Elbe, but that both powers should conclude a perpetual alliance with Germany for the whole of their respective domains. Here it was taken as a matter of course that Austria would resume possession of her provinces on the Upper Rhine. It was proposed further to invite Switzerland and the Netherlands to join the perpetual alliance. How tragical was the irony of destiny! Immediately after the Markers, Pomeranians, Prussians, and Silesians had given the signal to the other Germans for the War of Liberation, our leading statesmen seriously proposed to exclude from the Germanic Federation these lands which formed the kernel of the new Germany. The imperial knight's leading idea was the honourable intention to preserve for the people of the Rhenish Confederate states the rights of their provincial diets, and to furnish for them some security against "the sultanism" of their princes ; but Stein knew that the introduction of a constitution into the Old Prussian provinces was far from simple, and that in Austria it was almost impossible, and he therefore grasped at this desperate proposal regarding the frontiers of the Inn and the Elbe[1].

The Prussian statesman wished to reintroduce into this Germany westward of the Elbe and the Bohemian forest the circle-constitution of the old empire, so that the useless contingents of the smallest states might be welded together to constitute functionally capable masses. Consequently seven circles were to come into existence, and if possible the Netherlands also as an eighth (Burgundian) circle. Austria and Prussia in two circles each, Bavaria, Hanover, and Würtemberg in one circle each, were to assume the office of circle-governor, to undertake military leadership, and to exercise supervision for the carrying out of federal legislation ; the former electors of Baden and Hesse were each to receive in one of the circles the position of deputy circle-governor. Here, however, intruded the distressing problem whether it was permissible to grant enhanced power to the restless ambition of the courts of Munich and Stuttgart. All the petty neighbours trembled before the outrageous land-hunger of King Frederick ; the government of Hechingen implored the Prussian statesmen in moving terms[2] to take steps to preserve the little country from complete enclosure in the domain of Würtemberg, and to secure for it the retention of free access to the lake of Constance through Badenese territory. Consequently Stein proposed to allot to the Bavarian and Swabian circle the domains of Bavaria and Würtemberg exclusively; the petty states as a whole were to be subjected to the leadership of the three so-called German great powers, Austria, Prussia, and England-Hanover. These seven ancient electors were to constitute, in conjunction, a council of circle-governors which was to exercise executive authority, to control foreign policy, and to deal with military affairs ; no state in the federation was to treat with foreign countries independently. The council of electoral princes of the old empire, which had persisted even under the Rhenish Confederate constitution as the council of the

[1] This motive is manifest from the letters and memorials of Count Solms recently published by H. Baumgarten (*Im neuen Reich*, 1879, p. 549).

[2] Repeated petitions from the prince of Hohenzollern-Hechingen to the chancellor.

kings, was thus to be reconstituted with increased powers. Stein, like all the Prussian statesmen, wished to return as far as possible to the legal foundation which had been created by the princes' revolution of 1803. The directorate of the council of circle-governors was to be vested in Austria and Prussia in common ; in this manner Austria, as of old, would lead as president ; but Prussia was to exercise the real directorate, to control the conduct of business, just as at one time Electoral Mainz had been " mouth and pen " of the Reichstag of Ratisbon. The legislative authority was to be held, in common with the circle-governors, by a council of the princes and of the estates, which was to include all the less powerful princes, the free towns, and the mediatised. Every estate possessing a domain of more than 50,000 inhabitants received a vote indifferently whether it was still regarded as a sovereign power or not ; all the others, taken together, were to have six curiate votes.

In this way the imperial knight proposed to do justice to the unhappy victims of the *coup d'état* of 1806, without, however, restoring their territorial sovereignty. He repeatedly called the attention of his Prussian friends to the fact that they could not treat on equal terms all the mediatised, who differed so greatly in their respective importance.[1] There was Hohenlohe with 106,000 souls, Fürstenberg with 83,000 souls, and so on, until the list was closed by Aspremont which had ruled a populace of one hundred and ninety-five souls. The best part of the proposal was constituted by the sections upon the rights of the nation. In every federal state there should exist provincial diets with the right of granting supply, of representation, and of co-operation in legislation. For every German, the security of property must be guaranteed, the same with the freedom of the press, the right to petition for redress of grievances, the right to emigrate to other German states, and to secure an education at any German educational institution.

On September 13th, in Baden near Vienna, Hardenberg discussed this plan with Metternich, and it immediately became evident that Austria had no desire for so thoroughgoing a proposal. As Gentz declared to Karadja, the Hofburg was inclined to lay down in Vienna no more than the general principles of the federal constitution, and to leave everything else to the Frankfort Bundestag. They would not expect the sovereigns to do more than what was absolutely essential Then Metternich

[1] Stein to Humboldt, December 29, 1814.

demanded that Austria and Prussia should join the federation with all their original " German lands "; but Austria would on no account resume responsibility for guarding the Upper Rhine. Hardenberg gave way all the more readily since according to the Austrian proposal the legal basis of 1803 was to be re-established. The Austrian diplomats delighted to proclaim their confidence that henceforward in all warlike needs, with the possible exception of Italian affairs, the imperial state could rely upon German compulsory military service ; there existed somewhere in Galicia two ancient Silesian fiefs, the so-called duchies of Zator and Auschwitz, in consequence of which the Germanic Federation would be pledged for the defence of Austrian Poland ! In that *confusio divinitus ordinata* known as the Holy Roman Empire, no one had been able to determine which provinces of the two great powers were to be regarded as German territories, and even now the problem could not be accurately solved. It was not until four years later that the matter was settled—at least on paper. The only certain thing was that with the entrance into the Federation of the main mass of Cisleithania, any serious federal constitution became impossible, and this was precisely what Metternich desired.

Finally, the Austrian minister made urgent representations to his Prussian friend regarding the cumbrous nature of the two-headed directorate. How much simpler would it be if Austria, which could not be expected to renounce all her ancient imperial rights, should take over the sole presidency ; all German affairs would of course be harmoniously arranged in advance between the two leading great powers ; the presidency was to be " understood as a mere formal conduct of business." Hardenberg gave way ; he had from the first regarded Stein's plan as no more than an experiment, and not as a fixed programme. Just as blindly as at the outset of his diplomatic career he had believed in the friendship of France, so now did he trust in Austria ; he would no longer admit the possibility of a contest between the two powers, and he failed to recognise what an advantage the right of presidency would give should such a contest arise.[1] Since

---

[1] It has often been contended that Metternich gave a verbal promise that in the future the presidency should be divided. Not only, however, has no proof ever been brought forward in support of this remarkable view, but documents are forthcoming which compel the acceptance of the opposite conclusion. In the year 1816, immediately before the opening of the Bundestag, the federal deputy von Hänlein, upon his own initiative, made a belated attempt to secure for Prussia a share in the presidency. There occurred a long exchange of letters between him and Hardenberg, and in this confidential correspondence, in which all the reasons in support of Hänlein's demands are exposed in detail, there is no mention of any Austrian assent.

Münster also showed a decisive opposition to the two-headed directorate, the Prussian proposal was weakened and abbreviated in accordance with Austria's wishes, until the forty-one articles had shrunk to twelve. These twelve articles were, on October 14th, laid by the two leading states before the Committee of Five which, in accordance with the determination of the European powers, was to deliberate about the German constitution. Consequently the fate of the Germanic Federation was placed entirely in the hands of Austria, Prussia, England-Hanover, Bavaria, and Würtemberg; for the remaining states nothing but a supplementary assent was reserved.

Manifestly this attempt to form a German pentarchy was merely an arbitrary resource of embarrassment; for, as far as historical legal rights were concerned, and in accordance with the ancient prerogative of the council of electors, the electoral houses of Baden and Hesse ought not to have been excluded. In order to gloss over the arbitrary character of this action, Metternich appealed to that clause of the treaties of accession by which the petty states, from Baden downwards, were pledged to acquiesce in the requirements of the future federal constitution; but by this assent the right of joint deliberation was by no means excluded. The true motive for the arbitrary procedure of the two great powers was mere diplomatic convenience; they regarded it as impossible to attain to any result in a negotiation with all the German states. The event showed, however, that, in the extraordinary confusion of German politics, the apparently easy is often difficult, and the improbable is possible. The federal constitution did not come into existence until the variegated masses of all the petty states were summoned to the council. On the other hand, the negotiations of the Committee of Five, which were protracted until November 16th in thirteen stormy sittings, remained utterly without issue, for among the selected five states were the two most virulent enemies of German unity, Bavaria and Würtemberg.

Both of them had retained in security their complete sovereignty, Bavaria unconditionally, Würtemberg with an insignificant reservation. Encouraged by the unreasonable indulgence displayed towards them by the great powers, they immediately disclosed, as Stein angrily put it, their system " of isolation against the league, of ambition against the petty states, and of despotism against their own territories." As the Prussian statesmen immediately perceived, their aim was to defer

the settlement of the German constitutional question until their
own territorial demands had been settled to their satisfaction.[1]
With his accustomed brutal roughness, Wrede immediately
declared that Bavaria as a European power had no " personal
interest " in the Germanic Federation, for she could by adhesion
to France gain far greater advantages, and it was only from a
friendly compliance, and against the general wish, that she would
join the union of the German sovereigns. Even after the
congress, Montgelas declared to the Prussian envoy, von Küster,
his complete indifference towards the Germanic Federation.
" Why should not the German states live together like the
Italian, in complete independence, bound together only by
neighbourly feelings and mutual free accommodation ? "[2]

Nothing was further from the ideas of the Prussian statesmen
than a radically consolidating policy. Whilst in the eyes of Stein
the unified state always remained the ideal, Hardenberg and
Humboldt accepted with full conviction the general belief in the
civilising influence of particularism. Knesebeck, in his doctrinaire
way, repeatedly uttered the thought that only through the
variegated character of its political conditions did Germany
become competent to constitute the pivot of Europe ; he desired
that " this pivot should be characterised as the palladium for
free association and for preservation of the balance of power, by
exhibiting both these qualities within its own system."[3] Yet
however modest the desires of the Prussians, their anger was
aroused by the frivolous scorn for Germany displayed by Wrede.
The Bavarian roundly declared that his king was unwilling " to
renounce the practice of any governmental right dependent upon
sovereignty " ; and least of all to renounce the privilege of forming
alliances with foreign countries. In this right, the Bavarian
national pride found satisfaction. Were it to be renounced,
Bavaria "would lose prestige and dignity among foreign nations."
For the five circle-governors he demanded complete equality,
and consequently there was to be an annually changing directorate. For this reason also he wished to admit to the league
as few Austrian and Prussian provinces as possible. In any case,
neither of the two great powers must contribute more troops to
the federal army than did Bavaria.

[1] Thus writes Humboldt in the *Systematic Description* to which reference
has already been made.
[2] Küster's Report, Munich, August 28, 1815.
[3] Knesebeck's Memorial, January 7, 1814.

In this way was for the first time disclosed the intention of the middle-sized states to weaken the German army because of their jealousy of the great powers—a policy of envy which was unparalleled even in the history of Poland, and which for years to come was to make itself felt in the ludicrous military constitution of the Germanic Federation. Even more audaciously than the Bavarians, did the Würtemburger plenipotentiaries express themselves ; by their provocative speeches they stirred up once more all the horrible dregs of the old Rhenish Confederate sentiment. They would not hear a word of the fundamental rights of the nation if for no other reason than that the court of Stuttgart did not recognise the existence of a German nation. By a shameless falsification of history, which was already beginning to disseminate its poison in the schools of the Rhenish Confederate states, everything was roundly denied which had been common to the Germans for centuries, and out of the whole history of our people nothing was regarded as valid beyond the eight years of Napoleonic anarchy. "The aim of the Federation," declared von Linden dryly, "is antagonistic to the idea of building, as one may say, a nation out of its different populations, as, for example, those of Prussia and of Würtemberg!" On the other hand, the court of Stuttgart displayed an extremely suspicious zeal on behalf of military organisation. It desired that only circle-governors should become members of the federation, that all the other princes should be excluded as merely circle-estates subordinate to the five powers, and suggested as eminently desirable the enlargement of the south-western German circle, so that King Frederick might secure the desired new territory by a devious route, and might brandish the sword of the circle-governor over four millions of mediate or immediate subjects.

The Prussian plenipotentiaries led the struggle against this unworthy intrigue. Even Metternich was concerned to see how the seed disseminated at Ried and Fulda had sprung up all too luxuriantly ; nor could he restrain himself from occasionally contradicting his South German protégés, especially when they were inclined to infringe the rights of his co-estates, the mediatised. Finally, Münster greedily seized the opportunity of displaying before all the world the light of the celebrated Guelph freedom. The prince regent, in an arrogant circular to the European courts, announced the foundation of the kingdom of Hanover, and maintained the problematical opinion, " by its union with Great Britain, the House of Guelph has been able to give

much valuable protection and support to the German fatherland."
In a like boastful tone, Münster wrote a note attacking the
doctrines of Würtemberg sultanism. He showed that the rights
of the provincial diets had by no means been abrogated by the
sovereignty of the petty crowns ; and by the uncritical public
opinion of the time he was highly esteemed on account of his
noble liberal sentiments, whereas he had in reality merely broken
a lance on behalf of the feudal characteristics of the Hanoverian
nobles' regime. Before long, the state of affairs in the Committee
of Five seemed so hopeless that Stein, profoundly discontented,
appealed to the czar for help. Alexander expressed his cordial
approval of the proposals of the German great powers, and referred
the German states to the promises contained in the proclamation
of Kalisz. The despot of Stuttgart, however, could no longer
remain to look on at the criminal attack upon the absolute
sovereignty of his Rhenish Confederate crown. He was heard to
say : " People will soon be ashamed to declare themselves Würtembergers." On November 16th Würtemberg announced her
withdrawal from the Council of Five, and before the mocking
eyes of Europe the German pentarchy broke up in consequence
of its own internal disunion.

Meanwhile the minor states had also taken action, justly
embittered by the high-handed proceedings of the Five. On the
day of Würtemberg's withdrawal, Baden, which had vainly
demanded admission to the Council of Five, entered a formal
protest, reserving for the grand-duke all the rights of unrestricted
sovereignty. Von Hacke, the Badenese minister, profoundly
Bonapartist in sentiment, did not disdain to make use of the ill-
natured phrase, that his grand-duke had not thrown off foreign
chains in order to wear those forged at home. Gagern gathered
round himself the representatives of most of the petty states, from
Electoral Hesse downwards, and laid before them the necessity
" of making the great ones recognise that we are here, and that
we understand our craft," Here there was brought together an
extremely mixed society : honourable and intelligent patriots,
such as Smidt, and Plessen, the Mecklenburger ; impenitent particularists, like Marschall of Nassau ; and, finally, such visionaries
as Gagern himself, who dreaded, not the Rhenish Confederate
sentiments of Bavaria and Würtemberg, but " the masked
duumvirate " of Austria and Prussia. Many of the participators
were influenced only by jealousy of the mediatised ; they would
not allow themselves to be outbid by these discrowned persons,

who, as consistent legitimists, were enthusiasts for all the treasures from the lumber-room of the Holy Empire, and who besieged Emperor Francis with petitions to reassume the Carlovingian crown. There was only one thing in which the petty states were unanimous, their desire to break the dominion of the Five.

On this occasion, however, as so often in the history of the empire, the petty courts showed somewhat more patriotic senti- ment than the middle-sized states; several among them, con- scious of their own weakness, seriously desired a strong imperial authority which could protect them against the ambition of their greater neighbours. Consequently Stein determined to utilise this opposition of the petty princes for his own patriotic ends; he adroitly pushed the busy Gagern on one side, and on November 16th, the same day on which Würtemberg withdrew, he induced the union of the nine-and-twenty minor princes and towns to transmit a collective note to the two leading powers. In this document, Austria and Prussia were asked to lay before all the German states a new constitutional plan " upon the basis of equal rights and of a complete representation of all members of the federation "; but the federation must be headed by an emperor " as the protector of German freedom." However vague and obscure this imperial plan appeared, and however certain it was that several of the signatories utilised the idea of an emperor simply as a frivolous excuse for getting rid of the dominion of the Five, it is equally certain that the declaration of the petty states contained certain honourably designed concessions. In especial, they offered to concede to the Landtags a certain minimum of con- stitutional rights to be determined by the federation.

The German pentarchy, thus simultaneously attacked from within and from without, fell to pieces. For some months there- after there no longer existed a German constitutional committee. The ground was free for arbitrary plans of all kinds; Gagern and Plessen were already speaking of a federation of the middle- sized and petty states, without Austria and Prussia, but with Denmark and the inevitable Netherlands. Münster replied to the minor states in the name of the great powers, benevolently recognised their patriotic aims, and definitely declared that, in view of Austria's refusal, the reconstitution of the emperordom was altogether impossible. The Rhenish Confederate senti- ment, however, which had been so shamelessly expressed in the notes of Würtemberg and Baden, was one which the great powers were unwilling to leave unreproved. Austria and England-

Hanover still hoped from moment to moment to detach the Prussian court from Russia, and consequently in the German negotiations displayed towards the views of Prussia an accommodating spirit which did not indeed pledge them to anything serious. Münster drafted for Prussia and Austria an identical note which was to be handed to the court of Baden. In language of unexampled severity, he displayed to the government of Carlsruhe the register of its sins, enumerated all the acts of oppression performed by that government against its own people, " measures which must be classed with the most arbitrary of those characteristic of the French revolutionary system." Next the important principle was expounded that it was by no means left to the German states to decide whether they would or would not join the federation. The great powers did not appeal to the thousand years' existence of the German empire, which had never been legally abolished ; they held fast to that which was immediately under their hands, to the treaties of accession of the previous year. All those who had joined the great alliance were bound by the proclamation of Kalisz, which conceded to the German people the re-establishment of its constitution " with the necessary modifications." " The guarantee for the sovereignty of Baden which the allied powers have jointly given cannot be interpreted as an agreement to unconditional privileges which have never been conceded to your royal highness, and which would be in direct conflict with the intentions made known to the German nation by the allied powers as to the aims of the war, to whose fortunate conclusion their love for the fatherland and their courage, based upon this assurance, have so greatly contributed."[1] At the last moment Metternich hesitated, for such a tone seemed to him altogether too outspoken. He regarded it as sufficient to communicate to the Badenese minister, by word of mouth, the opinion of the great powers. But to the court of Würtemberg, on November 24th, a common answer was handed which, though couched in somewhat milder terms, corresponded to Münster's draft, and which declared with great definiteness that all the German states were pledged to join the federation. It was as if Stein himself had guided the pen of the great powers ; the only trouble was that neither Metternich nor Münster had any serious intention of backing up the fine words with action.

The dissolution of the Committee of Five was weighty with

[1] Münster's Proposal for an answer to the Badenese note, November 16, 1814.

consequences for many years, for it gave the stimulus to the establishment of constitutional political forms in South Germany. From the meanest motives, from the arrogance of sovereignty, and particularist dread of the intervention of the federal authority, the cabinets of the three middle-sized states of the south determined, upon their own initiative, to do what was necessary, and to grant a representative system to their respective countries. Moreover, it was easier for them to do this than it was for Prussia, for their Napoleonic prefectural administration had already been in existence for ten years, subjecting all portions of the country to an identical ordering, and checking all centrifugal tendencies. As early as September, Max Joseph had ordered a revision of the paper constitution of 1808; in October, as soon as he perceived in Vienna that the great powers wished from the federal side to force the sovereigns to grant a minimum of constitutional rights, he commanded his committee of revision to bring its labours to a conclusion as speedily as possible. Frederick of Würtemberg, in an unmannerly rejoinder dated November 24th, made his minister defend once more the inviolable sovereignty of the Swabian kingly crown. He stormed and raged against the usurpation of the great powers, and at Christmas left Vienna in high dudgeon. None the less, he was too prudent not to see that the days of undisturbed autocracy were over. The Swabians could hardly recognise the brutal tyrant any longer, so gentle and gracious did he appear immediately after his return, so obviously did he endeavour to keep the peace with his people ; he would no longer hear a word about Napoleon, but no less did he definitely declare that he would never obey any instructions from Vienna.[1] On January 11, 1815, he astonished his unhappy land by a proclamation which announced the speedy summoning of a Landtag. The king granted this long-designed benefit at the present moment in order to show that he " was not forced by any external necessity, or fulfilling any pledge entered into with others." He believed that in this way he would overreach the Germanic Federation ; he did not foresee how soon his ill-used people would itself exact a terrible penalty for the sins of the last decade. Nor did the sick grandduke Charles of Baden lack understanding. The masterful exhortations of the great powers terrified him out of his dull meditations ; on December 1st, in a definite note submitted to

---

[1] Report of the chargé d'affaires Jouffroy, Stuttgart, January 12 and March 7, 1815.

the Prussian chancellor, he indicated that he was prepared to concede to his people all the constitutional rights demanded in the Prussian federal plan, and that he had already appointed a constitutional committee. Such were the turbid sources from which sprang the constitutional movement in South Germany; but since this movement corresponded with the nature of things, it continued to progress even when the petty thrones had no longer anything to fear from the Germanic Federation.

At that moment, the anxiety of the middle-sized states was by no means devoid of foundation, for the Prussian statesmen, unaffrighted by the breaking up of the Committee of Five, pursued with unabated zeal the work of constructing the German constitution. To them the national political development was a matter in which they put their whole hearts. Again and again had they countered the unpatriotic talk of the Bavarians and Würtembergers with the declaration that the king of Prussia " regarded it as his duty as a ruler to bring his subjects once more into such unison that they might combine with Germany to constitute a nation." Humboldt at once set to work upon the elaboration of a fresh scheme, but encountered a new and wholly unexpected difficulty. The Austrian minister, who had hitherto expressed himself as in favour of the circle constitution, was now suddenly of another mind. He conjectured, as was certainly extremely probable, that the small North German contingents, subordinated to the Prussian circle-governors, would infallibly disappear in the Prussian army; and since in relation to the construction of the German constitution, which, for the rest, left him altogether cold, he pursued one aim alone, the limitation of Prussian power, he now declared himself opposed to any subdivision into circles. Münster, too, agreed with his Austrian friend when the latter evoked the spectre of North German hegemony.

The consequence was that Humboldt had now simultaneously to elaborate two proposals for the federal act, one with, and the other without, circles; in both of these the basic ideas of the twelve articles were retained. On December 9th the indefatigable man expounded in a memorial the advantages of the circle constitution. It was indispensable to secure for the smallest states orderly stages of procedure for their judicial system, and to enable them to prepare, even in time of peace, for the full utilisation of their military energies in war; the opposite was practicable only under the " Bonapartist system," which lived in a continuous state of war and had no scruples about the means employed. At the same time he endeavoured to meet the complaints of the petty states regarding oppression, and proposed to accept into the council of the circle-governors, in addition to Baden and Electoral Hesse, three members of the council of princes, subject to annual rotation.[1] Two days later he sent the completed proposals to the chancellor, insisting once more how essential was the circle constitution to Prussia's disintegrated situation ; but recommending, none the less, that too urgent an insistence should not be made on behalf of this demand, because our strength in Germany was always in part a moral one, and because " Prussia must not appear to the petty princes as a danger, but as a protection." Now, at length, after nearly three months of fruitless negotiations, the talented man began to gain an inkling, although nothing more than an inkling, of Austria's friendly intentions towards the federation. " In this German constitutional affair," he wrote, " others have gladly thrust us into the foreground, and, easily and readily, everything has given way before us, because (since it is known that we always desire a firm and vigorous constitution) there are those who would prefer that we should be made to appear disagreeable and dangerous to the princes to whom alone the fetters of a constitution are burdensome." Not even yet, however, was he able to recognise clearly that the Hofburg itself could not desire " a firm and vigorous constitution " ; on the contrary, he hoped to come to a speedy understanding with Austria and Hanover about one of the two proposals, and to be able in about a week to resume negotiations with Bavaria and Würtemberg.[2] While the Prussian statesmen, faithfully diligent and devoid of cunning, were thus drawing water in the German sieve of the Danaides, Metternich was secretly negotiating with Münster about the design for a Germanic Federation without Prussia !

Stein provided Humboldt's work with notes of his own, demanding greater rights for the mediatised and for the imperial knights, but also a larger measure of popular rights, especially the abolition of serfdom and of the corveé, as well as the abolition of statute labour throughout Germany. Serious umbrage was taken by Stein on one account only, because Humboldt, out of regard for Austria, had weakened the provisions regarding the

---

[1] Humboldt's Memorial upon the two new proposals for the federal act, December 9, 1814.

[2] Humboldt to Hardenberg, December 11, 1814

Landtags, and had given the provincial diets no more than a consultative voice. " This," declared Stein, " is a very retrograde step. Of all countries Prussia has least cause to take it and to induce others to take it. In this state are united all the elements which guarantee a peaceful and reasonable movement on the part of vigorously organised representative institutions ; nationality, custom, and proved readiness to furnish taxes and make sacrifices, circumspection, sound reasoning, general culture. For many reasons, Austria cannot express like principles, on account of the diversity of the constituents of the country, on account of the lower level of general culture, the maxims of the government and of the rulers, and for this reason Austria may be an exception. Let us leave this country to declare itself." [1] Thus even this ardent partisan of the Lorrainer emperordom felt himself obliged to demand a position of exception for Austria as soon as the practical consequences of federal life came under discussion.

The arduous work of these December weeks remained without issue, for meanwhile the dispute concerning the Saxon and Polish questions had become aggravated, and the imminence of war engaged all minds, so that during the first half of January the work of constructing the German constitution made no advance. As soon as the air had cleared a little, Humboldt immediately returned to his child of sorrow. Meanwhile he had been associating a great deal with the well-meaning Weimar minister, von Gersdorff, had become better acquainted with the desires of the petty states, and had acquired the conviction that since the dissolution of the empire there had come into existence at the German courts a colossal spirit of arrogance which it was necessary to take into account. The gradations of rank and of right which had existed in the old imperial constitution, had been forgotten ; the new sovereigns regarded one another as equals. If the federal act was to come into existence at all, there must not be imposed upon the petty states too marked a subordination to their greater rivals ; for, said Gersdorff, with that childlike innocence which has always been the privilege of the diplomatists of our minor states, " people love the semblance of freedom even if they cannot possess the reality." [1] Humboldt had from the first declared that a federation of states was possible only among a plurality of states. Moreover, every reason for the formation

[1] Stein's Remarks upon the proposal without circles, December 26 and 29, 1814.

[1] Gersdorff to Humboldt, December 6, 1814.

of a council of circle-governors fell to the ground if the circle sub-division itself was not to be accepted by the Hofburg. In view of the attitude which the middle-sized states had assumed in the Committee of Five and in the Saxon negotiations, it seemed extremely doubtful whether a council of five, seven, or ten states would manage the executive authority of the federation more harmoniously and more effectively than a Bundestag consisting of all the states.

For this reason, as early as January, Humboldt discussed with the chancellor the question whether, in view of the ill-humour of the minor states, it would not be better to drop the idea of the two councils, and instead to constitute a single federal assembly, which should discuss current affairs in committee, and deal with important questions in full assembly. In the full assembly every state should have at least one vote, whilst the mediatised should have a certain number of curiate votes. In view of the boundless jealousy of all against all, absolute parity seemed the only means of securing any kind of federal unity. The two statesmen thereupon composed a note to Metternich, begging for a definite declaration whether the imperial court finally refused to accept the circle constitution, and whether it would approve the formation of a single Bundestag instead of the two councils. When this had been answered, a new proposal could be elaborated. Prussia was prepared to make any concession. "There are only three points which must be regarded as absolutely essential : a powerful military authority, federal jurisdiction, and a representative constitution guaranteed by federal charter. Without federal jurisdiction, the German legal edifice would lack the last and most necessary keystone."[1] These were the three cardinal points which Hardenberg had indicated in Paris as the chief tasks of the federal constitution.

Thus did the faithful patriots worry over the hopeless task. Alone among all the German states did Prussia pursue the work of constructing the German constitution with persistent zeal ; her statesmen now indicated the only way which might lead at least to a certain degree of understanding. In all respects the Prussian policy was straightforward and devoid of *arrière pensée*, especially as regards the mediatised, who frequently expressed

---

[1] Hardenberg to Humboldt. Proposal for a note to Prince Metternich, relating to the new organisation of the Bundestag. The draft is undated, but must have been written in January, since several of the sentences in the document are reproduced word for word in the Prussian note of February 2nd-10th.

their thanks for the magnanimous protection which was extended to them by the Prussian crown alone.[1]

To get matters under way again quickly, on February 2nd the Prussian statesmen determined to send to the Austrian minister the only thing that was ready, Humboldt's two proposals of December. In a covering note they repeated the considerations expressed in Humboldt's confidential memorial for and against the circle constitution, and declared themselves prepared to accept any alteration, save only upon the three essential points : military authority, federal jurisdiction, and constitutional rights. By this compliant attitude they hoped all the sooner to secure a speedy understanding with the Hofburg, since Humboldt's two proposals contained merely a more detailed elaboration of the twelve articles which, in October, Metternich himself had laid before the Committee of Five. It was therefore very welcome to the Prussians that, at the same moment, the league of German princes and towns once more took action. Increased to the number of thirty-two members by the accession of Baden and some of the smaller states, on February 2nd the league invited the two leading powers to open as soon as possible the deliberations of all the states concerned. Hardenberg and Humboldt immediately declared themselves ready, and since Metternich also agreed, they now, on February 19th, despatched their note, with the two memorials, to the Austrian cabinet.

The Austrian statesman, however, who in the autumn had walked so pleasantly hand in hand with Prussia, now discovered endless scruples. During the Saxon negotiations he had learned to value the middle-sized states as useful allies against the North German rival, and wished to avoid anything which could wound their pride and infringe their sovereignty. The attitude towards the Germanic Federation taken by the Hofburg had been disclosed, as long ago as December, by Baron von Wessenberg, in a new federal scheme. This was the fifth proposal mooted in the weary affair. It was a senseless botch, wherein the German states were invited at their discretion to join a federation which was to preserve the common external and internal security ; whoever joined was not to secede without the assent of the other members. All the states of the federation were to have equal rights as members. A permanent Bundesrat was to be constituted out of the envoys of all the states, Austria holding the

---

[1] Count Solms-Laubach to Hardenberg, April 4, 1815 ; and several other similar memorials.

presidency. There was no trace of a genuine federal military authority. The only function of the Bundesrat was "to take care " that every state should adequately maintain its own contingent. The expenditure was to be met by proportionate contributions. In foreign affairs, the rights of the individual states of the federation were to remain unimpaired, except that their alliances with foreign powers were not to be directed against the federation itself. Diets were to be summoned within a year and a day, but their organisation was to be left to the suzerain lords. There was also an article about the mediatised, and about a few exceedingly modest liberties of the subjects, among which freedom of the press was not numbered. Finally came a promise that the federation would " care " for the freedom of commerce and navigation.[1] Now, at length, the Hofburg showed its colours. In October it had accepted the twelve articles, only because at that time it wished to keep Prussia in a good humour. Metternich's real opinion was still, as it had been in Teplitz, that the sovereignty of the German states must be limited only so far as was necessary to safeguard the European possessions of the House of Austria. Of the three points which Prussia regarded as essential to the federal constitution, one, federal jurisdiction, was entirely disregarded in Wessenberg's plan ; as for the other two, military authority and constitutional rights, Metternich's confidant eluded the issue with a few rhetorical artifices. So utterly divergent were the aims of the two powers, whose interests Hardenberg held to be harmonious.

The work of Wessenberg could quietly abide its hour, precisely because it was the emptiest and most colourless of all the proposals hitherto put forward. This became the basis of the German federal constitution, the egg out of which the cuckoo of the Frankfort Bundestag was hatched. For the moment, Metternich sagely refrained from presenting the work of his privy-councillor as a formal proposal of the Austrian government ; he contented himself with declaring that Humboldt's plans were impracticable. Since the two leading powers could not agree upon a proposal, the promised deliberations of all the states concerned could not be begun.

To complete the confusion, Stein now threw a new apple of discord among the disputants. The imperial knight could not

---

[1] The view of A. Schmidt (*Gesch. d.d. Verfassungsfrage*, p. 373) that Metternich desired to make use of this proposal in order to exclude Prussia from Germany, is unproved, and to me seems quite unprovable.

so speedily abandon his fine imperial dreams; too profoundly had he taken to heart the grandiose images of the days of the Hohenstaufen. As soon as he was assured that the petty states, in words at least, demanded the re-establishment of the imperial crown, he resumed his Teplitz plans, and on this occasion he even succeeded in convincing the czar. From the untoward experiences of the last weeks, Alexander had learned how readily an Austro-French alliance against Russia and Prussia could be formed, and he indulged the hope that the possession of the German imperial crown would, as of old, render difficult an approximation between the Hofburg and the Tuileries. But even now, as always during the congress of Vienna, he acted as a trustworthy friend of Frederick William, and would not support the imperial plan unless Prussia freely agreed. Consequently, from February 9th onwards there went on a lively exchange of notes between Stein and Capodistrias on the one side, and Humboldt on the other— to Hardenberg's profound annoyance. At first, as formerly in Teplitz, Stein put forward the confused idea that because Austria was not a purely German state the imperial state must be linked to Germany by an artificially constituted bond. The imperial knight and his Russian assistant marshalled incontestable grounds for the view that a monarch would be a more vigorous head than a council. No less incontrovertibly did Humboldt show the incapacity of Austria to utilise this monarchical power for the good of the nation. "Germany refuses to succumb to that Austrian immobility to which experience is nothing, and over which centuries pass without leaving a trace." The necessity of the Prussian emperordom, which seemed to be an obvious deduction from these pros and cons, could not be recognised in the then situation; the Lorrainers were once more so firmly established in the saddle that they sometimes even thought they would be able to unseat Prussia altogether from the back of the German steed! The result was that the imperial plan came to nought. Frederick William did not allow himself to be persuaded by Stein, although even his confidants Wittgenstein and Knesebeck did not conceal their longing for the re-establishment of the Hapsburg emperordom. Humboldt was right in his dry declaration that nothing but a federation now remained possible.

In these fruitless interludes four additional weeks were lost, and hardly had this period elapsed when, on March 7th, came the news of Napoleon's return. For many weeks, the European war-alliance and the question of preparations for war pressed all other problems into the background The German constitution seemed lost beyond the possibility of rescue. Even the German military committee, established at Prussia's instigation, and presided over by the crown prince of Würtemberg, broke up with nothing effected. With angry shame did Rühle von Lilienstern leave this assembly from which he had expected the introduction of universal military service for the whole of Germany. The conferences regarding German river navigation, which had also been summoned at Prussia's suggestion, proved a similar failure, for the Guelphs found it altogether unprecedented that purely German rivers should enjoy the same freedom as did those which belonged to several European powers in common. Münster wrote disdainfully to the prince-regent that Hanover would certainly not make financial sacrifices " in order to favour a vague idea of freedom of commerce." Honourable men among the German diplomats were overcome by an overwhelming sense of shame. What a spectacle had this Germany offered for six long months, Germany which had so recently filled the world with her warlike renown ! Nothing but quarrels and disputes, nothing but envy against the saviours of the nation, and still no issue ! Gersdorff, in distress of mind, informed the Prussians that, after all, nothing effective could be made out of Germany, that the hostile sentiments of Bavaria and her friends could not be mistaken ; it was better therefore that Prussia should conclude no more than an alliance with the south, but a firm federation with the smaller North German states, for this would offer a better future for the whole fatherland.[1]

Most of the territorial questions in dispute had been settled, the monarchs were preparing to depart, all looked impatiently for the close of the congress and tensely awaited news from the west ; the Rhenish Confederates once more impudently lifted their heads, and several of the middle-sized states hardly concealed their hope for a new victory of the Imperator. This was not the mood in which to look for the erection of a permanent national structure. Hardenberg, who as a rule had a secure sense of the favour of the moment, wished now to postpone the constitutional deliberations, until, after a new defeat of Napoleon, the arrogance of the Rhenish Confederates should have been broken, and the general sentiment should have once more become calm and collected. But how would the nation, from which new and severe sacrifices were once again demanded, receive

[1] Gersdorff to Humboldt, April 7, 1815.

its princes and ministers who, from this pomp of endless festivals, brought nothing, absolutely nothing, home? It seemed altogether too disgraceful; even Gentz issued warnings against the anger of public opinion. Moreover, Metternich was urgently desirous that the German federal act, which in his eyes was indeed no more than a European affair, should be included in the great final act of the congress, and should thus be effected under the guarantee of the whole of Europe. At a later date he regarded this point as of the highest value, and was glad to express the characteristic opinion that the Germanic Federation was a permanent league precisely for the reason that "its institution was the joint work of the European powers and of the German princes."[1] Strangely enough, this view was shared by all the Prussian statesmen, even by Humboldt. They hoped by the common guarantee of Europe to render a new felony more difficult for the middle-sized states, and they did not reflect how horribly the old empire had formerly suffered under the officious intervention of its foreign guarantors. The upshot was that Prussia was determined to resume the negotiations at this most unfavourable time conceivable.

For a long time, indeed, Humboldt had ceased to hope for the attainment of a tolerable ordering of German affairs. Of what use was dialectic skill against the ill-will of the middle-sized states and the calculated reserve of Austria? In his own words, nothing now remained but to bring the federation into existence in whatever way it might be possible. But he once more put his shoulder to the wheel, and in the beginning of April brought forward a new and notably abbreviated proposal. This was the sixth. But the negotiations were gain postponed; the middle-sized states displayed no inclination to discusss anything. During the latter half of the month, the general sentiment seemed once more somewhat more favourable. Immediately, Humboldt set to work with renewed courage,[2] and on May 1st brought forward a seventh and somewhat more detailed plan.

The Hofburg, however, declared both these proposals impossible. The House of Austria itself, was, of course, in accordance with its often displayed fidelity to the empire, prepared for every sacrifice; no one could possibly doubt this who listened to the ardent asseverations of the Austrian statesmen. It was only on account of the insuperable resistance of the minor kingly

---

[1] Metternich to Hruby, December 11, 1817.
[2] So he himself reports, in his *Systematic Description*.

courts, that the minister found himself compelled, to his profound regret, once more to reject the Prussian proposals. Metternich's rich diplomatic experience had taught him that long and wearisome disputes are ultimately decided through general exhaustion. Such a feeling now began to master everyone. All agreed with the Austrian when he declared, what had been his opinion as long ago as the previous September, that it was not yet a suitable time to think of a federal constitution, and that it would suffice if the " elements " of such a constitution could be established. He then produced once more Wessenberg's plan of December, which could indeed hardly be regarded as the element of an element, had this botch somewhat enlarged, and on May 7th handed the new elaboration to the Prussian statesmen as an eighth proposal. Regarding this proposal detailed negotiations were now at length entered upon between Metternich and Hardenberg. At the desire of Prussia, the Austrian incorporated a few strengthening clauses ; the chancellor, upon his own initiative, added an article about the mediatised, and thus there came into existence the ninth and last federal scheme, which, on May 23rd, in the name of Austria and Prussia, Metternich circulated among the plenipotentiaries of all the German states for their approval. Notwithstanding the twofold remodelling, the main articles of the Austrian proposal of December 1st remained unaltered, so that Wessenberg must be regarded as the true author of the German federal act. The amiable and highly cultured baron was regarded as one of the most open-minded politicians of Austria ; like his brother, the coadjutor, detested by the Catholics, he even cherished a certain enthusiasm for the German fatherland. But in matters of German policy, there could not exist any difference of opinion among Austrian statesmen ; whoever served the House of Austria must endeavour to give the German united state the character of a loose international alliance, because otherwise the imperial state could find no place in it.

On the previous day, May 22nd, Frederick William had signed the momentous ordinance regarding the representation of the people. The Prussian statesmen, as Humboldt often said, regarded it as an honour to them that no one in Vienna had been warmer than they in advocating the rights of the German diets. How, therefore, could Prussia lag behind the South German courts which had already instituted constitutional commissions ? Who could then have regarded it as even conceivable that the introduction of the representative system was in Prussia to encounter the most formidable obstacles, and was here to be longest delayed ? At least a formal pledge seemed inevitable ; Hardenberg had long been accustomed to compromise with the difficult duties of the legislator by means of high-sounding promises. Since 1808 the king himself had also been won over to the idea of constitutional reform, and at the same time he desired to give his faithful people a sign of grateful confidence. But with what criminal carelessness did the chancellor once more set to work ! He made the king promise that the provincial diets should be re-established, and where they were no longer in existence that they should be reintroduced, and that from them the general representation of the country should be derived by indirect election. In this way he tied in advance the hands of the absolute ruler, and this at a moment in which he himself had not even a superficial knowledge concerning the constitutional rights of those variegated territories which were newly entering the Prussian state ! Public opinion, thankful for everything which was regarded as open-minded, accepted the royal promise with delight ; and especial pleasure was exhibited at the promise of a written constitution, such as was now in fashion. All too soon was it to appear that Hardenberg had made a grave political mistake, that he had promised the impossible.

Humour was not to be lacking to the tragical failure of the hopes of our fatherland. The work of the German constitution which had been proceeding almost without result for seven months, must now at last be carried out with breathless and inconsiderate haste. When the oft-promised deliberations of all the states concerned were at length opened, Gentz had already almost completed the editing of the final act of the congress ; it was necessary to be speedy if the German federal act was still to find a place therein.

The result was that between May 23rd and June 10th, in eleven brief conferences, of which two were no more than opening and closing ceremonies, the most difficult of all European questions was settled. Never had the destiny of a great nation been played with in a more frivolous manner. Würtemberg was absent at the opening. Baron von Linden, writing in French, excused his absence upon a country visit. His colleague Wintzingerode pleaded indisposition, and the Würtembergers remained absent from all the subsequent sittings as well. A substitute was indeed present for the Badenese minister, who had already left Vienna, but the substitute had no credentials, and after a few days took his departure. All the others put in an appearance. At first the petty states were represented by five plenipotentiaries only, but from the third sitting onwards it was arranged that each state should have its own representative.

The real discussion began on May 26th. Bavaria immediately demanded, against the lively opposition of the Prussians, that the expression " sovereign " princes should be adopted in the introduction to the federal act. When the proposal was then discussed in detail, there arose in connection with every article so hopeless a confusion of fundamentally diverse demands, and such a mountain of notes, reservations, and considerations accumulated upon the president's table, that all possibility of an understanding came to an end. The session ended in ill-humour. The next day, Hardenberg and Humboldt wrote despairingly to Metternich and Münster a note,[1] in which they declared that in view of the brief time available, and of the experiences of the last sitting, the continuation of a genuine discussion seemed impossible ; views were too divergent ; moreover, Austria, Prussia, and Hanover—which in the eyes of the Prussian statesmen still seemed faithfully allied in sentiment—must not put themselves in a false position, must not for the sake of peace allow themselves to be forced to vote for the weakening of the federal authority. " The undersigned have in all the preliminary deliberations been throughout of the opinion of his grace Prince Metternich that what the previous proposals contained upon this matter can be sacrificed only to the necessity that the federation shall here and now be brought into existence ; and they freely admit that it is solely upon this ground, solely in order to avoid hindering or postponing any union of the princes of Germany, and in addition with very painful sentiments, that they have joined in bringing forward a proposal of which they feel only too keenly how little it corresponds to the important aims which had been entertained immediately after the liberation of Germany and even at the opening of the congress ; and what an unfavourable impression this will make upon the public. Should this proposal be yet further weakened by a discussion for which the present moment (in which speedy general agreement is the dominant need) remains extremely unfavourable, hardly any good result can be expected from the proceedings in

[1] Hardenberg and Humboldt to Metternich and Münster, May 27, 1815.

Frankfort." For this reason, Prussia demanded that the three great powers should present an ultimatum to the German states ; the three courts should accept the alterations which seemed unavoidable after the proceedings of the last conference, and they should declare in the next sitting that any further alterations were inadmissible ; the federation should be formed with all the princes prepared to accept this proposal ; the Bundestag of Frankfort could decide about matters of detail. The note concluded by saying that if this procedure were adopted, the majority of the states would immediately agree to the proposal, whilst some would not adhere till later, as soon as they became convinced that the federation would come into existence whether they adhered or not.

Here at length was a rapid and bold seizing of opportunity, after the old and proud Frederician manner ! If Austria and England-Hanover had accepted the Prussian proposal, success would have been assured ; federal jurisdiction, more incisive formulation of the article about the diets, and all the improvements which Prussia had effected in the Austrian proposal, would have been secured for the Germanic Federation, for not three weeks later the battle of Waterloo was fought, and after that battle how would the middle-sized states have dared to remain aloof from the Germanic Federation ? Moreover, the Prussian proposal was in perfect harmony with the well-grounded legal position which in November the three allied courts had maintained against the cabinets of Stuttgart and Carlsruhe—the position that the petty states were by the treaties of accession pledged to join the federation. It now, however, became manifest that the vigorous notes of the previous November had, for Austria and Hanover, been mere moves in the diplomatic game. Metternich would no longer recognise this secure legal aspect of the question. Just as Wessenberg's proposal had merely contained a modest "invitation" to the German princes to enter the federation at their pleasure, so now the Austrian minister declared that no kind of pressure, not even indirect pressure, should be exercised upon the German sovereigns to induce them to join the federation ! What did he care about federal jurisdiction and diets, these two fixed ideas of Prussian politics towards which the Hofburg was half indifferent and half suspicious ? Was Austria to forfeit the friendship of the middle-sized states for such things as these ?

Metternich rejected the Prussian proposal, and on May 29th

the conference was continued in the former chaotic style. The prospect became ever gloomier, for, at this sitting, Councillor von Globig, envoy of the finally reinstated king of Saxony, was introduced into the assembly; by his presence the centrifugal tendencies were notably reinforced. Globig naturally opened confidential deliberations with his old well-wisher Metternich. It was secretly discussed whether Saxony should not enter into a South German federation under the leadership of Austria, but the idea was speedily abandoned, for the Austrian was of opinion that in existing circumstances a united Germanic Federation was, after all, the most suitable means for effectively checking Prussian ambition! On May 30th the conference discussed the article about the Landtags. Since Austria had ruled out all the constitutional rights introduced into the Prussian proposals, this article now ran quite briefly, to the effect that a representative constitution must exist in all German states. Gagern, who was always an enthusiastic advocate of constitutional ideas, found this wording far too bald and unsatisfying. To others it appeared too strict and commanding; who could venture to issue an order to a sovereign prince? The majority decided: "In all German states a representative constitution will come into existence"— a prophecy instead of a command! Many of the voters hoped in their secret hearts that the prophecy would never be fulfilled.

On June 2nd came the catastrophe, the triumph of particularism. The German world was to learn what the restoration of the Albertine kingship signified for our national policy. There was no longer any dispute about the fact that the elements of the future federal constitution were being discussed. The federal act expressly declared that the first business of the Frankfort Bundestag would be: "The drafting of the fundamental laws of the federation and its organic institution." There thus still remained a faint hope that in Frankfort, after Napoleon's overthrow, a reasonable-minded majority might come into existence, and that some of the sins of Vienna might be atoned. But now Saxony demanded the *liberum veto*, unanimity for all resolutions of the plenum of the federal assembly. An ultimate vestige of shame prevented the conference from accepting this proposal in all its naked impudence. But the majority next day passed a resolution which amounted to the same thing, deciding that all decisions about fundamental laws, about organic federal institutions, concerning *jura singulorum*, and concerning the affairs of religion, could be passed only by a unanimous vote. In this way a new Polish Reichstag was founded, a permanent obstacle was imposed against the legislative development of the future German united state. The party of reform was forced into the paths of revolution. This was the first sign of life of the re-established Saxon kingdom. The fundamental laws of a federal constitution which had not yet come into existence, whose elements were only now being established, were to be subordinated to unanimous resolutions. This was merely to declare at the outset that the new Germany could be created only with the aid of the sword. And what was the meaning of the phrase " organic institution " ? Here also there was no general understanding, and all explanation was shunned.

This decision spoiled the little there was still left to spoil. Throughout, particularism and the arbitrary disputes of the petty thrones had retained the upper hand. It was natural for them to assert their right to independent diplomatic relations, and to independent alliances ; the only reservation in the latter case was that they might not enter into alliance with foreigners against the federation or its members. But this did not unconditionally exclude the possibility that Germans might take the field against Germans as accessory troops of foreign powers. And this danger was still imminent. The old and debased traffic in soldiers was resumed. Even during the congress, a Nassau regiment was sold to Holland, or, to use the official expression, was " lent." " Should a federal war be declared " no member of the federation might undertake individual negotiations with the enemy. But what a federal war might be, and whether the federation was pledged to take action in case of an attack upon the foreign possessions of any of its members—concerning these vital questions no agreement could be reached. The only thing that was certain was that the federation, in a more paltry position than a third-rank state, might not itself wage a war of offence, for the federal act spoke only of defence against the aggressor. When the rights of the diets had been dealt with in a phrase, the arrogance of the Napoleonic kings was diverted against the mediatised. Vainly did Prussia endeavour to secure a few curiate votes for the dethroned ; the middle-sized states carried the proposal that this question should be referred to the Bundestag and, after all that had passed here under everyone's eyes, the value of this consolation was obvious. Still worse was the case of the Jews. The original proposal had secured for them " the right which they already enjoyed *in* the individual states of the federation." This significant *in*, was now replaced by a *von*, so that they were guaranteed the rights they enjoyed *from* the individual states of the federation. The change gave Hanover and Electoral Hesse a free hand to repeal the laws of the kingdom of Westphalia, and to reintroduce the Jewish poll-tax ; the Jews of Frankfort forfeited the emancipation which they had recently acquired from the prince-primate Dalberg after purchasing the Judenschloss.

The hopes for a national reconstruction of the Catholic church of Germany also vanished little by little. How greatly had the German hierarchy been ill-used by the secularisation and the innumerable other arbitrary acts of the Napoleonic epoch. How profoundly had its political power declined. Instead of a crowd of spiritual princes, there now sat in the high council of the Germanic Federation only six Catholic sovereigns, Austria, Bavaria, and Saxony, two Hohenzollerns, and Liechtenstein. Both parties of the German clergy besieged the statesmen with petitions. Cardinal Consalvi and the Oratorians demanded the restoration of their ancient possessions, and wherever possible the restoration also of the ancient political power of the Church ; they demanded in any case the participation of ecclesiastical representatives in the negotiations concerning the Federation, and the restoration of the bereaved bishoprics by the pope. Heinrich Wessenberg, on the other hand, advocated the plan of a German national Church, under the leadership of a prince-primate ; he repeatedly brought forward the scheme in verbose memorials, and yet, in priestly fashion, remained ultramontane towards the Protestants ; it seemed to him hardly desirable that the Federation should recognise the rights of the Protestants. The two parties fought one another vigorously. To the Oratorians, Wessenberg was hardly better than a heretic. Count Spiegel, however, also a distinguished and highly-cultured prince of the Church, and a man of the old school, urgently warned the Prussian statesmen against the memorials of the Oratorians ; " They are," he said, " permeated by a purely ultramontane spirit, and contrast strongly with the ever-venerable sense of truth which animated the fathers at the Councils of Constance and of Basle." It is true that he desired the re-establishment of the Catholic church, but he desired also its further development through the influence of " liberal governments." [1]

Bavaria and Würtemberg were equally hostile to both

---

[1] Spiegel to Humboldt, December 2, 1815.

parties; each of them separately hoped to found provincial bishoprics in virtue of a concordat with Rome, and in this, as in everything else, to leave the Germanic Federation altogether out of account. The Prussians, finally, in this question, as throughout the federal negotiations at Vienna, showed themselves to be just, enlightened, and national-minded; they demanded that the Federation should give the Catholic church a common constitution for the whole of Germany, but that it should also guarantee the Protestant churches in the possession of their ancient rights. Such were the divergencies of view. Only in one respect were all in agreement, in the opinion that Austria must be left to herself, must remain outside the new ordering of our ecclesiastical life. As soon as any practical question came up for discussion, it always appeared that Austria lived apart from Germany. It was for this reason that Heinrich Wessenberg, admired by the liberal world, could live in Vienna with his brother the Austrian privy-councillor, and could even enjoy a certain favour in the circles of the Hofburg; what he was aiming at related to countries elsewhere in the empire and left the imperial hereditary dominions unaffected. Numerous conferences had been devoted to these ecclesiastical questions, the petitions and proposals relating to this matter had made a mountainous mass of writings; at length, presumably at the instigation of Wessenberg's elder brother, in the last Austrian federal proposal an article had been included, providing the Catholic church with a common constitution, and promising the Protestants the maintenance of their ancient rights. The majority agreed. Bavaria, however, was adverse, and maintained her position with such tenacity that Heinrich Wessenberg abandoned hope. On June 3rd he wrote to the chancellor[1] that since ecclesiastical affairs in Germany were still in a condition of unparalleled neglect, and since the congress had not been able to concern itself about matters of detail he would venture to propose that, within two months, the sovereigns concerned, the princes with Catholic subjects, should send representatives to Frankfort. There, in Frankfort, in free conferences, which to Bavarian pride might seem intolerably dangerous, the indefatigable man still hoped to bring his national church into being.

Meanwhile, Austria herself had attained to the view that matters must be brought to a conclusion. If the negotiations were to continue, there might be nothing left even of the Austrian

[1] Wessenberg's Memorial to Hardenberg, June 3, 1815.

proposal. Metternich therefore, on June 5th, declared to the conference—what he had already more than once hinted, but had not yet carried into effect out of regard for the feelings of the Rhenish Confederate courts—that the federal act had acquired a form which appeared to correspond to the views of most of the courts ; he then announced Austria's adhesion to the Germanic Federat on on the basis of the constitutional principles which had now been established, and begged the other states to follow this examp'e. Yet he gave no intimation that the Federation would, as Prussia had demanded, come into existence without the adhesion of all the states, but left it open to each to join or not at pleasure. Thereupon Prussia, Hanover, Denmark, Luxemburg, and some of the petty states, announced their adhesion. Most of them subsequently appended doleful written explanations. Prussia merely added that it was better, after all, " to form an imperfect federation than none at all " ; Hanover's explanation was to the same effect ; Luxemburg concluded a bond " which time, experience, and increasing confidence must improve "—and so on. But what an uproar there was in the assembly when Count Rechberg now dryly declared that he found it necessary for the present to withhold the adhesion of Bavaria ! He added some solemn and cryptic obervations from which everyone was forced to conclude that the court of Munich renounced the Federation. The dismay was general ; and, most unfortunately, the good Gagern now committed a folly weighty with consequences. He never could do anything without the accompaniment of imperial patriotic phrases, and therefore, whilst announcing the adhesion of Luxemburg, he added as a condition that the Federation must embrace the whole of Germany. Nassau, as always, took the same line as the Orange cousins. Gagern's proviso was unquestionably in part due to a federalistic whim, for the Luxemburg envoy remarked in an elucidatory note that his king could not admit that anything but the totality of the German states could constitute a Germanic Federation, and that therefore the garrisoning of the federal fortress of Luxemburg could only be effected by the Federation, that is to say, by all the states in rotation. The declaration of the garrulous visionary was certainly not made with malicious intent. He had no idea of how bad an example he was setting. What confusion would arise if some of the other states were to declare that they would join the Federation only if all the rest did ! And this in effect was what happened. The future of Germany was put up to tender, and was ultimately left to the decision of those who desired to do least for the fatherland.

It was decided that at the conference of June 8th the still remaining declarations of adhesion should be read, and the work should be concluded. The two intervening days passed in anxious excitement, in painful suspense. Count Rechberg gave no sign ; it was the general conviction that Bavaria would not join. Even the phlegmatic Humboldt was overwhelmed with all that he had had to endure in this environment. Profoundly discouraged, he was already drawing up the plan for a provisional federation without Bavaria.[1] Meanwhile, Gagern's mistake brought its fruit. Saxony, Darmstadt, and others, even Denmark and Mecklenburg, which had adhered on June 5th without reservation, now declared that they could only join a federation which embraced the whole of Germany. Several of these states expressly begged that the princes who still wished to remain outside should have adhesion made possible for them by new concessions. It was an endless screw. If Bavaria should refuse to join, everything would fly to pieces.

Thereupon, on the morning of June 8th, Count Rechberg announced that his new instructions had come to hand. Such was his assertion, but it seems by no means impossible that the Bavarian had in his creative imagination arranged the whole ridiculous climax of the unworthy intrigue, simply in order to secure thereby more effectively the granting of the ultimate wishes of the Wittelsbachs. However, everyone breathed more freely. Austria and Prussia immediately entered into confidential conversation with Rechberg. In addition to a few matters of trifling importance, he demanded the abolition of federal jurisdiction and of the article concerning the Catholic church. Thus was fulfilled Hardenberg's warning of May 27th. The two great powers were actually placed in the unpleasant position of having to secure peace by agreeing to the weakening of the federal authority—though this, indeed, was no sacrifice for Metternich. Federal jurisdiction was abandoned, although, as Humboldt had often said, this was the keystone of the German legal structure ; while of the enormous mass of paper which represented the ecclesiastical negotiations, nothing remained beyond an exiguous article decreeing what had long already been the law almost all over Germany, namely, that the differences between the Christian

[1] Humboldt's Proposal for a provisional treaty between the acceding German states.

sects should not involve any difference in the enlargement of civic and political rights. Then the conference was opened, and Metternich announced " with pleasure" that Bavaria wished only a few trifling alterations to be effected. These few trifling alterations were approved, and now the matter was really settled, for what more was there to excise from this act? On June 10th one more sitting was held in order to sign the federal act, and in order to celebrate with all diplomatic honours the interment of the corpse of German unity. When could its resurrection be expected?

The first eleven articles of the charter dated June 8th were further incorporated into the final act of the congress, just before its dissolution; henceforward victorious Germany had to revere all the princes of Europe, with the exception of the pope and the sultan, as the guarantors of her fundamental law. Nor were there lacking the protests which traditionally belong to every great German action of state. All the mediatised proclaimed their rights. Even more boldly did the princes of Isenburg and Knyphausen lift their heads; they regarded themselves as sovereigns, and as such declared their accession to the Germanic Federation. It was superfluous; eight-and-thirty German powers sufficed for the needs of German civilisation, which indeed, according to the general view, was rooted in the motley complexity of our national life. It suddenly appeared, however, that there was yet a thirty-ninth sovereign, the landgrave of Hesse-Homburg. He had been altogether forgotten; but since the patriotic old gentleman and his valiant son enjoyed the special favour of the two great powers, the Germans might hope that the Bundestag would still have pity on him. The loudest complaints of all came from the Roman see. In an energetic Latin note, Cardinal Consalvi appealed as a precedent to the action of the nuncio Chigi, who had once protested against the Peace of Westphalia, and entered a protest because neither the Holy Roman Empire, the centre of political unity consecrated by the holiness of faith, nor yet the power of the spiritual princes, had been re-established.

It was only in order that the Federation might certainly comprise the whole of Germany, that the better disposed cabinets had yielded to the last extravagant demands of Bavaria; and yet, notwithstanding all the chaffering and haggling, a federation of all the powers had not come into existence. Just as formerly North Carolina and Rhode Island had failed to participate in the establishment of the second federal union of North America, so Baden and Würtemberg remained apart from the foundation of the Germanic Federation, and did not join until Napoleon's overthrow had for the second time been decided. Baden adhered on July 26th, and Würtemberg on September 1st.

Thus came into existence the federal act, the most unworthy constitution which was ever imposed upon a great civilised nation by rulers of its own blood, a work which was in many respects even more lamentable than the structure of the old empire in the century of its extinction. It lacked that majesty of historical greatness which formed an atmosphere around the empire of the Othos even in its decay. This political artifact stood up in all its bareness and nudity, the work of a short-lived and self-centred diplomacy which had forgotten all the memories of its own nation ; there was here no rust of centuries to conceal the scanty hideousness of the forms. People sang and talked about emperor and empire ; but never has a German heart beat higher at the name of the Germanic Federation. Of the states of the federation, there were six only, and these among the smallest, whose territorial area had not undergone changes during the last twenty years ; even the most tolerant of nations could no longer believe in the legitimacy of a territorial distribution which was at once so new and so arbitrary. The same foreign dominion which had brought the old empire to destruction pressed now upon the new federation. Since the days of Frederick, the power of Austria had undergone a notable increase, and was now all the harder to break because Austria exercised her influence directly, without the masterful forms of the emperordom. The foreign diplomats smiled maliciously, saying that it was an excellent thing to have coupled Austria and Prussia in this way and thus to have weakened both ! The old imperial law had at least continued to speak of a German nation ; the idea that all Germans were loyal, attached to the emperor, and ready to serve him, had never completely disappeared. The new federal act knew nothing of a German nation ; it recognised only Bavarians, Waldeckers, Schwarzburg-Sondershauseners, subjects of those German princes who of their own free will had joined a legal union. The nation had to drain the cup of humiliation to the dregs ; the Würtemberger's saying that a nation, after all, is not to be constructed out of different peoples, had proved perfectly true. The Germans stood altogether out of relationship to the federal authority, and were not pledged in any way to obey it; only when a sovereign deigned to recognise a federal decree as a law of the land, were his subjects compelled to obey this law. The nation was mediatised by a league of princes. Like the revolution of 1803, this new constitution of Germany was created exclusively by the dynasts.

The new Bundestag was the Reichstag of Ratisbon in a somewhat more modern form, just as cumbrous and just as impracticable; it was a mere formality that it sometimes sat in committee and sometimes in plenum, for even in committee all the nine-and-thirty voted. The contrast between formal rights and living power was even more crudely conspicuous in the Germanic Federation than it had been in the Holy Empire. The arrogance of the petty crowns, stimulated by the enjoyment of sovereignty, effected in Vienna a distribution of votes which greatly exceeded all the enormities of the ancient imperial law, and which now in its turn helped this arrogance to rise to the degree of insanity. A certain preference for the smaller members of the federation lies in the nature of any federal constitution. But it went far beyond the measure of permissible injustice that in the full assembly of the Bundestag, seven great states, Austria, the five kingdoms, and Baden, which together contained more than five-sixths of the whole German people, should possess a minority of twenty-seven votes, as against forty-two votes possessed by the remaining sixth. This amounted to an open invitation to the great states to circumvent the federal decrees, or else to browbeat their smaller comrades. And then, in addition, came that gift of the crown of Saxony, the unanimity requisite for all important decisions—a prescription which in the Holy Empire had applied only to religious questions and to *jura singulorum*. Now Reuss of the younger line could prohibit all development of the Federation. But further such development would be made altogether impossible by the general adoption of a representative system. For if the Federation were to have any kind of effective life it must first attempt to limit the military authority and to control the foreign policy of the individual states; but these were the only sovereign rights which, after the introduction of the diets, would still remain undiminished to the petty princes, and a voluntary renunciation on their part of these rights was altogether impossible to expect.

This many-headed federal assembly, without a leader, possessed neither legal nor moral responsibility. It consisted of delegates, bound strictly to their instructions, and therefore able to shuffle off all blame from themselves upon their principals; whilst, on the other hand, the petty crowns learned all too soon how to take refuge behind the Bundestag against the anger of public opinion. Germany's internal politics became a struggle in the air; no one knew any longer where he was to seek his true opponent. The demoralising influence of such inveracity showed itself very speedily alike at the courts and among the people; cowardly anxiety on the one side; cuckoo-cloudland dreams of obscure bitterness upon the other. The hopeless confusion became all the more intolerable because a severe struggle between the federation and its members was impossible to avoid, for the central authority of the Federation was autocratic, was simply an organ of the princes, whereas in the individual states the power of the Landtags soon became operative.

The nation accepted the unhappy piece of work with sinister coldness. Whoever expressed any opinion at all about the matter showed savage anger. The few articles concerning popular rights, for which public opinion was for the most part prepared, contained such empty and windy promises, that even this good-natured nation was forced to begin to believe in the ill-will of its rulers. How strangely, beside the indefinite phrases about freedom of the press, freedom of trade, and diets, reads the precise enumeration of the privileges of the mediatised and of the post-office monopolies of Thurn and Taxis. Most lamentable of all, the federal act was not a constitution, but contained merely the elements so far formulated of a future federal law. Four years later, the honourable-minded Gagern wrote, not without repentance, to a conservative friend: "You speak of the maintenance of what exists. Vainly do I seek durability. I see a federal act which we first undertook to develop at Vienna."

In the territorial negotiations, the Prussian statesmen, thanks to the king's firmness, had attained at least a half-measure of success. In the federal negotiations, they were completely vanquished; they had not carried into effect a single part of their intentions. But the escutcheon of Prussian honour had remained untarnished. The attitude of the state which had saved us from the foreigner, served also in Vienna to shame all other Germans—if there was indeed any place for shame amid so savage a struggle of interests. Tenaciously and straightforwardly, and more consistently than Stein, had Hardenberg and Humboldt held fast to a definite plan, yielding only step by step in face of the united resistance of almost the whole of Germany. This plan of theirs was certainly affected by the general political obscurity of the epoch, but was at any rate more honourable and reasonable than were all the other proposals put forward in Vienna. It was not their fault that the form of their proposals underwent continual changes, for this was the inevitable outcome of the pressure of a hopeless struggle against opponents who could never be convinced by a word, but only by a blow. The one fault of both was their unsuspecting confidence in the false friends Austria and Hanover. But even a perfect statesman, who could have remained absolutely free from such weaknesses, would not have been able to conquer in this struggle. The whole course of German destiny during recent years had led inevitably to the tragical and yet necessary consequence that after the fall of Napoleon the configuration of the German state came to be decided, not by Napoleon's valiant enemy Prussia, but by his hesitating opponent Austria, and by his allies the Rhenish Confederates.

The czar manifested discontent at the lamentable issue, and not even Gentz had expected so ridiculous a botch. None the less, the new order of German affairs possessed three momentous advantages. The historical effects of the princes' revolution of 1803 remained undisturbed, the grotesque theocratic system was not restored. New Germany breathed the healthy air of a temporal state. Again, although the federal constitution did not impose an absolute barrier to the origination of a new Confederation of the Rhine, it rendered this far more difficult ; for this reason alone, as Hardenberg and Humboldt frequently declared, did Prussia's statesmen adopt a work as to whose defects they were under no illusion. Prussia joined the Federation in order to prevent the middle-sized states from repeating their treasons, whereas these states regarded the federal constitution merely as a bulwark against Prussian ambition. Finally, the Germanic Federation was so loosely organised and so feeble that neither in its internal nor in its external development could it appreciably disturb the state of Frederick. As soon as Prussia had thought the matter over, the shadowy federal constitution would be seen to offer a thousand ways and means of attaching the petty states to herself by separate alliances, and of showing them that in actual practice Austria did nothing for Germany, while Prussia alone was in a position to do justice to the longings of the nation and to the rightly understood interests of the petty courts. As we look back upon the life-history of the Germanic Federation we see that it is upon this that depends its historic renown : it did not possess power to prevent the increase in strength of the one really living German state, of the state that was destined at a later date to destroy that Federation, and to bestow upon our unhappy nation a new and worthy order.

CHAPTER II.

BELLE ALLIANCE (WATERLOO).

§ I.   THE BELGIAN CAMPAIGN.

ALTHOUGH it is a matter of daily experience that coming events
cast their shadows before, it very rarely happens that the heroes
of a closed chapter in history resume their places upon the
transformed stage of time.   In such a return of past greatness
there always inheres a wonderful and dream-like magic, because
there is involved a contradiction with the necessary and eternal
process of historic life.   Never has destiny assumed a more
fantastic form than during the Hundred Days, when the
men and the passions of an age of war emerged like a train of
spectres in clear noonday to trouble the life of a new and peace-
loving generation, and in which the grandiose adventure of the
Napoleonic emperordom found its appropriate and stormy
epilogue.   On March 1st Napoleon with his nine hundred faithful
followers landed on the coast near Cannes ; on the evening of
March 20th, the birthday of the king of Rome, his dusty carriage
drove to the Tuileries through the silent capital, and a crowd
of veterans drunk with joy greeted the returning hero on the
portals of the abandoned royal palace.   " The emperor has
appeared and the royal government no longer exists," he wrote
proudly to the foreign envoys.   Never before had the elemental
forces of genius and of reputation secured so brilliant a triumph ;
the bloodless victorious progress really seemed, as the Imperator
assured the princes of Europe, " the work of an irresistible force,
the unanimous will of a great nation aware of its duties and of its
rights."

Yet this miracle-like revolution proceeded almost exclusively
from the army.   The old corporals and sergeants who here, as in
all professional armies, controlled the spirit of the troops, regarded
with idolatrous worship the image of the democratic hero ; they
were the apostles of that Napoleonic religion whose titanic legends

had consoled the proud nation during its defeats. How would it have been possible for the fourth regiment of artillery in whose ranks Bonaparte had once served as lieutenant to resist the fiery appeal of the *gros papa*, who restored the glorious tricolor and the world-subduing eagles, and who dismissed the detested new officers belonging to the emigré nobility ? Carried away by the delirium of enthusiasm, overwhelmed by the power of wonderful memories, one regiment after another followed the alluring example : the times were to return in which the prætorian was everything, the civilian nothing. The old guard decorated their eagles with flowers, which were not to be removed until the honour of the empire had been avenged by brilliant victories over the Prussians and other foreigners. But no longer, as once in the days of the 18th Brumaire, was the army France. While even a portion of the officers, and among them some of the most capable of the marshals, like Oudinot and Macdonald, scorned to partici-pate in the great perjury, the peaceful middle classes were utterly perplexed by the re-emergence of this democratic tyrant, whose remarkable and ambiguous character made him at once welcome and ominous. The restoration had not effected any notable changes in the Napoleonic constitution ; it was nourished, as the Bonapartists insisted, upon the " capital of authority" which the First Consul had left for his successors. The effective machine of the prefectoral administration con-tinually extended its operations. The well-meaning king, on the other hand, who had been placed in the saddle by the favour of the tories, remained altogether estranged from the sentiments and customs of the new democratic society. He was surrounded by the Artois, the Blacas, the covetous pack of émigrés who were impatient for the re-establishment of the old nobles' regime. The hatred of the people for the Bourbons was dependent not only upon the mistakes of the crown, but also, and still more, upon the sinister intentions attributed to its supporters.

Beside those who now crowded round the banner of the lilies, the returning Napoleon seemed even to the bourgeois classes a national hero, a representative of the idolised ideas of '89. But at the same time his name signified war. The instinct of the business world immediately recognised that this man would never keep the peace, and that the neighbouring powers could never allow him to remain at peace. Immediately after his return, the advantageous position which Talleyrand's cunning had secured for the Bourbon crown in the society of states was once more lost ; France stood completely isolated, and before the eyes of a world which urgently needed peace there opened the gloomy prospect of new and interminable warlike storms. Moreover, the parliamentary institutions of the *Charte constitutionnelle de France* had quickly taken root. Hardly had the epoch of military glory passed away when, with admirable vitality, the nation one more threw itself into the party struggles of political and literary life. The country took pleasure in the oratorical arts displayed in the representative chamber, in the noisy criticisms of the free press. The constitutional doctrine again found honourable and convinced advocates. Thousands of persons honestly believed that it was the destiny of this liberated nation to vitalise parliamentary governnent after the English model with the incomparable Napoleonic administrative despotism, and in this way to found an exemplary constitutional state ; but the realisation of these ideals seemed far more readily possible under the weak rule of the Bourbons than under the iron dominion of the soldier emperor. Consequently the cultured and possessing classes held suspiciously aloof from the Imperator ; in a few days the national securities fell to fifty-three. It is true that only a few regiments of the south and of the west held firmly to the side of the royal house ; even the legitimist rising which broke out in La Vendée was devoid of danger, since it proceeded from the nobles rather than from the peasants. Napoleon's return was premature ; a few years later, when the memory of the horrors of the war-time had begun to fade, and when the hatred felt for the emigrés had become more powerful, the Imperator might perhaps have succeeded. In the existing situation of affairs, the majority of the nation remained sceptical, anxious, perplexed. It was only to the peasants in the eastern provinces, who have always been of a warlike disposition, and to the workmen of some of the larger towns, that the crowned plebeian was welcome. In the suburbs of Paris a Jacobin federation was formed, but the memories which were revived in this body had little in common with the Cæsarism of which the army made a cult.

Napoleon speedily noticed how greatly the country had changed. " The Bourbons," he said savagely, " have spoiled France for me." In order to win over the middle classes he had to coquet with liberal ideas. In cleverly composed manifestos he represented himself as the chosen of the people, laying stress upon the popular character of the empire, which had disciplined democracy, perfected equality, and paved the way for liberty. But promises no longer sufficed. He found himself compelled to constitute a cabinet out of men of the Revolution and to enlarge the constitution of the empire by a supplementary act, which guaranteed to the nation an electoral popular assembly, freedom of the press, the right of petition, and even the restriction of military jurisdiction. In this way he was forced to tie his own hands at a moment when nothing but an absolute dictatorship could compel the nation, greatly desirous of peace, to make a strong military effort. He appeared upon the Champ de Mars to gratify the Parisian love of spectacles by a great popular military display, and to make public profession of his democratic faith. " As Emperor, as First Consul, and as soldier, I owe everything to the people!" His favourite daughter Hortense and her little son Louis attended the display; but Marie Louise did not return to the Tuileries, for the loyalty of the Austrian woman was given to the child of fortune, not to the spouse.

The Imperator gradually came to realise that he was now only the leader of a great gang of military mutineers, and no longer the universally dreaded chief of the state. He was overwhelmed with shame and rage when he was forced to show himself at the window in response to the homage of the working-class Jacobins. From time to time he even asked himself whether he should not straightway don the red cap, take over the leadership of the revolutionary parties, dissolve the National Guard of the Parisian bourgeoisie, and constitute in place thereof a popular army composed of the federated manual workers. But his detestation of the Jacobins prevailed. Napoleon could not lay aside his old despotic habits; he issued lists of proscribed persons; and he re-established a twofold secret police, whose agents mutually watched one another. Notwithstanding the supplementary act, notwithstanding his liberal asseverations, notwithstanding his coldness towards the Jacobins, he did not succeed in acquiring the confidence of the bourgeoisie. The credulous doctrinaire Benjamin Constant did, indeed, take the side of the returned despot, and the organ of the constitutionalists, the *Censeur* of Dunoyer, extolled the supplementary act as the perfection of French liberty—a wonderful self-deception which for decades to come was to be the watchword of the opposition. But the mass of the constitutionalists remained obstinately mistrustful. In secret, they put their hopes on the cunning Louis Philippe of Orleans, who had for long been busily though quietly weaving nets to secure the citizen crown of France. When the deputies assembled in June, one of Napoleon's opponents, Lanjuinais, former president of the Convention, was elected president ; the revolutionary leaders opposed the emperor with relentless violence.

The worst of all was that Napoleon, in order to allay the bourgeois fear of war, had to display a hypocritical confidence in the maintenance of peace. At the moment, he said, nothing was further from his mind than the desire for war. It was not until the *grande armée* of the empire had been re-established, that the struggle for the inalienable ancient boundaries was to recommence. He repeatedly assured the European courts that nothing had been changed in France, that he renounced all designs of warlike aggrandisement, and that he now recognised one struggle only, the sacred struggle for the happiness of the nations. No one believed him. Unceasingly Old Europe pursued preparations for the annihilation of the usurper, and yet for a time he had to maintain the semblance that his empire was a realm of peace. Not for three weeks did he dare to command an increase in the army. On his arrival this had consisted of 115,000 men, and by the beginning of June it had enlarged only to 198,000 men. The same sense of insecurity also forced him to adopt an extremely venturesome plan of campaign. According to the experiences of the previous year, a vigorous defensive war in the interior of France might perhaps have been not altogether impossible ; but since the usurper could neither count upon a mass rising in his favour, nor yet dared to expose himself to the danger of a defeat upon French soil, he was constrained to undertake an attack upon his neighbours, and for this desperate venture had at his disposal only 128,000 men. The rest of the forces were distributed along the frontiers, this being a completely useless dispersal of military power, but the suspicions of the public would now allow the Imperator to leave any portion of French soil entirely undefended. Not until war was unavoidable did Napoleon drop the peaceful mask, displaying once more the ambitious ideas of the old imperial policy. His war minister Davoust had to summon to the colours all the old soldiers from the left bank of the Rhine. In his address to the army, the Imperator spoke as of old, as the protector of German particularism, exhorting to the struggle against the insatiable coalition which was already engaged in swallowing the petty German states. A proclamation discovered in Napoleon's carriage on the battle-field of Belle

Alliance announced to the Belgians and to the Rhinelanders the joyful tidings that they were worthy to be Frenchmen !

Since this Cæsar was once more at the head of his prætorians, it was inevitable that the old struggle between world dominion and national freedom should break out once more. In accordance with the letter of international law, Napoleon's taking up of arms was indeed nothing more than a legitimate war of conquest of the sovereign prince of Elba against the most Christian king. Vainly did Gentz, in the columns of the *Oesterreichischer Beobachter*, endeavour by the use of artificial sophisms to interpret away this incontestable legal right. But of what use to the despot were forms of international law, to the man who all his life had played with loyalty and faith, who had trodden under foot every sacred right of the society of nations ? To the millions in Germany, Russia, and England, the returning tyrant did not appear to be a prince making war, but simply a blood-stained criminal whose reckless breach of his word imperilled all the blessings of peace, so recently and so laboriously won. A cry of anger rang through Prussia. The old enemy was once more upon the spot ; like a hungry wolf he had broken into the peaceful fold of the liberated nations ; who could doubt that the German sword must once more hurl him down from his usurped throne ? This valiant nation which had suffered such unspeakable woes from the blows of the tyrant neither could, nor would, see anything of the moving and elevating incidents which embellished the Imperator's return, nor could it make allowances for the political confusion which explained the hopeless embarrassment of the French nation. To the Prussians, the French were simply a mob of traitors, the French army was composed of soldiers false to their oaths, who were conspiring with their old robber-chieftain to undertake fresh campaigns of plunder. On this occasion, too, a sense of happy pride was joined to a deadly hatred. Old Blucher spoke once more from the heart to his Prussians, when at the first news he joyfully exclaimed : " That is the best luck of all for us ; now the army can clear up the mess made by the diplomats." It was only in the course of the congress, and through Talleyrand's hostile machinations, that the mass of the patriots of the north had come clearly to understand what a flabby and feeble thing had been the peace of Paris, and how little was our western frontier secured. As soon as the prospect of a new war opened, the press, headed by the *Rheinische Merkur*, immediately declared that the time had at length arrived to draw the teeth of the Gallic beast of prey. In a thousand tones, far more loudly and more definitely than the year before, was the demand voiced: "Restore the plunder, restore Alsace and Lorraine!"

At the courts, too, there was not a moment's hesitation in recognising that the destruction of the peace of Paris could not be tolerated. Already on March 8th Stein resolved upon the outlawry of the disturber of the peace. On March 13th the eight powers which had signed the treaty of peace assembled and determined upon a public declaration announcing to the nations of Europe that Napoleon Bonaparte had placed himself outside civil and political rights and must be outlawed as an enemy and disturber of the peace of the world. The Bonapartists raised an outcry regarding this unprecedented, this cannibal resolution; yet it merely expressed what was imperiously demanded by the aroused feelings of all Germans and Russians, and by the great majority of the English nation. On March 25th the four allies of Chaumont renewed their former league, offered their support to the king of France and to any other land which might be attacked by Bonaparte, invited all the powers of Europe to join them, and pledged themselves not to lay down arms until Bonaparte was no longer in a position to excite new disturbances and again to seize the reins of power in France. The declaration of the eight did not directly exclude the possibility of a change in the French frontiers, for it expressly reserved for the powers the right to complete and strengthen the decisions of the treaty of Paris. But, like the war alliance of March 25th, it rested upon a momentous error of fact, upon the assumption that the Bourbons were maintaining themselves at least in some part of France, and that the allied armies would act as accessory troops coming to the assistance of the royal army.

A few days later, information reached Vienna that King Louis had had to evacuate his country down to the last village. The legitimate ruler was domiciled in Ghent as a prince without country, and was now almost entirely under the influence of the vengeance-breathing emigrés; while the outlawed disturber of the public peace, writing peaceful letters to his crowned brothers, informed them of the bloodless subdual of France, and offered to recognise the treaty of Paris immediately. The situation was altered in a moment, and the rancorous whigs in parliament did not hesitate to take advantage of the fact. Whitbread and Burdett enquired in thunderous speeches whether

England was to bleed again in order to force upon a free people a government, a dynasty, whose hopeless weakness had been so painfully displayed.

The tory government felt it necessary to appease the opposition, and therefore announced in Vienna that although the prince regent did indeed approve the treaty of March 25th, and would do all in his power to fight against Bonaparte, still he could not pledge himself to impose upon the French any definite government. On May 9th, Austria, Prussia, and Russia recognised that this interpretation of the treaty was well grounded, and also reserved a free hand for themselves in respect of the future government of France. There followed in the committee of the eight powers a tedious deliberation upon the question whether, in view of the actual success of Bonaparte and of his peaceful despatches, a new declaration were not desirable. Talleyrand had the audacity to lay before the allies a proposal for a manifesto in which they should modestly declare that Europe was fighting just as much for France as for her own safety, and would lay down arms immediately after the dethronement of Bonaparte.[1] But no one would any longer accede to such suggestions. The commission appointed to consider the question decided that the usurper's assurances were not worthy of belief; in extremely moderate language it maintained that the right of a nation to change its government was not unrestricted, but that it was within the competence of neighbouring states to take steps to prevent a misuse of this right which might involve danger to them all; it recalled the universally known fact that the allies had granted conquered France mild terms of peace only upon the express condition that the Corsican disturber of the peace should be dethroned; and it declared aptly and incisively that the formal assent of the French nation to Bonaparte's reaccession to the throne would be equivalent to a declaration of war against Europe. This formal assent to the usurper's *coup d'état* had in fact occurred almost at the same moment in which the commission's report was, on May 12th, laid before the Committee of Eight. The Napoleonic supplementary act was submitted to the nation for general approval; more than one and a quarter million voters expressed this approval, barely five thousand dared to vote against Napoleon's reinstatement, the great majority held aloof, letting matters take their own course. Thus the French nation had unquestionably recognised the

[1] Correspondance inédite de Talleyrand et de Louis XVIII, Paris, 1881, p. 383.

dynastic revolution, and for the eight powers the necessity was obvious, in accordance with the words of their commission, to drop the earlier declaration which had been directed against the person of Bonaparte alone, and to declare war against the state of France, as it had now actually undergone transformation. But this conclusion, the only logical one, was not drawn, for the intentions of the allied powers were extremely divergent.

The unctuous assurance of the tories that England did not desire to force any particular government upon France, was not honourably meant, but was simply a move in the parliamentary game. There had been no change in the obstinately legitimist sentiments of the tory cabinet ; in the eyes of that cabinet, the landless king was, and remained, the legitimate ruler of France, and it was the obvious duty of Europe to restore the king to the throne of his fathers by means of a royalist crusade, so that England, as the high-minded protector of the grateful Bourbon, could secure the dominant influence in the Tuileries. In this sense Wellington continually repeated : " France has no enemies ; this war is a war of Europe, including France, against Bonaparte and his army." Consequently no one could make any claims for territory against France. Filled with moral indignation, comfortably patting their well-filled pockets, the tories spoke about Prussian poverty and greed ; their envy of Germany was so detestably plain that even the good-natured Prussian patriots at length came clearly to understand the true character of British commercial policy, and many of those who for years had been ardent admirers of English magnanimity now expressed an adverse judgment. But however restricted, hypocritical, and narrow-minded the policy of the tories might appear, they alone among all the allies knew precisely what they wanted and followed their aims with tenacious obstinacy.

In the Hofburg there was no lack of fanatical legitimists to blow the *corno inglese*. To Adam Müller it seemed absolutely incontestable that Louis XVIII had been reigning for four-and-twenty years, and that Bonaparte was only a rebel ; if this were not so, the divine right of kings would be denied and " the ridiculous claim of the nations to have a will of their own would receive recognition ! " Metternich's views were more sober. He cherished no preference for the Bourbons, and was prepared to act as circumstances might dictate ; but since his peace-loving nature recoiled from every dubious innovation, and since the treaties of Paris and Vienna seemed to him an inviolable structure of exquisite diplomatic wisdom, the tories might hope that they would be able gradually to bring over their Austrian friend to their own point of view. Alexander, on the other hand, and Frederick William, could not forgive the Bourbons the war alliance of January 3rd. Among the Prussian generals the view was widely diffused that this ungrateful French royal house, which was at once weak and faithless, ought not to be restored; the czar spoke with warmth in favour of the liberal-minded duke of Orleans. But neither the court of St. Petersburg nor yet that of Berlin had hitherto conceived any definite plan for the re-establishment of the French throne; moreover, the two powers were by no means in agreement. Whilst the Prussian statesmen were from the first working to safeguard the western frontier of Germany, the czar had relapsed into a mood of extravagant generosity. The true ground of his magnanimity was betrayed by him on one occasion when he exclaimed: " Either I shall have a share in this cake, or the cake shall not be baked at all ! " Russia could gain nothing from this war, and what did he care about Germany when he could hope by liberal-mindedness and delicacy of feeling to overpower English influence in France ? On May 25th he directed his ambassador to write that there existed " a French nation whose justified interests must not be sacrificed without punishment; consequently there must neither be effected the re-establishment of the untenable old order nor yet a humiliation of France, a country indispensable to the well-being of Europe."

Owing to the existence of this far-reaching divergency of views, an unambiguous declaration of war against France, such as was desired by Hardenberg and Humboldt, could not be carried through. The coalition determined to make no further public declaration, and was all the more content with the adoption of this half-measure because the opportunity for more definite resolves might well be offered in the vicissitudes of the campaign. All the world anticipated a long and wearisome war; the leadership of the European army had been once more entrusted to Schwarzenberg and Langenau. Thus the powers opened the struggle in a situation which was extremely obscure from the point of view of international law. They had announced the struggle against " Buonaparte " (for so they continued to name the Imperator), and had subsequently declared that they did not pursue the aim of re-establishing the Bourbons. Unquestionably they were in a state of war against France, since international law recognises war only as between states; whether they regarded themselves as enemies of France was extremely doubtful, in face of their own contradictory declarations. Moreover, the proclamation to the French which Schwarzenberg issued when the army invaded France was extremely indefinite. With considerable difficulty Gagern had secured that from the sentence, "Europe desires peace," at least the dangerous conclusion, "and nothing but peace," should be excised.

This legal obscurity at the opening of the war was not, indeed, solely responsible for the unfortunate issue of the peace negotiations, for the decision in this matter was determined by the united resistance opposed by the rest of Europe to the German demands; but it unquestionably rendered the position of the German negotiators at the peace congress far more difficult. Suffice it to say that gradually all the powers of the second rank joined this ambiguous alliance against Bonaparte; a foolish and premature taking up of arms on the part of Murat in Italy, which was speedily quelled, strengthened the courts in the conviction that any negotiation with Bonapartism was impossible. Germany appeared, even at the beginning of the great war, completely united, an experience which had been unknown for three centuries. No one any longer ventured upon open treason, although the hostile sentiments of the courts of Munich and Stuttgart were manifested once again in a thousand disputes about commissariat. The nation was to learn painfully enough that harmony of views is not true unity. Since at the moment when war had been declared the Germanic Federation was not yet in existence, the German states could join the coalition only as isolated individuals; they did not receive any voice in the councils of the great powers, and immediately perceived how valueless was that right of independent diplomatic representation which they had regarded as the finest ornament of their crowns.

In view of the enormous superiority of the fighting forces of the allies, the prompt opening of the campaign offered a sure prospect of success; almost all the well-known generals of the coalition, Blucher and Gniesenau, Wellington, Toll, and Diebitsch, were here fully agreed. "Hesitation," declared Blucher, "will serve merely to provide Napoleon with armies which we must fight at the cost of our own blood." In Gneisenau's opinion, on May 1st three great armies, each comprising 200,000 men, could be ready, on the Upper, the Middle, and the Lower Rhine respectively, for the invasion of France. His statesmanlike vision enabled him to foresee what almost all the others regarded as impossible, that the Imperator would assume the offensive. All the more urgently did he advise the allies to take the offensive on their side. If the three armies should advance simultaneously on Paris, and if in the meanwhile the fourth army, that from Russia, should assemble in their rear, Napoleon would not be able to put into the field a force greater than that of any one of these armies ; should one of the invading armies suffer a mishap through the skill of its opponent, it could withdraw to the great reserve army, whilst the other two could continue the advance on Paris. Now, as in the previous year, Gneisenau indicated the hostile capital as the only possible goal of the campaign, whereas even men of courage like Humboldt held the timid view that history never repeated itself. Now, as before, Gneisenau issued warnings against any dispersal of forces. If Napoleon were overthrown, everything else would be thereby settled, including the fate of Italy.

In the Hofburg, on the other hand, the Italian theatre of war was regarded as so extremely important that even Radetzky declared that Austria must choose Switzerland for the central field of her operations in order to remain in communication with the Italian army. In the Italian peninsula things began to ferment. The Milanese were already repenting of the premature revolution of the previous year ; they were inclined to murmur against the rule of the *bastone tedesco*. Murat's fantastical manifesto, in which he spoke of Italian unity, made a certain impression ; moreover, the natural enthusiasm on behalf of their great countryman, who had once more manifested the miraculous power of the *antico senno* of Italy, was reawakened. Emperor Francis regarded it as necessary to send his brother John to the new Lombardo-Venetian kingdom which, six years earlier, had first summoned the Italians to freedom. The archduke was not lacking in integrity, or in good words, but upon the experienced southerners he made an extremely unfavourable impression. The court of Vienna felt by no means secure in its Adriatic possessions. In addition there was the old preference of the Austrian generals, a preference shared also by Knesebeck, for far-fetched and roundabout methods ; finally, and above all, there was an urgent desire to leave to the allies the dangers of the war so that Austria might stand forth with unbroken forces when peace should with difficulty be attained.

As a result of these considerations an astonishing plan of campaign was drawn up, in complexity excelling even that of 1814. In the Netherlands were to be 210,000 men under Blucher and Wellington; on the Middle Rhine, Barclay de Tolly with 150,000 Russians; on the Upper Rhine and in Switzerland, 200,000 Austrians; finally, in Piedmont, an army of 60,000 men. Here was a mass of troops which in the end of July was reinforced by supports of 170,000 men to reach a total of 800,000, the strength of the allies being thus three times as great as that of the enemy. Schwarzenberg regarded not Paris but Lyons as the immediate aim of operations. Of Napoleon, however, it might be anticipated with certainty that he would hurl himself upon the nearest foe, either upon the Netherlands army or upon that on the Middle Rhine; thus the Austrian troops were saved from the blows of the dreaded enemy. Since according to the Austrian plan the Russians were to take their place at once in the first rank of the fighters, Schwarzenberg demanded the postponement of the invasion till June 16th, then till June 27th, and finally even till July 1st. Although to all the other powers it seemed an extremely dubious policy to give their restless enemy three months' respite, in a coalition army the procrastinator always has the right of it. Austria obstinately maintained that her equipments could not be completed earlier, and consequently, on April 19th, the great war council of the coalition in Vienna adopted in essentials the proposals of the Hofburg, and agreed to a postponement of operations. The diplomatic world, and Hardenberg as well, believed that the decisive issue would be fought out in the centre of the allied army. It was thought that the army in the Netherlands would, like the Silesian army two years earlier, play the modest role of an accessory corps; and now, just as then, the course of events was to mock all prophecies.

With the deliberations about the plan of campaign was associated a lively struggle concerning the distribution of the smaller German contingents. The courts of the mid-German states all made it a point of honour as petty kings to place their troops under foreign command, if it were possible to do so, in preference to Prussian command. Count Münster considered that the hour had come for the realisation of his ancient ideal, an English-Hanoverian hegemony in North Germany, and he warned his smaller neighbours against joining Prussia. In fact, not only the Netherlanders, but also the Hanoverians, the Saxons, the Nassauers, and the Brunswickers, were assigned to Wellington's English army; only a small North German Federal army-corps, consisting chiefly of men from Electoral Hesse, was placed under Prussian command. The South German troops went with the Austrians and Russians to the Upper and Middle Rhine, so that on this occasion, too, it was impossible for any sentiment of national comradeship-in-arms to be generated.

Napoleon's army was the best that he had ever led into the field. The backbone of his regiments consisted of the veterans who had returned from the military prisons and fortresses in Germany. The common man looked up with idolatrous respect to the *petit caporal;* never before had the rank and file been so thoroughly permeated with prætorian pride and passionate lust for battle. But they had little confidence in their generals, for a portion of the marshals had remained loyal to the Bourbons; and if fortune should turn her back upon the Imperator, little moral power of resistance was to be expected from these valiant grey-beards, who had all been false to their oath to the flag and who had the worst to fear from the Bourbons.

How different was the feeling in the Prussian army! When in a vigorous appeal to his Prussians the king said: " Europe cannot tolerate the man who now occupies the French throne, the man who plainly announces that world-dominion is the aim of his ever-renewed wars," he obtained everywhere a ready response from his loyal people. Now, as two years before, the young men hastened to take up arms. The Landsturm and the detachment of the volunteer yagers were re-established; and now, as formerly, the fighters were inspired with the confident resolve that this holy war should not end in any other way than that of a complete victory. Prussia, still altogether exhausted by the colossal efforts of recent years, again placed 250,000 men with the colours; even the smaller North German neighbours showed, on this occasion, a lively zeal, sending 70,000 men. It is true that the national army could not be compared with the enemy in warlike experience and steadiness. At the moment when the unexpected call to arms was sounded, the army was in a dangerous state of transition. The Army Law and the acquirements of new territory had made it necessary to remodel a considerable |proportion of the forces; even in the Netherlands theatre of war individual battalions had to be separated from their old regiments. The whole of the cavalry was reconstructed, and the artillery was in need of men; for his 304 guns, Blucher had only 5,303 men; in one army-corps there were only eleven men per gun, whereas according to the regulations, there should have been thirty. The majority of the troops of the l'ne, which until the end of the previous year had still remained on the Rhine, had shortly before been sent back by the minister of war to the eastern provinces, partly because he wished to disburden the heavily pressed Rhinelanders of the cost of billeting, and partly because he was afraid of a war with Austria. When now the storm suddenly broke out in the west, and the king of the Netherlands urgently begged for immediate aid, it was necessary to despatch to the theatre of war whatever came first to hand. Half of the 116,000 men who were got together in Belgium belonged to the Landwehr, and of these a considerable proportion, the Landwehr from the Elbe, was composed of troops from the new province which had formerly belonged to Westphalia; these were men who had to get accustomed to Prussian service, and many of them had quite recently fought in Napoleon's army.

In March, the king bestowed the supreme command of the field army upon his grey-headed field-marshal; and Gneisenau, too, resumed the difficult confidential position at Blucher's side. In order to obviate the recurrence of disputes between the leaders, the command of the first three army-corps which were to open the Belgian campaign was entrusted to the generals Zieten, Borstell, and Thielmann, respectively, all three of them ranking in the service as junior to Gneisenau. Bülow commanded the fourth corps, which was to serve as a reserve, so that the headstrong man did not come too frequently in contact with his opponent Gneisenau. The North German Federal army-corps, which assembled on the German Lower Rhine, in the rear of Blucher's army, was placed under the command of Kleist, whose gentle and restrained nature rendered him especially suitable for the diplomatic tasks of a federal military commander. Finally, York and Tauentzien received the command of the two army-corps in the eastern provinces. General Grolman entered Blucher's headquarters staff as quartermaster-general, and appointed four of the most capable officers, Reiche, Aster, Clausewitz, and Valentini, as chiefs of staff in the Belgian army. The hero of Wartenberg was profoundly vexed; he several times demanded his dismissal, and in this distribution of roles could see nothing more than the partisan hatred of the " Tugendbund." All the military opponents of the reform party shared the views of York, complaining that with the appointment of Boyen and Grolman visionaries and demagogues gained control of the army. At court there recommenced malicious intrigues of secret suspicion against the Silesian headquarters staff. In the officers' circles definite assurances were exchanged to the effect that Duke Charles of Mecklenburg, who had once more greeted the field-marshal upon his departure—greeted him in the name of the Berlin garrison—had vainly begged for the command of a brigade in Blucher's army; the king's brother-in-law must be shielded from the dangerous influence of Gneisenau. General Knesebeck even undertook to advise the field-marshal that he should voluntarily renounce the supreme command; but hardly had Knesebeck begun to speak cautiously about Blucher's advanced age, when the old man burst out into loud laughter, and said, " What nonsense you are talking ! "

This was all that could be done ; who could venture to drive the hero of the nation from the position which belonged to him ? During the last inactive months he had, indeed, become an infirm old man, and at this moment the affectionate father received a cruel blow ; his favourite son Francis, a bold and talented cavalry officer, who in the last campaign had been severely wounded in the head, became hopelessly insane. But as soon as war was determined on, the magnificent old man speedily pulled himself together, like a noble charger at the sound of the trumpets, and no longer felt the burden of years and sorrow. Once more he had foreseen it all : why would not the accursed diplomats believe him when he had prophesied to them a year ago that the rascal would certainly break out of his cage ? Everywhere on the journey the masses thronged round the popular hero. Fresh and youthful looking, radiating confidence, he appeared amongst his rejoicing troops. How much good it did him to see the new East Frisian regiment, composed of the fellow-countrymen of his beloved wife, under his command. To the embittered Saxon officers he delivered a mighty speech, straight from the fullness of his German heart, saying that he knew nothing here of Prussians or Saxons, that he knew only of Germans who would and must fight for their great fatherland. With such an army, he said, he could conquer Tunis, Tripoli, and Algiers, if only the sea were not in the way. He could hardly await the hour of battle, and, certain of victory, he wrote to Heinen, the manager of his estate : " The French are before me, glory behind, and an explosion will come soon ! " [1]

[1] Blucher to Heinen, Liège, May 6, 1815.

He found the army administration in a painful quandary. The king of the Netherlands, who had so urgently begged for speedy help from the Prussians, now that he knew himself to be in safety did nothing whatever for the care of the allied armies in the rich country; he knew the contempt which the Prussian office's had cherished towards him since the Thuringian campaign; he responded to it by unconcealed dislike, and displayed so much ill-will that Gneisenau blamed him, certainly with injustice, on account of his French sympathies. Hard cash, of which Wellington had a superfluity, was altogether lacking to the Prussians; for a month and a half the army had received no pay. Ribbentrop, the admirable commissary-general, was at his wits' end. Blucher wrote angrily to the chancellor: " The king of the Netherlands is the most disobliging, secretive, and avaricious of men." [1] To meet the most urgent needs, he issued on his own authority bills of exchange, which were cashed by the merchants of Elberfeld on the strength of his great name. Meanwhile he had to have his troops provisioned by the peasants, and for this reason was compelled to disperse his forces between Fleurus, Namur, Cinay, and Hannut, farther north of the Meuse and the Sambre than was advisable. These troubles did not disturb his confidence of victory. At the first glance he recognised the internal weakness of the new empire, saying: " The French nation is by no means so devoted to Bonaparte as the French newspapers declare." With prophetic certainty he declared that the decision would be effected upon the Belgian theatre of war. " If we bring the war to a happy conclusion," he wrote to the chancellor, " all the great lords will be in my debt; and everything will in fact turn out well, for the great power which the over-cautious fellows on our side assign to Napoleon in their dreams, is a cobweb of the brain. He lacks everything and, above all, he has lost confidence in himself and his followers." [2]

Blucher was from the first clear as to the demands which, after the victory, Germany ought to impose upon France. As early as the beginning of May he wrote: " I hope that this war will be concluded in such a way that in the future France will no longer be so dangerous to Germany. Alsace and Lorraine must be surrendered to us." Yet it is a remarkable fact that this same man, in whom were embodied the national pride and ardour of the North German people, was at the same time a cosmopolitan in the

[1] Blucher to Hardenberg, Namur, May 27, 1815.
[2] Blucher to Hardenberg, Namur, June 2, 1815.

noblest sense of the word. It will for all time remain a proud memory for our nation that the magnanimous German cosmopolitan sentiment which had hitherto profited our culture alone, and for our political life had been merely a curse, was now at length, in the most extraordinary circumstances, to prove fruitful also in the political sphere, and was to enable Germany's commander-in-chief to enter into European politics in the grand style. In Blucher's eyes this was a holy war of the fraternal nations of Europe on behalf of their common freedom, and nothing seemed to him more self-evident than that brother must stand for brother to the last drop of blood. With a reckless self-forgetfulness which was possible only to German idealism, he declared himself ready to devote all the forces of his army to the cause of Europe. Full of confidence he came to meet his English comrade-in-arms, and loyally assumed that the Englishman would be animated by like sentiments. The blunt and trustworthy soldierly character of the English commander pleased him well. "Wellington is obliging-ness itself," he wrote with satisfaction; "he is an extremely resolute man, we shall get along very well together." Since, notwithstanding his angry demands and proposals, the opening of the war was continually postponed by the Viennese strategists, he wrote menacingly to the chancellor: "If the command to advance is not given, if the disturbances in France increase, I shall do what I did in Silesia, and take the matter into my own hands. Wellington will certainly join me in this." Gneisenau, prepared, like his old friend, for every sacrifice on behalf of the common cause, took another view of the Englishman's character; he con-sidered that from Wellington might be expected the most tenacious and valiant resistance to the enemy, but not any bold act of insubordination, nor yet any kind of sacrifice on behalf of the allies. Gneisenau's judgment was right, for while in Blucher's headquarters staff there prevailed a magnanimous enthusiasm on behalf of European freedom, Wellington was an Englishman from top to toe, in good things as in bad.

The six brief days of the Belgian campaign do not merely awaken the highest political and human sympathy through the restless, powerfully cumulative, and dramatic course of events, through the excess of magnificent struggles, passions, and changes of fortune which were pressed together within a few hours; they afford also a profound insight into the wonderfully multiform and unequal development of the western nations—for in the plains of Brabant there were simultaneously in the battle-field three fundamentally different epochs of European military history. Here was the eighteenth century, the mercenary army of old England ; there was the epoch of the Revolution, the professional soldiery of the democratic tyrant ; there again, finally, was the newest age, the Prussian nation in arms. Each one of the three armies developed its most characteristic art in a titanic struggle, and each was led by a commander appropriate to its character. Here were Blucher and Gneisenau, the heroes of the stormy national anger ; there was the crowned plebeian ; there again, finally, was Wellington, who was at that time extolled by Münster and the high tories as the greatest military commander of the century, but who to us of a later age seems the last great representative of a completely obsolete art of war.

Wellington is numbered among those rare men who, without creative genius, almost without talent, simply by force of character, by the power of will and of self-command, climb to the heights of historic fame. Who would ever have prophesied a world-wide reputation for this boy who was far from quick of comprehension, who was never really young, and who was greatly excelled in talent by his brothers Richard and Henry ? Son of a high-church tory family which had settled in Ireland as a member of the conquering race, and which amid the hostile Celts had preserved all the more obstinately the pride of race and caste, the good qualities and the bad of the English motherland, he had, in accordance with the old-established custom of English young men of family, rapidly passed through the subordinate ranks in the army with the help of money and favour, so that when he was only twenty-five years old, he commanded a regiment in the Revolutionary war. Subsequently in the East Indies he learned the art of military leadership under the eyes of his brother Richard Wellesley, the brilliant founder of British power in the East. Severe to himself and others, unswervingly obedient and faithful to duty, just and honourable, cold, trustworthy, and reasonable in all things, he showed himself completely competent for the difficult military and political tasks which Indian life imposed upon the military commander. How boldly the cautious man, who painfully weighed all possibilities beforehand, could at the right moment seize the favour of fortune, was shown by the brilliant victory of Assaye, over the sixfold superior force of the Hindus, and by the bold cavalry campaign in the Mahratta mountains. Having returned to Europe, he took part in the celebrated pillaging excursion to Copenhagen, brave and efficient as ever, but at the same time utterly indifferent about the tragical fate of the little power thus nefariously attacked— for never was son of Britain so completely permeated by the English national view: "My country, right or wrong!" Subsequently, having received the supreme command in Portugal, always full of a quiet confidence of victory, he dryly declared: "I shall hold my ground." Upon this sober head the theatrical display of the neo-French military glories made no impression whatever; he never doubted in the overthrow of Napoleon. Through the six years of the Peninsular War he trained his mercenaries to become virtuosi in all the methods of the traditional art of war.

He had no use for innovations or comprehensive improvements; he never gave favour for any service, never proposed any promotion out of order. Independent generals, men who thought for themselves, were inconvenient to him, whereas his more liberal-minded brother Richard allowed talented subordinates to do as they pleased; what Wellington needed was trustworthy and able tools, and he found these for himself with a secure knowledge of men. His aides-de-camp were for the most part young peers, who, mounted upon the best horses in the world, punctually carried the commander's orders and obediently avoided having any opinions of their own. He knew his own worth and said straight out to his friends in the tory cabinet, "You have no one except me"; had himself provided with extraordinary powers, which he never misused, but which enabled him to suspend and send home any officer at his own discretion. His generals, occupying the position assigned to them, could do whatever they thought fit during the battle, but the nearest obstacle in front of them was a barrier which they must not attempt to pass under pain of court-martial. His officers had little love for the severe man who never thawed into comradely cordiality, who never displayed any sign of benevolence or magnanimity, not even when the service would in no way have suffered had he done so. The piercing glance of the cold eyes, the proud features with the aquiline nose and the tightly closed, immobile mouth, the sharply commanding tones of the voice, forbade any confidential approach. But all obeyed him, all were proud if they could satisfy this man who was so hard to please; not even in private conversation did the officers venture to criticise or discuss the commander's measures. They followed Wellington's commands blindly, as if these commands had been unsearchable decrees of fate; seldom did he speak to them, and when he did so he communicated his intentions in slow, cumbrous, and inelegant language, but definitely and clearly.

So absolute a dependence was possible only in the small armies of the old time. In fact, Wellington found himself most at his ease when, like the lansquenet leaders of the sixteenth century, such as Frundsberg, Emser, and Leyva, he was himself the personal centre of the army, when his regiments were assembled round him in close array, and when he could practically see them all at once. Far beneath the officers of rank who had gained their commissions by purchase, separated from them by an impassable gulf, were the rude masses of the rank and file, " the scum of the English nation" as Wellington himself phrased it. These hirelings were held together by abundant pay and good diet, with the aid of a suitable use of the cat. It was wonderful what these athletic bodies could effect with the courage of the old English boxers ; it was wonderful what muscular energy and staying-power they could display when the drill-sergeant had had them under his thumb for a few years ; irresistible was the bayonet attack of the giants of the guard, irresistible the mighty charge of the heavy dragoons upon their grey chargers. But woe to the town which was taken by storm by these troops, as was the unhappy Badajoz ; in the delirium of victory, the cat-o'-nine-tails lost its terrors, the bonds of discipline were rent asunder, and lust of murder, greed for plunder, all bestial passions, were unchained. Thus the army resembled a great piece of clockwork, operating with the utmost precision, and yet it was something more than a machine, for in the officers' corps there persisted the knightly breeding and the national pride of the English nobility ; and the brutal rankers, after so many brilliant successes on the part of their unconquered commander, were wholly devoted to him, and followed his glorious banner with absolute confidence.

In Spain, Wellington economised his troops with extreme circumspection, venturing a bold attack only at considerable intervals when there was every prospect of success, but never staking the existence of his army. He had never encountered the Imperator upon the field of battle ; Napoleon's grandiose manner of making war, forcing victory by the use of colossal, massive blows, remained unknown to him. Quite unmoved, he continued the traditional cautious art of warfare which had proved so successful in the unusual circumstances of the Spanish theatre of war, regarding it as the only right method. He looked down upon the national army with all the contempt of the professional soldier ; to him such armies were no better than the Spanish guerrillas which had so often proved useless upon the battle-field, and never would he admit that the success of the peninsular campaign would after all have been impossible without the fanaticism of these undisciplined bands, which, operating in the rear of their enemies, wearied and weakened these by the terrors of petty warfare. " Enthusiasm," he wrote, in his clumsy manner, to Castlereagh, " is in fact no help in bringing anything to pass, and is only an excuse for the disorder with which everything is done, and for the lack of discipline and obedience in armies." These military views were inspired simultaneously by the anti-revolutionary sentiment of the high tory. In later years, as soon as his secure soldier's glance enabled him to recognise the absolute necessity for reform, Wellington ventured on several occasions to separate himself from his political friends, and, undisturbed by the anger of his party, to complete with a high hand what he had himself hitherto resisted as a dangerous innovation. In old age, crowned with fame, he stood high enough to live only for wider issues, to follow only the voice of serene patriotism. He said once : " I would willingly give my life if thereby I could save my country from a month's civil war." In the year 1815, he was still a conservative partisan through and through ; the world of war of those days appeared to him simply a struggle of legitimate authority against the Revolution.

He regarded half with suspicion and half with contempt the national passions which were surging through the nations of the Continent. He had passed the greater part of his life among the Irish, the Hindus, the Spaniards, and the Portuguese ; his experiences had convinced him that no other nation could be compared even distantly with the English. The old English sin of under-estimation of foreigners was, in this dry and unamiable hero, displayed in so injurious and coldly arrogant a form that even the Spaniards, who owed him so much, detested him cordially. Like his friend Castlereagh, he remained of the opinion that parliamentary freedom must be an exclusive possession of the favoured English stock, and that it was unsuitable for the immaturity of the continentals. Just as previously in India and in Spain he had combined the activities of the statesman with those of the soldier, so in Paris and Vienna after the peace he acted as envoy, and was taken by the ministers so deeply into their confidence that he was regarded as practically a member of the cabinet. He shared the mistrust of the tories for the rising powers of Prussia and Russia ; he was far more intimately acquainted with the secrets of the cabinets than was Blucher's headquarters staff, and from the first took over his command with a fixed, clear, and carefully thought-out political design, with the intention, that is to say, of restoring the legitimate king to the palace of his ancestors.

Among the 94,000 men of his army, 32,000, approximately one-third, were English ; 37,000 were Germans ; and 25,000 were Netherlanders. Of the Germans, it was only the famous regiments of the German legion, numbering about 7,000 men, which were as experienced in war as the well-drilled English veterans, the rank and file, in their case, being less rough than the English, whilst the officers, after the German manner, were more highly cultured ; the black troop of the duke of Brunswick also consisted for the most part of well-trained soldiers. On the other hand, among the Hanoverians and Nassauers the troops were for the most part raw, and the same was the case in the newly-formed Netherland regiments ; no trust at all could be placed in the Belgians, whose sentiments were French. Wellington had little confidence in this motley army, and endeavoured to give it a greater moral force by stiffening the young troops with detachments from the veteran forces. Nor had he much esteem for the warlike value of the Prussian army. From time to time, indeed, Blucher's powerful personality, the lofty spiritual impulses which were expressed by the words and glances of the old German, charmed even the sober Englishman ; on one occasion, looking after Blucher riding away, Wellington said, with unwonted warmth : " What a fine old boy he is." But the " republican spirit " of this national army seemed to him sinister. The passionate national pride and the impulse to activity of the Prussian army had now become a matter for suspicion to all the courts ; at this time even the czar was of opinion that he would some day find it necessary to protect his Prussian friend against the latter's own army.

Although Wellington, like most of his countrymen, was secretly of opinion that the overthrow of the world-empire had really been effected by the Spanish war, he was not without anxiety at the prospect of his first personal encounter with Napoleon. He would not and dared not expose himself to the danger of a defeat; for how could England effect the restoration of the Bourbons, undesired by the other courts, if his little army were beaten. Consequently he went to work with extreme caution. Since the council of war in Vienna had resolved to postpone the struggle, the English commander, in accordance with his custom, yielded unquestioning obedience, and prepared for a cautious defence. Whilst Blucher was compelled by commissariat difficulties to distribute his army through a wide region north-west of the Sambre (though still near enough to be able, in case of need, to collect his army with extreme punctuality within four-and-twenty hours), Wellington needlessly and intentionally distributed his forces throughout an even wider area. Being ignorant of Napoleon's character and methods of warfare, he assumed that the French would simultaneously enter Belgium at different places and in several columns; instead of massing his army near the Prussians, he distributed it upon the wide line from Quatre Bras westward to the vicinity of Ghent; whilst, after his strictly methodical manner, he retained his reserves at Brussels, so that he could send support to any threatened point, as circumstances might dictate. He believed that in this way he was prepared for any possible attack, that he could safeguard communications with England by way of Antwerp and Ostend, and that at the same time he could secure against surprise his protégés, the court of the fugitive king in Ghent and the little force of the Bourbon household troops at Alost. This widely extended distribution of his forces, however, hindered rapid co-operation with Blucher; it remained possible that Napoleon, being superior in strength to each individual section of the allies, might suddenly advance between the two armies, and might defeat the Prussians, who stood nearest to him, before Wellington could hasten to their assistance.

Shortly before the swords were actually drawn from the scabbards the German army suffered a new disaster. Not even this war, the first which the Germans had undertaken in complete harmony, was to begin without the flames of the old, fierce fratricidal hatred again springing to life. The unhappy Saxon negotiations had a tragic sequel in Belgium. As soon as the great powers had come to an agreement about the fate of Saxony, they determined to allow the imprisoned king to approach near to Vienna, so that he might accept the arrangement that had been made. The Prussian government learned from Dresden that the Saxon high nobility desired to take advantage of the passage of their tribal prince to make a noisy demonstration; it was informed also by the minister in Berlin that Frederick Augustus was determined to do everything he could in Vienna to secure a simple repudiation of the arrangement, and to begin the negotiations all over again.[1] Hardenberg immediately took his measures. The prisoner, who started on February 22nd upon the journey to Pressburg, had on his way to pass through Silesia. On the Austrian frontier he was received with the chiming of bells and with all the pomp due to a prince. More than such honours as this Emperor Francis was unable to offer to his protégé, for in view of the need to repel the new attack of the French, the contest about Saxony appeared in all its petty triviality as a nuisance which must be got rid of at all costs. Prussia now had the satisfaction to learn that all the principles of international law which Hardenberg had hitherto had to defend alone, amid the outcries of an outraged " Europe," were now formally recognised by Austria, England, and France. Unanimously the powers declared that inasmuch as a conquest of the entire country, a *debellatio*, had been effected, there was no legal ground for making peace with the dethroned prince; it was only as an act of grace that the conqueror was prepared to restore half of his land to Frederick Augustus, if he would first discharge the inhabitants of the other half from their oath, and accept the Viennese decision; until then the administration of the whole country must remain in Prussia's hands. It was with such proposals that, on March 12th, Metternich, Wellington, and Talleyrand met Frederick Augustus.

When he defiantly demanded the resumption of the negotiations, they answered in a sharply couched note that he completely misunderstood his position. Talleyrand gave an imposing assurance that Frederick Augustus had served " the most cruel enemy of Germany," and therefore deserved no consideration! The vacillations that followed (negotiations they can hardly be termed) aroused no more than a pathological interest. For two months the blinded old man put the powers off with demands for compensation by Warsaw or Lusatia, with appeals to law, with formal considerations, and a thousand petty shifts. Not till May 18th was peace restored between Prussia and Saxony, precisely in the

---

[1] Reports of the Saxon general government and of minister Geltz to the chancellor, dated January 2 and February 19, 1815.

terms arranged by the Committee of Five. At the courts the suspicion was aroused that Frederick Augustus was intentionally protracting the negotiations until a new victory of Napoleon might restore their old power to the Albertines. This view was not unreasonable. The Dresden mob, that of the nobles and that of the common people alike, hailed with delight the prospect of the great ally's return ! Then, as in the year 1866, the honourable feelings of these circles found faithful expression in the couplet :

> " Preussischer Kuckuck, warte !
> Uns hilft Bonaparte ! "

The court in Pressburg was inspired by different sentiments ; at that moment the return of the Napoleonic dominion would have been unwelcome to the old king, because it would have deprived him of the support of his powerful protector. The protracted and wearisome course of the final negotiations found sufficient explanation in the Albertine's legitimist obstinacy and pedantic adhesion to form ; to his petty royal pride what did it matter that the intolerable provisional conditions in his unfortunate country, which for a year and a half had known no rest, should be protracted for a few months more ?

The Prussian general government encountered similar sentiments in the Saxon officials. The supreme authorities offered obstinate opposition when the order was issued for the inevitable partition of the archives and registers ; the general government was even asked to furnish accounts. The privy council of Dresden, in a lengthy and ridiculous memorial, went so far as to maintain that it was " impossible for the partition to be effected by a general mutual understanding," and appealed to the parliamentary speeches " of Lord Castlereagh, who had personally co-operated in the composition of the Viennese protocols." All was in vain ; even the name of the English lord made no impression upon the chancellor. Hardenberg ordered that strict measures should be taken ; the partition had been irrevocably decided by the powers, and " there could be absolutely no question " of rendering an account for the administration of conquered territory.[1] Thus the country remained temporarily in Prussia's possession ; all the preparations necessary for the definitive partition were completed ; the hesitation of the old

[1] Instructions to the general government, March 24 and 27, 1815.

king led merely to fruitless disputes. Not even a glimmer of understanding, however, penetrated the minds of the Saxon legitimists when they finally saw the fruit of their conduct under their very eyes ; they never recognised that it was their own enmity to Prussia which had notably co-operated in bringing about the much-lamented partition of the country.

Frederick Augustus's obstinacy was to have momentous consequences for the little Saxon army. For a year and a half the war-lord had been a prisoner in Prussia's hands, whilst his soldiers had been auxiliary associates in the allied camp ; such was the perplexing and unnatural situation of the unfortunate Saxon regiments. It was their misfortune that they had enjoyed almost no share in the military glories of the allies ; the sentiments of the Prussian army were utterly strange to these long-service professional soldiers, and to them the name Landwehr was a term of abuse. After the peace, they remained for a long time in western Germany, far from their homes, but subject to continual influence from Dresden by letters and envoys. In the officers' corps the persistent uncertainty about the future of their country led to the formation of factions. An address in favour of the imprisoned king was drawn up, notwithstanding the vigorous opposition of the Prussian commanding officer. The legitimists could no longer endure to see upon the breast of their comrades the green cross, a distinction awarded by the Russian government ; in Coblentz there were actual affrays between Görres and the Saxon officers. The rank and file began to distrust their leaders, they felt that they had been betrayed and sold, for even the common soldier could not fail to perceive that the sudden removal of the army-corps to the neighbourhood of Prussian garrisons was dictated by political considerations. The troops suffered from all the evils of party strife. Anyone who takes an unbiassed view of the matter can merely wonder that under such unhappy conditions the bonds of German discipline had not been earlier dissolved.

Throughout the winter the discipline of the regiments remained beyond reproach, although old Rhenish Confederate memories were naturally revived, and here and there in the quarters of the Saxon soldiers the cry *vive l'empereur* might be heard. The two generals who rightly enjoyed the highest repute with the army, Zeschau and Le Coq, were strict legitimists, and therefore could not be left with the troops. By a disastrous error, the command of the corps was entrusted to General Theilmann, who was regarded with suspicion by his old comrades as a deserter; and he strengthened the ill-feeling towards him by endeavouring, after his theatrical manner and with unsoldierly loquacity, to win over the officers to the Prussian side by toasts and speeches. When the news came from Vienna of the partition of Saxony, he at once, on his own initiative, demanded of his comrades that they should choose between the Prussian and the Saxon service; thereupon ensued fresh dissensions among the officers and increasing disaffection among the troops. In this way the general, by his tactless and officious behaviour, was partially responsible for the failure of discipline in the little army.

It was the unavoidable duty of the king of Prussia to put an end to this hopeless confusion. As early as March, Boyen foresaw the risk of disturbances among the Saxon troops. Could affairs be left in their present condition until the Albertine was pleased to make up his mind to abandon his foolish resistance? On March 14th the king ordered General Gneisenau that he should immediately constitute new regiments out of the portion of the troops belonging to the Prussian subdivision of Saxony, and added: " It will be my pleasure henceforward to make no distinction between them and my other regiments."[1] The choice of service was left free to the officers. The king's conscientiousness led him to avoid entering into the painful question whether the earlier oath of the Saxons to their colours had not been dissolved by their desertion to the side of the allies. He merely ordered a reconstruction of the Saxon regiments, which was unquestionably within his rights, and wished to postpone the swearing-in of the troops that were to form part of the Prussian army until Frederick Augustus had discharged them from their old oath. On April 1st Hardenberg issued further strict injunctions to General Gneisenau to act on the royal order, since there could be no doubt, from the course of the negotiations, that Frederick Augustus would ultimately give way. The powers in Vienna were in harmony with the chancellor's procedure; they resolved to send the regiments that remained with the Saxon crown to join Wellington's army. The Prussian generals indulgently postponed the carrying out of the order for some additional weeks. To show his confidence in the Saxons, Blucher took up his headquarters among them in Liège. But his cordial address fell upon deaf ears; the discontent of the troops increased from day to day; and the billet-hosts of the Liège region, who were

[1] Cabinet Order to Gneisenau, March 14, 1815.

all Bonapartist in sentiment, still further increased the hostility of the blinded men.

When at length, by a new royal order, the division of the army was decreed, there was a terrible outbreak of the discontent which had so long been smouldering among the troops— discontent stimulated by emissaries from Dresden, and unquestionably fostered by a few unscrupulous officers. A crowd of drunken soldiers invaded the commanding officer's house, crying out, " We will not suffer ourselves to be divided." The old hero had to take to flight from his own soldiers ; he escaped death only through the bravery of his Saxon sentries. In such outbreaks everything depends upon the force of will and the moral prestige of the officers. The Saxon sentries in front of Blucher's door honourably fulfilled their military duty ; the cavalry and the artillery remained altogether aloof from the disorder. Even among the infantry the men were quiet wherever the leaders knew how to control them ; those officers who had already reported for Prussian service maintained their authority whenever they were efficient men. That battalion, however, which at the time of the battle of Dennewitz had gone over to the Prussians earlier than the other Saxons, now in Liège distinguished itself by a tragical lack of discipline.[1]

Lenity in face of this mutiny almost in sight of the enemy would have been disgraceful weakness. Military law took its course. The ringleaders were shot ; the colours of the Saxon guard were publicly burned. General Borstell, who out of sympathy with the unhappy men had refused to undertake the burning of the colours, had to pay for his disobedience by confinement in a fortress ; the command of the second army-corps was taken over by General Pirch. The Saxon corps had then to start upon the march home, for the Prussian soldiers, raging at the insult offered to " Marshal Forwards," would not fight beside the Saxons, and Wellington refused to accept the mutinous troops into his army. Guilty and innocent alike lost the glory of Ligny and Belle Alliance. Upon the return march the Saxons had what was perhaps the most horrible experience which has ever befallen German soldiers. Everywhere on the Rhine and in Westphalia there was displayed a fierce hatred and loathing of the mutineers ; in Aix-la-Chapelle armed citizens suspiciously occupied

[1] I avail myself here, among other sources, of the description given by my father who, as a very young officer, was attached to a Saxon regiment in the vicinity of Liège, and who was able to keep his men in order.

the guard-posts and the gates when the Saxon regiments were marching by. Everywhere the nation was rejoicing over the brilliant victory of Blucher and Gneisenau. The Prussian volunteers, on their way to join the victorious army, could not control their contempt for the " Saxon dogs "; after repeated sanguinary brawls had occurred, it was necessary on several occasions for the men to avoid the high-roads in order to escape ignominious encounters. For the officers, too, there was the bitter reflection that they might have taken part in the battle of Belle Alliance, and that there they would unquestionably have done their duty; but of course all the blame was cast upon the Prussian generals who, after all, had only carried out their king's command and who had not asked the Saxons to swear any new oath. Whilst the whole of Germany was uplifted in heart at the new glory of Prussian arms, in Saxony a profound gloom prevailed. After the division had finally been carried out, the little army had to suffer for decades from the consequences of this evil day; it was overloaded with officers, and promotion was completely arrested. The Napoleonic veterans gave the tone ; it was from these circles that a deadly hatred against Prussia was handed down as a sacred inheritance to the younger generation.

The distress of the old field-marshal verged upon despair. For five-and-fifty years he had worn the sword and had never spilt any blood but that of the enemy. Now came this disgrace ! Now was it necessary for him, the father of his soldiers, to undertake executions in his own army, and he had subsequently to exercise all his authority to protect the mutineers from the rage of the Prussians. The great man was shaken as if by an ague, and listened in a state of terrible distress for the roll of the musketry when the sentence of the court-martial was being carried out. To the king of Saxony, however, he wrote with his characteristic frankness, using such language as a military commander had never before ventured to use to a crowned head : " By your earlier proceedings your majesty has brought the profoundest disaster upon your subjects, a respected branch of the German nation. It may result from your subsequent conduct that this branch will be overwhelmed with shame. The blood that has been spilt will one day at God's judgment seat be visited upon him who was responsible ; and before the throne of the Almighty to have given commands and to have allowed commands to be given, will be regarded as identical. Your majesty is well aware that an old man of seventy-three can no longer have any other earthly desire than to make the voice of truth audible, and to make the right prevail. For this reason your majesty will have to receive this letter"![1] In his anger, Blucher may have said a word too much, for there is no proof that the mutiny was deliberately planned. But on the whole the old man was right; had it not been for the blind hesitation of Frederick Augustus, and for the scandalous incitements which for months past had been made by his aiders and abettors, the blood of the Saxon soldiers would not have flowed at Liège.

In the second week of June, skilfully concealing his march, Napoleon led his field army towards the Belgian frontier in order to cross the Sambre at Charleroi. From that town a road runs northward through Quatre Bras to Brussels, and thence passes eastward in a wide curve through Sombreffe to Namur. The Imperator had approximate knowledge regarding the position of the allies, being aware that Wellington's army was in the neighbourhood of Brussels, and that of the Prussians at Namur. Consequently the triangle between Charleroi, Quatre Bras, and Sombreffe was the natural place for the junction of the allied armies; should this junction be effected in good time, the victory of the 210,000 men of the two commanders over the 128,000 Frenchmen would be assured. Consequently Napoleon resolved to break in here between the two armies in order to defeat them separately. Although he was profoundly disturbed by the ferment in France, and by the almost hopeless difficulty of his military situation, and although on his own admission he could not during this campaign always maintain his customary calm sense of security, he still possessed his ancient arrogant contempt for his opponent. He hoped that his sudden appearance would suffice to press Blucher back towards the east, and to force Wellington to retreat northward, so that the interval between the two would be increased. He did not expect that the Prussians would immediately give battle, close to the frontier. But the unexpected happened. As soon as Gneisenau learned that the enemy was approaching Charleroi, he immediately, on the night of June 14-15th, ordered the concentration of the entire army at Sombreffe, to be completed on the 16th. The advance of the French began at dawn on June 15th. Their right wing attacked Zieten's

[1] Blucher to King Frederick Augustus, May 6, 1815. See Appendix II.

army-corps, which, after a bloody skirmish, withdrew along the road to Sombreffe.

Already in these opening struggles the terrible embitterment of the two nations was manifest. How often in the previous year had the Napoleonic veterans returning from the German fortresses begun brawls in blind anger when they met Prussian regiments on the road ; now they wanted to take revenge on these " Prussian dogs " who, on their side, responded with a no less cordial hatred. Simultaneously Napoleon's left wing marched northward upon the road to Quatre Bras, and since the outposts of the English army stood far further back than those of the Prussians, the French forces easily reached Frasnes. Thus the position of the Prussian army at Sombreffe was threatened on the right flank. Moreover, it was already doubtful whether on the next day Bülow's corps could reach the army in time. To spare the susceptibilities of the older general, Gneisenau had issued marching orders to Bülow in so polite a phraseology, that the command sounded almost like a mere suggestion. Bülow, always inclined to act on his own initiative, and still without information regarding the real outbreak of hostilities, stayed quietly in Liège, and postponed the ordered junction of his corps at Hannut until June 16th. Consequently a second urgent order to advance sent to him at Hannut failed to find him there ; at a time when every minute was valuable, the fourth corps lost an entire day, and was unable to join the army on the 16th. Extremely serious, therefore, was the situation of the three Prussian corps which formed a junction in the neighbourhood of Sombreffe, and although the members of Blucher's headquarters staff impetuously demanded that decisive action should be taken at once, on the morning of June 16th the question was earnestly debated whether it would be better to move the army farther to the north, nearer to the English forces to the right and to the rear ; there the junction of the allies could be completed undisturbed.

Whereas Gneisenau immediately saw through Napoleon's designs, Wellington held fast to his previous opinion that the enemy's advance would be effected in several columns, and dreaded an attack upon his right flank, upon the road from Mons. He disregarded the first news of the skirmish near Charleroi, for he believed that only a portion of Napoleon's army was there ; and even when, on the afternoon of June 15th, a whole day later than Blucher, he issued from Brussels orders for the concentration of his army, he did not simply command that the whole army should march to the left, to the important nodal point of Quatre Bras where the roads from Charleroi and Namur to Brussels meet and where a junction with the Prussians was possible, but he directed his corps to the line five miles in length from Enghien in the west through Nivelles to Genappe in the east, so that the English army touched the Charleroi road only by its extreme left. All the orders of the English commander were dictated by the utterly groundless anxiety of being outflanked to the west ; his reserves, which should have been sent to Genappe upon the Charleroi road, were kept by him on the 16th for five hours at Waterloo, because he doubted whether he ought not to employ them farther to the west. Fortunately Prince Bernard of Weimar with the Nassau brigade, acting on his own initiative, occupied the cross-roads of Quatre Bras on the afternoon of June 15th ; but even this weak advance-post of the left wing of the English was still several miles behind and to the right of the Prussian position, and would with difficulty be able to prevent Blucher's right flank from being turned.

Yet more disastrous was it that Wellington was himself completely deceived, and that he deceived the Prussian commander, regarding the position which the English army could assume on the 16th. At midnight on the 15th he wrote to Blucher that next day, at ten o'clock, 20,000 men of the English army would be at Quatre Bras, and this was simply impossible in view of the actual disposition of the forces. On June 16th, before the break of day, he left the brilliant ball which the duchess of Richmond was giving to the English officers, mounted his horse, and hastened on the Charleroi road, southward beyond Quatre Bras, to the heights of Frasnes, just opposite the French left wing. Thence at about half-past ten he wrote to Blucher saying that at noon his reserves would be at Genappe, about two miles behind Quatre Bras, and that at the same hour the English cavalry would reach Nivelles, six miles to the west of Quatre Bras. If this was accurate, Blucher could count with certainty upon the support of the English in the afternoon. At one o'clock the two commanders met upon the windmill hill of Bussy, in the rear of the Prussian position, and here Wellington promised that he would take part in the battle in the afternoon, attacking the French in the rear or in the flank, as circumstances might dictate, by way of Marbais or Frasnes. The duke parted from the Prussian commander with the words, " I shall he here at four o'clock."

Trusting in this promise, Blucher and Gneisenau resolved to offer battle. The two army-corps of Zieten and Pirch were facing southward upon the hills of Brye; and farther forward, in the low-lying and damp meadow-land of the Ligne brook, which extends along the foot of this gentle elevation, on the stream, were, to the right, the village of St. Amand, and to the left the village of Ligny, both occupied in force. Thielmann, with the third army-corps, did not reach the battle-field till noon, after an exhausting march, and placed his troops between Sombreffe and Tongrinelle, as a left wing facing westward, so that the lines of the centre and of the left wing met almost at a right angle, and the line of battle formed an angle, opening towards the south. The extreme right wing at Wagnelée was completely unprotected should an attack be made upon it from the west, from the neighbourhood of Frasnes. It was only the confident expectation that Wellington would arrive at the right moment to support the right wing that determined the Prussian commanders to give battle in so disadvantageous a position; they hoped to be able to maintain the fight through the afternoon, until, towards evening, the 40,000 men of the English army would arrive to determine the issue.

But the English commander was unable to keep his word. He was himself attacked at Quatre Bras by a superior force, and even at three o'clock in the afternoon he had only 7,000 men on the spot; then reinforcements began to arrive, but it was not until late in the evening that more than 30,000 men were assembled at Quatre Bras, just enough to repel the attack, so that there could no longer be any question of giving the promised support. Wellington had promised the impossible, unquestionably in good faith, and through an error; but, after all, what did it matter to him that he could not keep his word and that through his fault his allies suffered a reverse? They were only Germans, and never had Wellington had any regard for the foreign nations with whom his life as a warrior brought him in contact, whether they were called Hindus, Portuguese, or Prussians. His immediate task was to preserve the English army— such was his view of his duties. If his allies undertook to deliver the main assault upon the enemy, he would all the more certainly secure time to get his own troops together. It was the fault of the duke alone, it was due to the belated and defective assembling of his forces, and subsequently to his giving a promise it was impossible for him to keep, that instead of a battle with united forces there took place two simultaneous battles, separated from one another by fully five miles, both fought under extremely unfavourable conditions.[1]

Even as late as the morning of June 16th the Imperator remained under the delusion that the two armies of the coalition had withdrawn respectively to Brussels and Namur, and for this reason he did not grudge a long rest to his troops, which had been wearied by the fighting of the day before and by the prolonged marches of the previous days. Not until noon was he assured that the Prussians still maintained their position at Ligny and St. Amand la Haye, and he then determined upon an attack with the main body of his army, the right wing, and the reserves. Ney, however, who was at Frasnes upon the Brussels road, with the left wing, received orders to march away to the right, and to attack the Prussians upon the right flank ; in this way, on the evening of the long summer day, Blucher's army might be annihilated. This plan of battle presupposed that upon the Brussels road Ney would encounter no more than a weak hostile force, that the English had really withdrawn to Brussels.

Upon the battle-field of Ligny, Napoleon had about 75,000 men, and Blucher from 78,000 to 80,000. The unfortunate disposition of the Prussian forces enabled the Imperator to employ almost the whole of his forces against La Haye and Ligny, where the two army-corps of Zeiten and Pirch, numbering 56,000 men, had unaided to sustain the attack of a superior force. Thielmann, separated from Ligny by the winding stream of the Ligne, was occupied in repelling some feint attacks of the French ; he was indeed able to send a portion of his troops to the aid of the other two corps, but he could not take part in the principal struggle with the mass of his own corps. The main battle took place for the possession of La Haye and Ligny ; here, within this narrow area, was the issue to be decided, and here the Prussian left wing could take no part. Both armies fought with desperate valour, the hatred of years finding terrible expression. On neither side was quarter given ; one French general threatened to shoot any of his men who brought in Prussian prisoners. On the whole the French troops exhibited more self-command and steadiness ; the officers held their people more firmly in hand, whereas the passion of an

[1] Such are the essentials of the matter as presented by Clausewitz ; and the duke, in his well-known rejoinder to Clausewitz's book, does not attempt a contradiction. What Clausewitz merely indicated has now been proved in detail by the investigations of M. Lehmann (*Historische Zeitschrift, Neue Folge* II. p. 274), and H. Delbrück (*Zeitschrift f. Pr. Geschichte* 1877, p. 645).

impetuous lust of battle which flamed through the German national
army often led the Prussian commanders to premature expenditure of their forces. This region of the fertile plain of Brabant,
whose undulating surface made it resemble a sea in which the
waves had undergone solidification, covered with crops standing
as high as a man and interspersed with potato fields, gave opportunities for numerous surprises which the young Prussian troops,
and above all the Landwehr, were not always prepared to meet
with calmness. The day was oppressively hot ; under a fierce
sun and in a sultry atmosphere, the Prussian infantry, part of
which had been in action on the previous day, whilst another part
had been marching all night, had for six hours to sustain without
intermission a hand to hand fight for the villages. Many of them
were foaming at the mouth from the fury of the struggle and the
incredible exertion ; here one would be seen lapping up the foul
effluent from a manure heap, whilst another, unwounded, would
drop dead close by from sheer exhaustion.

Shortly before three o'clock, Vandamme began the attack
upon the Prussian right wing at La Haye, and occupied the
village after a bloody struggle lasting two hours. Then Blucher
himself led fresh troops to the assault ; the village was recon-
quered, but was lost once more when an attack, made by the
Prussian cavalry near by, miscarried. Here the fight now came
to a stand-still ; the French progress was arrested in the
village, beyond which they could not advance a foot. In vain
towards evening did Napoleon send a portion of the guard to support Vandamme ; Zieten's corps maintained its position immovably for six hours. Had the English now arrived to reinforce
the right wing, victory would have been decided. Meanwhile
Gérard, with the right wing of the French, had advanced against
the village of Ligny. There the Prussians had utilised the château
and the houses for defence ; their batteries effectively commanded the plain in front. Four times were the assailants repelled,
and when at length they made their way into the houses, they
gained only half the village. In the other half, across the stream,
the Prussians maintained their position ; and now within the
village there developed a fight of unprecedented obstinacy, for both
parties received extensive reinforcements from the thick masses
of infantry in the rear. Soon the château and a considerable
proportion of the village were in flames ; in the village street
the bodies were heaped up ; every house and every stable became
a little fortress, and men fought with bayonets on the stairs and

in the rooms. In this way the struggle continued indecisively for five terrible hours. But the Prussians were using up all their strength; 14,000 men, more than nineteen battalions, were gradually thrown into this single village, and finally there remained no more than one fresh regiment of infantry available for the decisive issue. As yet nothing was lost; the appearance of the English would have turned the scale. In the afternoon, Wellington had once more sent a message to the field-marshal by Lieutenant Wussow, to the effect that with the reinforcements just received he would attempt a vigorous offensive action in favour of the Prussian army; his representative upon Blucher's headquarters staff, Colonel Hardinge, still declared positively at seven o'clock that in half an hour at latest his countrymen would arrive. An hour later, Gneisenau sent a message to General Krafft, saying that the latter need only maintain his position in Ligny for a little while longer, for the help of the English could not then fail to arrive.

The sun was at the point of setting. Then Napoleon personally led against Ligny, in order to break through the Prussian centre, his well-spared reserves, consisting of the Old Guard and a powerful force of cavalry. Whilst the grenadiers pressed into the village street with fierce cries of, " Long live the emperor ! No quarter ! " and now at length compelled the wearied defenders to withdraw, several battalions of the guard, favoured by the fading light, surrounded the village from the east. Following them, riding through the stream, came seven regiments of heavy dragoons, the nucleus of the imperial cavalry, numbering 5,000 horse. They rode past Ligny towards the windmill hill of Bussy, attacking the second line of the Prussian position. Blucher recognised the danger, and endeavoured to repel the attack with his favourite arm. Just before, the old man had seemed exhausted by his exertions, and by the terrible doubts with which he was assailed so that he had the appearance of a broken man ; but now he flamed up once more with youthful fire, sending to the attack a cavalry brigade which was stationed on the flank behind Ligny. The cavalrymen shouted with delight when the old hero, brandishing his sabre, mounted on his magnificent white charger, placed himself at their head. Near him rode Lieutenant-colonel Lützow, the leader of volunteers of 1813, commanding the sixth regiment of Uhlans ; next came the West Prussian dragoons, those of the Electoral Mark, and the Landwehr cavalry of the Elbe ; in an extended line, the horses rode through the standing corn.

Then the animals were suddenly taken aback by a deep sunken lane which cut through the fields, and whilst the Uhlans were endeavouring to get across the unexpected obstacle, two well-aimed salvos of artillery struck their disordered ranks, Milhaud's cuirassiers advanced to the charge, and the Prussians withdrew. The cuirassiers in turn had to retire before the fire of a Prussian battalion ; the laughing Westphalians could see how the heavy dragoons disengaged themselves from their fallen horses and holding their cuirasses with both hands, fled on foot. The Uhlans and the Landwehr cavalry re-formed their ranks and advanced once more ; the masses of the contestants flowed hither and thither. Gneisenau was riding amid the wild confusion ; drawing his sabre, he said cheerfully to Major Bardeleben, who, weaponless, his arm in a sling, was riding beside him : " Keep close to me ; I will cut a way out for you ! " Simultaneously the regiments driven out of Ligny withdrew towards Brye, retreating slowly, firing unceasingly, but in disorder. The centre of the line of battle had now been almost broken through.

St. Amand la Haye was also at length evacuated ; unceasingly the enemy pressed forward towards the height of Bussy. Just before nightfall a thunder-storm broke over the battle-field ; for half an hour the rolling of the thunder and the howling of the storm completely drowned the noise of battle. Yet amid the obscurity the struggle continued ; the exhausted soldiers breathed more freely in the fresher air. The beaten forces made a fresh stand at Brye and the hill of Bussy, so that here the advance of the enemy was checked. Meanwhile the field-marshal had disappeared. In the first attack of the Uhlans, his horse had been shot, and he now was lying almost unconscious beneath the heavy beast ; several times friends and foes passed close by him in conflict without noticing him, only his faithful aide-de-camp, Count Nostitz, remaining with him, until at length, Major von dem Busche of the Landwehr cavalry of the Elbe came by, and brought away the stunned man upon a soldier's horse. In the confusion of the night several hours elapsed before the rescue of the commander became known.

Now, for the time being, the leadership of the army was entirely in the hands of Gneisenau, who remained for a while in deep reflection in the neighbourhood of Brye. Those who saw him in his majestic calm, had no suspicion of the difficult thoughts which were raging through his mind. Like Blucher and Grolman, he had trusted implicitly in Wellington's assurance, had counted securely upon victory an hour before, and thought with anger of the English commander who had kept his word so badly. What could seem more natural than to follow the Englishman's example, to care only for the security of his own army, and to direct its course in safety towards the German frontier ? The old Roman road, which in the rear of the battle-field leads north-eastward into the valley of the Meuse, offered the defeated army the most convenient line of retreat ; here a junction could soon be effected with Bülow, who was advancing from the east, whilst subsequently reinforcements could be secured from Germany. Instinctively a portion of the troops had already taken this route, which seemed at the first glance to be the only one open ; but if the army went towards the Meuse it would withdraw from its ally, and it might be expected with certainty that the cautious English commander would then retreat to Antwerp, and perhaps to his ships. In this way the Belgian campaign would be ended at a single blow, and who could tell whether the coalition, with its evil memories of the congress and its laboriously maintained dissensions, with its pusillanimous headquarters staff under the command of Schwarzenberg, would continue to find courage to carry on the war against France after the two best commanders had given up the game ? There was still another way out. If Wellington had not been willing to advance to join the Prussians, these could themselves withdraw in order to effect a junction with the English army. Should the army surrender its communication with the Rhine, and, disregarding all dangers, take the difficult path to the north in the direction of Wavre, the allies would draw nearer together, and it was possible that in two or three days, somewhere in the vicinity of Brussels, the battle could be resumed with renewed energy, that battle which had now proved a failure through the fault of Wellington. The momentous decision had to be made within a few minutes ; the fate of the next months of European history rested upon it. Gneisenau determined, as he was forced to determine, as Blucher alone of all military commanders of that day would have determined. After a glance at the map, he ordered a northward march through Tilly and Mellery to Wavre.

The aides-de-camp hastened to give the troops the right direction in the darkness. General Jagow covered the retreat, remaining upon the battle-field until two in the morning. The French were not confident of their own victory, and the guard stood under arms throughout the night. They neither ventured to pursue, nor yet even to ascertain the direction of the beaten army's retreat, and they completely lost touch with their opponents. The Prussian army had lost 12,000 men, somewhat more than the enemy. Zieten's corps had lost an entire fourth of its strength. So invincible, however, was the moral energy of this army, that after a few hours' rest during the night the regiments were at daybreak already once more in good order. There was not a trace of that feeling of depression which is apt after a defeat to overcome even the most valiant; the rank and file and the leaders all looked for a new battle which should wipe out the disgrace. A few thousand men of the newly-formed Westphalian regiment had, indeed, been dispersed, and strayed along the Roman road to the Meuse and to the Rhine. But of the tried troops from the old provinces hardly anyone was missing; the few among the veterans of 1813 who in the darkness of night had been separated from their regiments through going to the east, determined, as soon as they encountered Bülow's corps, to join this force, and were able to take part in the battle of Waterloo.

The English army had passed the hot day more successfully. When, towards two o'clock, Ney, with the left wing of the French army, advanced northward, as ordered, upon the Brussels road against Quatre Bras, he was soon to learn that the English force that opposed him was far stronger than Napoleon had assumed. The Netherland general Perponcher, recognising the significance of the situation, had, on his own initiative, and against Wellington's orders, remained with his division at Quatre Bras,[1] and had to repel the first attack. At the outset the force at Ney's disposal was more than twice as strong as that of the 7,000 Nassauers and Netherlanders who were placed here; and since in addition Ney was able unnoticed to advance his infantry through the wood of Bossu which lay upon his left, the allied forces were for some time hard pressed, and were already on the point of evacuating the important position at the cross-roads. Then, between three and four o'clock (several hours later than Wellington had calculated), came the first regiments of the reserve from Brussels; an English division, under General Picton, and Duke William with his Black Brunswickers. They were able to reinforce the position upon the left wing, and were already advancing beyond Quatre Bras, when a powerful onslaught of the French cavalry threw them into confusion. Wellington himself escaped death only by

---

[1] The importance of this brave decision was recognised by Gneisenau in a letter to the king dated June 12, 1817.

the speed of his charger. Meanwhile the valiant Guelph had been shot dead in the midst of his body-guard. He died at the best moment for his reputation; for henceforward he lived in the memory of his loyal people as a hero of the nation, as the leader of the black troop ; and the detestable traits of Guelph obstinacy and arrogance which had, during the brief months of his rule, been extremely conspicuous to the little land of Brunswick, were quickly forgotten.

At this dangerous moment, the English and Hanoverian regiments of General Alten came into contact with the right wing of the allies. Wellington would not withdraw from Nivelles more than this weak division, for he was still under the illusion that Napoleon would attempt to surround him on the west. Alten's division began to deploy in the wood of Bossu, and with the help of this force Ney's second attack was repelled. For a long time now Ney had abandoned the hope of being able to reach the battle-field of Ligny by overthrowing the English force ; it would be enough for him if he could only press his opponents back at this point from the Brussels road. The man who had hitherto always been distinguished above all his rivals by an unshaken soldierly courage, showed himself throughout this campaign to be in a condition of feverish disturbance ; it was plain that he was profoundly disturbed by the memory of the broken oath of a few weeks back, and by the fear of a shameful future. In passionate excitement he adjured his valiant Rhenish fellow-countryman Kellermann to give a decisive turn to the affair, as he had done once before at Marengo, by a powerful cavalry charge ; the whole future of France was at stake. This third attempt also failed, chiefly owing to the steadfastness of the English veterans under Picton. Meanwhile Alten's regiments had entered the wood of Bossu, while fresh reserves were advancing upon the Brussels road—the English guards and the remainder of the Brunswickers. Wellington now had at his disposal more than 30,000 men, against 21,000. Twilight fell as the whole line began to advance, and the battle ended almost on the same spot on which it had begun.

A remarkable piece of luck came to the aid of the English commander. General Erlon's corps had been assigned to Ney's army, but in the afternoon, before Erlon had been able to take part in the battle of Quatre Bras, he had been summoned by Napoleon to the battle-field of Ligny ; the regiments were already close to the right wing of the Prussians, when Ney recalled them to Quatre Bras; and thus throughout the afternoon this corps, which might readily have inflicted a decisive blow upon Wellington, wandered to and fro between the two battle-fields, and did not finally join Ney's army until the evening, when the matter was already settled. The marshal, although he had not been able to fulfil the impossible demands of the Imperator, had still secured a valuable success, for the junction of the two armies of the coalition had been temporarily prevented. Wellington, however, spoke with unpleasant arrogance of a victory which was, in truth, of extremely modest proportions, saying several times: " We have conquered; the Prussians have been beaten." Since he still failed to grasp Napoleon's plan, and on June 17th, and even on June 18th, believed it possible that he might be outflanked from the west, he was unable to grasp that he had himself been responsible for all the wretched confusion of this needless double engagement, and could not find a word of gratitude for the Prussians whose unselfish sacrifice had alone rendered it possible for him to give battle at Quatre Bras.

Late in the night, Blucher was discovered by his general staff officers in a peasant's hut at Mellery, on the road to Wavre. The old man lay upon the straw, quietly smoking his pipe; he had been shaken in every limb by his heavy fall, but his cheerful confidence was unabated. He immediately expressed his approval of the orders issued by his friend Gneisenau; the two had lived in such intimate association that Gneisenau was always sure that his own resolves would express the field-marshal's thoughts. In the morning the commander-in-chief rode in front of the army to Wavre; the soldiers shouted with delight as soon as they saw the rescued man, and they answered with a cheerful " yes," when, as he rode by, he asked them if they would like to fight again on the morrow. The scorching sunshine of the day before was followed by a grey, oppressive day, interspersed with thunder-showers; in the evening came pouring rain which lasted all through the night. The soldiers, who had now for three days been continuously marching or fighting, laboriously plodded over the saturated ground, helping to push the wheels of the cannon through the deep mud. In bivouac, sleep was impossible, and yet their courage remained imperturbable; on the morning of June 18th the Silesian fusiliers were dancing a merry waltz to the strains of their field music. A cordial appeal issued by the field-marshal exhorted the troops to offer up all their energies in the new struggle : " Do not forget that you are Prussians, and that our watchword is ' Death or victory ' ! "

In his report to the king, Gneisenau openly complained that Wellington, " contrary to all expectation and assurance," had not concentrated his forces at the right moment ; and in confidential letters he expressed his views still more incisively. In the published reports from Blucher's headquarters staff, the painful question was, however, carefully ignored, and after the war Gneisenau magnanimously avoided any paper warfare against the allies of Prussia, although the English commander's insincere accounts of the matter must have made this honourable soldier long to express his own views. It was not until twenty years later that the secret history of this campaign was elucidated in a posthumous historical work by Clausewitz, who had unquestionably utilised information imparted by his friend Gneisenau. At that moment nothing was further from Gneisenau's thoughts than fruitless squabbling about past errors ; he reported to the king that a battle with separate forces was no longer possible, and immediately made preparations for a junction with the English army. Hour by hour the feeling in the headquarters staff became more confident, for the hesitating attitude of the enemy showed clearly that the result of the fighting of June 16th had for the Prussians been a lost battle but not a defeat. Blucher was absolutely sure of the issue ; it was his wish that if Napoleon did not attack the English, he himself in conjunction with Wellington should immediately offer battle, and he welcomed the violence of the weather, speaking of it as " our old ally of the Katzbach." The Russian military attaché Toll had a bad time of it when he thought it necessary to offer consolation to these proud Prussians, and said soothingly that the great army under Schwarzenberg would soon put things right. Nostitz, Blucher's aide-de-camp, answered sharply : " Before you get back to your emperor either the Belgian campaign will have been completely lost, or else we shall have won the second battle and shall no longer have any need of your great army ! "

In answer to Blucher, the English commander declared that he would be ready to undertake a new battle on June 18th, on the Brussels road, if he could count on the help of about 25,000 Prussians. Blucher rejoined that he would come, and that he hoped to do so with his entire army. After a brief and brilliant cavalry skirmish, in which Lord Uxbridge with the giants of the English dragoon guards literally rode down the French lancers,

Wellington returned northward in the afternoon, and collected his army at Mont St. Jean, across the Brussels road, fronting southward. Even now he did not completely abandon his fear of being outflanked on the right, and therefore stationed at Hal, nine miles to the west of the battle-field, a force of 17,000 men, so that in the decisive hours nearly one-fifth of his army was lacking. In the night of June 17th-18th, the whole Prussian army was assembled in the neighbourhood of Wavre, from nine to ten miles to the east of Mont St. Jean, and the anxiously-awaited ammunition column also put in an appearance. But this short distance, which an aide-de-camp could traverse at a gallop in little more than an hour, offered serious difficulties, in the existing terrible conditions of the roads, to the movement of the cumbrous artillery of a great army. In addition, considerable delay was unavoidable, for the as yet untouched corps of Bülow was to take the lead, and would have to make its way through the more advanced portions of the army. If the English commander intended merely to make a demonstration, as Gneisenau for a time suspected, the position of the Prussians, whose left wing was exposed, might become extremely dangerous ; they could only undertake the venture confiding in the invincible staying-power of the English army. All that Wellington expected from the Prussian commander was that he could draw near to strengthen the left wing of the English. Gneisenau, however, in his great manner, chose a bolder and more difficult course, thinking rather of attacking the French in the rear and upon the right flank. Should this attack prove successful, Napoleon's army would be annihilated, and the war would be ended at a single blow.

It was only through the sins of omission of the conqueror that the conquered could venture to conceive such bold ideas. It would certainly have been a grave undertaking for Napoleon to pursue the Prussians with the main force of his army, but his desperate situation demanded bold resolves. Had he pressed on at the heels of the most active of his opponents, it was possible that the beaten army would during its retreat have been thrown into utter disorder, for the effect of a victory is usually redoubled by persistent pursuit. It was at least doubtful whether, in that case, Wellington would have ventured to attack Ney ; it is more probable that the English commander would have retreated upon Antwerp. It was not cowardice which prevented the Imperator from making up his mind to such a course, but his old error of overweening presumption. As formerly after the battle of

Dresden and after the victories in Champagne, so on this occasion did he esteem his opponents too lightly ; he fully believed that the Prussians were retreating in complete disorder towards the Rhine, and did not even regard it as necessary to have their retreat watched. If matters had happened as he imagined, he would, indeed, have had plenty of time to defeat the English. On the morning of June 17th he gave his army a comfortable rest. His thoughts were more in Paris than on the field of battle ; he asked his generals what the Jacobins would do after this new victory of the empire. Not till noon did he order Marshal Grouchy to pursue the Prussians in the direction eastward towards Gembloux and the Meuse, not to lose sight of them, and to complete their defeat ; for this purpose he assigned to the marshal 33,000 men, a force too strong for an observation corps and too weak to venture a battle against the whole Prussian army. During the latter half of the day, Grouchy moved eastward to the Irre, without getting in touch with the Prussians. It was not until the morning of June 18th that he found their trace, and turned towards Wavre. He guessed nothing of Gneisenau's plans, now thinking that the Prussian army was retreating upon Brussels ; just as little as the emperor did he imagine that a beaten army could regain order immediately after the battle, and prepare for a fresh onslaught. The Imperator no longer thought of pushing in between the two armies of the coalition, since the possibility of the retreat of the Prussians northward was altogether out of his calculations. He himself, on the afternoon of June 17th, formed a junction with Ney's army in the neighbourhood of Quatre Bras, and then, feeling perfectly secure, moved northward upon the Brussels road after the English, expecting on the 18th or the 19th to force them to join battle with him on one side or the other of Brussels.

Whilst the course of the double battle of June 16th was confused and obscure, the battle of June 18th was simple and imposing. With the eye of a master, Wellington had chosen a strong defensive position such as he had learned to love in the Spanish campaign. His army was placed near the centre of a line of low hills running from west to east, at the village of Mont St. Jean, which is traversed by the well-paved Brussels road cutting straight across the elevation. Upon this narrow space, over an extension of less than a mile, the troops were closely packed together. There were more than 30,000 Germans, 24,000 Englishmen, more than 13,000 Netherlanders, a force of 68,000 in all. Lord Hill commanded the right, the Prince of Orange the centre, and General Picton the left wing. A deeply sunken cross-road, enclosed by hedges, ran along the front. At the rear of the army the ground fell gently away, so that the majority of the regiments were hidden from the advancing enemy; further to the north there lay close to the road the thin wood of Soignes, traversed by numerous paths, and offering good cover in case of retreat. For many hours the duke remained with the centre at Mont St. Jean; here, beneath an elm tree, upon an elevation near the high-road, he could gain a comprehensive view of almost the entire field, and could, after his usual custom, direct everything in person. A few hundred yards to the front there lay, like the outworks of a fortress, three strongly occupied positions; in front of the right was the château of Hougomont, standing amid the ancient trees of its park and surrounded by high walls; in front of the centre, on the high road, was the farmstead of La Haye Sainte; before the extreme left wing were the white houses of Papelotte and La Haye. From Mont St. Jean the road declines gently southwards, then runs absolutely level through open fields, to ascend once more nearly three miles to the south, crossing another elevation close to the farm of La Belle Alliance. Thus the battle-field has the form of a wide and shallow basin, offering the freest possible opportunities for the utilisation of all arms.

Napoleon established his army upon the heights near La Belle Alliance, placing Reille to the left and Erlon to the right of the road, whilst his reserves were in the rear at Rossomme. It was his plan simply to break through the English lines by one or more frontal attacks, if possible at the enemy's weakest point, the English left wing. Since the firearms of those days allowed the attacking force to draw close to the defenders with unbroken energy, the Imperator hoped to fight down his tenacious opponent by colossal, massive blows. His method of warfare had, during the last ten years, become continually more violent; to-day at length, in the feverish passion of the desperate gamester, he showed all the savagery of the Jacobin, pressing thousands of his cavalrymen and whole divisions of his infantry into a single mass, which, like Alexander's phalanxes, were to trample everything down before them. It was in this way that the battle opened with a continual advance and withdrawal of the attacking forces, like the waves on a steep shore, until the appearance of the Prussians in Napoleon's rear and upon his right flank completely disordered the Imperator's plan of battle. The course of the struggle was like that of a deliberately planned tragedy: at first a simple development, then a violent tension and increase, and at length the intervention of a crushing destiny; among all the battles of modern history, only that of Königgrätz displays a similar character, that of a perfect work of art. Thus the ultimate issue left upon the world the impression of overwhelming and invincible necessity, because a wonderful destiny had allotted to each of the three nations, and to each of the commanders, the precise role which corresponded best to their peculiar energies : the British exhibited in the work of defence their phlegmatic and iron tenacity ; the French displayed their knightly and uncontrollable courage in attack ; finally the Prussians exhibited a similar stormy boldness in onslaught and, in addition, what counts more than all, the self-restraint of the inspired will.

Napoleon counted with certainty upon a speedy victory, for he believed that the Prussians were far away to the southeast at Namur. His army numbered more than 72,000 men, being superior to that of Wellington, above all in the strength of its cavalry and the preponderance of its artillery, for Napoleon had two hundred and forty heavy guns as against one hundred and fifty in Wellington's army. In such circumstances it seemed that there could be no harm in postponing the attack until noon, when the sun would have had some effect in drying the saturated ground. In order to alarm his opponent and to increase the confidence of his own army, the Imperator held a grand review under the very eyes of the English. Sick as he was, distressed by a thousand doubts and anxieties, he undoubtedly also felt that it was necessary to raise his own spirits by the sight of his faithful followers. Whenever, at a later date, in his lonely island prison, he thought of this hour, it was with rapture, and he would exclaim : " The earth was proud to carry so many brave men ! " Thus for the last time there appeared in parade before their warlord the veterans of the Pyramids, of Austerlitz, of Borodino, who had so long been the terror of the world, and who had now saved from the shipwreck of their old glories nothing more than their soldierly pride, their eagerness for revenge, and their untamable love for their hero. The drums sounded, the bands played *Partant pour la Syrie !* In long lines were extended the grenadiers in their bearskin caps, the cuirassiers with helmets decorated with horse-tails, the voltigeurs with tasselled shakos, the lancers with fluttering pennons—one of the most magnificent and bravest armies ever seen in history. All the boastful glory of the empire was exhibited once again, an overwhelming spectacle for the hearts of the veterans ; and in their midst once again the war-lord in his gloomy majesty. There was no end to the shouts of acclamation ; the idol of the soldiery had only two days before displayed his invincibility once more. Yet this convulsive jubilation, which contrasted so strangely with the absolute stillness of the English camp, came from oppressed hearts. The consciousness of guilt, the premonition of a tragical destiny, lay upon the most valiant spirits. Ten hours more, and the bold hope of the German strategist had been fulfilled ; this magnificent army, with its defiant spirit, its pride, and its savage strength of manhood, had been annihilated down to the last squadron.

Half an hour before noon Napoleon began the battle, sending his left wing against the château of Hougomont, whilst upon the right he made arrangements for a decisive blow. There four divisions of infantry were united to form a gigantic column ; the way was paved for the attack by the persistent artillery fire of a great battery placed at Belle Alliance. Towards one-thirty, General Erlon led the powerful force of infantry against the British left wing. But before this movement began, the calm security of the emperor's calculations had already been disturbed by the receipt of sinister news. Through an intercepted letter he learned at one o'clock that General Bülow was marching against the French right wing ; and whilst standing on the hill at Rossomme, behind the French centre, studying his map, he thought that already, far to the east, at the village of Chapelle St. Lambert (which stands on an elevation), he could discern dark masses of troops, which immediately afterwards disappeared among the undulations of the ground. An aide-de-camp was immediately despatched in this direction, and confirmed the observation. The emperor vigorously endeavoured to control his dismay, and for the moment sent two cavalry divisions eastward across the right wing of the battle-field. Surely it could only be the single corps of Bülow, perhaps only a portion of that corps, and before the Prussians could intervene in the battle, Wellington would certainly be defeated. To his officers Napoleon declared, with confident mien, that Marshal Grouchy was advancing to the support of the right wing—for the army must not suspect this danger. Meanwhile Erlon had moved forward with his four infantry divisions ; during the first advance he suffered severe losses, whole ranks of the deep columns being mowed down by the English artillery fire. The first outcome of the attack was to put a Netherland brigade to flight ; only part of the troops of the young kingdom maintained their position ; old Blucher had been right when he expressed the opinion that these Belgians were " by no means fierce animals." Now, however, the English and Hanoverian infantry emerged from behind the protecting hedges, surrounding with a long line the unwieldy masses of the French. After a murderous struggle, in which the valiant Picton found his death, the attacking force had to withdraw. Ponsonby's Scottish cavalry pursued them, dispersing the retreating men, and pressing forward irresistibly as far as the great French battery ; only here were they forced to turn by the French cavalry.

The great blow had miscarried. Now, too, it was no longer possible to avoid recognising that at least a considerable proportion of the Prussian army was advancing, and advancing towards the village of Planchenoit, in the rear of the French right wing. It was still possible for the Imperator to withdraw from the battle, but how could his pride endure so humiliating a resolve ? He despatched Lobau's corps to Planchenoit, so that his line was now no longer straight, but had the form of a curve bent backwards towards the right. The Prussians had spoiled his entire order of battle even before they had fired a single shot. The danger threatening the right was carefully concealed from the portions of the army which were fighting against the English. For this reason Napoleon did not allow Lobau's troops to advance further eastward, where they could easily have arrested the progress of Bülow's corps on the edge of the wide valley of the Lasne, but kept them close to Planchenoit, for the collision with the Prussians must be postponed as long as possible, so that the army's confidence of victory might not be shaken by the thunder of artillery upon the right. Influenced by his dread of the Prussian attack, the Imperator no longer ventured to send against the English the twenty-four battalions of his guard, which still remained untouched in reserve, but determined to break through Wellington's centre with the whole of his cavalry. This was a hopeless move, for the main body of the allied infantry was still unshaken.

In the morning Blucher had left camp at Wavre. He had by no means recovered from his severe fall on the previous day, but who could speak to the old hero of repose ? " I would rather," he exclaimed, " have myself tied on to my horse than miss this battle ! " In good spirits he rode among the regiments, which were labouring through the mire with incredible exertions ;

a conflagration in Wavre had seriously delayed the march. The soldiers rejoiced wherever the commander appeared, turning towards him with shouts, stroking his knee ; for every one of them he had an encouraging word, saying : " Children, I have promised my brother Wellington that we will come. You won't let me break my word ? " Thielmann remained at Wavre with the third army-corps in order to protect the rear of the army against an attack by Grouchy, who did in fact draw near to Wavre in the afternoon. The other three corps marched upon Chapelle St. Lambert ; at ten o'clock the advance-guard, and at one the main body of the army, arrived there from the heights. Now the army was divided. Zieten marched straight forward with the first corps to Ohain and beyond, to attack the French right wing. Bülow with the fourth corps, and behind him Pirch with the second corps, turned to the left, southwestward towards the rear of the French position. Fortunately the difficult defile of the valley of the Lasne was not occupied by the enemy ; the stream was crossed, and at about four o'clock Bülow's troops attained a well-protected position in and behind the wood of Frichemont ; the advance that was to take the French by surprise, was not to be begun until a sufficient force was on the spot. The regiments took up their positions in profound silence ; the generals went to the border of the wood and with tense glances followed the course of the battle. When one of the officers expressed the opinion that the enemy would now give up the attack upon the English, and, in order to secure their retreat, would throw their chief force against the Prussians, Gneisenau answered : " You ill know Napoleon. He will now endeavour to break the English line of battle at all costs, and will only employ what is absolutely necessary against us."

This actually took place. Even before the Prussians reached the wood of Frichemont, between three and four in the afternoon, the second great onslaught of the French had begun. Ney, with fourteen regiments of heavy cavalry, galloped along the west side of the road, to attack the squares of the English guard and Alten's division in the centre. For some time the struggle appeared indecisive, but the infantry held their position unshaken. The French attack was finally repulsed, and thereupon Ney joined to his force Kellermann's cavalry, so that now twenty-six cavalry regiments moved to the renewed attack, the greatest force of cavalry which this warlike age had ever seen in operation at a single spot. The ground shook with the hoofs of ten thousand horses, the basin of land was filled with a forest of sabres and lances, the struggle wavered for an hour, and the attack against individual battalions was renewed from ten to twelve times. But the firmness of the English and German infantry still retained the upper hand. This attack also came to nothing, the squadrons began to retreat, a bold advance on the part of the English and Hanoverian reserve cavalry threw them into complete confusion ; but even the victors were profoundly exhausted.

Meanwhile upon other parts of the battle-field the course of events was far more favourable for Napoleon. Quiot's division, which had already taken part in Erlon's great attack, advanced again along the high-road and stormed the farm of La Haye Sainte. Here was Major Baring, with a battalion of light infantry of the German legion, and a few Nassauers. Already at noon the green yagers had repelled Erlon's columns ; the faithful men were devoted to their officers, and every one of them, down to the last private, was determined never to retreat from this post of honour. But what a task was now theirs ! The roofs of the farm buildings were already on fire, and some of the soldiers must engage in the work of fighting the flames, whilst the others, behind the hedges and walls of the garden, were directing their fire against an overwhelmingly superior force. Powder and shot were exhausted. Vainly did Baring again and again send messengers to the rear to Mont St. Jean, urgently begging for ammunition. It was not until almost the last cartridge had been fired that the valiant little garrison evacuated the position. The French raged into the farmstead as the hostile force withdrew, shouting as they searched the rooms and the barns : " Pas de pardon à ces coquins verds ! " for how many of their comrades had fallen at noon, and more recently, before the well-aimed balls of the German yagers. The outwork of the English centre had been taken, and soon the attacking stream advanced further towards Mont St. Jean. The centre of Wellington's line of battle had been broken. Thereupon the duke himself led Kielmannsegg's Hanoverian brigade to the spot, and thus succeeded for a time in filling the gap in the centre. But only for a time, for the reserves had already been called up to the last man, and La Haye Sainte, the commanding position immediately in front of the centre, remained in the enemy's hands. At the same time the valiant Bernard of Weimar, upon the left wing, was unable any longer to maintain the outwork of La Haye and Papelotte against Durutte's division. He began to retreat. Wellington's anxiety increased. During the last few hours he had repeatedly sent aides-de-camp to Blucher with urgent requests for assistance. Cold and severe he stood among his officers, watch in hand, saying : " Blucher or nightfall ! " If Napoleon were now in a position to send his guards against Mont St. Jean, or against the shaken left wing of the English, he could not fail to gain the victory.

At this momentous instant the Prussian attack commenced. The thunder of artillery now began to sound over the battle-field from the east, plainly audible to both contending parties, this being the first intimation of the struggle which was going on at Wavre in the rear of Blucher's army, between Thielmann and Grouchy. At the same time the first shot was fired in front of the wood at Frichemont. It was half-past four in the afternoon ; Wellington's army had had to sustain the battle unaided for five hours. Bülow's batteries took up a position in echelon upon the heights in front of the wood. It was a magnificent spectacle, the way in which the brigades of the fourth corps, with drums sounding and banners flying, advanced, one after the other, out of the wood, and, passing between the batteries, made their way downwards into the plain towards Planchenoit. In the ever-young heart of Gneisenau, the impression produced on this occasion by the wild poesy of war was magical, and even in his official reports of the battle he could not refrain from dwelling upon the glorious characteristics of this spectacle.

The hero of Dennewitz did his best to atone for the errors of June 15th and 16th, leading the attack with admirable coolness, as in the great days of the northern army. At the very beginning of the struggle fell the universally-loved Colonel Schwerin, the man who a year earlier had brought the news of victory to the capital. Lobau's corps was forced back, and the Prussians advanced irresistibly to Planchenoit. Somewhat later, towards six o'clock, General Zieten had reached Chain with the advance-guard of the first corps, and then, as soon as he had received information of the pressing need of the English left wing, quickly advanced upon the outposts of La Haye and Papelotte, where Durutte's division had just installed itself. Prince Bernard of Weimar, with the remnants of his troops, was retreating into the protecting wood of Soignes, when Prussian reinforcements arrived ; by the prolonged and unequal struggle his valiant Nassauers had been completely incapacitated for further fighting. Steinmetz's brigade now drove the French out of both the outposts, the Brandenburg dragoons charged the retreating forces, the fire of the batteries of the first corps swept the enemy's right wing, and the terrible news spread as far as the French centre that upon the right all was lost.

By seven o'clock Napoleon's defeat was unquestionable. His left wing had again and again vainly attacked the château of Hougomont ; in the centre, the great cavalry onslaught had failed ; upon the right and in the rear, the Prussians were pressing nearer and nearer from two directions. It was no longer possible to maintain the solitary gain of the last phases of the struggle, the farmstead of La Haye Sainte. By a well-timed retreat, at least half the army might still be saved. It was, however, a necessary outcome of the Imperator's character and of his desperate political situation, that he should despise this way out, and should venture a third general attack, on this occasion on both sides simultaneously. At seven o'clock he summoned the twenty-four battalions of his guard, retaining only two in hand as a last reserve, and despatching twelve to Planchenoit against Bülow. The remaining ten were to be led by Ney in a fresh attack against the English centre, but on this occasion on the western side of the high-road, as far as possible from Zieten's force. With shouts of acclamation the battalions rode past the Imperator at Belle Alliance ; it was their task to decide the victory. Then they rode down into the sinister basin where thick masses of dead men and dead horses indicated the road of death to the French cavalry ; to the sound of the drums, they galloped on, regardless of the fire of the English batteries, and mounted the slope immediately in front of the British guards. Maitland's grenadiers were hidden there in the grass. When the first bear-skin caps appeared over the hill, there resounded Wellington's urgent command : " Up, Guards, and at 'em ! " At once before the eyes of the dismayed French there rose a red wall, the long line of the English guards, a terrible salvo was fired, at a range of a few paces, into the attacking ranks. There was a brief and fierce hand-to-hand fight, and then the blues were driven back down the declivity by the reds, at the point of the bayonet. Ney's horse, struck by a bullet, collapsed under its rider, and the French guards fled when they saw their leader fall. Ney, however, disengaged himself from his beast, sprang to his feet, and with an angry exclamation endeavoured to rally the routed men. Vainly, however, for meanwhile the other battalions had come between two fires on the left and were also retreating. The imperial guard broke up ; its unhappy commander wandered bare-headed upon the battle-field, with broken sword, vainly seeking a bullet which should relieve him from the pangs of conscience and from his gloomy anticipations.

Blucher meanwhile had led the attack which determined the annihilation of the Napoleonic army. Bülow's troops advanced in three columns upon Planchenoit, at the storming-pace. In and near the village were twelve fresh battalions of the imperial guard ; they fought with the greatest courage, for all felt that here was the decisive issue of the whole war. The advancing Prussians were exposed, without protection, in the open field, to the bullets of the defending force, which was concealed in the houses and behind the high walls of the churchyard. The last struggle was almost the bloodiest of this savage age ; in three and a half hours, Bülow's corps lost 6,353 men, more than a fifth of his whole strength, proportionally as great a loss as that of the English army during the entire battle. The first and the second attack were repulsed ; then Gneisenau himself led the Silesian and Pomeranian regiments in the third attack, and at length, towards eight o'clock, this proved successful. There was a last fierce resistance in the village street ; and then the guard fled in wild disorder ; pursued by Major Keller with the fusiliers of the 15th regiment, and then by other battalions. Along the whole line there sounded in long-drawn notes the beautiful signal to advance of the Prussian bugles. Simultaneously, farther to the north, Lobau's corps was attacked by Bülow's troops in front and by Zieten's cavalry on the flank, and was completely routed. Here the two portions of the Prussian army effected a junction ; the terrible girdle which was to surround the right wing of the French upon three sides, was closed. The English pressed on from the north, the Prussians from the east and from the south. Grolman indicated to Zieten's troops the way to the height behind the French centre, to the farm of La Belle Alliance, which with its white walls was as conspicuous as a lighthouse, looking down across the low-lying country. Thither also did the victors of Planchenoit take their way.

More than 40,000 Prussians had already taken part in the struggle ; and now, when the work was nearly finished, Pirch's army-corps came down from the heights behind Planchenoit. During this last hour Napoleon had hastened to La Haye Sainte, in order to urge Quiot's division to make yet another attempt upon Mont St. Jean. As soon as he noticed Ney's defeat upon the left and at the same time the break-up of the whole of the right wing, he said despairingly : " *Tout est perdu ; sauve qui peut !* " He then hastened back along the high-road, not without great danger, for the road was already commanded with a severe cross fire by the English army and by Zieten's batteries.

Wellington contemplated the terrible confusion in silence, immovable, with wonderful self-command. Not only was his army utterly exhausted, but also its tactical organisation was completely broken up ; by the prolonged struggle all sections of the troops had been shaken inextricably together ; from the remnants of the two magnificent cavalry brigades of Ponsonby and Somerset no more than two squadrons could be assembled. There was no possibility of sustaining another decisive battle with such troops. The duke was well aware that it was only the appearance of the Prussians which had preserved him from an unmistakable defeat ; his repeated urgent messages to Blucher leave no doubt about this matter, but he owed the last satisfaction to the military honour of his valiant troops ; and moreover he foresaw with statesmanlike intelligence how much more important would be England's word in the peace negotiations if it could be believed that the British arms alone had played a decisive part in the struggle. For this reason, as soon as he saw the whole of the French right wing exposed to the Prussian attack, he advanced all the available remnants of his army a little further. In this last advance, the Hanoverian colonel Halkett drove before him the only two squares of the imperial guard which still held together, and with his own hands took prisoner their general, Cambronne. But the forces of the wearied men were soon exhausted, and they got only a little beyond Belle Alliance. Wellington, having saved appearances, left the further pursuit entirely to the Prussians, who in any case were nearest to the enemy. The beaten forces were in a condition of absolute panic ; no orders were listened to any longer, everyone thought only of his own miserable life. Infantry and cavalry confusedly intermingled, the broken up masses streamed southward along and beside the high-road. The drivers cut the traces and rode off on the horses, so that of the two hundred and forty guns, all but twenty-seven fell into the hands of the conqueror. Even the call *l'empereur*, which hitherto had instantly opened every road for the imperial carriage, now lost its charm ; Napoleon, although he was ill and could hardly keep his seat, had to escape on horseback. It was only in order to save the colours that a few of the faithful still continued to fight ; four were lost in the battle but all the others were saved. Never in history was a brave army so suddenly thrown into complete disorder. After the superhuman exertions of the day, all courage of body and vigour of will collapsed in a moment ; the obscurity of the night, the superior strength of the conquerors, the extent of the attack, and the relentless pursuit, increased the confusion. A further decisive factor was that in this army, notwithstanding its stormy courage, there was lacking moral greatness. What held these mutineers together ? Nothing but the belief in their hero. Now that his star had paled, they were merely an undisciplined mob.

The sun had already sunk behind thick clouds when the two commanders met a little to the south of the farmstead of Belle Alliance ; they embraced one another cordially, the self-contained man of forty and the ardent grey-head. Gneisenau was close at hand. Now at length there had been gained the complete victory such as Gneisenau had often looked for in vain from Schwarzenberg ; now at length had come complete repayment for all the hatred and all the shame of those horrible seven years. His heart sang within him, there came to his mind thoughts of the most magnificent of the Frederician battle-fields, over which he had often ridden when in garrison in Silesia. " Is it not just like Leuthen ? " he said to Bardeleben, and regarded him with sparkling eyes. In truth, just as long ago at Leuthen, the trumpeters were blowing *Nun danket alle Gott,* and the soldiers were joining in. Gneisenau, however, thought also of the night of terror after the battle of Jena, of those hours in the wood of Webicht when he had shared the deadly anxiety of a beaten army, and had experienced the elemental force of a nocturnal pursuit. More thoroughly than on the Katzbach was the victory to be utilised to-day. " We have shown," he exclaimed, " how to conquer ; now we will show how to pursue." He ordered Bardeleben to keep upon the heels of the fugitives with a battery, continually shooting after them at haphazard in the darkness, so that the enemy could rest nowhere. He took under his own immediate command whatever troops were available : Brandenburg uhlans and dragoons, and infantry of the 15th and 25th and of the 1st Pomeranian regiments ; the elder Prince William, who led the reserve cavalry of Bülow's corps, joined him.

In this way the savage pursuit raged along the road throughout the night ; the fugitives could rest nowhere. Not until Genappe, where the road crosses the valley of the Dyle by a narrow bridge, did the fragments of the imperial guard endeavour to attack the uhlans; but towards eleven o'clock, directly they heard the Prussian infantry advancing to the assault, they broke up once more. Here General Lobau and more than 2,000 men were taken prisoners; Napoleon's carriage with his hat and sword were also seized. What a surprise came when the cushions of the seats were lifted; the great adventurer had wished to secure means for himself in case of flight, and had filled the carriage with gold and precious stones. The poor Pomeranian peasant lads were as perplexed by the brilliants as had long ago been the Swiss at Grandson by the jewels of the duke of Burgundy; many of them sold valuable stones for a few groschen. The Imperator's beautiful plate was retained by the officers of the 25th, and was given by them to the favourite daughter of their king as a table ornament.

After a brief halt, Gneisenau and Prince William continued the pursuit. Across the Dyle the French believed themselves to be in safety, and had arranged to bivouac. At least seven times they were driven away from their fires by the persistent Prussians. When the infantry could pursue no further, Gneisenau made a drummer mount a captured horse and beat his drum with all his might while the pursuit was continued with the uhlans and about fifty fusiliers who were still able to keep going. What a number of squads of the French ran away from the sound of this single drum! The road was littered with arms, knapsacks, and all kinds of discarded articles, as had once been the road from Rosbach to Erfurt. At dawn the pursuers reached the battle-field of Quatre Bras, and only when they had crossed this did they stop from exhaustion at Frasnes, after sunrise. They had increased the dispersal of the hostile army to complete dismemberment, so that of the French fighters at Belle Alliance only 10,000 men, in utterly disorganised masses, subsequently assembled in Paris.

Blucher proudly thanked his incomparable army, which had rendered possible what all great commanders had hitherto regarded as impossible: " As long as history lasts, your memory will persist. Upon you, the unshakable pillars of the Prussian monarchy, rests secure the fortune of your king and of his house. Never shall Prussia be overthrown if your sons and grandsons resemble you! " To Stein he wrote simply: " I hope, my honourable friend, that you will be satisfied with me," and expressed the desire " to live out quietly in the country " his remaining years, as Stein's neighbour. He ordered that the battle should be known as " La Belle Alliance," the significant name of

the farm where the two conquerors had met, " by the favour of
fortune ; and in commemoration of the alliance which now exists
between the British and the Prussian nations, an alliance dictated
by the very nature of things ; in commemoration of the union
of the two armies and the mutual trust of the two commanders."
Wellington would not yield to this fine thought, which gave well-
deserved honour to both nations.   The battle must appear as his
victory, and therefore he christened it after the name of the
village of Waterloo, where there had been no fighting at all ; for
there he had spent the night of June 17th, and from the days of
the Spanish campaign he had been accustomed to name his victories after the site of his last headquarters.   Whereas Gneisenau's
report of the battle gave a straightforward and modest description
of the actual course of events, as far as this was already known,
the duke's report made it appear as if his last feint-attack had
decided the issue, and as if the Prussians had merely afforded an
unquestionably valuable assistance.   Fortunately, little was as
yet manifest of these characteristics of English friendly alliance.
The relationship between the soldiers of the two armies remained
thoroughly amicable ; the valiant Highlanders who on the battle-
field embraced the men of the Prussian four-and-twentieth, had
joined with them in singing *Heil dir im Siegerkranz*, troubling themselves little about whose services were the greatest.

In the homeland, the unhappy news of Ligny had caused
profound dismay ; the people already began to foresee a new
age of unending wars.   All the more passionate was the joy when
the news of victory arrived.   How suddenly had the relationships
of power between the two neighbour peoples been changed !
Now the Germans met the enemy across the frontier ; half the
Prussian army and a part of the North German contingent sufficed,
in conjunction with about 60,000 Englishmen and Netherlanders,
to defeat the French army ; inevitably the thought sprang to life
that Prussia alone, without Austria, would be strong enough to
master this ill neighbour if only all the other German states would
join Prussia.   Gneisenau declared with satisfaction : " The French
do not merely fear, they now actually know, that we are
stronger than they."   In consciousness of such energy, the nation
like one man demanded a relentless utilisation of the victory,
and the complete liberation of the German river.   A contemporary poet wrote :

> " That chain of frontier forts by Vauban built for France—
> Seize them for Germany ! "

Yet never does the imperfection of all human activity display itself more conspicuously than in war. One last success which still seemed possible eluded the Prussians, and, as the officers considered, not without blame attaching to the two most learned men of the army. Grouchy's force escaped annihilation. On June 18th, when the marshal advanced against Wavre, Thielmann checked him at the Dyle, in the evening, by a bold and courageously led fight. In the early morning of June 19th Grouchy made a further attack, and Thielmann, who had only three brigades at his disposal against the superior force of the enemy, retreated upon Louvain. His chief of staff, the talented Clausewitz, considered the position more serious than it really was, and retreated too far to the north. Consequently when the French, on receiving the terrible news of Belle Alliance, suddenly turned and hastily retraced their steps to the Sambre, the Prussians had lost touch with them and could no longer get at them. Meanwhile the main army had also initiated an undertaking against Grouchy. When General Pirch, late in the evening of June 18th, reached Planchenoit, and found the battle already almost over, there occurred to Aster, his chief of staff, the fortunate idea that the second corps must now move eastward, in order, as circumstances might dictate, to pursue Grouchy's army or to cut off its retreat. In this proposal he merely suggested what he was immediately afterwards ordered to do by Gneisenau. The task offered great difficulties. The corps had been weakened by the fight of Ligny, and by the detachment of several bodies of troops, so that it now numbered only 16,000 men, its strength being half that which it had possessed three days earlier ; the soldiers were utterly weary ; and nothing definite was known as to Grouchy's position. It is not surprising that the night march was a slow one ; yet had his staff been sufficiently alert, the general would have been able to learn on the 19th where Grouchy was. But this activity was lacking. Not until June 20th did news arrive that in the previous night, without a shot being fired, the marshal had made his way to the Sambre, passing not far from the outposts, and had thus had the luck to slip through between the two corps of Pirch and Thielmann. Pirch hastened after him, encountered the rear-guard at Namur, and took the town after a sanguinary fight at the gates ; but Grouchy's main force was already in safety. The result was that, for the time being, the French still possessed a tolerably well-ordered force of 30,000 men, which perhaps might constitute the nucleus for a new army.

The two commanders-in-chief speedily came to an understanding as to a common invasion of France, in which the Prussians were again to take the lead ; but in this resolution they were guided by fundamentally different intentions. Blucher simply wished to complete the overthrow of the detested land, until the monarchs could make further arrangements ; Wellington desired to restore the legitimate king to the Tuileries as speedily as possible. How much more advantageous was the Englishman's political position ! Whilst Blucher, ignorant of the designs of his court, had to content himself with forbidding his generals any official intercourse with the Bourbons, Wellington, unconcerned about the wishes of his ally, quietly moved forward towards his definite goal, and demanded of the court at Ghent that it should follow the English army.

The decisive issue of the war had occurred with such wonderful speed that those powers which did not desire a new restoration could make no preparations to meet the altered situation. King Louis was still the king of France, recognised by all the powers ; the whole diplomatic corps had accompanied him to Ghent, and the representations of the foreign statesmen were fortunately able to overcome the dangerous influence of Count Blacas, and to induce the king to assume a more moderate attitude. A first unwise and arrogant proclamation was succeeded on June 28th by a second, full of friendly assurances. The Bourbon promised that he would henceforward place himself between the allied and the French armies " in the hope that the deference paid to me will turn to the advantage of France " ; he solemnly pledged himself not to re-establish tithes and seigneurial rights, and not to demand the return of the national goods. Wellington did not hesitate to declare to the peace deputation sent to him by the capital, that the conqueror's conditions would be very much harder if the nation did not summon back its king. Strangely enough, Pozzo di Borgo, the Russian ambassador, eagerly supported the efforts of the English commander ; and did this altogether on his own initiative, for at that time the czar was thinking of promoting the accession of the duke of Orleans. It was Pozzo's hope that through favouring the cause of the Bourbon he might for years to come be the most powerful man in the Tuileries. A portion of the possessing classes was also inclined to the view that a new restoration was the only possible issue from the hopeless confusion, and that in especial it would be advantageous to the position of France in Europe.

This was a matter of cool calculation which had nothing to do with any sentiments of dynastic loyalty.

The Imperator had immediately to learn that France had no place for an unlucky Napoleon. Acting on the advice of his entourage, on June 20th he left the army, which was his sole support, and hastened to Paris ; there he found himself so utterly abandoned by all the world that, two days later, he abdicated in favour of his son. The provisional government which had constituted itself under the leadership of the cunning Fouché, no longer regarded the words of the fallen man. Full of anxious doubts, he remained for a few days at Malmaison, where formerly the divorced Josephine had lived in solitude, and vainly offered the government his services as a simple general. At length he perceived that the game was finished ; the thought of getting control of the wheel of state with the aid of the Jacobin confederates in the suburbs, seemed to the despot too unsol-dierly. At the approach of the Prussians he left Paris, on June 29th, and hastened to the coast at Rochefort. The great play-actor now threw his toga into artistic folds, declared to the prince regent that he came like Themistocles to seek protection at the hospitable fireside of his magnanimous enemy, and on July 15th went on board the English line-of-battle ship "Bellerophon." Hardenberg now learned with satisfaction that the proposal he had himself so often made was approved without hesitation by all the powers ; nothing remained but to keep the dangerous man in safe custody far from Europe. Upon the lonely fortress-island of St. Helena the prisoner provided for himself with his own hands such a punishment as even his bitterest enemy could hardly have conceived. This titanic life came to a rogue's end. He filled his last years with idle quarrels and the professional diffusion of colossal lies ; he himself withdrew the veil from the boundless vulgarity of the giant spirit of the man who had once been so audacious as to set his foot upon the world's neck.

Not without difficulty did the two commanders come to an agreement concerning the fate of Napoleon. The contrast between the British and the German policy was displayed throughout. Wellington desired to spare the feelings of the French as much as possible, and since at heart he remained abso-lutely cold, he recognised rightly that it ill became the con-querors to besmirch their victory by a deed of violence. In Blucher's headquarters, on the other hand, the old hatred flamed violently forth ; so many Germans had met their deaths through the fault of this one man ! Blucher had gone so far as to determine that if he could capture the evil-doer, he would have him shot in the fortress of Vincennes, on the very spot where the duc d'Enghien had formerly been murdered ; otherwise what was the meaning of the Viennese declaration of outlawry against the disturber of the public peace ? Only upon Wellington's urgent request did he abandon the savage plan, acquiescing in the " theatrical magnanimity," as Gneisenau bitterly wrote, " out of respect for the character of the duke and—out of weakness." On the other hand, the Prussian commander insisted that the march must be continued as far as Paris, whereas the Englishman would have preferred to spare the capital this fresh humiliation, and wished to allow his Bourbon protégé to enter alone. Blucher stood firm, imposing such harsh conditions upon the peace envoys from Paris that the continuation of the war was unavoidable.

The Prussian army pushed on irresistibly, far in advance of the English. Siege operations were vigorously pressed, so that fourteen fortresses had to open their gates to the Germans. Everywhere the populace displayed intense hostility ; the French persisted in believing that this new war of the coalition was a monstrous injustice. The Prussians, too, behaved more harshly than in the previous year. Gneisenau hoped that on the Oise he would be able to cut off Grouchy's army from Paris. He did not succeed ; but by his persistent pursuit, the marshal's troops were broken up almost as completely as had been the conquered French after Belle Alliance. Major Frankenhausen, the bold military adventurer, gave them no rest, maintaining now the ancient glories of the Prussian cavalry which hitherto in this war had little opportunity of distinguishing itself. In the battles of Compiègne and Villers-Cotterets the French made but a feeble resistance. It was in dispersed fragments that the conquered reached the capital. With their accession, the force commanded by Davoust, the military governor of Paris, now amounted to over 70,000 men, but what could be expected from these discouraged and undisciplined hordes ? On June 29th Blucher reached Gonesse, a few hours' march to the north of Paris ; the charming basin of the Seine lay before him. His army had traversed the one hundred and sixty miles from the Belgian battle-field in eleven days, resting but one day on the march.

Here, in the headquarters at Gonesse, there came a bad time for Gneisenau. What draws all our hearts to the image of this great German is that in everything he was so simply human, and for this reason on occasion he could be humanly bitter and unjust. So was it with him to-day. He knew that he had been the real commander in this war, that the saving idea of the junction of the two armies had sprung from his head alone. Now he had to learn how the allies praised Wellington as the leading hero; this Englishman, who had indeed displayed upon the battle-field great circumspection and tenacity, but who in the conduct of the campaign had heaped error upon error. Gneisenau became profoundly embittered when he reflected upon his inglorious and inconspicuous activities, upon all the distresses of recent years which he had so long borne in silence ; how he had been the sport of fate from childhood upwards. He had been born at Schilda, the Saxon Abdera, amid the confusion of the war-camp of the imperial army, among the enemies of Prussia ; Prussian cannons were the child's lullaby, and during the nocturnal retreat after the battle of Torgau he would have perished under the hoofs of the horses, had not a compassionate grenadier picked ¡him up out of danger. Thereupon followed the weary, joyless time when as a barefooted lad he had to herd geese in Schilda, until at length his Catholic relatives in Würzburg took pity on him. The homeless man never really knew to what German stock, or to what Church, he properly belonged. Next came the wild, mad days of student life in Erfurt, a brief period of service in the Austrian cavalry, and a journey to America with the unhappy men whom the margarve of Ansbach sold to the British. Next he entered the Prussian service, at the outset with brilliant, exaggerated hopes, then to endure once more the utter futility of life as a subaltern, so miserable, so depressing, that this fiery sprit, which had once almost consumed itself in its own ardency, was in danger of degenerating into philistinism. But now, when a world-transforming destiny broke over Prussia, in Gneisenau, genius sprang to life ; it was through his work that the discouraged army gained the first success, and since Scharnhorst's death there had been no one to compare with Gneisenau. What was his reward ? The officers of the general staff who in daily intercourse experienced the magic of his genius, could not fail to know what Germany possessed in this man ; it seemed to them that they stood in a topsy-turvy world when they saw this born leader of men standing humbly beside the czar with his plumed hat in his hand. Yet when the soldiers greeted old Blucher with thunderous hurrahs, they hardly noticed the unknown general standing beside the field-marshal. Bülow had engraved his name in the tablets of history ; but of Gneisenau they knew nothing. He believed himself to be older than all the generals of infantry ; and still remained no more than lieutenant-general ; he had never led an independent command, and had received neither the order of the black eagle, nor that of the great iron cross. The king did not love him, the ill-natured gossip among the people of the court never ceased ; he felt so little secure of his position in the army that, shortly before, he had begged the chancellor to give him, when peace came, the position of postmaster-general. Vanity was far from his mind ; how often did he speak of himself as a mere soldier favoured by fortune ; but once at least his discontent had to find expression. In a single day, in a towering rage, he wrote to the chancellor three letters full of violent complaints, accusing in his anger even Stein and Blucher of ingratitude.[1] It was not long before the king did him ample justice ; he subsequently wore the star which had been found in Napoleon's carriage. Yet the majority of his contemporaries never assigned to him the historic renown to which he was in truth entitled ; it was only a later generation of his countrymen which recognised his greatness, and even to this day the French are not aware who was the greatest commander of allied Europe.

The ill-humour passed over Gneisenau's free spirit like a fugitive cloud. On this same June 30th the hero was once more fully himself when he laid before the two commanders his plan for taking the capital. Whilst Bülow kept the tolerably well-fortified north side of Paris busy by feint-attacks, Blucher marched to the right with the rest of the army, crossed the Seine below the town, and moved to attack the place from the south ; on July 2nd Bülow was relieved by the arrival of the English, and followed the field-marshal. The last fights on the open southern side of the city were left once more entirely to the Prussians. Vainly did Davoust, in a letter couched in moving terms, beg for a truce. The marshal's contention that after the fall of Napoleon there was no longer any reason for the war, sounded to the German commander like mockery ; in a peremptory reply he demanded that the detested oppressor of German citizens should capitulate : "Do you wish to bring upon yourself the maledictions of Paris, as you have already brought those of Hamburg ?" A skirmish in which his favourite arm came off badly, profoundly grieved old Blucher. The veteran Brandenburg and Pomeranian hussars, six hundred and fifty horse under

[1] Gneisenau to Hardenberg, three letters from Gonesse, June 30, 1815.

the leadership of Sohr, fell into an ambush at Versailles, set by the eleven cavalry regiments of General Excelman ; when they took to flight, they found their way into a blind alley, between high walls, in the village of Chesnoy. One-third of them cut their way out, but most of the others were killed. Among them was the youthful volunteer, Heinrich von York, the general's favourite son ; when the enemy offered him quarter, he shouted out : " My name is York ! " and went on fighting until he was killed. Thus the iron man who had begun the German war had to pay once more with his heart's blood just before the ultimate victory.

On July 2nd Zieten's corps, after a severe fight, made its way on to the plateau of Meudon. During the following night, the wild Vandamme, endeavouring to reconquer this position from Issy, was completely defeated ; the superiority of the Prussian arms was so manifest that on the next morning Davoust declared himself prepared to surrender. Blucher sent down Müffling to negotiate. He had once in Blucher's name signed the never-to-be-forgotten capitulation of Ratkau ; since then Blucher had never been able to look upon him without suppressed anger, and now sent him to arrange another capitulation so that the old blot might be wiped from his scutcheon. The town had to be evacuated within three days, and Davoust was to retire with the remnants of his army across the Loire. Blucher wrote in triumph to Knesebeck : " My day's work is completed, Paris is mine ! I owe everything to my brave troops, to their tenacity, and to my own iron will ! " Subsequently the whole of the west and north of the country was occupied by the allied armies. With what delight did Scharnhorst's son-in-law, Friedrich Dohna, make his cavalrymen water their horses in the Loire ; he thought proudly of his valiant ancestors who, in the wars of the Huguenots, had also borne the terror of German arms as far as the walls of Blois and Orleans.

On this occasion Blucher would not afford the detested town the honour of his visit, or the delightful spectacle of a ceremonial entry. They were to feel what war is. The regiments entered separately, and were all of them billeted, though the citizens complained bitterly of this ill-usage. The authorities and the inhabitants were profoundly incensed ; it seemed to them an incredible disgrace that in four days these Prussians had made an end of French military glories. The conqueror demanded the furnishing of two months' pay for the army, and the immediate delivery of two millions as a war tax ; those who complained were referred by him to Daru—he understood how to provide money. On the very first day the Danzig picture was removed from the Louvre by Prussian musketeers, and thus began the retaking of the spoil. Everything must be given up, to a single hair, said Blucher; and he pursued the work in haste so that the accursed diplomats might not again intervene. It was only to the hard will of the German commander that the world owed it that the European scandal of the great Parisian plunder-shop now came to an end. Altenstein, Eichhorn, and de Groote, the young connoisseur of Cologne, showed the Prussian soldiers the stolen goods; but notwithstanding the zeal with which the search was pursued by the German experts, a portion of the invaluable spoil was never recovered. After the Prussians had once set in hand the work of atonement, the other states also put in their claims. The manuscript treasures of the Heidelberg Palatina, which long before Tilly had removed to Rome, and subsequently Bonaparte to Paris, were at length returned to the Neckar. The artistic people of Florence received with songs and with a flower-decked procession their statues of the Gods, the Venus and the Apollo, when they were brought back to the magnificent Uffizi gallery. It was Blucher's wish to blow up the bridge of Jena, and this would have given him especial satisfaction if he could have done it while Talleyrand was on it; only the intervention of the monarch held Blucher in check.

The headquarters were established at St. Cloud. In the Salle de l'Orangerie, where the *coup d'état* of Brumaire had once been carried out, the Prussian regimental tailors established their workshop; on his departure the field-marshal took with him David's picture of Bonaparte crossing the Alps, and gave it to the king for the palace in Berlin. Governor Muffling ruled Paris with a firm hand, this applying equally to the troops and to the eternally complaining hosts of the billeted; second in command was Colonel Pfuel, a zealous Teutoniser, renowned in all the gymnastic and swimming places of the North German youth. It did not come amiss to the stalwart man to give a complaining Frenchman immediate satisfaction with the national weapon, the foil. His position was difficult among the feverishly excited people; the Prussian guard-posts were frequently attacked at night; on several occasions the Prussian guards had to make their way by force of arms into the arcades of the Palais Royal when the taunts of the guests in the coffee houses became too arrogant. Wellington's calculated lenity afforded a remarkable contrast to the severe, but by no means violent, conduct of the Prussians. The duke had his troops quartered in the open, in the Bois de Boulogne, and avoided everything which could offend Parisian vanity, whilst coolly completing a master-stroke of British diplomacy which would have done honour to the most adroit of the London stock-jobbers. From his point of view it seemed a matter of course that England's will should be alone decisive in this coalition war. Without even asking the allied courts, he arranged for the Bourbon to enter the Tuileries under the protection of English bayonets. On the afternoon of July 10th, when the three monarchs entered Paris, King Louis had already been two days re-established upon his throne, and received them as a courteous host. Fouché, who was quick to note which way the wind was blowing, had adhered to the Bourbon cause in good time, and saw to it that the chambers of the empire should not reassemble. What availed it to refuse all Louis's invitations or that the Prussian guards in the Tuileries would not notice the court ? The second restoration had been completed by England alone ; none of the other powers could seriously think of re-expelling the Bourbons. By this accomplished fact, British policy at the same time frustrated the just demands of the German nation. The detachment of Alsace-Lorraine from France would have been possible if the allies had first agreed among themselves, and had then summoned back the Bourbon king to the diminished kingdom ; it had become impossible now that it was necessary to negotiate on the question with a friendly monarch. With good reason did Hardenberg complain that the arbitrary procedure of the Englishman had forced the coalition into an " amphibious position."[1]

To the two emperors the brilliant success of the Belgian campaign was a surprise, and by no means an agreeable one. The czar's army had not been under fire at all. The Austrians and the South Germans, after an insignificant fight at Strasburg, began a lifeless investment of the fortresses of Alsace : the archduke John, having conquered Hüningen almost without bloodshed, was honoured by the grateful Baslers like a second Napoleon. All the other places still held out. The populace everywhere displayed fanatical hatred ; many stragglers from the allied army were killed with inhuman tortures. The mountain guards assembled in the Vosges ; after the war the people of Schlettstadt had the extremely mild horrors of the siege commemorated on

[1] Hardenberg's Diary, July 3, 1815.

their town-hall in pathetic pictures. In a word, Austrian military glories remained of an extremely modest character. Emperor Francis said in his wheedling way to the officers of Blucher's head-quarters staff : " You Prussians are devils of fellows " ; and Metternich declared to Baron von Stein that after the battle of Ligny an Austrian army would have required at least six weeks in which to recover, to which Stein bluntly answered : " You see, then, what moral energy can do." More faithfully than in such civilities were the true sentiments of the Hofburg manifested in the rancorous letters of Adam Müller, who could not vent his wit sufficiently about " Blucher's Berlinese soldiers who were strutting about the boulevards of Paris imagining themselves Romans."

The czar, too, hardly concealed how profoundly he was annoyed that his allies had deprived him in advance of all the military glory. As soon as he saw that the restoration of the Bourbons was beyond repair, he immediately abandoned his Orleanist plans, endorsed Pozzo di Borgo's arbitrary procedure, and once more endeavoured by generosity towards France to get the better of his English rival. The magnanimous sympathy which he had made it a pleasure to display, now assumed a peculiar mystical colouring. On the journey, while at Heidelberg, he had fallen into the nets of the bigoted enthusiast, Frau von Krüdener, who henceforward never let him escape. The nature of the cele-brated prophetess was fundamentally shallow ; when she died, Goethe exclaimed, " What a life ! Like shavings. You couldn't get a handful of ashes out of it for the soap-boiler ! " She knew, however, how to conduct herself gracefully in the fashionable speech and fashionable sentiments of the romantic age, and Alexander's heart, thirsty for love, longed for sweeter consolation than could be offered by the barren rationalism of his tutor Laharpe. In Paris, the czar was immediately received by a circle of ladies inspired with Christian enthusiasm, rendering homage to the new saviour of the world who was to found the realm of God's peace on earth, and who naturally, after the example of the Saviour, was to forget and forgive everything. It was just as much a matter of course that these generous intentions should once more coincide precisely with the reputed interests of Russian policy. Although Alexander, after his manner, was really a faithful ally of his western neighbour, it was by no means his desire that Prussia should become strong enough to dispense with Russian friendship : for this reason Germany must remain vulnerable on the western frontier. Even more vigorously than in the previous year did the czar advocate the cause of the French, and he remained altogether inaccessible to the suggestions of Stein. Metternich, too, quickly adapted himself to the new situation which Wellington's lack of consideration had brought about; he immediately abandoned the idea of establishing Napoleon II on the throne, with which Gentz had played for a time, and adhered cordially to the Bourbon. Since now, as before, he was of the opinion that Austria must on no account resume her dangerous position on the Upper Rhine, he desired a speedy conclusion of peace on mild terms. What did the court of Vienna care about the just claims of the German people?

Nowhere did these hopes of the Germans find warmer expression than in the letters of the Prussian generals. Four days after the decisive battle, Gneisenau wrote to the chancellor: " Woe to them, shame to them, if they do not seize this unique opportunity to safeguard Belgium, Prussia, Germany, to all eternity! " For Belgium he demanded certain fortresses in French Flanders; for Prussia, Mainz and Luxemburg, and also Nassau and Ansbach-Bayreuth; Bavaria was to receive compensation in Alsace-Lorraine, and the House of Nassau in French Luxemburg. " You know better than I, what language Prussia can and must use. Prussia has never before stood so high! " In a similar sense, Blucher begged the king " to tell the diplomatists that they must not lose once more what the soldier has gained at the cost of his blood! " The old man, like almost the entire German nation, cherished the naive belief that it would be impossible for the foreign powers to refuse the honourably earned reward of victory if only our diplomats should remain firm. The king was, personally speaking, in perfect harmony with the desires of his generals, and commissioned Gneisenau to take part beside Hardenberg and Humboldt as plenipotentiary at the peace congress; it gave immense satisfaction to the fiery hero that Talleyrand, who in Vienna had incited to the war of annihilation against Prussia, must now encounter him as a simple negotiator on behalf of the conquered. The sober spirit of Frederick William recognised, however, how little this harsh struggle for power would be decided on rational grounds, or in accordance with the manifest justice of the Prussian demands; " To pursue the interests of my own state alone," he wrote soothingly to the field-marshal, " will encounter difficulties in the concurrent interests of the other states."

In actual fact, the position of the Prussian negotiators was to-day even more unfavourable than it had been in the first peace congress ; in all important questions they encountered the united opposition of the other four powers. It is true that the old opponents at Vienna, the Netherlands, Baden, and Würtemberg, were on this occasion eloquent advocates of the Prussian claims, since it was far more important for them even than for Prussia that the French eastern frontier should be weakened. So markedly, however, had the system of the pentarchy already developed, that the memorials of the powers of the second rank were treated by the great powers as empty exercises in literary style, and were rarely regarded as worthy of an answer. The Prussian state stood alone ; the Prussian army had sacrificed itself heroically for the common cause of Europe, without in the end acquiring anything to speak of for its own country.

§ 2. THE SECOND PEACE OF PARIS.

When Hardenberg reached Paris on July 15th, the czar met him with violent reproaches regarding the undisciplined conduct of the Prussian army. Yet Blucher kept strict order, and punished relentlessly the isolated excesses of his troops. It was only the Netherlanders and, in accordance with their usual custom, the Bavarians, who could be accused of certain outbreaks of roughness ; sometimes, too, the intractable ill-feeling of those upon whom the soldiery were billeted was a contributory cause of misconduct. The prefect of the Seine himself incited the Parisians against the allies. When Müffling had the Venetian four-horse chariot taken down from the Arc de Triomphe in the Place du Carrousel, the workmen were several times driven away by the mob and by the body-guard of the Bourbon, until at length an Austrian battalion restored order. The chancellor immediately realised that the accusations directed by the czar against the Prussians, and the Prussians alone, masked a definite intention, and that this was to represent the Prussians as drunk with the pride of victory ; moreover, their warlike renown was diligently mini-mised and disputed.

In the great council of ministers there sat : Nesselrode, Capodistrias, and Pozzo ; Castlereagh, Wellington, and Stewart ; Metternich, Wessenberg, and Schwarzenberg—and there was not one of them who displayed a friendly disposition towards the three Prussian plenipotentiaries. The presidential power of the new Germanic Federation at first adopted an attitude of reserve, for it could not venture to contradict too obviously the unanimous desire of the German nation ; on the other hand, it did nothing at all to support the demand for the restoration of the Vosges frontier. Gentz from the first spoke with poisonous mockery of the " narrow-minded views" of the Prussians who wished to derive a selfish advantage from the war against the revolution. The proposal of Stein and of his friends that Alsace should be given to the archduke Charles, served merely to arouse the hostility of the emperor Francis, who always cherished a deep mistrust of this brother.

Between the two rivals, Russia and England, there now ensued a vigorous competition for the reward of generosity ; both powers hoped to secure the friendship of France in view of the threatening eastern complications. Among the British, too, there was operative the memory of the compact of January 3rd and of the *entente cordiale* which had then been established ; but the main factor in their conduct was the spiritual narrowness peculiar to the high tories. It was impossible for these islanders to attain to the wide outlooks of continental policy. Castlereagh frankly declared : " If we can take measures for the next five or seven years, the best has been effected that we can hope from diplomacy." The conquerors determined not to begin negotiations with the crown of France until they had come to an understanding among themselves. The unhappy land lay disarmed at the feet of the conqueror. Everywhere prevailed the frenzy of partisan hatred : in Paris there was profound hostility towards the king, the protégé of the foreigners ; in the south there was already beginning a civil war, the fierce struggle of the White Terror. In addition, the remnants of the Napoleonic army were now dissolved, upon Alexander's advice, because the czar wished to prove to the allies that there was no longer an enemy opposed to them and that the hour of forgiveness had arrived. The country was not in a position to offer any kind of opposition to the conditions of the conquerors. All the more difficult was it for the conquerors to arrive at an understanding among themselves. The deliberations were on this occasion as stormy as the negotiations for the first peace of Paris had been easy. For two entire months the Prussian statesmen carried on a diplomatic struggle against the whole of Europe, until at length they had to give way, and then, after the powers had come to their decision, the peace negotiation with France was opened.

As early as July 15th, Castlereagh had laid down the principles from which the allies ought to start[1] : " To discredit or weaken the prestige of King Louis, is tantamount to the diminution of the power of the allies themselves." It was also the duty of the powers to treat the nation with forbearance and conciliation, whilst the king should be supported in the reconstruction of the army and in the suppression of the conspirators. In sharp contrast with this view, in which the conqueror of Belle Alliance was regarded as no more than the devoted police officer of the Most Christian King, were the demands expressed by Hardenberg on July 22nd.[2] Three aims, he said, have to be attained by this peace : a guarantee for the peace of Europe ; indemnification for the cost of the war ; finally, the carrying out of the promises which were given at the first peace. The peace of the world can be secured only by the weakening of the eastern frontier of France, for the French will display themselves as hostile immediately our army is withdrawn. The last war had manifested the vulnerability of the Netherlands, just as the military weakness of High Germany was proved by the Napoleonic campaigns. Consequently the Netherlands must be strengthened by taking over a number of French fortresses ; Alsace must be restored to Germany, and its fortresses garrisoned by Austria ; Prussia must receive the fortresses on the Saar and the Upper Moselle ; Switzerland must be given a border fortress in the Jura ; Piedmont should have the whole of Savoy. From Dunkirk as far as Chambéry and the lakes of Savoy, a strip of land many miles wide, running along the whole of the eastern frontier, and including the three chains of fortresses constructed by Vauban, must be ceded, as was shown in detail by a map from the chancellery.

Just as throughout this war Prussia had displayed uncalculating self-sacrifice for the common cause of Europe, so now Hardenberg demanded very little directly for his own state as the reward of victory ; no more than Metz, Diedenhofen, and Saarlouis. Even Gneisenau had speedily recognised how strong was the general mistrust of Prussia, and therefore now advised that more should be asked for the Netherlands, Austria, and South Germany, than for Prussia herself. To the British, matters must be represented in this way ; that thus Prussia could be safeguarded in the west, and would consequently be better able to

[1] Castlereagh, Memorandum of July 5, 1815.
[2] Hardenberg, Memorial concerning the principles to be acted upon by the Committee of Four, July 22, 1815.

make head against Russia.[1] Finally, the chancellor suggested as possible that the Burgundian Franche Comté should be detached from France, since this urgently longed for its ancient freedom. In the general confusion of those days there were displayed isolated centrifugal tendencies which had long been supposed defunct. Even from Lyons envoys came to Emperor Francis begging that the town should be separated from France as an independent republic. In Franche Comté, the old Hapsburg traditions were still active ; Besançon, the birth-place of Granvelle, preserved in every street memories of the golden days of Charles V, and over the doors of the town-hall there still flaunted the eagle with the proud and ancient *Deo et Cæsari, semper fidelis.* But all this signified little ; the war of annihilation waged by the Convention against the provinces had ended in a complete victory of the unity of the state. In all the regions whose return was demanded by Hardenberg, the great majority of the people cherished hostile sentiments towards the allies. The only exception was the loyal Saarbrücken, which had twice ceremonially greeted the chancellor upon his journeys, and had subsequently urgently petitioned for union with Prussia ; [2] even the neighbouring Saarlouis, the home of Ney, was fanatically French in sentiment.

With regard to the question of war indemnity, Hardenberg remembered the vain and foolish generosity displayed by Prussia in the previous year, and declared : " It would be preposterous to act in this way again." Although the timid Altenstein had counselled him to content himself with 800,000,000 francs,[3] Hardenberg demanded the payment of 1,200,000,000 francs ; out of this came 200,000,000, first of all, for each of the conquerors of Paris, Prussia and England. The account given by the chancellery proceeded to show that France in the years from 1806 to 1812 had taken from Prussia alone 1,228,000,000 francs—an estimate which was considerably more than 300,000,000 below the truth.[4] Finally, a European commission must provide for the return of the art treasures and for the fulfilment of the other still unfulfilled promises of the previous year. The Prussian proposals were severe, but thoroughly just, in view of the complete overthrow of the Napoleonic army and of the unteachable hostility of the French. It was unfortunate that the renunciation which the

---

[1] Gneisenau to Hardenberg, July 27, 1815.
[2] Hardenberg's Diary, July 11, 1815.
[3] Altenstein's Memorial concerning the Contribution, Paris, July 21, 1815.
[4] *Vide supra*, Vol. I, pp. 375 and 460.

Prussian state displayed on its own behalf would render it difficult to safeguard the desired booty; for who but Prussia could manage with a strong hand the refractory Alsatians during the difficult time of transition, and until a new and good German generation had grown to maturity? Since Austria obstinately renounced her ancient inheritance, the most extraordinary proposals were made; one of them was that there should be a federal state with forty members, under the crown prince of Würtemberg. Gagern even desired that Alsace should join the Swiss confederacy, this while close at hand in France were 100,000 rancorous Napoleonic veterans. What a prospect for the future!

Meanwhile, however, this objection, the only valid one that could be made against Hardenberg's proposals, hardly received from the opposing party even a cursory attention. The great memorial which on July 28th was handed in by Capodistrias moved rather in the airy regions of political romanticism, since Russia could not reveal the true aims of her policy. The clever Greek had found it all the easier to adopt the unctuous tone which corresponded to Alexander's present mood because he himself was fond of great words and empty generalities. He began in moving terms by saying that no one had been waging war against France, but only against Bonaparte, consequently the right of conquest was inapplicable without sacrificing the legitimate royal house to hatred, and justifying in the eyes of posterity all the horrors of the Revolution. For this reason there must be a simple re-establishment of the peace of Paris, and to provide against the eventuality of a further revolution, a renewal of the alliance of Chaumont; finally, the country must be subjected for a brief period to military occupation, until the payment of the contribution had been completed, this contribution being employed by the neighbouring states chiefly for the institution of border fortresses.

These proposals, though adorned with the fine-sounding title of "A combination of moral and real guarantees," aroused great anger in the Prussian camp. On August 4th, Humboldt wrote to the chancellor: "The Russian plan is the most disastrous for Prussia that could possibly have been imagined. If it were to be adopted, Prussia would derive from the entire war, from her losses, from her colossal sacrifices, no other advantage than a share in the contribution which is to be employed chiefly for the construction of fortresses against France. On the other hand, Prussia would suffer from the great disadvantage of being unable to apply the moneys secured by the present war to the relief of her own exhausted country and to the safeguarding of her eastern frontier; she would have for years to endure the passage of Russian troops through her own territory and through Germany; in all her negotiations with France she would continue to be hampered by the influence of the Russian court." At any cost we must induce the allies to diminish the French domain, and thus counteract " the possible reproach that Prussia is pursuing her own advantage only. In actual fact, Prussia in her present situation is concerned more about safeguarding her frontiers than about aggrandisement." [1] In a second confidential memorial, he went on to expound the system which he had so often discussed with Metternich, that of " an intermediary Europe," a firm union between England, Austria, and Prussia, which was to keep within bounds the two threatening masses of France and Russia; in Vienna this system had already been shaken by the undue enlargement of Russia, and it would become altogether untenable if Prussia were to be left with her frontiers unsecured, opposed to the profoundly hostile French nation, and to the Bourbons who had already so clearly shown their hostility to Prussia. [2]

Humboldt then handed the Committee of Four a striking refutation of the Russian memorial; the task was, as it were, created for his pitiless dialectic. He showed how the war, though in truth it had not been begun with the aim of conquest, had now in fact eventuated in a state of conquest; how France must atone for France's errors; how the allies did, indeed, possess the right to safeguard themselves, but had not indisputably the right to interfere in the internal affairs of France; it was right to take from France what was indispensable for the military protection of her neighbours, but independence must then be immediately restored to the country, for Prussia knew, from her own experience, that nothing caused more profound embitterment to a nation than the presence of foreign troops in times of peace; if Europe proposed to take the French under her protectorate, the Revolution would never come to an end. At the same time, Hardenberg renewed his own proposals in a detailed memorial of August 4th, showing how, since the days of Louis XIV, France had transgressed her natural lines of defence, and that it was precisely through the possession of these outposts that she had been continually lured on to new wars of conquest. Even Knesebeck

---

[1] Humboldt to Hardenberg, August 4, 1815.
[2] Humboldt, *Mémoire très-confidentiel*, August 4, 1815.

agreed here, speaking quite soberly and without doctrinaire eccentricities; he insisted that even if the peace should be concluded upon terms of excessive lenity, this would afford no security for the persistence of the Bourbon rule, for the French people would never forgive the defeat in Brabant.

Meanwhile Stein came to Paris at Hardenberg's request. On the way the baron spent a few days on the Rhine with Goethe, and Arndt noted with profound emotion how the two best sons of the fatherland regarded one another in so friendly a manner, each endeavouring to make due allowance for the other's peculiarities. In Paris, Stein employed all his eloquence with the czar. In a terse memorial, dated August 18th, he refuted the Russian opinion that France was the ally of her conquerors. If France is our friend, he asked, why have we occupied the country, why are we requisitioning supplies from her? He concluded admonishingly: "England and Russia ought not to believe it to be to their advantage that Germany should be left continually in a state of excitement and distress." But what could Stein's words avail beside the tears and prayers of Frau von Krüdener and Frau von Lezay-Marnesia? The lightnings of his oratory were unable to penetrate the thick clouds of incense which surrounded the czar in the Hôtel Montchenu. If Stein no longer counted, what could be expected from the representatives of the powers of the second rank? The Bavarian ambassador, Rechberg, held back cautiously, for Bavaria needed the help of Austria for the attainment of her own plans of aggrandisement. The Badenese assumed an extremely modest attitude, describing in moving memorials the untenable situation on their Rhenish frontier, describing how recently the French had endeavoured to bridge the Rhine from Strasburg, and demanding that they should at least have exclusive possession of the Kehl bridge, and that the fortresses of Strasburg should be dismantled.[1] Far more audacious was the language of the ambitious crown prince of Würtemberg and of his minister Wintzingerode. In their letters and memorials they already referred to that opposition on the part of the middle-sized states to the great powers which for many years to come was to disturb German life. They declared threateningly that Europe could as little bear the new fourfold despotism as it had been able formerly to bear the single despotism of Napoleon, and the crown prince pro-

[1] Hacke to Hardenberg, August 19; Hacke and Berstett to Hardenberg, October 21, 1815.

phesied that which forty years later he repeated to Bismarck, the envoy of the Bundestag, that the unprotected condition of our south-western frontier would sooner or later compel the South German crowns to combine in a new Confederation of the Rhine.

No one worked more unweariedly than Gagern, the Netherland imperial patriot, for on this occasion the interests of the Netherlands coincided perfectly with those of Germany. The indefatigable man felt perfectly in his element when in innumerable memorials he displayed the entire armoury of his learning in the history of the empire, and when he enumerated the long series of French arbitrary acts since the days of Henry II and Maurice of Saxony. The pupil of Montesquieu, however fantastical might be his federalist dreams, was untouched by the romanticism of the legitimist doctrine of the state. The contention that the war had been waged against Bonaparte alone, he countered bluntly with the question whether it was at Bonaparte alone that the musket-balls and case-shot of Belle Alliance had been discharged, whether Bonaparte alone had been sabred there. " It is the nations which are at war ; upon nations must fall the fortunate as well as the unfortunate consequences of war." It was natural that the former barrister should also defend the petty states against the hegemony of the great powers. Don Labrador, the Spanish ambassador, formally demanded admission to the conferences.[1] But the impossibility of conducting these difficult negotiations before the forum of all the European states was obvious, and on August 10th the Committee of Four determined that the states of the second rank were to be admitted only to the actual negotiations with France, that is to say, after the issue had been really decided.

The inseparable community of interests between Prussia and the South German states was so plainly manifest that all the evil memories of Rhenish Confederate days seemed to have passed away without leaving a trace. Prussia resumed her natural role as protector of united Germany. All the legal and political grounds for the re-establishment of our ancient western march were brought forward exhaustively by the Prussian diplomats and their colleagues from the smaller states. With sound tact, the statesmen laid the greatest stress upon the point of view of military security, the only one which could make some impression upon an assembly of diplomats. Dr. Butte, on the other hand, in his widely read work upon the conditions of peace, and also

[1] Labrador to Hardenberg, September 15, 1815.

the majority of the German newspapers, once more took up the ideas of Arndt, and demanded the linguistic frontier as a neutral right of the nation. In view of the friendly disposition on both sides, no serious dispute about the division of the spoil need be feared if only the return of Alsace to the Germanic Federation could be assured. But this decision lay wholly in the hands of the great powers, and all too soon did it appear that in Paris, as shortly before in Vienna, Humboldt's dream of " an intermediary Europe " was an empty picture of fancy. England and Austria, which he had regarded as Prussia's natural allies, were just as strongly averse to the German demands as were Russia and France.

On August 6th, Metternich for the first time gave expression to his views, with the formal declaration that this war had been carried on against armed Jacobinism, and must not degenerate into a war of conquest. Consequently he sought guarantees of European peace chiefly in a reasonable ordering of the internal affairs of France, and in a provisional military occupation ; in addition, the fortresses of the most advanced line must either be ceded to the neighbouring states, " or must at least be dismantled." Coming down to details, he declared that Germany needed nothing more than the fortress of Landau, in compensation for the destroyed Philippsburg ; it would suffice, for the rest, that the fortresses in Alsace should be dismantled, and that Strasburg should retain only the citadel. To the experienced diplomatists of the Committee of Four, it was immediately obvious that in this " or at least," expressed at the very beginning of the negotiations, was to be found Metternich's true opinion ; in accordance with the rounding-off system of policy which he had for three years unerringly pursued, he could not desire the restoration of Alsace. It was only the Prussian statesmen, always inclined to believe the best of their Austrian friend, who could not grasp the true significance of Metternich's memorial ; they merely deplored " the vacillating attitude " of the court of Vienna, whereas the Russian and the English ministers immediately recognised that Austria dissociated herself from the common cause of Germany, and for this reason spoke only of " the Prussian demands."

For a time Hardenberg continued to cherish hopes also of English help ; yet everyone now knew that the attitude of Castlereagh and Wellington by no means corresponded to the wishes of their country. The London newspapers were loudly demanding a vigorous utilisation of the victory ; Castlereagh's political associates, the tories, who had always been the most decisive opponents of France, expressed their lively disapproval of any false generosity. Lord Liverpool wrote in the name of the cabinet that the manifest sentiments of the nation could not be overlooked. Even the prince regent expressed himself in favour of the German claims, and followed the advice of Count Münster, who, in Paris, to Stein's astonishment and delight, faithfully espoused the Prussian cause. Altogether undisturbed by the opposition of the nation, Castlereagh and Wellington went their own way. The duke insisted that the sole purpose of this war had been to bring the Revolution to a close, and that for this reason the only result could be an occupation for a few years. Castlereagh agreed with the duke, and held out hopes to the Prussians for a better reward after future wars : [1] " Continued disturbances in France may doubtless in the future render it necessary for Europe to undertake the partition of France, and Europe will effect this change in its territorial distribution, will carry it out with energy, and will maintain it with unanimity, should it ever appear in the eyes of humanity to be a necessary and a justified measure." The present war, however, had not been begun for such a purpose. In conclusion he wrote : " Should the allies prove deceived in their confidence, through the warlike ambition of France, they will then take up arms again, basing their strength, not alone upon commanding military positions, but also upon that moral energy which alone can hold together such a coalition."

Consequently the Germans, who were longing for peace, were to abandon this unique opportunity of safeguarding their frontiers, in the agreeable expectation of further shedding of blood and of fresh need for war ! Is it to be wondered at that this reference to future misery, and that these unctuous words on the moral energy of the coalition, sounded to the Germans like mockery ? Day by day they became more incensed. Even social intercourse between the statesmen of the two parties was brought to a standstill ; the British uttered bitter complaints regarding Humboldt's icy coldness and his cutting sarcasms. In this way the negotiations were carried on for a month and a half. Finally the chancellor determined to yield half a step ; on August 28th he offered to relinquish Upper Alsace, demanding for Germany no more than Diedenhofen and Saarlouis, Landau and Bitsch, and, finally, Strasburg as a free town.

[1] Castlereagh, confidential Note to Hardenberg, probably written in August.

Meanwhile Gneisenau had composed a memorial for the czar, which on August 31st he handed in on the command of the king; Frederick William expected that a certain impression would be created by the fiery words of the general, and hoped that on the next day, in a personal interview, he would be able to effect a complete change in his friend's mood.[1] Without entering in detail into the Prussian demands, Gneisenau endeavoured in the first place merely to win over the czar to the principle of the cession of territory. He showed that in fact France was responsible for the misfortune of the new war; without the assistance of all the energetic men in France, and without the dull-minded indifference of the masses, "the despised adventurer" would never have been able to complete the journey from Cannes to Paris. "Europe rightly expects from the allies the punishment of such misdeeds, and will learn with astonishment that it is proposed to conclude a new peace of Utrecht, to eternalise the sorrows of unfortunate Germany; this will bring the governments to despair and will embitter the nations. If of two neighbouring countries, one possesses a unified state authority and is physically and morally prepared for attack, whilst the other, through the natural defects of a federal constitution, and through the physical characteristics of its frontiers, is strictly limited to defence, it is easy to foresee which of the two will tend to become subordinate to the other. That which in the hands of one of these states becomes a means of attack will in the hands of the other be a means of defence. Unquestionably the Bourbon government will not be able to secure popular favour unless it completely gives itself up to the adventurous and revengeful spirit of the nation. Encouraged by the experience that their frontiers remain uninjured even after the greatest defeats, and that the calculations of a narrow-minded policy will secure the integrity of their domains under all conditions, the French will soon know no bounds to their arrogance. Ought we to give the French party in Germany new grounds for the belief that more is to be gained by adhesion to French plans of conquest than by the fulfilment of duties to the fatherland and by adhesion to the common cause of Europe? Powerful Russia stands, indeed, too high for petty considerations which do not correspond to the magnanimous character of the czar. If the frontier of France remains unaltered, it will be generally said that England desired to throw the continent into new confusions, so that time

[1] Boyen to Gneisenau, August 31, 1815. Gneisenau, Memorandum to his majesty Czar Alexander.

might not be given for the continental countries to defend themselves against British commercial policy." Such was the general trend of the long memorandum, couched in defective French, and yet written with the highest oratorical energy. Nor did Gneisenau hesitate to demand that Piedmont, the Netherlands, and the smaller German states, should be admitted to the conference, a demand which in the eyes of the other great powers was a terrible heresy.

The czar turned a deaf ear. Nor did his conversation with the king lead to any result. Alexander thanked the general, curtly and dryly, for his well-meant and zealous endeavours on behalf of the great interests of Europe,[1] and made Capodistrias compose a detailed refutation, which, whilst lacking in reasoned considerations, furnished an incredible abundance of moral commonplaces. " Is it for this reason that Europe has overthrown military despotism and annihilated the spirit of conquest, in order subsequently to make a victim of the king of France and to prepare a new desecration for the French kingdom ? To do this would be once for all to banish morality from all political negotiations. Force alone would become a principle, a means, and an end, of statecraft ! If France were to be debased, and by means of a series of arbitrary measures to be yet more morally corrupted, the country would be forced ultimately to throw itself into the arms of the strongest party. A transient occupation of the country would afford to the neighbours of France all the security they can desire." In conclusion, Capodistrias wrote : " Let us, in so decisive a moment, not fail to recognise the inalterable course of providence, which has allowed the cause of religion, morality, and justice, to stumble, only in order to prepare for that cause new triumphs, and in order to give a powerful and valuable stimulus alike to princes and to peoples."[2]

When this masterpiece of oriental pulpit oratory was handed to the Prussian statesmen on September 5th, they had already been forced to abandon their last hope from England. Castlereagh's brother, Lord Charles Stewart, had hastened to Windsor, and in the last days of August had returned with the joyful tidings that he had overcome the influence of Count Münster and had won over the prince regent entirely to the views of Castlereagh and Wellington. The two might now proceed with enhanced

---

[1] Czar Alexander to Gneisenau, September 5, 1815.

[2] Capodistrias, *Réponse au Mémoire du Général de Gneisenau*, September 5, 1815.

confidence. On August 31st the duke replied in brief and incisive terms to Hardenberg's last memorial, to the effect that any cession of territory would be unpolitic and illegal because it would not be in harmony with the Viennese declaration of the allies ; an occupation for a few years would suffice perfectly.[1] On September 2nd, Castlereagh, in the name of the prince regent, expressed England's complete agreement with the Russian proposals. Thus there was an absolute divergence of views : Russia and England objected on principle to all the Prussian demands for territory ; Austria, with her modest desire for the dismantlement of the Alsatian frontier fortresses, seemed to assume a middle position, but was in reality in close approximation with the Anglo-Russian opinion. Could Prussia, depleted of money and troops, now carry through her demands by force of arms ? It was not to be thought of .

Yet even the czar felt that he must not expose his best ally to an unconditional and humiliating defeat, for he had an urgent desire that the Prusso-Russian alliance should continue. He therefore determined on September 7th to give way a little, a very little, and ordered Nesselrode to declare to the chancellor that Russia, like England, held absolutely to the idea of a transient occupation (*le système des garantis temporaires*) ; but certain trifling cessions of territory were not irreconcilable with this system. Thus Landau could be ceded to Germany, Savoy to Piedmont, certain frontier fortresses to the Netherlands, perhaps even Hüningen to Switzerland ; but to Prussia nothing at all. This memorial, too, was full of the teachings of wisdom and virtue : " The duplex aim of the tranquillisation of Europe and of France cannot be attained unless the allies display in the peace negotiations the same purity of aims, the same unselfishness, the same spirit of moderation, which has hitherto constituted the irresistible energy of the European league." [2] Notwithstanding all this, the czar now did the very thing which two days before he had described as treason to religion and morality, abandoning the inviolability of French soil, which he had been advocating with so much sacred wrath, and thus opening the way to an understanding. In a confidential covering letter, Nesselrode implored the chancellor " to bring this unhappy affair to a speedy close. This would be the best birthday present you could give to the czar. There is nothing more

---

[1] Wellington's Memorial to Hardenberg, August 31, 1815.

[2] Nesselrode to Hardenberg, concerning Castlereagh's Memorial of September 2 (September 7, 1815).

painful to him and to us all than this difference of opinion between two courts whose relations are so intimate."[1]

Metternich immediately utilised the favour of the moment with extreme adroitness in order to play the part of mediator between the disputants. In a memorial dated September 8th, he gratefully recognised the moderate and conciliatory attitude of all the courts, and found it readily comprehensible that, none the less, in consequence of the differences in their respective geographical situations and national moods, their views might not perfectly harmonise. It was Austria's desire to secure the greatest possible safety with the least possible sacrifice for France, and she therefore proposed " a mixed system of permanent and temporary guarantees," therefore, above all, that France should return to the *status quo* of 1790 ; " the frontiers of 1790 "—here was a happy discovery of one of the convenient catchwords which the diplomacy of those days, still entirely French in sentiment, so greatly loved. The further proposals of the memorial were indeed extraordinarily inconsistent with these fine-sounding words : they showed clearly that Metternich was not mediating in an honourable spirit, but was really an adherent of the Anglo-Russian party. There was no longer any mention of the fourth part of Alsace which in the year 1790 had still been German ; on the contrary, Austria demanded in addition to Landau and those Netherland fortresses to whose cession the czar had already agreed, nothing more than Saarlouis ; and even this was not demanded unconditionally, since it was suggested that France might pay money to Prussia for the building of another fortress on the Saar. Finally, there was to be a war indemnity of 1,200,000,000 francs ; and for some years the country was to be occupied by 150,000 men, to constitute " a European police," under the supreme command of Wellington.[2]

Having thus been sacrificed by Austria, Hardenberg finally declared, on September 8th, that the king of Prussia, in order to secure harmony, would renounce his more extensive demands, and would accept the frontiers of 1790 ; but he understood that this principle was to be honourably interpreted, and demanded, in compensation for the German enclaves in Alsace, in addition to Landau and Saarlouis, Bitsch and the northern regions of Alsace, with Fort Louis, Weissenburg, and Hagenau. Not even England now found any objection to raise to a moderate demand

---

[1] Nesselrode to Hardenberg, September 7, 1815.
[2] Metternich, Memorial to the Committeee of Four, September 8, 1815.

for territory, and thus the negotiations ended, as had before the dispute about Saxony, with a repulsive chaffering about individual towns and fortresses. Hardenberg defended his ultimate demands with the utmost obstinacy, but since none of the other powers supported him, he could save for Germany no more than Landau, Saarlouis, and the coal-fields of Saarbrücken. Of Metternich's proposal to return to " the *status quo* of 1790 " there ultimately remained little more than the name, for the so-called mediator did not take his own proposal seriously. On September 19th, the four powers resolved that they would now open negotiations with France. Next day they handed in their joint ultimatum. They assumed that peace was assured, for what could unarmed France do to oppose these far too lenient conditions ? The Russian army was already preparing to depart. On September 23rd Blucher wrote home : " The peace has been arranged, not, unfortunately, upon the terms that ought to have been secured, upon the lines upon which I opened the matter ; but owing to the firm stand Hardenberg finally took, the terms are better than they seemed likely to be. We had to fight against all the others at once." [1]

In the eyes of the French, on the other hand, the allies' ultimatum was the beginning of the real negotiations. The whole of Paris eagerly endeavoured, as if by tacit conspiracy, to detach the high-minded czar from his allies. The distinguished world displayed a luxuriant abundance of those pious modes of speech which were agreeable to the new world-saviour, and admired the solemn phrase of Talleyrand : " There is nothing less aristocratic than unbelief." The czar was overwhelmed at once with skilful adulation and with gross flattery ; when he mustered his army to take leave of it upon the plain of Vertus, the Parisian newspapers, as if drunk with ecstasy, declared that the noble commander must feel himself so perfectly at home upon this field of virtue ! Wellington, on the other hand, notwithstanding his reserve, did not escape the most savage attacks, and on one occasion in the theatre was actually hissed out of the royal box. Finally, everyone displayed fierce enmity against the Prussians, What anger was manifested in Paris on August 3rd when the Prussian troops illuminated their quarters and barracks in honour of their national festival, and when upon the king's house the nscription was to be read : *Parcere subjectis et debellare superbos !* What petty quarrels there were, too, about the payment and

[1] Blucher to Hienen, September 23, 1815.

provisioning of the troops ! At first the Bourbons, owing to the general disorder, were hardly able to fulfil the duties imposed upon the conquered. But when Hardenberg had 5,000,000 francs brought from Prussia, in order to discharge the arrears of pay, Blucher refused to accept this new sacrifice from the hands of his fellow-citizens : " The army," he wrote proudly, " is not a mercenary army which must be bought off at any cost, it is one with the nation ! " At length an understanding was reached, in virtue of which France was to resume the administration of the occupied portions of the country, and was at the same time to undertake to pay and maintain the troops. But just as in the previous year the Bourbons had failed to carry out the promised restoration of the art treasures, so also on this occasion did they break their word. The czar, whose generosity was inexhaustible, immediately granted a postponement for the overdue payments ; wealthy England was not pressing ; while Austria lacked courage to separate herself from the other two. Prussia alone, devoid of all financial resources, was unable to display any consideration. When Louis, the minister of finance, wrote curtly and arrogantly to Humboldt, that the sums demanded for the clothing of the Prussian troops could not be paid, he received a letter saying that he would be responsible if Prussia should now help herself. The generals were ordered to make requisitions in the departments, and at length the Bourbon court resolved to meet its obligations.[1]

The note in which, on September 21st, Talleyrand answered the ultimatum of the allies was likewise couched in a tone of stubborn arrogance. The wily schemer had derived new hopes from the commencing departure of the Russian army, and began in a lofty strain to the effect that the Most Christian King had not been waging war against the four powers, his allies, and therefore could not agree that they possessed a right of conquest ; never could he cede a single scrap of land from " ancient France " ; if the four powers put forward such demands, the French plenipotentiaries were instructed not even to listen to them. Yet the allies were demanding from " ancient France " nothing more than Saarlouis, Landau, and a strip of land along the Meuse ; they were prepared to leave the Bourbons, in exchange, Avignon and the German quarter of Alsace, the conquests of the Revolution, so that " ancient France " would still secure an increase of several hundred thousand

---

[1] Louis to Humboldt, August 23. Humboldt's Annotations, August 24, 1815.

souls ! Two days earlier, Talleyrand had also declared that the return of the art treasures was inadmissible, for this would increase the hatred of the people for the Bourbons. Such language in the mouth of a completely disarmed state seemed intolerable even to the British and the Russians. Wellington, who had hitherto regarded the demand for the return of the art treasures as a dubious one, now expressed the opinion that this was necessary " in order to read the French a great moral lesson." The four powers replied on the following day, expressing sharp dissent. There was no question of conquests but merely of measures for the safety of Europe. Was the royal court desirous of upholding once more that principle of the intangibility of the French frontiers which had caused so much unhappiness under Napoleon ? In contrast with the Germans, the English and the Russians had at first unctuously defended the principle of the inviolability of France ; but now they abandoned this principle.

The answer caused profound dismay in the Tuileries. King Louis endeavoured once more by personal intervention to take the emotional spirit of the czar by storm. " In the bitterness of my heart," he wrote on September 23rd, " I take refuge in your majesty, to express to you with devotion the painful feelings with which I have read the proposals of the four powers. One thing, above all, disturbs me profoundly and leads me to despair in the well-being of unhappy France—the overwhelming thought that your majesty, upon whom I place my hopes, seems to have approved the note which was sent to me. I do not hesitate, Sire, to assure you, that I shall refuse to be an instrument in bringing about the destruction of my country, and to declare that I would rather abdicate than agree to besmirch the ancient glories of my throne by so unexampled a humiliation ! " In autograph notes, the attention of Emperor Francis and of King Frederick William III was drawn to this despairing despatch.[1] The threatened abdication was, however, utterly improbable, and the theatrical pathos of the letter was in ludicrous contrast with the fact that the allies were leaving ancient France in undisturbed possession of a notable enlargement of territory. Even the czar was estranged by the immeasurable distress of his protégé. Alexander did not, indeed, remain completely unaffected ; he secured that of the last demands of the coalition a trifle should still be abated. The allies renounced the important Meuse fortress of Givet, and also

[1] King Louis to Czar Alexander, September 23 ; to Emperor Francis, September 23, 1815.

Condé : the glorious name of this fortress was too dear to the House of the Capets.

A change of ministry in the Tuileries established the work of peace on a firmer foundation. Since the legitimist ultras had secured a victory in the elections to the chamber, through the adoption of the forcible methods of the White Terror, neither Fouché the regicide nor Talleyrand the mediator could maintain his position in the cabinet. Beneath the surface, the czar gave his aid to the change, for he regarded Fouché's intercourse with the English as suspect ; he even had serious thoughts of securing for Pozzo di Borgo, the declared enemy of the military Jacobins of Prussia, a place in the ministry, for Pozzo was a Frenchman by birth ; but in the end he regarded it as more prudent to leave his confidant in the secure position of Russian ambassador. On September 26th, the duc de Richelieu formed a new cabinet. Richelieu was a well-meaning statesman, but one totally unacquainted with France ; he had acquired the favour of the czar during a prolonged stay in Russia. Powerless as he was, and entirely dependent upon the favour of Alexander, he soon bowed before the inevitable ; and on October 2nd a decisive agreement between France and the four powers was effected. The protocol employed the high-sounding phrase that the frontier of 1790 was to constitute the rule ; but in reality all that France lost was a strip of land on the Belgian border with Marienburg and Philippeville, the remainder of Savoy and, finally, Landau and Saarlouis, with Saarbrücken.

Alexander could not abandon the scene of his deeds without once more astonishing the world by the display of his sublime sentiments. In the anxious days after the battle of Bautzen, Frederick William, upon a solitary ride with his friend, had once said with profound emotion : " Now God alone can save us ; if we conquer, we will render to Him the honour before all the world ! " How frequently since then had memories of that consecrated hour entered the czar's mind. Profoundly moved by the prophecies of Frau von Krüdener, and by a fantastic little work by the German philosopher Baader, he now resolved to transform after his own manner the thought thus uttered by his friend, and wrote with his own hand the charter of the Holy Alliance, a personal confession of faith which was to show the world that the new European three-starred constellation owed its glories solely to the sun of Christ. In this remarkable document were displayed all the nobility of sentiment and all the ardency of faith, but also all the obscure sentimentality and worldly vanity, of this suggestible character. The recognition that the European society of nations constitutes a living community, this old and half-forgotten truth which was now pressing vigorously for revival, after the horrors of the Napoleonic age, underwent a strange theocratic transformation in the language of the God-inspired man. The three monarchs of Austria, Prussia, and Russia (thus wrote the czar) regarded themselves as united by the bonds of a true and indissoluble brotherhood, and as occupying in relation to their subjects the position of fathers; they considered themselves appointed by providence to rule three branches of a single family, and they recognised as the sole sovereign of the Single Christian nation, " God, our divine Saviour Jesus Christ, the word of the Most High, the word of life." All states recognising these sacred truths were fraternally invited to enter the Holy Alliance.[1]

The enigmatical favour of fortune by which it always happened that Alexander's outbursts of emotional feeling coincided with his advantage, presided also over this outpouring of his most sacred sentiments. All the powers of Europe might accept his brotherly invitation, except those two which, in accordance with Russian policy, were traditionally regarded as Russia's irreconcilable enemies. The pope must necessarily hold aloof, because the vicegerent of Christ on earth could not recognise the *civitas Dei* except under the rule of the crowned priest. Again, the infidel sultan, as the czar expressly declared, was necessarily and for ever excluded from the great brotherly alliance of Europe. The oracular phrases in which Alexander earnestly and ceremoniously presented his proposals were extremely antipathetic to the sound sense of Frederick William; but why should the king refuse to oblige his old friend in a matter which, after all, imposed no obligations upon the Prussian state? The king, therefore, did as the czar desired, and signed the charter on September 26th. Emperor Francis found it less easy to make up his mind; he foresaw how distressing this Holy Alliance would be to his good friend in Constantinople. Since Metternich, however, smilingly declared the pious charter to be no more than empty talk, Austria also gave in her adhesion on the same day. All the states

---

[1] A reference in a parliamentary speech by Lord Liverpool has given occasion to the frequently repeated assertion that the charter of the Holy Alliance contains certain secret articles. Although the untenability of this assumption is manifest from internal considerations, the assurance may here be given, as a work of supererogation, that the original charter, preserved in the private state archives of Berlin, contains nothing more than the universally-known text.

of Europe subsequently joined the Holy Alliance, most of them
out of complaisance for the czar, but some also because the pious
words regarding the paternal government of the princes were well
suited to the ultra-conservative tendencies of the epoch of the
restoration.

Three only among the European powers withheld their assent :
the two ancient enemies of Russia—and England. Whilst the
prince regent, as ruler of Hanover, gladly signed the document,
Castlereagh declared in an incisive speech that Parliament consisted of practical statesmen, and therefore, while it was able to
approve a diplomatic treaty between states, it could not approve
a declaration of principles which would thrust England back into
the days of Cromwell and the Roundheads. The high tories'
true motive, however, was not regard for Parliament, with which
thay well knew how to deal, but mistrust of Russia, and regard
for the sultan, who was in fact greatly disturbed by the conclusion
of the Holy Alliance. The remarkable episode is not without
interest to the historian of civilisation, since the romantic moods
and the lively sentiment of European community characteristic
of the age are all therein reflected. But the Holy Alliance never
had any political significance ; such a significance was merely
assigned to it by poetic fiction in the opposition press of all the
countries, who soon took to speaking of " the system of the Holy
Alliance," and who directed to this imaginary address their complaints against the policy of the eastern powers.

Peace was at length signed on November 20th. Not even
this treaty, however, brought to the Germans the final conclusion
of their internal disputes about territory. Landau was ceded to
Austria, and by Austria to Bavaria, but this did not suffice to
satisfy the demands of the Wittelsbachs. Since Austria spurned
the reacquisition of Alsace, and had thus abandoned the simplest
means for the complete satisfaction of the court of Munich,
Metternich, in order that he might still have in his hands something to bargain with, made the great powers guarantee the future
" reversion " of Breisgau and the Badenese Palatinate—a promise
that was utterly illegal—and the unhappy territorial dispute
between Bavaria and Austria remained temporarily unsettled.
England was more fortunate. In addition to the abolition of
the slave trade, which to the British nation had already become an
object of national vanity, of general sport, the tories acquired a
protectorate over the Ionian islands, so that the island kingdom's
position of power in the Mediterranean was now established more

firmly than ever. France had to accept the military occupation of her north-western provinces for a period of from three to five years (the term being dependent upon her conduct), and had to pay an indemnity of 700,000,000 francs. ｜Of this sum 500,000,000 were allotted in sums of 100,000,000 to each of the four great powers and to the minor states taken as a unit ; in addition, England and Prussia received 25,000,000 each for the occupation of Paris. The remainder was ear-marked for the fortification of the territorial areas bordering on France, Bavaria receiving 15,000,000 and the Germanic Federation 25,000,000 for the Rhenish fortresses ; Prussia had to content herself with 20,000,000, since Saarlouis and the right of garrisoning Luxemburg were ceded to this country.

On the same day the four powers renewed their old alliance. England had desired a simple prolongation of the treaty of Chaumont for a period of twenty years. Russia, however, held that France ought to be treated as a suspected enemy only during the exceptional conditions of the period of occupation, and she secured that the four powers should guarantee, for a time that was not distinctly specified, the maintenance of the legitimate royal house and of the *Charte*,[1] for the czar considered that the greatest dangers for France would arise from the party fanaticism of the émigrés. The four powers solemnly promised one another to watch over the safety of Europe by repeated meetings of the monarchs or of their ministers. In this way the whole continent, and especially France, was placed under the police supervision of the coalition ; it was impossible to expect that the Bourbons would be content until they had secured release from this situation, so humiliating to a proud nation, and until they had effected the acceptance of France into the alliance of the great powers. Since the four powers, Austria and England not excepted, mistrusted the savage passion of the émigrés, when taking leave, they directed a note to Richelieu, exhorting him to combine moderation with firmness, and with strict loyalty to the constitution to oppose all enemies of the public peace in whatsoever form they might display themselves. It was with profound anxiety that the statesmen of the coalition left Paris. Not one of them believed in the vitality of the ancient royal house ; they all estimated the durability of the Bourbon dominion at no more than a few years. Yet such a state as this, whose future seemed altogether incalculable,

---

[1] Russian Memorial concerning the treaty of alliance, October 9-21, 1815.

had been re-established by allied Europe in a dominant position on the German Upper Rhine !

In the whole of modern history there was only one occasion on which, after brilliant successes in the field, a peace was concluded which in leniency could be compared with the treaty of November 20, 1815, and this was the peace of Prague of 1866. But that which in Prague was effected by free determination, and by the wise restraint of the conqueror, resulted in Paris from the common suspicions of the other allies towards the boldest and most active of their own comrades in victory. The great moment in which the balance of power in Europe, which since the days of Cardinal Richelieu had been so unnaturally disturbed, might have been restored, and in which their ancient inheritance might have been given back to the Germans, was wasted, because all the powers of the east and of the west were united in the resolve that the central region of the continent should be kept in a state of continuous suppression. It was by painful experience that the German nation bought the knowledge that they could expect atonement for ancient wrongs from their own good swords alone. All the gloomy prophecies of Hardenberg, Humboldt, and Gneisenau were literally fulfilled. Not only did the French feel, as was reasonable, that the presence of foreign troops for several years was an indelible disgrace, they also regarded a peace whose mildness was unexampled as a cruel wrong. It was not the loss of Saarbrücken or Landau which they took to heart ; what they could not forget was the defeat of Belle Alliance. Revenge for Waterloo—for decades to come this remained the watchword of the French nation. From this idea sprang the revolution of 1830, the threats of war of 1840, and the re-establishment of the empire ; until after more than half a century, the old and cherished wish found expression in a wicked war of conquest, and the German victor in this war at length atoned for the sins of omission of 1815.

Thus for many decades the relationship between the two neighbour peoples remained morbidly insecure and tense. It was with fierce anger that the Germans received intelligence of the ineffectual peace. It was in the name of the whole nation that Blucher exclaimed : " Notwithstanding all their exertions, Prussia and Germany once more stand before the world as betrayed." Thereupon he again vented his anger against the diplomats, asking fiercely how long " this extraordinary collection of subjects who rule their own monarchs" was to continue to exist. In their naive ignorance of the political situation, many Germans had seriously hoped that in Paris not only would the ancient frontiers of the fatherland be re-established, but also that all the errors of the federal constitution would be put to rights. Schenkendorf could not abandon the hope that the heirs of the Leopolds and the Ferdinands, who had so cold-bloodedly spurned the German crown, would now be forced to don the ancient purple. The loyal man could not await the hour in which the stony and pear-shaped countenance of Emperor Francis was once more to be surmounted by the crown of the Carlovingians, and he sang :

> "O be at length then wiser,
> You flock that lacks a herd,
> Choose ye at once your Kaiser,
> Make him by force your lord ! "

What wrath was now disseminated throughout this genera-tion of Teutonisers when it was learned that everything remained as before, that the imperial glories were buried, that Rappolts-weiler and Oberehnheim were again to be named Ribeauvillé and Obernai, that the ancient and powerful homeland of German civilisation was once more to be defiled with the slime of French ill-breeding, and was perhaps to sink therein for ever ! Through a thousand German hearts resounded the complaint of the poet :

> "There lies a long-lost treasure
> Among the hills of Vosges,
> 'Tis ours the task that German blood
> Be freed from hell's own yoke ! "

The sorest wound of all was that these same lost German lands, to which Germany had wished to bring freedom, rejoiced over the diplomatic success of the foreigner. Rückert despairingly exclaimed :

> "Fruitless the victory that we prized ;
> All France laughs in our face.
> And you, Alsace, de-Germanised,
> Mock, too ! Supreme disgrace ! "

In the *Rheinische Merkur* Görres thundered with all the savagery of his Jacobin anger against the basilisk's egg which the Gallic cock had laid, and which German folly had hatched. The incensed man would not see the obvious reasons for the great failure, assigning all the blame to Hardenberg's weakness and to " the

German lack of unity," which was to remain a persistent cause of complaint, a permanent grievance, of the disillusioned patriots. Yet the king and his statesmen had done their duty as best they could, and had received loyal support from the ministers of most of the middle-sized states. It was not the Germans who had failed to exhibit unity, but Austria which had fallen away from Germany. That traditional domestic policy which had so often sacrificed German imperial lands to foreigners in exchange for Hapsburg hereditary dominions, had, on this occasion, simply left the Germans in the lurch, because there was nothing desirable to gain for the House of Lorraine.

It was the curse of peaceful dualism that the Prussian government was henceforward blamed by public opinion for the sins of Austria, and that this government, simply in order to avoid offending the dear Austrian ally, refused on principle to justify itself before the nations. How wickedly and shamelessly, too, did the Hofburg now lie to the German people ! Gentz, who henceforward completely lost moral stability, declared with a brazen face in the *Osterreichischer Beobachter*, that there had never existed any difference of opinion between the great powers regarding the conditions of peace, and concluded by saying that if this were not the case " then we must have unwittingly or deliberately misinformed the public ! " Is it surprising that in face of such a policy the language of the patriots daily became more violent, and that Görres wrote in a fury : " Just as the Vendôme column is a perpetual sign of our disgrace, so in the *Rheinische Merkur* shall there be a perpetual protest on the part of the nation, so that posterity may recognise that our contemporaries were not all in agreement with what was done ! "

Not merely did the unhappy peace embitter the sentiments of the nation to such a degree that from the first there was not even a glimmer of joyful hope radiated over the youthful Germanic Federation. It resulted further in increasing the excessive self-esteem of " the people," which had originated during the war ; there could be no doubt about the matter that " the people " would have done everything very much better than the diplomats. The masses of the nation soon turned their backs on all political ideas ; they devoted themselves to the cares of domestic life, engaging in faithful work in order to heal the wounds of the titanic struggle. Whoever still preserved in his heart the ardent idealism of the War of Liberation, consoled himself with the belief that the hour had now arrived when the people must take over the conduct of the German state. It sounded like a prophecy of the struggles and sorrows of the coming decade, when one of the best of the younger generation, F. G. Dahlmann, the historian, of Kiel, uttered in commemoration of the victory words which in form and content were characteristic of the spirit of the time : " Peace and joy cannot return to earth until, just as wars have become national and thereby have become victorious, so also peace-times shall become national ; peace and joy cannot return until, in peace-time also, the national spirit is cultivated and held in honour, until the light of good constitutions is diffused over the paltry lamps of the cabinets."

MENTAL CURRENTS OF THE FIRST YEARS OF PEACE.

§ I. LITERARY CHARACTERISTICS OF THE EPOCH.

NOT every epoch understands its own nature. More especially in those weary periods which usually follow the decisive moments of national life, courageous and high-spirited individuals are apt to be completely deceived regarding the driving energies of the age. Before the war no one had imagined how much bravery and civic sense, how much power of self-sacrifice and noble passion, slumbered among the people of the German north ; now, when all these hidden virtues had manifested themselves so gloriously, the greatly moved spokesmen of the patriots were simply unable to believe that the high enthusiasm of the War of Liberation could evaporate as soon as its aim had been secured. Who could dispute the contention that the federal act and the conclusion of peace had miscarried only because the people had not been able to participate in the negotiations of the diplomats ? All the more certain was it that the nation, as soon as it had received the promised constitutional government, would attend to its own affairs with zeal and understanding, and would lead the errant cabinets back into the paths of national statecraft. It was in such a sense that Arndt wrote, at the beginning of the first year of peace : " In this year 1816, between the rulers and the peoples, the bond of love and obedience must be indissolubly tied." He saw the doors of a new epoch widely opened ; as soon as the beautiful new-born child of this year, constitutional freedom, should make its entry into all the German states, " those who had fallen in the field would exult, and widows and affianced maidens in their solitude would weep tears of joy."

The sanguine man was to learn all too soon how completely he had misunderstood the character and sentiments of his nation. Germany stood at the threshold of a lengthy period of political tutelage, full of error and disillusionment ; public opinion, which

Arndt esteemed as " the mightiest queen of life," showed but little understanding of the problems of constitutional government, and hardly even displayed any serious interest in the matter. The solitary widows and affianced maidens, the warriors who had returned to their homes to exchange the sword for the ploughshare or the carpenter's plane, were hard pressed by poverty ; their struggles were directed to providing a subsistence for themselves, to discovering how they could rebuild huts upon the plundered battle-fields of the national war. Germany was once again the most impoverished of all the lands of western Europe ; in many regions of the march of Brandenburg there began for the fifth time a fierce struggle for the first beginnings of civic welfare. With a quiet confidence in God, the common people returned to the arduous labours of the day, patiently bearing the lot of privation which came to them as the reward of so many victories. That spirit of restlessness and brutalisation, which after great struggles is apt for a time to persist in the sentiments of the masses, was nowhere seen among the pious and sober-minded men who had fought in this holy war. But amid the pressure of economic cares there was no room left for political passion. Even the memory of all the wonders of the last three years rarely found open expression, although it still persisted in loyal hearts. Twice or thrice in succession, on October 18th, bonfires flamed on the hill-tops ; but after that, in most cases, they were seen no longer, sometimes because they were forbidden by the police, sometimes because the masses became indifferent. In this generation, which was in general so passionately fond of writing, the number of popular books and woodcuts describing to the nation the most remarkable age of its recent history, remained extraordinarily small. An affected picture, " The Return of the Young Hero," was occasionally to be seen hanging on the walls in the houses of well-to-do bourgeois whose sons had gone to the front among the voluntary yagers ; at fairs, and in country inns, even the portrait of Blucher, the popular hero, was rarely to be seen.

Among the cultured classes, too, there were, generally speaking, only three sharply separated circles in which the elevated mood, the proud patriotic hopes, of the years of war, were still long preserved during peace : the Prussian officers' corps ; the students at the universities ; and finally, a moderate number of patriotic authors and men of learning, to whom people now began to apply the new Spanish party-name of liberals. Prussian officers lived and moved among memories of the campaigns ;

with a vigorous sense of self-approval they regarded the re-established glory of their flag, while contemplating with profound discontent the rickety structure of the Germanic Federation and the disastrous issue of the peace negotiations. During the struggle they had learned to respect the warlike energies of the bourgeoisie, and had adopted into their own circle many valiant comrades from the ranks of the volunteers. Now, by the new Army Law, the education of all young men fit for military service was entrusted to their hands; they came in contact with all classes of the population, and continued at the same time to preserve the free scientific spirit which had been awakened in them by Scharnhorst; it was only in cases of isolated reversion that they continued to exhibit the caste arrogance of earlier days. But although the foreign powers and the minor German courts regarded with great suspicion the national pride and the fresh intellectual life of this people's army, the strictly monarchical sentiments of the officers remained completely inaccessible to all party aspirations. Their comrades of the Russian guard had for the first time become acquainted with the ideas of the Revolution during their stay in France, and had thence taken home with them revolutionary views which were subsequently to bear fruit in foolish conspiracies. Upon the Prussian officers, on the contrary, the sight of the general perjury and the savage party struggles of the French exercised only a repellent influence; now, as in the nineties, they prided themselves on their opposition to the Revolution; they prided themselves on their antique Prussian loyalty to the throne, and were inclined to despise the new constitutional doctrine, if only for the reason that it was derived from France. Even Gneisenau, who, but a year before, had demanded the speedy completion of the Prussian constitution, returned home in a changed mood, and urgently advised that the carrying out of such proposals should be allowed to mature with extreme slowness.[1] The only political idea which was passionately discussed in the letters and conversations of the army, was the hope of a third Punic War, which should finally enable the Germans to secure their ancient western frontier and should restore to them a respected position among the nations.

Far more lively was the mood of the young volunteers who now returned from their regiments to the lecture theatres of the universities. Patriotic and religious enthusiasm, anger at the shameful peace, and obscure ideas regarding freedom and equality,

[1] Gneisenau to Muffling, March 25, 1816.

233

which had, unconsciously for the most part, been borrowed from the despised French—all this was simmering confusedly in the heads of these Teutonising youths, generating a noble barbarism, which regarded as valid only the virtues of the citizen, and which avowed adhesion to the saying of Fichte, that it was better to have life without science than science without life. Meanwhile the exaggerated national pride of Teutonism was too obviously in contradiction with the free broad-mindedness of our cosmopolitan people, to whom it was quite impossible to remain permanently unjust to a foreign nation ; the contempt displayed for all grace and for refined culture was too un-German, the aspect of this arrogant student-community, now childishly touching, now almost ludicrous, was too sectarian for its political fanaticism to be effective throughout wide circles. The old rule still held good that the men of fifty and sixty years of age govern the world. Whilst the political war-cries of the patriotic writers found, indeed, approval in isolated instances among the older men, they did not awaken the strong passion which eventuates in action

With more accuracy than Arndt did Hegel grasp the spirit of the time when he said that the nation had completed the work of rough-hewing, and could now once more turn its mind inward to the kingdom of God. The mighty harmonies to which the age of our classical poetry had given utterance were still resounding ; the rich treasures which during the last two generations the intellectual work of the nation had disclosed were by no means exhausted. The ambition of this thoroughly unpolitical generation continued, undisturbed by all the prose of external life, to concern itself almost exclusively with the things of the spirit. To its best men, the days of the Napoleonic wars soon came to seem no more than an episode, like a hailstorm which had broken over the blooming garden of German art and science. Just as the common people once more returned to their ploughs, so the men of culture again took their pens in hand, not, like the former, in quiet renunciation, but inspired with the joyful consciousness that they belonged once more to themselves and their own inmost life. With astonishing distinctness now became visible that inward contradiction which, since the flourishing of the new literature, had come to exist in the character of our nation : those valiant Teutons who in the sagas of primitive heathendom had continually dreamed of war and victory, and who since then in each successive century had deafened the world with the clash of their swords, now esteemed warlike renown less highly than did any other people ; they lived in the belief that Germany's sharpest weapon was German thought.

Throughout the world, the decade following the overthrow of Napoleon was a blossoming time of the sciences and the arts. The nations which had just been fighting so fiercely one with another, now engaged in a fine rivalry in respect of the fruits of their intellectual life ; never before had Europe approximated so closely to that ideal of a free world-literature of which Goethe dreamed. In this peaceful rivalry, Germany took the first place. What a change from the days of Louis XIV, when our nation had been forced to go humbly to school to all the other nations of the west. Now the whole world revered the name of Goethe. The quaint guest-chambers of the Erbprinzen and of the Adler in Weimar were always full of distinguished Englishmen who desired to pay their respects to the prince of the new poetry. In Paris, Alexander Humboldt enjoyed a repute which exceeded that of almost any native man of learning ; when a stranger entered a hackney-coach and gave the address of the great traveller, the driver respectfully lifted his hat and said : " Ah ! chez M. de Humboldt ! " When Niebuhr came to Rome as Prussian ambassador, no one in the world-city ventured to contest with him the glory of being the first among all men of learning.

Foreigners spoke little of our state, of its warlike deeds. To all the foreign powers the sudden revival in strength of the centre of Europe was disagreeable, and they all rivalled one another in the endeavour to consign to oblivion Prussia's share in the liberation of Europe. Not one of the foreign military historians who in these years of historical production described the most recent campaigns, did anything like adequate justice to the services of Blucher's headquarters staff. The old prestige of the Prussian army, which in the days of Frederick had been dreaded by all as the greatest army in the world, had by no means been re-established by the victories of Dennewitz and Belle Alliance. Since it is always difficult to gain a comprehensive view of the true course of a coalition war, the public opinion of Europe gladly contented itself with contemplating the simple conclusion that since the Prussians had been beaten when they fought alone at Jena they had been saved only by foreign help. For this reason, too, no one in foreign lands had any interest in the political institutions to which Prussia owed her freedom. Now, as before, Prussia remained the least known and the most completely misunderstood state of Europe. Moreover, the new Reichstag of Ratisbon, which now assembled in Frankfort, aroused the scorn of Europe by its fruitless disputes. Soon after the wonderful uprising of our nation, the old and convenient opinion became generally current that by a wise provision of nature the German nation was foreordained to eternal weakness and dissension. All the more willingly did people recognise the intellectual greatness of this powerless nation ; it was solely to their artists and to their men of learning that the Germans owed the fact that by all the civilised peoples of the west they were once more regarded as one among the great nations. In foreign lands, they were now spoken of as the nation of poets and thinkers ; in the partition of the earth they should be content with the lot of the poet which Schiller ascribed to them, and, intoxicated with the divine light, should be satisfied to lose the light of earth.

For the first time since the days of Martin Luther, the ideas of Germany once more made the round of the world, and now found a more willing acceptance than of old had the ideas of the Reformation. Germany alone had already got completely beyond the view of the world-order characteristic of the eighteenth century. The sensualism of the days of enlightenment had been long replaced by an idealist philosophy ; the dominion of reason by a profound religious sentiment ; cosmopolitanism by a delight in national peculiarity ; natural rights by a recognition of the living growth of the nations ; the rules of correct art by free poesy, bubbling up as by natural energy from the depths of the soul ; the preponderance of the exact sciences by the new historico-æsthetic culture. By the work of three generations, those of the classical and of the romanticist poets, this world of new ideas had slowly attained to maturity, whereas among the neighbour nations it had hitherto secured no more than isolated disciples, and only now at length made its way victoriously through all the lands.

With wonderful elasticity did France resume her intellectual labours after the long and heavy slumber of the imperial age. Madame de Staël's book upon Germany, which the Napoleonic censors had suppressed as an affront to the national pride, was now in everyone's hands, and gained everywhere adherents for German ideas, which were given the comprehensive name of romanticism. The dominion of the sensualist philosophy collapsed before the criticism of the doctrinaires ; a compact circle of men of talent, such men as Mignet, Guizot, and the Thierrys, opened to the French an understanding of the world of history. The age of Louis XIV, which even the revolutionary thinkers of the eighteenth century had still regarded as the epoch of classical beauty of form, began to lose its prestige, and soon there uprose a new school of poets to liberate France from the tyranny of academic rules, so that Victor Hugo could say with considerable truth of his own people that romanticism is in literature that which liberalism is in politics. Yet more vigorous and more direct was the exchange of ideas between Germany and England; the Germans now repaid to the British what they had once received from Shakespeare and Sterne. Walter Scott, the most fruitful and best-loved poet of the age, went to school to Bürger and Goethe, drawing from the profound spring of sagas and folk-songs which the Germans had unlocked for the world; by his historical romances the broad masses of the European reading public was first won over to romanticist ideals. Some of the Italians, too, above all Manzoni, entered the path of the new poetry; but among this semi-antique people of Italy, romanticist poetry could just as little attain to an undisputed dominion as had in former days the northern artistic form of Gothic architecture.

Everywhere there was an awakening of spirit. In Germany itself, the wealth of this fruitful epoch seemed less striking than in neighbouring countries, for the classical age of our poetry had barely come to an end, and the great majority of the younger poets regarded themselves, when compared with the heroes of those great days, as nothing better than a generation of epigones. All the more powerfully and fruitfully did the creative energy of the German spirit unfold itself in the domain of science. Almost simultaneously appeared the epoch-making writings of Savigny, the brothers Grimm, Boeckh, Lachmann, Bopp, Diez, and Ritter; whilst Niebuhr, the Humboldts, Eichhorn, Creuzer, and Gottfried Hermann, went vigorously forward along the paths they had already opened. The current of new ideas flowed everywhere unceasingly. There was an overplus of brilliant men, as there had been in former days when Klopstock led the revival of German poetry. And just as had previously been the case with the pioneers of our poetry, so now this new generation of learned men was permeated with an innocent and youthful enthusiasm, with a serene ambition which sought nothing more in the world than the blessedness of knowledge, and the increase of German glory through the activities of free investigation.

The dry dust which had so long lain upon the works of German learning was, as it were, wafted away; the new science felt itself to be the sister of art. Its disciples had all drunk from the cup of beauty, and many of them had even received the determinative impressions of their lives in the circles of the poets. Diez continued to cherish after many years the sheet of paper on which Goethe had once written for him the title of Reynouard's Provençal researches, and had thus indicated to the young man the way to his life work. Boeckh and Creuzer had idled, revelled, and caroused so many nights with the enthusiasts of Heidelberg romanticism; I. Bekker had delved with Uhland among the treasures of the Paris library; the impish Bettina Arnim sometimes played her mischievous tricks in the studies of Savigny and of the brothers Grimm. They all looked up with veneration to old Goethe, assembling round this central spirit to form as it were an invisible church, round this man who had received the veil of poesy from the hand of truth herself, and who incorporated the ideal of the age, the living unity of art and science, at once in his life and in his works. All endeavoured to express the results of their researches in a nobler and worthier form; the chaste simplicity of Savigny's writings, the powerful sentiment and the abundance of unsought, vivid, and intuitive images in the pithy style of Jacob Grimm, put to shame the sugary artificiality of many later poets. In all the works of these investigators, a warm heart and that creative imagination which reshapes historic life had just as great a share as had industrious research and critical acumen.

Just as the poetry of the previous generation had inspired the men of the rising generation, so the speculative work of the previous age made its way into the flesh and blood of the new science. It was only because the German spirit had so long been profoundly immersed in the problem of the unity of being and thinking, that that spirit now became able to diffuse itself throughout the world of history without becoming superficial and without losing itself in a mass of details. It was not in vain that all these young lawyers, philologists, and historians had sat at the feet of the philosophers. They wished to reach out through history into the secret of the human spirit itself; they endeavoured, as W. Humboldt declared of himself, to gain a view of how man had come to be, and thus to acquire some idea of what man may be and ought to be, to approach more closely to the ultimate questions of existence. Hence was derived the comprehensive outlook, the splendid multiplicity, of this generation of learned men. It was only so recently that the wide field of the world of history had been first occupied ; whoever drove his ploughshare through this virgin soil, subsequently scattered the seed with no niggard hand, so that it was dispersed also upon his neighbour's land. Almost all the notable men of learning were simultaneously at work in several fields, and every one of them, when immersing himself in some particular form of study, never failed to keep his glance fixed upon the great interconnection of the sciences. It was the pride of this fruit-bearing generation to propound brilliant hypotheses, and to illuminate wide prospects which the scientific researches of individual workers in two successive generations have since made accessible to the whole world.

Through the blossoming of science, the universities entered the foreground of the nation's spiritual life. They had ever taken a rich share in the struggles and transformations of German thought ; but now they assumed the leading position in the domain of the spirit, as they had done once before in the epoch of humanism and at the outset of the Reformation. University professors gradually acquired a determinative influence upon the activities and views of our nation, such an influence as they possessed in no other country ; among the leading authors of the ensuing decades, there were but few who had not held an academic position for a shorter or longer period. The university of Berlin soon outsoared all others ; here, during these years, there were at work the most ardent reforming minds in German science ; yet Berlin was never more than first among equals, for this country offered no opportunities for a centralisation of culture. Never have our universities been so truly free, fulfilled with such profound inward happiness, as in these quiet years of peace. The quarrelsome youths brought home from the battle-fields, in addition to their unmannerly Teutonism, to their arrogant political dreams, a fine enthusiasm, and a warm receptivity for ideals ; the deplorable roughness and intemperance of earlier times did not return. Education remained free from corporate coercion and corporate tendencies, for all felt that in science everything was still in a state of youthful growth. No one was astonished when a man of learning, even of mature age, changed from one faculty to another, or when a philologian like Dahlmann, who had never heard a historical lecture, was summoned to the chair of history. When a man displayed the stuff of which a master is made, no one asked whose pupil he had been. Most of the university lecturers did their professorial work with admirable zeal ; but if a fine spring day lured them into the neighbouring hills, even the most industrious among them did not hesitate to write up on the door of his lecture-theatre *hodie non legitur*.

The students of all faculties thronged round notable teachers of philosophy, history, and philology, and many of them continued to pursue such studies for years before thinking of engaging in a professional occupation for themselves. The classical state schools, avoiding mind-destroying polymathy, still knew how to awaken in their pupils a permanent delight in classical activity and an impulse towards free human culture. The disease of the universities of to-day, the dread of examinations, was still almost entirely unknown. The princely schools of Saxony, and the convent schools of Würtemberg, anciently celebrated homes of classical learning, sent their senior students to the university as soon as the teachers considered that the time was ripe, the state leaving them to do as they thought best. Entry into the state service and the ecclesiastical service of the petty states was for the most part secured by young men who had finished their university career, and was secured by patronage, in accordance with the ancient patriarchal manner. It was only in Prussia, after the reorganisation of the administration by Frederick William I, that a system of regular state-examinations had come into existence, and from Prussia this mechanical ordering, which was unquestionably juster, and was demanded by the manifold relationships of a great state, gradually made its way into the petty states. But here also a very moderate standard was exacted, for the state needed many young officials for its new provinces. The idealistic tendency of the time forbade that studies should be anxiously directed with the view to the earning of a living. Youth still enjoyed undisturbed academic freedom ; everyone listened and learned as fancy directed him, if he did not prefer to pass his golden student days in the sole pursuit of uncontrolled enjoyments.

Such was the life of the little learned republics, happy free states of absolute social equality and freedom from restraint, raised, as it were, above the pettiness of everyday life. Men of great talent, who in every other country would have demanded a wide stage for their activities, felt perfectly happy in the poverty and exiguity of these little university towns, with their ancient castles and narrow, winding streets, where every house had memories of some merry wit among the students, or of some distinguished professor. Here science was supreme ; the professor, revered by a grateful audience, regarded himself with frank self-satisfaction.

Often enough there occurred fierce intellectual disputes, after the German manner ; the scientific opponent was apt to be regarded as a desecrator of the temple, for everyone was whole-heartedly devoted to his own researches. But these straightforward and frugal-minded men were little troubled with vulgar ambition. They made it a point of honour to despise the display and comfort of material existence ; they still all firmly believed in the proud saying of Schiller : " In the end we are idealists, and would be ashamed that it could be said of us that things formed us, and not that we formed things."

Even after decades had passed, in Tübingen people used to speak of the wealthy bookseller Cotta, who had first introduced the unheard-of luxury of a sofa into the unpretentious town of the Muses. The youthful incompleteness of our civilisation, which still knew nothing of the many-sided social activities of the life of great towns, redounded to the advantage of reflectiveness and the peaceful pursuit of scientific work. Like the classical poetry of an earlier day, so now the new research remained perfectly free, almost untouched by the favour of the court and by official influence ; not even the prosecution of the demagogues was able to disturb the inner life of science. Although now almost all the German states, nobly competing one with another, endeavoured to secure the activities of leading teachers for their respective universities, in the eyes of the courts and of the bureaucracy even a professor of European reputation was merely a professor, without rank at court. The man of science, on the other hand, looked down with all the pride of idealism upon the aims of commercial life. Every teacher appealed to the best intelligences among his pupils to devote themselves entirely to science ; mediocrities were good enough for the handicraft work of the soldier and the official, and above all for the thoroughly despised world of business life. An incomparably greater preponderance of the spiritual energies of the nation devoted itself to learned activities, and it remains a fine testimony to the fertility of this generation that, none the less, the officialdom now numbered among its ranks an extraordinary abundance of men of talent.

Now, just as sixty years before, while the political life of the nation was flowing subdivided in innumerable streams and streamlets, it was only the authors and the men of learning who spoke directly to the nation as a whole. For this reason they regarded themselves as the chosen representatives of the people and of its highest goods; it was but very slowly that a few politicians gained general repute beside them. The whole epoch exhibited, for good and for evil, the characteristics of a literary age. Even now, a poem by Goethe, an incisive criticism, or a learned feud, such as that between the symbolists and the critical philologians, aroused far greater interest among the leading spirits of the nation than did any event in the world of politics. Karl Immermann voiced the very spirit of this romantic age when he declared that he could not follow a parliamentary debate with attention, because he could not form any mental picture of such void abstractions. The complete sacrifice of the free personality in the service of the state remained no less antipathetic to this generation than was the life of political parties, with its voluntary limitations and its fundamentally unjust hatreds. To the German, the highest of all aims was still to live out his own life, to develop his own ego, in its free peculiarities, in all possible directions, and, as W. Humboldt expressed it, to pay more attention to the doing than to the deed.

Although the dominant tendency of the age ran absolutely counter to the enlightened cosmopolitanism of the years before the Revolution, this romantic generation had none the less preserved many of the humanly lovable virtues of the philosophic century. The young Teutonisers might arrogantly decry French triviality; the leaders of science and art continued, after the old and genuine German manner, to exhibit gratitude and receptivity for every fine work of poetry and research, even if it came from much-abused France. Notwithstanding the mystical enthusiasm of the time, the old broad-minded tolerance still persisted. The contrasts of religious life had not yet become accentuated; they did not as yet exercise, as they do to-day, a falsifying and embittering influence in the sphere of politics. No one was surprised if a liberal was at the same time a strict church Christian. To everyone it seemed perfectly in order that Catholic ecclesiastics should attend the consecration of a Protestant church; even zealous converts like F. Schlegel, Stolberg, and Klinkowström remained on terms of cordial friendship with some of their old Protestant associates. The struggle of the literary parties did not render impossible the recognition of the human value of an opponent, nor exclude a genuine delight in every happy discovery. Uproarious youths prided themselves upon their Germanic strictness of morals;

mature men displayed in their moral judgments a fine and liberal mildness, which was in truth far more German. Exhibiting consideration for human weakness, they placed little value upon that correctness of conduct which to the prudish sense of the present day appears to be the only token of morality, and willingly let a hot-blooded friend go his own way, if he would but co-operate in the work of a free human culture, and if only he did not lose faith in the divine destiny of our race.

It was not without reason that the poets and men of learning looked down with contempt upon the prose of philistinism. They lived in a free and intelligent sociability which knew how to ennoble life by the serene play of art and which approximately realised Schiller's ideal of an æsthetic education. The exchange of ideas in correspondence and conversation, the natural means for the intercommunication of daily impressions, had not yet been rendered obsolete by newspapers. There yet existed the basis of all social charm, the frank and daily intercourse between the two sexes, for women were still able to follow in their entirety the thoughts of men. There was not a town in the realm without its connoisseurs, collectors, and critics, without its circles of lovers of the theatre and of the arts. When the cheerful populace of the smaller towns assembled for their simple meals by the gloomy flickering light of tallow candles, all contributed according to their respective capacities in the way of riddles and witticisms, songs and rhymed toasts—since for many years past every cultured German had known how to provide on his own initiative for the poetic needs of the household. Social life was warmed by cheerful pleasures ; in a game of forfeits a kiss was still permissible in all honour ; the free-spirited girls of the day, who were none the less carefully trained for domestic life, still frankly admitted that Käthchen of Heilbronn was a figure altogether after their taste. In the narrower circles of the initiates how much fine intelligence and wit, how much merry humour and eager enthusiasm, now prevailed—as when Ludwig Devreint and Callot-Hoffmann celebrated their extravagant bacchanals all through the night in the taverns of Lutter and Wegner ; or when Lobeck and the Königsberg philologians joined in a drinking-bout after the Greek manner, their heads crowned with roses, talking in Greek of the heroes of Homer and of the fortunate island of the Phaeacians. The social life of the day, notwithstanding its occasional beastliness and excesses, exhibited none the less an abundance of noble intellectual enjoyments, of which music almost alone has been preserved amid the dulness and the weary ostentation of modern society. The women who had been young during those years, seemed, even in advanced age, to the posterity of a duller generation, to be illumined as by a poetic charm ; they won the hearts of all by their inexhaustible amiability, by their refined understanding of everything that is human.

Doubtless there was also manifest at the same time an indication of the commencement of decay. Literature had for some time run to seed ; writers offered to readers what they thought the readers wanted, whereas the classical poets of earlier days had spontaneously expressed what already lay half-conscious in the soul of the nation. The love of novelty and the sensuality of the reading world were exploited by a mass of trivial light literature ; since a national style had not come into existence in any branch of creative literature, profounder natures readily lapsed into arbitrary and strained experiments, so that Goethe characterised these years as the epoch of forced talents. The fashionable intermingling of poetry and criticism rendered it easy for a barren dilettantism to increase beyond measure. Whoever moved in the circles of romanticism, repeating the catchwords of this school, and sometimes cudgelling his brains over the design for a drama or an epic poem, regarded himself as a poet, and forgot the consciousness of his incapacity in the favourite consolation that the artist was made in the world of thought and aspiration, and that Raphael, even if born without hands would have been the greatest of all painters. The terribly misused word " genius " was a charter for every folly, every extravagance. The straightforward human understanding was apt to be ruined by ingenious toying with new ideas and with surprising points of view. The belief in the boundless rights of the sovereign personality, the general desire to be something different from other men, led some to moral anarchy and others to vain self-admiration. With nervous sensitiveness, people watched every breath of their own beautiful spirits. In the letters of Gentz and in the memoirs of Rahel Varnhagen, the barometer plays the part of the mysterious elemental energy which bestows upon genius the dark and the bright hours.

The thoughts of the nation were still so completely dominated by literature, that even the great contrasts of political and religious life frequently found expression in learned disputes. Such was the nature of the struggles between Savigny and Thibaut, between Voss and Stolberg. When Gottfried Hermann took the field against Creuzer and the symbolists, he regarded himself as the champion of freedom against the *tenebriones*, the men of darkness in the state and in the church. Even the purely political parties, whose weak beginnings were now at length becoming manifest, emerged directly out of literary life. The immediate intervention of political theory in the destiny of states, which so strikingly distinguishes modern history from the more ingenuous days of antiquity and of the middle ages, was nowhere more conspicuous than here in the land of learning. German liberalism sprang, not from the class interests of the wealthy and self-conscious bourgeoisie, but from the academic ideas of the professors. With the indefinite historical yearning for the great days of the old emperordom, which had first come into existence in literary circles during the epoch of foreign dominion, there gradually became intermingled the doctrines of the new philosophy regarding the natural right of the free personality; to these were subsequently added a few phrases from Montesquieu and Rousseau; and finally, in addition, a large proportion of the unconscious prejudices of the learned caste. Thus there came into existence a system of ideas which were supposed to correspond with the law of reason, and were to lead our nation through freedom back to the attainment of its ancient power. In the writings of Rotteck this doctrine was produced in a condition of complete elaboration, like a philosopher's system and, just like such a system, put forward a claim to perpetuate itself through the world by the might of reason, by its theoretical incontrovertibility. The overthrow of the Napoleonic world-empire had been effected solely by the power of ideas which had been born in the circles of the brain-workers, had from these passed to the nation, had finally overpowered even the hostile crowns, and had led to the holy war—this view was assumed by literary politicians to be indisputable; thus it seemed that Germany's internal liberation would also be well secured if only all parties would fully accept the sacred truths of the new constitutional doctrine, and would hold firmly to this creed with the faithful conviction of the man of learning or of the martyr of the church. To this generation of well-meaning doctrinaires it still remained altogether unknown that the state has power, and belongs to the realm of the will. It was not until decades had passed, filled with crass confusions and profound disillusionments, that German party life could outgrow the cradle of doctrine and raise itself from a policy of belief to a policy of action.

In the Latin countries, poetry, when it had attained to classical perfection, had everywhere and for a long period given form and direction to the spirit of the nation. So extreme was the stubbornness of the Germans that even during the golden days of Weimar they would never yield to the dominion of a rule. Whilst Schiller and Goethe still stood at the summit of their creative activities, romanticism was already beginning a fierce attack upon the classical ideal. When the War of Liberation had reduced the literary struggle to silence, the anxiety about the fatherland repressed all other thoughts ; the few writings which ventured forth during this wild time seemed to unite in advocating Christian and patriotic enthusiasm. But hardly had peace been concluded when the sharp contrasts which the manifold life of Germany contained, once more and in a moment broke forth into active life. Even half-forgotten thoughts from the first years of the Revolution, ideas which had been supposed to have been long outgrown, re-emerged into the light of day ; for it is the lot of every literature which is no longer in its first youth to find that at times the past once more comes to life, and that the shades of the dead take part in the struggles of the living. Rationalism and religious sentiment, criticism and mysticism, natural rights and historical doctrines of the state, Nazarene and Hellenic ideals of nationalism and cosmopolitanism, liberal and feudal tendencies, struggled and intertwined in perpetual change.

It was not merely the timid Gentz who complained in alarm that the long-desired time of peace had brought to the Germans a war of all against all. Even Arndt, who was ever sanguine, could not conceal his disgust when at the court of the young crown prince of Prussia he saw Alexander Humboldt, the advocate of a purely scientific cosmopolitanism, and at the same time the brothers Gerlach, hotspurs of Christo-Germanic religious fanaticism. He anxiously asked how, in view of the immeasurable divergence of sentiments, this nation could ever attain to internal peace, to firm decision. In the long run, indeed, the healthy sense of the nation succeeded in grasping and retaining all that was genuine and viable in this anarchical confusion. Nevertheless, many a fine talent succumbed hopelessly amid the confusion of opinions ; and whoever found courage to take part in the struggles of the German spirit had to be prepared to accept a lot of renunciation. Every notable intelligence, even if high above the sectarian spirit, was forced, willingly or unwillingly, into the struggle of the literary parties and was extolled beyond measure by one faction, while being abused by the other with all the lack of restraint characteristic of German fault-finding ; those only who had attained to a great age might hope, like Savigny and Uhland, to secure belated recognition even from their opponents.

§ 2. POETRY AND THE FINE ARTS.

Even in the serene and youthful days of our classical literature, unrestrained criticism had frequently hampered the free natural growth of poetry. Now, when during seventy years Germany had experimented in almost all conceivable artistic styles and had made trial of even more manifold æsthetic theories, artistic creation showed itself to be affected with the disease of learned over-refinement. No branch of poetic art suffered more severely in this respect than the drama, which needs popular favour as flowers need the sun. Goethe had good reason for calling the arrogant spokesmen of romanticism " starvelings yearning for the unattainable " ; notwithstanding their talented flashes of thought and their high intentions, they completely lacked the gift of architectonic, the constructive and convincing energy of the creative genius. Although they had promised themselves to oust the classical ideal by a popular poetising, their works, after all, remained unknown to the people, and were the property of no more than a small circle of admiring connoisseurs. To them, art was, as it were, a magic philtre, one which the philistine was incapable of enjoying, and which was intoxicating to those alone who possessed divine grace ; under its influence these rare spirits forgot reality and smiled upon life as upon a foolish masque. This sovereign disdain which prided itself upon " pursuing sport as earnest and treating earnest as sport " conflicted with the healthy sentiment of the crowd.

Of the older German dramatists, the romanticist art-critic would allow a high rank to Goethe alone, and Goethe had hardly thought of writing his most mature works for presentation on the stage ; the peaceful sensual beauty of his *Iphigenia* and of his *Tasso* were not fully conceivable except to the mind of the reader. Lessing was no longer counted among the poets ; Schiller's tragic passion was mocked as empty rhetoric ; even Heinrich von Kleist, the one dramatist of genius whose outlook was closely akin to that of the romanticists, remained long unnoticed by the critics of this school. The two most efficient dramatists of the period, Iffland and Kotzebue, who continued to dominate the stage even for a decade after their death, were regarded by the arrogance of the romanticists with such unjustified contempt that youthful talent was necessarily frightened away from the drama. All that the romanticists could see in one of these writers was his honourable philistine sensibility, and all that they could see in the other was his insipidity and the commonness of his thought ; in neither could they recognise the exceptional technical talent, nor yet the fortunate gift of ready invention, whereby both put to shame their obscure critics. Of the dramatic endeavours of the romanticists themselves, but few ever appeared before the foot-lights, and all those that did thus appear stood the test badly. The leaders of the school soon turned their backs upon the stage, speaking with scorn of the common prose of theatrical success. Utterly regardless of the vital conditions of the modern theatre, which on five or seven nights a week had to satisfy an audience wearied by the cares of every-day life, dramatic theory constructed its stately cloud-pictures and made excessive demands, for which not even the splendid stage of the Hellenes could have furnished satisfaction.

The heroes of our classical poetry had never had the same intimate relationships with the stage as in earlier days Shakespeare or Molière. Now, however personal intercourse between dramatists and play-actors became ever rarer. Dramatic art forgot that, above all other arts, it is its fine destiny to constitute a bond of unity between the higher and the lower strata of society. There gradually came to exist within our nation a momentous cleavage which down to the present day has remained a grave evil of German civilisation : the reading public separated itself as an aristocracy from the onlooking and listening public. A large proportion of the daily needs of the theatre came to be supplied by literary journeymen ; spectacular plays and bad translations from the French appealed to the sightseeing spirit of the crowd. Whoever esteemed himself one of the select circle of true poets, commonly loaded himself too heavily with the impedimenta of the æsthetic doctrine to be able to act with that boldness, to laugh with that heartiness, which the stage demands from its rulers ; and such writers incorporated their dramatic ideas in bookish dramas. That mongrel type of poetry with which an over-elaborated modern culture cannot completely dispense, exhibited in Germany a more luxuriant growth than elsewhere. Here, upon the patient paper, all the complicated theorems and fantastical ideas of the wayward German intelligence found free play : tragicomedies and plays for *jeunes filles*, in which every conceivable metre recurred in riotous confusion ; hidden allusions comprehensible only to the poet himself and to his intimates ; literary satires which made art the object of art ; and, finally, exotic poems of all kinds, which had to be read as if they were translations.

Among foreign prototypes, Calderon, in the judgment of initiates, occupied the first place. The German cosmopolitans would not see that this purely national poet ranked as a classic writer precisely because he had given artistic expression to the ideals of his epoch and of his nation ; they slavishly imitated his southern forms which in our northern speech sounded operatic and simply undramatic, and they transported into the free Protestant world the conventional ideas of honour of the Catholic knighthood. Much intelligence and much energy were wasted in such artifices ; at long last these pretentious activities effected nothing more than the destruction of all traditional dramatic art-forms. But the poets grew accustomed to regard an ungrateful world with proud bitterness. Germany became the classic land of talent misunderstood. The excess of unsatisfied authors constituted a force of discontent in society, nourishing the national errors of fault-finding and hopeless moroseness. Subsequently, when political passions awakened, this contributed greatly to the embitterment of party struggles.

Pushed to the grotesque seemed the moral and æsthetic weaknesses of the romanticist epigones as displayed in the unsettled life of Zacharias Werner ; his dramatic talent failed to procure him fame because the virile art of the dramatist demands an entire man. Throughout life he vacillated restlessly to and fro between dissolute sensual desires and exaggerated ecstasy, between cynical commonness and lachrymose sentimentality, which could not refrain from praying beside the grave of a dog for the soul's peace of the deceased. Since his distracted spirit could find no consolation in " God and St. Rousseau," he ultimately took refuge in Rome, in the bosom of the ancient church, clinging in convulsive anxiety to the rock of Peter. Though the critical understanding of the East Prussian sometimes awakened in him, though the festival of the liquefaction of the blood of St. Januarius appeared to him like a Peruvian idolatrous service, he deafened his doubts with the turmoil of his own ecstatic outcries. Then he went to Vienna, in the days when the nimble-minded Father Hoffbauer had for the first time founded a strict ecclesiastical party in the pleasure-loving town, and had collected a crowd of converts around himself. Werner joyfully accepted all the views of this clerical circle, and countered the songs of freedom of the North German youth with the song " Let the watch-cry be, the old time becomes new ! " During the days of the Vienna congress he was the favourite preacher of the fashionable world. Half repentant and half diverted, elegant Vienna listened while the long, lean priest with the sinister dark eyes raised his powerful bass voice, now describing in glowing colours the molten sulphur pool of eternal damnation, and now depicting, with a thorough personal knowledge and with hardly concealed satisfaction, the aberrations of sensuality. Growth and nobility were lacking in his poetic creation as they were lacking in his life. His youthful dramas displayed strongly realistic talent and a living sense of historic greatness ; in isolated scenes of *Die Weihe der Kraft* the mighty figure of Martin Luther, and the high-spirited, richly-coloured life of our sixteenth century, are vigorously and vividly displayed. Intermingled therewith was, indeed, a morbid delight in the ghastly, the horrible, and the savage : that enigmatic combination of fervour and belief, voluptuousness and bloodthirst, which repels us in the natural religions of immature peoples, seemed to come to life once more in this unhappy man. After his conversion, with the zeal of the penitent, he recanted his finest drama, and wrote a pitiable work entitled *Die Weihe der Unkraft*. In his last play, *Die Mutter der Makkabäer*, he already displayed the lack of principle of a partially deranged mind, endeavouring to conceal the poverty of his religious sentiments behind turgid hymns and horrible images of martyrs.

More effective than Werner's historical tragedies, was his " fate-tragedy," published in 1815, *Der vierundzwanzigste Februar*, a master-work of its kind, aiming at the production of physical horror. The tragical destiny did not here arise by internal necessity out of the character of the actors, but out of the enigmatical sorcery of a momentous anniversary, and the astonished reader, notwithstanding the sublime insight afforded into the rationality of the moral world, bore away nothing but an impression of unaccountable horror. Since the novelty of this extravagant conceit attracted attention, and since in any case the romantic world was inclined to seek profound significance in mania, it was natural that an adroit producer should soon be found to elevate the whimsy into a system, with characteristic German wrongheadedness. Adolf Müllner, the lawyer of Weissenfels, composed a drama, *Die Schuld*, and subsequently in innumerable critical writings developed the theory of the new fate-tragedy. According to this theory, a higher world-order, more mysterious even than the blind destiny of the ancients, intervened in earthly life ; and by some foolish chance, by a broken string, by some sinister place or day, overwhelmed unsuspecting mortals with destruction. In this way, everything which the Protestant world had ever conceived regarding tragical blame and responsibility was once more placed in question by the unbridled love of innovation of the romanticist doctrine, and it seemed as if our art of tragedy was to end in self-annihilation. Müllner made himself at home in three literary periodicals at once, loudly trumpeted the long series of his own works, and alarmed his opponents by his filthy coarseness. For some years the fundamentally prosaic man continued to occupy the throne he had usurped, and the repute of German poetry was now so firmly established throughout the world that even foreign periodicals spoke with credulity of the new dramatic revelation. Then the fate-tragedy suffered the inevitable destiny of stilted nonentity : the public began to weary of it and turned to other fashions.

The art of dramatic presentation also suffered from the decline in dramatic poetry. How many talented monographs upon the theatre as a means of national education had already been published, and yet, among all German statesmen, Stein alone had made this idea his own, and had drawn the conclusion that it is the duty of the state to care for the stage. When, on his retirement, he sketched the plans of Prussian governmental reorganisation, he placed the theatre, as well as the academy of arts, under the control of the department of public instruction ; yet, barely two years later, they were by Hardenberg brought back into the domain of public amusement, and, with the exception of the court theatre, were subjected to police supervision.

In the royal capitals, the support of the court theatres was generally held to be a personal duty of the sovereign, and it soon became manifest that such theatres had more to expect from the free-handedness of artistically disposed princes than from the frugal petty-bourgeois sentiments of the new diets. Hardly had the Stuttgart stage, in the year 1816, been elevated to the position of a national theatre and had been nationally financed, when the diet began to complain of extravagance, and cheerfully acquiesced, three years later, when the king declared himself prepared to strike the maintenance of the court theatre out of the civil list. For the most part the monarchs cared with commendable zeal for the external equipment of their theatres, as well as for the employment of notable individual talent ; the old social prejudice against actors soon became mitigated when the stage was seen to be in such close association with the court.

None the less, the histrionic art gained little through the court theatres. After the death of Iffland, Frederick William entrusted Count Brühl with the management of the court theatre of Berlin. Brühl was an amiable and highly-cultured man, but neither dramatic poet nor actor, and he had merely assimilated, with the zeal of a talented connoisseur, the strict classical principles of the theatrical school of Weimar. The dangerous example was quickly followed ; soon at all the courts the office of theatre-intendant was reckoned among the high court dignities, the control of the greatest German theatres was taken out of the hands of skilled experts and placed in those of high-born dilettantes.

Yet the good traditions of earlier days still persisted for a time. The lack of fine new pieces was not yet too plainly perceptible, for the dramas of the classical epoch could still count upon general acceptance, and the works of Shakespeare now for the first time became fully established upon the German stage. The court theatres of Berlin, Munich, Carlsruhe, and Brunswick, were distinguished by many excellent performances, and the same was true of the long celebrated theatre of Hamburg and of the new municipal theatre of Leipzig. In Berlin, the realist tendency, which had here in former days gained dominion through the work of Fleck, found a talented representative in Ludwig Devrient. What sinister and diabolic energy was displayed in his Richard III, what an extravagance of exuberant humour in his Falstaff ! Almost more astonishing was the ability with which he played minor parts ; his Knecht Gottschalk, in *Käthchen von Heilbronn*, so admirably presented simple loyalty and truthfulness that in the souls of the audience there was awakened in a moment an understanding of the pristine energy and greatness of old German life. None the less, the firm artistic discipline of the stage became gradually more and more relaxed. The new romanticist ethics encouraged every man of talent to press recklessly towards the front, and to emphasise his own peculiarities; while the distinguished intendants had neither the technical knowledge which might have empowered them by their own example to maintain in the company a unity of style, nor yet had they sufficient prestige to enable them to keep the individual members within bounds. The brilliant new court theatres were no longer able to display such equably cultured and harmonious performances as had formerly produced delight in Hamburg in the days of Ekhof, and in Berlin in the days of Iffland. Moreover, dramatic criticism had for some time established itself like a noxious fungus upon the healthy tree of dramatic art. It had already become the rule that every aspiring senior school-boy or university student should win his literary spurs by dramatic criticism; almost every man of culture occasionally exercised his powers in the tragical handicraft of the critical spoil-sport. By far the majority of these notices had the sole aim of winning renown for the writer by arrogant distribution of blame; or else of giving rise to party struggles in theatrical spheres, struggles in which the populace in the small towns took part with passionate zeal. The trouble became still greater when the political prosecutions began. Thenceforward theatrical criticism remained the only domain in which the pens of the newspaper writers could run freely, for Count Bernstorff, the minister of state, said " the snappish dogs must be left at least one bone to worry! "

There were but two poets of this epoch who succeeded in enriching the theatre with works at once suitable for the stage and possessed of permanent artistic value. These were the first two Austrians since the Thirty Years' War to win for themselves an honourable place in the history of German poesy. Just as, long ago in the thirteenth century, the remote lands of the Danube had fortunately preserved the ancient German national epic, when the rest of Germany had long turned already to knightly poetry, so now these same regions had remained almost untouched by the wealth of thought, but untouched also by the errors of the doctrinaire over-refinement of our literary revolution. When now at length a few fine intelligences in

Austria became aware of the world of new ideas which had been opened up in Germany, they occupied a position of fortunate freedom in relation to the catchwords of our literary parties. From a distance, more unrestrainedly than the Germans in the German realm, they could discover that which was genuine and great in the powerful movement. Their public was one which loved spectacles and was gratefully receptive, a public whose naive and vigorous sensuality had not yet been corrupted by learned criticism. They had also before their eyes the fine example of the great musicians of Austria, who all held in honour the golden soil of handicraft, and who did not think themselves too good to work straightforwardly for the stage.

It was just at this time that the Burgtheater, under the skilful management of Schreyvogel, began to outsoar all the theatres of Germany. Here the Viennese learned to know the finest dramas of Germany, presented artistically and yet simply; the admirable dramaturge knew so well how to bring even foreign works near to the German spirit by clever adaptation, that such a play as Moreto's *Donna Diana* seemed almost as homelike to the audience as a native comedy. Here there was no field for subtle artificiality. The result was that even Franz Grillparzer was infected, on one occasion only, by the theoretical priggishness of German romanticism. His first work, *Die Ahnfrau*, was a fate-tragedy; the tragical issue arose, not out of the free activity of the hero, but from " intimately concealed and obscure powers." But the beauty of the language and the ardour of the passion, the stormy progress of the action, and the remarkable and precocious security of the technique, make us almost forget the perversity of the fundamental idea. Soon, too, the sound sense of the poet broke completely loose from the fetters of the artistic theories of Müllner. In his tragedies *Sappho* and *Das goldene Vliess* there were displayed purity of form, precision of character-drawing, German seriousness, and the fine and truthful sensuality of the old Austrians—a happy fusion of classic and of romantic ideals. To him, henceforward, Goethe remained the master beloved with childish veneration, and Weimar the consecrated focus of German life. In the historical dramas of a later period of his activity, Grillparzer created nothing greater than the elemental character of Medea in *Das goldene Vliess*; notwithstanding his high artistic diligence he was denied continuous development. Not his one of those mighty spirits which in irresistible progress gradually come to illumine wider and ever wider circles of the world with the light of their ideas ; but his was an amiable and modest artist's nature, he was a true poet, who, even in the days of the decadence, preserved with invaluable loyalty the traditional ancient principles of dramatic idealism, and was the worthy herald of the new German poetry in Austria.

Soon afterwards another Austrian, Ferdinand Raimund, conquered a new domain for German dramatic art. For years, upon the boards of the Leopoldstadt theatre, he had delighted the audience by his masterly acting as a comedian ; and when now in all modesty he devoted himself to providing his little stage with new matter elaborated by himself, he did not produce, as have done the majority of actor-playwrights, pieces carefully designed to draw a full house and possessing grateful roles, but created works of national art. He was the originator of the new fairy extravaganza, and since the days of Hans Sachs was the first German poet who really understood how to enthral the whole population with the stage, and who delighted the masses by poetic works in which even cultured persons could take cordial pleasure for a time. In this child of Vienna, the delight in telling stories was inborn ; from the medley of folk-life he drew his merry figures, having an inexhaustible supply of those genial jests and foolish conceits which the Austrians and the Upper Saxons are accustomed to greet with the delighted exclamation, " Look here, that is really *too* absurd ! " But behind the unrestrained and sportive action, there was the half-hidden humour of a profound disposition smiling through tears. How firmly, too, was the ancient German moral idealism still established in those blameless days of social peace ! Raimund continually returned to the question of what is the true happiness of life, which to the oppressed man of the common people remains the highest of all moral problems ; and ever and again, whether he was representing the spendthrift, the misanthrope, or the peasant as millionaire, he allowed the audience to perceive that happiness is to be found only in peace of the soul. The masses believed him ; the old German folk-songs extolling cheerful poverty had not yet been forgotten. Among the numerous imitators of the unpretentious folk-poet none came near to the master. The folk-comedy rapidly became brutalised ; pithy bluntness degenerated into slovenliness, kindly wit became tedious punning, ingenuous simplicity sank to dulness. It was not until a much later period, during an epoch of embittered political and social struggles, that in North Germany a new form of farce came into existence, which in wit and incisiveness excelled these innocent fairy-tales just as much as it was inferior to them in humour and poetic content.

As far as narrative poetry was concerned, the insatiable passion for writing and reading characteristic of the epoch became a source of severe temptation. Never before had so vast a number of busy pens been simultaneously at work in all branches of literature. The catalogue of the books which the Leipzig booksellers had on sale at the fair, swelled to become a volume of inconvenient size. In every town a lending library provided for the needs of the reading public. The customs characteristic of an old-established prosperity could not yet become developed in this impoverished land; the Germans found no shame in the fact that they read more and bought fewer books than any other people. Nevertheless certain works already secured a sale which was unheard-of according to the ideas of the old times: for instance, Rotteck's *Allgemeine Weltgeschichte*, Zschokke's *Stunden der Andacht*, and the translations of Walter Scott's novels. In the year 1817, Friedrich König, the inventor of the cylinder-press, returned home, and at Oberzell near Würzburg founded his great printing establishment which rendered it possible for the book-trade to work for the needs of the masses. Since people gradually became accustomed to accept greedily every novelty in the domain of science and art, discontent was soon felt with the simple classical education upon whose fruitful soil the new German civilisation had flourished. No longer did it suffice to give the mind a strictly formal culture, rendering it possible, starting from a narrow circle of well-secured knowledge, to develop gradually, but freely and continuously, and to acquire new knowledge through independent work. Under the high-sounding name of " realistic culture," there was now demanded a variegated abundance of disconnected memoranda, which might enable everyone to converse about everything. People were ashamed of the frank admission of ignorance ; no one wished to remain in the background when conversation flitted rapidly from the fate-tragedy to the Spanish constitution or from phrenology to the new English steam-engine.

The alert F. A. Brockhaus, with the secure insight of the experienced bookseller, noted this powerful impulse of the time, and from the year 1818 onwards engaged in the elaboration of an older and hitherto little noticed compilation, to constitute a great encyclopædia which, in a convenient alphabetic arrangement, placed at the disposal of cultured Germans "all that it was desirable to know." This was the beginning of that gigantic *pons asinorum* literature which distinguished the nineteenth century, by no means to its advantage. The undertaking, which was as un-German as its name (*Konversationslexikon*), none the less found acceptance in wide circles, and there speedily followed numerous imitations; this generation, burdened with the heritage of so many centuries, could no longer get along without such crutches. Neibuhr watched with unconcealed disgust the transformation which was gradually taking place in national customs; he foresaw how uneasy, empty-headed, and desultory, how dependent in its modes of thought, the modern world must become, if the empty arrogance of half knowledge and of polymathy, if the desire for continually changing impressions, should get the upper hand. In a world so fond of reading, a refined sense of form speedily became blunted. What was desired above all was material stimulation, and since every epoch has the authors which it demands and deserves, there was to be found an army of busy romance writers satisfied to provide for the needs of the moment, and to have their names current for a few years in the critical periodicals. It remained henceforward a distinctive characteristic of the new century that works of true poetry lay, like isolated nuggets, dispersed throughout a colossal rubbish-heap of worthless light literature, and that they were discovered only after a considerable time amid the masses of inferior matter. In those unpretentious days, however, it was not, as in our own time, the money-making impulse which led so many interlopers to the German Parnassus; it was as a rule vanity and literary fashion. Just as in the drama, so also in the field of romance and novel-writing, those of a truly poetic nature seldom displayed a talent for composition, whilst the virtuosi of absorbing and fascinating narrative just as rarely exhibited the formative energy of the poet.

In consequence of the stern realism of the war, that lachrymose sentimentality which had before been chiefly nourished by the writings of Jean Paul, had for a brief period been forced into the background. Now, however, it regained its sway; in many of the houses of North Germany there prevailed a tasteless, sickly-sweet tone. Many vigorous men of the present generation who grew up in this sentimental atmosphere were filled thereby with such loathing that throughout life they earnestly avoided every expression of aroused sensibilities. The insipid scribbler H. Clauren was the writer best suited to the taste of the great reading public. Fashionable ladies delighted in the heavenly steel engravings and the moving novelettes of the pocket-companions which were then in fashion : " Urania," " Aurora," " Alpine Roses," " Forget-me-Not," or " Evergreen," stood upon the title-page of the elegant gilt-edged volumes. Upper Saxony, which in former days had so often intervened decisively in the mental development of the nation through the activities of vigorous reforming spirits, was for some decades the principal seat of this light literature ; it was as if the " Gottshed-Weisse-Gellert flood " once mocked at by the young Goethe, had again broken over the beautiful country. In Dresden, Friedrich Kind and Theodor Hell, with a few other equally meek and gentle poets, met weekly at a " poets' tea," displaying for mutual admiration and regarding with invincible mutual politeness their dull novels, which were worthy of the Chinese beverage—novels that were then published in the widely-read *Abendzeitung*. Carl Böttiger, most prolific of critics, then hastened, as Goethe said, " to hail as masterpieces the pap of these bunglers and scrawlers."

Ludwig Tieck, who had also removed to the charming town on the Elbe, distinguished himself by holding aloof from this void activity. It was plain to him that the mysterious " poesy of poesy," upon which the romanticists prided themselves, was essentially nothing more than ingenious connoisseurship. Although his admirers ranked him immediately after Goethe, he was numbered among those who *are* rather than *do*. Since in these days he was but rarely seized with the overwhelming creative impulse of the poet, he threw himself with a fine zeal, and with his highly-praised " powers of rapid perception," into the study of the Shakespearian drama. What he effected by word of mouth, and by his pen, in the elucidation and imitation of the great Englishman, was in reality more fruitful for German life than were the shapeless romances and the literary-satirical dramatised tales of his youth, which failed to appear as the ingenuous children of fancy, precisely because they themselves declared with conscious intention that " they were completely unreasonable." How many youthful poets and dramatists gained their first inkling of the true nature of art in the old house in the Altmarkt, when the poet, in his celebrated evening readings, displayed to his hearers, with a truly sympathetic energy, the whole world of Shakespeare's figures in all their abundant vitality. Tieck early attained celebrity, and while still in his prime was regarded as a patriarch of German poetry. The paralytic man with the clear eyes of the poet received good-naturedly and with sympathetic understanding the young men who came to him on pilgrimage, and although his inspired words now and again conveyed strange impressions, his gaze remained ever directed towards the altitudes of humanity; again and again he referred his young admirers to the sacred four, the masters of the new art—Dante, Cervantes, Shakespeare, and Goethe. It was not until after many years that he himself resumed the writing of poetry. Even more than Tieck had the brothers Schlegel become estranged from poetic creation. Friedrich Schlegel was completely immersed in the intrigues of ultramontane policy. August Wilhelm Schlegel pursued his historical and philological studies in Bonn, an ornament of the new Rhenish university; the small foppish old gentleman was always venerated by the students as the representative of a prolific epoch which had given birth to the new science.

It was only in the young poets who had formerly assembled in Heidelberg that the poetic vein did not run dry. No one had wandered farther into the labyrinths of the romantic dream-life than had Clemens Brentano. Half rogue, half enthusiast, to-day high-spirited to the verge of insanity, to-morrow crushed and contrite, a riddle to himself and to the world, the restless man now wandered from one town to another in the Catholic south, and now turned up in Berlin in order to read to the brothers Gerlach and to the other Christo-Germanic members of the *Maikäfer-Gesellschaft* his essay upon the philistines, the audacious declaration of war of the romanticists against the world of reality. He greeted the War of Liberation with loud rejoicing, but just as little as Zacharias Werner could he accommodate himself to the North German Protestant tone of the movement; how strangely forced and artificial seemed his war poems, mostly written for the glorification of Austria:

> Through God and thee, Francis, 'tis shown,
> What Austria wills, she can do!

Subsequently his mystical tendency led him into vulgar superstition; he spent several years by the sick-bed of the stigmatised nun of Dulmen, and recorded his observations upon the miraculous woman in ecstatic writings. And yet the serene, heavenly light of poetry again and again made its way through the mists in which his sick spirit was enveloped. Hardly had he finished giving free rein to his distorted fancy in the wild fantasia of *Die Gründung Prags,* an unhappy imitation of Kleist's *Penthesilea,* when he pulled himself together, and actually succeeded in doing that which men of learning had hitherto vainly demanded of romanticism—in producing popular matter in a popular form. He created his masterpiece, *Geschichte vom braven Kaspar und dem schönen Annerl,* the prototype of German village stories. With perfect justice Freiligrath subsequently praised him in the following words : " Well did Brentano know the feelings of the lowly. No other writer has described so frankly and faithfully that which gives its simple greatness to the mental life of the common people—the pent-up energy of untutored passion, vainly struggling for expression and then suddenly breaking out into consuming flame." No less unequal remained Brentano's activities in subsequent years. The romanticist epicures admired his story of the barn-door fowls, Gockel, Hinkel, and Gackeleia ; they could not prize enough the way in which here an artificial conceit was hunted to death, the way in which the life of fowls and the life of human beings were confused one with another in childish sportiveness. Meanwhile, in his better hours, he wrote his *Märchen,* valuable stories of Father Rhine ; of the nixies, and of the crystal castle down beneath the green waters, pictures displaying roguish charm, as dreamily lovable as the Rhenish summer night.

The far stronger and clearer spirit of his friend Achim von Arnim found no satisfaction in the world of fable. At an earlier date, in *Gräfin Dolores,* Arnim had manifested high realistic talent ; now, in his romance *Die Kronenwächter,* he ventured on to the high seas of historic life, vigorously incorporating with his energetic and invincible realism the figures of German antiquity, displaying all the racy frankness, the rough sensuality of old Germany, the uncultivated rudeness of its camp morals, and the disputatiously defiant spirit of the burghers of its imperial towns, showing these to his readers sharply and clearly, like the figures of Dürer's wood-cuts. Yet even to this favoured disciple of the romanticist school there was denied that orderly artist-sense which controls the abundance of the matter. In his romances, the simple and the rare pass immediately into one another without transition, as in life ; the narrative is choked by a thick brambly growth of episodes ; sometimes the writer loses all interest, and sweeps the figures from the board like an impatient chess-player. Despite all its greatness of thought and all its depth of feeling, his work lacks the balance and the unity of the highest art.

Far greater approval was secured among the mass of the reading world by Amadeus Hoffmann, the only novel writer who in fertility and resource could compete with the busy little writers of the pocket-companions. In his extraordinary double life was incorporated the contradictory romanticist morality, which wantonly broke down every bridge between the ideal and the real, and disdained on principle the use of art to glorify life. When he had spent the day in cross-examining the arrested demagogues and in the conscientious and thorough study of the criminal records of the Court of Appeal, the time came with the evening for the sun of his dream-world to rise. Not a word then must any longer remind him of the phantasmagoria of life, then he passed his time carousing with merry intimates or extemporising with musical friends. Thus inspired, he wrote fantasies after the manner of Callot, such as *Die Elixiere des Teufels*, and *Die Nachtstücke*, weird stories of demons and spectres, of dreams and wonders, of madness and crime—the most uncanny ever produced by an over-wrought imagination. It was as if the devil-faced gargoyles had descended from the gutters of our ancient cathedrals. The hideous spectre came so threateningly close, was so plainly perceptible to the senses, that the reader, as if paralysed by a nightmare, was spellbound, accepting everything presented by the bold humour and the diabolical charm of the masterly story-teller. Yet ultimately of the crazy sport nothing remained but the dull numbness of physical terror.

Whilst in the fields of drama and romance so much that was impish was pursuing its restless activities, the lyrical poetry of romanticism attained perfection in Ludwig Uhland. When his poems were published in the year 1814, the matter-of-fact man was ignored by the critics of this school. This worthy pettybourgeois seemed the very antithesis of the romanticist itch for genius. In Paris he passed his days in diligent study of the manuscripts of old French poetry, spending his evenings silently pacing the boulevards in the company of the no less silent Immanuel Bekker, mouth open and eyes closed, quite unaffected by the alluring brilliancy and the temptations by which he was surrounded. Subsequently leading a simple and well ordered life in his native town on the Neckar, he did not think himself too good to participate in word and action in the prosaic constitutional struggles of Würtemberg. Yet it was precisely this healthy naturalness and bourgeois efficiency which enabled the Swabian poet to keep wisely within the limits of artistic form, and to provide for romanticist ideals a lively configuration which was in harmony with the consciousness of the age. A thoughtful artist, he remained completely indifferent to the literary disputes and æsthetic doctrines of the schools, waiting patiently for the coming of the time of poetic ecstasy which brought to him the blessing of song. He then applied inexorably to his own works the critical acumen which other poets dissipated in the literary newspapers; alone among German writers he exhibited an inflexible artist's pride in retaining in his desk all that was half finished or half successful. His poetic energies were first awakened by the heroic figures of our ancient poetry, by Walther von der Vogelweide, and by those in the *Nibelungenlied*. In the poems of antiquity he deplored the absence of the profound background which allures the fancy into the distances, but an inborn and strictly schooled sense of form preserved him from the obscure exuberance of mediæval poetry. This classicist of romanticism presents his figures to our minds in firm and secure lineaments.

Whereas the earlier romanticists were for the most part attracted to the German primæval age by the fantastic stimulus of the strange and of the antique, what Uhland sought in the past was the purely human, that which was ever living, and above all that which was homely—the simple energy and cordiality of the uncultured Teutonic nature. To him the study of the sagas and songs of old Germany seemed " a real migration into the profounder nature of German folk-life." He felt that the poet, when dealing with matter belonging to a remote period, must give expression to such sensations only as will find an echo in the souls of his contemporaries, and he remained ever clearly conscious of the wide separation between the ages. Never did his delight in the multi-coloured beauties of the middle ages estrange him from the Protestant and democratic ideas of the new century. The same poet who sang so movingly of the heroes of the crusades, sang also with enthusiasm of the Tree of Wittenberg, which, with giant branches thrusting upward towards the light, grew through the roof of the monk's cell; he gladly associated himself, too, with the martial singers of the

War of Liberation, and bowed himself humbly before the heroic greatness of the new-risen fatherland :

> " After such heroic sacrifices
> What are these songs worth to thee ? "

With vigorous scorn he turned his back upon the pseudo-muse of the sugary romanticist masters, of the tricksters with assonance, and of the sonneteers, holding firmly to the saying of the earliest writers, " Plain speaking and good feeling make the true German song." Vivid popular expressions streamed spontaneously forth from this master of vigorous language. So easily did his unaffected verses seem to run, so freshly and serenely did his figures move, that readers failed to notice how much artist's diligence was concealed behind the purity of these simple forms, how deeply the poet had had to explore the wells of knowledge before Roland and Taillefer, Eberhard der Rauschebart, and Schenk von Limburg could be presented in so familiar and convincing a manner. He chose by preference for his narratives the form of the dramatic ballad, so well suited to the passionate Teuton temperament; on rare occasions, where the nature of the matter demanded it, he employed the quietly-recording minutely-descriptive southland romance form. It was not detail which seemed to him important, but its reflection in the aroused human heart. The most intimate recesses of the German temperament lay open to him, and with extraordinary success at times, in a few unpretentious words, he was able to disclose some intimate secret of our people. More simply than in the poem of Der gute Kamarad there has never been given an account of the way in which the contentious Teutons have always been ready for the fray, from the days of the Cimbri to the days of the French wars—eager for battle and devotedly pious, so kind hearted and so loyal.

Even in his narrative verses the power of sentiment was so strongly displayed that many poems which he himself termed ballads soon became popular as songs. It was on account of his songs in especial that he was beloved of the people, who hailed him joyfully, at first in his Swabian home, and afterwards throughout Germany, so that he ultimately became the most popular of all our great poets. In the straightforward, profoundly felt words describing the joys and the sorrows of love, the happiness of the wanderer and the pain of parting, the pleasures of wine and of arms, everyone, whether gentle or simple, rediscovered memories of his own life. The High Germans, more particularly, were reminded of home when from between the lines of the poems there always seemed to greet them the Swabian land with its vine-clad hills and sunny rivers, with its cheerful and song-loving inhabitants. The simple strains, resembling those of folk-songs, involuntarily challenged the reader to sing them ; before long, composers rivalled one another in setting them to music. All the youth of the land followed suit. Uhland's songs were heard wherever German soldiers were marching, wherever students, singers, and gymnasts, assembled in happy festival ; they became a power of blessing in the freshly blossoming and vigorous folk-life of the new century. The younger generation, steeled in war, pressed forth from the imprisoned chamber air of the good old time, forth into freedom ; the German *wanderlust* demanded its rights ; old and half forgotten popular festivals were once again honoured. The new folk-songs threw a bridge across the deep chasm which separated the cultured from the uncultured, and led the masses, who read nothing, for the first time to an appreciation of the poetry of their own day. Even though that priceless unbroken unity of national civilisation which had once existed in the days of the Hohenstaufen remained ever unattainable to the learned culture of the modern world, there nevertheless ensued a wholesome return to nature, so that by degrees a portion at least of the finest German poems became dear to the whole nation and comprehensible to all. How fast beat the heart of the Swabian poet when he saw the joy of song newly awakening among his people ; full of confidence he issued to his comrades the spirited exhortation :

> " Sing who can, your song forth-giving
>   In German poets' forest-ground !
> Rejoicing all and truly living,
>   When songs from every twig resound ! "

The homely man could never have too much of the noisy thronging of popular festivals, and he secured at times the highest reward of the poet when upon a journey in the Rhineland he came by chance in the forest upon young people singing his own songs with their clear voices ; or when a senior student of Tübingen was taking ceremonial departure across the Neckar bridge, and the parting song *Es ziehet der Bursch in die Weite* reverberated as far as the vineyard of the poet's house on the Oesterberg.

It is true that his poems embraced a comparatively narrow circle of ideas ; he sang, as had formerly sung the knightly poet with the golden harp, almost exclusively of "God's love, of the hero's courage, of the gentleness of love, of the sweet may-blossom." In his tragedies, too, he preferred to extol the tenacious loyalty of ancient German friendship ; his plays lack the compelling force of dramatic passion. His patriotic poems do not attain to the vigorous political emotion of his favourite Walther von der Vogelweide ; the fine Promethean impulse to fathom the highest problem of existence, the whence and whither of mankind, rarely touched his peaceful imagination. For this reason, Goethe would hear nothing of the roses and the wall-flowers, the blond maidens and mournful knights, of the Swabian singer ; he failed to recognise that in the writing of songs and ballads no one rivalled him so nearly as did Uhland, and he expressed the acrimonious view that in all this there was nothing which went to the fashioning of human destiny. The Germans, however, had long before tacitly conspired to follow the old master's own precepts, saying to themselves, if I love you that is my own affair. The faithful Swabian knew how impossible it is to convince a master of his error. His own love was unaffected by the old man's injustice. He was never weary of sending Goethe his poet's greeting, and of telling the nation how, long ago, in the golden springtime this king's son had awakened the sleeping princess of German poesy, and how the sculptured foliage of Strasburg cathedral once rustled when the young poet mounted the winding stair of the tower—" the poet who now for half a century has been singing the world of the beautiful."

Although after the age of thirty the taciturn man published few and isolated poems, and was content as a talented investigator and collector to participate in the great work of the rediscovery of our primæval age, his reputation as a poet nevertheless continued to increase from year to year. The songs of his youth could never grow old. Highly cultured and yet inconspicuous ; an enthusiast for the ancient glories of the empire and of the Austrian imperial race, and yet a democrat, to whom " the princes' counsellors and court chamberlains decorated with dull stars upon their cold bosoms " always remained objects of suspicion ; in the political struggle fearless and loyal, as the motto on the national coat-of-arms demands, to the point of defiant obstinacy—he seemed to the Swabians the typical representative of his country, the best of the tribal fellowship. They revered him, declaring : " Every word which Uhland has spoken has been justified by the event."

A crowd of young poets followed in the master's footsteps, and soon came to speak of itself as the Swabian school of poets. Here for the first time in the history of modern German poetry was the attempt ventured at the foundation of a separate territorial culture, taking, however, the form of a perfectly harmless particularism. Nothing was further from the mind of these poets than the intention to cut themselves adrift from the common work of the nation ; they merely felt cordially happy and proud because they belonged to this cheerful land of wine and song, to this stock which had once borne the war-standard of the Holy Empire, and which was more intimately associated than any other with the great memories of our middle age. Amiable serenity and natural freshness were characteristic of the countless ballads and songs of these poets, they remained German and chaste, and continued to preserve the pure forms of lyrical poetry even at a later date when the new cosmopolitan revolutionary spirit, disturbing nobility of artistic form and innocence of mind, invaded German poetry. Yet the marvellous poetical mood of the songs of Uhland was as inimitable as was the roguish humour which enabled him to depict so happily the valiant spirit of the German heroic age. Many of the Swabian ballad-singers gradually lapsed into the rhymed prose of the meistersingers ; their dull amiability could offer no ideas to the new century.

By far the most distinguished spirit in this circle was Justinus Kerner, a man of thoroughly poetic nature, full of droll humour and profound sensibility. His hospitable home among the vineyards close by the ancient castle of Weibertreu near Weinsberg, celebrated in song and story, remained for years the meeting place of all fine intelligences from the highlands. Whoever had been cordially received there by the poet and his wife " Rickele," whoever had heard him over his Neckar wines telling extravagant anecdotes, or had listened to him reciting his brilliant and intensely felt songs, was hardly surprised to learn that even this thoroughly Protestant and modern man did not remain untouched by the mystical tendency of romanticism. Just as Brentano revered the wonder-worker Katherina

Emmerich, so Kerner honoured the prophetess of Prevorst, a sick peasant woman of the neighbourhood, believing that through her instrumentality he could overhear the harmonies of two worlds. That which drove him into these obscure regions was not the anxiety of conscience of an enchained and unstable soul, but the poetical enthusiasm of a childlike temperament which could find no peace in the dry rationalism of the Enlightenment.

Meanwhile the nation first began fully to understand what it possessed in its greatest poet. Ever more powerfully and commandingly did the figure of Goethe rise before their eyes, as the excitement of the war time passed away, and as the three first parts of *Dichtung und Wahrheit*, which were published during the years of 1811 to 1814, gradually made their way through wider circles. Among the autobiographies of notable men, this book occupies as isolated a position as does *Faust* in the realm of poetry. Since St. Augustine's *Confessions*, no autobiographical work had described so profoundly, so truthfully, and so powerfully the most beautiful secret of human life, the growth of genius. To the severe saint, the forms of the life of this world seemed to disappear completely in face of the crushing thought of the sinfulness of all creatures, and in face of the yearning after the living God ; but through *Dichtung und Wahrheit* there breathes the spirit of a poet who finds joy in this world, who endeavours to contemplate eternal love in the abundant life of creation, and who from the highest flights of thought returns ever to the simple faith of the artist : " What can be the use of all this array of suns and planets and moons, of stars and milky ways, of comets and nebulæ, of worlds that have been and worlds that are yet to be, if in the end a happy man is not instinctively to rejoice in its existence ? " As honestly as had Rousseau, Goethe recognised the faults and errors of his youth ; but his secure sense of style preserved him from Rousseau's forced and artificial outspokenness which led the Genevese author into shamelessness. Goethe did not, like Rousseau, lay bare even those half-unconscious and contradictory surgings of sentiment which are endurable only because they are fugitive, and which when subjected to detailed analysis appear grotesque, but gave merely the important essentials of his life, relating how he had become a poet.

Whilst of Rousseau's *Confessions* there remains in the end nothing more than the painful recognition of the sinfulness of man, who oscillates unsupported between his archetype and his caricature, between God and beast, the readers of *Dichtung und Wahrheit* attain to the happy feeling that the German writer has in a twofold sense succeeded in doing what Milton once demanded of the poet, namely, in transfiguring his own life to make it a true work of art. Just as he had inherited talent from his mother and character from his father, and now little by little, but with unequalled steadfastness, diffused his energies throughout the entire domain of human contemplation, imagination, and cognition, so at each stage of his development, did his spirit appear healthy, exemplary, accordant with nature, and therewith extraordinarily simple in all its wonderful transformations. The talented Fanny Mendelssohn expressed the feeling of all readers when she prophesied: " God will not summon this man home prematurely ; he must remain on earth until he has attained an advanced age, and must show his people what living means." Reverence for Goethe was a bond of unity between the best men of this distracted nation ; the higher the culture of any German, the more profoundly did he venerate the poet. The tone of the book manifested the feeling which Goethe had once expressed in youth : that he would not have been astonished if people had placed a crown upon his head. Yet he stood far too high to be tainted by those involuntary tendencies to self-conceit which are found in almost all confessions. The mighty self-consciousness which found expression in these memoirs was the serene repose of a spirit perfectly at one with itself, the happy frankness of a poet who all his life had been engaged in writing nothing but confessions, and who had long been accustomed to answer censorious and envious spirits by saying : " I did not make myself."

Whenever he had intervened in German life he had furnished the highest. Now, too, the figures which he conjured out of memory were illuminated by a spiritual warmth which can be paralleled only by that of the finest of his own free imaginary figures. From the parsonage of Sesenheim there shone a ray of love penetrating the youthful dreams of every German heart, and whoever recalled the happy days of his own childhood, instantly pictured the rambling old house in the Hirschgraben, the fountain in the courtyard, saw and looked into the deep laughing eyes of Goethe's joyous mother. The poet said in the words of his own old man : " We wander among the shades in the form in which we have left earth." To him another destiny was allotted, for so enthralling was the charm of this book that even to-day when Goethe is named almost everyone thinks first of the kingly youth ; his years of manhood, which he did not himself describe for us, are in the shade when contrasted with the sunshine of these early days of his history.

Just as Rousseau intertwined contemporary history with the narrative of his life, so Goethe, with incomparably greater profundity and thoroughness, gave a comprehensive historical picture of the spiritual life of the Frederician age. Flaming up once more in youthful fire, the old man described the springtime of German art, filled with joyful hopes, described how everything was germinating and pressing upward, how the fresh aroma of the soil filled the atmosphere as it arose from the freshly tilled fields, how one tree stood bare beside another which had already burst forth into leaf. How often had Niebuhr and other contemporaries of Goethe refused to admit that the poet possessed the historic sense, taking this view because he was so fond of immersing himself in nature. Now, however, he performed the two highest tasks of the historian, the artistic and the scientific, showing by his work that the two are one. So vividly did he recall the past for his readers that they all felt as if they were themselves living among the events described, and yet at the same time he enabled them to understand what had happened, to recognise the necessary sequence of events. The work was composed in the days of the Napoleonic world-dominion, at a time when the writer seemed to despair of the political re-establishment of the fatherland ; and yet from every sentence there spoke the confident and hopeful mood of the Frederician epoch. Not a word showed that after the recent defeats the poet had abandoned faith in Germany's great future. Even now, when all the world gave up the Prussian state for lost, and when even the Teutonising enthusiasts turned away with indifference from the image of Frederick, Goethe showed for the first time in stirring words how intimately the new art was associated with the heroic glories of Prussia : in Germany there had never been a lack of talented men, but a national strength, a veritable content, was first given to our imaginative life by the deeds of Frederick. Thus the poet had never inwardly become unfaithful to his nation. He said once in those weary days that there now remained only one sacred duty, to maintain spiritual mastery, and amid the general ruin to preserve the palladium of our literature !

It was a terrible misfortune that Goethe had absolutely no confidence in the awakening political life of the nation. Painfully enough did he experience the truth of his own saying, that the poet is by nature unpartisan, and therefore in times of political passion can hardly escape a tragical fate. At times, indeed, he had intimations of a happier future. When the *grande armée* passed through on the way to Russia, and those who were disheartened expressed the opinion that now the world-empire had gained completion, he rejoined, " Wait a while, and see how many of them will return ! " Yet when there did indeed return no more than pitiable remnants of the innumerable host, and when the Prussian nation arose like one man, the poet shuddered at the rough enthusiasms of the " undisciplined volunteers." He never forgot how little the Germans had in former days understood the lofty patriotic sentiments of *Hermann und Dorothea,* and he did not believe that his fellow-countrymen possessed the enduring energy of political will. From the first he had exchanged ideas with the ancient civilisation of the west, and now contemplated with sinister forebodings the passage of the peoples of the east across the peaceful land of Central Germany, the coming of the " Cossacks, Croats, Cassubians, and Samlanders, brown and other hussars." He strictly forbade his son to join the army of the allies, and had then to suffer the experience of seeing the passionate youth, ashamed and desperate, undergo a sudden change of sentiments which led him to display in his father's house an idolatrous veneration for Napoleon.

It was the news of peace which first delivered the poet from his mood of dull depression. He breathed more freely, and wrote for the peace festival *Das Epimenides Erwachen,* in order, after his manner, to unburden himself by a poetical confession. The masses, who on such an occasion had rightly expected a popular and generally comprehensible work, did not know what to make of this allegorical figure ; yet anyone who was capable of unriddling the meaning of the fable was profoundly moved to hear how the wise dreamer, " who had slept through this night of horror," greeted the victorious fighters, and expressed shame for his long slumber, " for by the sufferings you have endured you have become greater than I." This was ˜an admission which put criticism to shame : but it was by ˜no means an abasement, for at the same time Epimenides thanked the gods who during these stormy years had preserved for him the purity of his feelings. Henceforward Goethe looked back upon the War of Liberation with a freer and serener glance, and for the statue which the estates of Mecklenburg erected to Blucher in Rostock he wrote the verses :

> " In tarrying and in war,
> In defeat and in victory,
> Self-contained and great,
> He delivered us
> From our foes ! "

As soon as arms had been laid down he went " to the Rhine's long lines of hills and favoured plains." Two happy summers, that of 1814 and that of 1815, were spent by him in the liberated Rhineland whose sunny life made it seem more homelike to him than any other region of Germany. His heart leapt when he saw everywhere reawakening the old Rhenish cheerfulness of spirit, and the old friendly intercourse between the two banks, and when upon the Rochusberg at Bingen, where the French outposts had so long kept watch, he saw the people assembling once more in a cheerful church-festival. In the pages he penned in commemoration of these happy days, the old man seemed to regain the *joie de vivre* which had formerly characterised him as a Strasburg student. Reminiscences of his Strasburg studies were regained, too, in friendly intercourse with Bertram and the brothers Boisserée. He delighted in visiting the cathedral of Cologne, went to see all the ancient buildings on the Main and the Rhine, and spent a long time in Heidelberg. Here was now to be seen the collection of ancient German paintings which had been made by the brothers Boisserée, with the altar-piece of St. Bartholomew and the great St. Christopher—this was a shrine of pilgrimage for all youthful Teutons and the cradle of our new artistic research. The figures drawn by Dürer, " their vigorous life and virility, their inner energy and steadfastness," had powerfully attracted the poet in youth ; what pleasure it now gave him to be able to admire in the works of the old Dutch painters and of those of the school of Cologne, the industry, the rich significance, and the simplicity of our German forefathers. " How stupid we are," he exclaimed ; " we actually imagine that our grandmothers were not beautiful like ourselves ! " He made a point, too, of his admiration for the *Nibelungenlied*, in opposition to Kotzebue and the other dullards who cracked jokes about the heroic greatness of Teutonic antiquity. To his three friends in Cologne, Bertram and the two Boisserées, " who turned back courageously to the past," he sent his portrait with friendly verses. The Christo-Germanic enthusiasts exulted, for now the mountain had come down into the valley, now the old pagan king had paid homage to the cathedral of Cologne ; they already regarded the poet as one of themselves, and hoped for the speedy appearance of a Christian *Iphigenia*.

How little did they know the many-sided spirit of the man who at this very moment was saying with quiet self-confidence :

> " Who knows not how for years three thousand
> To himself account to give,
> May remain in darkness unenlightened,
> May from day to day still live ! "

When Goethe frankly recognised the sound nucleus of German romanticism, it was far from his intention in advanced age to return to the circle of ideas of his *Goetz von Berlichingen*. He remained the classicist, the man who had translated Benvenuto Cellini, and who in his work on Winckelmann had announced the evangel of the German renaissance. Dürer was so dear to him precisely because this brilliant spirit resembled himself in the combination of Teutonic wealth of ideas with southern beauty of form. The experienced man, who had often humbly described himself as " a man of narrow views," knew only too well how readily the claims of life mislead into an involuntary one-sidedness, and saw therefore with disapproval how the conscious and deliberate one-sidedness of the Teutonist movement threatened to atrophy in the Germans their best good, their free outlook on the world, their frank receptivity. When the younger generation actually undertook to spoil his beloved language by an arrogant process of purification, to rob it of fertilising intercourse with foreign civilisation, he broke forth into titanic wrath. The " discontented, opinionated, and rough-shod " methods of the new generation repelled him—these clumsy unkempt characteristics, this strangely composed and shapeless amalgam of natural Teutonic roughness and artificial Jacobin insolence. It was especially in the young painters who had established their studio in the monastery on the Quirinal, that Goethe speedily noted that inadequacy which is ever characteristic of fanaticism. The fruitful early years of mediæval enthusiasm were over. Now the watchword was " piety and genius ! " Diligence was despised, and many of the works of the Nazarene school seemed as bald and empty as were the monastery cells of San Isidoro. This tendency was strongly opposed by the poet. He did not even grant a word of acknowledgment for the illustrations to *Faust* by Peter von Cornelius, for he felt that the great painter had understood but one side of his poem, and had hardly noticed the classic ideas which were subsequently to be more fully developed in the second part of the work.

Above all, the free spirit of the old classicist was repelled by what he termed " the baby's pap," by the artificial neo-Catholic characteristics of romanticism in its decay. A momentous influence upon the whole later course of German civilisation down to our own day was exercised by the fact that Goethe never came into contact with a free and spiritual form of the positive Christian faith. In his youth he had associated for a time with the fine spirits of the pietist movement, but their narrow outlook was one which could not enthral the man of genius. In old age he never came into close association with the adherents of that profound, broad-minded, and highly cultured Christianity which had gradually ripened during the terrible years of suffering and of battle. Had he done so, it would hardly have escaped his keen insight that such men as Stein and Arndt derived their imperturbable hopefulness, their moral superiority, when compared with Hardenberg or Gentz, chiefly from the energy of living faith. Thus it came to pass that the last and greatest representative of our classic age noticed little of the reawakening religious life of the nation, and for several decades a contempt for religion was in the circles of highest culture regarded as an almost essential index of the liberal mind. The lath-like figures of the painters of the Nazarene school, with their strained simplicity, and the now sugary and now extravagant utterances of the romanticist apostates, necessarily aroused Goethe's anger ; and when he saw the elderly Frau von Krüdener playing the part of the illuminate, of the God-inspired prophetess, his Protestant blood boiled over. The falsification of science by religious sentiments and mystical leanings always remained an offence to him, and he hailed with delight Gottfried Hermann's " critical, hellenistic, and patriotic " campaigns against Creuzer's symbolism. He felt strongly that all our German characteristics would perish should we ever completely abandon our cosmopolitan sense ; he was never weary of speaking of the necessity for a world-literature, never weary of commending all that was genuine and good in the works of the neighbour nations ; and he even found words of approval when Uvaroff, the talented Russian, proposed that every science should be represented only in a congenial tongue, and archæology therefore in German alone.

The new constitutional doctrines met with Goethe's approval just as little as did exaggerated Teutonism. In the simple and genial relationships of life he ever preserved a touching kindness and consideration for the common man, and had a profound veneration for the strong and secure instincts of popular sentiment. He often repeated that those whom we speak of as the lower classes are unquestionably the highest classes to God. While actually engaged in writing his *Iphigenia*, his kindly heart was continually disturbed by the thought of the hungry hosiery workers of Apolda. But in the state, in art, and in science, he displayed the aristocratic disposition characteristic of every notable intelligence, and vigorously defended the natural privileges of culture. In the popular scenes of his *Egmont* he had long before plainly expressed his views regarding the political capacity of the masses. "It brings disorder if we listen to the crowd," such was his answer when the spokesmen of liberalism confidently declared that the infallible wisdom of the people would know how to heal all the troubles of German political life. The un-German characteristics of the liberal journalists, their dependence on the doctrines of the French, seemed contemptible to his German sentiments; their rationalist lucidity reminded him of Christoph Friedrich Nicolai, and at the same time filled him with concern, for he lived in the belief that a culture based upon pure reason must lead to anarchy, since reason possesses no authority. Soon, too, he observed with disgust how the young liberals became infected with the same intolerant spirit as had formerly been exhibited by the heretic hunters of the Berlinese Enlightenment, and how they despised all who held other opinions, regarding them as serfs of princes or of priests. In opposition to these slaves of faction, he maintained that there existed but one true liberalism, that of the sentiments, of the living emotion.

The growth of journalism filled him with unconquerable disgust. He saw how superficialising and stifling was the influence exercised upon general culture by this itch for the news of the day, this unwholesome mingling of idle gossip with political information, how much effrontery and futility would flourish luxuriantly beneath the irresponsible anonymity of all those who sat here in judgment over men and things. "A profound scorn for public opinion" seemed to him the only outcome of the highly prized freedom of the press. Shrugging his shoulders he turned his back upon the idols of the day : " Should one who lives in world history concern himself about the passing moment ? " How solitary, too, had the old man become. Herder and Wieland had passed away, and an ignoble humiliation had disturbed the fine relationship between him and his friend the grand duke. The poet could not endure that a trained dog should show off his tricks " where the crowned darling of the Muses had poured forth the consecrated fire of the inner world." The grand duke, however, held fast to his whim ; Goethe had to give way before Aubry's dog, and withdrew from the direction of the Weimar theatre.

Yet nothing disturbed the free serenity of his nature. With youthful zeal, in his new periodical *Kunst und Altertum,* he defended the classical ideals as he had formerly defended them in the *Propyläen.* In this campaign against what he termed " the new cant of non-art " (*die neue frömmelnde Unkunst*) he was supported by many of his artist friends at Weimar. It is true that the poet stood on the dividing line between two epochs, and the proud and confident tone of his polemic concealed at times a sense of insecurity. Just as formerly Winckelmann had simultaneously exhibited an enthusiasm for the classical sculptures in the Villa Albani and for the frosty elegance of a Raphael Mengs, so also Goethe did not break entirely with his old comrade Tischbein, and adorned a stiff painting by his friend, which displayed little or no natural truth, with commendatory verses of his own ! Yet he remained in touch with all the freely aspiring talents of German art, and greeted with warm praise the first bold efforts of Christian Rauch.

More effective than this critical activity was the appearance of *Die Italienische Reise* in 1817. For a long time these memorials of his Italian journey had been circulated by the poet among his friends ; now, collected and revised, they were published with the deliberate intention of throwing light upon Rome, upon the works of classical antiquity, and upon those of the Renaissance. The Germans were to be brought to share the feeling, the unconquerable yearnings, which had once driven him to the Eternal City, were to learn that he could not tarry even in Florence, how in Assisi he had eyes only for the slender columns of the temple of Minerva, and could not vouchsafe a glance at the " gloomy dome " of St. Francis, the consecrated spot where Giotto's art had once awakened, and how finally beneath the Porta del

Popolo he at length felt secure of Rome. Then readers had
to follow him through all those rich days, the most beautiful and
most fertile of his life : when in the morning the sun rose over
the jagged summits of the Sabine hills, and the poet walked
alone along the Tiber to the springs of the Campagna ; when
amid the vestiges of the Forum, as a partner in the councils
of destiny, he learned to know history from within outwards ;
when in cool and solitary halls he was inspired with the joys of
artistic creation, when his imagination was impressed with the
figures of Iphigenia, Egmont, Tasso, and Wilhelm Meister ; when
at length, beneath the orange trees on the sunny strand of
Taormina, he seemed to see vividly wandering before him the
figures of Nausicaa and the much enduring Odysseus. Again
and again recurs a humble admission from the man who had long
before written *Goetz* and *Werther* that here he was reborn,
that here for the first time he attained to the clarity of vision
and the repose of the artist, that here he first learned to
work on the grand scale. The ancient Teutonic yearning for the
south, the gratitude of the men of the north to the beautiful
homeland of all civilisation, had never found warmer expression.
The impression was deep and enduring. The poet had the joy of
knowing that several of the most talented among the younger artists
devoted themselves soon afterwards to the study of the antique.
It was not the Nazarenes alone, however, who resented the
pagan book; Niebuhr himself and many other men of a worldly
and liberal intelligence were estranged by it. This purely
æsthetic view of the world-order, one which on principle turned
away from political life, expressed the sentiments of the
eighties. Notwithstanding the recent powerful revival of literary
tendencies, such an outlook could no longer suffice for the
generation which had fought at Leipzig and Belle Alliance.

It was only a few years before that Goethe had written
some of his most youthful convivial lays, such as the merry
student song *Ergo bibamus*. Gradually, however, as he approached
the seventies, there became active in him the sentiments of
age, mild contemplativeness, calm resignation, an inclination
to the didactic, the symbolic, and the mystical ; and according
to his custom he let nature have free play. It was in such a
mood that he read Hammer's translation of Hafiz. The impulse
towards the remote which the world-voyages of romanticism
had awakened among the Germans, seized him also ; he felt how
the quiet and serene wisdom of the east corresponded to his age,

and how the natural religion of Persia harmonised with his own love of earth. Yet it was impossible for him to " adopt anything immediate " into his works ; he would not and could not, like Schiller, forcibly take possession of foreign matter in order to refashion it. Easily and gradually he familiarised himself with the forms and images of Persian poetry, until his own ideas came involuntarily to assume something of the aroma of the land of the morning.

It was at this juncture that a friendly destiny brought him into contact with Marianne von Willemer, during his journey to his Rhenish home. It seemed as if to him alone the sad words were not to apply which he had written two years before. " For a man must know, be he who he may, a final pleasure, and a last day." His youth revived in those sunny autumn days when he wandered with the beautiful young woman through the avenues along the terraces of the castle of Heidelberg, and scratched the Arabic signature of his Suleika on the basin of the fountain : " Once again does Goethe feel the breath of springtime and the sunshine's warmth." What now filled him with happiness was not such an overpowering passion as he had once felt for Frau von Stein, but a warm and deep inclination of the heart for a charming woman, who through the love of the poet became herself an artist. Docilely she entered into the orientalist conceits of her friend ; in an interchange of songs with Hatem, Suleika wrote those melodious poems full of sweet yearning and yielding humility which for half a century were regarded as Goethe's finest work. His answers were now full of the play of intellect, now lighted up with passion. In glowing and mystical verses he sang the most delightful of all God's thoughts, the power of that love moving between two worlds, and bringing together those who belong to one another :

> " Allah need create no longer,
> We ourselves create his world ! "

Thus there gradually came into existence the poet's last great lyrical work, *Westöstliche Divan*, a posy of love-songs and drinking songs, of sayings and observations, of old and new confessions, held together merely by the bond of their oriental form. Contentious words are not lacking, for, as the master himself declared : " I have been a man, and that means a fighter." Unsparingly he described the power of the base among men, and in sharp contrast with the unrestrained love of song of the Swabian poets he foresaw that the excessive yearning for song would ultimately disillusionise German life : "Who drives the art of poetry from the world ? The poets !" The key-note of the collection is, however, constituted by a quiet serenity, freely contemplating earthly activity : "Enough remains, remains still thought and love." The artistic prosody of the *Divan,* in which freedoms hitherto unprecedented were allowed, served as an example for the more thoughtful among the lyrical writers of the succeeding generation. Here and there, it is true, there was lacking that charm of direct inspiration which gave all the youthful works of Goethe their compelling force ; certain stiff and affected turns of phrase appeared elaborately thought out rather than truthfully felt, and many artificial arabesques seemed to be introduced merely to increase the exotic stimulus of the general picture. Nevertheless in the *Divan,* in *Commentar über die Orphischen Urworten,* and in the countless sayings of his last years, Goethe unlocked a treasure-house of wisdom which yielded the apt word for almost every vital problem of the emotional life and of culture, a treasure-house which only the present generation has learned to appreciate. Many of the poems of his old age recalled the cryptic runes of Teutonic antiquity over which the heroes might reflect and dream throughout life. At times he ventured into the ultimate mysterious profound of existence, up to the very limits of the expressible, where the articulate word becomes dumb and music takes its place—as for instance in that marvellous song which ever resounds softly through the soul when a ray of heavenly happiness falls into our poor life :

> "Until thou too canst pass this test,
>   'Dying, live again : '
> Art thou but a gloomy guest
> On this earth of pain."

Thus he lived on in solitary greatness, unceasingly contemplating, collecting, investigating, writing, advancing through the finite in all directions in order to plumb the infinite, rejoicing in every bright day of the springtime and in every gift of the fruitful autumn, and rejoicing no less in every fresh work of art and in every new discovery in the wide domain of human knowledge. Schiller's more delicate frame had been prematurely worn out in the hard service of the Kantian conception of duty ; to the fortunate and thoroughly healthy nature of Goethe, his titanic and many-sided activities seemed merely the natural and easy unfolding of inborn energies. Those who were not in contact with him, hardly suspected how earnestly he had taken to heart his own severe words: " He only can work who always works ; soon comes the night wherein no one can work ! " Still less did they imagine what a firm faith in God sustained the notorious pagan throughout his old age, how carefully he guarded himself against forestalling Providence, and how in every chance occurrence of the day he recognised the immediate intervention of God—for thus only to the artist was the divine governance of the world conceivable. And since he himself continued to grow day by day, as if this life were never to come to an end, youth always remained especially dear to him. Even though the arrogant roughness of the younger generation was at times an offence to him, in the end he could not be angry when he looked into the ardent eyes of the inspired hotheads ; and he expressed the kindly sentiment that it would be foolish to demand of them, " Come, be an old man with me." To young poets he knew how to hand on the counsel which he had himself received from nature ; they should strive in the first place to become men rich alike in heart and in head, and should keep their minds open to every breath of the times. " The content of poetry is the content of one's own life ; we must advance continually with advancing years, and must examine ourselves from time to time to make sure that we are really alive ! "

Certain zealous renegades, such as Friedrich Schlegel, ventured to speak of the overthrown old god, but men of nobler nature knew that to attack this man was to abuse the nation itself. When Baron von Stein complained of Goethe's holding back in the Napoleonic days, he added modestly, " But after all the man is too great to find fault with." Nowhere had the poet warmer admirers than among intelligent circles in Berlin. Here the veneration of Goethe became a cult ; the ever-enthusiastic high-priestess Rahel Varnhagen continually announced in oracular speeches the fame of the divine poet. The old man regarded from a distance, and with equanimity, the clouds of incense which arose before his altar on the Spree, and from time to time, in his formal, privy councillor's style vouchsafed a civil answer. But he would not permit these worshippers to draw nearer to his person ; he felt that they were making a pretentious doctrine of that which nature had granted to him in the cradle. In the bosom of the elvish little Rahel there beat a grateful, pious, and kindly heart ; amid the artificial ecstasy of this dilettantist adept and demi-artist there was still preserved a woman's secure sense of what is great and strong ; at one time, and for many years, Fichte had been her idol as well as Goethe. But side by side with such amiable characteristics she exhibited a half unconscious and for that very reason immeasurable vanity, so that her admiration for the greatest of German poets was in effect no more than a source of egoistic personal gratification ; she consoled herself for her secret sense of barrenness with the sublime thought that the great spirit of Goethe, reaching out towards the infinite, had scorned to confine its energies within the domain of philology ! " Why should I not be natural," she asked naively, " I could gain nothing better or more manifold by affectation ? " Yet how little real content was there in all the cultured conversation of this æsthetic tea-drinking circle. Much which was there spoken of as talent depended in essentials upon nothing more than the misuse of the German speech, upon the preposterous apposition of unsuitable words. When Rahel spoke of a nobly conceived and ardently executed piece of music as " ein gebildeter Sturmwind," the circle of priests of the higher culture shouted with delight, and her husband inscribed the foolish phrase in his diary in his most beautiful script. But the old hero in Weimar knew the great gulf that is fixed between knowing and doing. Where among his admirers he encountered creative faculty, he was not slow to thaw. How fatherly was his attitude towards the wonder-child Felix Mendelssohn-Bartholdy ; he rejoiced with the happy parents over the magnificent combination of refined culture and genuine talent.

Whilst poetry had entered the season of autumn, for the fine arts there now came the time of blossoming. As long as the enthusiasm of the years of war lasted, Gothic art was generally esteemed the only veritable German art. Our youth seemed to have turned away for ever from classical ideals, and Schenkendorf exclaimed commandingly : " No more on any German wall must pagan images be seen ! " Many of the volunteers from the east first learned upon the march to the Rhine to know the wealth of form characteristic of our earlier history. It seemed to them that these ancient cathedrals were the only valid examples for the art of the fatherland, and they hardly noticed that in the churches of detested France they everywhere encountered the same " Old German " style. When they gazed up at the old crane upon the unfinished spire of the cathedral of Cologne, they thought with the knightly singer, " that the conclusion of the work had been postponed until the coming of the right masters ! " The crown prince was utterly overcome at the sight of the majestic pile that was falling into decay ; at his instigation Schinkel was sent to Cologne, and declared that to preserve such a building meant to complete it.

King Frederick William was also touched by this mood of the time when, after the first peace of Paris, he determined to commemorate the German victories by the construction of a magnificent Old German cathedral in Berlin. Soon afterwards, in Old Prussia, the demand was heard on all sides that the beautiful grand master's castle of Marienburg which had been so shamefully mutilated by the rough hands of the Poles and by the prosaic coldness of the Frederician officials, should be restored in its antique glories as a monument of victory for the ancient Ordensland which prided itself on having aroused the other Germans to the holy war. Schön, the zealous representative of Old Prussian local pride, was the leader in this undertaking ; it was his hope that this finest of the secular buildings of our middle ages could be made a Prussian Westminster, and that every member of the nation should take his share in the work. The king accepted the idea of restoration ; the thin partition walls which a Philistine generation had erected across the gigantic halls were removed ; above the slender pillars of the refectory there could be once more seen rising lightly and freely the palm-like tracery of the ancient Gothic arches. The decoration of the castle was left to the nation. No money was accepted ; whoever wished to help must himself co-operate in the artistic treatment of a portion of the building. The nobility, the towns, and the corporations of the impoverished province, rivalled one another in gifts, and patriots from all the territories of the state participated. Soon the stained glass windows displayed pictures from Prussia's older and more recent history, for during these years was revived the art of glass-staining which, with so many other acquirements of civilisation, had perished amid the storms of the Thirty Years' War. There, beneath the black and white banner, were figured the knight of the Teutonic order and the soldier of the War of Liberation ; the schools of the frontier-land presented a window showing David's sword and harp and bearing the inscription, " He who is no warrior can be no shepherd." All the most intimate secrets of the romantic generation came to light in these activities; how happy did the Germans feel that they were once more entitled to look the heroes of their great past in the face. It was amid universal rejoicing that the young crown prince held high festival in the great halls of the old fortress, and, after his enthusiastic manner, proposed the toast : "May all that is great and worthy rise up like this building!"

Nevertheless the Gothic tendency in art was just as little able to gain the upper hand as were the Swabian poets in the field of poetry. The ideas of Winckelmann and Goethe still held sway, and nowhere more than in Berlin. Here the best works of the German late renaissance, the palace, the arsenal, and the Elector's monument by Schlüter, the memorials of a classically cultured and yet national art, were more comprehensible to modern sentiment than were the buildings of the middle ages. At this central point of a great but recent history, the return to the architectural forms of the fourteenth century necessarily appeared arbitrary and artificial. Now, too, for the first time did people begin to become familiar with the genuine works of the Hellenes. Winckelmann had formerly learned to know almost exclusively the Roman imitations of Greek art, and had failed to observe what a wide course had been run in antiquity from the Dorian age and the golden days of Pericles down to the second blossoming of the epoch of Hadrian. Since the opening of the new century, the treasures of ancient Greece had been unearthed ; the Elgin marbles found their way to London in 1816, and in the same year the Æginetan sculptures were transferred to Munich. Admiration grew concurrently with the understanding for the antique. At this time too was working in Rome that late-born Hellene who lived as did no other modern in the world of classical forms, and who seemed to have been transferred into this new century by the enigmatical sport of destiny. Yet through Thorwaldsen's mighty spirit ran a strong Teutonic vein. To the hearts of the Germans his art made a direct appeal; they counted the Icelander as half their own ; he had been greatly influenced by the German, Asmus Carstens, the bold rebel against academic art, and from him had learned what was truly living and of permanent value in the works of classical antiquity.

While the Old German and the classical tendencies were thus still engaged in an undecided struggle, a change weighty with consequence occurred in Berlin. During the difficult

years in which the Prussian state was on the verge of bankruptcy, the construction of monumental works of art was
obviously impossible. There was only one artistic plan which
the king could not relinquish. He desired to erect a worthy
monument to his wife, and his sound natural feeling led him
here also in the right path, although he was modestly accustomed to speak of himself as no more than a layman in
matters of art. He longed for an appropriate memorial of his
beloved ; and since he felt obscurely that Gothic, which in
any case to his sober sense seemed unduly fantastical, did not
do full justice to the majesty of the human form, he would
not hear of an Old German mortuary chapel. Schinkel, who
during the years of war was still completely absorbed by
Teutonising views, vainly assured him that the architecture of
paganism was cold, and that the hard religion of destiny of
the ancients could not possibly represent the idea of death
with the loving and consoling serenity of Christianity. Frederick
William had a small Doric temple built amid the sombre pines
of the Charlottenburg park, to constitute a simple and serious
setting for the queen's tomb. Christian Rauch was entrusted
with the execution of the actual monument, Rauch who had
once been in the queen's service, had been introduced by her
to art, and who undertook the work with the enthusiasm of
artistic inspiration and of personal regard. Thousands assembled
when this mausoleum was opened in the spring of 1815, most
of them at first coming only to gaze once more upon the
countenance of the beloved princess. But when they saw the
recumbent figure, the charming form in its peaceful grandeur,
so life-like that it almost seemed to breathe, beautiful as a woman
of ancient Greece, but pious and peaceful as a Christian, every
vein in the hands and every fold of the white marble vesture
treated with the highest technical certainty and accuracy, even
these northerners, to whom of all the arts sculpture seems most
remote, were inspired by a breath from the spirit of the antique.
Year by year pilgrims continued to flock to this shrine.
Everyone felt that German art had taken one of its great steps
forward. The classically trained and strictly formal realism of
Rauch gained a decisive success. The enthusiasm for Gothic
disappeared from Berlin society; even the romanticist crown
prince gradually turned towards classical ideals.

Meanwhile the statesmen had returned from Paris,
Hardenberg greatly influenced by the powerful impressions

received at the Louvre, while Altenstein and Eichhorn had on the return journey visited the Boisserées' collection at Heidelberg. All frankly expressed their feeling that the artistic life of Berlin seemed extremely poor when compared with the wealth of the west, and were at one with the king in the determination that the state must never relapse into the banality of the past century. When Altenstein soon afterwards became chief of the educational system he proposed to continue the work which had been begun by Wilhelm Humboldt with the foundation of the Berlin University, and to make the Prussian capital a centre of German art. Frederick I, inspired with the spirit of a Mæcenas, had always thought first of the glory of the court ; now, when the Prussian crown devoted itself zealously for the second time to the advance of the fine arts, it had at length become conscious of the great civilising duties of the state. It was now recognised that the cultivation of art was a necessary part of national education ; a lofty idea was held regarding the artist's freedom, and it was considered enough to provide worthy tasks for men of creative intelligence without endeavouring to control them in the exercise of their peculiar gifts. But the king's admirable sentiments in this respect by no means corresponded with the resources of the exhausted exchequer. Once again, as so often before, Prussia was forced to attempt great things with insufficient means, and at the right moment the right man was forthcoming.

A universal genius such as German art had not known since the days of Dürer, at once architect, sculptor, painter, musician, and when he took up the pen always sure to use the noblest and most efficient words, Carl Friedrich Schinkel kept his gaze steadfastly directed towards the loftiest aims : to him a work of art was " an image of the moral ideals of the time." Continually engaged in active creation, despising sloth, he spoke of indolence as sinful in times of culture, and bestial in times of barbarism. He was whole-heartedly devoted to his Brandenburg home. When he saw this state resplendent in the pride of victorious arms, and when there came a glorious end to the struggle of light against darkness which had so often occupied his own artist's dreams, it seemed to him that the time had arrived for the introduction into Prussian life of the charm and fulness of a ripe civilisation, and for the transformation of Berlin into a splendid seat of the muses. It was his idea that as Palladio had once stamped his genius upon Vicenza, so might he stamp his own upon the

Prussian capital. In the centre of the town should be the palace, the university, the theatre, and the museums ; round about these, instead of the monotonous lines of lowly houses, there should be grouped stately mansions and charming villas, interspersed with fountains and amid abundant foliage ; magnificent gates in the town wall, and in front of the Leipziger Platz a great Gothic cathedral, a monument of victory of the War of Liberation. But whereas the fortunate Palladio was furnished with inexhaustible means by a race of wealthy seigneurs, and while his native city was placed in his hands like a lump of potter's clay to be moulded according to his will, the Prussian artist had all through life to contend with the enforced economy of the monarch and his officials. "We must put a bridle on him!" said the king with a smile whenever the indefatigable man came forward with fresh proposals. Hardly the twentieth part of his bold designs were carried into effect. What a struggle he had merely to save the dilapidated statues on the roof of the palace which the officials wished to clear away. Instead of the noble freestone which had delighted him in Italy, he was forced for the most part to content himself with glazed brick, and in place of bronze he had to use zinc castings. None the less this poor fraction of his scheme, together with the works of the epoch of Schlüter, served to imprint permanent characteristics upon the architecture of Berlin.

Schinkel soon freed his mind from the Teutonist intoxication of the years of war. He recognised that the multiform culture of our day cannot be restricted to a single style of architecture, and was willing to employ the artistic forms of the middle ages when their use seemed demanded by the position and significance of the edifice. But for his own intimate ideals he found true expression in a new form of renaissance, which adhered more closely to the works of classical antiquity and above all to those of Greece than had done the art of the sixteenth and seventeenth centuries, and yet always understood how to do justice to the sense and purpose of modern buildings. In his first great work, the new main guardhouse, the warlike function of the building was so vigorously and defiantly expressed by the severe, compact, Doric forms, that the beholder almost forgot the extremely modest proportions, and was involuntarily reminded of Sanmicheli's majestic fortifications. When, soon afterwards, in the year 1817, the theatre was burned, and the frugal officials insisted that the old walls of the building should be utilised in the reconstruction, he knew once more how to make a virtue of necessity, and soon there arose between the two charming cupolas of the Gendarmenkirche, above a tall perron, a calm and formal Ionic temple, the stonework adorned with rich carving (for Schinkel's designs involved the co-operation of all the arts)—the entire structure a faithful image of this epoch, so rich in intellect, but so poor in financial resources, inspired with brilliant designs, but perforce in many cases narrow and inadequate in execution.

Henceforward Schinkel was firmly established in the king's favour, and he assumed the leadership of artistic activity in Prussia, although the wings of his genius were continually clipped by lack of means. Throughout North Germany and as far as Scandinavia his classical tendency prevailed. The designs for the Berlin cathedral had to be abandoned, since funds were lacking. His fine monument of victory was however erected on the Kreuzberg. This was conceived by Schinkel in those Gothic forms which were still regarded as characteristically national; it was only in the sculptures with which Rauch and Tieck adorned the columns that the new classic style was given free play. But on all the battle-fields where the Prussian army had fought, upon the windmill hill at Grossbeeren as upon the high tumulus at Planchenoit in the plain of Brabant, everywhere the impoverished state erected the same miserable Gothic columns with the inscription : " The fallen heroes are held in grateful memory by king and fatherland. They rest in peace." Schinkel knew that monumental art leads a hothouse existence as long as the daily life of the people remains unadorned and ugly. He contemplated with pain the bald, barrack style of the dwelling-houses, the wretched furnishing of the narrow rooms. In what a deplorable condition was the craftsmanship of German art, which had once gloriously rivalled that of the Italians ; for every great artistic undertaking it was necessary to summon workmen from abroad, stonemasons from Carrara, engravers on copper from Milan, bronze-founders from France. But he was proud to be the apostle of beauty among the northern nations, and therefore, when in the year 1821 the industrial institute of Berlin had been founded, he issued, in conjunction with the talented technician Beuth, *Vorbilder für Fabrikanten und Handwerker*, a collection of standard types for domestic furnishing, which, in numberless imitations, gradually found its way into every workshop and served to reawaken the sense of form in German handicraft, even though some of the designs may to the modern artistic sense appear unduly poor and simple.

Meanwhile Rauch had established his studio in the Lagerhaus, the old margravial castle, and there, a strict teacher, trained a succession of devoted pupils and skilled handicraftsmen, so that German art gradually learned how to dispense with foreign aid. Just as he himself, without preliminary scientific training, had first become familiar with the world of ideas through the work of artistic creation, so in the case of his pupils he looked only to their capabilities; efficient tinsmiths, stone-masons, woodworkers, steady of eye and adroit of hand, were more welcome to him than young men of learning. Thus sculpture was preserved from that overculture which not infrequently led our poets into aberrant paths.

Rauch advanced with a firm and steady pace in the course he had begun; Teutonist dreams never led him astray. He felt at one with the Prussian state and its ruling house, and it was his rare good fortune to be able to incorporate in his political ideals everything that was dear to him in his works of art. How splendid that the whole nation could once again unite in rejoicing over a great achievement. Whereas in former days it was the rulers only who had from time to time erected a memorial, there now awakened among the people the desire to honour the heroes of the nation. First of all, the Mecklenburgers combined, and made Gottfried Schadow execute a statue of their countryman Blucher, the first great work of the revived German art of bronze-founding. Subsequently money was raised in Silesia, and Rauch was commissioned to design a monument to the commander of the Silesian army, to be erected close by the Ring of Breslau where the volunteers had once assembled. Then the king also demanded monuments for his generals, first of all for Scharnhorst and Bülow, dead before their time. A wide field of great and fruitful tasks opened to the artist, who had simultaneously to contribute to the ornamentation of Schinkel's architectural works, and to produce statues in bronze and in marble, materials he knew so well how to use to the best advantage. His statues of the heroes were serious, virile, and noble, at once true to nature and conceived in the grand style; even that slight tendency to stiffness characteristic of Rauch is not open to serious criticism, for it corresponded to the character of the Prussian army. In his most powerful works, the reliefs for the monuments of Scharnhorst and

Bülow, Rauch attained to a heroic height which our sculpture has never since excelled, displaying with the simplest means and in a few majestic lineaments the whole course of the struggle from the days when the youths of Prussia cut their lances from the stems of pine trees, down to the proud and victorious flight of their eagle over the fortresses of the Netherlands and France. Rauch became the historian of the German War of Liberation, just as in former days Rembrandt and Bol, Van der Helst and Flinck, had handed down to posterity the spirit and meaning of the eighty years' war of the Netherlanders.

Now also the first steps were taken to realise the design of founding a great museum in the capital. The idea had been conceived in the first years of the reign of Frederick William, and had subsequently been considered more seriously when W. Humboldt was minister of education. The king, in order to spare the state treasury, bought from his private purse Giustiniani's and Solly's great collections of paintings, and presented them to the state. He instructed the officials to conduct the negotiations for the purchase in strict secrecy, for the designs of his government to encourage the arts at first secured approval only from a small circle of connoisseurs, and it was feared that in the depressed mood of the public, which was inclined to take a pessimistic pleasure in depicting the condition of the state in the gloomiest colours, the monarch would be blamed for extravagance instead of being thanked for generosity. It had also been proposed to purchase the Boisserées' collection, but this could not now be effected, for the rebuilding of the theatre after its destruction by fire monopolised all available means. But the best pieces of the collection were reproduced by the new art of lithography, recently discovered by Senefelder, and were widely diffused ; they constituted the first artistic adornments of the impoverished German households.

In Rome, meanwhile, the German painters had found an enterprising patron in Bartholdy, a relative of the gifted house of Mendelssohn. He placed at their disposal the walls of his palace in the Via Sistina, for experiments in the art of fresco, which had completely passed into disuse since the time of Raphael Mengs. Cornelius, Overbeck, Veit, and Wilhelm Schadow, encouraged by Niebuhr's approbation, now rivalled one another in the production of finely conceived pictures from the story of Joseph. Cornelius joyfully hailed fresco-painting as " a beacon upon the mountains announcing a new and noble awakening of art," because it once more offered painters a field for monumental works, and because its harsh strength was absolutely incompatible with poverty of spirit or bungling execution. "Art," he exclaimed in the terrorist tone characteristic of the young Teutonisers, "art must at length cease to be a lazy handmaiden of luxurious grandees, must cease to be a trader and base fashion-monger." Like Schinkel he foresaw the day when art, adorning the walls of our towns and decorating our houses within and without, would transform and consecrate the whole life of the nation. With the assured pride of a reformer of national civilisation, he took his way homeward over the Alps when summoned to Munich by the young crown prince, Louis of Bavaria.

The heir of the wealthy Wittelsbachs, a race ever fond of architectural exploits, believed himself foreordained to establish a brilliant court of the muses in Bavaria, which had so recently re-entered the intellectual life of the nation. A pure enthusiasm for art and for the glory of his idolised German fatherland inspired the talented but visionary prince. The diplomatic world related with much headshaking how in Rome he had visited the museums and the churches arm in arm with the dangerous demagogue, the poet Friedrich Rückert ; how he had familiarly hailed the German painters in his own uncouth verses, and how at their artists' festivals he had noisily joined in acclaiming the annihilation of philistinism and the unity of Germany. In all his artistic plans there co-operated an unstable dynastic ambition : he hoped to outbid the Prussian starvelings and parvenus whom he so heartily despised, and by a grandly conceived system of artistic patronage to secure for the Bavarian house the leading position in Germany. What a contrast to the artistic activity in Berlin ! There, what was done was no more than the inevitable outcome of the history and the vital needs of a powerful state richly endowed with spiritual forces ; the works created by great artists in undisturbed freedom all displayed the characteristic of inevitability. In Munich, they built simply for the sake of building, upon a soil that offered little in the way of great memories ; the artists summoned from abroad enjoyed the fruits of a royal freehandedness which contrasted brilliantly with Prussian thrift, but they felt themselves to be in a foreign land and had long to endure the mistrust of the native population ; they were controlled by the capricious and incalculable will of a single individual, who leapt impatiently from scheme to scheme, and who naively regarded what he had bought and paid for as his own work. The peaceful rivalry of the two towns favoured the many-sided development of German art. It ultimately led to the natural result that the chiefly monumental arts of architecture and sculpture attained their greatest successes upon the historic soil of Berlin; whilst painting, freer and less dependent upon the favour of the environment, found its home in Munich.

The crown prince had for years been undertaking excavations in Greece, and in Italy he had purchased everything that could be bought of the best works of antique sculpture. Now, for his collection, which was the finest on this side of the Alps, he had a worthy temple built by Klenze just outside the gates of Old Munich, the Glyptotek, constructed entirely of marble, and exhibiting the massive beauty of southern architecture. The building as a whole cannot rival the brilliant individuality of Schinkel's work, but on the walls and ceilings of the magnificent halls, Cornelius for the first time displayed the whole wealth of his talent. Here, writing an epic in colour, he produced the first of those great picture-cycles in which the wealth of his restlessly probing spirit could alone find adequate scope— grandly conceived images from the world of Hellenic saga. The mass of the Munichers mocked at the crazy building of the crown prince; they did not know what to make of the profoundly conceived symbolism of this artistry of ideas, which for the most part completed its work in cartoon, and almost completely renounced the stimulus of colour. Men of more serious mind admired the way in which the bold idealist had so faithfully reproduced the chaste loftiness of the antique, and who yet conveyed in his pictures a power of passion inconceivable to the ancients; for never had an artist of antiquity created any form so utterly transfigured with misery as was that of the mourning Hecuba. The Christo-Germanic hotspurs of the circle of artists at Rome observed with disgust that their leading representative was approximating in his work to the detested pagans Winckelmann and Goethe, and that the neo-classicist tendency which had originated in Berlin was everywhere gaining the victory. The school of San Isidoro, once so fruitful, gradually broke up; its members returned home, most to devote themselves to a purely ecclesiastical art which lived only in anachronisms. Of the notable men among them, Overbeck alone remained on the Tiber, continuing faithfully to observe the old Nazarene principles.

So well, however, was he able to illuminate by the depth and the warmth of his faith the narrow world of Christian figures which to him was the only world of real existence, that even the Italians ultimately came to honour him as a new Fra Angelico, and it was a delight to the pious convert to adorn with his grave pictures the oratory of St. Francis in the Portiuncula at Assisi. Munich, like Berlin, must have its great gallery of paintings. The Boisserées' collection, which was too costly for the Prussians, was at length acquired for Bavaria. Its principal works, together with those of the Düsseldorf gallery, which during the revolutionary years had been illegally removed to Munich, constituted the groundwork of the collection of the Munich Pinakothek.

Thus within a few years a multiform new life awakened in the domain of the fine arts, and almost all the German courts gradually began to cherish these youthful energies; it was felt to be a duty to compensate the nation in any way that was possible for the painful failure of its political hopes. Even the venerable remnants of ancient German art, which had suffered so terribly during the Enlightenment mania of the previous century, now found faithful guardians on all hands, and when in the year 1820 the town of Goslar had its cathedral, the richest in memories of all the Saxon land, pulled down, this was everywhere considered a piece of almost incredible vandalism.

During the period of German romanticism no other art bore such ripe and thoroughly sound fruits as music, which had ever been the most closely akin to the German genius. In music the sense of form of the Teutons always displayed its activity with a frank primitiveness, altogether undisturbed by the hostile criticism which in other departments so often interfered with the freedom of creation. Music remained faithful to the Germans even at a time when our intellectual life seemed almost defunct; even the arid century which preceded the peace of Westphalia enheartened itself by the thrilling strains of Luther's hymnal. At a later date, when the new national culture had as yet hardly begun, Handel and Bach composed their classic works; until at length during the blossoming time of our poetry, through the labours of Gluck, Haydn, and Mozart, music was in Germany raised to a height which that of no other nation has ever attained. The most many-sided of all composers came to stand by the side of the most many-sided of the poets. Both owed to the mysterious energy of immediate environment a wonderful ease of creation; but how far simpler and more natural was the lot of Mozart. He produced for an audience which followed him with grateful receptivity, and lived in confidential intercourse with the singers and other musicians whose parts he wrote expressly for them. In this way every one of his works became a well-rounded whole; he was spared all the fragmentary attempts and false starts which Goethe in his loneliness was unable to avoid. Music united even more than literature all of German blood in a common joy; the majority of the great composers belonged by birth or by long residence to those Austrian lands which had so little share in the work of our poesy, and found there, above all, the most happy understanding.

Even during Mozart's lifetime there became manifest that opposition between the naive and the sentimental which, based upon the very nature of all the arts, must inevitably manifest itself in their periods of richest development. Like, Michelangelo beside Raphael, like Schiller beside Goethe, Beethoven appeared beside Mozart, an emotional genius who with elemental energy pressed forward towards the infinite almost beyond the limits of his art, a singer of freedom, of virile pride, filled with ideas of the rights of man. His *Eroica* had been dedicated to Bonaparte, the heir of the Revolution, but he tore up this dedication and trampled it under foot when he heard of the arbitrary acts of the despot. Never did he compose more greatly than when he was describing the anciently cherished idea of the free Teutons, the victory of the serene spirit over the obscurity of destiny, as in the *Symphony in C minor*. The composer himself, the deaf master of sound, was a living witness to the miraculous energy of the god-inspired will. He was able to move even the blasé society of the Vienna congress by his lofty song of faithfulness, *Fidelio;* but the ability to follow in its entirety the bold flight of his *Symphonies* was reserved for a later generation.

From the very first, the development of our music exhibited a purely national character, and it was therefore impossible that it could remain untouched by the romantic moods and great events of the age. Immediately after the war, Carl Maria von Weber composed music for the *Sword Song, Lützows wilder Jagd,* and other poems of Körner whose musical setting first assured their imperishability, and kept alive in thousands of youthful hearts the enthusiasm of the War of Liberation. A deliberate advocate of patriotic sentiment and culture, he then undertook the leadership of the newly established German Operatic Society in Dresden, and succeeded in throwing altogether into the shade Italian opera, which the court, after the custom of the previous century, still favoured as the more genteel ; he even summoned the press to his aid in order to initiate his countrymen into the the understanding of German art. Born in Holstein but by blood and temperament a genuine Austrian, he became during his extensive wanderings intimately acquainted with the land and the people of almost every corner of German soil ; it was from the very heart of the nation that he created the first German romantic opera, *Der Freischütz*, a work of youthful freshness, describing so ingenuously and faithfully all the atmosphere and all the haunting charm of the German forest, that we of a later generation find it difficult to realise that a time ever existed when the German woodman did not sing to the strains of the French horn, " What is there on earth like the hunter's delight ? " At the same time German song attained its highest development through the work of a pious and modest Viennese composer, Franz Schubert ; the entire gamut of the most secret moods of the soul was at his command, and above all he was attracted by the gentle beauty of Goethe's verse. Soon afterwards, Uhland's songs found a congenial composer in the Swabian Conradin Kreutzer.

Romanticist music remained completely free from the catholicising tendency by which so many of the poets of the romantic school were affected, and this despite the fact that most of our notable composers were members of the Catholic church. It expressed plainly and straightforwardly that which was common to all ; it realised the ideal of popular art so often praised by the romanticist poets, but truly attained among them by Uhland alone ; and since in no art has dilettantism so good a right as in music it soon drew the people also into free co-operation. Already in the seventeen-nineties, lovers of music had assembled in the singing academy of Berlin to act as choir in the performance of Handel's splendid oratorios and similar works. Zelter, Goethe's unpolished and warm-hearted friend, founded in Berlin in the year 1808 the first German choral society, a small circle of poets, singers, and composers, to cultivate the art of song. Several other North German states followed this example. In the Prussian national army there was no end to cheerful singing during the war ;

Lützow's volunteers had a trained choir, and their example was, after the peace, imitated by many of the Prussian regiments.

Then, at the right moment (1817), Nägeli, the Swiss musician, published his *Gesangbilderngslehre für Männerchor* ; he spoke of choral singing as "the one kind of national life of common interest to all that is possible in the realm of the higher art," and summoned the whole nation to participate in it. Seven years later originated the Stuttgart choral society, the prototype of the numerous choral societies of South and Central Germany. In accordance with the free democratic methods of the highlands, they counted from the first upon a greater membership than did the comparatively domestic choral societies of the north, and did not hesitate to give public performances and to appear in choral festivals. Music became the social art of the new century, became what oratory had been in the days of the Cinquecento, an indispensable ornament of every German festival, a genuine pride of the nation. The love of song awakened in every district to a degree which had never been known since the days of the meistersingers. There was a vivid sense that with this new and nobler form of sociability a breath of freer air entered the national life, and the boast was gladly made that "before the power of song the ridiculous limitations of class fall to the ground." It was through song alone that countless members of the common people received an intimation of a pure and sublime world, uplifted above the dust and sweat of daily life ; and when this valuable gift is taken into consideration it seems of comparatively little account that the vague enthusiasm which characterless music awakens, confirmed many a German dreamer in the disordered enthusiasm of his sentimental political ideas.

Yet it was not in vain that the new generation had steeled its energies in a national war, nor was it in vain that subsequently, at every stage in the development of the new poesy, the return to nature was preached, the return to the simply human. On all sides, the national customs became more manly, more vigorous, and more natural, and everywhere, too, they became unconsciously more democratic ; the epoch of excessive domesticity, of carefully closed clubs and private circles, was drawing to an end. Since the peace, it had become possible to resume the long interrupted practice of travelling. Whilst rich foreigners undertook the grand tour through Europe, whose principal romantic attractions had been indicated by Lord Byron in *Childe Harold*, the easily contented Germans preferred to visit the modest charms of their native central mountains. The crags of the Meissener highlands, which pastor Götzinger had recently made accessible, became esteemed under the name of the Saxon Switzerland. Gottschalck's guidebook to the Hartz mountains was the first to give advice to mountaineers, and after Reichard had published his *Passagier*, the number of guide-books for travellers continued gradually to increase. The travellers of the two preceding centuries had sought out the works of man, everything that was rare and remarkable ; the new age preferred the romantic charms of picturesque landscape and regions memorable in the history of the fatherland. Travelling on horseback, which had formerly been so greatly preferred, became rare, owing to the general impoverishment. When Arndt in youth wandered through Germany on foot he found for the most part only journeymen as companions on the road ; now the poesy of foot-travel had become a delight to cultured youth as well, and the true gymnast must be a hardy pedestrian. A new world of blameless joys was opened to the young men of Germany when throughout Thuringia and Franconia, and on the Rhine, happy troops of students or artists went singing on their way through the summer time. Every ruined fortress and every mountain top commanding a fine view was visited ; at night the jolly comrades settled down cheerfully in the straw in peasants' inns, or they quartered themselves on a hospitable pastor. Guitar slung over his shoulder, August von Binzer, the pride of the Jena Burschenschaft, wandered happily all over Germany, and the young people flocked together in all the villages in order to listen to the playing and singing of the new troubadour.

The political sentiments of the rising generation were gradually transformed by this joyous life of wandering. The young men became familiar with the thought of national unity, feeling at home everywhere upon German soil, they learned that the kernel of our nationality is the same throughout Germany, notwithstanding the multiplicity of the forms of life ; and they looked with increasing hostility upon the artificial barriers which political forms had established amid this single people. Unfortunately the recognition was made almost exclusively by the North Germans. Since North Germany had little to offer in the way of the romantic glories which to this generation seemed alone worthy of regard, the South Germans seldom left their beautiful native mountains. Whereas in the north it was soon hardly possible to find a man of culture who had seen nothing of the land and people of the south, in the highlands particularist self-satisfaction, the child of ignorance, continued to flourish. For a long time to come South Germany remained the Acropolis of hateful tribal prejudices. In the north there were now to be found, outside Berlin, no more than a few isolated fools who denied understanding and culture to the South Germans. Far more often in the south was to be heard the accusation that the North Germans were lacking in kindliness ; many an excellent highlander believed that the lands northward of the Main were an interminable dreary plain, and was of opinion that under this wintry sky the only things that could continue to thrive were sand and æsthetic tea, criticism and junkerdom.

§ 3. SCIENCE.

The mighty revolution of the general world-outlook which had begun within German science since its entry into historic life, the whole contrast between the old century and the new, found memorable expression in a learned dispute whose profound significance was not understood at all abroad, and even in Germany was understood by very few. The greatly desired re-establishment of the Germanic Empire had been prevented by the rapid course of the war. All the more passionately did the disappointed patriots cling to those hopes whose fulfilment still appeared possible under the Germanic Federation ; and of these there was none which seemed so reasonable and so modest as the demand for unification of the national law. Rulers and ruled were at this moment agreed as to the necessity for abolishing the enforced *code Napoléon*. Was the old common law to be reintroduced in place of the French law books, that law of the Roman jurists which the Teutonising zealots regarded as the deadly enemy of general Teutonic freedom ? Was there also to be re-introduced that tangle of local laws whose variegated complexity was uncongenial at once to patriots and to philosophers? The hour seemed to have arrived for the simultaneous overthrow of the foreign system and of particularism by the introduction of a national code. The great basic ideas of natural law had long ago been established by the philosophical jurists of the previous century; if only a wise and vigorous legislator could be found, it ought not to be difficult to apply these ideas to Germany. It was by such views that public opinion was dominated when Thibaut, the celebrated teacher of the Pandects at Heidelberg, in a little work full of patriotic fire, expounded the deplorable consequences of the existing dismemberment of the country and " the necessity for a general civil law for Germany "; he proposed that the future German legal code should be placed, like a state treaty, under the general guarantee of the allied powers. Almost the entire patriotic press expressed its agreement with this view.

Then, in the autumn of 1814, appeared the opposing work of Carl Friedrich von Savigny, *Vom Beruf unserer Zeit für Gesetzgebung und Rechtswissenschaft*, the scientific programme of the historical school of law. Its influence was all the more powerful because even those of contrary view could not but feel that this work did not convey the opinion of a single man, but expounded the well-established data of that profounder and freer conception of national life which had first been elucidated in the talented foreshadowings of Herder aud of Möser, and in the anti-revolutionary earlier writings of Gentz and of Wilhelm Humboldt, which had subsequently undergone scientific elaboration at the hands of Niebuhr and Eichhorn, and had then found practical application in the laws of Stein and Scharnhorst. Among the professors of civil law, Gustav Hugo of Göttingen was the first to take up a decisive attitude in opposition to the doctrines of the eighteenth century. His keen understanding made it impossible for him to rest in the insoluble dualism of the doctrine of natural rights; it seemed to him unthinkable that a fixed and unchangeable natural law could be opposed to the plastic positive law. Consequently he abruptly expelled from the domain of speculation, law and the state as phenomena of the historic world, and put before jurisprudence the task of pursuing positive law backwards through its transformations up to its ultimate roots, and thus learning to understand it historically. Supported by a thorough study of original sources, such as had long been unknown to arrested German jurisprudence, he began to expound the development of Roman legal history, and showed that the much lamented adoption of Roman law in Germany was to be regarded, not as the outcome of chance or confusion, but as a natural act of the German spirit, as a natural outcome of the civilisation of the German renaissance. Hugo the Kantian did not propound the deeper problem, why the configuration of positive law is at once so manifold and so mobile.

It was here that Savigny set to work, Savigny who was master of the wider outlook of the romanticist philosophy of history. With that convincing calm which made the obscurest matters seem lucid, he showed that the development of law was not determined by subjective ideas, but by the spirit of the nations as manifested in universal history. Law does not exist once for all, but comes into existence and continues to grow, like language, with the nations, with their beliefs, their customs, their whole mental furniture. Consequently the body of the laws comes into existence, not, as had been believed during the seventeenth and eighteenth centuries, solely or preponderantly through legislation, but through the continuous co-operation of the people themselves, who actively participate in the establishment of customary laws, and, as their culture becomes maturer, in the deliberate work of jurisprudence. It is precisely in the youngest nations that the law-fashioning energy is the most powerful, that the restricted but vigorous individuality of the law has not yet been atrophied by the indefinite generality which seems characteristic of the law of aging nations. Savigny then shows, referring to analogies in the history of art, that not every time is called to every work, and proceeds to demonstrate the utterly unripe condition of German jurisprudence. How far had German legal science, alike in its richness of ideas and in the development of its terminology, lagged behind the advance of general literature, and how clumsy would be a legal code established with the aid of such defective powers! What we need, said the writer in conclusion, is an organically progressive system of jurisprudence common to the entire nation, based upon a study of existing law traced back to its earliest sources, in order to discriminate between what is still living and what belongs to an outworn past ; herein we shall find the temporarily attainable unity of German law. If this unity undergoes such a degree of independent development as to exercise an intellectual control over existing law, the demand for codification (which among the Romans first became manifest in the days of decadence) will spontaneously disappear.

It was owing to this work that the science of positive law became enabled to assume once more an equal standing with the other mental and moral sciences. In the previous century it was only the ideas of the philosophers regarding law which were received with respect ; the study of actual law had been contemptuously left to the formal acuteness of juristic handicraftsmen. Now the science of positive jurisprudence came to recognise that upon it also was imposed a philosophic task, that it had to teach how the rationale of history is manifested and unfolded in the evolution of legislation, and that it had thus to participate in the best intellectual work of the epoch, whose glory it was to endeavour to awaken humanity to a consciousness of its historic growth and thus to an understanding of its own nature. In the remoter distance, there at length became apparent a still higher task, which Savigny merely indicated, leaving coming generations to deal with it. If it should become possible to demonstrate in every individual case the internal necessity of the configuration of law, to demonstrate its causal interconnection with the national economy and the general civilisation of the various peoples, then, last of all, the laws of legislation itself must be discovered. The little book threw a striking light upon many of the most difficult problems of historical science, which to the philosophical century had still seemed incomprehensible. No one had hitherto shown so vividly how the past continues to exercise an influence over the present even without the knowledge and in opposition to the desire of the living, how the energy and the will of the individual are subordinated to the mass-acquirements of his epoch, how every growth of civilisation necessarily brings with it a certain loss, and how consequently the proud doctrine which was so easily accepted by the age of the Revolution, the doctrine of the eternal progress of humanity, has the value merely of an unproved assertion. No one before had so victoriously refuted the darling illusion of the day, which sought freedom in forms of government. Freedon and despotism, said Savigny, are possible in every kind of constitution : freedom is found everywhere where the state authority respects nature and history in the living energies of the people ; despotism is found everywhere where the government proceeds in accordance with the dictates of subjective arbitrariness.

Eleven years earlier, in his first published work, *Das Recht des Besitzes*, Savigny had written a book comparable with the best performances of the great French civil jurists of the sixteenth century. Now, with his *Geschichte des Römischen Rechts im Mittelalter*, he entered a domain hitherto entirely unworked, disclosing for the first time the intimate connection between ancient and modern law. By the mysterious favour of destiny, which it is impossible to regard as chance, it invariably happens that as soon as definite intimations of a great new discovery are manifested in science, help comes to the hand of the investigator. Thus at Verona in 1816, Niebuhr discovered the palimpsest of the *Institutes* of Gaius ; the classic age of Roman jurisprudence, which had hitherto been known almost exclusively through the scanty fragments given in the *Pandects*, came suddenly to life before the eyes of an astonished later generation. The history of Roman law was reconstituted by a long series of thorough individual researches, whilst simultaneously Eichhorn continued his history of German law, and Jacob Grimm and a number of other young men of talent studied the sources of Teutonic law. The *Zeitschrift für geschichtliche Rechtswissenschaften*, issued by Savigny and Eichhorn, became the forum of the continually growing historical school of law, a school of which Savigny remained the recognised chief and most efficient exponent The compelling force of academic eloquence and the creative energy of genius, so rarely found united, were united in Savigny. Whilst his somewhat haughty manner seemed at first repellent anyone who came into closer contact with the jurist was soon encouraged by the amiable mildness of his judgments, and learned that in science also modest gifts have their place if they avoid unscientific presumption. Advancing along the paths traced by Savigny, German jurisprudence gradually became at home once more in the field of positive law, and after two generations felt strong enough to comfute the master himself, and to demonstrate in actual practice, " the vocation of our age for legislation."

The historical doctrine of law ran absolutely counter to the prevailing opinions of the day. The patriots were annoyed because their cherished dream was disturbed, and profound injury was inflicted even upon the self-satisfaction of the philosophers. Hegel spoke of Savigny's work as an affront to the epoch, and Schön, the liberal Kantian, could never see in the mighty thought-work of the historical science of law anything more than " jottings from chronicles." On the other hand, the bureaucracy of the Confederation of the Rhine listened with horror to phrases about the law-constructing energy of the national spirit, which left so little scope for the wisdom of the boardroom ; Gönner, the Bavarian councillor, went so far in a malicious lampoon as to accuse the adherents of the historical school of being men of demagogic views. In reality, the fundamental ideas of the new doctrine stood high above the realm of party struggle. If it remained true to itself it would be forced to condemn with equal vigour obstinate adhesion to the established order and frivolous attempts at revolutionary legislation, whilst its critical strength and sobriety had absolutely nothing in common with the mystical dreams of the neo-Catholic romanticists. None the less, Savigny could not disavow his romanticist comrades. Just as all the science of that day despised epochs of clear and conscious culture in comparison with the twilit early life of the nations, just as the brothers Grimm preferred folksongs to more highly developed poetry, whilst Arnim approvingly exclaimed to them, " You pay respect to that which no one can claim as his own, to spontaneous growth,'' so also the master of the historical doctrine of law preferred to devote himself to periods of half-unconscious legislation, when law and custom were still but partially distinguished one from another, and when law, like language, seemed to arise by spontaneous growth. The entire epoch was dominated by the æsthetic view of the world, and thus it was that Savigny involuntarily applied the measure of art to law, demanding from the legislator what the writers of the *Xenien* had once justly demanded of the artist, that he should be silent if he was unable to realise the ideal. He failed to see that in political life it is determined by the dictates of hard necessity that the statesman must provide, not what is perfect, but what is indispensable Dahlmann replied to Savigny with good reason when he said : " If the roof falls in over my head, my vocation to reconstruction is decided for me."

Like all the romanticists, Savigny had acquired his culture in a struggle with the ideas of the Revolution, and although as a statesman he was never a man of extreme views, he was unable to do historical justice to this most recent epoch, which itself also belonged to history, and took a manifestly unfair view of the *code Napoléon*. In his detestation of the shallow love of novelty characteristic of the modern world, he failed to recognise that law is ultimately determined, not by the national intelligence but by the national will, which in periods of higher civilisation can find expression through the mouth of the state alone. He did not always notice that the great transformations of national life, which to the historian have an aspect of inevitable necessity, were after all rendered possible only by the will of the doers, by the choice and the stress of free resolve. One who blindly followed Savigny might readily lapse into a dull fatalism, and be tempted to erase completely from history the most priceless energy of the historic world, the power of the will. The saying " A constitution cannot be made, it must grow," the equivocal praise of " organic development," and similar favourite phrases of the historical school, served those inspired with an unreflective love of repose as a welcome excuse for refraining from all exertion. The consequence was that an achievement of German science which should have filled the whole nation with pride, was soon diverted into the sphere of the petty contentions of the day. The mass of the liberals long continued to cleave to the obsolete doctrine of natural rights, and nevertheless in individual cases exhibited more historical sense and a better understanding of the signs of the times than their opponents. The conservative parties adopted the ideas of the historical school more or less in good faith, and looked down with the consciousness of scientific superiority upon the superficiality of liberal teaching. " Rational law" and " historical law " were the catchwords of the two sides in a fundamentally unmeaning dispute which for decades continued to increase the embitterment of our public life, and which at times lost its way in a hopeless confusion of terminology. The rough experiences of the year 1848 were needed before those of one party could learn to envisage history as an eternal process of becoming, and before those of the other party could recognise that in the life of the state that only is rational which has historical foundations. Not until then did the name of the historical school lose the offensive significance of a party label ; not until then did the indestructible nucleus of its doctrines gradually become the common property of all moderate politicians.

Among the pioneers of the new historic culture, no other commanded so wide a circle of history as Barthold Niebuhr. No one regarded with such incisive contempt the literary arrogance of the old school, whose members were learned in books but knew little of life, for Niebuhr was a man of almost universal knowledge, who followed with luminous understanding every European movement in politics, science, and art. The unpolitical generation of the last few decades had esteemed Schiller's romantic historical tales and the experiments of Herder and Schlegel in the philosophy of history more highly than Spittler's objective political presentation ; Niebuhr was not

merely the founder of the new critical method of writing history
(through the brilliant independence of his research, which never
failed to investigate the original sources of information), but
further, he placed the state in its proper position, in the very
centre of the historic stage, carrying out in action the opinion
of the Greeks that the historian must be endowed before all
with a political intelligence. He knew how rapidly the civilisation and the moral energy of a nation withers when it lacks
power to enforce respect from the world, and he described with
pitiless severity the atrophy of the German character that
resulted from the empty semblance of life characteristic of
particularism ; he knew how petty, backbiting, and slanderous
this generation had become, to which " honour is a horribly
oppressive sentiment." In the narrow worlds of antiquity and
of the middle ages, it was possible for petty states to maintain
themselves as transmitters of civilisation ; but to-day " only in
great states whose structure is homogeneous is a full life attainable." He had formed his views of the state from experience
of actual life, from contemplation of the anciently established
peasant freedom of his native Ditmarsh, through journeys in
England and Holland and through prolonged activities as a
bank manager and as an administrator. Consequently he was,
like Stein, a declared enemy of every search for political systems
and, once more like Stein, found the corner stone of freedom
in self-government, which accustoms the citizen to stand manfully upon his own feet, and to learn the art of government
after the manner of the ancients by laying his own hand upon
the tiller. It is of more importance, he said, whether the
subjects in individual communes are or are not kept in a state
of tutelage, than whether the boundaries between authoritative
and representative government move this way or that. Consequently he recognised immediately that, notwithstanding the
Charte of the Bourbons, France was still a despotic land, because
the Napoleonic administrative order persisted unchanged. In
order to warn his compatriots against one-sided and excessive
esteem for constitutional forms of government, and in order to
remind them once more of the sound basic ideas of Stein's
reforms, he published soon after the establishment of peace that
treatise by Vincke upon the British constitution which had
come into existence under Stein's eyes,[1] saying bluntly in his

---

[1] See Vol. I., p. 319.

preface, to the horror of the liberal world, " freedom depends far more upon administration than upon constitution."

His *Roman History*, too, was quite as much a work of personal experience, as a testimony to his powers as an investigator, and for this reason even his contemporaries counted it among those classic books which never become obsolete, even though it may be refuted in every detail. When calling the past into existence he enjoyed the happiness of creation ; and since he could never engage in activity with but a single energy of his soul, he threw all the intimacy of his own passionate powers of perception, all the earnestness of his moral judgment, into the exposition of those struggles in Rome which to most of his predecessors had been merely the dry materials of learning ; every turn of the often severe but always noble and original style reflected the profound movements of a great spirit. He tells us himself that he would never have been able to write the initial volume without an actual first-hand view of the English state ; subsequently, shaken to the soul, he had seen the storms of a titanic epoch break over the country of his election ; through such experiences there had resulted a continued growth of his understanding of Roman history, which had of old absorbed into itself the history of all nations as rivers are absorbed by the sea. Then his diplomatic career led him to Rome. He lived here for years, and although he never overcame his longing for home, his historic imagination, which loved to elucidate the distant and the strange with the aid of the near and the familiar, was continually and powerfully stimulated. The ancient world took form before his senses : in the shape of the fields he could recognise the technical skill of the ancient land-surveyors, in the misery of the modern *métayers* he perceived the curse of the Roman latifundial system in persistent operation ; and when in the Vatican he saw the ancient sarcophagus with the touching image of the faithful spouses it seemed to him as if he were contemplating himself and his transfigured first wife.

Thus the slowly maturing re-elaboration and continuation of the work received that characteristically warm tone which gave the charm of life even to dry lists of figures and to circumstantial critical excursuses. The world of antiquity had hitherto appeared to be something utterly disparate from our own ; but here everything seemed intimate and comprehensible. The historian described the fate of Pontius and of Pyrrhus in the same simply human spirit in which, shortly before, in a masterly sketch, he had related the life of his father, the great traveller, Carsten Niebuhr. To the orthodox philologists of the old school, the bold critic who had disturbed the traditions of the history of the Roman kings was for long a thorn in the side. What a storm was raised, finally, when with statesmanlike insight he traced the necessity of that slow revolution which led the plebs to dominion, and even demonstrated the justice of the notorious agrarian laws. He did not hesitate to apply even to the classic poets of ancient Rome the new doctrine of the romanticists that national poetry alone is truly living, and said in plain terms : " If form can *per se* be fatal, this is true above all of a foreign form ; and for this reason Roman literature was in a certain sense stillborn ! "

Yet, even this free spirit was prone to suffer from a gloomy timorousness which sometimes led him completely to misunderstand the living energies of the time. In his darker hours he would passionately complain that the epicurean *Zeitgeist* of these easy-going days ruined all scientific work ! So sensitive was his temperament that he was inspired with horror by the decivilising forces of the Revolution. In his student days, when reading Fichte's defence of the Revolution, he had exclaimed : "What remains for us but death if such principles should become dominant ? " The son of a distinguished father, and at the same time one of those rare juvenile prodigies who fulfil in manhood the promise of childhood, he was accustomed from his earliest days to the admiration of his entourage, and was renowned on his own account even before he had written anything ; a man of affectionate disposition, he was throughout life on terms of tender and intimate friendship with such brilliant intelligences as Count Moltke, Dahlmann, and Count Dessere. He could never endure the proximity of the common or the base. Is it surprising that to this aristocrat of the spirit nothing seemed more detestable than the power of broad mediocrity which invariably tends to predominate in democratic epochs ?

When he contemplated the political immaturity of his nation and the triviality of the current constitutional doctrines, it seemed to him that for the time being Stein's administrative reforms had gone far enough ; and he agreed with the criticism of the stout-hearted Dahlmann, " organisation and administration do not proceed on parallel lines ; a moment inevitably comes in which they coalesce, to separate no longer." Although he recognised the worthlessness of the Italian governments, and openly declared that Rome had been far happier under Napoleon than under the restored papal administration, when the ill-treated population first ventured to rise in revolt he was overcome by his hatred of the Revolution, and angrily exclaimed that in this country no one but a fool or a knave could speak of freedom. The far-seeing thinker, who was already with marvellous precision able to foresee the war between the southern and the northern states of the American union, showed nevertheless in his plan for the constitution of the Netherlands that the most thorough knowledge of the past by no means excludes a complete misunderstanding of the present. He knew the extraordinary state-structure of the republic of the seven provinces down to its remotest corners and recesses, and he knew why it had crumbled to pieces. But when, in November, 1813, the prince of Orange asked him to write proposals for the reconstruction of the Netherlands, the enemy of the Revolution could not make up his mind to recognise as an accomplished fact the notable transformation which had taken place in the country since the year 1794. The unified state, created by French arms, but for which the way had long been prepared in history, seemed to him to display a revolutionary uniformity; in all earnestness he proposed to reanimate the utterly defunct federalism, and demanded the re-establishment of the old federation of states. Thus historical reverence led him to put forward a scheme which, notwithstanding its profoundly learned character, was just as impossible, and in its essence no less unhistorical than were the hastily conceived constitutional structures of the Jacobin benefactors.

Through Niebuhr's researches the uncritical and unconditional veneration of antiquity became undermined; the antique world was reintroduced into the current of time. Simultaneously a new conception of mediæval history began to prevail. By the philosophical century, the civilisation of the middle ages had been passionately assailed, whereas by youthful romanticism it had been blindly admired; now the attempt was made to understand it. Public sentiment was, indeed, still profoundly influenced by the old rationalism; a considerable lapse of time was yet needed before a scientific judgment of the detested and obscure middle ages became endurable. When young Johannes Voigt wrote his *Hildebrand as Pope Gregory VII and his*

Epoch, he was severely criticised in the press; this faithful Protestant was reproached for the display of Catholic sentiments because he had honourably recognised Hildebrand's personal greatness. Meanwhile Friedrich von Raumer was engaged in the preliminary work for his *History of the Hohenstaufen ;* and just as Schön was working at the restoration of the Marienburg, Stein was devoting the best energies of his old age to the collection of the sources of our primitive history. In the new year of 1819 he founded the society for the publication of the *Monumenta Germaniae.* The distinctive motto of the great undertaking was *Sanctus Amor Patriae dat Animum.* Gradually it produced a line of historical investigators, and thus laid a secure foundation for the knowledge of the German middle ages. But all this was still in its inception ; during the first years of peace it was in Niebuhr alone that the political treatment of history found a classic representative.

All the more extensive was the success of the philologists, who now first gained a clear understanding of their historic task. Boeckh's saying, " There is no philology which is not history," was in everyone's mouth. The philologists fulfilled what the romanticist poets had promised. The time now really came whose coming Novalis had once prophesied, " when in fables and poems there is recognised the undying course of world-history." That bold saying, too, of Friedrich Schlegel, in which the historian had been termed a " skilful prophet whose gaze is directed backwards," now found its justification; for suddenly the remote youth of the Indo-Germanic peoples, which had hitherto been inaccessible to research, was illuminated by science, and from this in turn was diffused a reflected light upon the foundations of contemporary European civilisation. The same tendency of the age which dominated the historical school of political science and the historical doctrine of law, led the philologists also to conceive of language as a continuous growth. They too, like Niebuhr and Savigny, opened a campaign against the abstractions of the previous century, preparing the way for a less presumptuous and consequently freer view of the universe. The arrogant illusion that the great objective course of historic life proceeds from the free preferences of individual men, the belief in natural rights and the universally valid religion of reason, collapsed hopelessly as soon as philology showed that which can most readily be proved from the history of language, that the human being lives only in and with his nation.

Wilhelm Humboldt, in one of his brilliant minor essays, had already given expression to the pregnant thought that the formation of language, like folk-poesy, is completed by the instrumentality of individuals, and yet proceeds always from the whole. To this truth, which in its ultimate profundity unquestionably involves an ever-insoluble enigma, Jacob Grimm continually returned. He showed how the higher forms of poetry issue from the folk-song, " which is of spontaneous origin," and he found in the ancient folk-epic a content which was neither purely mythical nor purely historical, but one exhibiting a fusion of divine and human history.

Here, strangely enough, he was opposed by A. W. Schlegel. The old romanticist could not break completely loose from the rationalism of the previous century, which sought throughout history for evidence of calculation and purpose. Just as he struggled against Niebuhr's critical boldness, so also he maintained in opposition to Grimm that the folk-epic was the conscious work of poets who endeavoured in artistic rivalry to outbid one another by remarkable productions. There was, in fact, danger that youthful German science might succumb to that mythical tendency which dominated the younger school of romanticism. Delighted by the great discovery of the creative energy of the folk-genius, Grimm followed with such joy the dominion of the unconscious, of the spontaneously natural, in intellectual creation, that he almost completely lost sight of the free activity of artistic genius. Weaker heads became utterly immersed in foolish fantasies ; von der Hagen imagined that in the *Nibelungenlied* he could rediscover the myths of the Creation and the Fall.

Yet the clear spirit of Jacob Grimm, Protestant to the core, could not long linger in the dreamy borderland of science, and he soon turned to a province of research which promised incomparably more definite results. In the year 1819, with his *Deutsche Grammatik*, he founded the science of historical grammar. Others had philosophised about language or endeavoured to establish its laws ; he contented himself with studying its growth step by step, and since he had already recognised the primitive unity of the Teutonic languages, he utilised for comparison all the subdivisions of this group of tongues. Here also, influenced by a brilliant suggestion of Wilhelm Humboldt, he established the important difference between the accented root-syllables which contain the sense of words, and the purely formal constituents of the vocabulary. Thus law and life were soon given to the study of the development of our language, which had hitherto seemed so enigmatical and so much a matter of chance. In the innocent, poetic, physically fresh youth of the nation—thus wrote Grimm with artistic vividness—language also displays a sensual energy and obviousness. It loves form for form's sake and luxuriates in the sound of euphonious inflections. But as civilisation matures, language becomes more intellectual and abstract, and aims at clearness and brevity ; the ear is more obtuse and has lost pleasure in form ; the soberer understanding is no longer concerned about the sensuous images which underlie the words, and gradually everything is rejected or polished away beyond what is immediately necessary to make the meaning clear. It will be readily understood that Grimm's poetic sensibilities made him give the preference to the older speech, characterised by formal richness, and that his own style, as the years passed, became continually more sensuous and figurative. Yet he did not fail to recognise that a completed evolution cannot retrace its steps, and he therefore strenuously resisted those meddlesome attempts to " purify " the language which the Teutonising zealots advocated on patriotic grounds, for this, he considered, would be to treat our ancient speech as if it had been a chance product of to-day.

A year after the appearance of the first volume of his *Grammatik*, Grimm discovered the law of consonantal change, and thus at length secured for etymology, which had hitherto been insecurely based upon the recognition of similarity in sounds, a firm scientific foundation. Meanwhile the unresting workings of his intelligence had led him to recognise the primitive kinship of all the Indo-Germanic languages, and he regarded with delight the unending prospect which was opened from this newly attained attitude. If the identical word could be discovered in Sanscrit and in all the younger languages of the allied nations, the proof was afforded that the object which this word was used to denote must already have been known to the enigmatical primitive nation of the Indo-Germans. Thus it became possible to withdraw from the darkness the mysterious national cradle of India. It was possible to ascertain by research what stage of civilisation had been reached by the peoples of Europe before their dispersal, before their westward migration began ; to discover what was common to them from the first, and what they had subsequently acquired in their separate courses. The historical sciences were immediately faced by an interminable series of new tasks, involving the most intimate spiritual life of all nations and epochs. In the two generations which have elapsed, little more than the fringe of the subject has been touched.

Whilst Jacob Grimm, a most fortunate investigator, thus advanced from discovery to discovery, his brother Wilhelm found satisfaction in quieter courses. It was his delight to offer the new generation the works of our ancient poetry in graceful editions with a thoughtful commentary; after the poet's fashion he loved at times to lose himself amid the yearnings of happy dreams; it was through his gentler pen, too, that the fairy tales secured their amiable form. In the two brothers there were incorporated two equally valuable tendencies of science. The elder cared only for learning and research as a form of poietic activity; the younger did not scorn to provide for the intimate needs of those thirsting for knowledge by exercising the function of teacher. It was through their collection of fairy tales that the Grimms secured from the populace that affection which is so rarely accorded to the severe investigator. Throughout the country everyone knew good-natured anecdotes of the two brothers, who needed only to strike the ground with their magic wand in order to bring to light the rich treasure of ancient sagas. People told one another about their deep and tranquil mutual affection: how they walked through life uprightly and serenely side by side, and how, notwithstanding their great love for the fatherland, they would never abandon their snug Hessian home, would never leave the red mountains of the Fulda valley. Both were so unpretentious, and yet were so severe in their opposition to the fashionable idolatries of the day, so clear in their condemnation of all vanity, artificiality, and untruth. It was told how their work-tables stood side by side in the same room, and how with an innocent joy they shared every new discovery. No riddle, no old wives' tale, and no child's lullaby, was too trifling for them; everything derived from the sacred shrine of German speech gained life under their eyes; Jacob was profoundly moved at the sight of any old fragment of the kind. But while engaged in their arduous labours they never interrupted their cordial intercourse with men of worth; no conflict of opinion ever disturbed the faithfulness of their friendships; how charmingly did Wilhelm know how to converse in his letters with the strictly Catholic Haxthausens, while occasionally Jacob would chime in with his deeper tones. It was a moving picture of simple greatness which afforded even to the uncultured some indication of the moral force of living science.

Jacob Grimm valued words only on account of things. His work found a fortunate complement in that of Cari Lachmann of Brunswick, the classically trained and strict representative of formal philology, who valued things only on account of words, and who imposed upon the still rambling youthful science the strict discipline of method. Equally at home in classical and in Teutonic tongues, he was the founder of Old German textual criticism and prosody, an editor of unequalled acumen and accuracy. What F. A. Wolf had once taught regarding the origin of the Homeric poems. Lachmann applied to German epic poetry, and endeavoured, not without some violence, to dissolve the *Nibelungenlied* into a series of independent poems. When August Zeune had presented to the volunteers of 1815 his *Zelt- und Feldausgabe der Nibelungen* [Tent and Field edition of the Nibelungen], a superficial study of Old German poetry became a passion of Teutonising youth. It was fortunate for science that Lachmann frightened away the immature by the seriousness of his pitiless criticism, and thus before long completely expelled dilettantism from the domain of German philology. Meanwhile Benecke undertook his lexicographic labours, and the unassuming Friedrich Diez was quietly collecting the first materials for the majestic structure of his grammar of the Romance languages. Diez, like Lachmann, had been a volunteer with the German army in France ; in Giessen he had often sat at board with Follen and the wildest hotheads of the Teutonist movement, and had yet remained so free in spirit that just as well as a born Provençal was he able to see into the heart of the beautiful language of the troubadours.

The unequal mental equipment of different generations is not explicable by the varying favour of external circumstances alone ; the times educate the genius, but do not create him. Whenever a great transformation of spiritual life has been preparing beneath the surface, a mysterious dispensation, whose counsels no human eye can fathom, gives rise to a highly gifted generation. At the right moment the right men emerge, discovery follows discovery, one keen spirit provides materials for another to work upon, though the former knows nothing of the latter. Thus was it now, when a great hour had struck for the philosophico-historical sciences.

Whilst the brothers Grimm were still engaged in indefinite speculations regarding the common origin of the European tongues, Franz Bopp of Mainz, working quite independently, had already laid the foundations of the new science of comparative linguistics. For many years Wilhelm Humboldt had lived in the belief that the philosophy of language and the philosophy of history must mingle in the profoundest depths of humanity. How often in his letters to Schiller had he declared that language is a living organism intimately associated with the personality of the speaker. He had long known that the peculiar character of individual languages may be chiefly recognised in their grammatical structure ; it was only the burdens of his diplomatic career which had prevented his following up these ideas. Influenced by similar intimations, young Bopp had early acquired a knowledge of the classic tongues and of most of the languages of modern Europe ; he hoped to discover a hidden harmony in the linguistic treasury of our race. The first thing was to establish beyond dispute the genealogical relationship of several languages, and this could be done only by means of the precise examination of a very ancient language which had preserved the character of the lost primitive tongue in a condition of comparative purity, so that in case of need it might itself be utilised in place of the primitive tongue.

Bopp therefore resolved to start from Sanscrit, for the high antiquity of Indian literature was indisputable, and since the publication of Friedrich Schlegel's brilliant amateur work *Die Weisheit der Inder*, the kinship of Sanscrit with the Persian, the classical, and the Teutonic languages had generally been assumed, though proof was still lacking. In 1816 appeared Bopp's booklet upon the verbal conjugations of Sanscrit. In a detailed consideration of the grammatical structure of this oldest of languages, it was shown how the future was formed by the combination of an auxiliary verb with a root syllable, and so on, and the author went on to show incontrovertibly the essential identity of the forms and roots of the verb *sein* in Sanscrit and in the ancient Teutonic tongues. The fortunate discoverer recognised in the Gothic language the link between the Old Indian and the German : " When I read the Venerable Ulfilas I fancied that I had Sanscrit before my eyes." Thus was the ball set rolling, for in questions of this nature it is the first blow which is decisive. A definite starting-point had now been won for the delimitation of the boundaries of the Indo-Germanic group of languages, for the ascertainment of the closer or more distant relationships between each individual member of this group and its oldest sister, and hence for the establishment of the genealogical tree of the nations themselves. Thus in the circle of the historical sciences comparative linguistics gradually came to occupy a similar position to that acquired by comparative anatomy among the natural sciences. The next step was to subject other families of language to comparative study, and to reduce words to their simplest elements ; in this way an ascent might be made to the great problem of the origin of language itself, and an approach to those limits which the wisdom of nature has imposed upon all human enquiry.

In the philology of the classical languages a freer life became awakened as early as the year 1795. Shortly before, in his *Prolegomena ad Homerum*, Friedrich August Wolf showed that the Homeric poems had arisen out of rhapsodies, works of popular poesy which had been handed down and developed during the centuries. Goethe rejoiced, saying that the Homeric light was rising with renewed vigour. But Wolf's permanent significance was found, less in this particular hypothesis (which still left much in obscurity, and subsequently gave rise to numerous tasteless aberrations of an over-refined and over-learned acumen), than in his completely new views regarding the nature and aims of philology. He rescued classical litera-ture from the hands of the æsthetes, and transferred it to the domain of historical criticism ; he demanded of philology that it should become enlarged to constitute the science of antiquity, that it should endeavour in all directions to render vividly realisable the entire life of the classical world. Language and literature were to be conceived as no more than isolated mani-festations of this general life. In his masterly lectures at Halle, Wolf showed how this problem was to be solved.

Among the younger men who adopted this historical concep-tion, August Boeckh of Carlsruhe, the universally loved and outspoken teacher of the students at Berlin, occupied the first place. In the Bacchanalia of the romanticists of Heidelberg he had not lost his thorough-going diligence, but had merely enlarged his outlook and developed his understanding for all that is human. For many years he had been occupied with the design of presenting in a comprehensive work, *Hellen*, the unity of Greek life in all its manifestations. Unfortunately this grandly conceived structure never attained completion. A fragment merely was published in the year 1817, *Die Staatshaushaltung der Athener*, the first successful attempt to comprehend Greek history (following Niebuhr's example in respect of the history of Rome) as life that had been actually lived. Historians rejoiced when from forgotten and overlooked sources the complicated activities of Attic home life and political economy were displayed in their intimate interconnection; but the economists did not yet understand how to derive advantage from the inductive methods of the talented philologian. Among all the historical sciences, political economy had remained the most backward. It still reposed upon the misunderstood theories of Adam Smith, and still fancied that, after the manner of the doctrine of natural rights, it could harness the historic life of the nations in the yoke of eternally valid abstract rules.

A similar relationship to that occupied by Lachmann to Jacob Grimm, was occupied towards Boeckh's circumstantial historical tendency by the school of formal classical philology, which maintained a fruitful centre of cultivation for nearly half a century at Leipzig in Gottfried Hermann's *Griechische Gesellschaft*. Here flourished grammatical study, prosody, and strictly methodical textual criticism. In their distinguished teacher was found a union of everything characteristic of the old Upper Saxon learning : thorough knowledge and penetrating acuteness, unflagging diligence and urbane tolerance, but also a jejune rationalism which refused on principle to recognise the enigmatical night-side of historic life. Both schools had learned from Wolf and had much in common ; Immanuel Bekker of Berlin had also grown up under the eyes of Wolf, Bekker, the taciturn master of criticism, who ably revised the text of so many of the Greek classics without troubling himself to offer interpretations.

Independently of both these tendencies, the high-romantic school of the symbolists, led by Friedrich Creuzer, pursued its strange career. Creuzer's lively imagination was from the first strongly attracted towards the world of the supersensual and the mysterious. At the beginning of the seventeen-eighties, long before the rise of romanticism, this born romanticist was filled with enthusiasm at his home in Marburg when contemplating the lofty Gothic pillars of the Elisabethkirche ; he formed a friendship with Novalis, with Görres, with the Heidelberg circle of poets, but also with Savigny and Boeckh, and advanced into the dream-world of natural philosophy farther than any of the professional experts. Like Schelling, he prided himself upon the inborn miraculous gift of "immediate intuition," which can neither be taught nor learned. This faculty, he imagined, would enable him to discover that natural speech which manifests itself among all nations in mysterious religious symbols, and he fancied that this would reveal a bond of unity between the myths of all ages. His symbolism offered numerous brilliant hints for subsequent investigators ; even the theologians owed him thanks, for he showed them the importance of the forgotten neo-Platonists. He was the first to disclose what a world of misery and horror was concealed beneath the beautiful myths of antiquity ; and he immersed himself with such zeal in these sinister mysteries that little was left to him of the clear joy of life which was the dominant characteristic of the Greek national faith. He also was the first to detect the vestiges of ancient oriental priestly wisdom in the beginnings of Hellenic culture ; but his airy bridge between the east and the west was constructed before the soil for its foundation on either shore had been adequately explored. Notwithstanding the wealth of his learning, the brilliant enthusiast never attained secure results, because he always approached historical facts with a preconceived opinion ; he loved especially to dwell upon the Pelasgians and other unknown primitive peoples, for here the brilliant caprices of "immediate intuition" found free play.

The mysticism of his doctrine aroused the hostility of the enlightened world. First of all, Gottfried Hermann attacked Creuzer's *Symbolik* with his customary dignified calm ; next, old Johann Heinrich Voss rushed into the fray, his fierce battle-cry sounding like a voice from the tomb. How wonderfully swift had been the life of this generation ; how remote now seemed the day when Voss's translation of Homer had been justly celebrated as a pioneer work ! All the new ideas which had since then been given forth by German genius, had passed over the hard-shelled old rationalist without leaving a trace. His culture was still rooted in the Wolffian philosophy, which imagined that the world-all could be comprehended through the principle of sufficient reason. He had already entered the lists against Herder and Wolf ; Kant himself was not immune from attack, for the philosopher of Königsberg had admitted a justification for intuitive belief, and considered that the scientific explanation of the world in the end explained nothing. Now, in Heidelberg, in the world of the romanticist enthusiasts, this prosaic reason seemed to have been betrayed and sold. All the talk about the unconsciously creating energies of the popular spirit was to Voss empty fantasy; and who was to speak to him of dogmas and symbols, when it had been proved that morality alone contains the nucleus of all religions? He was convinced that Germany was threatened by a great conspiracy of priests and junkers, that the two red-headed rascals, Görres and Creuzer, desired to lead Luther's children back to Rome. All who boasted the name of enlightened and liberal shouted in joyful chorus when the angry man launched his rough polemics against the symbolists. It was Voss who first accustomed the liberals to the hateful tone of a terrorism of opinion, which behind an opponent's views sought always for evidence of base designs. In this dispute, right and wrong seemed as strangely mingled as in the simultaneous struggles of the political parties. Whilst Voss and Hermann could boast of clearness and definiteness, Creuzer unquestionably displayed more genius; whilst the two former proved themselves keener critics, the latter manifested an incomparably profounder understanding of religion, of the hidden emotional life of the nations. Upon many of the paths along which the symbolists first hastened with fantastic leaps, the better equipped science of to-day is now advancing with steady stride.

Thus the philologists wrangled one with another, hardly noticing the growth of an enemy common to them all, the mercantile spirit of the business world. Since the exclusively classical education given in the gymnasia was no longer adequate to the growing needs of economic life, after the war a demand for reform speedily arose. To the fanatics of utilitarianism that only seemed worthy of study which was immediately utilisable in business and conversation; the modern preference for superficial polymathy, and the "enlightened" hatred of tradition, played their part. In Baden, a demand for the restriction of classical education soon became one of the principal items of the liberal party-programme. In Prussia, Schön was the zealous advocate of this movement, which threatened the very foundations of German culture, and which was not to undergo mitigation for many years to come.

The fertility of the new generation of men of learning seemed inexhaustible. Almost at the very moment when the historical doctrine of law, historical grammar, and comparative linguistics, came into existence, Karl Ritter created the science of comparative geography. Notwithstanding the great discoveries of the sixteenth and eighteenth centuries, geography had hitherto been nothing more than an abundant collection of statistical, historical, and physical items, lacking all internal unity. No one asked any longer what Strabo could have meant when he demanded for geography a philosophical treatment, and when he expressed esteem for "multiform Europe" in comparison with the simpler coast line of Asia. Not until these days of a growing historical sense did the insight also awaken that the earth is the school of humanity and the theatre of human activities, and that the first aim of geographical science is to learn how the configuration of the globe has exercised a determinative influence upon human history. When Ritter, in the year 1817, expounded these new ideas in the first volume of his comparative geography, he raised geography to the rank of an independent science. There was at work in him the same impulse towards the recognition of the determinism of historic life which finds expression in the works of Savigny and Bopp; and like both these writers he frequently referred to the example of comparative anatomy. The forms of the earth became animated under his eyes as did word-forms to Jacob Grimm. In the different continents he saw the great individuals of the earth; and he taught that every country represents a moral energy, supervises the education of its inhabitants, lives out its necessary history. With enormous diligence, he brought together everything which natural philosophers, travellers, and historians had ever reported about lands and peoples, in order to display, first as regards Asia, the eternal mutual interaction of nature and history. If his work were ever to attain to its goal (and when an old man he continued to speak of geography in modest terms as a youthful science), the entire evolution of humanity would be represented as a locally conditioned natural phenomenon. Men of weaker intelligence engaged in so difficult a path could readily have been misled into a materialistic conception of history, but Ritter was not exposed to this temptation. As a grown man he remained at heart the simple and pious child who formerly at Schnepfenthal had sat at the feet of the good Salzmann. It was not blind natural laws, but the will of the living God, which he hoped to reveal by his researches; a sacred feeling of devotion overpowered him whenever he had an intimation of the profound significance of this sublime undertaking, and he frequently spoke of his book as his " hymn of thanksgiving to the Lord."

Few sciences are so intimately connected as geography with the power and the wealth of the nations. In the dawn of history this science follows always in the footsteps of the conqueror and the venturesome trader ; and even in more civilised times the geographer is dependent on royal patronage. To the Germans alone has it been possible on two separate occasions to acquire a leading position in geographical science by the unaided force of genius. When the Spaniards and the Portuguese were dividing the domain of the two Indies and the old commercial greatness of Germany collapsed, Copernicus came to take equal rank with Columbus. How many circumnavigators and discoverers had since then secured free-handed support from the state-authorities of England, France, and even Russia. In Germany, the land without colonies and almost without international trade, nothing of the kind happened. The nation and its governments hardly looked beyond the poor limits of their quiet home-life. Alexander von Humboldt and Leopold von Buch had to undertake their bold journeys at their own expense. When Adalbert von Chamisso returned in those days from his voyage round the world, and at the sight of the lighthouse of Swinemund was moved to the depths of his soul, feeling he had become a German, and that here his beloved home was welcoming him, it was the Russian and not the Prussian flag which waved over his head. Yet it was a son of this inland nation who now rebuilt the foundations of geographical science ; seldom indeed has German idealism secured a more astonishing success.

Hitherto in the historical sciences Germany had moved far in advance of the neighbour nations, but natural science lagged correspondingly far in the rear of the achievements of the French and the English. For a long time after this date Paris was with justice regarded as the home of the exact sciences. It is true that a few men of leading intelligence, influenced by the teeming poetic and philosophic culture of the previous generation, were enabled to recognise the highest aims of nature-study, to grasp nature as a unity, as a cosmos. In his *Metamorphosis of Plants*, Goethe had given a concrete demonstration that the idea can permeate and illuminate natural phenomena without arbitrarily distorting them. Alexander Humboldt

always gratefully acknowledged that through Goethe he was first
equipped with new organs for the understanding of nature; it
was only because he had once drunk deep draughts at the
source which flowed from Jena and Weimar that he was able
to display such an astonishing many-sidedness in his researches
in natural science. Ritter, too, would never in the absence
of natural philosophy have arrived at the idea of uniting in his
geography all the branches of historical and positive research
in a joint creative work. But to the mass of those who were
less highly endowed, the venturesomeness of philosophy proved
disastrous.

Not in vain had Schelling uttered the bold saying that since
the nature of light had been understood, Newton's purely empirical
theory of colour had become obsolete. Not in vain had the
volatile Hendrik Steffens, still more audaciously, demanded that
nature-study should rise to the level of speculation, and in all
sensuous experience should recognise straightway nothing but
the spiritual. Every young puppy in whose head a new idea
was fermenting now considered himself justified in putting the
world to rights in accordance with some preconceived plan;
Lorenz Oken was only in the fourth term of his medical studies
when he published his *Grundriss der Naturphilosophie*. Respect
for reality was lost, the chemist must not dirty his hands, the
physicist scorned to test the data of " apperception " by experiment. Confused images replaced clear conceptions. In the
tones of the prophet, Schelling spoke of the two principles of
darkness and light, whose pivot is fire. The diamond was a
flint become conscious; forests were the hair of the earth-
beast; and at the equator was displayed the swollen belly of
nature. It is true that amid these saturnalia the good
Oken continued to preserve his delight in observation and comparison, and that he enriched science by thorough investigations
into the developmental history of mammals; but many a fine
talent succumbed completely amid the play of these extravagant
fancies. How much of his youthful energy had young Justus
Liebig to waste before he at length mastered his romanticist
pride and made up his mind to approach the world of reality
frankly as an ignoramus.

Natural philosophy saw in nature, unconscious spirit; in
the forces of nature, the organs of obscure powers of the will;
and endeavoured therefore to demonstrate everywhere the
mutual interplay of conscious and unconscious life. Here, in

the enigmatic borderland of natural science, natural philosophy came into contact with the religious enthusiasm of the time, and with the esoteric doctrines of those thaumaturges and swindlers who since the days of Swedenborg had throughout the eighteenth century busily pursued their activities at the courts. Down to the year 1815 old Mesmer still lived in Switzerland, the wonder-worker whose doctrines Lavater had once diffused through the circles of the awakened. He knew the secret natural energy of the magnetic universal fluid, the veritable vital principle, which was to cure all diseases and even to prevent their occurrence. Wohlfahrt now brought into renewed circulation this half forgotten "evangel of nature." Everywhere appeared sleepwalking women and magnetic healers ; everywhere in the drawing-rooms of the fashionable world esctatic gentlemen and ladies formed a magnetic chain. Hufeland and several other physicians of note were friendly towards the new revelation, but the fashion of the day stormed blindly over and beyond these moderates.

The grain of truth which the doctrines of animal magnetism concealed soon disappeared in the turbid slime of vulgar superstition. A morbid impulse towards the unsearchable led the science astray before it had really made itself at home in the searchable ; fantastical books disclosed the secret of " vital force," which was regarded as a specific substance. Gall's doctrine of the skull also regained numerous supporters, especially now that the court natural philosopher Carus knew how to advocate it in the fashionable world. When young officers entered the military academy of Berlin, General Müffling regularly had their heads examined by a phrenologist in order to discover their special talents. If a portrait painter became fashionable, he ornamented his figures with unnaturally high foreheads, in token of genius. An English admirer once sent Goethe a bust whose head strongly suggested water on the brain ; it seemed to the poet as if the sculptor, from a study of the principles of the doctrine of the skull, had had an infallible *a priori* knowledge what [the prince of poetry looked like. Men of all parties became immersed in this dream-life. The clever Jewish physician Koreff lured the aging Prussian chancellor into the labyrinth of mesmerism ; and Wangenheim, too, the leader of the liberals in the Bundestag, was one of the high priests of natural philospohy. Rationalism predominated, however, in the liberal world ; the faith in wonders found most of its disciples in the ranks of the conservative parties. In France also the two most zealous apostles of somnambulism, Bergosse and Puységur were numbered among the hotspurs of legitimacy. The academic teaching bodies could never completely overcome their mistrust of the fantastic caprices of the natural philosophers: the university of Berlin obstinately refused an appointment to the talented enthusiast Steffens; and for the first time a serious dispute broke out between the state authority and the young university when Hardenberg despotically appointed his favourites Koreff and Wohlfahrt as ordinary professors. Quite undisturbed, meanwhile, about the approval of the great world, Heinrich Schubert pursued his modest way, the most lovable and most guileless of the students of natural philosophy, traditionally pious, as was the custom at home in the parsonage in the Erzgebirge, a worthy example of Christian love and tolerance. When in his thoughtful and amiable manner he wrote about the *Symbolism of Dreams* and the *Night-side of Nature*, the pious were greatly edified.

The figure of Alexander von Humboldt rose like a mountain peak out of the fog-laden sea of romanticist natural science, a peak already illuminated by the sunshine of a new day. When still quite young, pressing forward far in advance of his time, he had spontaneously moved from the æsthetic to the scientific view of the universe. The genuine precision of inductive research, which the natural sciences had altogether lost, and which was first regained by historians through the work of Savigny and Niebuhr, was in Humboldt's blood. So strong was his tendency towards objective knowledge that from the first to him facts alone were valid. He sharply distinguished that which had been proved from that which was merely hypothetical, and nothing distressed him more profoundly than the arrogance of the speculator who will never admit ignorance, who will never modestly leave a phenomenon unexplained. Consequently in the circles of the æsthetic idealists, where reality was despised as a burdensome restriction imposed upon the free spirit, he appeared at first like a stranger from another world. Schiller regarded the brother of his beloved Wilhelm as a mere collector, and complained that this naked, incisive intelligence, utterly devoid of imaginative power, shamelessly supposed itself to have taken the measure of nature. Since that time the Germans had long recognised what a power of imagination animated this genius of empirical science.

Alexander Humboldt was not indeed capable of masterly prediction of the course of research, but his mind was one which could combine thousands of carefully investigated details to constitute a living unity, so that with fraternal pride Wilhelm Humboldt exclaimed to his younger brother: "From that which you have so brilliantly observed, you weave a magnificent girdle encompassing the world-all!" Moreover, Alexander Humboldt stood far nearer to Wilhelm's idealism than Schiller had believed, for the younger, like the elder, found the only genuine content of universal history in the evolution of the human spirit, the sole difference being that, in Alexander's estimation, contemplation, construction, and imaginative reproduction were of less importance than research. Alexander, too, like Wilhelm, could boast of "a free spirit, never restricted by the present," a spirit which ever worked on great lines, and which amid the laborious investigation of details never lost sight of the whole. "He really endeavours," said Wilhelm Humboldt of his brother, "to comprehend all solely in order to search out one thing which is accessible only from all sides at once." Knowledge seemed to him the highest of all goods; all the energies of his soul were dominated, absorbed, as it were, by the one comprehensive impulse for knowledge. Neither love nor any other strong personal passion ever disturbed his investigations; he never chose anyone for a friend who could not collaborate with him in the great work of his life.

Thus the fine and intimate relationship between the brothers remained rather a community of spirits than a league of hearts. Their mutual confidence increased with the years, in proportion as Wilhelm passed from his æsthetic labours to the study of comparative philology, and thus approximated to his brother's circle of ideas. In the friendly alliance between the two, the idea of the *universitas literarum* gained flesh and blood; this alliance displayed to the world the indestructible unity of the exact and the historical sciences, of the enmity between which petty minds are accustomed to prate. Alexander could not probe so deeply into the hidden abysses of the spiritual life as could the weightier and more strongly equipped genius of Wilhelm, nor could the younger brother climb so boldly to the heights of speculation as could the elder, whilst pure mathematics were remote from the direction of Alexander's mind. On the other hand he excelled his brother and all his contemporaries in the wonderful mobility and receptivity of a restless intelligence, which was able to adopt and assimilate everything which men had ever studied and thought.

In Alexander Humboldt the cosmopolitan tendency of the German spirit found fuller expression than ever before except in the case of Leibnitz. He regarded it as his vocation to store up and to master the entire intellectual content of the epoch, to serve all nations as an intermediator of modern culture, as a teacher of humanity. No one understood so perfectly how to discover and encourage men of talent. With unwearied and amiable zeal he gave to all out of the abundance of his ever living and ever ready knowledge. Goethe compared him to a fountain with many jets, under any one of which a vessel may be held to secure an immediate, fresh, and inexhaustible supply. Even the weaknesses of character which he shared with Leibnitz were advantageous to his vocation as intermediator. When like a supple courtier he agreed with everyone, overwhelming all without distinction with a flood of adulation, he unceasingly acquired thereby new well-wishers and assistants for the cause of universal culture, which could thrive only through the work of all. When he enjoyed and fostered his own world-wide reputation with unconcealed vanity, his brilliant name served him as a means to direct the attention of the great ones of the earth to the value of the innumerable scientific undertakings he supported with cordial advocacy. In case of need he intervened on behalf of the threatened freedom of research far more courageously than had Leibnitz, and whilst the whole world paid him homage, at heart he always remained a German. No one knew better than he the defects of our young civilisation, our poverty and pettiness, and he watched with quiet joy how step by step the Germans approximated more closely to the older civilisation of the neighbour peoples.

Like all great travellers he began in early childhood to yearn for the immeasurably remote. When in the palm-house at Potsdam he looked up at the magnificent expanse of fans, the wonder-world of the tropics rose alluringly before his vision. The boy's dreams were gloriously fulfilled by the man. Accompanied by his faithful comrade Bonpland, he wandered during five rich years through the interior of South and Central America ; the friends climbed Chimborazo, and passed many months, cut off from the world, in the untrodden primæval forest of the Orinoco. When Humboldt returned, he was the one and only German who in those Napoleonic days acquired the undivided admiration of the foreign world. Even among the French conquerors his reputation maintained the honour of the German name ; Bonpland's fellow countrymen could find no higher praise for their compatriot than to describe him as the collaborator of the German investigator. Humboldt now settled in Paris, where intercourse with Laplace, Arago, Cuvier, and Gay-Lussac offered him a fruitful exchange of ideas, such as a student of nature could as yet find nowhere in Germany. All thronged round the bewitching conversationist, when he appeared in the salon at the close of a laborious day, and when by brilliant observations, anecdotes of travel, novelties of the day, and mischievous jokes, he entertained the company far into the night.

His repute rose still higher when intercourse between France and Germany revived after the war. He was now regarded by the Parisians as the natural representative of German science ; on the Seine all his fellow countrymen sought his protection, and his favourable word was often of more account than that of the official diplomats. In twenty-nine great volumes he gradually communicated to the world the results of his American travels. The record of his journey was an unrivalled specimen of strictly scientific descriptive work. Here were first demonstrated the geognostic differences between the two hemispheres; here first was taught the drawing of geographical sections displaying elevation, and how to determine the mean altitude of continents, the astonished readers being shown how trifling is the elevation of the mountains in comparison with the general elevation of the mainland. Humboldt founded the science of the geography of plants, and by the recognition of isotherms (1817) he opened the road for the new science of meteorology. In discovery and inventive genius Humboldt was rivalled by some of his Parisian friends, but not one of them could command so wide an outlook. The same man who astonished experts by the detailed precision of his barometrical observations of altitude, was the first to give historians an insight into the civilisation of the American aborigines, and also a clear picture of Spanish colonial policy ; and, like Boeckh, he put the political economists to shame by a masterpiece of comparative statistics, his investigations into the available supply of the precious metals. To Humboldt's example and personal instruction, Ritter, too, owed his first intimations regarding the true task of geography.

Like Humboldt, his fellow countryman Leopold von Buch

had amid the philosophical intoxication of the time retained desire and energy for the observation of reality. He also was an aristocrat, preserved by great wealth from the pettiness of the life of German learning, but was of an utterly different disposition from the brilliant conversationist of the Parisian salons—an untutored genius, candid, solid, blunt, a plain-spoken junker of the Mark. The vigorous pedestrian was at home in all the mountainous corners of Europe from Lapland to the Abruzzi; the minute ramifications of the mountains along the much indented fiord of Christiania stood up as clearly before his eyes as the modest sand-hills of his native Fläming. Through his work and that of Humboldt geology was completely transformed: they refuted the Neptunian theory of their common teacher Werner, and proved the Plutonic origin of the highest mountains. Goethe was distressed to see how his beloved "realm of Poseidon" was thus demolished by the "mad inrush" of Plutonism. The poet's love of earth was rooted in his emotions. High as he stood above the fantastic imaginings of the great mass of natural philosophers, it was his poetical view of the universe which impelled him to the study of nature. Not wholly without preconceptions did he approach geology and the theory of colour, and however faithfully he observed every natural phenomenon, ultimately he could accept nothing as proved which conflicted with the fundamental conceptions of his imperturbable wisdom of life. The Plutonic theory seemed to him sinister, for he felt that the vesture of earth must have been slowly formed, without any sudden cataclysms, out of the moisture of life.

If German nature-study could but succeed in restraining philosophy within its proper bounds, it might well hope to overtake the science of the neighbour nations. There was now no lack of men of talent. Meckel of Halle had in comparative anatomy now advanced far beyond Cuvier; Soemmering of Munich had as early as 1810 maintained the possibility of the electric telegraph; whilst in Göttingen the mathematician Gauss was already at work—despising the drudgery of teaching, completely immersed in the ultimate problems of pure theory, one to whom even Humboldt looked up with profound respect, a man of all time, one of those thinkers whose work first secures full appreciation in the life of subsequent generations. He knew that mathematics was the queen of the sciences and that his theory of numbers was the queen of mathematics.

When in those days Hegel gave utterance to the saying that philosophy brings forth ideas suited to the epoch, he had at any rate rightly understood the character of his own time. The powerful influence of the ideas of Schelling is displayed in almost all the intellectual work of his day, alike in the fantastic aberrations of natural science and in the fruitful discoveries of the historian. His philosophical doctrines continued to dominate German thought until in the twenties they were dethroned by Hegel's system; even the peculiarly dignified demeanour of this generation of learned men recalls the example of the proud philosopher who so masterfully expelled the profane from the threshold of the temple. In fact for the thinkers' pride of the Germans it was hardly possible to furnish greater satisfaction than was furnished by the teaching of this ever impressionable spirit who maintained the identity of the real and of the ideal, explaining nature as spirit made visible, and spirit as nature invisible. The great problem of German philosophy seemed to have been solved, the identity of being and thinking to have been finally established. Fichte had seen in nature no more than the stage for the ego, without elucidating nature's independent life; Schelling undertook to show the twofold revelation of God in the concurrent spheres of nature and history. In this way everything that was and is to be became to him a living unity; in the endless succession of phenomena, the divine self-consciousness was unfolded. " From the first wrestling of obscure forces down to the outpouring of the highest juices of life there is at work an energy, a mutual interplay, an unceasing impulse towards higher life." When compared with Fichte's one-sided idealism, this all-embracing system seemed to exhibit the same magnificent superiority as did the figure of Goethe beside that of Schiller—so long as the observer failed to notice that the great edifice of thought was not based on any secure foundation of proof, but reposed merely upon the bold assumptions of a brilliant intelligence.

With Schelling began that morbid insolence of speculation which was subsequently carried to a climax by Hegel, and which was to become extremely deleterious to the austerity of our science and even to the probity of our nation. Rejoicing in its brilliant success, philosophy soon overstepped the secure boundaries which the Kantian criticism had established. Scorning to restrict itself to the province of enquiry and examination, not content, as the love of wisdom, to occupy the

domain allotted to it by the ancients, philosophy now maintained itself to be one with its own object, with primal knowledge, to be one with morality, one even with poesy, from
which it had sprung, and to which it would ultimately return.
Whoever had attained to this lofty conception of the universe
no longer needed those proofs which the men of atomistic
learning had laboriously excavated from the mine-shafts of the
empirical world; from the contemplation of this conception he
gained energy for the direct creation of nature, for the animation
of its mechanism with freedom.

During his stay in Jena, Schelling had for a long time
devoted himself entirely to the development of his system of
natural philosophy. It was not until in the year 1803 he
delivered his brilliant lectures upon *The Method of Academic
Study*, that he turned to consider the second revelation of God,
the world of history. A happy instinct held him in harmony
with the general movement of the time. He now recognised
" that religion, the public belief, life in the state, is the point
round which everything moves "; and subsequently, in Würzburg, Erlangen, and Munich, he worked at the foundation of his
" historical philosophy." Natural philosophy was henceforward
left to his pupils, and soon degenerated completely into
mystical and magical trifling. Ennemoser, the thaumaturge,
foresaw the speedy coming of the day when the priests, the
fortunate and exclusive possessors of the magnetic art of
healing, would once more rule the people body and soul. The
master himself, however, entering the historic world, attained to
the most fertile and soundest idea of his life; to his artist
spirit there truly came moments of illumination in which the
nature of things became directly manifest to his eyes.

From the contemplation of the eternal development of
historic life he derived with definite assurance that of which
Herder had had no more than a shadowy intimation, the
knowledge that law and religion are to be understood as manifestations of the world-constructive intelligence, and therefore
as necessary growths. The completed world of history was found
by him in the state, the great work of art which, lifted high
above the individual will, was an end in itself, realising the
harmony of necessity and freedom in the external life of reality.
Many valuable sayings enable us to recognise how profoundly he
had entered into the inner life of history. To his century,
proud of its culture, he uttered the warning: " An enlightened

nation for which thought has become a universal solvent, when getting rid of obscurity foregoes also strength, and loses that barbaric principle which is the basis of all greatness and beauty." But his philosophy of history was never completed. The early acquirement of fame had in youth frequently misled him into hasty production, and now that he had attained to maturity this inclined him to a cautious silence. His proud spirit could satisfy itself and a wondering world in no other way than by the production of a perfect work. Again and again, amid the scornful cries of his liberal opponents, he exclaimed, " Now will be seen what I have to say"; again and again was his great work upon the epoch announced but it was never completed. For in the long run the hard facts of history were uncongenial to his restless imagination. Of all the epochs in world-history that of " the future," which gives such free scope for foreshadowing and prophecy, attracted him far more power- fully than did the world of actual history. More than all, he loved to devote himself to the contemplation of " the primæval age," describing, in sharp contrast to the absolute faith in progress displayed by the apostles of " enlightenment," how in that epoch of primitive innocence fortunate mankind had absorbed the secrets of religion from the instruction of lofty spirits. Before long the inconstant man thrust history aside to lose himself in the theosophical problems of the philosophy of revelation. His ideas upon the history of philosophy lived on, however, in the works of Savigny, Ritter, and Creuzer.

Schelling, even when his fancy roamed into the infinite, could never completely repudiate the mentality of the Swabian Protestant. In the " Christian philosophy " of the Bavarian Franz Baader, on the other hand, was revived all the bondage of mediæval scholasticism. The brilliant eccentric accepted Catholic dogma as at once the precondition and the goal of his thought, and yet attacked the papacy and the Jesuits just as passionately as he attacked liberalism, the enlightenment, and the omnipotence of the state ; he considered that he had discovered the mystical triangle, the true Catholicism, in the union of the Roman, the Greek, and the Protestant churches. He thought out a dynamic philosophy which was to replace what he regarded as the mechanical systems of his predecessors. For the ethics of Kant, not based upon the teaching of the Saviour, and therefore ncapable of bringing salvation, he pro- posed to substitute a new system of ethics, based upon physics and religion; and although he refuted with apt phrases many of the aberrations of superficial liberal reasoning, he involved himself in such a tangle of magic ideas, that even Steffens, most enthusiastic and faithful of romanticists, found it impossible to accept the grotesque imaginings of the Munich mystagogue. Just as at one time he had incited Czar Alexander to found the Holy Alliance, so throughout life he sought salvation for the nations in an obscure mingling of religious and political ideas; his ideal of the state was "genuine theocracy." From Kant, most German of philosophers, romanticist extravagance turned away in alarm. In place of Kant, Jacob Boehme was once again honoured as the *philosophus teutonicus*, Boehme, the thoughtful theosophist enthusiast, who had long before preached to the disorderly generation of the Thirty Years' War his mystical "Everywhere canst thou see God!" In the spring campaign of 1813, when Fouqué's regiment was engaged in a skirmish near Landskrone, the romanticist poet exclaimed in ecstasy: "Here it would be sweet to die, in view of this sacred mountain upon whose summit God Almighty first appeared to the shoemaker of Görlitz.

Whither had they vanished, those days of the all-powerful enlightenment, when the conflicting creeds seemed about to expire, when all ecclesiastical life seemed overgrown by temporal culture, and when the possible disappearance of Christianity was discussed with philosophic unconcern by its friends and its enemies alike! The shattering experiences of the epoch of the Revolution had reawakened the religious sentiment slumbering in every nation; but together with the living faith there reawakened hierarchical aims which had long been supposed extinct, and the gloomy passions of religious hatred, fanaticism, and superstition were revived. With each successive year, the new century proved to be in sharper contrast with its predecessor, to be an epoch of unending religious contentions, confused and riven asunder to a degree which had hardly been exceeded by any other century in religious history. It was rich in healthy spiritual life, but was no less rich in unbelief, worldly-mindedness, indifference, and despair; it was full of quiet yearning for a purer form of Christianity, and yet was at the same time incompetent to effect a reconciliation between the embittered religious and anti-religious parties, which were held within bounds only by the sense of their own weakness and by the imperious need for repose in civic life. Nowhere was the confusion of these religious contrasts so motley and multiform as in the homeland of the Reformation, which had of old been used to treat questions of faith with serious earnestness, and to express conscientious convictions with perfect freedom. The German nation became divided into two camps of straightforward believers and straightforward freethinkers ; in this country the number of deliberate hypocrites remained small.

Since average culture invariably lags a few paces behind the advance of science, among the mass of Protestant pastors and among the cultured laity there still prevailed that easy-going philanthropic rationalism which, with a rigidly working intelligence, simply discarded from the realm of dogma everything that was " irrational," and which in its self-complacency failed to observe that in throwing away the husk it had also thrown away the kernel of the Christian faith, had thrown away even the profound doctrines of sin and redemption which had ever been dear to the Germanic temperament. It was through this doctrine of salvation that in former days Christianity had made its first appeal to the hearts of the Teutons, who alone among all the pagan peoples already believed in the coming rebirth of the sinful world. When Luther undertook the purification of the secularised Church, he started from the contrite recognition of personal sin ; in what definite terms, too, had Kant spoken of the essential sinfulness of the human race. Ordinary rationalism now hardly remembered these fundamental ideas of Christianity, but cherished an ingenuous belief in the goodness of human nature, finding satisfaction in a mundane doctrine of salvation by works, salvation through bourgeois business honesty. Yet this rationalism was devoid alike of the courage and of the scientific energy requisite for advance along the steep path which had once been indicated by Lessing and the *Wolfenbüttel Fragments,* and for the assimilation of the critical methods of the new philological study of saga ; it did not venture a serious examination of the historical origins of the New Testament, but took the Bible for granted, and contented itself with the reinterpretation of texts in such a way as to make them exhibit a specious harmony with the laws of nature.

The loudest and most intolerant representative of this tendency was Paulus, professor at Heidelberg. Born some years before Schelling, in the parsonage at Leonberg in Swabia,

Schelling's own birthplace, he was the deadly enemy of his countryman, and of all doctrines which in any way transcended plain reason. What a delight it was to him as a free-thinker to explain the Resurrection as the awakening from an apparent death, and the miracle of Cana as the successful practical joke of a frolicsome wedding guest. Many rationalistic teachers even called to their aid the esoteric doctrines of the natural philosophers, describing the Saviour as a physician with magnetic powers, for to minds of this order the natural miracle always seems more endurable than the supernatural. The old faith-inspired hymns alarmed their jejune faintheartedness ; these hymns were weakened by foolish modifications, or cut altogether out of the hymnal. How much more decent than the forceful " eternity, thou thunder-word " sounded the new and well-bred rationalist hymn, " Death ends not all, this reasons prove ! " From the first the Protestant church had neglected ritual for doctrine. Under the dominion of rationalism, religious service lost everything which quickened the emotions and roused the imagination, and at the same time spiritual teaching sank to the level of mere secular instruction. The pulpit orators no longer understood how to fortify and uplift burdened consciences, how to provide consolation from the wealth of scriptural promise ; they devoted themselves to broad moral considerations, elucidating what the rational Christian must think about individual dogmas, and did not even despise the use of consecrated buildings for giving well-meant advice on the cultivation of potatoes and the breeding of sheep. The churches were deserted, men of intelligence could no longer breathe in this thin atmosphere. The duty of caring for souls was neglected ; upon any trifling excuse the enlightened pastors and consistories would grant permission for divorce. The old supernaturalism with its faith in revelation, which had flourished especially in Würtemberg under the leadership of the prelate Bengel, also became infected with the arid rationalism of the day. Both schools lived on terms of false peace with science, tacitly assuming the existence of a necessary harmony between faith and knowledge. Both continued to move in a circle of ideas which the living forces of literature had long since abandoned. The barren dispute regarding the rationality of individual dogmas touched the externals only of religion, not its essence.

Meanwhile Schleiermacher educated a new school of theologians who learned from the master how to keep pace once more with the young scientific life of the nation. He had formerly uttered the rousing call which summoned the cultured despisers of religion back to the faith, and which lifted the consciousness of God into the world of feeling, above the domain of knowledge and activity. Now, furnishing a scientific equipment for this fruitful basic idea in numerous writings and in his masterly lectures at Berlin, he became the renovator of theology, the greatest of all our theologians since the century of the Reformation ; and even to-day no German theologian gains internal freedom unless he has first come to terms with the ideas of Schleiermacher.

The secret of enduring spiritual efficiency is found chiefly in the harmonious conjunction of apparently conflicting gifts, and rarely indeed has a creative mind been at once so multiform and so harmoniously constructed as that of this Proteus who in three fundamentally diverse epochs, the æsthetic, the patriotic, and the scientific, faithfully reflected all the transformations of Berlin life, and yet never sacrificed his own individuality. He received his first decisive impressions among the contemplative enthusiasts of the Herrnhut Brotherhood, and to the end of his life he enjoyed the consciousness of personal communion with the Saviour ; but his religious fervour was kept within bounds by an incisive understanding which was master of all dialectic arts, and was prone to manifest itself in the form of sarcasm. At one time, when he wrote his *Letters upon Schlegel's Lucinde*, he had wandered far afield in the false sentimental enthusiasm of romanticism, but had none the less preserved a purity of heart which as the years passed gradually came to illumine his entire nature, and made the inconspicuous little man seem like a patriarch. The translator of Plato was at home in all the depths of speculation, and was consequently in a position to fight philosophy with its own weapons, as soon as it was audacious enough to substitute the derivative for the primary and to base its explanation of the world of sensation upon the world of concepts. Everything that is human he endeavoured to treat from the religious outlook, and to utilise on behalf of theology all the science of the age ; and yet he could not live without fulfilling the popular function of the preacher. Around his pulpit there continued to assemble the best society of Berlin, but his heartfelt oratory edified even the poor in spirit. How admirable did he seem to everyone when he personally delivered the funeral oration over the coffin of his little son Nathanael, so profoundly afflicted concerning the fragment of his own life which lay before him, and yet so strong in the consolation which alone consoles. Whoever read his profoundly moving letters to the good Gass, the Breslau theologian, or whoever saw him in personal intercourse with his numerous friends, so lovingly considerate of each one's peculiarities, could readily believe that this impressionable nature demanded nothing more than the intimacies of private intercourse ; and yet Schleiermacher could not do full justice to his powers anywhere else than in public life, and in the days of political lassitude his sense of the state remained just as keen as it had been in the period of patriotic enthusiasm. His opponents, and those unfamiliar with his personality, censured him for his chameleonic changes of colour, and yet whenever it seemed to him that some sacred possession of the nation was in danger he showed himself a man true as steel, perfectly consistent in character, as with thoughtful candour he tranquilly took his place in the arena.

The fundamental thought of the *Reden über die Religion* was closely akin with the ideas of the new historical science. If the roots of religion were to be sought in the emotional life, it inevitably followed that the manifestations of the consciousness of God must be manifold. Consequently dogmas assumed the aspect of subjective emotional truths, of utterances of the pious emotional sensibility regarding its conceptions of God. Upon theology was imposed the new task of comprehending in their historical necessity these configurations of Christian sensibility. Theology was no longer to engage in a hateful polemic, contesting and condemning individual creeds of Christendom, but was to endeavour to understand them all as higher or lower forms of Christian self-consciousness—for Schleiermacher also after his own manner, and independently of Schelling and Savigny, had acquired an understanding of historical development, and had drawn a sharp distinction between that which had come into existence through human nature, and that which man himself had made.

Therewith he effected in the domain of theology a similar rectification of frontiers to that which Kant had once effected in the domain of philosophy ; he secured for theology a ground upon which it could acquire no less incontestable scientific results than were acquired by all the other historical disciplines. He conceived Christian freedom in a spirit as wide as that exhibited by Luther in his first writings, for he held that the living consciousness of God had nothing to fear from free historical and philosophical research. Christian sentiment was to him nothing else than humanity in full perfection, and it was therefore impossible that this sentiment could come into conflict with any justified human aim. Just as emphatically did he insist on the truth that all religion is positive, and that the pious sense of dependence can be kept alert only in the community of the faithful. In ethics, with a freer spirit than Kant's, he allowed personality its full rights : it was not suppression of nature which to him seemed moral, but the enlightenment of nature by the living spirit ; nor did he conceal his opinion that the virtue of Christian self-denial must be supplemented by the classical virtue of self-assertion. The weaknesses of his teaching were displayed as soon as he endeavoured to demonstrate which of the facts of sacred history are necessarily contained in the Christian consciousness ; then he was betrayed into subtleties, and had to learn how impossible it is to deduce positive dogmas directly from the abstract idea. Yet how little significance for him had dogmas and ritual when compared with the blessing of religious community ! When the struggles about evangelical union broke out he was the most valiant defender of a free ecclesiastical constitution and of the alliance of the Protestant confessions.

Among the laity also, signs of a more active Christian life showed on all hands that the dominion of rationalism was passing. It could not be forgotten how thoughtfully in the days of the great news of victory the German army had listened to the words of the poet : " Canst grasp the word of blessing that comes from near and far ? Art not thereby overwhelmed, thou people of the Lord ? " Even the children of this world had then felt to the depths of their souls the simple truth that pious nations alone are free and valiant. The spirited hymns to " the old German God " did not anywhere breathe a definite religious party spirit, but they displayed a profound joy in the consciousness of God which had nothing in common with the inner poverty of rationalism. In most of the men who with a clear consciousness had lived through that epoch of God's judgment there remained for all time a heightened religious feeling, equally whether, like Stein, Arndt, Savigny, and Aster, they found peace in the faith of their fathers, or, like Niebuhr, sought longingly for faith. Martial-minded youths, finally, wore silver crosses in their Teutonic caps, and were overwhelmed by enthusiasm for Christianity; since the days of the Reformation the German universities had not seen any generation of students so seriously concerned about questions of religion. It was true that the Christianity of the ardent Teutonisers was free neither from disagreeable boasting nor from a Puritan lack of good taste: the prayer at the opening of the evening wine party did not always prevent the meeting so reverently begun from degenerating into a wild carouse; and with full justice did the Berlin public take forcible measures against the young barbarians when the students on the occasion of a representation of Zacharias Werner's *Weihe der Kraft*, greeted the appearance of Martin Luther with the loud cry, " The reformer of the stage ! " To many of the noisy Christo-Germanic enthusiasts religion served merely as a political catchword now that Germanism and Christianism were regarded as synonymous; while to some it was simply a cloak for the hatred of the Jews which was now in fashion.

Nevertheless there was a sound kernel to the religious enthusiasm of the younger generation. The Germans at length recognised how intimately their entire civilisation was linked with Christianity, and the effects of this recognition were so far-reaching that frankly pagan sentiments like those which had formerly been cherished by Winckelmann soon became impossible to the children of the new time. Young men thronged round the teachers who displayed an understanding of the yearning for religious emotion. In Heidelberg, Daub, a pious and brilliant mystic and an intimate friend of Creuzer, endeavouring to re-establish dogma through speculation, soon had more adherents among the students than had the rationalists. His followers compared him with Hamann, and spoke of him as the " Magus of the South." In Jena, Fries, a philosopher devoid of acuteness or profundity, nevertheless won the hearts of the students because with honest patriotism and scientific earnestness he combined a no less upright piety. For some years his dialogue *Julius and Euagoras* remained the favourite work of edification of the Teutonising students, for here the philosophy of Kant and the religious fervour of the Herrnhut Moravians were juxtaposed with the same innocence and immediacy as in the heads of the youthful readers.

Almost in every German province there still existed a few strictly religious communities which adhered faithfully to their thoroughly orthodox pastors, opposing a passive but insuperable resistance to the ill-favour of the rationalistic consistories. This was the case especially in the Wupper valley and among the pensive Swabians, but also in Saxony, Pomerania, and Old Prussia. In Breslau, those of strict religious views assembled round Hendrik Steffens, the worthy but unstable enthusiast who knew how to fuse the rigid Lutheranism of his Norwegian home with the imaginative pictures of German romanticist philosophy. In the fashionable society of Berlin, certain gifted young men, who formerly as officers " had in war been led to the Lord," founded a private circle of believers : this numbered among its members the brothers Gerlach, Lancizolle, Le Coq, Thadden, Senfft-Pilsach, Goetze, and Carl von Roeder. Here the crown prince passed edifying hours which were to prove momentous in the formation of his religious and political views ; here he secured assistance for his unwearying works of benevolence ; and here also the plan for the foundation of the Berlin missionary union was first mooted. In all works of Christian charity the religious tendency showed itself far superior to a flabby rationalism ; strongly religious was Oberlin the Alsatian, the never-to-be-forgotten benefactor of the Steintal, and a religious man was Falk of Weimar, who was the first to open a home for orphan children. Nor was there any lack of highly gifted preachers ; in Holstein, the memory persisted for decades of the vigorous eloquence with which Clause Harms, the fiery Lutheran zealot, discoursed to his peasants in the local dialect. In the north, the " Wandsbecker Bote," the tender-hearted old Claudius, and on the Upper Rhine the devout Jung Stilling, were regarded as the leaders of the pious. Both of these men died at the very beginning of the years of peace, but their words and example continued to exercise a powerful influence. Pietism and the strict religious parties gained ground more and more, especially in the country districts, until at length the authorities of the Church were forced to take these new powers into account.

The natural reaction against the superficiality of rationalism had begun, but even in this first stage of a vigorous religious life there were manifest certain morbid tendencies which must inevitably prove injurious to the religious peace of our nation with its parity of creeds. While many of the orthodox encountered the free manifestations of Protestantism with unchristian severity, and passionately opposed evangelical union, they were attracted, consciously or unconsciously, towards the Roman church. In 1818, Beckedorff of Bernburg, tutor in the princely family, and one of the most notable of the Lutheran pietists, published letters upon the reunion of the Christian Churches, and although Roman Catholic sentiment was expressed in every line he secured the warmest approval of his co-religionists—until, a few years later, he went over to Rome. The convert Friedrich Stolberg wrote a *Geschichte der Religion Jesu Christi*, Catholic through and through, but it was loudly praised in the conventicles of the Evangelical pietists, and the bookseller Perthes, a faithful Protestant, son-in-law of the "Wandsbecker Bote," zealously circulated the work. Max von Schenkendorf, singer of the War of Liberation and an intimate friend of Jung Stilling, went so far as to voice the glories in enthusiastic poems of the fanatical leader of the Catholic league, "the firm and faithful Max of Bavaria." In addition, now in one place and now in another, people were disturbed by the ghost-seeing, the second sight, and the prophetic ecstasies, of all kinds of enthusiasts. Most of them were connected in some way with the Moravian Brethren ; they flourished luxuriantly where the soil had been aptly prepared by rationalism. The vague excitement which in periods of great and fateful transformation always seizes the mass of the people, co-operated with the follies of the natural philosophers. Just as, after Luther's appearance, the peasants dreamed of the millennium, so, after the overthrow of Napoleon, revivalist preachers spoke of the fall of the black angel and of the beast with seven horns. In all German-speaking lands, from the Upper Rhine to Livonia, a few mysterious exorcists and pious sleep-walkers made their appearance ; in many instances the emotional enthusiasm increased to the point of lunacy. Frau von Krüdener travelled through Switzerland, Alsace, and Baden, exhorting the people to repent and to feed the poor. Although her sermons were as futile and maudlin as had been her romance *Valerie*, she found adherents among the masses ; Metternich complained to her friend Czar Alexander that she was disturbing the public peace,[1] and the Badenese police had ultimately to expel her as a demagogue. A lust for the miraculous was in the air and thoughtful natures succumbed to it most readily. Even Schleiermacher's excellent wife could not do without edifying intercourse with a wonderful female somnambulist, and her husband himself was not altogether immune from this woman's influence.

---

[1] Krusemark's Report, Vienna, October 4, 1817.

Just as rich in contrasts was the life of the Catholic church. The majority of Protestants were under the delusion that the power of the papacy had now been completely broken. How was the Roman See ever to resume its designs for world-dominion? Only a few years before, the Catholic church in France had been restored solely by the power of the secular arm, and it was by the grace of the allies that the sovereign pontiff had so recently regained the heritage of Peter. The much-tried pope Pius VII was generally regarded with good-natured compassion, not unmixed with contempt; the conservative parties hailed him as a useful ally in the struggle with the revolution. Not even the protest of the Curia against the decisions of the Vienna congress disturbed the unsuspecting security of the governments. In all seriousness the question was being discussed whether after the death of Pius VII another pope would ever be elected.

In fact the well-bred mildness of the distinguished prelates of the eighteenth century lived on in a certain section of the clergy. Whoever moved in these crcles might readily imagine that the antagonism of the creeds would by degrees spontaneously disappear. The Bible-societies of Kreuznach and Neuwied were vigorously supported by many Catholic priests of the bishopric of Treves.[1] In Breslau the members of each of the two theological faculties were accustomed to attend the disputations held by the " sister church," and as late as the year 1828 the prize in a competition instituted by the Catholic faculty of Tübingen was won by the Protestant theologian David Friedrich Strauss. Amongst priests and laity Hontheim's dream of a German national church continued to gain numerous adherents, and there was frequently voiced a demand for the introduction of a German liturgy and for the abolition of the celibacy of the priesthood. Many defenders of the omnipotence of the state wished to apply to the Catholic church the territorial system of Thomasius, and to treat priests as nothing more than " most honourable state-servants." Heinrich Wessenberg, the spokesman of the movement for a national church, had already introduced German hymns into his diocese of Constance; he regarded the Protestants tolerantly as " the church of the left." Sailer, the excellent prelate who by example and precept reawakened a living piety in the Catholic church of Bavaria, was more guarded

[1] Report of President von Ingersleben upon the state of affairs in the grand duchy of the Lower Rhine, July 26, 1817.

in his dealings with the Roman See. But he also did not hesitate to appeal publicly to the writings of Protestant theologians. He lived on terms of intimate friendship with many Protestants, sharing with them a veneration for Thomas à Kempis, a knowledge of whom was revived in German Catholic congregations through Sailer's translation. Overberg, too, the Catholic pedagogue of Münster, secured Stein's respect by his apostolic gentleness; and the no less strongly religious Boisserées, who looked upon art as merely the daughter of religion, continued to keep in touch with the works of Protestant science. Just as these men stood near to the views of the Evangelical pietists, so on the other side Hermes, the theologian of Bonn, had adopted the methods of Protestant rationalism, and attempted the impossible task of upholding Catholic dogma by the rational demonstrations of the Kantian philosophy. His adherents dominated the educational institutions on the Rhine, and honourably endeavoured to preserve religious peace.

What a gulf between the ideas of these peace-loving men and the plans of dominion which animated the Roman See. Hardly had Pius VII returned to the holy city when in the bull of August 7, 1814, *Sollicitudo omnium ecclesiarum*, he re-established the Jesuit order, and personally read the mass *In nomine Jesu* at the altar of St. Ignatius Loyola, where the chisel of Le Gros had celebrated in boastful sculpture the triumph of the church over heresy. When subsequently Czar Alexander invited him to join the Holy Alliance, the pope rejected the proposal, which could hardly have been seriously meant, with all the pride of the rightful ruler of the world. Soon afterwards, the Inquisition and the Index of prohibited books were reintroduced, and the Bible-societies were declared to be the work of the devil. In the days of revolutionary oppression the ancient church had displayed marvellous moral courage, and had learned by experience that its most powerful energies sprang from suffering. Now it shone with all the glory of martyrdom; the romantic yearning of public opinion, and the dread which the courts felt for the revolution, were to her advantage. In anti-papal England, for the first time since the days of James II, a cardinal was able to appear in full canonicals. The pleasing illusion of those enlightened persons who believed that the new century had outgrown the passions of the religious wars had just been plainly refuted by the Spanish War of Liberation; and now, while the monarchs were still in Paris, there broke over southern France the madness of the White Terror : the Catholic mob stormed the houses of the Protestants and murdered the heretics to the cry of, " Let us make black-puddings of Calvin's blood ! "

With such a favourable wind, the bark of Peter was once more in full sail. By the nature of things, the Roman See was compelled, despite the pope's tender-heartedness, and despite the prudence of his secretary Consalvi, to return step by step to the ideas of the epoch of the counter-reformation. Quite inconspicuously the first Jesuits insinuated themselves once again into Germany ; and the two-edged influence of secularisation was soon manifest. The increasingly plebeian clergy had neither possessions nor home, and was no longer, as had been the wealthy and noble cathedral chapters of old, bound to the fatherland by political interest. When, at the Vienna congress, Helfferich and the two other orators of the Catholic church gave expression to their ultramontane views, they secured but little support from the German clergy ; but since then, unnoticed, the clerical party had grown from year to year. This party still proceeded with cautious steps, for in all the German states the officialdom regarded it with mistrust ; even Emperor Francis and Metternich, although they looked on militant Catholicism as the natural ally of the Austrian party in the German realm, were still, as strict absolutists, unwilling to listen to a word about the independence of the church. The Jesuits, in order to curry favour with the courts, now refurbished those Jacobite doctrines which had once led the House of Stuart to destruction : the Reformation, they said, was the ultimate source of all revolutions, whereas the church was the fortress and support of kingship, for the church taught passive obedience, and by her mystical consecration she released the king-by-God's-grace of all duties towards his subjects.

The most zealous adherents of the ultramontane party were the numerous proselytes whom romanticism had led into the Roman camp. Among these were numbered the talented brothers Schlosser in Frankfort ; Count Stolberg in Holstein, who was in close relationship with the clericals of the Münster region ; and all the members of that powerful group of converts who from Vienna despatched vigorous envoys into the German realm. What a lamentable picture of intellectual decay was now exhibited by Friedrich Schlegel ! In the days of his æsthetic pride he had once said boastfully : " I think of founding a new religion; it is time!" This same æsthetic intoxication drove him, when he had given up the idea of founding a new religion, into the arms of the Roman church, accompanied by his brilliant wife Dorothea Mendelssohn and her son Veit the Nazarene painter, and he was now fast-fixed in the shackles of a complete system which had an answer ready for every question that could be proposed. Wilhelm Humboldt observed with disgust how this once open mind had become tightly closed to everything; how Schlegel could now discern nothing but heretics on the one hand and faithful disciples on the other, and could no longer take part in a free conversation, modestly searching for truth. Owing to his increasing slothfulness Schlegel was of little use to the ultramontane propaganda. Far more effective work was done by the Pomeranian Klinckowström, an amiable romanticist enthusiast; his school in Vienna became the nursery of the clerical Austrian nobility. His brother-in-law, Pilat of Augsburg, Catholic by birth, and married to a convert, was editor of the *Oesterreichischer Beobachter*, Metternich's official journal. But in talent, activity, and fanaticism, Adam Müller excelled all the rest; it seemed as if the brilliant but fundamentally false sophist desired to wipe out the stain of his Berlin origin by his raging fury against heretics; his hand was at work wherever there was evidence of Jesuit intrigues throughout the north; most of the pens which defended the German policy of the Hofburg, belonged to this circle of converts. Gentz alone could not make up his mind to go over to Rome (although his detestation for Luther, the archrevolutionary, became ever more violent), for the nucleus of his culture was too intimately associated with the Kantian philosophy.

Enlightened Protestants had long become accustomed to these numerous conversions, and they were first startled out of their thoughtless indifference when it was reported that C. L. von Haller of Berne had gone over to Rome. Who could take it amiss in the case of the valiant publicist, the passionate enemy of the Revolution, that as a logical outcome of his political views he should be forced to a change of faith? But Haller kept his conversion secret, with the approval of the bishop of Fribourg. Subsequently, as member of the council of Berne, he took the official oath which pledged him to the protection of the Reformed Church; and when the unsavoury secret was at length disclosed by others, in an open *Letter to my Family* (1821) he declared unashamedly that he had remained silent on excellent grounds, in order that his new volume, *Die Geistlichen Staaten*, might exercise a stronger influence upon its readers, " because it was apparently written by a Protestant "! Seldom have the moral principles of Jesuitry been more impudently enunciated. A fine prospect now opened for religious peace, when the apostate, amid the acclamations of the French legitimist press, triumphantly declared that the world was now divided between Catholics and the godless, that this one conversion would be followed by thousands of others, until humanity would be completely delivered from the powers of the ecclesiastical and of the political revolution. A flood of polemic writings appeared. The gentle pulpit-orator Tzschirner of Leipzig, the rationalist philosopher Krug, and other Protestants, expressed their naive astonishment in straightforward words. People began to recognise upon how weak a foundation had been established the dominion of the much-vaunted " rational Christianity."

The Catholic church, like the Protestant, was afflicted with the extravagances of crude superstition. Munich was the acropolis of the Catholic Magians. In Bavaria, the exorcisms of the deceased Gassmer were still remembered ; now Baader could boast of a daughter possessed of the devil. In Franconia, a cardinal of peasant origin made a progress through the villages accompanied by a girl who was about to give birth to the Saviour ; in the Black Forest, in Alpgau, among the rough Hotzeners, the fanaticism of the Saltpeterers once more became active ; out of Austria the fanatical sect of the Pöschlianers invaded Bavaria, a disorderly rout which did not shrink from religious murder and which could be controlled in no other way than by severe punishments. Among the crowd of pious sorcerers a priest of distinguished origin, Prince Alexander Hohenlohe, made himself conspicuous by impudent self-assurance. When Pius VII was informed that by the power of prayer the prince could heal those who were sick unto death, and that the Franconian country-folk came to him in crowds, the pope, who knew his man, said, shrugging his shoulders : " Questo far' dei miracoli ! " In a boastful appeal, the miracle-monger informed the princes of the Holy Alliance that it was not by force of arms that the revolution would now be conquered, that education must be reformed, that youth must be led back into the bosom of the church. Here pious illusion proved no less irresistibly infective than among the Protestants; even Sailer once prayed devoutly at the bedside of the miraculous nun of Dülmen.

The irreconcilable harshness of religious contrasts, the utter lack of peace characteristic of our religious life, was displayed with terrible clearness when a literary quarrel once more broke out upon the fervid soil of Heidelberg. So many notable representatives of fundamentally diverse tendencies lived in close contact in this little town, where differences of opinion were always fought out with deplorable bitterness. In order to make head against his opponents, Daub and Creuzer, Paulus had founded the periodical *Sophronizon;* it was ably edited, and soon attracted attention by its frank criticism of numerous defects in state and church. Particularist liberalism, which divined nothing of the conditions of national power, and rationalism, which would never take into account the religious sentiments of the believing temperament, both found here a platform. When now Count Friedrich Stolberg published in Adam Müller's ultra-conservative *Staatsanzeiger* an incisive essay upon the aberrations of the *Zeitgeist*, Voss, writing in *Sophronizon* in 1819, gave vent to his feelings against the companion of his youth. "How did Fritz Stolberg come to put himself on the side of slavery?" he fiercely demanded. As an old man he wished to bear witness against the old man, because he would soon have to answer for himself on the other shore "where neither knight nor parson rules." Consequently he considered himself discharged from all loyalty, from all obligations, towards the old friend to whom forty years earlier he had dedicated his translation of the *Odyssey;* and with heartless roughness, shamelessly disclosing the details of domestic life, he described how the count, even in the days when they had together been youthful and enthusiastic members of the Hainbund [Poets' Club] at Göttingen, had secretly inclined towards "hierarchic and aristocratic coercive rule," until at length his pride of nobility and his disordered imagination had driven him into the wilderness of Hildebrandian uncleanliness, "for the black barbarism of the junkers, raging more fiercely than the Turk of old, now threatens the enlightened nations." Apt observations upon the futility of conversions, and upon the pious self-admiration of the Stolberg circle, were lost in a sea of false accusations. For beyond question Stolberg had been attracted to the Roman church, not like Haller from the force of political conviction, but through the religious impulse of a weakly temperament, which could never find support in its own strength. The keen insight of Goethe had long ago led him to regard the soft-hearted man as an unconscious Catholic.

Like most of his contemporaries, Voss had formerly been an enthusiast for the rights of man championed by the Revolution. Now, after the overthrow of the foreign dominion, the old man's revolutionary sentiments, which during the War of Liberation had not been openly displayed, flamed violently forth once again. He mockingly spoke of Napoleon as the destroying angel of the high-born, and addressed to the friend of his youth the question :

" Nobler the sons of the long sword whom in the ages long vanished Virtues of dogs then adorned, shall we say virtues of wolves ? "

With this fanatical hatred of the nobility was associated the mistrust of the rationalist for every form of religious life which was not characterised by a limpid clarity. The grand inquisitor of rationalism could account for the reawakening of the religious sentiment in no other way than by regarding it as the result of reckless agitation on the part of a secret society of parsons and nobles. Not even the death of his old friend Stolberg, which occurred shortly afterwards, softened his mood. Fierce rejoinders from the intimates of the man he had attacked, and new blusterous polemic writings by Voss, Paulus and Schott, and Varnhagen, showed how impossible was any adjustment of this disorderly dispute. Goethe found once more the right word when he said :

" I feel confined, sadly I muse,
'Twixt flame and wave I dwell,
Like feelings as when I peruse
Dante's account of Hell."

This detestable feud had a profound and disastrous influence upon German liberalism. Voss and his associates on the *Sophronizon* were the first to maintain the opinion that traditional religious belief is intimately connected with belief in the value of a hereditary nobility, that the free man respects only " the truth which his mind has acquired for itself, and merit which is won by personal service." Although the folly of this proposition must have been manifest to everyone who knew the religious fervour of the North American democracy, among the Germans, with their love for systematised thinking, it secured a considerable amount of support, and there gradually ensued a morbid confusion of speech which has continued to falsify German party-life down to the present day. People began to believe that which immediately after the holy war no one had ventured to maintain, that rationalistic or even anti-religious sentiments were the unmistakable index of political liberalism ; the two were simultaneously designated by the fine-sounding name of free thought and in this way the governments, being by nature conservative, were forced into close approximation to the strictly religious parties. Even more deplorable in its effects was the unfortunate example of a spirit of " enlightened " intolerance, which discovered everywhere priestly tyranny, blue-blooded arrogance, or servile obedience, and which subsequently secured its natural response in the animosity displayed in the prosecution of the demagogues.

The most influential publicists of those days were likewise animated by this spirit of narrow-minded intolerance. For twenty years Carl von Rotteck was the highly esteemed political teacher of the South German bourgeoisie, simply because he had neither energy nor desire to rise above the average middle-class outlook. Although the honest man did not woo popular favour, his views never failed to exhibit a spontaneous harmony with " the imperious *Zeitgeist*." He took the word from the mouths of the well-to-do townsmen and peasants of the south, and with invincible courage, with the fervent eloquence of conviction, announced what all were obscurely feeling. To his mother's French blood he owed a facility of expression rare at that time among German men of learning ; never wearying, he turned this way and that his extremely modest provision of ideas, until to his readers everything he alleged seemed luminous and incontestable. The democratic ideas which had found their way into High Germany in the days of the taking of the Bastille had since then undergone a quiet process of invigoration and had been widely diffused ; the whole traditional ordering of the state had been destroyed by the princes' revolution of the Napoleonic epoch, while among the middle classes, resentment of the arbitrary rule of the Rhenish confederate officials increased from year to year. Out of such ideas and wishes, Rotteck, at a remarkably early date, immediately after the conclusion of peace, constructed his finished ideal picture of an exemplary constitutional state. He believed himself to stand in the foremost front of time, and did not suspect how strongly his own doctrine was influenced by the traditional ideas which continued to live on in the nation with wonderful tenacity; like the feudal nobility in the good old days, he regarded the centralised authority of the state as the natural enemy of liberty. All who did not share his views were numbered among those "to whom a smile from a powerful minister, a ribbon and a star, or a comfortable appointment, are dearer than the common weal." When compared with Savigny and Niebuhr, Rotteck had the aspect of a scientific reactionary, for the fundamental ideas of his theory belonged essentially to the eighteenth century; but with great adroitness he deduced from these antiquated propositions certain consequences which did in fact correspond with the practical needs of the day. A partisan from top to toe, accustomed from the first to measure men and things solely with the foot-rule of political doctrine, he had lived through the great age of our literature entirely without understanding it; to him Marquis Posa's enthusiasm for freedom was still the crown of German poesy—what could Goethe, the prince's lackey, show to equal this?

Nevertheless, even this political zealot could not deny the literary origin of German liberalism, for he too was irresistibly attracted to that Frenchman who among the predecessors of the Revolution had had the weakest political intelligence, but had at the same time been the most moving artist, and who was therefore the most intimately akin to German culture. From Rousseau he learned the doctrines of popular sovereignty and universal equality, and also the childlike belief in the natural innocence of man. With the aid of the Kantian natural law, which approximated very closely to the views of the Genevese philosopher, he then endeavoured to incorporate these ideas into a system, although he regarded philosophy as no more than the interpreter of the healthy human understanding. The third source of his doctrine was the work upon the limits of papal authority written by Hontheim under the pen-name of Febronius. Here Rotteck found a remarkable mixture of zeal for enlightenment and faith in Catholic doctrine, one which was in conformity with his own sentiments; here too he found the prototype for the method of his artificial political demonstration. Just as Hontheim, a well-meaning precursor of the advocates of a national church, simply ignored the last centuries of ecclesiastical history, ascribed to the pope no more than a few modest honorary rights, and yet was by no means inclined to attack the papacy as an institution, so Rotteck deprived kingship of all its important prerogatives, and yet believed that he was not anti-monarchical. In all innocence and without any revolutionary *arrière pensée*, he preached a revolutionary theory which was utterly irreconcilable with the characteristics of the German state system.

The son of a loyal Austrian, he grew to manhood in the beautiful district of Breisgau, during the days when the reforms of Joseph II aroused enthusiasm among the enlightened Upper Austrians. The system of making people happy by force always remained for him the true expression of liberal policy. Subsequently he had had to endure the painful experience of seeing his homeland united to Baden, and he now lived under a government which he long continued to regard mistrustfully as semi-foreign, in a state without a history, a state whose institutions seemed the outcome of chance or caprice. Even under the pressure of the Napoleonic censorship, he had continued manfully to express his love for the German fatherland ; when the liberators entered Baden he immediately took over the editorship of the *Teutschen Blätter*, and placed the paper at the disposal of the allied headquarters. But he felt quite at home only among his Alemannic fellow-countrymen; to them were primarily devoted all his energies of tongue and pen, and with genuine delight he dedicated one of his books " to all the worthy citizens of Freiburg." When the homely little man, in the afternoons, as soon as his work at the university was finished, climbed vigorously up the foot-hills of the Black Forest to his little vineyard of Schönehof, and thence looked down over the charming valley and the beautiful towers of the minster, he felt that the pearl of Germany lay beneath his eyes. Now that this magnificent country was blessed with the long-desired rational constitution, he could think only with contempt of the distant north, which naturally, after the manner of his countrymen, he had never taken the trouble to visit. He asked with pride whether sunny Rhineland could rest content with political rights which might indeed suffice for gloomy Pomerania. The Alemanni of Baden found in Rotteck, as the Swabians found in Uhland, all the characteristics of their own nature : hardy candour, democratic obstinacy, Josephan enlightenment, but also provincial limitations, naive ignorance of all the conditions of political power, and the self-satisfaction of ingenuous particularism. "We must go and see Rotteck about it," said the peasants of the Black Forest, when complaints made to the officials proved unavailing.

Rotteck's reputation was first established among the middle class by his *Allgemeine Weltgeschichte*. The book began to appear in 1812, and the sale increased with each successive volume; in the bourgeois houses of many small southern towns the entire library consisted of Bible, prayer book, and Rotteck. To the profoundly dissatisfied and yet politically helpless peoples of the petty states, what could sound more agreeable than the self-satisfied triviality of this historical wisdom, which knew absolutely nothing of the determinism of historic life, but deduced all the misfortunes of the nations solely from the wickedness and the blindness of their rulers, and which frankly declared that its highest aim was "to give expression to that public opinion which is now manifesting itself with such force, and whose manifestation affords such promise of salvation." The arid rationalism of the eighteenth century historians was here fused with the party passion of the new age. Rotteck regarded the state only from beneath, with the eyes of the ruled. He never asked himself how human affairs appear from above, what ideas determine the actions of rulers, and what obstacles rulers have to overcome. To him every prince, every person in authority, was an object of suspicion. Even in personal intercourse, the inveterate bourgeois could not endure men of noble birth, and the sight of a uniform or of a decoration made him uncomfortable. As Rotteck admitted in one of his letters, his sympathies were alienated from Blucher as soon as the old hero came to bear the princely title.

Never before had a German book voiced so bluntly the worst weakness of modern democracy, the envious hatred of everything that transcends vulgar mediocrity. In set terms, the popular historian reproves Alexander the Great because this "man of dust and clay made crushed nations the pedestal of his fame"; he angrily demands of the heroes of the crusades, "by what right was Palestine conquered?" To him the entire course of universal history displayed in detestable monotony the same painful tragedy: the ever-innocent people had all through the centuries been maltreated by bloody tyrants, and misled into wars to their common hurt; then came the middle ages to afflict mankind, "ten centuries of barbarism, savagery, and gloom, a period equally lacking in charm and interest "; until finally the darkness was lightened by the popular heroes of the American and French revolutions, and the imperious *Zeitgeist* came into its own.

The frank self-complacency of the philosophical century was here revived, but now it indued a political dress. In Rotteck's *Universal History*, the republican ideal of the state was for the first time preached to the German middle classes. During the American War of Independence, enthusiasm for the youthful republic of the west had been restricted to the narrow circles of cultured youth, and during the storms of the Napoleonic days America had been utterly forgotten. Now Rotteck directed the gaze of the discontented once again towards the west. " In the west," he exclaimed, " in the youthful New World, natural, rational right is building its chosen realm." It is true that as a law-abiding citizen he appeasingly added : " But it is not the republican form which we regard as the sun of this day, but the republican spirit "; he even went so far as to maintain that in a rational monarchy the republican spirit can get most vigorously to work. But since his exemplary state was based upon the republican idea of popular sovereignty, the impression was left in the minds of his readers that the republic alone was the rational state, was alone the " free state " (for these two expressions were already used as practically synonymous). This doctrine found acceptance all the more readily, because everyone had now begun to learn at school the philologists' fable of the wonderful freedom of the republics of antiquity.

Just as misleading was the partisan description of the recent past. How powerful was still the mythopœic faculty of the popular intelligence, even in this century proud of its cultural attainments. Immediately after the conclusion of peace, the image of the experiences so recently lived through became distorted and confused in the popular memory. Just as the French universally believed that they had been conquered only by a force ten times as strong as their own, so among the discontented of Germany there soon became current a whole world of strange partisan fables. Rotteck expressed the heartfelt feelings of the southern liberals when he confidently maintained that of all the European powers it was the two constitutional states of England and Spain, miraculously strengthened by the freedom of their institutions, which alone had been able to withstand the Napoleonic world-empire. Nobody alluded to the fact that Russia had displayed the same power of resistance, for after the foundation of the Holy Alliance this state, but now so loudly praised, became the object of the liberals' passionate hatred, and Rotteck exhorted Prussia to devote herself to the task of serving the cause of European freedom by constituting herself a bulwark against the threatening Muscovite slavery. On the other hand, praise was showered upon the Cortes constitution of 1812, which was supposed to have inspired the Spanish nation for its heroic struggle ; for a whole decade this constitution remained the favourite child of the liberals, because, having come into existence in the absence of the monarch, it imposed extreme restrictions upon the power of the crown, and seemed therefore to approximate to the highest ideal, that of American freedom.

A still more extraordinary story was soon in circulation regarding the German War of Liberation. It was said that by the appeal of Kalisz and the promise of a Prussian constitution the allied princes had filled the German people with false hopes. " Allured by a flattering tale " (it was thus that Rotteck spoke of the Kalisz proclamation), they had hastened by hundreds of thousands to take up arms ! The inveracity of this view could be sufficiently proved by an appeal to the calendar. The ordinance respecting the future constitution of Prussia was signed on May 22, 1815, and was not published until July 8th, when the last war against Napoleon was already drawing to a close. As regards the appeal of Kalisz, the mass of the men of the Prussian Landwehr had known little or nothing about it. Yet this partisan fable found credence, at first in the south, and subsequently, when discontent became more rife, even in Prussia. People felt they had been betrayed and sold ; it seemed impossible to explain the deplorable state of Germany after such enormous sacrifices as the outcome of a great deception. Soon everyone was regarded as a reactionary who continued to recognise otherwise than the truth, that the Prussians had simply risen up, in response to their king's appeal, to free the soil of their homeland from the enemy and to re-establish the honour of their old royal flag. Those thus blinded, no longer noticed how insulting their allegations were to the Prussian nation.

Even in Prussia the performances of the Landwehr were overestimated. The liberals of the highlands at length came to recount miracles of Lützow's yagers and of the other volunteers, although these had contributed but little to the victories of the allies. Those, indeed, who had a first-hand knowledge of the art of war held other views. Speckbacher, one of the brave leaders of the Tyrolese insurgents of 1809, remarked to York's aide-de-camp Carl von Roeder : " Among us peasants there was a vigorous spirit, but no discipline ; among the Austrian imperial troops, it was the other way about; with Blucher and York, the soldiers had both, discipline and courage—I wish I had been there ! " The morose party-feeling of the liberals deprived them of all ear for this language of the straightforward human reason ; the name of voluntary army (*Freischar*) was to them as irresistible as that of free state (*Freistaat*). The insignificant Prussian volunteer corps were compared with the Spanish guerillas, and the " holy volunteers " were regarded as the true conquerors of Napoleon. The fiery verses of *Lützows wilde verwegene Jagd*, which young Körner had unreflectingly composed in the fulness of his inspired heart, gradually acquired the sense of a partisan song. The poem was repeated in a challenging tone, as if to bring the regular troops into contempt ; and before long King Frederick William could not endure the vigorous strains, because they seemed to him to convey an affront to his valiant army. This discontented generation seemed no longer able to take an innocent delight in the great deeds of German history.

All the embitterment of liberalism found expression in Rotteck's work, published in 1816, *Uber stehende Heere und Nationalmiliz* [Standing Armies and a National Militia]. What a contrast to Rühle von Lilienstern's patriotic book *Vom Kriege* ! The Prussian officer, with statesmanlike moderation, had proposed to nationalise the army and to militarise the nation as well ; whereas Rotteck, the partisan, propounded a revolutionary alternative, asking whether the nation was itself to be made an army, or whether the soldiers were to be made citizens. This, he said, was the great question of a momentous hour. Hardly a year after the army of the line and the Landwehr had fought together so gloriously at Belle Alliance, he attacked the Prussian Army Law with fanatical rage, declaring with arrogant confidence : " Any state which endeavours to gain strength through a standing army, renounces the possibility of a vigorous Landwehr." He described a standing army as the bulwark of despotism. He declared : " When all our young men are summoned to the army, the entire nation will be permeated with the sentiments of the hireling." In conclusion, he bluntly demanded the abolition of standing armies, so that in time of peace no more than a small force of recruited troops should be maintained, and the Landwehr was to have a scanty training lasting a few weeks. Whilst thus flourishing revolutionary catchwords, he demanded with ingenuous class-selfishness that the system of substitution should be introduced into his Landwehr; entire groups were to be liberated from service, and above all the students. He ends with the proud prophecy: " Whatever prince carries out this idea will shine by the light of his own glory, and should he be a German he would be the leader of his race!"

Such was the blindness displayed even in its first beginnings by the excessive self-esteem of particularist liberalism. The princes of Germany, rivalling one another in liberal deeds, were to compete humbly for the gift of the crown of the future empire at the hands of the sole representatives of the masterful *Zeitgeist*. When, about this time, Duke Charles Augustus disbanded the army of Weimar, and contented himself with an armed watch, praises were showered upon him, and the *Allgemeine Zeitung* wrote with delight: " Here, in the most exquisite manner was the action performed, whilst there was its glorification uttered, each unconsciously of the other." It is true that another leader of Badenese liberalism, Baron von Liebenstein, opposed his Freiburg comrade in a thoughtful work, but now as always Rotteck had spoken for the great majority of the party. Need for peace and economic stringency, provincial ignorance of the relationships between the European powers, mistrust of the courts, and, not least, subconscious doubt of the military efficiency of the isolated petty contingents in the minor states— all these things combined to make liberal sentiment more and more definitely adverse to the army. Rotteck's angry declamation against the hireling spirit of the soldiery awakened loud echoes, although everyone must have known that the German soldier was removed from civic life only for a brief period by the compulsion of the military law, and that he had to content himself unwillingly enough with his poor pay of two groschen a day. Fervent abuse of the mercenaries was regarded for an entire generation as an unmistakable sign of sound liberal sentiments, and the inevitable result was that the officers' corps inclined more and more to rigid conservative views.

The mistrust of the army felt by the liberals was closely

associated with their fierce hatred of the nobility, which found expression in all the periodicals and pamphlets of the parties of opposition. The particularist spirit of the various territorial areas and estates had been the ancient curse of Germany; all classes, and by no means the nobility alone, had shared in this ancient national sin. Just as at the close of the middle ages the defiant spirit of the great communes contributed to destroy the prestige of the imperial authority, and throughout the sixteenth century to frustrate all attempts at imperial reform, so now the bourgeoisie was certainly no less to blame than the nobility for the reawakening of a detestable class-hostility. In this matter also the literary origin of German liberalism had to be atoned for. Since very few men of noble birth had co-operated in the rise of the new art and science, in the cultured middle classes, side by side with justified feelings of self-complacency, there came into existence a sentiment of deplorable contempt for the nobility, and people talked as if nature had denied understanding to noblemen. Many of the literary leaders of the nation, in the humiliating circumstances of a poverty-stricken youth, had learned to know and to loathe pride of caste, for not a few of them had been tutors in noble houses. Detestation of the high-born found expression, above all, in many of the works of the new poesy, such as *Emilia Galotti*, and *Kabale und Liebe*. Among the members of the Hainbund this feeling was deeply rooted. Whoever read *The Pastor's Daughter of Taubenheim* and similar poems by Bürger, might well believe that the seduction of poor girls was the principal occupation of the German nobleman. Voss, the issue of Mecklenburg serfs, cherished from childhood an inextinguishable hatred of the junkers, and with unconcealed satisfaction, in one of his *Idyllen*, made Michel the peasant say of the nobles: "Rascals are they; the best place for them to idle is under the gallows-tree."

In our literary circles the night of the fourth of August, and all the other blows which the French Revolution directed against the aristocracy, were hailed with delight. Since then, the power of the German nobility had been profoundly shaken. By the principal resolution of the Diet of Deputation the nobles had been completely despoiled of their share in the government of the empire; while by the reforms of Stein and Hardenberg and by the laws of the Confederation of the Rhine they had to a large extent been deprived of their dominant position in the country districts. But they yet retained many privileges which were offensive to the pride of the bourgeoisie. In the feudal minor states of the north, Saxony, Hanover, and Mecklenburg, the nobles still controlled the government and the diet ; here for the most part the nobles' benches of the supreme court of justice were still in existence ; and in the Old Prussian provinces patrimonial jurisdiction and the manorial police served in addition to maintain the power of the nobility, since landowners of bourgeois origin were still in the minority. In the army and in the civil service, the nobleman everywhere, in actual practice, received the preference. The personal entourage of the princes consisted exclusively of nobles, and Voss scornfully exclaimed : " The nobleman is the born curator of the royal stud, the royal chase, the royal board, and the royal pleasures." After the overthrow of the crowned plebeian, the arrogance of the nobility often assumed an extremely provocative form ; even Niebuhr complained that never for forty years had the nobleman treated the bourgeois with such contempt. In official usage, the tasteless title of *demoiselle* was obstinately retained in speaking of bourgeois girls. The rules of precedence of the petty courts also gave expression to a ridiculous caste pride. Not even the highest state official could take his wife to court if she was of bourgeois origin ; in Hesse, the ministers could gain audience of the sovereign only through the instrumentality of an aide-de-camp of noble birth. The theatre in Weimar had its special boxes for the nobility ; and in the banqueting hall of the castle of Pillnitz there were separate galleries for the nobles and for the bourgeois who attended as spectators at the king's banquets. In the eyes of the pure-blooded junker, the only seemly occupations were those of military officer, court chamberlain, equerry, and forest ranger. A nobleman could interest himself in science and in art only as an amateur ; there was immense excitement in Breslau when a *gnädiger Herr* appeared on the boards of the town theatre among the ordinary players. Marriages between men of noble birth and well-dowered bourgeois girls were common enough ; but very rarely, and only in defiance of much opposition from her class, did a girl of the quality throw herself away upon a man of the bourgeoisie.

These vestiges of an obsolete social order were naturally grievous to the bourgeoisie ; but it was rank ingratitude to forget how brilliantly the talents, the loyalty, and the bravery of the Prussian nobility had been manifested during recent

anxious years. The great majority of the commanders and statesmen to whom Germany owed her liberation were men of noble
birth. Whilst the French aristocracy, enraged at the loss of
their class privileges, had during the war made common cause
with the enemies of their fatherland, the Prussian nobles,
although they had vigorously opposed Hardenberg's legislation,
had magnanimously forgotten their ill-feeling directly the king
issued his summons, and had sacrificed everything for the rescue
of the country. Had it not been for the devotion of the
landed gentry it would have been impossible to provide the
Landwehr with officers or to make use of this force in the
open field. Nevertheless these patriotic soldiers were by the
liberal press compared to the émigrés ; Béranger's mischievous
verses *je suis vilain et très-vilain* found an echo on this side of
the Rhine as if they had been equally applicable to Germany.
In the speeches and writings of the liberals, the Prussian state
of 1806 was invariably described as the embodiment of all
possible political sins. Before long it was repeated everywhere
that the junkers had led Prussia to destruction, and that seven
years later the country had been rescued by " the people."
After the war, the nobility endeavoured to recover a portion of
its ancient power. The mediatised besieged the Bundestag and
the courts with their grievances ; in Prussia the feudal party
closed its ranks. Proposals for the reconstitution of the
influence of the nobles' order were voiced on all hands. During
the congress of Vienna, the plan to form a " league of nobles "
(*Adelskette*) was much discussed. This was to be a great
association which throughout Germany should safeguard the
interests of the titled class and should keep alive the sentiment of
knightly honour, but the proposal came to nothing, and a later
plan of the same kind, mooted by the nobles of East Prussia,
had a similar fate. Many of the romanticist authors broke out
into extravagant laudation of the nobility. According to
Friedrich Schlegel this class was the foundation of civil society,
the foundation upon which all the other classes had been built.
A defiant little poem of Schlegel's exhorted noblemen to
stick to the sword and the plough and to shun the babble of
the towns.

These endeavours, and in addition the foolish intrigues of
the French émigrés after their return home, increased the anger of
the middle classes. People relapsed into those views of unmiti-
gated class-envy which at the time of the peace of Tilsit had

been promulgated by the Bonapartist Friedrich Buchholz in his *Researches concerning Hereditary Nobility*. How incontrovertible it seemed when this political Nicolai showed that virtue was not transmissible by inheritance, and that a nobility of service like the French Legion of Honour was the only rational form of nobility. " It is impossible," said Buchholz," to be at the same time a patriot and a feudal aristocrat." Von Diericke, an old Frederician general, modestly undertook the defence of his order, and in his *A Word concerning the Prussian Nobility* (1818) showed how many sons of the despised junkerdom had co-operated in camp and council to consolidate Prussia's greatness. His book aroused all the more anger because his facts could not be contradicted. In many learned circles the childish hatred of the aristocracy rose to such a height that even students took it into their calculations. In Breslau, when young Carl von Holtei was writing his examination paper, and did not feel quite sure of his knowledge, he shrewdly omitted the " von " from his signature, and was then delighted to observe how the professors put their heads together, showing to one another with satisfied smiles this admirable product of the young bourgeois intelligence. The discreet phrases in which, in his letters *Concerning the Nobility*, Perthes expressed his opposition to Fouqué the enthusiast for the knighthood, now seemed to incensed public opinion as little adequate as had at an earlier date the writings of the bourgeoisphile but conservative Rehberg.

Thus by its great literary successes the German bourgeoisie was misled into excessive self-esteem such as formerly in France had actuated the third estate, the only difference being that in the case of Germany, bourgeois arrogance still remained entirely restricted to the field of theory. Liberal newspapers asked with a light heart what it would matter if by general bankruptcy the entire nobility should lose its territorial possessions, and its place be taken by a new class of landowners. Rationalism had no understanding of the moral energy proper to an independent aristocracy intimately associated with the history of the land. These revolutionary ideas were voiced with especial openness by Voss and Rotteck. Consciously or unconsciously, behind such notions there lurked particularist anger against Prussia, for hardly had Prussia with its national army liberated the fatherland, when from South Germany were once more raised the old false accusations against " the classic land of junkerdom and the corporal's cane."

Animated with such views, Rotteck, in the year 1819, when the Badenese diet opened, penned his *Ideas concerning Representative Institutions*, the scientific programme of the new liberalism. The idea of deducing demands for the future from the nature and history of the existing state, was all the more remote from the minds of the liberals because their culture was still entirely dominated by abstract philosophy, and because every publicist had a proud sense that he was tribune of the people for all Germany. Amid the anarchy of the Germanic Federation, little was left of the common German constitutional law ; no one could find permanent satisfaction in the contemplation of any single one of the nine-and-thirty separate sovereign states ; hence it resulted that all political writers involuntarily lapsed into the abstractions of the so-called " general constitutional law." Yet no one else spurned the historic world so presumptuously as did Rotteck. The enlightened man distinguished a threefold law, that of the past, the present, and " the future." The law of the future was without preamble esteemed as " the noblest of the three, and in essence the only valid law," whilst historic law was lightly dismissed as historic injustice. Consequently rational law must be the only rule for the state, rational law meaning the personal preferences of the Freiburg professor and his French teachers ; but of course, he modestly added, reality can never be more than an approximation to philosophic theory.

Just as Sieyès had combined the fire of Rousseau's theory of popular sovereignty with the water of Montesquieu's doctrine of tripartite authority, so Rotteck tried to dilute the doctrine of the *Contrat Social* with some of the ideas of monarchical constitutionalism. Briefly and clearly, in Rousseau's manner, he explained that the people is the natural possessor of the authority of the state, while the government is the artificial organ of the general will, its powers being the outcome of delegation. Consequently, in all circumstances, legislative authority is vested in the people, whose personality is otherwise lost ; hence diets can exercise all the rights which the people, when delegating governmental authority, may be reasonably conjectured to have tacitly reserved for itself. Therefore the bi-cammeral system is unjust even when the upper chamber represents, in capital and landed property, just as much share in the state as does the lower chamber. Naturally the people always knows what it desires, and always desires what is best :

" where the popular will rules, it is impossible for conditions to arise which conflict with natural rights." With these republican ideas, certain feudal conceptions are then combined. For instance, the representative represents nothing but his own constituency, since he has received no mandate from any other. All such contradictions are explained by the one dominant thought, by the intention to transfer the centre of gravity of political life ever downwards. Faithful to the views of his Breisgau peasants, Rotteck was willing, in case of need, to make a distinction between freeholders and copyholders, but unquestionably universal suffrage was the logical deduction from his theory. Indeed, the Berlin historian Woltmann had voiced this last demand as early as the year 1810, in his *Spirit of the New Prussian State Organisation.*

Thus powerful was the influence of abstract doctrine upon this loyal and obedient populace, as yet completely untouched by revolutionary greed. When barely out of its cradle, South German liberalism was already advocating the very same ideas which in France had created the ephemeral constitution of 1791, and soon afterwards had actually destroyed the monarchy ! The only thing peculiar to the good-natured Freiburger, in contradistinction with his French predecessors, was his hum-drum innocence, owing to which he had absolutely no conception of the consequences of his teaching, and his clear understanding of the municipal foundation of the organisation of the state. The ideas of the Prussian towns' ordinance arising from the depths of the German spirit, had long since quietly made the round of Germany ; even Rotteck could imagine the establishment of his constitutional splendours only upon the basis of local autonomy. Nevertheless it was impossible to over-look the French origin of his doctrines. For him also, the whole life of the state subsisted entirely in the forms of the constitution ; he also regarded equality, not liberty, as the highest of political goods, and therefore took a far more lenient view of the pseudo-constitution of the kingdom of Westphalia than of the Old German feudal order.

For this reason, his teaching also secured approval from the rigid Bonapartists in Munich. Here the *Alemannia* of Aretin and Hörmann continued to preach a shameless particularism. It asseverated : " Sooner will lions and eagles mate, than southerners and northerners unite." It instanced conversations between a " genuine Bavarian " and a preposterous soldier of the Pomeranian Landwehr who could hardly speak German. It mocked and calumniated everything that was North German, and bluntly declared that the general name of *deutsch* was utterly unmeaning. But the Old Bavarian particularism was now adorned with new feathers. Adroitly mingling true and false, Aretin described the Alemanni (for thus he termed all the South Germans) as the sole representatives of constitutional freedom, whereas the north was the land of feudalism—and this in the year 1816, long before the new South German constitutions had been promulgated. Subsequently he wrote a text-book of constitutional law, in which he endeavoured to fuse the principles of the new rational law with the views of the Rhenish Confederate bureaucracy; and when Aretin died while the work was in progress, Rotteck brought the old Bonapartist's book to completion.

Very different was the mental atmosphere surrounding the beginnings of North German liberalism. Here the concatenation of the times had not been completely interrupted; many of the ancient feudal institutions still persisted; a cordial sentiment of historic piety was active almost everywhere among the people. In this region the ideas of the Revolution had never struck such deep roots; the liberals did not propose to remodel the state completely in accordance with the abstractions of rational law, but demanded merely the revitalising and the progressive development of the old feudal order. The *Kieler Blätter* was the organ of this moderate tendency. Nowhere was the intimate relationship between the new liberalism and the idealistic enthusiasm of our classical literature so admirably displayed as in the circle of refined and amiable men who thronged round this journal, the most vigorous in the German north. At the hospitable board of Countess Rentzau on the Seeburg, and at that of Frau Schleiden on the Ascherberger See, there assembled the leading men of the university of Kiel, Dahlmann, Falck, Twesten, C. T. Welcker, with the physician Franz Hegewisch, the brilliantly witty hotspur, and the leaders of the Schleswig-Holstein nobility, Reventlow, Rumohr, Baudissin, and Moltke. They were all Goethe enthusiasts; it was a matter of pride to them all, here in the extreme northern march of Germany, to defend the German system against the growing arrogance of the Danish crown; and if they were fervent advocates of constitutional rights, their aim was simply to realise that ideal of free and humane culture which had formerly been enunciated in Weimar.

It was from this little world full of talent and charm that in 1815 was issued Dahlmann's essay *A Word concerning Constitution*, which in form and content was the precise opposite of Rotteck's writings. Dahlmann's work was as thoughtful and pithy as that of the Freiburg professor was thin and diffuse. Whereas Rotteck contested the validity of historic law, Dahlmann exhorted the Germans to realise fully the existence of their fathers in order to effect their own moral regeneration. Whilst Rotteck would tolerate monarchy only as a provisional institution, Dahlmann frankly displayed his strictly monarchical inclinations, and declared, to the horror of the philologists, that the Greeks and the Romans had failed to recognise the moment when it would have been advantageous to adopt a monarchical system. He looked for his ideal of the state in England, not in France. " In England the foundations of the political organisation towards which all the neo-European nations are striving are most purely developed and preserved." Since Montesquieu's *Esprit des Lois* had found its way into Germany, vague praise of English liberty had indeed never been lacking. At this very moment Rückert made the returning spirit of freedom exclaim: " Oh, build for me a temple after Albion's example ! " But Dahlmann was the first among publicists who, with a thorough knowledge of his subject and without any desire for blind imitation, held up the English parliament as [an example to Germany, just as Vincke shortly before had done with the British system of self-government. Such men as Niebuhr, Schleiermacher, and Thibaut, expressed their cheerful accord with the historian of Kiel, but it was many years before his ideas obtained wider support. The *Kieler Blätter* had little circulation outside Schleswig-Holstein, for the mass of the population of North Germany was oppressed by economic cares, while those in South Germany who might have been receptive to constitutional ideas preferred the more convenient catechism of Rotteck's rational law.

Opposed to both these tendencies of liberalism, separated from them by the breadth of the heavens, was Carl Ludwig von Haller, the dreaded " restorer of political science." The Bernese aristocrat had seen the power of the Swiss patricians collapse amid the storms of the Revolution, and subsequently, as an exile in Austrian service, had constructed the political system which was " to re-establish monarchy upon its true foundations, to overthrow the presumptuous revolutionary science of the godless eighteenth century, and to make the Catholic church shine with renewed effulgence." With the proud consciousness of his claim to rank as a universal historian, he announced his doctrine, first of all in *Allgemeine Staatskunde* (1808), and subsequently, from 1816 onwards, in *Restauration der Staatswissenschaft*. It seemed to him a wonderful dispensation of Providence that from him in particular, the born republican and Protestant, should proceed the anti-revolutionary doctrine of salvation. And indeed the sledge-hammer dialectical blows of his severe reasoning fell with crushing force upon the imaginative structures of the doctrine of natural rights. It was the incontrovertible demonstrations of this blustering naturalist which first shattered the belief in the state of nature, in the social contract, and in the innate sovereignty of the people, even in those circles of the uninstructed who were unable to follow the ideas of the historical school of law. Yet all that he advanced in place of this obsolete doctrine was a crude popularisation of the principles of patrimonial law upon which had been based the authority of the Bernese aristocracy. Just as in former days the rulers of Berne had treated the conquered subject lands of Aargau and Vaud simply as the property of their glorious republic, so Haller founded the state solely upon the right of the stronger. Land belongs to a prince, a corporation, or a church ; upon this property of a suzerain lord, and under his protection, settlers appear ; if the people should disappear, the state would still continue to exist in the person of the prince, who can readily find new subjects. Consequently the state resembles any other association based on civil law, differing from others only because it is more powerful and independent, and because its prince is " an owner, a man equipped with absolutely independent rights " ; he rules the nation through the instrumentality of his personal servants, is entitled to regard (it is even his duty to regard) himself and his house as the principal aim for which the state exists, but he must resist the dispersion of his own property and must protect his subjects with his own soldiers. A caricature of the ancient feudal state, which even in the fourteenth century existed nowhere in such crudity as this, was now propounded as the universally valid political ideal, was announced with the same air of infallibility that had characterised the writers who constructed the model imaginary constitutions of the Revolution. The subordination of the citizen, established by constitutional law, became degraded to a state of servitude defined in terms of civil law. In a word, the restorer of political science practically abolished the state.

Nowhere did his doctrine seem more utterly devoid of foundation, nowhere did it seem to conflict more hopelessly with facts, than in Prussia, for nowhere else had the majesty of the state-idea been esteemed so highly as in Prussia, where the princes had always been the first servants of the state. It was precisely upon this that depended Haller's fierce hatred of Frederick the Great, of that enlightened Prussian absolutism which had discovered the detestable conscription, and of the *Allgemeines Landrecht* [Prussian System of Common Law promulgated in 1794]. "Except on the title-page," said Haller, "there is nothing to show that this system of laws may not be intended rather for Japan and China than for the Prussian state." Yet it was in Prussia that Haller secured numerous and powerful adherents. The crown prince and his romanticist friends considered that in the idea of the state as private property they could rediscover the motley glories of the middle ages. Marwitz and the feudalists among the knighthood of the Mark hailed with delight this resolute thinker who reduced the monarch once more to the ranks of the land-owners, who divided society once again into the three castes of teachers, warriors, and manual workers, and assigned such valuable privileges to those "who had the freedom of the land." The absolutists found it satisfactory that in Haller's state the prince was above all the people. The ultramontanes were delighted with the praise of theocracy, which the convert had extolled as the freest and best of all political forms. The timid found their own fears confirmed by the complaints of the Bernese fanatic who imagined that the entire world was endangered by the great conspiracy of the freemasons, the illuminati, and the revolutionaries. To all opponents of the Revolution, the victorious polemic against natural rights was welcome. Whereas amid the simpler and wider relationships of French political life, the feudal and clerical party was already the open enemy of bureaucratic absolutism, in Germany all the aspects of the counter-revolution were still indistinguishably confused.

Far less support was secured by the purely ultramontane political doctrine of the skilled sophist, Adam Müller. The Roman Catholic system could not truly flourish in the homeland of heresy ; not one of our clerical authors could go so far as the Savoyard noble Joseph de Maistre, who, glowing with all the ardour and religious fanaticism of the Latin races, demanded, now half jestingly and now again wrathfully, that the sinful world should be subjected to the pope, and who fiercely contested the " bestial " science of " the century of folly." The able German convert lacked this emotional impulse, this crusadering enthusiasm. Adam Müller, with clear insight, descried indeed many of the weaknesses of liberalism, especially in respect of its economic doctrines ; he showed incisively how inadequate was the system of *laissez-faire* amid the struggles of social interest, how impossible was the complete international division of labour between independent nations, and prophesied that from the modern economic system would proceed a new plutocratic nobility more contemptible and more dangerous than the old aristocracy of birth. But in his *Theologische Grundlegung der Staatswissenschaft* we find no more than a repetition of Haller's doctrines, adorned with some of the frippery of theology and natural philosophy. In a manner even more arbitrary than that of Haller, he artificially effected a " natural " classification of society, sometimes distinguishing the teachers, the warriors, and the manual workers as the respective representatives of faith, love, and hope, and sometimes classifying the population into nobles, burghers, and rulers. Müller, like Haller, denied the distinction between constitutional law and civil law, and declared that every state must to all eternity be composed of a union of states. His ideal was a rational feudalism ; he hoped to solve the contradiction between politics and law by the power of faith, elevated to the rank of law.

Thus everything which German political science had secured during the last century and a half, since Puffendorf had delivered our political thinkers from the yoke of the theologians, was once more put in question, and political doctrine was degraded anew to the level of the theocratic conceptions of the middle ages. Friedrich Schlegel hailed the church as the greatest of all guilds, after whose example all the other corporations of civil society should be reconstituted. Baader spoke of the teaching caste, the warrior caste, and the caste of manual workers, as the three orders of every nation, rejecting the expression " the state " as an impious modern discovery. " Corporation, not association," was the catchword of the political romanticists, most of whom associated with this term no more than the indefinite conception of a debile state authority, limited by the power of guilds, diets of nobles, and self-governing communes, and in spiritual matters subjected to the control of the church. The sober-minded Gentz felt utterly alien from this dream-world of politics as understood by theologians, and declared to his friend Müller that everything characteristic of science—clearness, method, and consistency—was conspicuous by its absence. His secular sentiments were profoundly irritated when his friend asseverated that the peace of the world was dependent upon belief in God's incarnation. It was only when he imagined that he could himself recognise the precursors of the imminent revolution, that in an access of nervous anxiety he wrote : " You are perfectly right, all is lost unless religion should become established *pas seulement comme foi mais comme loi.*" But this contrite mood did not persist ; the first of German publicists stood on too lofty a plane to abandon for long his recognition of the secular nature of the state.

An abyss of centuries seemed to be established between the romanticist theory of the state and the doctrines of liberalism. The great majority of writers of note, the superior advantages of scientific culture, seemed to be on the conservative side ; and yet liberalism, notwithstanding its youthful immaturity, displayed more understanding of the needs of the present, had a better grasp of the just claims of the middle classes whose strength was increasing. Those who endeavoured to intermediate between these crudely contrasted views earned only suspicion for their pains. Even Steffens was accused of being a reactionary because in his brilliant though confused political writings, whilst demanding representative institutions, he nevertheless, after his fantastical manner, explained that " the communion of saints " represented the idea of the state, and regarded the privileges of the nobility as founded upon " the mystical depths of all those born of earth." To the patriots it seemed as if they were being mocked when the sanguine Steffens actually hailed as an advantage the feeble multiformity of the distracted political life of Germany, saying that every constitution was defective, and nothing but a plurality of constitutions could guarantee a higher spiritual unity ! Still less could Ancillon appease the angry spirits. His numerous works on political science looked down with distinguished contempt upon the shallow worshippers of the *Zeitgeist*, and yet manifested such poverty of ideas as to make Rotteck's limpid clarity seem in comparison an outpouring of genius, whilst he displayed in addition a chameleon-like vagueness of thought and of expression in order to leave always open a way of retreat. When in profound humility he acclaimed the

Holy Alliance as the reconciliation between politics and ethics, or when with unctuous prolixity he showed that there was no essential difference between an advisory diet and one which possessed powers of independent action, the liberals were all the more furious because they knew that the author, a cautious intermediary, was engaged at the Prussian court in the persistent support of the aims of the reactionary party.

Even before the return of the victorious armies, a disagreeable incident, trifling in itself, had greatly accentuated political differences, poisoning for a long time to come that party life which was now for the first time awakening. For years the Napoleonic fables of the Tugendbund and of the Jacobin intrigues of the Prussian patriots had been busily circulated in the Hofburg and among the Rhenish Confederate cabinets. Moreover, the well-disposed minor courts had been alarmed by the noisy terrorist language of the spokesmen of the Teutonising movement. All the governments felt insecure, realising how little the terms of peace and the federal act could satisfy the desires of the nation. In Prussia, the old opponents of Stein and of the Silesian headquarters-staff began once more to become active. As early as during the congress of Vienna a certain councillor named Janke endeavoured to arouse the suspicions of the chancellor on account of " the wild clamour for liberty " which proceeded from Arndt and Görres. When the monarchs were for the second time assembled in Paris, Schmalz, professor at Berlin, published a pamphlet entitled *Berichtigung einer Stelle in der Bredow-Venturinischen Chronik vom Jahre 1808.*[1] The passage in question had been emended by the author years before at Schmalz's instigation, and the Berlin professor merely availed himself of this excuse as a text on which to hang stories about the old Tugendbund, and to give a sinister picture of the subterranean intrigues of the secret societies which " perchance " had issued from the Tugendbund. Schmalz was Scharnhorst's brother-in-law and had always lived on good terms with the general ; during the period of French dominion he had preserved his patriotic courage ; and he had taken a vigorous part in the foundation of the Berlin university. In his innumerable writings on political science he displays a limited and hard intelligence ; hating the ideas of the Revolution, he was

[1] Rectification of a Passage in the Bredow-Venturini Chronicle of the Year 1808.

yet unable to offer a scientific refutation of their foundation, the doctrine of natural rights. His reputation was hitherto unstained. What a scandal, when this highly respected patriot suddenly launched a long series of furious accusations against the new Germanism. Just as formerly the Jacobins had held up before us the mirror of humanity, so now did these conspirators hold up the mirror of Teutonism to lead the people astray, to make us perjure ourselves in the endeavour to realise the insane notion of a single German nation. It was above all against Arndt, the most modest and moderate of the Teutonist orators that Schmalz directed his furious invectives. In his priceless *Catechism for the German Landwehrmann* Arndt had made use of the biblical phraseology: " Protect the defenceless and wives and children, for this is Christian and humane." From this Schmalz drew the conclusion that these reckless offenders " advocated murder, pillage, and rape, the last in express terms." Beyond question, as even the professor's opponents admitted, the unhappy man was acting in good faith.

For the first time for three hundred years a genuinely national movement was manifest in the quiet land of North Germany ; the contemplation of all the elemental energies which are unchained in such a stormy epoch had obscured and bemused many a weak nature. Just as in England in the days of Charles II thousands of excellent persons were convinced of the reality of the purely fictitious popish plot, so now in Germany a gloomy delusion spread like a devastating pestilence, and it was not the base and the stupid alone who believed in the secret conspiracies of demagogic leagues. The malicious half-truths of the Schmalzian pamphlet were even more wounding than its manifest absurdities. In defiance of the literary sense of self-complacency, he declared that the mass of the nation had never read a line of the writings of the publicists. From the magnificent unpretentiousness of the Prussian nation, which performed colossal deeds as if they were a matter of course, the denunciator drew the conclusion that there had nowhere been any extraordinary enthusiasm, but that the Prussians had hastened to the colours in the spirit in which neighbours come to extinguish a fire. When Arndt's writing on *Preussens rheinische Mark* declared " Prussia must be everywhere, and Prussia's Germany everywhere," and when it named the state of the Hohenzollerns the only German land capable of raising Germany from futility to glory, these vague prophecies seemed to the accuser sufficient proof of a deliberate design for the dethronement of all the minor German princes.

The best men of the nation were moved to the soul when they saw the repute of the most splendid period of modern German history thus shamefully soiled. The book-market was flooded with rejoinders, and during the last months of the year 1815 almost the whole of cultured Germany was breathlessly engaged in this wretched dispute. Even foreigners intervened. The *Times* took it upon itself to hold up obedient Hanover as an example to the unruly Prussians. Niebuhr and Schleiermacher refuted the pitiful attack, the former in a profoundly serious manner, the latter with unsparing ridicule. Some of the other rejoinders unquestionably displayed the blind self-conceit of youthful liberalism. Ludwig Wieland, son of the poet, bluntly answered the defender of absolute monarchy in the words : " The representative system is the true method, and indeed the only method, which legally disposed and patriotic men can publicly recognise ! " Councillor Kappe in Aix-la-Chapelle, a distinguished Prussian official, confidently maintained that German unity could be secured by the talisman-like word " constitution," for, he said, " on all hands the national will is striving towards such unity, and all divergences therefrom are dependent upon the excessive power of governmental authority as contrasted with that of the popular will ! "

These disputes came at a very inopportune moment for the king. Just before, when taking over the new provinces he had repeatedly declared that he was concerned solely with the future of the state, regarding the past as past. He had a keen, appreciation of all that he owed to the love and devotion of his Prussians, and confidentially assured the czar that he regarded it as his sacred duty to ensure the happiness of this loyal people. But the contemplation of the party struggles of the Parisians had disquieted him profoundly, and when he learned that the municipal representatives of Berlin had made the unheard-of proposal to subject the civic and defensive companies to the sole supervision of the municipality, he ordered the chancellor to take strict measures lest this party spirit which was unknown to the Prussian nation should gain the upper hand.[1] In the spring of 1816 he put an end to the literary dispute by an admirably conceived and amiably worded ordinance.

[1] King Frederick William to Czar Alexander, March, 1816. Cabinet Order to Hardenberg, September 1, 1815. Further details in Appendix IV.

The king publicly recognised that the same sentiments which had led to the formation of the old Tugendbund had in the year 1813 animated the majority of the Prussian nation and had led to the salvation of the fatherland, but now, in time of peace, the effect of secret societies could not fail to be deleterious. The old prohibition of such societies was therefore renewed. The continuance of the dispute was prohibited, and an enquiry which Niebuhr and his friends had demanded for their own justification was refused as superfluous. The turmoil now subsided, but everyone felt that the bad seed sown by the accuser (who, at this juncture, was distinguished by a Prussian order and by one from Würtemberg) had not fallen upon perfectly sterile soil.—Such were the sentiments amid which the German princes and the German peoples entered the greatly desired epoch of peace. On one side there prevailed a tacit and causeless mood of suspicion ; on the other there existed a blind faith in the magic influence of constitutional political forms, a childlike confidence in the unerring wisdom of the people. Among the masses, finally, there predominated a profound longing for repose and peaceful labour.

CHAPTER IV

OPENING OF THE GERMAN BUNDESTAG.

§ I. THE EUROPEAN SITUATION.

THE world-empire had fallen, and upon its ruins there was re-established a peaceful society of states. The old system of European politics, which endeavoured by means of mutable alliances and counter-alliances to preserve a balance of power between the five leading states, did not, however, at first return. As Gentz said, all the nations of Europe now constituted a great union under the supervision of the four powers which had carried on the war against Napoleon and had just renewed their alliances in Paris. Through so many years of work, during the weary time of waiting and of suffering, had this saving alliance been brought into existence; now in three terrible years of war it had stood the test. During their close and prolonged association, the monarchs and the leading statesmen had become accustomed to confidential personal intercourse, such as had hitherto been unprecedented among the crowned heads : they determined that in the future also they would consider all the great problems of European politics in personal interviews. The Quadruple Alliance regarded itself as the supreme court of justice of Europe ; it considered that its first duty was to preserve from a breach of the peace the new ordering of the society of states, and consequently that the great powers must exercise a common supervision over France, a country whose actions could not be counted upon, a focus of revolution and of wars. Whilst the European army of occupation, under the supreme command of Wellington, was to preserve order in France, the four ambassadors in Paris, meeting in regular conferences, were to deal with the current affairs of the great alliance, and to support the court of the Tuileries with their counsel ; in isolated cases the four even invited the duc de Richelieu to join their deliberations. All the contentious problems which had resulted from the

Viennese and Parisian negotiations, were referred to this conference of ambassadors; it was only the unravelling of the complex German territorial questions which was reserved for special discussion at Frankfort.

Never before had the system of states constituted so firmly ordered a federal community. The protectorate of the four powers dominated Europe, less forcibly than, but just as unrestrainedly as, formerly the will of Napoleon. The states of the second rank (in the diplomatic circles of the quadruple alliance, they were jestingly spoken of as *les Sous-Alliés*) were completely excluded from all the affairs of high politics; when the haughty Spanish court, which could not forget the days of Philip II, demanded admission to the Parisian conference of ambassadors, it was met with a brusque refusal, Prussia's negative being the bluntest of all. Nowhere was the predominance of the four powers felt more painfully than in France. Although the French had no certain information regarding the extraordinary powers of the conference of ambassadors, in questions of national honour the instinct of the masses rarely goes altogether astray. The nation felt obscurely that its government was supervised by the foreign powers, and it was inspired with an overwhelming hatred for the " lord-proconsul," Wellington. It was impossible for the old royal regime to strike deep roots once more, for the very reason that it was regarded by the people as a foreign dominion. At the peace congress of Paris, Humboldt had declared that the Revolution would never come to an end if Europe were to take France under her guardianship. All too soon was the admonition justified.

The four powers were at one in regarding the existence of the legitimate dynasty as a strong support of the newly-ordered society of states, and for this reason they treated the French court with an upright and careful benevolence. Hardly had the congress of Paris settled the question of the cession of territory, when Gneisenau, as early as October, 1815, began secret negotiations with the Tuileries. Accustomed in politics, as on the battle-field, to choose his means with little circumspection, he had in the days of the Saxon negotiations seriously considered whether Prussia might not be able to carry her claims through with the aid of the returned Napoleon. Now, once more, even an adventurous way seemed to him permissible, if only he could secure the aim of establishing on a firm foundation the new system of states. His negotiator, Major von

Royer, a legitimist in Prussian service, went so far, with Hardenberg's approval, as to offer the duc de Richelieu a secret alliance. Prussia, as France's nearest neighbour, was to pledge herself in case of a revolution to help the Bourbons with her entire military force. The negotiations led to nothing, plainly because Frederick William ultimately hesitated to undertake such far-reaching and dangerous responsibilities; but they afforded sufficient proof that Prussia was determined to forget alike the intrigues of Talleyrand and all the other proofs of Bourbon ingratitude, and to live on terms of friendship with her western neighbour.[1]

The savage struggles of the French parties aroused all the more anxiety in the conference of ambassadors because the wealthy land recovered with wonderful rapidity from its economic struggles, and soon appeared capable of undertaking a new war. According to the irreconcilable opposition, France consisted of two nations, the conquerors and the conquered of Waterloo. Where was to be found any common platform for the democratic masses, intoxicated by the glories of the world-ruling tricolour, and the émigrés, these " pilgrims to the shrine," who dreamed of the oriflamme and St. Louis ? Mockingly did Béranger exhibit to the old nobility the image of the Marquis de Carabas ; his satirical song, " C'est le roi, le roi, le roi," held kingship up to contempt. The whole country was covered with a network of secret societies ; every veteran of the *grande armée* who returned to his native village preached the Napoleonic legend. Even the talented doctrinaires who expressed their liberal views in the *Minerve*, undermined the prestige of the crown by a malicious mistrust. Yet more dangerous than the passion of the opposition seemed the fanatical infatuation of the royalist ultras who ruled the chamber of deputies. The hotspurs of the *Chambre introuvable* were aiming directly at the restoration of the ancient feudal order ; they demanded a sanguinary revenge against the regicides and the murderers of God. When King Louis endeavoured to moderate the savage zeal of the émigrés, they too turned against the crown, no less defiantly than did those Polish magnates who had

---

[1] Information gathered from Royer's letters to Gneisenau, October 3, 1815, and subsequent dates, kindly communicated to me by Dr. H. Delbrück. The reason for the failure of the negotiations was not expressly given in the letters, but can hardly have been other than that suggested in the text. On November 9, Royer reports that King Frederick William must now be let into the secret, since everything depends upon his decision ; whilst a few days later, the whole affair vanishes from the correspondence.

once exclaimed to their King Sigismund, *rege sed non impera!*
The feudal ideas of unbridled licence for the nobles reappeared,
adorned with the catchwords of the new parliamentary doctrine.
In the name of constitutional freedom, Chateaubriand demanded
that the crown should be subordinated to the will of the
chambers, and in his writings he already advocated that revolutionary theory of parliamentarism which the liberals subsequently
made their own, epitomised in the words, *le roi règne, mais il
ne gouverne pas.*

All the members of the conference of ambassadors, led by
Pozzo di Borgo, supported the king in his resistance of the
ultras. Even the high tory English statesmen disapproved of
the partisan fury of the émigrés, although the liberal zeal of the
" Jacobin " czar and of his obtrusive ambassador always
remained suspicious to them. When Wellington contemplated
the insane activities of the ultras, who received their instructions in the Pavillon Marsan from the comte d'Artois, he said
with concern that the offspring of Louis XV would not be able
to rule France, and that for this Artois would be to blame !
Metternich wrote warningly : " The return to a past order of
affairs constitutes one of the greatest dangers for a state which
has come into existence out of a revolution." Subsequently
he allowed the uneasy exclamation to escape him : " The
legitimists are legitimising the Revolution." The Prussian
ambassador, von der Goltz, an old member of Blucher's headquarters-staff, displayed himself a diplomat of worthy conduct
and sound judgment ; he was never weary of warning his court
concerning the suicidal party-rage of the royalists. The result
was that Hardenberg declared, as early as March, 1816, that
the established order in France could be secured only by the
dissolution of the *Chambre introuvable.* The other three powers
hesitated at first to recommend so bold a measure to the
Tuileries. But when the infatuation of the ultras remained
incurable, King Louis at length plucked up courage. On
September 5th the dissolution was effected, amid general rejoicing ; the elections returned the moderate parties in a majority,
and the Richelieu-Decazes ministry was on tolerable terms with
the new chamber. Henceforward the four powers began to
contemplate the future of France with somewhat more confidence. In a note of February 10, 1817, they informed the
duc de Richelieu that his oft-repeated request for a diminution
of the burden of the military occupation could not be acceded

to, and that Wellington's army was to be reduced by one-fifth, by 30,000 men ; but they did not refrain from adding that the praiseworthy principles of the duke and his colleagues had contributed greatly to this resolve. So profoundly was proud France humiliated : her first minister had to accept the formal praise of the high council of Europe.

It soon became apparent that the independence of modern states cannot permanently endure so intimate a community as had been established by the Quadruple Alliance. The old contrast between Russian and Austro-English policy continually recurred, and Czar Alexander did all he could to increase the suspicion of the courts of Vienna and of London. Without consulting his allies, in February, 1816, he published the charter of the Holy Alliance ; the world was to admire him, him alone, as the saviour and the leader of allied Europe. Whilst the other powers reduced their armaments, the Russian army was increased, and in serried masses was moved nearer to the frontier. The czar took delight in exaggerated descriptions of Russian military power, and notwithstanding the experiences of the last campaigns, this power was, in fact, incredibly overestimated by everyone ; even Gneisenau believed that Russia had more than a million soldiers at her disposal, and that she was in a position to begin a war of offence with the immediate use of 500,000 men. Metternich anxiously declared that the burden of these armaments, and his orthodox enthusiasm, might readily mislead the czar into warlike adventures ; the Austrian minister believed that everywhere, in France and Spain, in Italy and Turkey, he came upon traces of the secret intrigues of Russian agents.[1] This restless, ambitious policy sailed under the liberal flag ! In all the courts the Russian ambassador put in a plea for a system of " wise freedom," whilst the English ambassadors were just as zealous in the issue of warnings against the " dangerous folly " of liberal attempts at a constitution. In Poland, Alexander promulgated a constitution at Christmas in 1815. Although this fundamental law made no important alterations in the cancer of Polish affairs or in the enslavement of the country-folk, and although it placed all political power in the hands of the nobility, nevertheless the name of constitution exercised its magic charm. Uncritical liberals triumphantly acclaimed the gracious gift of the czar, and asked impatiently

[1] Krusemark's Reports, dated February 24, 1816, February 1 and March 23, 1817, March 7 and April 9, 1818.

when Germany's princes were going to follow the example of the enlightened autocrat, who was secretly preparing a charter even for Russia herself. Of the two statesmen whom the czar consulted in foreign affairs, the insignificant Nesselrode remained devoted to his friend Metternich ; all the more suspicious, therefore, to the court of Vienna seemed the liberal philhellene Capodistrias. The Austrian general Steigentesch soon found himself in just as painful a situation at St. Petersburg as was the Russian ambassador Stackelberg at Vienna. *Caveat consul!* was the continual exclamation in Stackelberg's reports ; in alarmed phrases he warned his imperial master against the cunning of these Viennese " Dalai-Lama." The secret compact of January 3, 1815, remained unforgotten in St. Petersburg, and the chief blame in this matter was ascribed to Prince Metternich by all Russian statesmen.

The profound mistrust of the tory cabinet for the czar was plainly shown in a proposal which in August, 1816, Lord Cathcart transmitted to the court of St. Petersburg. A conference of officers was to assemble, to consult about a simultaneous reduction of armaments on the part of all the powers, and to prescribe to each state the strength of its peace army. It was unmistakable that this pacific proposal was directed against the Russian armaments. Hence Metternich eagerly accepted the suggestion, and rejoined, with a friendly side-thrust at the Prussian army, that the diminution of armies was especially desirable in a period " in which even revolutionaries assume a military mask." Alexander gave a sympathetic but non-committal answer. The English proposal was shelved, for it was felt that so unnatural a limitation of the most important suzerain right of independent states could not seriously be carried into effect. Prussia, in especial, could never allow the extent of her national army to depend upon the preferences of powerful neighbours.[1] Meanwhile at the Austrian court anxiety grew from month to month, and at the new year of 1818 Metternich directly proposed to privy-councillor von Jordan, Hardenberg's confidant, who was in Vienna at the time upon the affairs of the Germanic Federation, that Prussia should conclude with Austria a secret defensive alliance, in case of a Russian attack. Hardenberg was immediately prepared to accede to this idea, for to him

---

[1] Memorial of the English government upon the European situation; Metternich's *Aperçu sur le mémoire anglais*. (Sent to Hardenberg by Krusemark in August and October, 1816.)

the friendship of Austria outweighed all other considerations. The king, however, refused. Why should Prussia abandon her old ally (who, besides, had already penetrated the secret designs of Metternich) on account of the indefinite fears of the Hofburg? The chancellor was profoundly displeased by this refusal; in his opinionated way he believed that Frederick William was once more playing a part similar to that which he had played in the tragical epoch of 1805. Vainly did he appeal for aid to Prince Wittgenstein, who was an unconditional adherent of Austria; vainly did he complain that his royal master displayed so little confidence. The monarch held firm, and on May 2nd Hardenberg was forced to refuse the Austrian offer.[1]

The English court was especially suspicious regarding the many-sided activities of Russian diplomacy in Spain. Here, as in France, the four powers were earnestly endeavouring to keep the re-established monarchy within bounds, in so far as their regard for the irritable Spanish national pride rendered this possible. They all felt how greatly the common cause of the European restoration was being damaged by the sins of King Ferdinand. The whole liberal world was in an uproar, and Byron wrote flaming verses against the Catholic Moloch, when the most profligate of the European princes re-established the inquisition immediately after his return, when he visited horrible punishments upon the heroes of that national war which had restored the Bourbon throne, when from the ranks of his monkish adherents the insane cry arose, " Long live chains, long live oppression, long live King Ferdinand, death to the nation!" But whilst all the powers were united in condemning the Spanish government, Russia at the same time endeavoured to undermine the position of power which England had acquired in the peninsula during the war of independence. The Russian ambassador, Tatischtschew, gradually acquired in Madrid even greater influence than Pozzo di Borgo enjoyed in Paris. It was soon observed that Russia desired the renewal of the old Bourbon family-treaty, in order to be able to employ against England the naval power of the two crowns. The unwearied Russian patron at length went so far as to sell a portion of his own fleet to Spain, and demanded that by common intervention the European powers should reconcile the revolted South American colonies with the Spanish motherland. All the powers rejected this adventurous proposal; England and Austria

[1] Hardenberg's Diary, January 14, March 12, May 2, 1818.

observed the Mediterranean policy of the czar with anxiety, an anxiety which was all the more lively because new disturbances were now threatening in the Balkan peninsula.

How often did Metternich complain that his "best and firmest ally," Turkey, remained the only state in Europe which could not secure recognition from the great powers. Through slothful arrogance, the Porte had refrained from demanding from Europe a guarantee for her territorial dominion; now, by the conclusion of the Holy Alliance, she found herself formally excluded from the society of European states. The hatred of the Mohammedans against the Giaours flamed up powerfully once more; Sultan Mahmud intentionally left certain articles of the treaty of Bucharest unfulfilled, and confidently awaited the reopening of the Russian war.[1] Meanwhile the inevitable rising of the unhappy Rayahs had already begun. The Serbs would not lay down their arms, and, under the leadership of Milosch, acquired the status of a semi-independent Christian national community whose very existence conflicted with the fundamental idea of the Ottoman empire; envoys from the dissatisfied Greeks assembled in St. Petersburg, and had a friendly reception from Capodistrias. Neither in London nor in Vienna was there any recognition of the inevitability of the wars of independence which were here preparing. In the circles of the high tories, the maintenance of Turkey was absolutely an article of political faith, especially since English interests in the east seemed to have been safeguarded by the aquirement of the Ionian islands. Notwithstanding all reasons to the contrary, people still appealed to the saying of Pitt, who declared that he would not talk politics with a man who did not regard the maintenance of the Porte as essential. Metternich, in his turn, unhesitatingly applied to the foreign dominion of the Turks his doctrine of the inviolable rights of legitimate authority. He detested the despairing Christian nations of the Balkan peninsula, not merely as protégés of Russia, but also as rascally rebels. In his concern he failed to notice that the unsteady ambition of the liberal autocrat, whilst playing at times with high-flying resolves, nevertheless lacked the resolution requisite to bring his schemes to perfection. To the anxious enquiries of General Steigentesch, the czar replied scornfully that it would be opposed to his conscience to shed the blood of a single soldier in a

---

[1] Krusemark's Report, January 8, 1817.

struggle against these Turkish swine.[1] To his ambassador in Vienna he had a despatch sent, to the effect that the European ministers had not yet liberated their minds from antiquated and pusillanimous ideas, the reason being that their hearts were untouched by the morality of the gospel. From this arose their mistrust of Russia, but to-day in accordance with the counsels of divine providence, there prevailed the rule of public opinion, based upon truth and justice.

Thus, while the Hofburg was trembling in contemplation of the imagined secret plans of the czar, the Austrian government was itself animated by a genuine desire for peace. How miraculously had this ancient Austria, after so many defeats and so many losses, risen once more to a height of power which recalled the days of Wallenstein ; rarely indeed, at the issue of a world war, had any state found itself so completely at the goal of its desires. Metternich could pride himself on the extent to which, by prudent husbanding and well-timed utilisation of the energies of the realm, he had personally contributed to this brilliant result ; and since even as quite a young man he had always wished to be regarded as one who had foreseen and prophesied everything that happened, his self-satisfaction now increased to the degree of immeasurable arrogance. To him it seemed that the whole new ordering of European affairs was his personal work, and that its preservation was the sole task of his life, since he himself and his state could not but lose by any change. The profound inveracity of his spirit made it easy for him to explain facts in a way agreeable to himself ; the images of the past became rearranged in his mind, and before long, in the history of the generation that had just come to a close, he could see nothing but a colossal welter of madness and crime ; amid the general confusion, he alone had remained free from passion, free from error, and above all, as he was always glad to maintain, free from self-love. He spoke contemptuously about " politicians of the breed of Richelieu and Mazarin."

The foreign diplomats soon observed how difficult it was to carry on a business conversation with him ; it was his custom to deliver long and learned addresses, in which he expounded his infallible opinion to the ears of respectful listeners. Monotonously, unctuously, verbosely, and grandiloquently, did his letters and despatches continue to revolve in innumerable

[1] Krusemark's Report, April 17 and May 13, 1816.

circumlocutions around the single idea of the maintenance of the *status quo*. Yet behind this proud confidence there was concealed a secret anxiety. Metternich dreaded war because he knew the weakness of the neglected Austrian military system, and still more did he dread revolution. He never doubted the excellence of the system which drained the life-blood of the two great nations of Central Europe ; but he saw that the party of revolution, which had alarmed him all his life, continued to prowl around in obscurity ; he regarded it as prepared to hurl a fire-brand upon his artificial structure. Since he had always been convinced that the Tugendbund had for long fostered revolution in the Prussian army, it was with great anxiety that he contemplated the party struggles in France and the convulsive movements of national feeling in Germany and Italy. He learned with horror that even in England, the citadel of the counter-revolution, the idea of parliamentary reform was reawakening, that the fiery Cobbett was widely circulating his *Political Register* among the masses, and that the long-neglected lower classes were remembering their human rights. The master of diplomacy had hitherto troubled himself as little regarding the problems of constitutional government and of administration, as he had about the great civilising aims of national life, whose fulfilment the genuine statesman regards as his highest duty. He even stood so remote from the internal life of his country as to sum up his judgment upon the character of the Austrian monarchy in the phrase that without being a federative state Austria still had the advantages as well as the disadvantages of the federative structure. Utterly void of poietic ideas, his policy was one which lived from hand to mouth. It was his view that enough was done by always running promptly to the spot with fire-buckets as soon as the flames of revolution broke out anywhere. His policy swore as unconditionally by the idea of stability as did that of youthful liberalism by the abstractions of the law of reason, and the enemy of the doctrinaires himself ultimately fell into a doctrinairism which was far more barren than were the theories of Rotteck. The more clearly it became manifest year by year that the living energies of history could not stand still in front of the limits imposed by the treaties of Vienna, the more desperate became this peace-lover's fear of the revolution ; until at length, in almost all his despatches, the spectre of the impending world-conflagration recurred like the fixed idea of a lunatic.

In one region alone of her dominions had Austria failed to carry out all her intentions; the plan for the Italian alliance had been frustrated in Vienna by the opposition of Piedmont. In order to win over the court of Turin for this idea, the Hofburg now put forward claims to the western shore of Lake Maggiore and to the important road over the Simplon, but since Russia and Prussia supported the threatened Piedmontese,[1] Metternich let this plan drop for a time, and contented himself with the actual dominion over Italy, which for the nonce seemed tolerably well-established. It was true that the delight with which the invading Austrians had been greeted in Lombardy had long since evaporated; the people murmured at the relentless dismissal of so many old officials; at the severe methods of a government completely unacquainted with the peculiarities of the country; at the malpractices of the secret police, and at the roughness of the *bastone tedesco*. In February, 1816, when Emperor Francis made his ceremonial progress through the new Lombardo-Venetian kingdom, he was received everywhere with unmistakable coldness; even the Prussian ambassador, General von Krusemark, a warm friend of Austria, had to report to the king that the Austrian officials and officers were one and all detested, and that all Italians " to whom the idea of an independent nation had become dear " were disaffected towards the new government. There was no breach of order anywhere, and Metternich, when Hardenberg communicated to him the names of certain suspected Italian patriots, confidently replied that the Italians, notwithstanding their hostile sentiments, lacked courage for conspiracy.[2] What was there to fear? In every court throughout the peninsula there prevailed a rigid absolutist spirit in conformity with the fundamental principles of the Hofburg; moreover, by a secret treaty signed on June 12, 1815, the Bourbons of Naples had pledged themselves to maintain the ancient monarchical institutions, and to report to the court of Vienna anything which seemed to threaten the peace of Italy.

In relation to German affairs, above all, the Hofburg was altogether without plan and without ideas. It would be enough if the Germanic Federation could be held together at all, and if in case of war it could give military help to the House of

---

[1] Krusemark's Report, April 10, 1816.
[2] Krusemark's Report from Milan, February 28, March 8, 1816; from Vienna, January 4, 1817.

Austria ; as long as this was done it mattered little if the deliberations of the Bundestag of Frankfort were as vain as had been those of the Reichstag of Ratisbon. Metternich cordially despised the petty German courts, and unhesitatingly appealed to the czar whenever " some of the German princes desiring to make a trade in inhabitants " could not come to terms about their territorial disputes. He knew, however, that these petty princes remained of the Austrian party solely because they revered the Hofburg as the benevolent protector of their sovereignty. Consequently he proposed to leave them as free as possible. Even the inconvenient article 13 of the federal act, the promise to summon diets, did not at first seem very dangerous, since the majority of the German courts were above all suspicion of liberal sentiments. The prudent Austrian statesman had never been misled into imagining that the imperial house could participate in the political life of the German nation, or could do anything on behalf of German rights and German well-being. In his memoirs he wrote unreservedly : " As far as Austria is concerned, the expression ' German senti-ment ' (especially in the sense in which the term has been employed among the higher circles of the population in North Germany since the disasters to Prussia and the North) is simply a myth." In his view every awakening of national ideas in Germany involved a danger to the dominion of Austria. Emperor Francis, finally, regarded patriotism with direct sus-picion, considering it a dangerous revolutionary passion, and he would never hear of an Austrian fatherland, since all the order of the state reposed simply upon the obedience of subjects to the person of the ruler; when there was laid before him a proposal for sending a letter of thanks to Schwarzenberg and the army, he carefully erased the word " fatherland," writing in its place, " my people " and " my state."

A good understanding with Prussia was essential, if the Germans were to remain in a loose defensive alliance without ever awakening to a strong national life. Metternich had not failed to recognise this, but how differently from Hardenberg did he understand the idea of peaceful dualism ! He had formed his views of the Prussian state in accordance with the contemptuous and hostile judgments which were current in the circles of the Catholic imperial nobility, and, subsequently as ambassador to Berlin in the years before 1805, he had observed, close at hand, the weakest period in the history of the

Frederician monarchy. He never could overcome the repellent impressions of those days. To him the Prussian state always remained no more than a chance structure, a household of different nations that had been thrown together. " Everything seems contradictory in the history of Prussia, and her annals embrace barely a century ! " Consequently he believed throughout life that the world-empire of Napoleon would have endured if only the Imperator had treated the state of Frederick with somewhat more intelligence, and had accepted it, as a modest middle-sized state, into the ranks of the Confederation of the Rhine. In the year 1811, he definitely counted upon the destruction of Prussia, and hoped with the help of Napoleon to gain Silesia for the House of Austria.

When this expectation was frustrated and Prussia experienced a glorious resurrection, Metternich still failed to have any understanding of the moral energies which had rendered the humiliated state capable of the unequal struggle. He delighted in regarding Prussian affairs in the gloomiest light, and spoke disdainfully of the narrow, irresolute king, and of Hardenberg's credulous weakness ; he persuaded himself that at the time of the truce the Prussian army had " existed only in name " ; he even thought it possible to decry the fame of Blucher, Gneisenau, and York, by a few silly jokes about the grammatical blunders of Marshal Forwards. In the Hofburg there was no doubt whatever that Prussia had been saved from destruction by Austria alone ; Metternich had never recognised the existence of more than three great powers upon the continent. Re-established Prussia was ever to remain the first auxiliary of the House of Austria ; in the view of the court of Vienna, the meaning of German dualism was the dominion of Austria with the voluntary co-operation of Prussia. Metternich, however, had a masterly understanding of the way in which he could deceive Hardenberg about the latter's own heart-felt opinions ; he preserved forms so carefully that the statesmen of Berlin remained firmly convinced that Prussia was regarded in Vienna as a thoroughly equal and friendly great power. During twenty years it happened once only, and this on a comparatively trifling occasion, that Metternich permitted himself to make any observation to the Prussian ambassador regarding the internal affairs of the allied state. Such questions were always discussed solely in confidential letters to Prince Wittgenstein, the most trustworthy of Metternich's friends in Berlin, or were cautiously touched on in friendly conversation during the personal meetings of the monarchs.

This carefully calculated reserve did not come easily to the prudent man, for in the bottom of his heart he was far more uneasy about the internal condition of Prussia than he was about the situation in France. He could not conceal from himself that Prussia had laid down her arms filled with bitter memories of an undeserved diplomatic reverse, and that it would be impossible for her to content herself permanently with the ridiculous disintegrated state of her territory. He held firmly to the belief that the administration of his deadly enemy Stein had filled young Prussia with dangerous ideas, with a revolutionary lust of conquest, and his suspicions were confirmed by the writings of Arndt and Görres. Most sinister of all seemed the unprecedented emergence of the Prussian national army; not one of the statesmen of the old school could believe that so much unconsidered candour, so much noisy patriotic enthusiasm, could go hand in hand with invincible loyalty to the crown. Moreover, the Prussian officers by no means concealed their contemptuous opinion of the Austrian army and Austrian military leadership. Many were of the same view with their gallant General Steinmetz, of York's corps, who at the time of the second peace of Paris wrote bluntly : " Austria no longer belongs to the German household ; the supreme dominion in Germany falls to the Prussians." During the first two years after the conclusion of peace, all the courts of the Quadruple Alliance continually suffered from the fear that Prussia might be led into revolutionary adventures by her fanatical army. Wellington declared that Prussia was worse than France, since in the former authority no longer existed. Alexander excused his military preparations by the need for protecting Germany against the revolution. " Prussia, in especial, is in a bad condition," he said to Steigentesch, " and the king of Prussia will be the first to whom I shall have to furnish assistance."[1]

In reality, nothing was further from the court of Berlin than the ambition of a revolutionary war policy. Everyone throughout the country knew that the king was firmly determined that never again, if he could possibly help it, would he draw the sword. No doubt among the younger officials and officers there were not wanting a few men of far-seeing intelligence who recognised the untenability of the configuration of the state

[1] Krusemark's Report, April 17, 1816.

domain, and who demanded speedy redress. In an able memorial, president von Motz, in Erfurt, maintained that the leading position in the north, for which Hardenberg was working, could be secured only if Prussia could acquire Upper Hesse and Fulda in exchange for portions of her Rhenish Westphalian provinces, and thus regain on the Lower Main what had been lost on the Upper Main in Ansbach-Bayreuth ; in this way the whole of North Germany would be surrounded by Prussian territory, and the important military position of the Kinzig defile, together with the chief commercial artery of Germany, the road from Frankfort to Leipzig, would pass into the possession of Prussia. He referred warningly to the hostile sentiments of the Rhenish Confederate states of the south : " As regards both Germany and France, these states seem to be animated by but one interest, namely, the dispersal and isolation of the German national energy and the hindering of all unity." For this reason he implored the chancellor to thrust a wedge of Prussian territory between Hesse and Bavaria, so that the North German central states might not be exposed " to pressure from the south."[1] But how could so bold a plan be realised without war ? The government rejected the proposal, being honourably resolved to content itself with the new arrangement of frontiers, more especially since the king spurned any territorial exchange as a disregard of his duties as a ruler. Hardenberg's German policy was content with the more modest task of favouring the development of the federal constitution which had been promised in Vienna and, above all, of firmly establishing the federal military system.

Alike to the king and to the chancellor, the friendship of the eastern powers seemed indispensable to the carrying out of these peaceful plans ; the only difference was that now, as before, Frederick William regarded the czar as his most trusty ally, whereas Hardenberg relied especially on Austria. The union of the royal house with the Russian court became even more intimate when Alexander's brother, the grand duke Nicholas, was betrothed to the amiable princess Charlotte. The marriage took place two years later, in June, 1817 ; and the Prussians learned with justified resentment that the princess had been received into the Greek church. The gentle spirit of the king made it impossible for him to contradict the heart-felt inclination of his

[1] Motz's Memorial concerning the geographical union of the eastern with the western half of the Prussian state, 1817. Humboldt's Reply, March 18, 1819.

beautiful favourite daughter ; through paternal tenderness the faithful Protestant was led to make a sacrifice to Russian arrogance, a sacrifice which had long seemed a trifle to the minor Protestant courts, but which was unexampled in the House of the Hohenzollerns, and which comported ill with the pride of a great power. Notwithstanding the friendship between the courts, the two nations became speedily estranged after the war, and indeed almost hostile. The enthusiasm displayed for the Cossacks in the spring of 1813 had passed away, and no permanent friendliness resulted from the long-continued military co-operation of the two armies. The Prussian liberals put little trust in the emotional utterances of the liberal-minded autocrat, and detested Muscovy as one of the powers of darkness ; while in the border provinces, everyone execrated the petty and dishonourable spitefulness of the Russian customs officials.

§ 2. THE FRANKFORT NEGOTIATIONS.

Such were the relationships among the great powers when the first envoys to the Bundestag arrived in the ancient coronation town. The curse of ludicrousness which was to rest upon the federal assembly throughout its activities, was attached to it from its very birth. First of all, the opening, which by the Paris congress had been announced for September 1, 1815, was postponed for three months. Then the envoys, who assembled in the course of November, had still to wait a whole year, exposed to the mockery of the inhabitants of Frankfort, before the proceedings began. The reason for this delay was that the two great powers wished first of all to settle the difficult problems involved in the German territorial disputes, and, more especially, the hopelessly confused Bavario-Austrian negotiations.

At the congress of Vienna, the court of Munich had not secured the promised continuous domain, and consequently remained in temporary possession of Salzburg and the regions along the lower Inn, which were to be handed over to Austria. In order to secure a compromise which should be in its own favour, it had since then persistently supported the policy of the Hofburg ; in Paris, the Bavarian minister Rechberg had given but lukewarm support to the demands of Prussia and of the petty German states, because Austria did not desire that

France should be diminished. It was in gratitude for this that Metternich, in the sitting of the Paris congress of November 3rd, had secured the assent of the great powers to the "reversion" of Breisgau and of the Badenese Palatinate. Thus, without even reporting the matter to the cabinet of Carlsruhe, the four powers arbitrarily disposed of the future of certain Badenese territories. The reversion of the Badenese Palatinate was absolutely illegal, and there was no more than an artificial and specious ground for the reversion of Breisgau. The grand duke of Baden possessed Breisgau in virtue of the peace of Pressburg, " in the same manner and with the same rights " as had formerly the duke of Modena. Since the imperial house was the next heir of its Modenese cousins, the court of Vienna put forward the preposterous claim that not only could it demand the Italian possessions of the House of Modena when that house became extinct, but that it could also demand the return of Breisgau when the direct Zähringen line died out. The great powers recognised this groundless claim because the statesmen of England and Russia had absolutely no knowledge of German affairs, and Hardenberg countenanced it because he continued to hope that Austria would take over the guardianship of the Upper Rhine.

With this means of negotiation in his hands, Metternich now demanded the immediate exchange of Salzburg for the Palatinate on the left bank of the Rhine. Seeing that Bavaria still hesitated, he finally lost patience, and in December sent General Vacquant to Munich to enforce the cession in any circumstances; simultaneously General Bianchi advanced to the Bavarian frontier with an Austrian army. The court of Munich recognised too late how foolishly Wrede had acted, when by his spiteful attitude in the Saxon negotiations, he had alienated Prussian sympathies. King Max Joseph and Montgelas now implored the Prussian ambassador Küster to forget the Viennese quarrels. The chancellor answered coolly that time would show, that if the Bavarian court should in the future display friendly sentiments, the king of Prussia would not be relentless towards the king of Bavaria. The chancellor then instructed the ambassador to join with England and Russia in supporting the Austrian negotiator.[1]

[1] Küster's Report, September 2 ; Hardenberg's Instructions, October 5 and December 1, 1815.

In Bavaria the news of Austria's demands aroused passionate anger. For centuries, with one brief intermission, the region of the lower Inn had belonged to the Wittelsbachs; Salzburg had always been part of the Bavarian realm, and had carried on friendly intercourse with the neighbours in the electorate. These two territories, with a purely Bavarian population, were to be exchanged for the remote Trans-Rhenish Palatinate, whose fickle and light-minded inhabitants had from remote antiquity been unsympathetic towards the ponderous Bavarians! The old tribal hatred against the Austrians once more became active; memories of the struggles of 1705 and of the legendary smith of Cochel were in everyone's mouth. The Salzburgers were forbidden, under pain of severe punishment, even to speak of the cession of the land. Marshal Wrede stormed and threatened, and in military circles the bitter complaint was heard: "We lack the protection of Napoleon." Loudest of all stormed Crown Prince Louis. He regarded it as a dishonour to the new kingly crown that the exchange should not be made by his house of its own free will, but that it should be enforced by the Quadruple Alliance. The literary incendiaries of the Wittelsbachs once more set to work. A fierce pamphlet, *Entweder—oder*, composed by Aretin, and widely circulated by Prince Charles, demanded vociferously of all true Bavarians that " they should beat their plough-shares into swords in order to resist the joint dominion of Austria and Prussia." In the Salzburg region a petition was circulated for signature by the Bavarian officials, suggesting that there should be placed at the disposal of the court " hundreds of thousands of bayonets " in the hands of Salzburg volunteers. " The people, not enervated by over-culture, rejoices in the plenitude of youth; our princely house is older than all the others! Must we suffer from Austria the very wrong which so recently, when Prussia designed to mutilate Saxony, was opposed by Austria upon the noblest and justest grounds of principle? " Yet while the Bavarian people were thus venting their ancient spite against the North German great power, Max Joseph was saying to Küster that he hoped before long there would be a new war between Austria and Prussia, and declaring that in that case Bavaria would faithfully take Prussia's side![1]

It almost seemed as if the history of the Germanic Federation was to begin with a civil war. The condition of the

[1] Küster's Report, January 25, 1816.

Bavarian army was, however, deplorable, and Metternich held firmly to his demands. He declared dryly that the promised " contiguity " of the Bavarian domain had been rendered impossible by the opposition of the South German neighbour states, and thus admitted with his customary ease of conscience that in Ried and Paris he had deceived his Bavarian friends with promises which could not possibly be fulfilled. The Wittelsbachs ventured one final attempt. The king wrote to Czar Alexander (who had urgently advised him to yield " out of regard for the peace of the Germanic Federation ") and was not ashamed to praise the czar for having preserved Alsace for the French. " It is to the magnanimous, continuous, and persistent labours of your majesty, that Europe chiefly owes her liberation ; it is your foresight, above all, which has preserved France for the political system of Europe, in opposition to the sophisms of ambition and the outcries of exaggeration. You will not deny the like protection to an ally who asks merely for preservation." [1] Shortly afterwards, in February, 1816, Crown Prince Louis went to Milan, to win over Emperor Francis by a personal interview. At the same time, however, Baron von Berckheim was despatched to Milan on behalf of the Badenese court, for in the meanwhile intelligence had been received in Carlsruhe, as to what had been determined in Paris regarding the future of Breisgau and the Badenese Palatinate, so that the Austrian court was now between two fires. The Badenese minister entered a formal protest against any infringement of the rights of his prince ; in his excitable manner, the Bavarian crown prince reminded Emperor Francis of his pledged word, and stormily demanded the promised contiguous domain ; the true-hearted emperor, shrugging his shoulders, answered the disputants, by saying, " I am body and soul at one with my allies, and can do nothing without them." Metternich, too, imperturbably appealed to the decision of the great powers ; and although he sharply censured the Badenese statesman for the irritable tone of his protest, Berckheim soon perceived that it was the intention of Austria to enforce nothing more than the cession of Salzburg, and that there was no serious intention of handing over Breisgau and the Badenese Palatinate to Bavaria.[2]

[1] Czar Alexander to King Max Joseph, December 24, 1815. The king's Reply, January 6, 1816.
[2] Berckheim's Report to the Badenese ministry, Milan, February 14. Berckheim's Protest, February 10. Metternich's Reply, February 22, 1816.

Louis returned home with nothing effected. Since the four powers urgently demanded that these unsavoury negotiations should at length be brought to a conclusion, negotiations in which the duplicity of the Hofburg played a hardly less detestable part than the arrogant greed of Bavaria, the court of Munich yielded a step, and by the treaty of April 14, 1816, surrendered Salzburg and the region of the lower Inn, in exchange for the Palatinate on the left bank of the Rhine and certain still masterless areas in Odenwald. It was with profound discontent that the Bavarians of Salzburg passed under Austrian rule, but a great part of the country was crown-land, so that the welfare of the inhabitants was wholly dependent upon the new suzerainty, which exercised its powers mildly ; the consequence was that the excitement gradually subsided, and to the inhabitants the unnatural separation from their fellow tribesmen soon came to seem a matter of course.

Since the Bavarian state had, by the treaty of exchange, gained an accession of 85,000 inhabitants, no just grievance any longer existed Nevertheless the failure to secure an unbroken territorial area continued to rankle at the court of Munich, and a demand was therefore made that, in the secret articles of the treaty, Bavaria should be allotted still further compensations. Metternich had no objection to display himself as a free-handed giver at the cost of Baden, for he foresaw what insuperable obstacles would arise to the fulfilment of his promise. It was agreed in the secret articles that after the extinction of the direct line of the Zähringens, the Badenese Palatinate should lapse to Bavaria ; in addition, in compensation for the lost contiguity, Bavaria was to receive as soon as possible the Badenese Main-Tauber circle, and until this cession could be effected she was to be paid by Austria an annual rent of 100,000 florins. Here was another frivolous and arbitrary act, and Bavaria did not hesitate to push her reputed claims by all possible means. Whilst in the Frankfort territorial negotiations the Bavarian envoy demanded the cession of the Main-Tauber circle as an incontestable right, Count Bray courted the favour of the czar. The alarmed Badenese court armed itself with similar weapons. Berstett hastened for help to London ; to St. Petersburg there had already been despatched a prince of the new collateral line, Count William of Hochberg. Subsequently, on the Neva, the most fortunate member of the Badenese cabinet, the young baron von Blittersdorff, won his diplomatic spurs, endeavouring with the aid of the empress Elizabeth to dislodge the Bavarian ambassador from Alexander's favour. Thus the disgraceful rivalry of the two German courts for foreign protection persisted for many months, and Capodistrias exclaimed contemptuously to the Badenese envoy: " You are always lying before the door of the great powers!"[1] Meanwhile the Bavarian government had increased its demands, at the instigation of the crown prince, who was unwilling to postpone his entry into the castle of the counts-palatine at Heidelberg; in February, 1817, Bavaria actually demanded from the great powers the immediate cession of the Badenese Palatinate.

This new and presumptuous claim on the part of Bavaria at length drove the Prussian chancellor from his reserve. Hitherto Hardenberg had moved with great caution, for he did not wish to wound Austria, and he felt that on his own account he was to some extent bound by the agreements of Ried and Paris. Yet such a manifestation of illegal land-hunger seemed to him " utterly opposed to the aims of the Germanic Federation "; he would never consent that Bavaria should cut off the minor South German states from the north. He therefore immediately altered his tone; having a decisive declaration made in Vienna and in Munich that Prussia would not tolerate any kind of forcible measures against Baden, and he remained henceforward the loyal protector of the court of Carlsruhe. The king of Würtemberg gratefully recognised the altered attitude of the cabinet of Berlin, and in secret even the Hofburg was pleased at Prussia's intervention, for Metternich did not fail to recognise that should Bavaria acquire an excess of power in the German south this would run counter to Austrian interests; but he could not formally repudiate his own underhand promise.[2] The ultimate decision of all territorial questions remained, however, with the Quadruple Alliance; and since Alexander had not as yet made any definite decision, and even for a time showed himself favourable to the Bavarian claims, the hateful negotiations still hung in the balance; from month to month they became more embittered, and exercised a profound and enduring influence upon the neighbourly relationships of the South German states, and also upon the course of their

[1] Blittersdorff's Reports, St. Petersburg, June 5, et seq., September 4, 1818.
[2] Krusemark's Report of March 5. Küster's Report of March 14. Hardenberg's Instructions of February 28, March 4, and April 12, 1817.

constitutional life. But the two German great powers had already recognised in September, 1816, that the Bundestag must now be opened before the territorial disputes had been settled.

To the general astonishment of the diplomatic world, the court of Vienna twice offered Stein the position of Austrian federal envoy. What a low opinion Metternich must continue to hold regarding the importance of the Bundestag if he could offer the leadership of this assembly to the man whom he detested as leader of the German Jacobins, and whom in addition he despised on account of his extravagant ideas! Stein refused, hardly to the surprise of the Hofburg; he knew that as Metternich's subordinate he would not find a worthy field of activity. The choice of the Viennese cabinet then fell upon the elderly minister Albini, the last presidential envoy from electoral Mainz to the old Reichstag. The intrigues of Ratisbon were to be comfortably pursued in Frankfort; the man who had guided the old empire to the grave was the right man to hold the new federation at the font. But Albini, already weakened with old age, died in January, 1816, before he had taken up office, and now the Austrian envoy in Cassel, Count Buol, was appointed to the vacant post. Buol was a man of mediocre intelligence, lacking both judgment and principle, but he was cunning enough to conduct a petty intrigue with a good-natured air, or to gain over the servile diplomats of the petty states by an excess of flattery and by occasional lies.

For the post of Prussian envoy, Hardenberg, too, thought first of Stein; in this position the dreaded rival, it seemed, would not be dangerous; his great name was to assure the nation of the Prussian government's German sentiments. At first the baron was inclined to assent, but after the second peace of Paris, he definitely refused the proposal. During the last few months his old mistrust of the chancellor had increased to unjustified contempt, and he no longer expected any good from the Bundestag. After prolonged hesitation, Hardenberg ultimately turned to the Prussian minister in Cassel, von Hänlein, an elderly diplomat of the Franconian school of officials, who, like Albini, had acquired his knowledge of German affairs in the Reichstag of Ratisbon. The unlucky choice soon brought its own revenge. Even before the opening of the Bundestag, the new envoy prepared a painful defeat for his state, a defeat which long continued to accentuate the difficulties of Prussia in the Federation. This was a worthy prelude to and symbol of the whole course of the history of the Federation.

On January 23, 1816, Hänlein accepted the position. Although still sceptical regarding the stability and value of the Bundestag, he relied upon his rich experiences in Ratisbon, as well as upon the friendship of Count Buol, his close associate and trusted colleague in Cassel, and immediately transmitted to the chancellor a memorial, *What are we to expect from the German Bundestag at Frankfort?* Hänlein, intimately acquainted with the old imperial constitution, did not fail to see that Austria, " which could not take more than a half interest in Germany," had gained a position of supremacy altogether intolerable for Prussia : the new presidential power, carrying with it the conduct of affairs, must soon become enormously greater than had formerly been the power of the emperor over the Reichstag. He then drew attention to the way in which the stipulation that there should be unanimity in respect of all vital decisions would hinder the peaceful development of the Federation, so that it seemed " as if it had been desired to choke the life and effective activity of the Federation in its very birth." Under such conditions, the North German people, becoming desperate, might readily be led to determine that the domination of the Prussian state in Germany should be secured by a revolution. To avert this danger one means only remained, the partition of dominion between the two great powers. Austria should resume the imperial dignity, whilst Prussia should receive the title of King of Germany ; then both states, closely allied and with perfectly equal rights, should take over the joint leadership of the Federation, with the power and prestige of a genuine " supreme head."[1]

In March, when Hänlein came to Frankfort for a brief visit, he was received by Buol with open arms, and at once laid his memorial before his faithful friend, and subsequently showed it also to old Wessenberg, who was in Frankfort as member of the territorial commission. In his usual gushing manner, Buol gave verbal assurance of his cordial approval. Wessenberg, in a complimentary note, thanked Hänlein for his admirable memoir, and concluded by saying : " It is to be hoped that your excellency will soon return with instructions in accordance with your views, for this will already gain much ! " Delighted with such success, Hänlein now hastened to Berlin, developed his great

---

[1] Hänlein's Report and Memorial to the chancellor, January 23, 1816.

plan once again in a detailed memorial,[1] and gave his solemn assurance that Prussia could rely upon the assent of the court of Vienna. Hardenberg took the improbable assurance at its face value ; where his Austrian friends were concerned, the experienced man was ever childishly unsuspicious, and he could not believe that Metternich's oft-repeated confidential utterances regarding the necessity of the German dual dominion had been no more than empty words. He therefore made Hänlein draw up a formal treaty for the immediate acceptance of the two great powers, which was subsequently to be laid as an accomplished fact before the friendly minor courts. Since the chancellor, faithful to his old view, had struck out the clause relating to the titles of emperor and king of Germany, the proposal had become restricted to two main demands : equality of the two great powers in the Bundestag, on such lines that Austria should take over the presidency, whilst Prussia, like electoral Mainz in the old Reichstag, should keep the minutes and draft the resolutions ; all the minor North German military contingents were to be under Prussia's orders, while the South German contingents were to be under the supreme command of Austria. The latter proposal was further elaborated in a memorial by Boyen, the minister of war. In this document, all offence to the self-respect of the middle-sized states was sedulously avoided, and nothing more was demanded than was absolutely essential to preserve the German federal army from sheer anarchy : Mecklenburg, Electoral Hesse, Anhalt, Nassau, and part of the Thuringian states, were to join Prussia, while Baden, Darmstadt, and Liechtenstein, were to join the Austrian army ; the remaining trifling contingents were partly allotted to the four small kingdoms, and partly combined to form a special Low German corps.[2] Such were the instructions with which, towards the end of June, Hänlein returned to Frankfort ; amid the accumulated business of this period of transition, it had taken Hardenberg all this time to find a free moment to devote to federal affairs.

Meanwhile Count Buol had made an adroit use of the absence of his Prussian colleague, scattering the seeds of Austrian federal sentiments freely over the grateful soil of Frankfort. The minor envoys reported with delight how affable the

[1] Wessenberg to Hänlein, March 11 ; Hänlein, Report and Memorial to Hardenberg, March 24, 1816.
[2] Boyen, Instructions concerning the military constitution of Germany.

Austrian seemed : he did not wish to be styled even *primus inter pares*, but only *servus servorum* ! Even more satisfactory was the joyful certainty that Austria had not the remotest thought of any transformation or enlargement of the hastily-drafted constitution. " The federal act," said Buol, " is like the Bible ; it may be expounded but not altered." Berstett, the Badenese envoy, a fat and easy-going man, who in the corvée at Frankfort often yearned for Paris and the well-supplied tables of the Frères Provençaux, wrote home well satisfied that no one ventured any longer to touch the master-piece, that the federal act was regarded as a sacred object, especially by the minor states.[1] Several of the middle-sized states showed themselves determined from the first never to allow the Bundestag to acquire serious efficiency. The king of Würtemberg now announced his accession to the Federation, adding in set terms that the latter half of the federal act seemed unessential. Similar views were held by the elector of Hesse, who was represented in Frankfort by his favourite, Buderus von Carlshausen, a notorious skinflint, who had gained the confidence of his prince by artful manipulation of the fractions of a heller in the accounts of the electoral war treasury. Berstett could give satisfactory reports of most of the other envoys as well ; they were all agreed in the determination not to tolerate even the semblance of a dangerous influence ; should Austria and Prussia come forward with plans for a federal military system, some kind of counter-project must immediately be proposed, for " its impracticability must first be proved before it can be rejected."[2] No one, however, knew better how to express the ideas of impenitent particularism than did Baron von Marschall, the envoy of Nassau ; at home, an all-powerful minister, he ruled with Rhenish Confederate official arbitrariness, and occasionally visited his post at Frankfort in order to strengthen the weaker spirits against the Germanising demagogues by his despotic manners and blunt invectives.

The hidden thoughts of these courts were immediately brought to light when it was learned that England and Russia intended to accredit as envoys to the Bundestag their diplomats who had been occupied in the territorial commission. Everyone knew that this headless Federation could not conduct any foreign policy, or that at most, in some special emergency, it might

---

[1] Berstett's Reports, December 16 and 18, 1815.
[2] Berstett's Report, November 12, 1816.

send an ambassador abroad ; could it, then, tolerate the regular attendance of foreign diplomats ? Meanwhile Count Reinhard had already been appointed French envoy to the still unopened Bundestag. This talented German-Frenchman was one of those strange characters, exhibiting a mixture of idealism with half-unconscious mendacity, frequently produced by the homeless life of Old German particularism. In the bottom of his heart he always remained the learned Swabian theologian, and sympa-thetically followed the bold flights of German genius ; he really believed that he was acting as a good German when, in earlier days, in Napoleon's service, he had kept a strict eye upon the Rhenish Confederate states, and had now no hesitation in employing, in the name of the Most Christian King and against victorious Germany, language which recalled the time of Louis XIV. In a memorial communicated to the federal envoys, he asked scornfully whether the Germanic Federation proposed to renounce all foreign relationships, like Turkey in former days, or like the Convention under Robespierre. What an unjust privilege it would be if the foreign powers, Austria, Prussia, England, the Netherlands, and Denmark, were to be represented at the Bundestag, while the other powers were excluded. A Germanic Federation without regular intercourse with foreign lands would be nothing more than a new Confederation of the Rhine, for in that case Germany's foreign policy would be decided in Vienna and Berlin alone. "The presence of foreign envoys in Frankfort will assist the Federation to conduct its affairs in accordance with the true spirit of the federal act." Finally, Reinhard claimed admission as a right, for if it should be decided in Frankfort to replace the federal act " by a better ordering of affairs," all the European powers were entitled to co-operate in this change in the treaties of Vienna !

Well did the Frenchman know how far he could allow him-self to go in dealing with the minor German princes ; to all of them the demand of the court of the Tuileries seemed a matter of course. The Badenese minister, von Hacke, immediately wrote to Berstett to the effect that the envoys of France, Russia, and England, must certainly remain in Frankfort, " for these powers are always a protection and a support for the German sovereigns against Austria and Prussia."[1] That which the court of Baden concealed in secret instructions, was openly

[1] Reinhard, *Mémoire sur les légations à Francfort*. Hacke, Instructions to Berstett, March 6, 1816.

expressed by Aretin in the *Alemannia*. Crome, too, the statistician of Giessen, an old Bonapartist who had now assumed the mantle of a German patriot, also proved, in a writing upon the political and national interests of Germany and Europe, that the unity of Europe and Germany could be secured only if every European power had the right to speak at the German Bundestag!

The court of Berlin alone decisively opposed these foreign claims, and now began to maintain a view (unfortunately far from incontestable from the legal standpoint) to which Prussia subsequently ever adhered. This was the contention that the European powers, since they had accepted the first articles of the federal act in the final act of the Viennese congress, had indeed recognised the status of the Germanic Federation, but had by no means given any guarantee for its constitution. As early as February, in a Prussian memorial, the unfortunate experiences of the last days at Ratisbon were recalled: the Germanic Federation was now only a federation of states, without a genuine centralised authority; " the life of this federation as such, and vis-à-vis the foreign world, must consist in the idea of repose." Hardenberg made an urgent representation to the court of Vienna to the effect that the continued presence of foreign envoys in such a federal assembly could not fail to lead to dangerous attempts at interference."[1] Czar Alexander, however, took the side of France, and in order to allay the anxieties of the Prussian court, laid before Berlin the instructions which had been sent to Anstett, the Russian envoy at Frankfort. With childlike innocence they ran: " As minister of the czar you have no opinion regarding the internal affairs of the Germanic Federation. It is useful, it is necessary, that personally, too, you should have no opinion upon these matters. Such is the czar's wish." [2] Therewith, for the patriots of the Bundestag, was proved the complete harmlessness of the admission of foreign envoys. It could already be foreseen that Prussian opposition would remain fruitless, and that in matters also of foreign politics the Bundestag was to be the worthy successor of the Reichstag of Ratisbon: it was itself unrepresented abroad and was to be exposed without defence to the secret intrigues of the foreign powers.

Beside the representatives of unconcealed particularism were

[1] Hardenberg, Memorial concerning the foreign envoyships, February, 1816. Instructions to Krusemark, March 11, 1816.
[2] Ministerial Despatch to Anstett, St. Petersburg, August 9, 1816.

ranked numerous well-meaning patriotic statesmen from the petty states : such as Smidt and Hach, from the Hansa towns ; Plessen from Mecklenburg, who had made himself known in Vienna as a well-informed and upright man of business ; Eyben of Holstein ; and, by no means last, the inevitable Gagern. How happy had the indefatigable man been during these first months, when there was as yet no business to do, and everyone could follow his own preferences in paving the way to hell with good intentions for the unborn Bundestag! With his customary complacency, and undisturbed by coldly-worded replies, he laid before the statesmen of Vienna and Berlin his interminable proposals. "The plague, slavery, the Jewish problem, fanaticism, embargoes on trade, colonisation, literature and the arts, handicrafts, praise of our great men"—all these and countless other affairs were to occupy the Bundestag, upon whose table the delighted Luxemburger already in imagination saw crown and sceptre lying.[1] Even the quieter members of this particularist circle were filled with boundless conceit. The ancient illusion of German liberty decked itself with new plumes. Through unrestricted sovereignty, Lippe, Lübeck, and Prussia, were placed upon an exactly equal footing ; consequently there could be no doubt that this approximation of nine-and-thirty completely equal and completely independent states would spontaneously, and solely through the miraculous power of unity, develop magnificent political efficiency, if only each individual member of the federation should be scrupulously prevented from exercising dangerous and excessive influence !

Even Smidt, the moderate republican, who in the affairs of his beloved Bremen had always preserved the secure and comprehensive outlook of the true statesman, even this leading intelligence of the Frankfort assembly, soon entered the dream-world of federalism, and innocently assumed that his colleagues were animated by the same upright patriotic zeal as that with which his own mind was filled. How splendid it was that henceforward the whole of Germany was to constitute a great republic of states, wherein sovereignty emanated from individuals. The only thing needed was that these sovereign individuals should, in the republican manner, be treated as perfectly equal, for why was it impossible that in Germany too "salvation should come just as well from Nazareth as from Jerusalem"?

[1] Gagern to Metternich and Hardenberg, May 3. Hardenberg's Reply, June 18, 1816.

The sovereign Hansa towns, too, must at length " emerge from the commons," they must no longer content themselves with modest transitional forms. In such a federation of equals, the sanguine man considered that the German great powers would be educated in the ways of justice, and he maintained that while " great states bring energy and strength to a federation, minor states bring love of justice and capacity for constitutional government." Yet he carefully avoided explaining why Mecklenburg was more capable of constitutional government than Prussia, or what sort of justice the king of Prussia was to learn from the elector of Hesse, the prince-regent of Hanover, or the king of Würtemberg.

The views of this well-meaning federalist found their literary echo in Heeren's work, *The Germanic Federation in relation to the European System of States.* The Göttingen historian, a distinguished representative of the old book-learning remote from practical life, had recently spent a short period in Frankfort, had associated freely with Smidt and the other federal envoys, and now sketched an entrancing picture of the great future of the Germanic Federation, but one which evoked little response from the depressed nation. The world had had to endure an epoch of blood and horror because Germany, in its dismembered condition, had been unable to defend itself. In face of such experiences, Heeren once more declared, in almost the same words as had been used by Johannes Müller at the time of the league of princes, that the freedom of Europe depended upon the loose ordering of Germany, for what foreign power could quietly enjoy its possessions if Germany should become united to constitute a great monarchy ? The motley characteristics of German internal affairs were also regarded by him as thoroughly wholesome ; the continual contemplation of " experiments " in various political institutions preserved Germans from narrow-mindedness. Yet this museum of political experiments (which to the professors of constitutional law was certainly of inestimable value) was to be recognised by all the great powers as the ruling central force, as " the peace-state of Europe." To the man of Göttingen this seemed self-evident ; before long Frankfort would become what the Hague had once been, " the centre of the system of states," and the Bundestag would enlarge itself to become a European senate !

At the courts of the great powers a definite opinion regarding the Frankfort assembly had already been formed ; but this opinion was less flattering than Heeren imagined. The Bundestag from now onwards and until the day of its dissolution, was regarded as the great mart for the second-rate diplomatic gossip of Europe. For many months a swarm of unoccupied minor diplomats had been buzzing about Frankfort. What was there for the poor devils to do other than to constitute petty cabals, to engage in tale-bearing, and to rival one another in the attempt to glean information from the plentipotentiaries of the Quadruple Alliance who were occupied in the great territorial commission, from Wessenberg, Humboldt, Clancarty, and Anstett? Whoever wished to remain on top in this busy idleness must make himself indispensable by piquant novelties, or by keeping an elaborate table. How often did the senate of Bremen send the faithful Smidt a present from its renowned town-hall cellar in order that Count Buol might better relish the turtle-soup, lampreys, and other delicacies of the Hanseatic envoy's dining-table. Yet of the secrets of the great courts the minor diplomats learned so little that even the real pith of Hänlein's unhappy proposal remained concealed from them.

All the more luxuriantly flourished the formation of myths, and this myth-making was inevitably directed above all against the state which, with its national army and its brilliant warlike renown, seemed the natural enemy of the newly re-established glories of Ratisbon. Moreover, among the envoys of the four powers, Humboldt understood least how to spare the vanity of the minor diplomats; only too often did he display his superiority by the use of cutting sarcasms and repellent coldness. Most of them stood before him with similar feelings to those felt by a dog before a glass of wine. It was known that Humboldt hoped to become minister of foreign affairs, but that he was unable to carry this wish into effect owing to Hardenberg's irreconcilable mistrust. It was natural that the purely personal opposition between the two statesmen should immediately be interpreted as political hostility, and that Humboldt should be falsely regarded as the secret leader of the Prussian revolutionary party. There was not a single revolutionary folly which was not ascribed to him. The diplomats in Wessenberg's house were perfectly certain that Prussia was preparing for a life-and-death struggle against the middle-sized states. Humboldt had already elaborated a constitutional plan " of an unprecedentedly liberal character "; as soon as Blucher returned to Berlin, " this army run mad " was to hand in a petition to the king, demanding that the army, like Cromwell's dragoons of old, should be represented in the Prussian Reichstag by army deputies.[1] Wangenheim, the liberal minister of Würtemberg, having certain proposals to make to his king regarding the Würtemberg constitution, accompanied them with a letter, which he promptly published. This letter hugely delighted the federal envoys, for in it Prussia was described as a state utterly disordered by the work of secret societies, and the alluring prospect was then held out to the despot of Stuttgart, that if a revolution should break out in Prussia and at the same time in the south, and a German state with a free constitution should come into existence, a change in the condition of affairs would be rendered possible, so extensive as to be hardly conceivable to the boldest imagination !

Such was the mood of the Bundestag when Hänlein returned with his confidential instructions. Count Buol possessed an infallible means for the immediate defeat of the Prussian plans ; it was merely necessary for him to communicate them to his minor colleagues, and he did not hesitate to employ this weapon. The affectionate friend, who, in the winter, had met the first proposals in so kindly a spirit, now (June 30th) received the new approach, as Hänlein said, in an extremely tragical mood ; he regarded it as his duty to discuss the matter immediately with the other envoys, and in this way forced Prussia to disclose the secret on her side also. The result was instantaneous and complete. An outcry of horror arose from the entire Bundestag. Was it possible that this revolutionary state should propose to violate the so recently concluded federal act (Buol's Bible), and should even demand the supreme command of the warlike forces of some of the sovereign powers ? Everyone overwhelmed the most maladroit of all Prussian diplomats with reproaches ; even the peaceful Plessen said openly to him that the federation could get along without Prussia. The chancellor was painfully surprised when in Carlsbad he heard of this incident in Frankfort, and when at the same time he received direct information from Vienna that Metternich would not accept the Prussian proposals. What was left but to withdraw from the false position which had been entered into almost as much on account of Hardenberg's credulousness as on account of Hänlein's blundering ? On August 9th Hänlein was recalled. His enraged chief reproached him with having by erroneous

[1] Berstett's Reports, December 16, 1815; March 6, 1816.

reports misled the Prussian court, and of having subsequently, by making the matter public, excited an extremely disadvantageous sensation. " The success of the federation depends upon the fullest understanding between Prussia and Austria ; no one must even hint at a divergence of views between the two courts which are so closely allied for the well-being of Europe and Germany." [1] At the same time Humboldt was temporarily commissioned to represent Prussia at the Bundestag, and by a resolute attitude he was able so far to re-establish the shattered prestige of Prussia that in the preparatory sittings of the Bundestag Count Buol did not venture to take any steps without his approval. But the evil consequences of the defeat that had been sustained, long continued. Prussia and the land-hungry Bavaria were for three years generally regarded with suspicion as ambitious disturbers of the peace of the Federation. Whereas in Ratisbon a Prussian party had never been completely wanting, in Frankfort at first there was no trace of anything of the kind, and the influence of the North German great power upon the federal negotiations remained so trifling that the South German statesmen were subsequently accustomed to describe these first years as the golden age of the Bundestag. [2]

Humboldt, from his experience of these first weeks, formed a hopeless, and unhappily altogether just, view of the Germanic Federation. He expounded this view in a lengthy memorial dated September 30, 1816, which subsequently formed the basis of the instructions of the Prussian federal envoy. [3] Here was given a drastic description of the federal constitution, " an utterly shapeless structure, resting upon no secure foundation " ; " the enormous difficulty " of all decisions was explained, so that " it is hardly possible to see how, about certain matters, any resolution can be passed." It follows from this that Prussia must indeed preserve a good understanding with Austria, but must be content at the Bundestag to deal only in generalities. The true carrying into effect of institutions of common utility can be secured only " in isolated intercourse with the individual German states. It must be the policy of Prussia to interweave these neighbour states to a certain extent into her own political system and even into her own administrative

[1] Hänlein's Report, July 2 ; Hardenberg's Answer, August 9 ; Berstett's Report, July 1, 1816.
[2] Blittersdorff, for instance, in his Memorial upon federal policy, dated February 18, 1822.
[3] Published by C. Rossler, *Zeitschrift für preussische Geschichte*, 1872.

system." These words contain the entire programme of Prussian
federal policy. Even before the Bundestag had come into
existence, Humboldt expressed that which the experience of half
a century was to confirm, namely, that in Frankfort only the
verbiage of German policy could thrive ; that all the affairs of
national statecraft must be managed from Berlin through negotiations with the individual states.

On November 5, 1816, the federal assembly was at length
opened. After Hänlein's defeat, Buol, in the preparatory
sittings, had without protest assumed the entire formal leadership. Upon Humboldt's demand, the recording of the minutes
was entrusted, not to Friedrich Schlegel, who at the Vienna
congress had aroused the anger of the Prussians by his clerical
zeal and his doggerel verses against the *Nord- und Morddeutschen*,
but to a harmless Austrian privy councillor named von
Handel, whose detestable German made the empty proceedings
seem even more ridiculous than before. The high council of
the German nation assembled in the Thurn and Taxis palace in
the Eschenheimer Gasse, where the Austrian embassy was lodged,
and henceforward for fifty years remained the modest tenant of
the princely house of Taxis. Since the middle-sized states would
not hear a word of the revival of the ancient imperial eagle,
the published minutes bore the Austrian arms upon their title-
page, with the inscription *Kaiserlich Oesterreichische Bundes-
kanzley.* It seemed as if there was really sitting here nothing
more than an Austrian provincial board. The president, moreover, was to blame for the fact that, at the opening of this
new epoch in German history, the blessing of God was not
called down upon the assembly. Buol refused to participate in
a Protestant service, and demanded High Mass in the ancient
imperial cathedral, although five-sixths of the sovereigns of new
Germany were Protestant. Since there was no ecclesiastical
ceremony, he proposed a theatrical festival, but Humboldt's good
sense fortunately brought this scheme to nought.

When the members of the Bundestag, saluted by the guard
with a present-arms and with the waving of flags, had all
assembled before the Austrian embassy, Count Buol read a
speech whose senseless verbosity could not fail to give offence to
cultured hearers, for it vividly displayed into what barbarism
heartless and mindless politicians fall as soon as they endeavour
to display pathos The address had been drafted by Metternich,
who had not thought it worth while to employ the classic pen

of Gentz ; even Buol regarded it as unsuitable, and out of consideration for his audience, read a portion only.[1] The most callow among the Teutonising students had never used emptier phrases than were here employed by the Viennese court when it declared : "In the German as human being, in the absence of all arbitrary political forms, there already exist the lineaments of the fundamental character of the Germans as a nation. National need is the creatress and guiding star of all national forms, and therewith is guaranteed progress towards the true, towards the highest goal!" The speech then went on to describe the decay of Germany during the last centuries, and then expressed gratification that, thanks to the Germanic Federation, Germany was once more taking its place as "a power among the ranks of the nations." . . . "Thus we hold fast to the summit where a great nation, in the manifoldedness of its civic forms, advances freely forward towards the glorious destiny of mankind and of its own development, and at the same time becomes a single whole in national relationships!" In conclusion, the envoy gives fervent assurances of "the Germanity of his sentiments"; he once more declares that his emperor regards himself "as a completely equal member of the Federation," and recalls (with a friendly dig at Prussia which everyone in the audience immediately understood) "the fortunate circumstance, one justifying mutual confidence, that Austria neither will nor can aspire either to conquest upon German soil or to the aggrandisement of her own position in the Germanic Federation!"

Humboldt's response was brief and dignified. Most of the other envoys merely commended themselves to the good will of those present, or else expressed the venturesome hope "that in subsequent years, and even in remote generations, this day would be accounted one of the most joyful that had ever dawned for the united fatherland." Gagern could not refrain from delivering a long speech, extolling the German sentiments of the House of Orange, and promising that Luxemburg should for ever be the natural mediator in Germany. He considered it a suitable occasion "in this illustrious German senate, to hold a trial of the dead, somewhat after the manner of the most remarkable nation of antiquity"; in glowing language he spoke of the prince of Nassau-Weilburg, of the Guelphs who had fallen for Germany, and, "to escape the reproach that

[1] Humboldt's Reports, November 1 and 8, 1816.

I am celebrating princely rank alone," also of Andreas Hofer, and of Palm. In conclusion he appealed enthusiastically to his inevitable *Je maintiendray!* It was an indescribably tasteless ceremony, the worthy opening of a political farce from which the entire nation was to turn away with loathing.

Six days later, Count Buol delivered his first presidential address, and dwelt with emotion upon the benefits which might accrue for the Germans from the realisation of the indefinite promises of the federal act. Of article 19, which promised the regulation of national commerce, the Austrian boasted in his extraordinary German " this article purposes to estrange [*entfremden*] the German federal states in respect alike of commerce and intercourse and of navigation "—an unintentional prophecy which was to be completely realised. In the empty words, the only point of political significance was the definite declaration that the Germanic Federation was not a federal state but a federation of states, for the former " would conflict with the unalterable course of the ages advancing ever towards higher directions ! " The catchwords " federation of states " and " federal state," now began to make frequent appearance in the press, although no definite legal sense was as yet attached to these phrases. How far had the political culture of the nation lagged behind its advance in other branches of knowledge ! Hardly a thought had as yet been given to the fundamental principles of the public law of federal states ; the classic American work, which a generation earlier had illuminated these questions with a combination of talent and knowledge of affairs *The Federalist*, written by Hamilton, Madison, and Jay, was still hardly known to the learned of Germany. Even J. L. Klüber, who soon after the opening of the Bundestag published his *Oeffentliches Recht des Deutschen Bundes*, had but little to say regarding the political characteristics of the different forms of federal life. By " federal state " was meant any kind of powerful, highly respected, federal authority which might raise the German name to honour ; the young Teutonisers enthusiastically agreed with their teacher Fries when, in his work *Vom Deutschen Bunde und deutscher Staatsverfassung*, with the audacity of the well-meaning dilettante he roundly declared, " we do not desire a lax federation of states, but a firmly united federal state." The Austrian envoy now displayed his direct opposition to all such vague aspirations, and he had the spirit and the letter of the federal act upon his side. Since unanimity was demanded for any change of the federal act, the further development of the federal constitution was rendered *a priori* impossible, and even before the opening of the Bundestag, the envoys, good and bad alike, began tacitly to recognise that even the drafting of the fundamental laws of the federation, which in accordance with article 10 of the federal act was to be the first business of the Bundestag, would necessarily suffer shipwreck upon this shoal.

Humboldt left the Bundestag immediately after the first sitting, and, in a very bad humour, went first to Berlin, to attend the sittings of the council of state, and then left for London as ambassador; the post of ambassador in Paris, which he desired, was denied to him because, since the last congress, the caustic Prussian had been a *persona ingrata* to the Bourbons. His place at Frankfort was taken by von der Goltz, the same man who, in the spring of 1813, had been president of the unlucky governmental committee of Berlin, a loyal official, pleasant and good-natured, but quite devoid of independent ideas. The choice showed how little Hardenberg expected from the pseudo-activities of the Frankfort assembly. The personal intercourse between the envoys of the two great powers continued to be effected upon the most courteous terms, and they even mutually exchanged their instructions.[1] Yet it was none the less plain how widely divergent in two important respects were the intentions of the two courts. In the Austrian instructions, the federal act was declared sacred and inviolable; Hardenberg, on the other hand, expressed his lively regret that it had not been possible in Vienna to secure for the Federation "something more in the nature of a federal state," and proposed to effect every reform that was still possible. Whilst Count Buol, acting on Metternich's orders, assured the minor envoys that in federal affairs his court would never enter into separate negotiations, the Prussian chancellor continued to repeat to his Viennese friend that it was only by direct understanding between Austria and Prussia " that the Federation could acquire consistency, and party-spirit be destroyed."[2]

The unacknowledged divergence of views between the two leading courts was at first but little perceptible, since the activity of the federal assembly was for a long time almost entirely

[1] Austrian Instructions of October 24. Prussian Instructions of November 30, 1816.
[2] Metternich to Buol, August 2; Hardenberg to Metternich, November 30, 1816.

devoted to the settlement of claims for pensions and to other private matters. The Bundestag was overwhelmed by a flood of petitions and grievances; all the unfortunates whose rights had suffered through the wild times of war sought help in Frankfort. Thither came bishops and priests from the left bank of the Rhine, demanding pensions upon the ground of the principal resolution of the Diet of Deputation; similar demands were made by the Teutonic Knights, and by the members of the dissolved cathedral chapters; next came the advocates and procurators of the imperial court of chancery; next Joseph Fahrenkopf of Mainz, who in the year 1796 had carried out building operations for the imperial fortress of Mainz, and whose bill was still unpaid; with him came hosts of creditors of the old imperial treasury, that bad paymaster which during the revolutionary war was always in want of money; there came, too, the holders of certain Electoral Palatinate bonds, a notorious government stock, regarding the payment of the interest on which Bavaria and Baden, the legal successors of the Electoral Palatinate, continued to dispute fiercely for a generation; there came an unending series of suitors, down to minor handicraftsmen, creditors of serene highnesses who obstinately refused to pay their bootmakers' bills.

With praiseworthy zeal, the Bundestag undertook to deal with all these distresses. But how could an assembly of diplomats decide with certainty all the complicated legal questions which were here involved? Fortunately they had at least one able lawyer in their ranks, the Hanoverian envoy Martens, the well-known authority on international law. Another difficulty was the ever-recurring doubt as to the competence of the federal assembly. This doubt was not definitely dispelled even when, in June, 1817, the federal assembly passed certain provisional resolutions upon this question of competence. Where, in difficult cases, was the Bundestag to secure the necessary information as to matters of fact? Since it possessed no executive authority, it always remained dependent upon the goodwill of the governments concerned. A final difficulty arose from the ludicrously cumbrous mode of procedure. Hardenberg had proposed that, after a brief delay, the assembly should pass its resolutions regardless of absent members or of those who had not received instructions. Goltz very speedily perceived how unacceptable this idea was to the arrogance of the minor courts, puffed up with the pride of sovereignty; the Würtemberg envoy, von Linden, roundly declared that a unanimous resolution was impossible if even one envoy should be absent. Owing to the negligent business methods of the Viennese authorities, and also to Metternich's indifference towards the Federation, the instructions of the Austrian envoy were almost always the longest delayed. Since the presidential court thus set a bad example, it soon became the custom to postpone and repostpone the decisions until the last envoy had received his instructions, and thus the fate of the federal resolutions fell into the hands of the most slothful and most ill-affected of the sovereigns.

The consequence was that even those private petitions towards which the majority of the envoys displayed sympathetic sentiments were granted only after scandalous delay. The trans-Rhenish priests, whose claims were, in accordance with the federal act, to have been settled within a year, did not receive an award until 1824 ; the procurators of the imperial court of chancery had to wait until 1831 ; the fortunate grandsons of the creditors of the old imperial treasury received in the year 1843 payment for the work done by their grandfathers during the years 1793 to 1796 ; finally, in the year 1844, the settlement of the debts of the Electoral Palatinate and of the Upper Rhine was at length ordered, through the intermediation of the crown of Prussia, which received the warm thanks of the Bundestag for this speedily rendered assistance. Many of the envoys became agreeably accustomed to these subordinate activities, and soon within the assembly there developed a peculiar class of federal bureaucrats, diligent and experienced men of business, whose spirits were never disturbed by any political ideas, but who for this reason could deal all the more effectively with the affairs of Joseph Fahrenkopf and of the holders of the Electoral Palatinate bonds. The prototype of these extraneous elements in the Bundestag was the representative of the sixteenth vote, von Leonhardi. At the close of the first session, the good Goltz also wrote home in high content that though the promised establishment of the fundamental laws of the Federation had unfortunately proved impossible, none the less, the federal assembly had displayed its efficiency in its internal working, and had therefore served to secure internal repose.[1]

In view of this contented futility, many of the political anxieties which had at first filled Hardenberg's mind spontaneously

[1] Goltz, Retrospect of the first session of the federal assembly, August 5, 1817.

fell to the ground. The chancellor withdrew his opposition to
the presence of foreign diplomats as soon as he had learned
the character of the Bundestag, for what was there to fear
from the agents of foreign powers in so powerless an assembly?
Moreover, what answer was there to be made to the great
powers when they demanded that their envoys should be
admitted in order to avert the danger of possible war, for the
federal act had, after all, given the Bundestag the right of
declaring war. In actual fact, the envoys of the great powers
in Frankfort at first found nothing whatever to do. What did
it matter that the petty diplomats went busily in and out of
the Red House, the Malepardus of the cunning Russian, Anstett?
Serious questions, in which the influence of the foreign world
might have had an injurious effect, did not come before the
Bundestag in these two quiet opening years. Even the fear, which
was at first widespread that a secret Sonderbund of the old
central lands of the Confederation of the Rhine, might come into
existence, showed itself to have been premature. It is true
that King Frederick of Würtemberg, when he received news of
Hänlein's appearance, immediately journeyed to Carlsruhe, in
order to gain over the grand duke of Baden and the king of
Bavaria, who was staying in Baden, for a common South
German policy, to protect their undiminished sovereignty;
but Bavaria and Baden were bitterly hostile one to another,
and both were mistrustful of their neighbour of Würtemberg.
The attempt miscarried completely; [1] and since King Frederick
died shortly afterwards, nothing more was heard for a time of
these Rhenish Confederate plans. Even the Saxon federal
envoy, the punctilious old Count Görtz, displayed throughout a
blameless innocence, since his king never ventured to contradict
the House of Austria.

Meanwhile the Bundestag could not deal with the most
harmless of the claims that have been enumerated without
coming into violent conflict with the arrogant sovereignty of the
petty princes. At the very beginning of the proceedings,
Bavaria expressed doubt whether the federal assembly was
competent to deal with the grievances of German subjects
against their suzerain lords; but the Bavarian vote was temporarily interred in a secret minute. Yet, as the Bundestag was
soon to learn, to permit of such grievances to be brought before

[1] Jouffroy's Report, Stuttgart, July 20; Küster's Report, Baden, July 25,
1816.

its forum was to expose itself without redress to a gross affront. From no country were so many complaints received as from unfortunate Electoral Hesse, which had had to suffer a regime of shameless arbitrariness and greed under the elector whose restoration had been so ardently desired. Among the innumerable persons whose rights had been denied by William of Hesse, was a land-owner named Hofmann. This man had purchased from the royal treasury a secularised estate which had belonged to the Teutonic Knights; in August, 1815, two years after the return of the old sovereign prince, the purchase had been inscribed in the cadaster by the electoral authorities. Nevertheless, six months later, the purchaser received orders to restore the lands, which meanwhile he had subdivided and had disposed of to twenty other persons. The elector, he was bluntly told, could not tolerate that state property should remain in the hands of private persons. The federal assembly adopted the mildest resolution possible in such a case; it referred the petitioner to the elector, saying " should he, contrary to all the best expectations of the federal assembly, fail to secure redress," he was to appeal once more to the Federation. The elector was in a fury when he heard of this scandalous infringement of his sovereign rights, and had a rejoinder read in Frankfort which was immediately to be printed in the published minutes (March 17, 1817). In this document he declared that the last resolution was " very remarkable," expressed to the envoys his " astonishment at conduct which could hardly have received the approval of their principals," and concluded by saying threateningly that he forbade all interference in the internal affairs of his country.

Even to the patience of the Bundestag this language seemed intolerable. All the envoys broke off social relations with the elector's representative; it was definitely expected that both the great powers would recall their representatives from Cassel, and would secure for the Federation a striking satisfaction for the affront that had been suffered.[1] Count Buol made a vigorous reply; the position of the Bundestag would have been affected in a manner most injurious to the common weal if he had permitted an unsatisfied member of the Federation to address him in such a tone. " The federal assembly," he said, " can never be subordinated to any single member of the Federation." He concluded with an assurance which for one in this circle

[1] Berstett's Report, March 16, 1817.

was couched in language of unprecedented enthusiasm, by saying that the Bundestag " was determined to establish in the minds of oppressed subjects the assurance that, as the outcome of the liberation of Germany from a foreign yoke through the blood of the nation, a condition of legal justice should everywhere prevail in place of the exercise of arbitrary power." Count Goltz announced the unconditional assent of his king to the resolution which was passed. Even Gagern, in an extremely emotional and confused speech, declared that the right of property infringed by the elector " contained a *noli me tangere* of almost virgin sanctity." With the exception of the two Hessian plenipotentiaries, the whole Bundestag seemed united.

Unfortunately, however, Count Buol had acted on his own initiative. His instructions, after the usual practice of the Hofburg, were once more in arrear. Consequently in the beginning of April he returned home in order to be able, on his return, to assure the Bundestag of the support of the court of Vienna. But what a reception was awaiting the unfortunate man ! The elector had immediately complained to Emperor Francis, and Metternich overwhelmed the presidential envoy with reproaches, asking how he could possibly have undertaken to infringe the dignity of a sovereign in such a manner ! He threatened him with recall, and with a formal disavowal of the resolution of the Bundestag. This extreme step was, indeed, averted by Hardenberg's intermediation. The chancellor made urgent representations to his Viennese friend to the effect that the Bundestag was right and must not be exposed to public contempt.[1] Metternich therefore contented himself with a severe reprimand, and Buol returned to his post in a mood of profound humiliation. Thereupon the Bundestag confirmed its previous decision by a new but extremely guarded resolution, and Hofmann's grievance was quietly settled by the elector. But there was no talk of any atonement for the affront that had been endured ; the German sovereigns now knew how far they might venture to go against the Federation. The envoys all felt that they had been shamed and browbeaten, and henceforward it became their custom to ask for definite instructions even regarding the most trifling questions, so that all decisive action was indefinitely postponed.

The case of Hofmann was but one of a long series of infringements of justice which continued to occupy the

[1] Hardenberg to Metternich, April 12, 1817.

Bundestag for many years, and which abroad, especially in France, gave the German name an evil reputation. A severe penalty had to be paid because, after the dissolution of the kingdom of Westphalia, the great alliance had trustingly restored the old territorial suzerains without imposing any conditions. The crown of Prussia, indeed, acted with strict legality in her own Westphalian provinces ; in the Treaty of Tilsit, Prussia had recognised the kingdom of Westphalia, and henceforward regarded as legally valid all the actions of the Westphalian government which accorded with the treaty. The princes of Hanover, Brunswick, and Electoral Hesse, on the other hand, had been deprived of their lands only *de facto* and without any peace having been signed, so that they regarded King Jerome as merely a usurper. Vainly did the court of Berlin represent to them that they had been re-established, not by their own power, but by the arms of the allies, and that for this reason they were not entitled to treat simply as an illegal order that Napoleonic kingdom which had once received recognition from all the great powers. Prussia desired, by means of friendly negotiations between the four states concerned, to secure common legal principles for the recognition of the Westphalian laws and ordinances.[1] But none of the other three courts would act on this reasonable suggestion. In Hanover and Brunswick, the Westphalian laws were all declared null ; it was only the well-established liberties of the subject which were treated with respect.

All the more audaciously did the elector of Hesse take action. Everything in his country was to be restored to the status of the autumn of 1806, and the avaricious prince entered upon this colossal undertaking, not like the king of Sardinia at the same moment with the ingenuous honesty of the legitimist fanatic, but after the manner of the manifest cheat. What his " administrator Jerome " had acquired for the royal treasury was retained as legitimate spoils of war, what he had disbursed was demanded back as stolen goods. The workmen who had decorated the rooms of the gay Napoleonid, received no pay, but the furniture which had been delivered was retained in the electoral palaces. Hardly in the days of the Polish Augustus had long-suffering Germany witnessed such gross acts of despotism. Most of all suffered the purchasers of the numerous domains

[1] Goltz's Report, July 19 ; Memorial by the chancellor concerning the kingdom of Westphalia, November 18, 1817.

which had been sold by Jerome. They were expelled from their properties, and besieged the Federation with complaints. When these grievances came up for discussion at Frankfort, the Hessian envoy harped on the usual string, and spoke about the " abominable lies " which were being circulated. Martens, the representative of Brunswick, was brazen-faced enough to exclaim threateningly to the loyal people of those Guelph-Hessian lands which had sacrificed and suffered so enormously for their tribal prince, that it was necessary, by the maintenance of strictly legitimist principles, " to deprive German subjects of the desire to give any assistance to a possible invader ! " The majority of the Bundestag, having learned wisdom from bitter experience in the Hofmann affair, was content on this occasion to commend the complainants to the grace of the elector (July 17, 1817). This merely served to postpone the decision, for soon additional victims of the electoral tyranny came to state their grievances.

While the Bundestag was thus wasting its time, Hardenberg was honourably endeavouring to carry into effect the only politically significant article of the federal act which still seemed capable of realisation, if goodwill were forthcoming—article 11, which promised the federal states common aid against hostile attack. From the time of the Vienna congress down to the dissolution of the Federation, the hopes of Prussia regarding the military system of the Germanic Federation remained unaltered. The court of Berlin desired the bipartition of the federal army, and it was only when the resistance of the German courts was not to be overcome in any other way that Prussia became willing to agree that the middle-sized states should form independent army-corps. Unaffrighted by the experiences of Hänlein, the chancellor immediately began confidential negotiations with the court of Vienna, although he was already aware, from the instructions issued to the presidential envoy, that the Hofburg was by no means disposed to incur the resentment of the minor sovereigns by separate negotiations. At the very beginning of these consultations, a preliminary question came up for settlement which displayed the hopelessly fictitious character of the federal constitution. The boundaries of the federal domain had to be defined before it was possible to decide upon the supply of men to be demanded from the members as their respective contributions to the federal army. The federal act had

been satisfied with the obscure statement that the rulers of
Austria and Prussia entered the Federation "for their entire
possessions in so far as these had formerly belonged to the
Germanic empire." Since Metternich had from the first determined that he would never allow the Bundestag to exercise any
influence in the internal affairs of the crown-lands, he considered
the matter of no importance. He declared unhesitatingly that
his emperor intended to assign to the Federation a domain
containing about 8,000,000 inhabitants—the lands of the crown
of Bohemia, the archduchy, Tyrol and Salzburg, Styria,
Carinthia, and Carniola. Hardenberg held fast to his favourite
idea, the complete equality of the two great powers, and therefore proposed to the king that the Prussian contribution to the
Federation should contain an equal population ; in addition to
the indisputably imperial lands of the crown of Hohenzollern,
Guelderland, which for two hundred years had had nothing to do
with the empire, and the sovereign duchy of Silesia, together
with Lusatia, were to be declared federal lands.

Frederick William, however, took the matter very much in
earnest, and surprised the chancellor by making a definite
rejoinder that he thought of entering the Germanic Federation
with the whole of his territorial domain. He knew the incalculable vicissitudes of European politics, and notwithstanding his
friendship for the czar, he prudently bore in mind the possibility
of a war against Russia. But since he regarded himself as
simply a German prince, and was loyally determined to
resist with the entire force of his monarchy any violation of
federal territory, it seemed to him only reasonable that the
Federation should on its side be pledged to defend the Prussian
state against every attack ; in this connection he thought first
of all of Posen, and of the unconcealed greed of the Poles in
Warsaw. In case the formal incorporation of the entire state
territory into the Federation could not be effected, the king
demanded that at least there should be concluded a permanent
defensive alliance between Prussia and the Federation. As
early as the autumn of 1816, the monarch's intention in this
respect had found expression in the instructions to the federal
envoy, and since then, to Hardenberg's despair, for a year and
a half Frederick William had obstinately held to this view.
German affairs were still in so confused a condition that
even the simplest and best-intentioned political idea appeared
premature and actually dangerous. However certain it was

that the European interests of Prussia coincided with those of the rest of Germany, it was just as certain that the Prussian crown must not renounce its independence in foreign policy in favour of the Bundestag. And however indisputable it was that the loyal German Ordensland belonged by blood and by history to the great fatherland, it might be foreseen with equal certainty that neither Austria nor the middle-sized states would ever voluntarily accept this eastern march into the Germanic Federation, for every one of them regarded limitation of Prussian power as the primary aim of federal policy.

The chancellor therefore implored his royal master not to arouse a general and painful sensation by such a proposal, and not in this way " to step out of the ranks of the European powers "; he artfully enquired, " would not this action serve especially to foster the idea of Germanity which prevails among the giddy heads of the time ? "[1] Humboldt agreed with the chancellor, pointedly recalling the difficulty with which Prussia had acquired her position within the European pentarchy. Goltz, too, reported from Frankfort, that all the petty states desired that the Federation should play only a passive part in European politics, and that they would never tolerate the entry of the entire Prussian state. Hardenberg further represented to the king what mistrust the plan would arouse in St. Petersburg and in the minor courts.[2] Yet the possibility that Prussia might some day, by a majority of the Bundestag inspired with Austrian sentiments, be dragged against her will into an Italian war waged by the Hapsburgs, was not yet mooted in any of these memorials; such a contingency lay far beyond the horizon of the time. If Austria should be attacked in Lombardy, it was the unanimous opinion of the statesmen of Berlin that Prussia was unquestionably pledged to support her federal ally; for who else than France could undertake the attack ? No one as yet ventured to dream of the Piedmontese taking up arms on their own behalf.

The king remained firm. In answer to the chancellor he said: " In this extremely important matter it is impossible for me to come to any other decision, for I am too keenly aware of the danger which may befall the state."[3] Hence, with a heavy heart, Hardenberg, through the instrumentality,

[1] Hardenberg to the king, February 23, 1817.
[2] Humboldt's Opinion, July 12 ; Hardenberg's Memorial, December 1 ; Goltz's Memorial, December 30, 1817.
[3] King Frederick William to Hardenberg, December 1, 1817.

of privy councillor Jordan, had to communicate the king's plan to the Hofburg, together with a detailed memorial by Ancillon. Metternich did not hesitate. Nothing was further from his mind than to outbid the Prussian proposal by offering that Austria should enter the Federation as a whole; such bold resolutions were then generally regarded as impracticable, since they conflicted with the fundamental ideas of the policy of stability, and to the court of Vienna they appeared all the more foolish because the plan of forming an Italian Federation had not yet been abandoned. The Austrian statesman sent his Prussian friend an affectionate letter, couched in extremely moving terms (January 9, 1818), which was to remain absolutely and permanently secret except to the king and the chancellor. He declared that the happy harmony of the two powers depended solely upon the complete equality of their position. " To destroy this equality would result in the overthrow of the entire structure. Let us guard ourselves, my prince, against making any change in this happy situation!" An appended memorial maintained with proud confidence that if any one of the states of the Federation should be illegally assailed in its non-German domains " it would hardly need a defensive alliance in order to set the Federation in motion, for its own interest would dictate this step. The case of Austria or Prussia being separately attacked by Russia without the other power coming to the aid of its ally, is so remote from possibility that it would be superfluous to waste time over its consideration." The king was not convinced either by the assurances of Austria or by a new memorial from the chancellor, and demanded, although Hardenberg urgently advised to the contrary, an opinion from the foreign section of his council of state.[1] After lively discussions, all the members of this body agreed that, in view of the sentiments of the German federated states, the king's proposal was for the time being impracticable. Even the monarch's confidant, Colonel Witzleben, who had at first advocated the views of his royal friend, was convinced by the superior reasoning of the other side. Now at length the king yielded, and on April 24th approved that, in addition to the ancient imperial lands, only Guelderland, Silesia, and Lusatia should join the Federation; he added ill-humouredly that this

[1] Ancillon's Memorial to the court of Vienna, December 5, 1817; Metternich's Letter and Memorial to Hardenberg, January 9, 1818; Hardenberg's Memorial, February 22, 1818. Cabinet Order to the Council of State, March 8, 1818.

was done against his own conviction.[1] Consequently Frederick William's intention to restore to the political union of the nation the land anciently colonised by the Germans in the middle ages, was for the present frustrated. It was not till a generation later, amid the storms of the revolution, that the plan was to be revived; not until eighteen years later still, when the dominion of Austria collapsed, was it permanently realised.

Just as unfortunate was the course of the negotiations about the federal army. Frederick William engaged in these with unwearied zeal, for since Prussia herself had five per cent. of her population in the army, he considered that he was justified in demanding from his allies an effort of similar intensity. Metternich, on the other hand, held the organisation of the smaller German armies to be a matter of trifling importance, because he was sure of the Prussian alliance. The matter did not seem to him of sufficient account to induce him to excite for its sake the suspicion of the middle-sized states; should a war break out, the smaller contingents would, in one way or another, be forced, as they had been in the last campaigns, to join the greater masses. Apart from this, the court of Vienna completely lacked military sense and failed to understand the moral significance of military organisation. Although the defects of the cumbrous Austrian military system had been lamentably displayed during the recent wars, there had been no improvement since peace had been declared; the suspicious emperor made it a matter of principle that no officer who had distinguished himself in the war should ever be given any position of influence, and he left Radetzky, the most capable of his generals, rusting for ten years in command of the fortress at Olmütz. The machine got more and more out of gear. The young officers made an open mock of military philistinism, and chuckled over an ill-natured satire which appeared in the year 1816, *Das standhafte Kriegs- Dienst- und Exerzierreglement der Reichsstadt Riblingen;* for how often had the Austrian army, like the armada of Riblingen, had to put up with a commander utterly devoid of energy and resource! In addition it was the urgent desire of the emperor to avoid all provocative negotiations in Frankfort. When for the first time the Bundestag sent him congratulations on his birthday, he expressed his thanks through Metternich (March 2, 1817). The augurs of the Eschenheimer

---

[1] The two Opinions of Witzleben reported by Dorow, *J. von Witzleben*, pp. 115 et seq. Hardenberg's Diary, April 24, 1818.

Gasse learned with a satisfied smile that the good kaiser admonished them not to forget that as a permanent assembly they had no reason to do anything in a hurry; never again by " excessive pressure of business " was a " disadvantageous outbreak " to be induced in the Bundestag.

Whilst Emperor Francis thus expressed his concern regarding the possible impetuosity of the youthful Bundestag, the middle-sized states all displayed their determination to reject everything which might even approximate to the unity of a genuine army. In no other question did the still unimpaired Rhenish Confederate sentiment of these courts display itself so shamelessly. Not the defence of the fatherland against foreign enemies, but the safeguarding of petty sovereignty against the power of their own great allies, was openly declared to be their aim. As Berstett reported to his court with much satisfaction, all the middle-sized and petty states desired the formation of a purely federal army consisting of several corps made up out of the small contingents, under the direction of an elected federal commander-in-chief ; in addition, one Austrian and one Prussian corps might be tolerated as independent accessory troops.[1] The German army was to be intentionally weakened, so that the numerical preponderance of the Austrians and the Prussians might not prove a danger to their smaller neighbours. If this, the highest, aim could not be achieved, the petty states must at least be preserved against any subordination to the great powers. The very same courts which so recently, when the question was that of the admission of foreign envoys, had acclaimed the European power of the Germanic Federation, now humbly declared that their task was not to take a decisive position in the European system of states, but simply to maintain a defensive position with dignity—such was the wording of the first report of the committee of the Bundestag appointed to deal with military affairs. Baden and Darmstadt went even further, and actually declared, in opposition to the spirit and the letter of the federal act, that neutrality was the one and only principle of the Federation. Since the minor courts all confidently hoped for a long period of undisturbed peace, they wished to impose no more than trifling military demands upon their wearied peoples and their disordered finances. The professional pride of the Rhenish Confederate officers led them to look down with contempt upon the Landwehr, which most of

[1] Berstett's Report, January 29, 1817.

the minor states had during the war constituted upon the Prussian model, more especially since this force, with the exception of the Hanoverian Landwehr, had very rarely come into action. Nor was there any lack of suspicion, for Stein's detested central administration had led to the arming of the people! After the peace, in all the petty states, the Landwehr was abolished, or was allowed to fall into desuetude, so that it appeared only occasionally for a few hours at a time, on days of festival, as for instance in the case of the greatly ridiculed " Corpus Christi soldiers " of Bavaria; and soon Prussia was the only German state which still possessed a Landwehr fit for war.

The thoughtless selfishness of the minor states and the hatred of militarism characteristic of liberalism were united in demanding disarmament. The middle-sized states were also agreed in the view that although a moderate contribution of military force must be promised in case of war, a supervision of this force by the Federation in time of peace could never be tolerated. At the courts of Darmstadt and Carlsruhe it was openly asked why sacrifices should be made for a federal army which could after all be of no use whatever to the narrow fatherland. Long before the Austrians and the Prussians could come to the help of the south-west, the French army would have flowed over the German frontier lands. So speedily had the brilliant victories of recent years been forgotten! So paralysing to German pride was the effect of the proximity of those Alsatian fortresses which the unworthy peace had left in the hands of France! On this occasion the elector of Hesse once more exhibited his fondness for the good old time, and gave strict instructions to his envoy, saying that Hesse had never contributed more than 800 men to the army of the Holy Empire, but that out of his special consideration for the Germanic Federation he would in an extreme case provide 2,500 men, but he must not be bothered with the " domestic wars " of Austria and Prussia. Already in the introductory negotiations upon military affairs these views of the minor courts were expressed with cynical openness. Bavaria asked bluntly why any arrangement at all should be made for the peace strength of the contingents. It would be enough if the relationships between the military forces to be supplied by the different members of the Federation should be laid down in case of war. Once an agreement had been attained about this simple matter, everything else could be left to circumstances, and to the free agreement of the states. In fact on May 29, 1817, the Bundestag merely came to the determination to appoint a committee to draw up a provisional register. But was population alone to form the measure for the register, or were extent of territory and amount of revenue also to be taken into account? Even upon these points no unanimity had as yet been attained. The wealthy Hansa towns vigorously recommended that population should be the determining factor, for this seemed to them advantageous from a business point of view; on the other hand, thickly populated Würtemberg was just as definitely opposed to the idea.

In face of such experiences, Hardenberg placed his last hope upon an understanding with Austria. As early as the middle of May, 1817, he proposed separate negotiations to the court of Vienna,[1] but it was not until July that Metternich, with manifest unwillingness, commissioned General Steigentesch to meet Boyen and General Wolzogen in Carlsbad. There the two old friends, Steigentesch and Wolzogen, came into sharp conflict, and a partial understanding was at length secured only through the quiet strength of Boyen. As soon as matters of detail came under discussion, it was at once apparent how completely Hardenberg had deceived himself regarding the intentions of the Hofburg. To the Viennese statesmen, the Prussian proposal for the bipartition of the federal army was absolutely unacceptable. This plan did, indeed, offer to Prussia the military command of the numerous North German petty states; but what had Austria to gain thereby, since the subjection of the Bavarian and the Würtemberg kingly crowns to the supreme imperial command was altogether inconceivable? The plan was the outcome of the policy of peaceful dualism; but in the existing posture of affairs, it could serve only to strengthen Prussia to the disadvantage of Austria. For this very reason it received the warm support of the only notable Prussian statesman who was already advocating the separation from Austria. President von Motz sent at this time a memorial to the chancellor, wherein with the boldness of genius he threw light on the gigantic fraud of German federal law. In this document, the Federation was spoken of as " a mere political expedient " which the jealousy of the German princes, in unison with Austria, Russia, and France, had brought into existence, " in order to keep Germany in a state of perpetual disintegration

[1] Hardenberg's Instructions to Krusemark, May 13, 1817.

of energies." Motz continued by saying that Prussia must now begin to look forward to the time " when the flimsy Federation would fall to pieces of itself," and must therefore, in the meanwhile, so long as a united German army was still impossible, endeavour to combine the North German contingents with her own army by military conventions.[1] How could Austria entertain a proposal which gave occasion for such hopes ?

At length, on August 10th, after vigorous resistance, the Austrian plenipotentiary signed at Carlsbad a convention regarding the federal fortress of Mainz ; each of the two great powers was to provide half of the garrison, and each in turn was to appoint the governor or the commandant for the term of five years. This formal equality did not, indeed, serve to establish harmony in the principal German fortress, for since Austria from the first, in opposition to the spirit of the federal act, sent non-German regiments into the Rhenish town, dissensions soon broke out between the German and the foreign troops, and as long as the Germanic Federation lasted, the continued broils in the garrison of Mainz afforded a cheerful counterpart to the bloodless disputes of Frankfort. Some time before, on March 12th, a treaty had been entered into with the Netherlands, in virtue of which King Frederick William pledged himself to provide for the second federal fortress of Luxemberg, three-fourths of the garrison, the governor, and the commandant. Simultaneously Prussia, under the able superintendence of Aster, began the construction of her Rhenish fortresses of Coblentz, Cologne, Wesel, Jülich, and Saarlouis, utilising gradually for this purpose, in addition to the 20,000,000 francs allotted by the treaty of Paris, a considerable sum from her own resources. The fortress of Ehrenbreitstein was re-established, and before long the beautiful heights overlooking the confluence of the Moselle and the Rhine were crowned by that powerful mass of fortifications which aroused the admiration of Wellington, the old stormer of fortresses, and which put to shame the French art of fortification, still entangled in the ideas of Vauban. Whilst, in thus providing for the safety of the Lower Rhine, Prussia went far beyond the duties imposed by her connection with the Federation, the southwest continued to remain utterly defenceless before the sally-ports of the Alsatian fortresses. In Paris, it had been

---

[1] Motz, Reflections concerning the Military Organisation of the Germanic Federation, especially in respect of Treaties with the minor North German states, September 24, 1817.

agreed that Landau, as a third federal fortress, should be handed over to the Federation, but the promise still remained unfulfilled. Frcs. 20,000,000 out of the French contribution had been earmarked for a fourth federal fortress on the Upper Rhine, but the South German courts were disputing about its site. Baden and Würtemberg demanded a fortress close by the Rhine, perhaps in Rastatt, for the protection of their own domain ; Austria, on the other hand, desired to close the road along the Danube by the fortification of Ulm, and thus prevent any recurrence of the campaign of Austerlitz. Since the position of Ulm was suitable for the erection of a great Upper German fortress, and since Austria would not consider the equality of the two great powers in the fortress of Mainz on any other terms, Boyen agreed that in the Bundestag Prussia should vote for Ulm.

The negotiators in Carlsbad could not come to an agreement regarding the division of the federal army. No more than an extremely general understanding, the mere sketch of a sketch, could be effected. The federal states pledged themselves that in time of war two per cent. of the population should be allotted to the federal army, and that in addition they would supply one per cent. for supplementary troops ; should a federal war be declared, the contingents of the federal states would wear a distinctive badge, and the Bundestag was to choose the state which should nominate the federal commander-in-chief. This state could only be Austria. Boyen made this concession because he foresaw that, as in the last campaign, the nature of things would enforce a subdivision of the theatre of war. In order to supplement the pitiful outcome of the conference of Carlsbad by a more definite arrangement, and in order to unite the two great powers upon a common procedure at the Bundestag, in December Privy-councillor Jordan was again sent to Vienna, but could obtain no more than vague assurances.

Meanwhile the Austrian diplomats had long ago betrayed to the minor courts the secret of the Carlsbad convention. As early as fourteen days after it had been concluded, and long before the Prussian federal envoy had himself any inkling of the Carlsbad negotiations, the South German cabinets had already been informed. The sovereigns were terrified, the spectre of German duarchy stood threateningly at their gates. The elector of Hesse immediately hastened to Darmstadt, and the grand duke of Baden to Homburg, to the king of Würtemberg ; the four princes pledged themselves to combine in resisting every encroachment by the great powers. In the autumn, when the Bundestag reassembled after its first recess, Count Goltz, who had not been officially informed of the matter until November, found the mood of the assembly extraordinarily excited and embittered.[1] It was not until January 15, 1818, that Buol ventured to lay the Carlsbad convention before the Bundestag, as a presidential proposal. In order to conciliate his incensed hearers, he gave the assurance that in doing this he wished merely to open the field for free discussion. Two points of view should dominate the negotiations : " The completest respect for the sovereignty of the German states, and the necessary regard for an effective system of defence." He then handed in, in addition, an extraordinary proposal for the subdivision of the federal army, which required a peace strength of no more than 120,000 men, each of the two great powers providing an army of 41,500 ; the remaining 37,000 were to be enrolled in nine corps, so that each of the middle-sized states, from Bavaria down to Luxemburg, could enjoy the privilege of having a general-in-chief. The pearl of these eleven corps was the eleventh, which was to consist of 2,606 Luxemburgers, Nassauers, and Hanseats, under the leadership of a Netherland general. Prussia gave a provisional assent to this remarkable proposal only because it was impossible that in case of war these trifling corps could maintain their independence beside the armies of the two great powers, and the step could not yet be ventured of directly advocating bipartition of the army.

Yet however sedulously Austria had respected the sovereignty of the petty potentates, and however modest her proposals might sound, to the heirs of the Confederation of the Rhine even this nothing seemed intolerably oppressive. Vainly in January did Hardenberg send General Wolzogen to Stuttgart to explain to the new king that only an army of not less than two per cent. of the population would be adequate to resist a French attack ; King William's selfishness was stronger than his soldierly judgment. When the voting began, on February 16th, Bavaria, Saxony, Würtemberg, Baden, and the two Hesses, were unanimously opposed to the great powers. Almost with one voice they demanded that the war strength should be reduced to one-half, declaring that more than one per cent. for

---

[1] Goltz's Reports, October 8 and November 25, 1817. Goltz's Sketch of the Proceedings of the Federation, April 13, 1819.

the active forces, and one-half per cent. for the supplementary troops, was out of the question. They further insisted that the federal commander ought to be directly chosen by the Bundestag, for this would make it possible for Marshal Wrede, or one of the petty princes, to be appointed to the supreme command of the German army. It was regarded as a matter of course that this German field-marshal would not be empowered to alter the distribution of the corps, even in war time ; he was also to enjoy the benefit of a sort of parliamentary headquarters-staff, an assembly of officers from all the contingents, whose business it would be to represent the interests of their respective sovereigns. There was to be no inspection from the federal side in peace time, nor were there to be any definite regulations about the Landwehr ; speaking generally, the carrying out of the future federal law was to be left exclusively to the individual states. This prospect was all the more cheering since the elector of Hesse expressly added that he must not be asked to keep the cadres and the necessary equipment for the war-strength ready prepared in time of peace. A distinctive federal badge was to be tolerated in war, but it must be nothing more than a sign of recognition, like the white brassard which the soldiers of allied Europe had formerly worn in France, without prejudice to their national independence. As regards the subdivision of the federal army, it was demanded as an inviolable rule that no state which provided a complete army corps should mingle other troops with its own ; the mixed corps should be constituted " in accordance with geographical relationships and ties of kinship." The elector of Hesse also announced that he had agreed with his cousin of Darmstadt to unite with him " in constituting a joint force in opposition to the enemies of their common and peculiar fatherland," and everyone knew that when he spoke of the enemies of their " peculiar fatherland," he meant Prussia alone.

In the first heat of his anger, Hardenberg wished to demand reparation from Hesse ; [1] the well-meaning man was completely helpless in face of the display of a particularism which so openly avowed that the protection of the great powers was desired without rendering anything in exchange, and which declared that, in case of need, it would not hesitate to join with the enemies of the country. Disheartening, too, was the deplorable mendacity of the whole discussion. Not one of the federal associates

---

[1] Hardenberg to Goltz, February 21, 1818.

could possibly imagine that either Austria or Prussia would ever consent to divide her army into two fragments, and consequently all dispute about the federal contingents of the two powers was unmeaning. Yet Metternich was far from being alienated by the behaviour of the middle-sized states. He negotiated in secret with the South German courts, and promised the king of Würtemberg that in addition to the closed masses of the Austrian, Prussian, and Bavarian armies, two or three mixed corps should be formed, so that Würtemberg, Hanover, and perhaps also Saxony, should each have the command of a separate corps. Meanwhile the South German envoys were also at work upon Buol ; Berckheim, the Badenese envoy, asked him reproachfully why Austria was allowing herself to be dragged at the heels of Prussia.[1] In the sitting of April 9, 1818, the presidential envoy at length openly went over to the side of the middle-sized states, and laid before the Bundestag certain " leading points " of federal military organisation, which in all important matters corresponded to the proposals of the South German courts. The assembly joyfully agreed ; Prussia was completely isolated, and accepted the inevitable.

Not even by this experience was the chancellor enlightened regarding the untrustworthiness of Austrian friendship, although Boyen, Wolzogen, and even the harmless Goltz, repeatedly drew his attention to the manifest duplicity of Viennese policy. He continued to regard Metternich as a faithful friend, whose only fault was an unduly yielding disposition, whereas Metternich (like the middle-sized states) was in reality tenaciously and astutely advancing towards a single goal, the prevention of any increase in the military strength of Prussia. A committee of the Bundestag was formed to carry these " leading points " into effect, and in addition there was established a military commission consisting of officers of the larger states, so that military affairs had always to run the gauntlet of three authorities. A new dispute began when Prussia declared herself prepared to contribute just as many troops to the federal army as Austria, although the population of her lands in the Federation was somewhat less. In his innocence, the king had hoped that the Federation would thank him for this patriotic sacrifice, and was profoundly disappointed when Metternich answered the Prussian envoy, in terms of friendly regret, that the acceptance of this " generous offer " by the Bundestag was unfortunately extremely improbable,

---

[1] Berckheim's Report, April 8 ; Boyen to Hardenberg, March 31, 1818.

especially if the dreaded Austria were to express herself in favour of the proposal. In fact the federal envoys, led by Martens the Hanoverian, expressed their well-grounded hostility to the unprecedented proposal as soon as Goltz ventured to bring it forward in the summer.[1]

The dispute concerning the subdivision of the federal army continued even longer. The " leading points " merely laid down that the minor contingents must be completely safeguarded from any contact with the armies of the three great states. Prussia now demanded that Electoral Hesse, in view of her geographical situation, should join a North German corps ; but the elector held, in opposition to this, that " the ties of kingship " were of greater importance, and wished, in conjunction with his cousin of Darmstadt, to join Würtemberg. The quarrel had become utterly intolerable since General Langenau, the new representative of Austria in the military commission, had secretly been adding fuel to the flames ; in Schwarzenberg's headquarters and at the congress of Vienna the versatile Saxon had already displayed his hatred for Prussia, and in all the petty arts which were decisive in the Bundestag he showed himself far more adept than the learned Prussian, Wolzogen. At length, in August, an agreement was secured that population should constitute the standard for the provisional military register of the Federation— for in the course of half a century, the Germanic Federation never attained to a permanent military register. Now recommenced the haggling of the petty states : Hildburghausen reckoned its population upon the basis of a census of the year 1807, Gotha and Altenburg were shown to have estimated their population at a figure which was 12,000 below the actual—and so on.

When the Germanic Federation entered its third year, the military organisation had not yet been decided, the Carlsbad convention regarding the fortress of Mainz had not been approved by the Bundestag, neither Luxemberg nor Landau had been made over to the Federation, nor had any agreement been secured regarding the fourth federal fortress. Meanwhile the French millions, purchased with the blood of those who had fought at Waterloo, lay at moderate interest in the hands of Rothschild, and enriched this house, whose greatness had first

---

[1] Instructions to Krusemark, May 20 ; Krusemark's Report, June 10 ; Goltz's Report, August 21, 1818.
[2] Goltz's Report, April 28, 1818,

been founded by the blood-money of the elector of Hesse; which since the year 1813 had rapidly risen to the position of a world power; and which within a few years had made over more than 1,200,000,000 gulden in subsidies and loans to the deeply indebted courts of Europe. German economic life secured but little gain from the treasures of the Rothschilds, for the firm was not German, as had been those of the Fugger and the Welser, but showed from the first the cosmopolitan character of the modern Jew. The five sons of old Amschel Rothschild, who had been raised to the baronage by the grateful emperor Francis, settled in the principal capitals of Western Europe, and were all guided by that simple principle which their father had once voiced to the elector of Hesse: " He who takes my money, takes my honour, and my honour is my life." The Frankfort branch of the house remained a faithful helper of the Hofburg in its eternal financial need, and was a powerful ally of Austria in her German policy. There was little to be gained by the Rothschilds in Berlin, for Prussian finances were once more in order ten years after the peace. Yet Friedrich Gentz, full of unselfish enthusiasm, wrote a long essay for the Brockhaus encyclopædia, wherein, in a thoroughly servile manner, he glorified the incomparable wisdom and virtue of the brothers Rothschild.

When the Bundestag so shamefully neglected the nearest and most important of its duties, how little could it do justice to the numerous other tasks which the ambiguous words of the federal act assigned to the assembly. All the parties of the opposition were united in demanding the speedy fulfilment of article 13, which promised the introduction of diets, and nothing seemed less easy to forgive the Bundestag than its unconcern about this promise. Yet article 13 was no more than a vague prophecy which by no means justified the federal assembly in interfering in the constitutional struggles of the individual states. Although Hardenberg had strictly enjoined upon Count Goltz that, after all the tribulations of the years of war, failure to provide the promised constitution might prove extremely dangerous, the federal envoys had speedily united in a tacit determination not to touch this thorny question. The cabinets soon learned that the realisation of the promise was far more difficult than the liberals, in their impatience, imagined; all the states jealously preserved their sovereignty vis-à-vis the Federation, and many of them had secretly determined to avoid the execution of this inconvenient pledge.

Nevertheless the Bundestag was compelled to deal with the matter. Charles Augustus of Weimar had, as early as May, 1816, been the first among the rulers to promulgate a constitution for his little country ; and in December of the same year he demanded a federal guarantee for this fundamental law. The level-headed prince openly expressed his willingness to realise in his own land the hopes that had arisen in Germany, and the liberal press loudly acclaimed " the only German prince who had kept his word." The majority of the Bundestag received the proposal of Weimar with unconcealed anger ; why should this minor prince press forward so arrogantly and, in order to curry popular favour, throw other sovereigns into the shade ? Violent altercations followed. When Bavaria expressed doubts regarding the competence of the Bundestag, the envoy of the Ernestines sharply replied that such a contention served only to confirm the widely diffused and groundless accusation that the Federation troubled itself solely about the new rights of sovereignty , but desired to withhold from subjects the rights formerly secured to them by the imperial constitution. The innocent Gagern increased the ill-feeling when he expressed to the grand duke his cordial thanks for this action, which would be an additional stimulus to other princes. Vienna was painfully embarrassed, for Austria desired neither to accord recognition to the princely demagogue in Weimar, nor yet to admit that the Bundestag possessed an arbitrator's authority. Hardenberg, on the other hand, who still confidently expected the success of his own constitutional plans, espoused the cause of the grand duke, praised the patriotic sentiments manifested in the proposal of Weimar, and in a confidential letter temporarily appeased Metternich's concern. With customary ceremonious slowness, the Bundestag at length did what it was not able to leave undone, and after more than four months voted the requisite guarantee in the driest possible terms ; but the Austrian envoy expressly added that, in such questions, everything must on principle be left to a free understanding between the princes and the estates.

At the same time, a lawyer named Beck, of Löwenstein, had in Odenwald prepared a harmless petition which asked the Bundestag to carry quickly into effect the cherished article 13. Certain hotspurs among the students of Jena and Heidelberg

went from place to place endeavouring to secure signatures
for the petition. Beck himself came to Frankfort, visited some
of the envoys, and according to the reports which the alarmed
representatives despatched home, used extremely revolutionary
language. Notwithstanding the zeal of the students and the
approval of the liberal press, the petition secured barely a
thousand signatures throughout Germany; but it was the first
example since immemorial times of a political agitation embracing several German states at once, and the official corporation
continued to regard the old rule as inviolable, that every petition
is permissible, but not the collection of signatures. Consequently
this tentative awakening of party-life aroused general alarm at
the courts; even Hardenberg, greatly moved, ordered the envoy
in Frankfort to keep a wary eye upon such dangerous demagogic
activity.[1]

Now, as before, Metternich was determined to keep the
Bundestag altogether aloof from these difficult questions. He
saw with satisfaction that in the Austrian crown lands the
promise of the federal act had long before been gloriously fulfilled; here there still existed those mummified postulate-diets
whose visible life and history was usually played in three acts:
the arrival of the estates in their state chariots; the reading,
and unanimous approval, of the sovereign's postulates; and,
finally, the driving away of the estates in the same
state chariots. Once only, in the autumn of 1817, did it
occur to Metternich that it might be advisable to assemble
some of the deputies to this diet, together with the heads of
the officialdom, to form a Reichsrat; but since Emperor Francis
kept the bold and innovating proposal lying in his desk for
eighteen years, until the day of his death, the minister pursued
the idea no further, and continued to adhere to the tried principles of stability. Why, then, should he awaken the suspicion
of the German sovereigns on account of this article 13, which,
after all, had found its way into the federal act only on the
initiative of the idealogues Hardenberg and Humboldt? As
soon as Rechberg, the Bavarian minister, alarmed by the vote
upon the Weimar proposal, expressed his lively concern regarding
possible encroachments on the part of the federal assembly,
Metternich gladly availed himself of the opportunity to satisfy
the minor courts regarding the harmlessness of the Bundestag,
and sent to Hruby, Austrian ambassador in Munich, a long

---

[1] Instructions to Goltz, December 8, 1818.

memorial, which was communicated also to the other cabinets, under the title of a " manifesto." After a moving description of the incomparable advantages of the German " federative state," this document went on to show that the Bundestag could not exercise an independent authority unless all the princes personally participated ; it would suffice to recall a single demagogic, and therefore disloyal, envoy, in order to obviate all risk of mischief. " The emperor is convinced that the small state of Weimar has up to the present hour managed to invoke more misfortune upon Germany than the federal assembly could possibly bring to pass in its present legal situation, even in hardly conceivable eventualities." Least of all need the Federation trouble about carrying out article 13. " A natural and extremely simple consideration of the activities which to-day disturbers of the peace of all kinds are permitting themselves to arouse in the designs of the *Zeitgeist*, demands unconditionally that the federal assembly shall refrain from taking any initiative. The law exists ; this must suffice for the moment ; the application of the law must be left to the wisdom of each individual government."[1]

So far was it still from the intention of the court of Vienna to interfere with the constitutional movement by federal resolutions. The first incitement to a reactionary federal policy came rather from the monarch who at that time, next to Charles Augustus, stood highest in popular favour. The ambitious young William of Würtemberg had since his accession to the throne honourably endeavoured to bring to a close the vexatious constitutional dispute which he had inherited from his ill-conditioned father, and had twice vainly laid before the estates liberal proposals for a constitution. But repentance overcame him in the autumn of 1817, and he determined to seek assistance from the Federation against his own liberalism. His envoys, Wangenheim in Frankfort and Wintzingerode in Vienna, received instructions to ask from the Federation an authentic interpretation of article 13, " so that firm and immovable limits may be imposed upon all excessive demands." Naturally, neither of them was to betray the true ground of the petition. They declared that the king was bound by his word, but that the disorderly mood prevailing in Prussia and among Würtemberg's neighbours called for restraint, and (this was a harmless addition by the prolix Wangenheim) that the constitutional

[1] Metternich to Hruby, December 11, 1817.

plans of Würtemberg were likely to constitute a momentous example for the whole of Germany.[1]   The proposal, however, was received with such coolness by the federal envoys, that Wangenheim had to agree that his motion, which he had brought forward in a secret sitting (December 18th), should not appear in the minutes.   Wintzingerode fared no better in Vienna.   It is true that in confidential intercourse Metternich declared that the diets spoken of in article 13 had nothing in common with the revolutionary design of general popular representation, and thus early disclosed a cherished idea of his policy which was subsequently to lead to grave discontent in German political life.   But were it only out of regard for Prussia and Bavaria, it seemed to him impossible that the Federation should exercise any influence in the matter of the diets.   King William's scheme had miscarried, but in Vienna it had not been forgotten. Metternich had learned how little lasting resistance was to be expected from the minor crowns if once it were determined to use the power of the Federation against the diets.   The constitutional king, who was hailed by the ingenuous press as the hero of liberalism, was the first to show the Hofburg the way to stifle German freedom.

In the interim, the unfortunate article 13 had once more come up for discussion in Frankfort, for the dukes of Mecklenburg also demanded the guarantee of the Federation for a constitutional law which was to serve for the enlargement of their venerable hereditary claims.   In this negotiation, Count Goltz, acting on instructions from Hardenberg, gave a detailed report of what had hitherto been done in Prussia to fulfil the promise of a constitution ; he advised against the regulation of the question of the diets by the federal assembly, since this body could do nothing more than " lay down general principles " ; but suggested that the individual states should, within a year, report once more to the Bundestag on their plans for a constitution.   At first Frederick William was extremely averse to this action on the part of the chancellor, because he foresaw that the Prussian constitution could not possibly be completed for years to come ; and what right had the Federation to demand an account of these matters ?   But the king's anxieties were

---

[1] Berckheim's Reports of November 18, 23, and 30, December 13 and 29, 1817, harmonising perfectly with the communications which Count W. Wintzingerode furnishes from Würtemberg documents (cf. *E. L. Wintzingerode, A Statesman of Würtemberg*, Gotha, 1866, pp. 31 et seq.).

allayed when Hardenberg represented to him that the introduction of new representative institutions in place of the obsolete
provincial diets was a matter which had, after all, already
been determined : " To-day cannot go back to yesterday." [1]
The Bundestag now gave the Mecklenburgers the desired
guarantee, and accepted the Prussian proposal. The crown of
Würtemberg, however, could not refrain from once again displaying before the nation the light of its incomparable liberalism.
The very same Wangenheim who had just secretly demanded a
restrictive interpretation of article 13, declared, according to the
published minute of April 6th : " His majesty's liveliest anxiety
is directed towards the establishment of a representative constitution based upon the most liberal principles." This was the
first sample of that hypocritical and false policy of vacillation
between the Bundestag and the local estates which for a generation to come was to be pursued by the constitutional middle-
sized states.

Next to a representative constitution, the freedom of the
press was the most cherished wish of the liberals ; they hoped
all the more securely for the fulfilment of this desire since
article 18 of the federal act prescribed for the Bundestag that
at its first assembly it should prepare uniform dispositions
regarding the freedom of the press and dealing with the question
of literary piracy. This hope also was to prove illusory. The
comparatively unrestricted freedom which German literature
enjoyed in its classic days rested upon the supposition that
writers would always hold aloof from politics. But when,
after 1813, a political press suddenly came into existence,
honourable and warm-hearted, but also muddle-headed, noisy, and
characterised by youthful ill-breeding, the old official corporation
was for a while alarmed and helpless in face of the new
manifestation ; there was no diplomat who, in his confidential letters, failed to complain of the unbridled freedom of the
" political scribblers." Among the few who, amid the general
alarm, were able to preserve some equanimity, was Hardenberg.
Whilst still in Paris, he wrote to the minister of justice that
he desired the approval of a regulated freedom of the press,
but also some restriction of the tendency to unbridled licence ;
it seemed to him that the revision of the numerous inadequate
laws of censorship which still prevailed in various parts of

---

[1] Cabinet Order of February 18 ; Hardenberg's Reply, March 10 ; the
king's Rejoinder, March 21, 1818.

Prussia, was urgently needed. Unfortunately, amid the enormous mass of administrative business of these days of transition, he could not find leisure to pursue the plan. Meanwhile the censorship was not severe; and literary piracy, which on the left bank of the Rhine flourished luxuriantly, was strictly suppressed in Prussia, although the petty neighbours did not follow this good example. In Reutlingen, above all, under the protection of the crown of Würtemberg, piracy was practised altogether without restraint. Once only did the chancellor, most unwillingly, allow himself to be moved to an act of injustice which inflicted a severe wound upon the repute of Prussia. Since the war, the *Rheinische Merkur* had rapidly fallen from its high estate; fiery patriotic emotion was no longer adequate for the sober needs of the years of peace. Since Görres had nothing to say about the business questions of organisation and administration, he soon declined into aimless terrorist blustering. From all the courts, German and foreign alike, there came complaints against the incorrigible *gazettier de Coblence*. When he wrote scornfully that the government's dread of the freedom of the press was strictly comparable to the hatred of public prostitutes for the lighting of the streets; when after the appearance of the Schmalzian pamphlet he broke out into incredible exaggeration, into offensive images (saying that now the seven stenches of the Prussian state had united to form a single Schmalz-stench, and that the general reaction had broken loose), this tone was too strong for the sensitive ears of the day. After repeated private warnings, Hardenberg resolved, in January, 1816, to suppress the *Rheinische Merkur*, a few days after Görres had hailed the new year with the confident prophecy that the *Merkur* would be the guiding star of the year that was then opening. The suppression made everywhere a painful impression. What a strange way to show gratitude towards the paper which, in a great time, had so courageously represented the German cause; and what folly to offend in this way an incalculably passionate publicist who still remained true to the German flag, but who, in his fantastic manner, might at any time go over to the other side! In general, however, the Prussian press was left comparatively unmolested.

Not until the spring of 1817 did the Bundestag remember the promise of article 18, and thereupon commissioned von Berg, the envoy of Oldenburg, to compile a statistical statement

of the German press laws. This man of cumbrous learning
undertook his laborious task with all the pomp and circumstance
of an old-time Göttingen professor. Hardenberg recognised that
in this way the goal would never be attained, and since complaints against the unbridled press, and especially against the
rough tone of the Jena newspapers, became increasingly frequent,
he decided, in the summer of 1817, to secure a federal press
law by common proposals from the two great powers. He
therefore had a memorial upon the freedom of the press
elaborated by Privy-councillor von Raumer, and when his
confidant Jordan went to Vienna in the winter, he was instructed
to come to an understanding with Metternich about this question.
The memorial already displayed some anxiety, but did not
exceed the measure of compulsion which appeared indispensable
to most of the governments of that day : it demanded absolute
freedom for all great scientific works, but strict censorship for
newspapers.[1] Here also, however, it became plain how widely
divergent were the views of the two great powers. Although
Metternich instructed Gentz to draw up a memorial on the press,
and expressed a vigorous demand that Germany should be free
from " the dictatorship of such men as Jahn, Arndt, Oken, and
Fries," he was once more deeply influenced by his respect for
the sovereignty of the individual states, and Jordan brought
nothing home beyond a few vague assurances.[2] Then, in April,
1818, Grand Duke Charles Augustus endeavoured to hasten the
activity of the Bundestag, and urgently demanded the imposition of uniform principles applying to the German press, because
he had often had the painful experience that the constitutional
freedom of the press of his country was regarded with ill-feeling
by his neighbours. This was a vain demand. It was not until
October, 1818, after more than a year and a half, that Berg
had compiled his report ; and now the Bundestag plucked
up courage to appoint a commission to draw up further
schemes. Thus, through shameful procrastination, was lost the
last opportunity for the securing of a tolerably reasonable German
press-law.

To the masses of the nation, the hopeless futility of the
Bundestag first became manifest when the assembly at length

[1] Hardenberg to Krusemark, June 12 ; Raumer's Memorial concerning
article 18, with Remarks by the chancellor, November 18, 1817.
[2] Jordan to Hardenberg, January 13 ; Metternich to Hardenberg, January
5, 1818.

came to deal with article 19 of the federal act, which promised the regulation of trade relationships. So anarchical a confusion as this impoverished and exhausted people had now to endure in its commercial intercourse, had never yet been known, even in the distressing history of Germany. The detested customs-houses and *droits réunis* of the French had everywhere been abolished immediately after the overthrow of the foreign dominion, and had not yet been replaced by a new system of indirect taxation. Consequently a great part of Germany lay exposed without defence to the overwhelming competition of the richer foreign world. The factories of Rhineland, which had only just begun to develop under the Napoleonic mercantile system, suddenly lost their market in France, Holland, and Italy, whilst they were cut off from access to their own country-men by the numerous state and district customs-barriers which intersected Germany. It was a topsy-turvy section of the world. As soon as the Continental System fell, English goods, which had for years been shut out from the continent, were poured over in vast quantities; crowds of English commercial travellers invaded German towns. In one year, English manufacturing industry sent goods to the continent to the value of 388,000,000 gulden, and of these, 129,000,000 gulden came to Germany alone. Parliament then proceeded to re-establish the metallic currency. Silver was reminted, quantities of new gold coin were issued, and the bank was pledged to the gradual resumption of specie payments. England needed gold at all costs, and endeavoured to supply this need by extensive exports, so that British cotton goods were frequently offered on the German market at from thirty to forty per cent. below the cost of manufacture. In addition, the high corn duties of England prevented the export of German grain, and during the famine years of 1816 and 1817, German manufacturers lost also the sole advantage which they had had over their English competitors, namely, the low rate of wages.

Embittered by so hopeless a state of affairs, public opinion ran to extremes. Anxious manufacturers demanded a severe prohibitive system for the protection of German labour, and those inspired with an exaggerated Teutonism agreed. In Berlin, the members of the town council and a number of burghers of high position pledged themselves to buy only German clothing and household requisites; unions for similar purposes came into existence in Silesia and Saxony. On the other hand, the revolutionary free-traders, who, like Brunner the Bavarian, condemned all customs-dues as an attack upon natural freedom, raised a clamour; a scientifically elaborated system of free-trade principles first came into existence in a small circle of professors and among the best heads of Prussian officialdom. The abolition, or at least the restriction, of the internal customs-dues, was the universal desire; as early as the year 1816, at the Leipzig fair, C. Weber summoned a meeting of manufacturers and merchants to send in a petition to this effect to the Bundestag, but very few combined any clear idea with the high-sounding words; hardly anyone recognised what enormous difficulties were imposed by nature herself against the economic unity of Germany. No other civilised nation was so homogeneous in character, but no other comprised within its boundaries such a variety of climatic conditions, of modes of consumption, and of methods of labour. What a contrast between the great manufacturing industry of the Lower Rhine, and the semi-Polish provinces where, with a rise in the price of grain, wages usually sank, because nothing but hunger would force the lazy populace to work; and what a contrast, again, between the northerly climate of East Prussia, where elks lived in the forests, and the happy vine-lands of the Rhine. No man of poietic intelligence had yet appeared competent to do justice to interests so fundamentally divergent.

Least of all could the Bundestag venture upon such a task. But one immediately pressing evil of German commercial relationships could be, and must be, allayed by the federal assembly, when in the summer of 1816 a famine, whose like had not been seen since the year 1772, afflicted the impoverished country. Rain fell almost continuously for months, all the rivers overflowed their banks, in Central and West Germany almost the entire harvest was destroyed; in Rhineland, as late as the spring of 1817, pale and miserable beings were to be seen wandering through the fields digging up the rotten potatoes of the previous year. The few roads which then existed had been so completely spoiled by the war, that it was impossible to transport grain any distance through the country; in winter even the mail coaches could in many cases only get along with a supplementary team of from sixteen to twenty horses. Consequently, in the year 1818, the price of the scheffel (one and a half bushels) of wheat was, on the Rhine, 2 tlr. 9 sgr. 6 pfg. higher than in Prussia, whereas in the previous fifty years the highest difference in price within the Prussian monarchy had amounted to only 10 sgr. 7 pfg. Internal trade, already pitifully small, was now completely destroyed by the foolish enmities of particularism. Austria, in accordance with her antediluvian economic principles, forbade all export of grain immediately the rise in price began, and thus gave the signal for a general tariff war throughout South Germany. Bavaria, Würtemberg, Baden, and Darmstadt, also closed their frontiers; in the highlands, the grain trade was completely arrested. In Frankfort, there was a shortage of fodder, the federal envoys trembled for their carriage horses, and Count Buol had, in the name of his colleagues, to send a request to the crown of Bavaria that a vessel laden with oats, which lay at Wertheim on the Main, might at length be allowed to pass by the Bavarian customs.[1] In the north, too, many grievous errors were committed. Bülow made such a careless use of the 2,000,000 thalers which the king had allotted for the purchase of grain from the Baltic, that the severely afflicted Rhineland derived little advantage from the money. None the less, the majority of the North German governments, by facilitating intercourse, honourably did their best to overcome the distress. After the South German courts had overwhelmed one another for several months with contradictory reproaches, and had mutually starved one another's countries, Würtemberg at length applied to the Federation, and demanded a speedy raising of the embargoes by federal action (May 19, 1817). With the manifest design of frustrating this idea, Bavaria made a counter-proposal to the effect that the measure must be extended to the non-German provinces of Austria, Prussia, and the Netherlands. Prussia, and the majority of the other states, voted for the proposal of Würtemberg; but the Hofburg, following its usual custom, left the presidential envoy for eight weeks without instructions.

Then the kindness of nature came to the assistance of the Bundestag; the fields displayed promise of a bountiful harvest, the price of grain fell, and, on July 14th, Buol was gratified to be able to announce to the assembly, in his classic German, that though he was still without information as to the intentions of his court, this after all was a matter of little importance, " since the prospect of so bountiful a harvest is itself raising the embargo." In the following year the question of common measures for the future was again discussed, and once more

---

[1] Berstett's Report, May 20, 1817.

Bavaria displayed her ill-will, until at length (on July 9, 1818) the presidential envoy closed this drama of federal unity by saying that the negotiations had, indeed, led to no definite result, but, he continued, " I still cherish the hope that before long this question will once more be agitated." This prophecy of Austria was to be brilliantly fulfilled; article 19 was to estrange the federal states one from another! An epilogue, which could have been possible only on German soil, was not lacking, for there exists a certain frankness of stupidity and baseness which can thrive only in the narrows of particularism. During the famine, the elector of Hesse had ordered Baltic grain through the faithful Rothschild; but the shipment arrived too late, when prices had already fallen. In order that his privy purse should not suffer in any way, the wealthy prince now forced the bakers of Cassel to take this grain off his hands at a price of 12 tlr. 2 gr., when the market price was only 7 tlr. In this way, for the burghers of the Hessian capital, the period of famine was artificially prolonged for several months by the affectionate father of the country.

What, finally, could the foreign trade of the nation expect from the Bundestag in a distressing emergency which was very loosely handled even by the naval powers ? Like Turkey herself, the Barbary states (Turkish protectorates) owed their continued existence chiefly to the disunion of the European powers ; the excess of contrasts which characterised the multiform civilisation of the west, redounded to the advantage of the barbarism of Islam. Since no European power would allow any of the others to take determined action against the Porte, the people had long been accustomed to regard the proceedings of the Barbary corsairs in the Mediterranean as legitimate campaigns ; every sea power protected itself by its own arms, or by the payment of tribute. After the peace, when naval commerce revived, the pirates ventured into more distant seas, and even as far as the Baltic, where, within sight of the German coasts, German ships were seized and their crews carried off to slavery ; in addition there was danger of infection from the plague-stricken lands of North Africa. The vessels of Hanover and Schleswig-Holstein still enjoyed a certain amount of security under the protection of the English and Danish flags, for a British fleet had recently threatened the dey of Algiers in his capital and had forced him to liberate his Christian slaves. All the more severely did the Hansa towns and the Prussian seaports suffer : a great part of their ships had to sail under foreign flags. At length, in September, 1816, Czar Alexander suggested in London the formation of a European naval alliance for a common attack upon the sea-robbers ; but the English government once more suspected hidden designs, and would not tolerate the appearance of Russian warships in the Mediterranean. The weary negotiations led to no result, although Prussia supported the Russian proposals, and declared herself prepared to contribute some frigates to the European fleet. In this matter, as in all questions of commercial policy, Austria displayed imperturbable indifference. When the corsairs of the sultan of Morocco had once more seized a Prussian ship, Gentz wrote scornfully : " Is this good man not to be granted the right possessed by other sovereigns of taking hostile action when he is injured ? "

Meanwhile the Hansa towns appealed for help to the Federation (June 16, 1817), and the Bundestag became emboldened to the appointment of a special committee. Count Goltz thought it necessary to offer an excuse for this unprecedented audacity, and assured his king that " Neither now nor in the future is it or can it be the intention of the assembly to intervene unasked in matters of European policy ; this action is not taken out of presumption, but in the firm conviction that your majesty and the great powers of Europe will be inclined to excuse what has been done in view of its purpose and of the good faith which guides our action."[1] No less humble than the wording of this excuse, was the committee's proposal that the Bundestag should request Austria and Prussia, in their turn, with the assistance of France, Russia, and the other naval powers, to induce the English court to join in common measures against the Barbary corsairs. Among all the German courts there was one only which felt all the shame of such a proposal. Presumably an opinion had been despatched by Nebenius, or another of the numerous capable young officials in Carlsruhe, to Mandelsloh of Würtemberg, who held Baden's proxy at the Bundestag ; however this may be, in the name of Baden, Mandelsloh was the first to moot the idea of a German navy, although as yet in extremely indefinite outlines. He asked whether it could be considered proper to suggest to the naval powers that they should protect German commerce at their expense ; and whether the nation which had once destroyed the pirate league of the Vitalie Brethren was not in a position to launch a

---

[1] Goltz, Report to the king, June 17, 1817.

few frigates of its own, and to drive " one or two miserable
pirate ships " from the German seas ? Why, even little Portugal knew how to protect her own skin against the Barbary
corsairs ! The inland stupidity of German federal policy found
no answer for such questions. Six months later (December
22nd) the Bundestag requested the committee to continue its
labours, and therewith the matter was shelved as far as the
Federation was concerned, although Prussia had declared herself
ready to despatch a few war-ships to the Mediterranean.[1] The
Barbary corsairs continued to rob at pleasure. Vainly did the
Anti-Pirate League which had been constituted in the naval
harbours besiege the Viennese ministerial conferences three
years later with its petitions. After repeated severe losses, the
Hansa towns wrote at length, in the year 1829, a humbly
worded despatch " to the sublime and glorious monarch, the
mighty and most noble prince, his imperial majesty Sultan
Abd-ur-Rahman " of Morocco, offering through England's mediation to negotiate for the payment of tribute. But before this
negotiation had been completed, the French conquerors entered
Algiers, enforced peace upon the North African coast, and thus
brought to a conclusion the most odious episode in the odious
history of the eastern question.

The Bundestag was likewise intolerably remiss in its dealings
with the numerous grievances and petitions of the mediatised
imperial estates. At the Vienna congress, Prussia had proposed
that the mediatised should be given a few curiate or collective
votes at the Bundestag, so that the much misused high nobility
might become reconciled with the new order of German affairs,
and might emerge once more from its unnaturally isolated
position. The proposal was shipwrecked by the jealousy of
the Rhenish Confederate courts. By article 14, the federal act
promised the mediatised a long series of privileges in matters
of taxation, jurisdiction, etc.—privileges which conflicted with
modern ideas of national unity and equality before the law, and
thus made public opinion adverse even to the just claims of
the old estates of the realm. Regarding the curiate votes,
article 6 of the federal act merely declared that the federal
assembly should take this question into consideration when
discussing the fundamental laws. The promises of article 14
were, it will readily be understood, far more cheerfully carried
out by the great states than by the petty princes, to whom the

[1] Raumer's Memorial concerning the Barbary corsairs, December, 1817.

mediatised seemed dangerous rivals. In Austria, the classic land of the privileges of caste, the high imperial nobility had always been graciously favoured, if only for the reason that from early days its members had invariably belonged to the imperial party. The king of Prussia, too, regarded it as his princely duty to compensate the discrowned for the injustice they had suffered; and on July 21, 1815, he issued an ordinance which went far beyond the promises of the federal act, and granted to the mediatised, in almost too generous a spirit, very notable privileges, including enfranchisement from all direct taxation. Less favourable was their situation in Bavaria. Montgelas and his bureaucracy could not refrain from making these serene highnesses feel at times the collar of subjection; they were forced to have their patents of nobility entered at the herald's office on the payment of high fees, and when the prince of Waldburg-Zeil refused to pay the fee, he was officially addressed as plain Herr Waldburg. None the less the Bavarian mediatised nobles continued to possess a tolerably secure legal basis, in a royal ordinance of the year 1807, which had served as an example in the prescriptions of the federal act.

In Würtemberg, on the other hand, and in Baden, Nassau, and the two Hesses, the dispute was interminable; all these courts foresaw that the Fürstenbergs, Leiningens, Löwensteins, and Hohenlohes, could never regard themselves simply as Badenese or Würtemberg subjects. With brutal roughness, King Frederick of Würtemberg had ordered the princes and counts of Waldburg and Königsegg to hold their tongues, when they combined to remind him in an address of " the glorious example of the king of Prussia." Thereupon " the most humble estates of the realm of Würtemberg, offering themselves up as innocent sacrifices to the state," under the leadership of the prince of Waldburg-Zeil, combined for the common defence of the rights of the estates; they applied to their " sometime overlord of the realm who diffuses general happiness," Emperor Francis, and to many other sovereigns as well, demanding that the Federation should give them curiate votes, and should arrange to carry article 14 into effect. Undeniably some of their wishes went beyond the rights which a well-ordered state can allow its subjects. But the Swabian despot had his ears everywhere; he learned of the intrigues of his high nobility from his plenipotentiary at the Bundestag, von Linden, a notorious emissary of the Napoleonic police, who had recently made his appearance in Berlin as ambassador, and had been unceremoniously given his papers by Hardenberg. The king immediately intervened with a *dehortatorium*, had Prince Waldburg roughly cross-examined, and then suppressed the union of the mediatised as " null and treasonable." At the same time he raised the alarm at the courts of his neighbours, and Hacke, the Badenese minister, gladly declared his willingness to adopt common measures " against the spirit of revolt and insubordination which is manifesting itself among the large proportion of the nobility." Prince Waldburg had actually ventured to address the sovereign prince of Bückeburg as " highly honoured cousin " ![1]

When the Bundestag was opened, the great majority of the federal states showed themselves so suspicious of the rebels among the high nobility, that Hardenberg instructed his envoy to drop, for the time being, the proposal to secure curiate votes for the mediatised, since it was completely hopeless. The petitions of the mediatised were shelved. It was not until January, 1818, that the envoys to the Bundestag began, in their reports home, to discuss the carrying into effect of article 14, and subsequently, on October 2nd, the inevitable committee was appointed to draw up common principles of action. There was no longer any talk of curiate votes, and since the desired common principles of action were never discovered, the rights of the mediatised were left to the laws of the individual states, although the majority of the old houses which had formerly constituted estates of the empire had territory in several of the federated states. The particularist spirit which had already destroyed so many of the priceless energies of our nation, had no idea what to make of an aristocracy which belonged only to the whole of Germany, and which stood above the pettiness of the system of little states. The mediatised were forced to withdraw in dudgeon from political life, so that all they could do was from time to time to give the German nation unwelcome reminders of their forgotten existence, by complaints about the infringement of their privileges.

In the first two years of its existence the Bundestag succeeded in bringing to fruition only one moderately useful law, the arbitral ordinance of June 16, 1817. Even this determina-

---

[1] Petition of the prince of Waldburg-Zeil to the king of Würtemberg, September 29, 1815 ; to Emperor Francis, April 2, 1816 ; to the prince of Bückeburg, March 23 ; Minister von Hacke to Count Wintzingerode, April 8, 1816.

tion bore, indeed, the stamp of the loosest federalism; no one ventured to return to the idea of a permament federal jurisdiction which Prussia had so obstinately defended in Vienna. None the less it was a distinct gain that the members of the Federation should undertake a mutual pledge that in the first instance their disputes should be referred to the mediation of the Bundestag; should this mediation fail of effect, the decision was to be left to the supreme court of one of the federated states, to be selected by joint agreement between the disputants. In this manner, numerous minor negotiations between the federated states were in fact peacefully settled, and settled more promptly than of yore by the imperial courts. But this applied only to disputes of trifling importance. For Prussia, at the very first discussion of the matter, laid down the principle which since then has always been firmly maintained by Berlin, that the arbitral authority was entitled to decide upon legal questions alone, and had no jurisdiction where political interests were concerned. This reservation, which was adopted by the minor states only after lively protest, was legally contestable, but politically necessary; for never could a European power agree that the major questions of its policy should be decided in accordance with the principles of civil jurisdiction, by such a body as the court of appeal of Zerbst or Jena.

If a conference of delegates pursues serious aims, the party attitude of the members is in the long run always determined by the sentiments of their mandataries; but at the Bundestag the personality of the individual envoys found free play, for the courts concerned themselves little about the futilities of Frankfort. Thus there gradually came into existence an extremely unnatural arrangement of parties, which rested solely upon the personal views of the envoys. Smidt and Berg were both regarded in Vienna as " a thoroughly bad lot," although neither the senate of Bremen nor the grand duke of Oldenburg deserved the reproach of possessing liberal sentiments. With these were associated Plessen, Eyben, Martens, and Wangenheim, and the new Bavarian envoy Aretin, also inclined to liberal views. But it was the inexhaustible garrulousness of the good Gagern which gave the greatest trouble to the presidential envoy. This remarkable legitimist of the ancient imperial law was willing to recognise " only the abdication of an emperor, but not that of an empire," and ingenuously demanded for the Germanic Federation all the powers that had been possessed by the imperial majesty. " Everything that is German " was to be at the disposal of the federal assembly. He even considered that emigration should be subject to the supervision of the Bundestag ; and in his zeal for duty " in the service of the human species," he sent an agent to America to study this new social phenomenon, whose significance the talented man had understood earlier than most of his contemporaries. In many cases it was difficult for the audience to preserve its gravity when, in his learned speeches, packed with quotations and allusions, he revived all the imperial patriotic phrases of the days of Ratisbon, all the intricate flourishes of the legal system of the Holy Empire, dragged in even the ox that was roasted whole at the coronation festival ! No failure disturbed the good-natured man in the confidence of his patriotic hopes. In the summer of 1817, when the Bundestag began its first recess, the envoy of Luxemburg made an emotional closing speech in honour of the federal constitution, exclaiming with enthusiasm : " This Federation is not so much apprehensive as formidable." To the dissatisfied liberals he said : " What have we gained ? We have gained this, that the mother carries her child cheerfully beneath her heart, relieved of the anxiety that she will have to bring up a slave, and foreseeing that she will give a free man to the fatherland ! " To this Luden's *Nemesis* bitterly rejoined : " What have we lost ? We have lost our belief in the honesty of all chiefs and leaders ! "

The muddle-headed enthusiasm of the imperial patriot could not fail at times to come into sharp conflict with the obstinate reality of German particularism. This happened, for example, in the deliberations concerning article 18 of the federal act. The article promised German subjects freedom of domicile, provided that " another federal state should declare its willingness to accept them as subjects." These were empty phrases which sounded like mockery ; Gagern maintained that they constituted a general German civil right ; this civil right could, however, be secured only if all Germans should adequately fulfil their military duties in one federal state as in another ; " if the fatherland were defended here as it is defended there ! " What a demand to make of Prussia, so long as in one part of Germany universal military service and in another part substitution or recruiting, so long as in one part a term of service of nineteen years and in another of six years, was valid ! When

Goltz raised this counter-consideration, Gagern innocently rejoined : " Why should not the Federation determine that with the completion of, say, the seven-and-twentieth year of life, the principal military duty of every German should be regarded as fulfilled ? " He added, with all the pride of a Luxemburger : " Changes in this or that special muster-roll are indeed of trifling significance, in comparison with the most important national rights ! " Naturally Goltz stood firm, and the childishly innocent attack upon the foundation of the Prussian military system was repulsed. Notwithstanding all this, Hardenberg continued to regard his old Viennese comrade with easy-going humour, and instructed Count Goltz on several occasions to treat the excellent patriot with respect, for he could do no serious harm.[1]

The other courts were less considerate. When Gagern had repeatedly called attention to the promise of representative institutions, when he had annoyed the sensitive new king of Würtemberg by sharp observations regarding the Swabian constitutional struggle, and had, unasked, offered his services as mediator,[2] when by the infantile ignorance of the liberal press he was even hailed as a tribune of the people, the faithful advocate of federalism, the saviour of particularism, soon came into the odour of Jacobinism, and Metternich determined to suppress the dangerous demagogue. A hint to the Netherland court sufficed. For a little while the king of the Netherlands had been in serious difficulties, for it had just come to light that the ambitious prince of Orange, hardly without prior knowledge on the part of his royal father, had been engaged with the French refugees in Brussels in a revolutionary conspiracy against the throne of the Bourbons. All the more gladly did the monarch seize the opportunity of proving to the great powers that he was animated with conservative sentiments, and without hesitation he cashiered the statesman who had contributed so much to the formation of the new united state of the Netherlands. What did he care for the Bundestag, and for the dreams of German imperial patriots ? In April, 1818, Gagern was recalled, and took his leave with the naive declaration that the cause of his dismissal was rather to be regarded as a compliment to himself than as a manifestation of contempt for his office. He was replaced by Count Grünne, a Dutchman,

---

[1] Instructions to Goltz, April 21 and July 12, 1817.
[2] Hatzfeldt's Report, The Hague, November 29, 1817.

who had so profound a knowledge of German affairs that he proposed in all seriousness that France should be accepted into the Germanic Federation on account of Alsace. The Hofburg had no objection to offer to Gagern's recall. The threat uttered by Metternich in December, 1817, was now for the first time fulfilled. The Bundestag knew henceforward that every " mutinous " word would speedily lead to " the recall of the unfaithful envoy."

Shortly after his departure, Gagern, in his invincible good humour, published a work entitled *Germany's Future and Germany's Federal Constitution*, designed to reconcile the Germans with their Bundestag. The motto of the book was *Ut amaris amabilis esto* ! The nation accepted the confident appeal in a mood of fierce mockery. Even men of moderate views had long ago turned away full of disgust from the spectre of the Eschenheimer Gasse ; and the time had already arrived when, to this loyal and law-abiding people, no expression of scorn seemed too strong, no insult too gross, to apply to the one and only authority whose name recalled the unity of Germany.

CHAPTER V.

RECONSTRUCTION OF THE PRUSSIAN STATE.

I. PERSONALITIES AND PARTIES AT THE COURT.

AFTER the conclusion of peace there began for Prussia, as formerly in the days of Frederick William I, a period of repose, uninteresting and jejune, poor in great events, but rich in work and tranquil prosperity, a period in which the entire political life of the nation was absorbed in the work of administration, and in which the royal officialdom once more exhibited its fine state-constructive energy. Notwithstanding its diplomatic defeats, the Prussian state was associated more closely than ever before with the life of the entire nation. Prussia now ruled over no more than 2,000,000 Slav subjects; with the exception of the Bavarians and the Swabians, all the German stocks were represented within her frontiers; she was, in addition, affected more strongly than before by the contrasts in the religious life of the nation, for now two-fifths of her population belonged to the Catholic church; finally, in the great communities on the shores of the Baltic and in Rhineland, Prussia acquired new civilising elements which brought the country into closer approximation with the neighbouring German lands, and which, rapidly increasing in population, were gradually to exercise a transforming influence upon the entire character of the national life. But what a gigantic piece of work to fuse with the old provinces this new domain, almost all of which passed unwillingly under Prussian rule. Never in recent history has a great power had such difficult administrative problems to solve; even the position of the kingdom of Italy after the annexations of 1860 was incomparably less difficult.

To the 5,000,000 inhabitants who were still left to the monarchy in the year 1814, there was now suddenly added a population of 5,500,000,—dwellers in a confusion of territorial

445

fragments dispersed from the Prosna to the Meuse, which until quite recently had belonged to more than one hundred distinct governmental areas, and which subsequently had been subjected to the laws of France, Sweden, Saxony, Westphalia, Berg, Danzig, Darmstadt, and Nassau. In addition, there were numerous minor areas which Prussia had secured by exchange with her neighbours, in order to round off her territory; the smallest of the new governmental districts, that of Erfurt, contained fragments from eight different states. Moreover, the Old Prussian provinces which now returned to Prussian rule, had, under the Napoleonic dominion, lost their ancient institutions, almost to the uttermost trace. Already in the actual occupation of the new provinces there broke out everywhere disputes with ill-wishing neighbours. As late as the spring of the year 1815, the Russian government in Warsaw ordered extensive sales of the domains in Posen; Darmstadt did the same thing in the duchy of Westphalia; while the Austro-Bavarian administration in the territories on the Moselle and the Nahe, before withdrawing, collected rents and taxes in advance, and had the forests at Boppard cut down. Nassau, in defiance of the treaties, refused to evacuate the circle of Siegen, until Hardenberg threatened to occupy the land in the absence of any formal cession. It was with reluctance that even Danzig was handed over by the Russians; while in Thorn, notwithstanding urgent representations, the Russian garrison remained until September 19, 1815. Years elapsed before the new territorial status could be legally secured by treaties with the rancorous neighbour states. It was not until 1816 that a boundary agreement was concluded with the Netherlands, and not until 1817 with Russia; with the profoundly mortified court of Dresden, minute and laborious negotiations regarding the new frontier had to be carried on until the year 1819, and it was not until 1825 that all the outstanding property disputes between the two neighbours were finally settled.

The task now presented itself of subjecting to a uniform administration the domain thus laboriously wrung from the jealousy of Europe; what was needed was to overcome the pro-foreign spirit in home life, the particularist spirit in the great state, to inspire with a living sense of the state all these fragments of the German nation which as yet had in common one with another little more than German speech. If the work of political fusion could be effected in this half of Germany, an actual demonstration would have been given of the futility of particularism, and the soil would have been prepared for the upbuilding of the German united state; it was the completion of the Prussian unified state which gave its true significance to this epoch in our political history. The task was all the more difficult because the monarchy, at the time when these new provinces were acquired, was itself undergoing a dangerous process of transition; in almost all the fields of legislation, comprehensive reforms had been but half completed, and there was lacking the true guiding hand of one strong enough to subject to a single will the overplus of talents which served the state. No other country of those days numbered among its officials such a crowd of exceptional men : men of high administrative ability, such as Vincke, Schön, Merckel, Sack, Hippel, and Bassewitz; financiers, such as Maassen and Hoffman; technicians, such as Beuth and Hartig; jurists, such as Daniels and Sethe; among diplomats, Humboldt, Eichhorn, and Niebuhr; and in addition to all these, the generals of the War of Liberation, and the great figures of science and art. All of them were accustomed to give utterance to relentlessly frank criticism in respect of the actions of the government this being regarded as a privilege of the high officialdom, as a substitute at once for popular representation and for freedom of the press; and they now carried over as an evil inheritance into the days of peace, the old party struggle which had never been completely stilled during the time of the war—a mass of personal hatred and of opposition in respect of matters of detail. From these circles, fault-finding and scandal made their way through every class of society; the state, which with all its errors and defects still possessed the best and most thrifty administration in Europe, was, in the letters and talk of its own faithful servants, criticised with immeasurable severity, as if, under the guidance of a rout of knaves and fools, it was going down hopelessly to destruction.

Four parties, by no means clearly distinguished one from another, contended within the government. The old school of absolutist courtiers and officials had now but few adherents, but it gained powerful allies from among the ancient opponents of Hardenberg, the feudalists, who secured their principal support from among the nobles of the Electoral Mark, and who were led by Marwitz and the ex-minister Voss-Buch. The youthful officials, on the other hand, and nearly all the privy-councillors, were adherents of Hardenberg's bureaucratic liberalism, though this did not prevent them in many cases from being violent personal opponents of the chancellor. Yet another line was taken by the small body of aristocratic reformers who still clung firmly to the ideas of Stein. Among the experienced business men of the high officialdom, the enthusiasm of the Teutonising youth found many indulgent judges, but not a single whole-hearted disciple. Nevertheless that gloomy suspicion which all the courts, both in Germany and abroad, cherished against the Prussian people and the Prussian army, had an inevitable reaction upon Prussia herself. Since Schmalz had raised his cry of disaster, there had been no end to calumnies and poisoned whispers. Not merely Stein, Arndt's outspoken well-wisher, but even the chancellor himself, was accused of a secret understanding with the Teutonomaniacs, although Hardenberg regarded the youthful enthusiasts for unity as inconvenient disturbers of his dualistic policy, and, even in his private journal, always referred to them in terms of angry criticism.

The considerate good-nature of Frederick William rendered it impossible for him to keep such sharp contrasts under firm discipline. With undue tenderness for his counsellors, he allowed the party struggle at the court to go on far too long, intervening only at intervals with a word of warning. If some new talent was summoned to the government, it was usual to divide a ministerial department in two, simply to avoid offending the old minister, who was often an opponent of the new one. Complete unanimity among the ministers was still regarded as indispensable, for in the end the monarch decided according to his own free judgment. How many storms had passed across the country in the brief twenty years since Frederick William had assumed the crown ; in retrospect it seemed as if the opening of his reign must have been several generations back. The loyal population of the old provinces already spoke of the king, although he was still in his prime, as "the old gentleman," and had a thousand stories to tell of his embarrassed and yet so cordially benevolent kindliness. His Berliners lived with him, and regarded it as a right that he should often walk through the Thiergarten in a simple military uniform; that at mid-day, when the guard was changed, he should show himself at the well-known corner window of his inconspicuous palace ; and that in the evening, half hidden in his box, he should attend a comedy, an opera, or a ballet—for he cared little for tragedy, of which he had had more than enough in his own life.

The experiences of a great epoch had somewhat strengthened his self-confidence ; he seemed firmer and more secure, but also more serious and more taciturn, than in former years. His friendly features exhibited a tranquil sadness, an expression which disappeared only on rare occasions, as when he gave a picnic to his happy children and to the grand duke Nicholas upon the Pfaueninsel. The easy-going rationalism instilled into him in youth had long ceased to satisfy his mind ; already during the heavy days in Königsberg he had found consolation in a firm faith in Holy Writ, and had formed a friendship with the excellent bishop Borowski. Now, from year to year, his yearning towards the eternal increased ; pious reflections and theological studies occupied a considerable proportion of his leisure hours. Although he never overcame his sorrow for his lost wife, there happened in his case also what so frequently happens to profoundly distressed widowers ; the solitude of unmarried life became intolerable to him. He displayed a lively inclination for an amiable young Frenchwoman, the Countess Dillon, who passionately responded to his affection, and for a considerable time he seriously thought of contracting with her a morganatic marriage—since for his people Queen Louise was always to remain the queen. But he was unwilling to do anything that his Prussians might take amiss ; and since in matters of conscience he had no confidence in the counsels of the light-minded chancellor, he privately enquired of Gneisenau and Schön, two men from whom he expected to receive a perfectly frank answer, how his marriage with the Catholic Frenchwoman would be regarded by the army and the nation. Since both his advisers gave strongly adverse advice, the king, profoundly affected, gave up his design. His days passed sadly and monotonously. He answered all petitions with the old punctuality, after a conscientious examination, and continued to retain the rudder in his own hand ; but personal association with his highest officials remained uncongenial to his retiring spirit ; he seldom saw the chancellor, and still more rarely the other ministers.

In a far more intimate personal relationship with the king was his daily companion, Colonel Job von Witzleben, who in the year 1816, at the age of thirty-three, was made leader of the military cabinet, and who two years later was appointed major-general and adjutant-general. What a contrast between the solid efficiency of this man and the indolent pedant Köckritz, who, up till 1806, had enjoyed the monarch's confidence; the very choice of his friends showed that Frederick William had grown with the growing time. The king's attention was first attracted by Witzleben's military gifts, and only gradually did he learn how many-sided was the culture of the young guardsman; how he was on friendly terms with Wilhelm Humboldt and other great men of science; how as a musician he displayed exceptional talent; how he was also well instructed in the theological matters in which the king was so greatly interested; and how, with all these endowments, he remained so unpretentious, utterly free from a self-seeking spirit, pious without any wordy display, a happy father of a family. The new adjutant-general soon acquired the king's absolute confidence. He could say everything to the monarch, because he always knew how to control the natural vivacity which flashed out of his dark eyes, and because in his honourable frankness he never forgot his cordial respect for his royal friend. He served as intermediary between the king and his ministers, was asked advice in important affairs of state, and day after day, smoking in his simple room, got through a colossal amount of work with an unceasing diligence which wore out his frame prematurely after a couple of decades. In the pressure of business, he rarely found time to describe the experiences of the day; often for months in succession his diary exhibits nothing but blank pages or brief records of journeys; but where political matters are mentioned, there is always displayed a level soldierly understanding, a sound knowledge of detail, and perfect uprightness. Although he did not consider himself a statesman, and although he cautiously held aloof from the parties of the court, none the less he did not hide his light under a bushel. With sound political judgment, he regarded the new military constitution as the firm bond of the unity of the state; he considered the completion of the reforms of Stein and Hardenberg to be indispensable; and (a thing which in these days of secret whispers, counted most) he knew and loved the Prussian people. Nothing seemed to him more contemptible than an attempt " to awaken suspicion in the pure soul of the king"; nothing disturbed his confident belief that there was no more sterling loyalty than that which was to be found in Prussia.

The tranquil influence of this faithful intermediary was all the more valuable because, since the ill-success of the congress of Vienna, the king had no longer treated the chancellor with his old confidence, and yet found him indispensable. When Hardenberg celebrated his seventieth birthday, Goethe wrote to his old fellow-student :

> " Thought transcends the power of speech
> When we contemplate your life,
> Spirit free, spite bonds of earth,
> In action firm and confident."

And unquestionably to the end of his life, Hardenberg remained a free spirit. Just as under the oppression of the foreign dominion he had held with unalterable firmness to the idea of the liberation of the fatherland, so now he unceasingly pursued the plan of crowning the work of internal reform by the promised representative constitution ; this was to be his political legacy, the conclusion of his long career. In personal intercourse he continued to preserve his charming amiability, and displayed so youthful an enthusiasm for all that is beautiful and great, adopted every new idea so lovingly and so intelligently, that even severe judges like Gneisenau and Clausewitz could not, despite numerous occasions for discord, feel ill-disposed towards this man of many services. But even in his more vigorous days he had not always succeeded in acting firmly ; and now that in old age he clung to his high office he rarely found courage to show a bold front to his enemies, and frequently believed that he was leading, when his opponents were making a tool of him. The dictatorial power of the chancellor had worked for good so long as he himself continued to hold in his own hands all the ministries with one or two exceptions ; but since he had limited himself to the conduct of the ministry for foreign affairs, and had had five separate ministers as his subordinates, he had gradually lapsed into a position no less untenable than that held in former days by the reporting cabinet councillors. Disputes with the ministers, and complaints regarding the postponement of business, became unavoidable, for the chancellor alone (with the exception of Boyen, Witzleben, and the cabinet councillor Albrecht) reported regularly to the monarch, and yet Hardenberg demanded from the ministers that they should assume full responsibility for their respective branches of the administration.

It was only an ignorant and fault-finding spirit which could accuse the old statesman of sloth. All well-informed persons knew what an enormous number of memorials and marginal notes, orders and reports, this rapid pen, always brilliant and adroit, committed to paper. But he had never had a talent for punctuality, and the burden of these activities, comprehending the entire life of the state, became too heavy for his shoulders after the enlargement of the Prussian domain. Urgent work was often shelved for months when the prince buried himself in his castle at Glienicke, and then by fits and starts, as chance or caprice might dictate, took up this paper or that from the mountain of accumulated documents. Anyone who there beside the dreamy Havel Lake wandered through the beautiful park, or who at Neuhardenberg in Neumark contemplated the choice art collection, and the new church built by Schinkel, could not but feel that a noble and highly-cultured man dwelt here. But how mortifying to contemplate the loose society of the frequenters of these distinguished places, who made a mock of the large-minded host at his own well-supplied table : the scandal-mongers of literature, Schöll and Dorow ; the magnetic healers, Koreff and Wohlfart ; the somnambulist, Friederike Hähnel, later Frau von Kimsky. Hähnel was a cunning cheat who had first met the prince at a séance at Wohlfart's, and by her convulsive ecstasies had taken his soft heart by storm.[1] Since then she had never left him, and she became the curse of his old age. Inexhaustibly skilled in the production of mysteries and morbid phenomena, and in the gentle art of plunder, she accompanied him everywhere, even to the congresses of the monarchs, and did not rest until his third marriage, like the two first, had actually been broken. About this time the chancellor arranged a marriage between his only daughter, the divorced countess Pappenheim, now of mature age, and the virtuoso of elegant profligacy, young Prince Pückler-Muskau. The evil reputation of the Hardenberg household offered abundant material for the numerous spies whom Metternich maintained in Berlin, and furnished the enemies of the chancellor with a dangerous weapon. They observed with delight how the king became more and more estranged from the statesman who respected his own white hairs so little ; and since the busy Koreff also sometimes occupied himself as a liberal author, there actually came into existence at court the party-fable that Hardenberg's constitutional plans were the work

[1] Hardenberg's Diary, February, 1816.

of his notorious plebeian entourage. When one of the prince's friends warned him against this rabble, Hardenberg answered with a smile: "Even if I am often cheated, it is such a delightful feeling to display confidence."

Among the ministers, Hardenberg had only one enlightened adherent, Boyen, and even Boyen was too independent in his views to follow the prince's leadership unconditionally. Kircheisen showed himself expert in the organisation of the courts of justice in the new provinces, and held aloof from politics. Schuckmann, on the other hand, minister of the interior, a rigid bureaucrat, active, well-informed, autocratic, " the philistine of the old time," as W. Humboldt termed him, resisted all plans for reform just as suspiciously as did Metternich's confidant, the police minister, Wittgenstein. How many years did the unsuspicious Hardenberg require before he saw through the blunt roughness of the last-named sly courtier, who long ago, by the overthrow of the Dohna ministry had opened Hardenberg's own way to power, and who therefore seemed to the chancellor worthy of the most faithful friendship. To the monarch, Wittgenstein was indispensable as an able administrator of the royal private property. He was highly respected, too, at the other German courts, being asked to advise in all sorts of princely family affairs, so that even the opinionated elector of Hesse sometimes listened to his counsels. To innocent observers the lively old gentleman with his trivial jokes seemed perfectly harmless ; even Heim, the popular Berlin physician with a profound knowledge of men, was completely deceived by the prince's agreeable manners, and was devoted to him. But nothing escaped the watchful glance of these false blue eyes. With irreconcilable, silent hatred, Wittgenstein tracked everything which recalled Stein and the stormy national movement of the years of war, and before long this led him to regard even the chancellor as suspect of Teutonising Jacobinism, so that Wittgenstein began unnoticed to follow all Hardenberg's footsteps. It is true that after the peace the infamous " hired" police, which Justus Gruner had once instituted as a last resort against the Napoleonic spies, had been abolished ; but many of the secret agents of this force still remained actively at work, and it was upon their reports that Wittgenstein based his opinions of the sentiments of the nation.

The young minister of finance, Count Bülow, Hardenberg's cousin, stood alone among his colleagues. This was a handsome blonde man who, with his distinguished worldly charm and his easy, even frivolous, adroitness in affairs, reminded the chancellor of his own youth, so that Hardenberg loved him like a son. After the peace of Tilsit, like many another excellent official of the Magdeburg region, he had unwillingly entered King Jerome's service, since his old home had no occupation for him and, as Westphalian minister, he had done much to facilitate internal intercourse and to carry into effect the principles of a reasonable commercial policy, until he was at length dismissed from office on account of his German sentiments and his independent way. Nevertheless he was regarded as a traitor by the Old Prussian officials ; nor could Prussian arrogance forgive Hardenberg for having introduced one of Jerome's servants into the ministry while the war against Napoleon was still in progress. Bülow had not remained altogether unaffected by the views of the French bureaucracy ; he admired the Napoleonic fiscal system, and among the Westphalian prefects had acquired a dictatorial tone, and had become accustomed to arbitrary methods of carrying out his views which seemed unendurable to the Prussian officials. Before long he had quarrelled with several of the lord-lieutenants ; he quarrelled even with his cousin and well-wisher, for an orderly national economy was utterly impossible so long as the chancellor could dispose freely of whatever sums he pleased without consulting the minister of finance. This continuous friction embittered the irascible man, and soon in his irritable and quarrelsome manner it was hardly possible to recognise any longer the old amiability.

The reactionary party of the ministry found powerful support at court in the commanding officer of the guard, Duke Charles of Mecklenburg. The brother of Queen Louise had distinguished himself on the battle-field and on the drill-ground as an efficient officer, but he completely lacked understanding for the reforming ideas of his sister's friends. He had a handsome and distinguished appearance, in social life he was agreeable and well-informed, at court festivals he was much admired as a talented poet and amateur actor, was an extremely vigorous worker in the council of state, as he was in his profession as a soldier, but he was disliked by most of the officers, and was utterly detested in the cultured society of the capital. For, in the officers' corps of the guard, he encouraged arrogant manners which were repulsive alike to civilians and to the troops of the line ; and, though still a young man, he remained a professional soldier of the old school, a firm opponent of the new military organisation. In politics he adhered closely to Wittgenstein, and, like the latter, resisted every innovation which might possibly be displeasing to the court of Vienna.

Still more powerful was the quiet influence of Ancillon. This theologian, an all-round man, was, in the year 1814, as privy-councillor, placed in charge of foreign affairs, and now once more floated contentedly on the surface, although the success of the war had given the lie to all his pusillanimous warnings. Hardenberg imagined that this nomination served to build a bridge between science and politics, for Ancillon owed to his learning, which though shallow was many-sided and well-equipped for drawing-room conversation, a high repute, and was able to impose upon men of considerably greater intelligence. The diplomats admired his Socratic composure, the urbane mildness of his manners ; even Schön, who criticised everybody, thought well of Ancillon, whilst in later years, young Leopold Ranke looked up to him with admiration. At the close of the old century, he had adroitly suited the effeminate taste of the time as fashionable preacher to the French congregation, and subsequently, as professor of political science at the military academy, he had advanced his commonplaces in so ceremoniously stilted a manner, voicing them with a smile of such convinced statesmanlike superiority, that Nesselrode, one of his audience, was altogether charmed. At court he understood how to maintain his place among men of fashion by a servile zeal. It was of momentous importance for a later day that even Queen Louise and Baron von Stein were blinded by the fraudulently acquired reputation of the smooth-tongued semi-Frenchman, and entrusted to him the education of the young heir to the throne. Thus it happened that the extravagantly-gifted but over-imaginative and arbitrary spirit of the prince, who needed above all strict discipline, and instruction regarding the hard realities of life, passed under the control of a characterless rhetorician, who hardly knew himself how much of his activities were the outcome of inborn timidity, and how much of worldly-wise calculation. Since then, Ancillon had frequently been asked advice in political matters, and now, in his cramped and inelastic handwriting, he unweariedly wrote a mass of memorials, diffuse observations without energy or incisiveness, all of which seem just as empty as his books, and yet continually arouse the impression that some profound meaning must be concealed amid the torrent of verbosity. It was through his instrumentality that the art of weaving empty words to constitute a glittering tissue was first introduced into Prussian politics—an art altogether unknown under the strict old absolutism, but one which at a later date, in the parliamentary epoch, was to display its most luxuriant blossoms. Innately a lover of repose and of the traditional order, in June, 1789, he had personally seen at Versailles how the representatives of the third estate arrogated to themselves the rights of a National Assembly, and thus prepared the overthrow of the monarchy. Since then he had been filled with dread of the revolution, and when the revolutionary world-empire had at length been overthrown, without, indeed, any co-operation on Ancillon's part, the faintheart immediately adopted the views of Metternich, and obediently followed every hint given by the Hofburg. He diligently promulgated in court society the accusations voiced by the Schmalzian pamphlet, and since although he refrained from open opposition to the chancellor, he now spoke with suspicious zeal of the immeasurable difficulties in the way of the constitutional plan, no one who knew the man could fail to recognise that he secretly belonged to Wittgenstein's party.

The nation first began to notice the covert party-struggle at court when, soon after the peace, certain unexpected changes took place in the Rhenish provinces. On the Rhine, the glorious mood of the years of war had not been dissipated so quickly. The Prussian officers and officials, who were now to incorporate into German national life this French land which had been bought at so high a price, looked around them with the lofty feelings of the conqueror; they luxuriated in the charms of the beautiful landscape and in the serene and lively atmosphere of Rhenish society. It seemed to them as if the heroic energy of the north was here being happily wedded to the grace of the rich south. Around Gneisenau, who commanded in Coblenz, there assembled a happy circle of distinguished men and beautiful women, who forced even from the frivolous inhabitants of the ancient episcopal town the admission that the new rulers had at their disposal very different intellectual forces from those formerly exhibited by the electoral court of Treves, or by the prefect of Napoleon. Here were Clausewitz and Bärsch, one of Schill's companions, Hellwig, the foolhardy hussar, and the gigantic Carl von der Gröben, who formerly as Gneisenau's confidant had travelled from land to land in order to pave the way for the holy war, leading a life almost as adventurous as that of his ancestor the African hero of the days of the Great Elector; here also were the romanticist enthusiasts, Max von Schenkendorf, Werner von Haxthausen, Sixt von Arnim, the pedagogue Johannes Schulze, and the learned collector Meusebach. When at eventide Gneisenau had the ladies fetched in Napoleon's carriage, booty taken at Belle Alliance, and serene in his greatness, masterful and yet modest, blushing at his own fame, sat at the festive board, when the songs of Arndt and Körner resounded, when the warriors related their experiences, and Meusebach made everyone roar with laughter with the primitively forceful humour of his brilliant verses, Schenkendorf exclaimed in his delight:

> "Such figures moved through boyhood's dreams—
> Ladies and knights of yore!"

In the countryside, too, the frank hero had won all hearts; when he went up the Moselle, the countrymen rowed out from every village, singing choruses, to offer him a ceremonial cup of welcome.

This joyful aftermath of the great war-time was not long to endure. When the Schmalzian pamphlet appeared, Gneisenau warned the chancellor that this first blow would be followed by heavier ones, and had now to learn that at court he was himself slandered as the chief of the Tugendbund, whilst his hospitable table was described as "Wallenstein's Lager." These calumnies cut him all the more profoundly because at this moment he was attacked by that morbid relaxation of tension which so often afflicts men of action when quiet days come; in peace service he felt like a fish out of water, and as early as September, 1816, he resigned his Rhenish command, partly for reasons of health, partly in order to prove to his opponents that he did not cherish any ambitious designs.[1] Not even then did the backbiting at court cease; but the king remained inaccessible to these malicious whispers, and little more than two years later, Gneisenau, after he had restored his health in the Silesian mountains, was appointed governor of Berlin.

At the same time Lord-lieutenant Sack was transferred from the Rhine to Stettin. For a year and a half he had

---

[1] Gneisenau to Hardenberg, March 26 and April 21, 1816; February 6, 1821.

carried on the provisional government of his Rhenish home with ability and circumspection ; but just as once before, when lord-lieutenant of Brandenburg, he had been at odds with the feudal nobility, so now it was impossible that the rough and vigorous official should lack enemies. Wittgenstein, Schuckmann, and Bülow, complained of his insubordination ; he was in open feud with the military governor, General Dobschütz. Baron von Mirbach, and other members of the proud nobility of the Lower Rhine, complained of his bureaucratic harshness and of his disdainful treatment of the nobles ; not even his friends could deny that he allowed himself to be praised in the newspapers more than was proper for a Prussian official, and that he had given too many of his numerous relatives posts in the Rhenish administration. Complaints were so numerous that Hardenberg found it advisable to transfer the deserving man to another sphere of activity ; he persisted in this intention although Sack felt profoundly injured, although the great majority of the Rhinelanders were annoyed at the withdrawal of their compatriot, and although numerous communes in the province urgently petitioned that his transfer should be cancelled.[1]

The ardent patriot Justus Gruner, who had hitherto administered Berg in the name of the allied powers, was coolly received when, with Gneisenau's warm recommendation, he desired to re-enter the Prussian state-service. It was a remark-able turn of fate that the founder of the Prussian secret police should suffer most of all from the reports of secret agents. In the Hofburg he was regarded, next to Stein and Görres, as the chief of the German Jacobins. In the summer of 1812, on Metternich's orders, he was sent to the fortress of Peterwardein, because from Prague he had planned a rising against Napoleon, and because he was in secret correspondence with Jahn's "Deutscher Bund."[2] He was not set at liberty until October, 1813, and subsequently, as governor of Berg, he alarmed the Austrians and the Rhenish Confederates once more by the passionate language of his speeches and manifestoes, while at the outbreak of the war of 1815 he had actually founded a secret league, which indeed never did any practical work, and which broke up soon after the peace, but which through its motto, "Germany's unity under Prussia," had filled all timid

[1] Kircheisen to Hardenberg, June 5 ; Cabinet Orders to Sack, January 15 and March 13 ; Sack to the king, March 24, to Hardenberg, March 24 and May 16, 1816 ; Mirbach to Hardenberg, November 29, 1815.
[2] Gruner to Hardenberg, November 27, 1819.

souls with horror. In view of all this, the chancellor considered it impossible to entrust the much-abused man with an influential administrative post, and Gruner had to content himself with the modest position of envoy in Berne. All these incidents made a very painful impression upon public opinion, especially since they were almost simultaneous with the suppression of the *Rheinische Merkur*, and since they followed so closely upon the publication of the Schmalzian pamphlet. The suspicious world sought for a secret connection, although Gneisenau regarded the prohibition of Görres's paper as perfectly in order while Sack was a declared opponent of Gruner. The atmosphere became more troubled day by day. Whilst at court the current talk was of the secret intrigues of the demagogues, the liberals were complaining of the outbreak of reaction.

§ 2. REORGANISATION OF THE ADMINISTRATION.

Notwithstanding this friction within the government, the work of reorganising the administration, so inconspicuous and yet so weighty with consequence, made steady and secure progress. As soon as the extent of the newly-acquired territory could to some extent be foreseen, the king while still in Vienna, on April 30, 1815, approved an ordinance concerning the better organisation of the provincial governments effecting a division of the state domain into ten provinces and twenty-eight districts. Two of the provinces, Lower Rhine and West Prussia, were subsequently united with the neighbouring provinces of Jülich-Cleves-Berg and East Prussia respectively. The six others, Brandenburg, Pomerania, Silesia, Posen, Saxony, and Westphalia, remain unaltered to this day. It was the work of the king that the office of lord-lieutenant, which in the year 1810 had been abolished by Hardenberg, was re-established. Frederick William desired that the peculiarities of land and people should be allowed free development, in great and vigorous provinces ; it was his wish that the cautious impartiality of the collegial governments should be supplemented by the individual prestige of the officials placed at their head, so that the administration should thus combine the advantages of the collegial and of the bureaucratic systems. At the same time he already cherished the design of placing a commanding general beside the lord-lieutenant, in such a way that, as in

Austria and Russia, the military subdivision of the country should be adapted to the civil administration. Bülow's proposal that the governmental colleges should be replaced by prefects, was definitely rejected by the king, and he also rejected the plan of instituting independent financial colleges beside the governmental colleges.[1] They retained their collegial form ; but were immediately subdivided into two sections, one of which dealt with matters of prerogative, police, and communal affairs, under the supervision of the minister of the interior, whilst the other dealt with finance and industry, under the supervision of the minister of finance, so that each minister should have, as far as possible, instruments connected with the work of his own department and dependent upon him alone.

In the delimitation of the new administrative districts, the government proceeded with extreme caution, with that regard for the historic past which has from the first been characteristic of Prussian statecraft. Whenever a village was to be separated from its old circle, two ministries had to give their opinions upon the matter ; the king himself made the final decision, and did this wherever possible with due respect to the wishes of the inhabitants. Nevertheless, the disturbance of many customary relationships was inevitable, for the newly-acquired territorial areas were confusedly intermingled with one another and with the older domains. Not one of the ancient provinces could retain its former boundaries unaltered. Immediately, therefore, there began an outcry against the government. The incredible force of particularism, just as strong in Prussia as in the petty German states, uprose in alarm ; the myriad tenacious interests of local life, which the storms of this gigantic age had passed over unnoticed, now clamoured for help. In innumerable petitions, this rigid conservative sentiment resounded on all hands. Everywhere was voiced the same cry of distress : " We do not wish to be separated from our brothers who have shared with us the joys and sorrows of this arduous time." When it was proposed to remove the central authority of the Freystadt circle to Neusalz, there was a rain of petitions, and a deputation was even sent to the king ; old Kalckreuth wrote to Hardenberg that it would be the ruin of him if the board was no longer to meet in the neighbourhood of his property, the tramps would steal the cabbages and potatoes from his fields. In a

---

[1] Proposal for an " Ordinance for the Institution of Provincial Governments and Financial Colleges," spring, 1815.

word, there was an insuperable passive resistance. The monarchy learned in a hundred instances what was subsequently again to be shown in the case of all reforms of local administration, that in Germany it is far easier to fuse two states than two circles or communes.

Everywhere, in the nation as upon the thrones, the differences between the various territorial areas and the distinctive national subdivisions were still grossly exaggerated. When the royal officials in Pomerania expressed the modest hope that in the course of long years "a gradual approximation between the two nations" of Swedish Pomerania and Old Pomerania might become possible, when even Sack in his administrative reports declared that the population of Jülich, Aix-la-Chapelle, Cologne, and the lands of the Moselle, differed from one another in character as completely "as if they had been different nations," it is not surprising that among the common people neighbourly ill-will frequently increased to the pitch of passionate aversion.

All the territorial divisions of Old Prussia regarded it as a scandal when it was proposed to incorporate them in the new provinces. When the government desired to allot Lower Lusatia and the Old Brandenburg domain of Beeskow to the province of Saxony, the estates of the Beeskow-Storkow circle assailed the king with such loud and stormy complaints as had been voiced from the same region long before, under Marwitz's leadership, against Hardenberg's agrarian laws. "First of all we have to speak of the matter which is to us the most sacred and the most important, which, however, is quite left out of account by your majesty's officials, and is perhaps even regarded by them as an advantage, because they are not accustomed to consider the sentiments of the people—we are to cease to be Brandenburgers and Prussians! Are we to remain Brandenburgers and to preserve our nationality? In that case it would fare with us as it once fared with the remnant of the Wendish people in our neighbourhood, who still continue to spend their lives in a state of unceasing mistrust, in a state of eternal separation from their neighbours, and subject to the continual hostility of the latter. Are we, on the other hand, to assume the Saxon national characteristics? But this would be impossible, not because we regard the Saxons as unworthy, but because we are Brandenburgers!" [1] Since the estates of

---

[1] Petition of the Circle-Estates of Beeskow-Storkow to the king, October 31, 1815.

the reacquired territory of Kottbus were in no less fierce revolt against any community with the Saxons, the chancellor gave way, and had the boundary of the province of Brandenburg moved further south. The inhabitants of Altmark were less fortunate. They also demanded their reunion with the Electoral Mark, demanded it as an incontestable right. The government, however, held fast to its determination to incorporate the cradle of the Brandenburg state with the province of Saxony, for by its geographical position the region was associated with Magdeburg, and since the fall of the Westphalian government had had nothing more to do with the administration of the public debt, which was a matter of so much importance to the Electoral Mark ; moreover its methods of local government were no longer in accordance with Brandenburg customs.

In the duchy of Prussia it was still remembered that long ago the towns of the Vistula had been the first to raise the banner of revolt against the Teutonic knights, and that they had summoned the Poles into the country ; the valiant people were accustomed to look down upon their West Prussian neighbours as traitors, and were profoundly hurt in their feelings when a portion of East Prussia was allotted to the province of the Vistula. Through vehement appeals to the king, the circles at least of Mohrungen and Neidenburg secured permission to remain in East Prussia. On the other hand, a petition of the Polish nobility in Michelau and Culmerland, demanded that this ancient tribal land of the Teutonic knights should be assigned to the grand duchy of Posen. The loyal German towns, however, opposed a vigorous contradiction, and the government rejected the suspicious proposal.[1] The inhabitants of New Hither Pomerania also adhered obstinately to their " rights, privileges, and liberties " which, in the treaties with Sweden and Denmark, the king had promised to maintain. After the German manner, they understood by these terms all existing institutions, the Swedish customs-system, and the old coinage, as well as the old officials, and they defended their independence so obstinately that not until the year 1818 did the chancellor venture to incorporate the small governmental district of Stralsund with the province of Pomerania ; in addition, the deputies of the circles and towns complained bitterly to the king about infringements of privilege. They declared that the

[1] Report of President von Hippel to the chancellor, Marienwerder, June 21, 1815.

government order issued by the Swedish chancellery in 1669 was inviolable, and did not cease to complain until the king had given them a definite answer to the effect that no province could, under the excuse of especial rights, demand for itself a position of exception from the general administrative ordering of the state.[1]   In the western provinces, the introduction of the new administrative districts encountered less resistance, since the separatist spirit of the towns and the territorial areas had in this region long before been broken by the hard fist of Napoleonic officialdom ; yet even here there was a passionate struggle about the meeting place of the authorities, and the attempt was occasionally made to disinter long forgotten feudal claims from the dust of centuries. County Werden did not desire to be separated from County Mark ; the town of Herford declared to the chancellor, in a pompous address, that it neither could nor would belong to any circle, for it possessed a legal right to continued independence and immediacy, adding that it was only under this proviso that Herford had once paid homage to the Great Elector.[2]

By far the greatest difficulties were offered by the reorgani-sation of what had formerly been Saxon territory. This was a region where in any case there was almost as much hostility to the new regime as that manifested by the Poles. Everyone complained bitterly about the destruction of the Saxon nation. In Naumburg, the mob tore down the black eagles and threw them into the mud ; even those of more quiet spirit regretfully described themselves as *Musspreussen* [Must-be-Prussians], a phrase which remained in use in a number of regions for many years to come. As long as there was still a prospect of acquir-ing the entire kingdom of Saxony, Hardenberg had ventured to think only of a personal union under the sovereign. Now, when it had been necessary to accept half of the country instead of the whole, it was obvious from the first that this fragment could not remain as a separate province. Under the sleepy feudal regime of Electoral Saxony, hardly the beginnings of national unity, or of a uniform modern political order, had been created ; the lands which were spoken of as the duchy of Saxony, consisted in reality of seven loosely associated territories : the margravates of Upper and Lower Lusatia, the two bishoprics

---

[1] Report of the Circles and Towns to the king, January 9, 1819. Cabinet Order of May 24, 1819.
[2] Petition of the Town of Herford to Hardenberg, November 6, 1816.

of Merseburg and Naumburg, the princedom of Querfurt, the county of Henneberg, and a portion of the Saxon patrimonial dominions. Nevertheless the representatives of the nobility, when in the autumn of 1815 a Saxon deputation went to Berlin, petitioned for " the maintenance of the integrity and nationality of the duchy of Saxony." Others, among them the burgo-masters, protested against this, declaring that they had complete confidence in the friendly government of Prussia.[1] At the same time the estates of Lower Lusatia petitioned for the preservation of their privileges; whilst the estates of Upper Lusatia demanded that the province of Lusatia, should not be united with any other portion of the monarchy, but that the two Lusatias should combine to form an independent realm, with Görlitz as the capital.[2]

How was it possible to do justice to all these particularist clamours, many of which were absolutely contradictory? More-over, the territories were widely dispersed from Görlitz to Langensalza, detached from their natural centre, the region of Meissen, which had remained with Saxony. After long hesita-tion the government therefore determined to unite with Branden-burg the region of Lower Lusatia, which lay far to the east, to allot Upper Lusatia to Silesia, and to unite the remaining portions of the duchy of Saxony with Altmark, the duchy of Magdeburg, and Eichsfeld (formerly part of Electoral Mainz), to constitute a new province. Thus the regions which had previously formed part of Saxony came to constitute three provinces and six governmental districts. Is it surprising that they complained loudly, and that they felt that all the distresses of the partition of their homeland had to be experienced once again? Petitions and complaints continued for a long time. The Saxon official district of Belzig, close to Potsdam, stormily demanded that it should remain part of the Wittenberg circle; all the landowners of Eichsfeld, claimed as a chartered right, that a court of appeal for Eichsfeld should be established in Heiligenstadt. Even three years later, the principal landlord of the region, Count Schulenburg, expressed to Klewitz the expectation that all the Old Saxon domains should be united to constitute a single province, for otherwise " these wounds will continue to bleed for ever." Even to the present day the town of Görlitz feels itself part of Upper Lusatia, and not of

[1] Schuckmann's Report to Hardenberg, November 15, 1815.
[2] Petition of the estates of Upper Lusatia to the chancellor, June 28, 1815.

Silesia. As a matter of fact, the province of Saxony was the only thoroughly artificial structure among the new great administrative districts. Whereas in the constitution of all the other provinces scrupulous regard was paid to local interests and memories, so that every one of them displayed a well-marked tribal character, here, thanks to the unhappy half-measures which had been adopted at the congress of Vienna, many an ancient historical bond was forcibly severed, Thuringian, Upper Saxon, and Lower Saxon tribal stocks being arbitrarily jumbled together. Yet even here, by the enduring patience, the loyalty, and the justice of the officials, the wilderness was gradually cleared, and the hostile populations were trained to feel a healthy spirit of community. In this way the idea of practical German unity gradually established itself in a struggle daily and hourly renewed against the remnants of particularism.

As soon as the administration of the provinces had been fairly settled, Hardenberg resumed the long interrupted work of legislation. By the ordinance of March 20, 1817, there was at length instituted the council of state, that supreme advisory board to the monarchy which had been repeatedly promised since the year 1808—although its powers were less extensive than Stein had formerly planned. All legislative proposals were submitted to the deliberations of the council of state, and so were the general principles of administration ; the same with disputes regarding the spheres of activity of the different ministries, with the dismissal of officials, and with all the grievances of subjects when these were assigned by the king to the council for consideration, so that effective limitations might be imposed upon the power of the new specialised ministers, which was liable to abuse. The king himself, or the chancellor, was president, whilst the formal conduct of business was in the hands of von Klewitz, the new secretary to the council. The members were : the royal princes, the ministers and the chiefs of the other independent central authorities, the field-marshals, the commanding generals and the lord-lieutenants, and, finally, thirty-four men honoured by the king with his special confidence and selected from all branches of the public service—the best energies of the officialdom, for there were very few among them who had not, in one way or another, displayed [qualities above the average. Among statesmen of note, two only had been passed over, men whose ruggedness seemed dangerous to the chancellor: Stein, and the ultra-conservative ex-minister Voss-Buch. The two churches were represented by the bishops, Sack and Spiegel; science, by Savigny. Thus was revived the old privy council, which had continued to exist from the days of the elector Joachim Frederick to those of Stein, although lately only as a shadow; but it was revived in new forms which assured the legal course of the administration without paralysing its speed and efficiency. It was to the new council of state that Prussia owed the advantage that the laws of the last years of Frederick William III were stronger, more thorough-going, and more practical than the labours, sometimes over-hasty, of the great period of reform, and that yet, notwithstanding the abundant deliberation of which they were the outcome, they were not, as were subsequently the laws of the parliamentary epoch, stamped with the contradictory characteristics of laboriously secured party compromises. This was the last brilliant embodiment of the ancient absolute monarchy, a union of talent, knowledge of affairs, and imperturbable straightforwardness, such as could not be displayed by any other state of those days except England, a body whose efficiency sufficed to show that all the odious criticisms against Prussia, which now again were freely circulated throughout the German minor states, were unfounded. But the work of the council of state was done in private, and even in Prussia the nation knew little of its existence.

On March 30, 1817, Hardenberg opened the sittings of the council of state with a speech in which there once again was sounded the confident tone of earlier years. He said that the task which lay before them was "wisely to accommodate the traditional order to the present circumstances of the state, to the culture of the nation, and to the demands of the age. The Prussian state," he said in conclusion, "must prove to the world that true freedom and legal ordering, that equality before the law and personal security, that the well-being of the individual and of the whole, that science and art, that, finally, if it should prove inevitable, bravery and endurance in a struggle for the fatherland, thrive best and most certainly under a just monarchy." [1] Thereupon the finance minister's proposals for a new finance law were handed over to a committee.

Meanwhile the lord-lieutenants, assembled in the council of state, engaged in confidential deliberations regarding the results

[1] Minutes of the Council of State, first sitting.

of the new administration. Stein's work, the unity of the supreme administration, was not as yet generally accepted as an irrevocable fact; the true dividing line between the inalienable rights of the central authority and the excess of centrifugal energies, was so difficult to discover that, even within the bosom of the government, lively disputes upon the subject still prevailed. Shortly before, Klewitz, a well-meaning man, thoroughly experienced as an official of the old school in the provincial administration of his Magdeburg homeland, had proposed in all good faith to the chancellor a terribly retrograde step, the restoration of the provincial ministries. The state, he said, in its great lack of homogeneity, could not endure a more rigid centralisation, and the power of the new specialised ministers might very readily degenerate into dangerous despotism.[1] This demand for the re-establishment of the provincial ministries soon became the war-cry of the feudal nobles, whose party was the stronghold of particularism, and gained some support also from the lord-lieutenants. These high officials all felt uneasy in their difficult intermediate position, whose boundaries were as yet far from clearly established, between the ministries and the district governments. Proud of the energy they had displayed, they opposed their chiefs with that defiant official zeal which had from the first been characteristic of Prussian officialdom, and since in their provinces they had received almost nothing but complaints regarding the unaccustomed conditions, they outbade one another in melancholy reports, reinforced one another mutually in their discontent, and gradually passed under the leadership of Schön, the man in whom were embodied all the fruitless vexations of this period of transition.

In the early days of Hardenberg's administration, Schön, like Sack and numerous other vigorous officials, had advised the introduction of the prefectoral system. Since he had himself become lord-lieutenant of West Prussia, he recommended no less zealously an almost unrestricted independence for the provincial authorities. What attitude, therefore, could satisfy this ever-discontented man? Dependence upon the ministers was all the more disagreeable to his excessive self-satisfaction because he had already constructed for himself an ideal picture of the history of recent years, in the foreground of which he

---

[1] Klewitz, Memorials to Hardenberg, September 24, 1816, and February 20, 1817.

occupied a conspicuous position amid his Old Prussian friends. In his mind, a restless, imaginative energy was strangely associated with dialectical perspicuity. When he was talking, which he often did for hours at a stretch with inexhaustible liveliness and ardour, his hearers speedily came to feel that his imagination was running away with him. It was through his work, he declared, that Stein, a man without ideas, had been furnished with the leading thoughts of the whole work of reform ; whereas Schön in reality had taken an effective part in one only of these fundamental laws, the edict regarding the abolition of hereditary servitude. He alone, he declared, in the spring of 1813, had rescued the province of Prussia from Stein's Muscovite plans of conquest ; it was through his friends, the leaders of the Königsberg diet, that the great soldier of the line, Scharnhorst, had against his will been compelled to undertake the formation of the Landwehr. Such fables he was accustomed obstinately to repeat, in writing and by word of mouth, until at length he had come to believe them himself. He hardly understood what a crime he was committing against the reputation of greater men. Luxuriating in vain self-praise, he ingenuously applied to himself the saying : "Do good and throw it into the sea ; if the fishes don't see it, God will ! " Talented, eloquent, a man of many-sided culture, pupil of Kant, friend of Fichte and Niebuhr, he was in regular and lively intercourse with the learned world, so that even in the minor states of Germany, where in general people paid little attention to Prussian men and things, the name of Schön was everywhere mentioned with respect ; yet at the same time he remained a man of affairs, with a thorough knowledge of agriculture and industry, an active official, one who did justice to the good schooling of the admirable old provincial minister von Schrötter, and one who on occasions would act inconsiderately and even despotically. Almost the whole of his years of service were spent in the administration of his Old Prussian homeland ; there was not a farm held by the Salzburg exiles in Lithuania, or a fisherman's hut upon the dunes of the Kurische Nehrung, with which he was not acquainted. Thus it was that with the twofold pride of the Kantian and of the experienced man of practice, he looked down contemptuously upon the dusty wisdom of the boardroom, and since all the Prussian statesmen, Stein just as much as Wittgenstein, were found by him to be of short weight when tried in the balance of his categorical imperative, he overwhelmed them all, with very few exceptions, with the caustic fires of a fierce criticism which had little in common with Kant's philanthropic wisdom. We need men, he said again and again, who are inspired by the force of ideas, men who stand before the people and live with the people. The religious excitement of the years of war left his spirit critical through and through, left him just as cold as did the patriotic enthusiasm of the Teutonisers, for he was never willing to recognise anything more in "nationality" than a blind force of nature which must be kept in control by the "idea" of the state.

Some years before, he had set forth his programme in the so-called political testament of Stein. This memorial, heretofore known only to a few high officials, had just (1817) been published by an unknown hand (though hardly without the author's knowledge) in the *Oppositionsblatt* of Weimar, and had been loudly acclaimed by the South German liberals. A declared enemy of all the privileges of the nobles, Schön regarded it as indisputable that the promises of this testament —the right of representation for all active citizens, the abolition of the territorial police and of patrimonial jurisdiction—voiced the wishes of the entire nation ; it was his pleasure to conclude his fierce attacks against those "who wish to force the nation back into the machine-service of the days before the year 1806," with the exclamation, *vox populi, vox Dei.* Even his fanatical hatred of Russia added to his reputation in the liberal world. How often in his letters to Hardenberg did he express the desire for a fortunate war against these barbarians, "who stand at the lowest stage of development, who are only among the prolegomena." On one occasion, when reporting to the chancellor the rumour of an attempted assassination of the czar, he triumphantly declared to his friend his delight " that this people imposes such terrible burdens upon itself, and spreads abroad intelligence of its own doings, which express the greatest shame of the nation. Praise be to God!"[1] His fellow-countrymen of Old Prussia esteemed him highly, although his bluntness was pleasing to no one. The rationalistic tendency of his spirit expressed the sentiments which had long prevailed in the town of pure reason, and all were aware how ardently he loved his home and with what perspicuity and courage he advocated

[1] Schön to Hardenberg, February 14, 1816 ; September 26, 1818 ; November 1, 1819.

before the throne all the interests of his native region. The example of his depreciative criticism had an unfortunate effect upon the people of this region, naturally prone to fault-finding ; it was through the administration of Schön, lasting for many years, that the excess of power of the extreme party in our eastern march first became established. In Berlin, people secretly made fun of his immeasurable arrogance, reporting to one another with a smile how, on one occasion, immediately before his homeward journey, he had refused an invitation of Hardenberg, with the words : " My province cannot do without me for an hour longer." Yet no one willingly came out into the open field against this contentious man with the severely critical glance. Witzleben, Klewitz, and Vincke, had a high opinion of him ; even the king, knowing Schön's devotion, put up with many a sharp word.

As soon as Schön learned from the proceedings of the council of state about the disunion among the ministers, he immediately regarded the situation of Prussia as no less desperate than it had been before the battle of Jena, and he urgently advised the chancellor to form a new ministry, which, like that of the English cabinet, should consist only of persons of the same way of thinking, and which, like the English cabinet, would be sustained by " the respect of the nation." To Schön, England always remained the archetype of liberalism, although the high tory cabinet of that day could not be more indifferent to anything than it was to the respect of the nation. To give expression to his proposals, Schön then laid before the assembled lord-lieutenants the draft of a common petition which should enlighten the monarch regarding " the atrophied state of the administration." This remarkable writing, full of drastic phraseology, described in crude colours, arbitrarily mingling true with false, how the composite state could be held together only by the spirit, whilst this spirit was now suppressed. The police were manifesting themselves only as a force of oppression, universal military service was burdening the country, justice was now no more than a laboriously working machine in the hand of the ministers, whilst nothing whatever was being done for church or school. There were added serious complaints regarding the arbitrary and negligent procedure of the minister of finance and also an expression of the justified grievances regarding " the French practice, in accordance with which all the current affairs of provincial administration are unrestrainedly attracted towards the centre." So powerful was the peevish discontent of the time that seven of the ten lord-lieutenants agreed to subscribe this long register of indefinite and to a large extent groundless complaints (June 30th). Zerboni, a friend of Hardenberg, and the ultra-conservative Heydebreck, refused their signatures, while the lord-lieutenant of Saxony, brother of the finance minister, was not approached.

The chancellor was at first much incensed at the opposition of the leading provincial officials, and among his confidants actually spoke of their intervention as a conspiracy. But he soon recovered self-command, recognised that some of the grievances were justified, and demanded in the case of others more exact proof, whereupon the complainants were forced to withdraw their accusations. The king, too, contented himself with a gentle criticism of the exaggerations of the memorial, thanked the signatories for this new proof of their zeal in the service, and announced to them that he had just provided a remedy for the complaints regarding over-centralisation.[1] The monarch in fact, in order to effect at length a definite delimitation of the activities of the provincial authorities, issued on October 23, 1817, instructions for the lord-lieutenants and the governments, two admirable laws, which had already for a long time been in preparation, concluding the reconstruction of the supreme administration, and establishing administrative principles which held good for half a century to come. Hardenberg, cured of his preference for Napoleonic administration, now returned to the ideas of Stein. The new administrative law was closely similar to, and even verbally identical with, the legislation of the year 1808. The lord-lieutenants were to travel through the entire province at least once a year, everywhere remedying defects and redressing grievances with the guidance of personal observation; they received such wide powers of independent activity that Vincke in Westphalia, Merckel in Silesia, and Sack in Pomerania, were soon revered much as if they had been sovereigns, and were enabled to leave permanent traces of their activity in almost the entire public life of their respective provinces. But when, in June, 1818, Hardenberg asked the higher administrative officials of the provinces to express candid opinions regarding the working

[1] Memorial of the lord-lieutenants, dated June 30, 1817, with Marginal Notes by the chancellor. Memorandum of Justification by Ingersleben, September 14, by Auerswald, October 15, 1818, etc. Cabinet Order to the lord-lieutenants, November 3, 1817.

of the new instructions, objections made themselves heard in all directions. Schön after his manner, expressed his discontent with "the bureaucratic abortion." Vincke could now see salvation only in the re-establishment of the provincial ministries. Motz, on the other hand, recommended a change to a moderate prefectoral system; collegial administration was suited only to an absolute monarchy, whereas Prussia was in the act of undergoing transformation into a constitutional state.[1] The task of holding together the artificial state by an administration which was not to suffer from lack of liberty, seemed to this generation one of insuperable difficulty. Many years were still to pass before the officialdom could recognise that the chancellor had once again displayed his secure political insight, and had happily adopted a middle course between the bureaucratic and the collegial systems.

Meanwhile, in the committee and in the plenum of the council of state, a struggle was being fought out more serious and more weighty with consequences than many of the much-admired parliamentary proceedings of those days. Nor were there lacking here the passion and the oratorical stimulus of parliamentary debates. How astonished was Gneisenau when he first became acquainted with the graceful and yet perfectly relevant oratory of Humboldt, Maassen, Eichhorn, and Ferber; and when he saw so striking a refutation of the general prejudices of the day which denied to the shy Germans the gift of fluent oratory. Immediately after the peace, the king had demanded of the finance minister the compilation of a comprehensive plan of fiscal reform; "the new subjects," he wrote, "must feel that they belong to me." As soon as the task was approached, it speedily became apparent that the only possible thing was a juster distribution of the burden of taxation, since no alleviation was possible. The extraordinary expenditure of the state for war purposes had been, as was subsequently established, 206,000,000 thalers for the years 1806-1815; in the next four years, additional sums amounting to 81,000,000 thalers were disbursed. The national debt had already increased to 132,000,000 thalers in the year 1812, and since then, by the War of Liberation, and by the addition of 45,000,000 of foreign debts which had had to be taken over with the new provinces, had (in 1818) increased to 217,000,000. The credit of the state

---

[1] Motz, Memorial to the chancellor regarding the governments, November, 1818.

was so profoundly depressed that Hardenberg, in the year 1817, had to regard himself as lucky when he was able to secure a five per cent. loan from England at a discount of 72 ; at the same time, the four per cent. state bonds were quoted at 71-73 on the Berlin bourse, and yet later were even lower, having fallen to 65. What a venture was it, in this condition of general impoverishment, to impose new burdens upon the exhausted nation, which, after the German manner, always bore fiscal pressure less patiently than police coercion. The realisable value of the great landed properties was now hardly half as high as it had been in the year 1806, whilst in certain regions it had fallen to a quarter of its former amount. When in June, 1816, the king at length withdrew the moratorium which had been granted during the years of war, he had, in the case of the indebted ground-landlords of the eastern provinces, to approve a special alleviation of payment down to the year 1819, and in Old Prussia even down to 1822.

The worst of it was that no one supervised the condition of the national economy. It was still quite impossible to calculate the arrears of payment due for war services and supplies and for manifold obligations taken over with the new provinces ; even three years later the government of the little district of Erfurt had unpaid bills belonging to the war period to the number of 2,141.[1] Count Bülow therefore declared that it was impossible for him to give the council of state any detailed valuation ; and without precise calculation he reckoned the deficit for the year 1817 at 1,900,000 thalers. The members of the committee, accustomed to the painfully precise Old Prussian methods of calculation, were simply unable to believe the unwelcome communication ; they sought the cause of the deficits solely in Bülow's neglect, and put forward an opposing estimate which furnished a surplus of 4,000,000 in extraordinary and 2,000,000 in ordinary income. Thus, in a budget of about 50,000,000, the estimates of the ablest financiers differed one from another to the extent of 8,000,000.[2] Schön, always immoderate in controversy, even wished to demonstrate the existence of a surplus of 21,000,000. The event proved that Bülow, who was supported by Schuckmann alone, had judged the position more accurately than had his confident opponents. But he was

---

[1] Motz, Memorial regarding the simplification of the administration, Erfurt, June 29, 1820.

[2] Schuckmann's Report to Hardenberg, July 11, 1817.

now unable to prove that he was right, and when the referendary
of the committee, Councillor Friese, came to examine the
details of the budget with a penetrating knowledge of the
situation, there was made manifest in all branches of the financial
administration the existence of gross disorder which could no
longer find excuse in the confusions of the years of war. Led
by Humboldt, the entire committee massed itself like one man
in opposition to the minister of finance, overwhelming him with
reproaches. Bülow rejected the accusations in a passionate
speech, throwing all the blame upon the intolerable cost of the
new military system, and in his anger gave vent to some sharp
expressions regarding the careless extravagance of his cousin.
Here was a strange transposition of parties! Simultaneously
Hardenberg was attacked by his favourite Bülow, and defended
by his rival Humboldt.

The minister of war at once accepted the challenge. He
noticed with concern that the secret struggle on the part of
the civil officialdom against the army, which in the decade
prior to 1806 had done so much harm, now threatened to be
renewed when the war was over; he knew also that Bülow had
already asked an opinion from General Lingelsheim regarding
the re-establishment of the Frederician military organisation.
In order to check such efforts, and to enlighten the council
of state once for all regarding the economic advantages of the
new military system, Boyen composed a brilliant memorial
*Exposition of the Principles of the Former and of the Present
Prussian Military Organisation* (May, 1817), which demonstrated
with convincing clearness that Prussia had never before possessed
an army at once so strong and so inexpensive. But the state
had gradually expanded; with each increase of its domain the
convulsive hypertension of its physical forces diminished. Under
Frederick William I the army had cost five times as much, and
under Frederick the Great almost thrice as much, as the whole
of the rest of the administration; now for the first time the
civil service, including, indeed, the costly administration of the
national debt, absorbed the larger moiety of the national income.
Boyen estimated the cost of the military system at 21,000,000
(this figure being somewhat too low), and showed that the state
could put 238,000 more men in the field than had been
possible in the year 1806, and yet in time of peace, if the
various payments in kind of the old time were estimated at
their value in money, the total cost of the army was now

2,000,000 thalers less than it had been in 1806. He concluded
with the energetic declaration that the strength of the forces
could not be determined by financial considerations alone,
since it must depend upon the position of the state in the
world, and upon the power and the disposition of its neighbours.

The chancellor, too, was wounded by Bülow's accusations,
"wounded as chief, friend, and near relative," and took his
accuser seriously to task. Since the alarmed minister of finance
thereupon saw his last prop trembling, he cautiously changed
front, and refrained from bringing before the throne his by no
means groundless complaints regarding Hardenberg's negligence.
"I would rather," he wrote, "that the king should visit me
with his displeasure, I would rather lose everything in the world,
than burden my soul with ingratitude, and enter into open
dispute with your excellency." [1] But the friendly relationship
between the cousins had been disturbed, and Bülow's position
became more untenable day by day.

Simultaneously the council of state was conducting equally
stormy discussions regarding fiscal reform. Of the two proposals
for legislation which the minister of finance brought forward,
one, the customs-law, secured almost universal support, whereas
the other, the law regarding internal taxation, was immediately
received with hostility. Bülow's idea was that, in addition to
the trade licences and stamp duties, the existing land taxes
should also be temporarily maintained, until the provincial diets
had been summoned ; the oppressive old excise, on the other
hand, which in any case could no longer be continued after
the introduction of industrial freedom and of the customs-law,
was to be abolished, and in its place taxes upon flour at the mill
and upon meat were to be introduced both for town and country,
and also on tobacco, beer, and brandy. His proposals were
closely similar to the system of taxation of the Frederician
days, which had raised seventy per cent. of the entire revenue
by indirect taxes. They displayed the hand of a skilled man of
business who, without any thoughts of reform, simply desired
to fill the state treasury in the customary manner ; and to the
opposition, whose leadership was resumed by Humboldt, they
seemed all the more suspicious since they proceeded from a
Napoleonic minister, and agreed almost word for word with the
views which Bülow's former colleague Malchus had recently

[1] Bülow to Hardenberg, July 10, 13, 14, and 16 ; Hardenberg to Bülow,
July 12 and 17, 1817.

expressed in his work upon the financial administration of Westphalia.

Among the Prussian officials, who had almost all received their economic training in the school of Adam Smith and Kraus, the indirect taxes of Bonapartism were in evil repute; Adam Smith, for example, had described a tax on flour at the mill as "this most ruinous of all taxes." The committee therefore expressly attacked the taxes on articles of consumption, and based its criticism more especially on the ground that the minister of finance had not also proposed a law for the institution of direct taxes; for the objectors held that to effect a just distribution of the burden of taxation, the inequality of the land taxes must first of all be abolished, or must at least be charged to the individual provinces. In putting forward these views, they expressed merely what the great majority of the bourgeoisie desired. The extraordinary variety of the land taxes was an old complaint. Therein was seen most clearly of all how laboriously this state had grown into existence out of a medley of independent territories. The more strictly the kings of Prussia pursued the idea of national unity in the uppermost strata of the administration, the more carelessly had the old feudal methods been tolerated in the country districts. In the monarchy there were no less than thirty-three distinct systems of land taxation, most of them extremely old; in the province of Saxony alone, there were eight, each of which exhibited numerous local differences and privileges. East and West Prussia paid a land tax of 639 thalers per square mile [German], while Rhineland paid 4,969 thalers, certainly upon a much more valuable soil. It is not surprising that the Rhinelanders murmured loudly about the comparative exemption of the east from taxation, and that Silesia, where in the days of Frederick II a cadaster had been instituted, regarded itself as placed at a disadvantage when compared with the other old provinces where no cadaster had been undertaken. And yet for the moment reform was impossible. Since in the course of centuries the old land taxes had assumed the characteristics of rent, equalisation could be effected only after compensation of the enfranchised. But where were the means for such compensation now to be obtained? Where was to be found the technical aptitude necessary to effect a cadaster for the entire land? Moreover, would it be right that the landed gentry, who in the eastern provinces still had to bear almost unaided the costs of the territorial police, patrimonial jurisdiction, and the patronage of the church, should have new burdens imposed upon them at a moment when, exhausted by severe sacrifices on behalf of their country, they were hardly able to maintain themselves in possession of their properties ? Humboldt would not hear a word of all these serious considerations. He contented himself with unsparing criticism, describing the inequality of the existing land taxation and insisting on the defects of all indirect taxation, doing this not without doctrinaire exaggeration.

Nor was the opposition entirely devoid of particularist *arrières pensées*. In Saxony, Posen, and on the Rhine, the inhabitants hoped that taxation would be allotted in such a way that the estates of each province might contribute to the necessities of the state a share to be decided by their own estimate. This incredible proposal, which threatened to transform the monarchy into a loose federation of states, was approved by several of the lord-lieutenants, and above all by Count Solms-Laubach in Jülich-Cleves-Berg.[1] The plan, however, failed to secure a majority in the council of state, for Bülow intervened vigorously on behalf of the threatened national unity, and Schuckmann showed in a lengthy memorial that if the Prussian state were to leave this vital question to the discretion of ten provincial diets, the country would soon find itself in a similar situation to that occupied by France in the days of Calonne.[2] Nor did the committee venture to adopt Humboldt's proposal that the co-operation of the diets should be invited in the establishment of the new fiscal system ; it was felt that the intelligence of the crown still greatly exceeded the political sagacity of the nation, and that a thorough-going fiscal reform could be effected only by the direct exercise of royal authority. Moreover, the promised new diets did not as yet exist, and there was absolutely no prospect of successful negotiation with the old estates of New Hither Pomerania and Saxony, which defiantly appealed to their chartered freedom from taxation. Consequently, to the report of the committee there was merely appended the extremely ambiguous conclusion that in order to tranquillise the nation it appeared to be necessary " to bring the new plan of taxation into some sort of connection

[1] Solms-Laubach, Memorial concerning the system of taxation on the Rhine, January, 1817.

[2] Schuckmann, Memorial to the ministry of state, June 4, 1817.

with the measures concerning the diets." On June 20th the report was sent to the king; he approved the customs-law, and the drawing up of a new and comprehensive plan for internal taxation.

The king did not conceal from the committee that he had expected not merely keen criticism but definite counter-proposals; none the less, he approved the plans, and ordered the lord-lieutenants to ask the opinions of inhabitants of repute, so that public feeling in the provinces might be ascertained regarding the plan of taxation. In August and September, assemblies of notables were held in all ten provinces, and every one of them expressed itself strongly adverse to the taxes on flour at the mill and on meat. Stormy incidents were not lacking. The notables of the grand-duchy of Posen, nine Polish nobles and three German bourgeois, maintained with Sarmatian exaggeration that this tax would destroy " all civic or human freedom, and that an attack upon such a sanctuary would dissolve the bonds of human society." They then bluntly asserted the gross untruth that the yield of taxation in Posen was employed to enrich the old provinces. " Muskets have been laid aside, people have shaken hands; is the duchy to have no share in the advantages of peace ? " The Silesian notables even added to their opinion a significant legal protest. They declared, upon the proposal of Count Dyhrn, that they were expressing only their personal opinion; that approval of the new tax laws must be reserved for the future diets.[1] Here was seen a shadow of coming events, the first evil indication of the political confusion which was to result from the premature promise of constitutional rights.

None the less a great deal of sound intelligence was displayed; and ultimately, although each province brought forward its own peculiar grievances, there was manifest a remarkable harmony of views. The notables first answered the difficult question what was to be instituted in place of the rejected indirect taxation. During recent years the thought of a poll-tax, graduated in a few great classes, had quietly made its way—an idea which had been mooted in the days of Hardenberg's first administration by one of the permanent officials of the treasury, von Prittwitz-Quilitz, an agriculturist of repute. This proposal was in harmony with the dominant

[1] Memorial of the notables of Posen to the chancellor, August 17, 1817. Proceedings of the Silesian notables, Wuttke, *The Silesian Estates*, pp. 219 et seq.

economic doctrine, as well as with the general detestation of the French indirect system of taxation, and it seemed as if it would be easy to carry it out, since the mass of the population was still immovably fixed in patriarchal conditions of life. No one ventured to think of an income tax, for by the idolised Adam Smith, and recently also by von Raumer, this had been branded as tyrannical, and had been completely discredited when the attempt at its introduction, in the bitter need of the year 1812, had ended in failure. In the council of state, the learned statistician, J. G. Hoffmann, first expressly proposed a graduated poll-tax, and secured support from most of the lord-lieutenants. When the assemblies of notables were vainly seeking some tax to replace those on flour at the mill and on meat, their chairmen directed their attention to this way out. Thus it happened that the majority of the assemblies recommended the introduction of a graduated poll-tax—" a fixed tax on consumption," as the Silesians termed it. Supported by these opinions, Hoffmann thereupon (October 27th) drew up a memorial upon the graduated poll-tax, and thus opened for Prussian fiscal policy a new path, which was, indeed, not entered without hesitation, and then only after two years of negotiation. Whilst all the other great powers continued, in various ways, to depend predominantly upon indirect taxation, Prussia devoted herself more and more to the development of direct taxation. The fiscal policy thus initiated was the proposal of a profoundly impoverished state which had to find money where it could ; it was the policy of a benevolent despotism, which had, indeed, already created the beginnings of self-government, but which did not as yet possess any clear idea of the monetary needs of great towns ; it was the method of a peace-loving government which reckoned upon long years of undisturbed repose, and therefore was not afraid of utilising in time of peace that system of direct taxation which is apt to be the last resource of times of war.

The long struggle in the council of state had, to Schuckmann's distress, not remained unknown to " the listeners at the door, listeners with writers' talons." The Berlinese mocked loudly at the unhappy minister of finance, half of whose fiscal plans had been frustrated, whose entire method of conducting business had been pitilessly exposed, and who, by the roughness of his methods and by his attacks upon the new military organisation, had increased the hostility of the opposition to the degree of hatred. The members of Humboldt's party had for a long time not concealed their feeling that nothing but the dismissal of Bülow could satisfy them. It was in this sense that Schön and Klewitz wrote several times to the chancellor, whilst Sack demanded that at least the arbitrariness of the minister of finance should be restricted by a co-ordinate committee. Schuckmann who throughout the dispute had stood by Bülow, was involved in his colleague's defeat. Since now there suddenly appeared a prospect of a complete change of ministry, Schön, the hotspur of the opposition, directed a passionate attack against Wittgenstein, who had taken hardly any part in the negotiations of the council of state. Once again with boundless exaggeration, he reproached Wittgenstein, not merely with the evil arts of the secret police, but also with the maintenance of the gendarmerie instituted in the year 1812. This was everywhere working satisfactorily, but Schön insisted that the force was a weapon for making war upon the people, and that it was utterly superfluous considering the size of the army.

When Hardenberg saw that a concession to the general discontent of the high officialdom was inevitable, he first endeavoured to induce his old opponent Humboldt to enter the government. But Humboldt, on July 14th, made a sharp rejoinder, to the effect that he could never agree with Bülow and Schuckmann, could not even come to any understanding with them, "since by one the material interests, and by the other the moral energies, of the state are endangered"; only Hardenberg himself and Boyen still possessed the confidence of the nation, only in military affairs were seriousness, order, and a patriotic spirit still displayed; the ministry lacked internal unity and independence vis-à-vis the chancellor. Boyen's exhortations were yet more urgent: "The *Zeitgeist* demands that trustworthy men should occupy the higher posts"; it would never do to wait until the nation itself demanded Bülow's dismissal; "such an administration, such a man, cannot fail in the long run to work indescribable injury to the fatherland."[1]

Hardenberg, however, was unwilling to abandon the rights of his office as chancellor; and he had no wish to sacrifice his cousin, nor yet Wittgenstein, who had made himself indispensable at court and in whom he himself continued to retain

[1] Humboldt to Hardenberg, July 14; Boyen's opinion regarding the financial administration, August 10, 1817.

absolute confidence. Still less did the king desire a thorough change of ministry : " In effecting changes of office," he declared, " great caution is necessary, for we run the danger of being unjust." In September, Humboldt, to his astonishment, received orders to betake himself to his post in London. On November 3rd and December 2nd there followed a reconstruction of the ministry, which effected changes in every department except those of war and police, and yet only half corresponded to the wishes of the opposition. Bülow handed over the ministry of finance to Klewitz, and was himself assigned, under the title of minister of commerce, the simple conduct of commercial policy—a task which corresponded better with his gifts and experience. The department of public instruction, which had been completely neglected under Schuckmann, was separated from the ministry of the interior as a ministry of spiritual and educational affairs, and was placed under the leadership of Altenstein. In like manner, a ministry for the revision of the laws and for the organisation of justice in the new provinces, was detached from the ministry of justice ; Beyme was appointed head of the new department, a man who had long possessed the confidence of the king, who had been cabinet councillor, and who now was generally considered a decided liberal. Finally, in order to secure unity of will in the reform of the national finances, Hardenberg established a board of control for the scrutiny of all national expenditure, and also a ministry of the treasury, to deal with exchequer, debt, and extraordinary expenses, retaining for himself the supreme leadership of both these departments.

Thus not one of the ministers was completely dismissed from office. The men who had heaped the severest reproaches upon one another agreed to remain in office, because the chancellor had after all to decide independently, irrespective of the majority of votes. In the committee of the council of state which had to complete the reform of the fiscal system, the two opponents, Bülow and Klewitz, sat jointly as presidents. The dissensions in the government were accentuated rather than moderated ; above all, the subdivision of the ministry of finance into three departments possessed of equal authority soon proved to be a grave mistake. Since the energies of the chancellor were inadequate for the performance of this excess of work, he abandoned the administration of the national debt entirely to his confidant Rother, an able financier, whose gifts had raised him from the position of a yellow hussar to one of the highest offices of state. In the board of control, the president, Privy-councillor von Ladenberg, soon gained unrestricted power. He was an official of the old school, a man of iron diligence and imperturbable self-confidence, who obstinately opposed fiscal reform, and desired to return to the old excise system. German wilfulness and German zeal for duty had always evoked violent friction among the Prussian authorities. Now, when the natural connection of the national finances had been arbitrarily severed, embittered disputes became inevitable. Klewitz, the minister of finance, did not secure the necessary respect from the other ministers, because they did not need his approval for their expenditure, and he therefore found it impossible to draw up any precise estimates for the budget as a whole. The times were full of ill-humour and suspicion, and public opinion consequently gave ready credence to every detestable fable that was circulated regarding the mysterious situation of financial affairs.

None the less it was under this extraordinarily disintegrated administration that was effected the great transformation of Prussian commercial policy, the most momentous political deed of the epoch. The services of the new minister of finance were appraised at their full value only in the circle of his intimate advisers; the ugly little man, with his good-natured philistine countenance, could not do justice to himself, and often served the young crown prince as a butt for unrestrained jests. A man of conservative nature, slow to decide, poor in original ideas, Klewitz nevertheless understood how to elaborate the reforming schemes of others with thoroughness and thoughtful deliberation; what he had once made his own, he retained firmly, with tenacious patience and imperturbable equanimity. Just as formerly in Königsberg he had cheerfully co-operated in the abolition of hereditary servitude, so now he saved from the shipwreck of Bülow's proposals the most valuable portion, the customs-law, and unconcernedly conducted the revolutionary innovation to harbour in spite of the passionate opposition he encountered both at home and abroad.[1]

Amid the storms of the great period of reform, little had

---

[1] Among other sources of information I here avail myself of a manuscript essay by L. Kühne, entitled *Who was the Founder of the Customs-Union?* (1841), from the papers of von Motz.

been effected for the transformation of the old excise system ; it had seemed enough to impose a few of the urban taxes in the country districts, and in Old Prussia to permit the introduction of articles of foreign manufacture upon the payment of an *ad valorem* duty of 8⅓ per cent. In addition, in the old provinces, there still existed seven-and-sixty different tariffs, dealing with approximately three thousand different commodities ; there was also the Electoral Saxon general excise in the duchy of Saxony, the Swedish customs-system in New Hither Pomerania, and, finally, in Rhineland, since the abolition of the Napoleonic *douanes*, there had existed absolute anarchy. And yet, since any regular control of imports on the frontier was still lacking, this intolerable burdening of commerce failed to secure any protection against foreign competition. A chaotic monetary system served also to accentuate the dependence of the impoverished state upon the foreign world : in Posen and Pomerania forty-eight, and in the provinces leftward of the Elbe seventy-one, foreign varieties of money were officially recognised and valued. The king had long noted with concern how profoundly the law-abiding sentiments of the nation were injured by the persistence of the obsolete prohibitive system. Since the establishment of bourgeois industry in the lowlands, smuggling had increased to an incredible extent. In the year 1815 the taxes paid on coffee in the old provinces were levied on no more than two pounds per grocer's shop per diem.

The intolerable state of affairs on the eastern frontier also required immediate attention. As soon as Prussia, Poland, and Russia began at Warsaw, in March, 1816, to negotiate regarding the carrying out of the treaty of Vienna of May 3, 1815, it speedily became clear that in Vienna Hardenberg had been outwitted by Prince Czartoryski. The apparently harmless clauses in the treaty regarding free transit and free trade in the domestic produce of all the territories which had formerly been Polish, served almost exclusively to impose obligations upon the Prussian state, without any corresponding advantages, since Prussian territory constituted the land of transit. In order to carry out the agreement to the letter, Prussia would have had to separate her Polish provinces from the rest of her territory by a customs-barrier, whereas Russia, in conflict with the terms of the treaty, left unaltered her old customs-barrier which separated Polish Lithuania from Warsaw, whilst Austria, too, was by no means inclined to permit commercial independence to her Polish crown-lands. The Polish negotiators saw in the treaty a welcome means for conducting a nationalist propaganda in Prussia's Polish territories through the intermediation of commercial agents settling in the country. They were arrogant enough even to dispute Prussia's unrestricted sovereignty over Danzig, and they put forward such preposterous demands that the king answered with a definite refusal when Czar Alexander, after his manner, in an affectionate and friendly letter endeavoured to sustain the claims of the Poles. The unsatisfying course of these negotiations enforced the determination to place the Polish territories on exactly the same footing as the other provinces of the east. On the other hand, the experiences at Frankfort showed that a federal customs-law was quite impossible of attainment, and that Prussia must therefore in the first place secure order in her own household.

In the year 1816, the initial steps to this end were taken. The prohibition of the export of money was withdrawn, the royalty on salt was equalised throughout all the provinces. The ordinance of June 11th abolished on principle all water-dues and all inland and provincial duties, and promised the introduction of a general and simple frontier customs-system. At the beginning of the following year the new customs-law was completed. But as soon as reports were spread regarding the details of the proposal, a cry of distress from the alarmed producers arose throughout the country. Impassioned petitions from the cotton-spinners and weavers of Silesia and Berlin, although they suffered severely under the existing order of affairs, confirmed the old truth that the selfishness of men is the worst enemy of their own interests. The agitation became so threatening that the king thought it necessary to appoint a special commission to examine this question. On this commission the old Frederician school once more gained the upper hand. The chairman, Lord-lieutenant von Heydebreck, regarded it as the highest task of national policy " to maintain the standard of the currency "; the majority determined to advise the crown to re-establish the old prohibitive system, as it had existed down to the year 1806. But to the majority report was attached a vigorous minority report, compiled by Councillor Kunth, the tutor of the brothers Humboldt, a worthy representative of Old Prussian official pride, who had often defended the rights of the bureaucracy against the aristocratic contempt of his friend Stein. Thoroughly acquainted with manufacturing conditions, as the outcome of personal observation, he lived and worked amid the ideas of the new economic doctrine. " Property and freedom, this comprises everything ; there is nothing more wanted "—such was his pithy phrase. It seemed to him that the worst defect of Prussian industry was the astonishingly inadequate culture of most of the manufacturers, and this he regarded as an evil fruit of the preponderance of the learned classes, a preponderance which could be remedied by degrees only, through the influence of foreign competition ; even among the leading manufacturers of Berlin there were some who found it hard work to write their names.

Kunth's opinion secured almost undivided support in the council of state ; it could no longer be ignored that the removal of the prohibitions of trade were no more than the necessary completion of the reforms of 1808. On July 3rd, when the plenum of the council of state was discussing the customs-law, the political opponents Gneisenau and Schuckmann unanimously advocated the liberation of commerce. Lord-lieutenant Merckel and Privy-councillor Ferber, an able political economist formerly in Saxon service, declared that the impoverished condition of industry in Silesia and Saxony could be remedied in no other way than by freedom. In the end, three only of the fifty-six who were present voted against the law—Heydebreck, Ladenberg, and Beguelin.[1] On August 1st, the king, who was at Carlsbad, approved " the principle of free import for all future time." New and arduous negotiations now followed, for at first it seemed impossible to introduce the new order simultaneously in both halves of the Prussian domain. Finally, on May 26, 1818, the customs-law came into effect, for the entire monarchy.

Its author was the director general, Carl Georg Maassen, an official of wide knowledge, devoted body and soul to affairs, a man who concealed beneath a childlike and unpretentious manner the bold daring of the reformer, and who was inspired with a profound and free conception of social life. Born at Cleves, he had first been a Prussian official in his homeland ; had then for a time, when in the service of Berg, studied the great manufacturing industries of the Lower Rhine ; and subsequently, under the Potsdam government, had acquired a knowledge of the economic life of the north-east ; he had thus learned by widespread practical experience to supplement the theories of Adam Smith, to which he had early adhered. The result was that his proposals for a customs-law were not the

---

[1] Minutes of the council of state. Fouth sitting, July 3, 1817.

outcome of a ready-made doctrine, but proceeded from the experience acquired in three different fields of practical statecraft. The problem to be solved was, first of all, to establish a lively community of interests throughout the entire monarchy by the liberation of internal trade; secondly, to open new sources of income for the state; and finally, to secure for domestic manufacture an effective protection against the superior force of English industry, and yet to avoid completely removing the wholesome stimulus of foreign competition. Where the wishes of the manufacturers were in conflict with the requirements of the state treasury, the interests of national finance must come first; this preference was dictated by the needs of the national economy.

The two first paragraphs of the law announced freedom of ingress, egress, and transit, for the entire territory of the state. In this way a full half of non-Austrian Germany was united to form a free market, to constitute an economic community, which, if results were favourable, could extend to the other half of the nation. For the crassest contrasts of our multiform social life lay within the Prussian borders. If it should prove possible to subject Posen and Rhineland to the same economic regime without injuriously affecting their economic peculiarities, this would suffice to prove that such a regime, with a few alterations, would suffice for Baden and Hanover. As Maassen frequently said, Prussia had precisely the same problems to solve as all the other German states seriously desiring customs-unity; and owing to the multiplicity of her economic interests, Prussia could more readily than the other states find the true solution. But the carrying out of the idea, the removal of all customs-dues to the boundary of the state, was more difficult in Prussia than in any other realm; at first, indeed, it seemed altogether impracticable. It was necessary to supervise a customs-line of 1,073 German miles (there was a mile of frontier for every square mile of national territory); and this had to be effected under the most unfavourable circumstances conceivable, for the minor German states, whose boundaries marched with those of Prussia, possessed for the most part no ordered customs-system, and many of them even favoured smuggling on principle. The necessities of the case compelled the Prussian ministers of finance to establish a simple and lucidly arranged tariff, by which commodities were classified in a small number of extensive groups. A comprehensive and complicated tariff, like that of England or France, would have required a numerous staff of officials, such as in Prussia would have cost more than the yield of the duties. For the same reason, Maassen decided that the duties should be regulated by the weight of the goods, whereas in all other states there prevailed the system of *ad valorem* duties which alone was in accordance with the dominant economic theory. The gradation of payments by value would have enormously increased the cost of the customs administration; moreover the levying of a high tax on valuable goods offered a strong temptation to smuggling, and this could not be ventured by a state whose frontiers were so difficult to supervise.

In the great question also of commercial policy, financial considerations were determinative. The state had the choice open between two ways.[1] It was possible to follow the example of England and France and to introduce prohibitive duties, in order subsequently to use these as a means of negotiation with the western powers, and in this way, step by step, to facilitate trade through differential tariffs. The other alternative was immediately to establish in Prussia a system of moderate duties, in the hope that the pressure of circumstances would force a similar course upon the great neighbour realms. Maassen had sufficient courage to follow the latter method, being guided especially by the consideration that the exiguous yield of high protective duties would be likely to prove inadequate for the needs of the state treasury. The only commodities whose import was prohibited were salt and playing-cards; raw materials were as a rule duty-free, or paid very trifling duties. A moderate protective duty, not exceeding ten per cent., was imposed on manufactured articles, this figure being about the usual profit upon smuggling transactions. Colonial produce, on the other hand, was subjected to a more lucrative duty, rising to twenty per cent., for Prussia was able to tax these products effectively on her easily watched sea-coast.

This economic law, the freest and most advanced of the epoch, differed so widely from dominant prejudices that in foreign countries people at first made a mock of the good-natured weakness of the Prussian doctrinaires. The statesman's lot in an absolute monarchy is an ungrateful one. How greatly esteemed in modern England is William Huskisson,

[1] It was thus that in retrospect Eichhorn described the situation, in a ministerial despatch dated February 7, 1834.

spoken of as " one of the world's great spirits " ; all civilised nations admire the free trade speeches of the great Englishman. But the name of Maassen is to this hour known in the fatherland only to a small circle of learned men. Yet the great free trade movement of our century was initiated not in England, but in Prussia. The restored French monarchy, in the tariff established in 1816, obstinately maintained the Napoleonic prohibitive tariff against foreign manufactured articles. The selfishness of the émigrés led to the imposition of yet more severe duties upon all the produce of the land, especially upon beeves and upon wool. Even in England it was only a small section of the commercial classes which had been won over to the doctrines of free trade. The landlord class was still faithful to the high corn-duties, shippers continued to support Cromwell's navigation act, and manufacturers held fast to the rigid prohibitive duties. The majority of the cultured classes continued to take the same view of Adam Smith as had formerly been taken by Burke, namely, that such abstract theories were good enough for the Glasgow professorial chair. It was the bold proceedings of the statesmen of Berlin which first encouraged the English free-traders to speak their minds openly. The free-traders' petition from the city of London, which Baring sent to parliament in May, 1820, appealed to the " shining example which Prussia had set the world." It was of Prussia that Huskisson thought when he made the famous observation : " Commerce is not an end in itself ; it is a means for the diffusion of well-being and comfort among the nations," and when he exclaimed to his fellow-countrymen : " England cannot stand still when other countries are advancing in culture and industry."

The new law seemed inadequate to the free trade views of the Prussian statesmen. In the ministry of finance, people were well aware, as J. G. Hoffmann frequently admitted, that the greater part of the yield of the tariffs was derived from the most marketable colonial goods, and that the treasury secured but little advantage from the other duties. But it was also recognised that rigid limits are imposed upon every system of taxation by the sentiments of those who have to pay the taxes ; public opinion of those days would never have pardoned the government if it had taxed coffee and left tea free of duty. Maassen rejected one-sided favouring of one branch of production ; he counted upon the harmonious co-operation of agriculture, industry, and commerce, and regarded protective duties as no more than a temporary expedient, adopted in order to enable German industry gradually to attain to its full powers. Even on the occasion of the first revision of the tariff in the year 1821, a further step was taken towards free trade, the tariff being simplified and several duties abrogated. Whilst the law of 1818 had established a special tariff for the western provinces, with somewhat lower rates, now all difference between the provinces was abolished. In form and application, the tariff of 1821 constituted the basis for all the subsequent tariffs of the customs-union.

While the council of state was engaged upon this reform, the economic immaturity of the age led to the outburst of numerous complaints. The masses declared that it would be impossible to endure the rise in the cost of living; manufacturers considered that the door was being opened " to English commercial despotism," and besieged the throne with such despairing petitions that the king, although he was personally quite in agreement with Maassen's plans, nevertheless commanded a further examination of the law which had already been signed. It was not until September 1, 1818, that the customs-law was published, and the new frontier custom-house officers did not enter upon their functions until the new year of 1819. On February 8, 1819, was issued the supplementary law regarding the taxation of articles of consumption produced at home, in accordance with which only wine, beer, brandy, and tobacco were subject to taxation, the taxes in question having to be paid by the producer, so that the consumer was relieved from direct taxation.

On the whole, the new legislation adopted a happy middle course between free trade and protection. In one direction only did it depart strikingly from the principles of moderate free trade ; it burdened transit commerce with comparative severity. The hundredweight of transit goods had on the average to pay a toll of half a thaler, but on certain important commercial routes a great deal more than this—unquestionably an extremely oppressive burden for ordinary commodities, especially when they had to cross Prussian territory several times. The immediate cause of this severity was to be found in financial needs. Prussia controlled some of the most important commercial routes of Central Europe : the connection between Holland and the highlands of Central Europe ; the old route of export of Polish grain; the intercourse of Leipzig with the sea, with Poland, and with Frankfort. It was calculated that fully one-half of the goods entering Prussia were in transit merely. The exhausted treasury was not in a position to renounce the sole advantage which could be secured from the inconvenient extension characteristic of the Prussian domain. Moreover, all those well acquainted with customs affairs were agreed in the opinion, which at that time was well founded, that it was only by the taxation of transit trade that the financial yield of the frontier tariff system could be secured. If duty-free transit were permitted, the door would be opened to all kinds of fraud, and an enormous smuggling traffic from Hamburg, Frankfort, and Leipzig would actually be invited, so that the whole success of the reform would be endangered. But the inequitable severity of the transit dues and the tenacious insistence of the government upon rates which were intolerable for the German neighbouring lands, are explicable on political grounds alone. Transit dues served the cabinet of Berlin as an effective means of negotiation in order to induce the minor German states to adhere to the Prussian commercial policy.

The dreams of a universal German commercial policy, which during the Vienna congress had been entertained by the Prussian plenipotentiaries, had in Berlin long been abandoned. The impossibility of such plans was manifest, not alone from the futility of the federal constitution, but owing to the internal relationships of the federated states. Hardenberg knew that the court of Vienna would make no change in its traditional system of provincial duties, and that it would be simply impossible for Austria to subordinate its non-German crown-lands to a federal customs-system. But the rest of Germany also preserved numerous vestiges of the shameful cosmopolitan epoch of our past. Hanover was still dependent upon England, and Schleswig-Holstein upon Denmark; Luxemburg remained in immediate geographical union with the unified state of the Netherlands. How was a general German customs-system conceivable so long as such foreign dominion persisted? Moreover, the constitutions of several of the states of the Germanic Federation offered insuperable hindrances. Prussian tariff reform rested upon the idea of the common law. Who could expect the Mecklenburg nobles to renounce their freedom from duties, or the Saxon nobles to abandon the general excise which was so closely associated with their feudal privileges, so long as the feudal oligarchy continued in these countries to rule undisturbed? How was it possible to introduce into Hanover the Prussian tariffs which presupposed the unity of the national economy, since in Hanover the royal domain-treasury and the feudal tax-treasury continued to exist independently side by side? Moreover, the customs-system was closely connected with the taxation of articles of home consumption; only if the minor states should determine to establish a system of indirect taxation upon the Prussian model, or should at least approximate to the Prussian method with an honourable system of mutual accommodation, would a permanent customs community become possible. Was such a willingness for sacrifice to be expected at a time when the Confederation of the Rhine and the intrigues of the congress of Vienna had morbidly stimulated the selfish arrogance of the dynasties and had deprived them of all shame? Even those states to which goodwill was not lacking, could not immediately accept the severe proposals which Prussia had to put before them in order to secure an adequate yield from her taxes. As Eichhorn subsequently declared, people had to get used to the changed situation, had to make a rough estimate of the politico-economical needs of their respective countries, and of the sacrifices necessary to cover the national expenditure: "Before clarity upon these matters had been secured, no useful results could be expected from common deliberations, and least of all from a discussion at the Bundestag concerning Germany as a whole."[1]

In such a situation, Prussia was forced to take independent action without any consideration for her German neighbours. Among good-natured folk the opinion prevailed that Prussia ought to leave her frontiers open to imports from all the rest of Germany, and to impose duties only on the produce of foreign lands. This childish proposal, if carried out, would have made all control of imports on the frontier impossible, and would have absolutely frustrated the financial and economic aims of customs reform. It was even impossible to tax German products less severely than others. It was indeed the German petty states, with their intricate, defective, and sometimes quite uncontrolled frontiers, which seemed the most dangerous enemies to the Prussian treasury. Certificates of origin, furnished by such authorities, could give no adequate security to the precise calculations of the Berlin bureau. Every alleviation of duty

[1] Eichhorn, Instructions for the envoys at the German courts, March 25, 1828.

along these frontiers would encourage frauds, so long as a perfectly ordered customs administration was lacking in the neighbour states. Moreover, if Prussia were to give special advantages to the minor German states, unquestionably foreign countries would retaliate, and the nation would gradually be forced into a system of differential tariffs which was absolutely contrary to the aims of the Prussian statesmen. To the ministry of finance, differential tariffs seemed far more undesirable than protective tariffs, for the latter burden trade for the advantage of native producers, while differential tariffs do so for the advantage of foreign producers.

If the new customs-system was to come into existence at all, the only possible way was, that, to begin with, all non-Prussian goods must be treated on equal footing. It was true that by this measure the German neighbours would be very hard hit. They were accustomed to carry on a lively smuggling traffic into Prussia, but this was now prevented by the strict supervision of the frontiers. The customs-barriers on the frontier of the new provinces disturbed old established commerce in many ways. The kingdom of Saxony suffered severely when Prussian customs-barriers were erected just outside the gates of Leipzig. The small Rhenish states were witnessing close at hand the increase in strength of the Prussian national economy ; what was on one side an advantage was on the other a disadvantage. It will readily be understood that it was precisely in the immediate neighbourhood of Prussia that ill-feeling was most marked. Moreover, the institution of the tariff by weight was especially burdensome to the German neighbour states, for foreign countries for the most part sent bulky commodities to Prussia, whilst from other parts of Germany the imports were usually heavy goods.

Nevertheless, if it was not possible for the moment to give special privileges to the minor states, the reform of the customs was from the first designed to draw the German neighbours gradually into the Prussian customs-union. " Recognising the impossibility of a union for the entire Federation, Prussia endeavoured to secure the same end by means of separate agreements "—such was the brief and exhaustive phrase in which, ten years later, Eichhorn summed up the essential ideas of Prussian commercial policy. The disintegration of its territory forced Prussia to pursue a German policy, making it impossible for her self-sufficingly to sever herself from her German neighbours, or to conduct her administration without coming to an understanding with these. For the moment, a considerable part of Prussia's Thuringian possessions, forty-one square miles [German] in extent, had to be excluded from the customs-line. It was absolutely essential to extend the customs-barriers at least so far that the entire domain of the state could be equably taxed. In the customs-law itself (section 5) the intention was declared to favour mutual trade by means of commercial treaties. The severe taxation of transit trade gave palpable expression to this hint. Hardenberg spoke still more definitely concerning the aims of the law before it actually passed into operation. When the manufacturers of Rheidt and other Rhenish towns petitioned the chancellor to abolish the German internal customs-dues, he answered, on June 3, 1818, that the government was not unaware of the advantages which might proceed from the union of several German states to constitute a common manufacturing and commercial system, and that the king's plan was pursued with unceasing consideration for this point. "It is in the very spirit of this design, at once to retaliate against foreign restrictions of commerce, to repay complaisance, and to favour a neighbourly co-operation for the common good." Similarly he declared to the manufacturers of Elberfeld that the Prussian customs-barriers were intended "to pave the way for a general extension, or for a union effected in some other way."

Here was a definite announcement that the state which for a long time had wielded the sword of the old emperordom, was now also resuming the commercio-political reforming ideas of the imperial policy of the sixteenth century, and was ready, by gradual steps, to secure for the nation that unity of economic life which had hitherto been lacking throughout the course of its history. Hardenberg hoped that this goal, which could not be attained in a single leap, would be reached step by step through a process of cautious approximation, by means of agreements between separate states. In this century of toil, Mars and Mercury are the stars which chiefly determine the destiny of nations. The military system and the commercial policy of the Hohenzollerns henceforward constituted the two titles upon which Prussia's claim to hegemony in Germany reposed. This commercial policy was the exclusive work of the crown and its officialdom. Even at a later date, when its ultimate aims had been fully disclosed, it always encountered a blind resistance from the nation. In the epoch of the Reformation, the economic unification of the fatherland had been frustrated by the resistance of the imperial towns; in the nineteenth century, unification was recommenced and completed in definite opposition to the desires of the majority of the Germans.

All parties in Germany were united in the struggle against the Prussian customs-law, Kotzebue's *Wochenblatt* no less than Luden's *Nemesis*. Vainly did J. G. Hoffmann, in the *Preussische Staatszeitung*, employ his thorough knowledge of the subject in the refutation of the almost invariably valueless politico-economical diatribes of the press. The very same protectionists who were demanding help for German industry, inveighed against the intolerable rates of the Prussian tariff, which now provided the protection they desired. The very same liberals who mocked the Bundestag as an utterly useless institution, demanded from this institution a creative act of commercial policy. When Hoffmann proved that the new law was a benefit for Germany, Pölitz, Krug, and other Saxon publicists rejoined that no state had the right to force benefits upon its neighbours. Ridiculous stories were retailed with the most absolute assurance, and were greedily accepted by ignorant readers. In one place it was asserted that a poor hawker of Reuss, pushing his barrow laden with vegetables to the weekly market of Leipzig, had had to pay a thaler for transit dues to the Prussian customs—the only lack of verisimilitude about the story being that the Prussian tariff did not impose any duty upon these goods. Sentiment was also called into the field against Prussia, for the Germans always have recourse to sentiment when ideas fail them. It was reported that on the very first day on which the unhappy law passed into operation, a custom-house officer in Langensalza had been stabbed by an infuriated patriot of Gotha, whereas the man had really committed suicide. It was distressfully declared that King Frederick William undoubtedly cherished philanthropic intentions, but that " financial considerations poison the best intentions " ; no one seemed to have any understanding of the hard necessity of these financial considerations. Among the liberal patriots there was general agreement that the desired unity of the German market could be attained only if the already completed unification of half Germany should be once more disturbed.

Unaffected by the general hostility, Klewitz firmly upheld

the work of customs reform. But in its industrial policy the government displayed less firmness against the ultra-conservative prejudices of the time. In the *Staatszeitung*, expert officials had again and again to describe to incredulous readers the advantages of free industry. Nevertheless it was not ventured to introduce into the new provinces the industrial law of 1811, and a contradictory state of affairs, which was out of harmony with the unity of the Prussian market, was allowed to persist untouched during an entire generation; in Saxony the old guild system was retained; in the Rhenish Westphalian territories and in the old provinces, industrial freedom prevailed, in the former in accordance with Prussian, and in the latter in accordance with French laws.

The last epoch of the reign of Frederick William III resembled the reign of the first Frederick William in this respect also, that the legal system of the country was least of all influenced by the reforming activities of the national authority. The old rule remained in operation that this state was never in a position to effect vigorous progress in all domains of life simultaneously. Savigny was right when he denied to his own age the vocation for effecting a reform of the civil law. The great codification of the common law was now a generation old, and by the majority of members of the Old Prussian knighthood was still regarded with comprehensible pride as a master-work; but while science had long outgrown the views of Suarez, no new acquisitions had hitherto been made. With his usual sound sense, the king was aware that the old subdivision of the estates, which underlay the civil code, had long before been abolished by the reforms of 1807; and since civil and criminal legal procedure were both urgently in need of reconstitution, Beyme was charged with the revision of the Frederician law-books. But notwithstanding Beyme's reputation as a liberal, his work now proved just as barren as it had formerly been in the Dohna-Altenstein ministry, when the king had so often vainly exhorted him to abolish patrimonial jurisdiction; and during two years in office he effected nothing of importance. The time was not ripe for a thorough transformation of the Frederician law-books, and yet it would not do to impose upon the entire state-domain this half obsolete legislation, whose defects the crown itself did not deny. Consequently, in the regained old provinces, the Prussian civil code was, indeed, immediately introduced, side by side with the ancient organisation of the law courts, but not without numerous exceptions. In Westphalia, patrimonial jurisdiction was to be restored only when those authorised to exercise it made a special demand to that effect, and this took place in no more than four instances. In Posen, owing to the untrustworthy character of the Polish nobles, the establishment of these patrimonial courts was entirely renounced; whilst oral procedure was permitted in the case of simple legal disputes. In Saxony, on the other hand, a country with a reputation for interminable litigation, everyone was pleased when the legal system was directly established upon the Old Prussian footing; it was only the innumerable lawyers who complained loudly about the decline of their industry. Finally, in New Hither Pomerania, the common law and the anciently celebrated court of appeal of Greifswald were retained, because the people regarded these institutions as among their ancient liberties, guaranteed in the peace of Kiel.

Great and unexpected difficulties appeared in the way of the reconstitution of the legal system on the Rhine. President Sethe was entrusted with the temporary organisation of the Rhenish law courts. This was a loyal Prussian patriot from Cleves, who had once, with a heavy heart, entered the state service of Berg, and had there become intimately acquainted with French law. He discharged his task with insight and freedom from bias, unconcerned by the anger of the feudal party, which accused him of Bonapartism, and equally unconcerned about the endless complaints of the Rhenish populace, which, with memories still fresh of the days of the Cologne clique, was everywhere suspicious of nepotist intrigues.[1] Shortly afterwards, in June, 1816, a special commission assembled in Cologne, of which Sethe was president, and of which Simon, a former judge of the territory, was also a member. Its function was to examine whether it was possible to harmonise the Rhenish law with the Prussian, and it received express instructions from the king " to make use of what was good wherever it could be found."

In the early days of the intoxication of victory, the abolition of the *code Napoléon* was by all Germanophils, even in Rhineland, regarded as an indispensable demand of national honour. Everyone had agreed with Savigny when he spoke

[1] Kircheisen to Hardenberg, December 7, 1815; to Sethe, January 5, 1816.

of the five codes as a political disease which had been lived through. So completely had the legal history of the fatherland been forgotten, that to the zealous Teutonisers even the public oral procedure characteristic of the ancient Teutons, which had been revived in the French legal system, seemed an arbitrary revolutionary innovation. In the interim, however, the sentiment of the country had completely changed. The provincial spirit had awakened, and had begun to extol everything that existed as a valuable peculiarity of the homeland; the *code* was the Rhenish law, and for this reason it was admirable if only legal procedure had been less costly. If anyone spoke about Prussian law, people thought immediately of that cumbrous legal organisation which had formerly existed in Electoral Cologne and Electoral Treves; never again was Rhineland to relapse into this chaos. The publicity of the proceedings seemed, above all, the bulwark of territorial freedom, for, amid the restless changes of their political destiny, the inhabitants of Rhineland had long ago learned to distrust every government, simply because it was a government. When the crown now summoned local experts to give their opinions, as had been done in Prussia before the promulgation of the civil code, the great majority declared themselves in favour of retaining the *code Napoléon*. The town councils of Cologne, Treves, Coblenz, and Cleves, appealed directly to the king, and even Lord-lieutenant Solms-Laubauch, an opponent of the French legal system, expressly declared that, in view of the general sentiment of the province, the abolition of public procedure was impossible.[1] Sethe earnestly desired a unified legal system for the entire state, but he also saw that this goal was still remote, and gladly recognised the great advantages of the neo-French legal system. The *code Napoléon*, which had arisen out of an amalgamation of Roman law with the general customs (mainly of Teutonic origin), could not, on German soil, be regarded simply as a foreign legal system, for Roman law had long been domiciled with us; its precision and brevity, its incisiveness and logical clearness, bore comparison extremely well with the casuistic verbosity of the Prussian civil code; and in these thoroughly bourgeois Rhenish territories where was now to be discovered a foundation for the patrimonial courts, or for the rigid feudal law of Frederician days?

[1] Solms-Laubach, Account of the conditions in Jülich-Cleves-Berg, August 18, 1819.

After deliberating for two years, the commission laid before the monarch the result of its negotiations. It recommended that the Rhenish legal system should be maintained until the Prussian law-books had been revised, and in a detailed opinion it described how trial by jury kept the legal idea alive among the people, inspired love for the law, restricted the arbitrariness of officials, and enlarged the narrowness of juristic culture by that free knowledge of the world and of men which was characteristic of the laity. Kircheisen, who lived and moved amid the ideas of the old judiciary, was profoundly disturbed by this memorial. He feared more especially that in the old provinces public confidence in the courts would be impaired if the jury system were to be retained on the Rhine, and, in a rejoinder, he angrily criticised the "detestable distinction between public and private procedure." Even in the old provinces, he said, the decisions were not private; the old German adage "where the courts are, there shall the best be," was more adequately fulfilled in Prussia, where judges were selected with so much care, than it was in France; in every question of fact a legal question was also involved, and the latter was comprehensible to the legal expert alone; it could never be allowed that the judge should arbitrarily enfeeble the laws when they conflicted with public opinion; and how could the state renounce the right, in case of incomplete proof, of visiting the accused with extraordinary punishment? [1] The minister carefully marshalled all the sound and unsound technical objections to trial by jury which were dominant in the minds of jurists of the old school accustomed to definite rules of evidence. He was not influenced by political anxieties, for the jury system had not yet been adopted as part of the liberal programme.

Beyme, however, took the side of the commission, and secured the king's approval. Upon the left bank of the Rhine, and in Berg, the French legal system remained temporarily in operation; and on June 21st a supreme court of appeal for the Rhenish land was constituted in Berlin, under the presidency of Sethe. Daniels, equally distinguished as judge and as man of learning, became president of the court of appeal in Cologne. Everyone on the Rhine was acquainted with the talented man; all spoke of his personal resemblance to Socrates; everyone related anecdotes of his colossal memory, and of his

[1] Kircheisen, Opinion concerning the organisation of justice in the Rhenish provinces, July, 1818.

Ulpian-like penetration. In his personality was incorporated that remarkable combination of German and of French culture which the Rhinelanders were at that time still accustomed to claim. So profound was his knowledge of French law that by the French themselves Daniels was regarded as the leading expert in this subject, and yet he remained a German jurist, for everyone who wished to find his way through the labyrinth of the ancient law of Electoral Cologne had recourse to Daniels' university note-books, now yellow with age. Under his leadership, there gradually came into existence the modern caste of Rhenish lawyers, men richly endowed with talent, proud of the legal system of the Rhine, and of the forensic eloquence which flourished in this region ; but men who, while extremely receptive for the formal political wisdom of the French, were without understanding of the just peculiarities of the German north-east. This caste constituted an entirely new force in Prussian political life, and one whose power increased as the years passed, and as liberalism began to extol trial by jury as a palladium of popular freedom.

Among the numerous pressing cares of Prussian policy was the question whether the bold venture of an inspired and warlike time, the army law of 1814, would now stand the test in the days of relaxation and poverty. The great majority of the generals held firmly to the ideas of Scharnhorst and Boyen. Gneisenau, more particularly, was never weary of referring to the Landwehr as the " sanatorium " which alone could keep the state on its feet amid its stronger neighbours ; no other nation could rival Prussia in this respect, for no other possessed so loyal, self-sacrificing, and highly-cultured a population. On the other hand, the foreign envoys all expressed adverse opinions against the new military organisation—some because they secretly feared universal military service and the incalculable force of this national army, and others because they genuinely regarded the bold innovation as an idealistic dream. Scharnhorst's ideas had as yet found no acceptance in foreign lands. The old professional soldiers of France, forgetful of the blows they had recently suffered, regarded the Prussian " army of children " with contempt. Czar Alexander spoke in good faith when he continually warned the Prussian generals that with such half-soldiers it was impossible either to conduct a war or to repress a rising.

Even the high officials had been by no means completely convinced by Boyen's able memorial. ⸢Whilst Bülow and Beyme openly demanded a return to the old military system, others, without distinction of party, came forward with bland proposals to make things easier for the upper classes. Schuckmann regarded it as indisputable that a young man of culture could be transformed into an efficient infantry soldier in six weeks at most; Solms-Laubach advised that the students of Bonn and Düsseldorf should be summoned merely to occasional drills on Sunday. Schön looked down with philosophic disdain upon the parade-ground arts of the handicraftsmen of war; he desired that all the officers of the Landwehr up to the colonels should be appointed by the circle-estates, and was of opinion that three days' training per annum was amply sufficient for the military education of a volunteer.[1] So profoundly had the contempt for a strict military training which found expression in Rotteck's works, permeated the circles of the statesmen.

Among the notable publicists of Prussia there was hardly one to be found who displayed an understanding of the essential preconditions of a military system truly fit for war. Even Benzenberg, the intelligent Rhenish patriot, wrote bluntly to his well-wisher Gneisenau to the effect that Belle Alliance had taught the nation how unnecessary was all the torment of the parade ground. Arndt desired wherever possible to content himself in peace-time with a permanent general staff; the Landwehr would do the rest. The no less patriotic author of the widely-read writing *Preussen über Alles wenn es will* (1817) also regarded a standing army as superfluous, and thought that the country could get along very well with a Landwehr maintained by the communes. Even the particularists who enthusiastically advocated the proportional allotment of taxation, endeavoured to exploit the national army for their special purpose, and recommended the construction of ten independent provincial Landwehr corps under the supervision of the provincial diets. The Polish nobility, in particular, took up the idea with suspicious zeal. " Without national sentiment a Landwehr is impossible "—such were the words employed by von Bojanowski and other landlords of Posen in repeated memorials;

---

[1] Memorials to Hardenberg sent by Schuckmann, July 11, 1817; Schön, June 21; Solms-Laubach, September 21, 1818. Schön to General Borstell, June 29, 1818.

if the king would grant the grand duchy an independent Landwehr the Polish nobles would joyfully flock to the colours.[1]

When the authorities began to put the army law into operation, nowhere was less resistance displayed than on the Rhine, this being contrary to all expectation. In Rhineland the common people regarded the short period of service as an alleviation after the severe Napoleonic conscription, and even the upper classes accepted their military obligations without murmuring, since these were in accordance with the idea of general equality before the law. Loud, on the other hand, were the complaints voiced by those in the east who had formerly enjoyed special privileges, by the great towns which had been free from military obligations, and by the proud nobility of New Hither Pomerania and Saxony. Three times did the municipal delegates of Berlin defiantly demand the re-establishment of the ancient military freedom of their commune, until the king threatened to publish the names of the signatories in the newspapers ; and when, in the summer of 1817, the time came for the Landwehr of Breslau to take the military oath, disorders broke out in the streets, though unquestionably the maladroitness of some of the officials and the notorious pugnacity of the Breslau mob were larger factors in these disturbances than any resistance on the part of the men called to arms. Nothing but the authority of the absolute crown could make a way through this thorny thicket of opposition, nothing else could rescue for Germany the principles of the new military organisation. Beyond question, a general Prussian diet, if summoned at such a moment, would have immediately begun a fight against universal military service.

In carrying out the work, serious technical difficulties were encountered, which seemed to confirm all the doubts and anxious considerations of the foreign world. The mere provision of weapons for the Landwehr had to proceed at a very slow pace owing to the deplorable condition of the finances. For the first levy, Boyen, in a continual struggle with the minister of finance, had at length secured the necessary means, so that, in December, 1819, of the prescribed equipment of arms there were still lacking no more than 8,415, muskets ; many circles voluntarily furnished their soldiers with side-arms and busbies. But nothing had yet been done to supply the needs of

[1] Klewitz, Report from Poland, September 24, 1817.

the second levy, which of 174,080 muskets, still required 135,559.[1]

It was owing to the same lack of funds that the strength of the standing army was from the first established at too low a figure. The army law had promised that the number of the troops of the line should be regulated by the existing circumstances of the nation. The supplementary Landwehr-ordinance of November 21, 1815, declared more modestly: "To the standing army of moderate size will, in the future, be superadded the Landwehr." Consequently the peace strength of the army was temporarily established at barely one per cent. of the population; including the army corps in France, this strength was 115,000 men, no more than in the year 1806. Beyond question, the men who were now summoned received, in three years of uninterrupted service, a far more careful training than had been effected during the closing years of the older army organisation, when furloughs became so frequent that the majority of the soldiers, notwithstanding their liability to service for twenty years, remained only about twenty-two months with the colours. Moreover, the concentration of the army in fortresses and large towns was beneficial to training, and this concentration was maintained, although the abandoned minor garrison towns besieged the throne with petitions. But this weak peace army, with its thirty-eight (subsequently forty-four) infantry regiments, was far from making adequate provision for the military education of the entire youth competent to bear arms. It was all the more inadequate because the population underwent a very rapid increase, as regularly happens in the case of vigorous nations at the close of devastating wars. In addition, an entire third of the standing army was still composed of re-enlisted men, of those who voluntarily continued to serve after their three years' term had expired; the ancient customs of the professional soldiery continued to operate, and in this time in which it was difficult to gain a livelihood, military service seemed to many a tolerably satisfactory occupation. Consequently a very large proportion of those fit to bear arms could not be accepted for service, and at the outset the rejections were often effected with a lamentable lack of consistency. In one place the supernumeraries were by an easy-going committee completely discharged from further military service, whilst in another, an officer in whose blood the old Prussian

[1] Arms-report of the Landwehr, December, 1819.

preference for "the tall fellows" still lingered would select his men by their stature. Ultimately, selection by lot was introduced, and those who were thus discharged from the regular term of three years' service were scantily trained for three months, as Landwehr recruits, by officers of the line specially appointed for the purpose, and were then apportioned to the Landwehr.

Consequently the Landwehr consisted in part of veteran soldiers, in part of imperfectly trained reservists, whilst its officers' corps, which still existed quite independently beside that of the army of the line, deteriorated year by year. The officers experienced in warfare were gradually eliminated, whilst the young *Einjährigers* [*Einjährige-Freiwilligen*, soldiers serving one year at their own expense], who now obtained commissions after one year of service and a few short drills, showed themselves, in most cases, to be even more inexperienced than their troops. The sole connecting link between the army of the line and the Landwehr was constituted by the Landwehr-inspectors, who were subordinate to the commanding generals of the line, there being one inspector to each governmental district. The king did all he could to increase the military self-confidence of the Landwehr ; he bestowed colours on this body, constituted a Landwehr-guard, and nominated the princes of the blood as commanders of the squadrons of this force. The generals became accustomed after manœuvres to shower praise upon the Landwehr, this offering a remarkable contrast with the strict discipline that obtained in the army of the line. The old fables of the battles fought by the Landwehr in the War of Liberation had gradually obtained credence throughout the nation ; the Landwehr was considered the true national army, the supporting pillar of Prussian power. Delighted crowds gathered to watch the Landwehr manœuvres, and the bureaucracy shared this preference, for a considerable proportion of the Landwehr officers were derived from the class of the officials.

But, to the keen military insight of the king, it was clearly evident to what an extent these national troops were still inadequately characterised by warlike efficiency ; even General Kleist and other friends of the Landwehr could not conceal from the war-lord that the cavalry was not worth much, and that even the infantry, when extensive manœuvres were in progress, showed itself efficient only under the leadership of specially assigned officers of the line.[1] Yet, owing to the small size of the army of the line, the reserve army would in case of war have immediately to be led against the enemy. That which in the summer of 1813 had been a policy enforced by the extremest need, was now to become the rule. Should mobilisation be ordered, the field army would immediately be increased to 298,000 men, of which the larger moiety (seven classes among twelve) would consist of Landwehr men of the first levy ; even if nothing more were in view than a military demonstration for diplomatic reasons, the state would be forced to call immediately to the colours all those fit to bear arms up to the age of three-and-thirty, to deprive thousands of families of their bread-winners, and seriously to disturb the entire civic life of the country. It is true that, owing to the cumbrous means of communication of those days, the greater part of the army would be at least five weeks on the march before it could draw near the enemy ; but would this brief respite suffice to supplement the defective training of the Landwehr recruits ? How much more unfavourable, too, was now the military situation of the national territory ; the state was no longer protected against the first hostile onslaught by the old outworks of Poland and the Rhenish lands, for its frontiers now marched directly with those of three great powers. Here was ground enough for serious anxiety. Profoundly concerned, the king unceasingly endeavoured to discover the right solution for all the military, political, and economic problems which were comprised in the one great question of universal military service, and discussed the matter with Witzleben. The most deplorable defect of the new system, the impossibility of passing the entire youth of the country through the school of the army, was unfortunately at present irremediable ; the outlay requisite for the necessary increase of the army of the line was disproportionate to the national revenue and the economic capacity of the people. But was it impossible in peace-time to weld the Landwehr with the army of the line in so intimate a fashion that the field army would no longer consist of two quite unequal portions ? The organisers of the Prussian army had now to face the same task which formerly Carnot had solved after his manner when he amalgamated the white regiments of the line, dating from the old regime, with the blue

[1] Kleist's Report to the king concerning the Landwehr manœuvres in Saxony, November 24, 1817.

national guards of the republic, to constitute his new half-brigades.

In these discussions there soon became manifest a difference of opinion between the king and the ministers of war. Although, naturally, Boyen did not believe the popular fables about the Landwehr, he overestimated the military efficiency of this body. His judgments were based upon his experiences in Bülow's corps; here the Landwehr had always made a good showing, for under the slack leadership of Bernadotte, and subsequently in the easy Dutch campaign, the troops had rarely had to undertake forced marches or to suffer any extraordinary hardships. The king, on the other hand, still clearly remembered how little tenacity had been displayed by the Landwehr of Kleist's corps during the terrible rainy days after the battle of Dresden; he knew also that in the campaign of 1815, of the troops which had been dispersed by the enemy, three-fourths had belonged to the Landwehr. In order to avoid the recurrence of such disasters, it was the king's wish that the Landwehr should always drill and manœuvre in co-operation with troops of the line, that one brigade of the line and one of the Landwehr should combine to form a single division, that numerous officers of the line should be detached for command of the Landwehr, and that the higher commands in the Landwehr service should be regularly entrusted to officers of the line; whereas Boyen advised that the system of complete separation of the two officers' corps should be retained, that friction between soldiers and civilians might be avoided, and that the peculiar spirit of the Landwehr might remain undisturbed.

Meanwhile Duke Charles of Mecklenburg ventured the first open attack against the principles of the new military system. In the spring of 1818, he sent his royal brother-in-law a lengthy memorial wherein, without putting forward any proposals of his own, he described in gloomy colours the serious dangers threatening the throne, the licence of the press, the presumption of the students, and, above all, Boyen's system of military organisation; this system was pressing arms into the hands of those who were likely to rise in revolt; the Landwehr arsenals were not forgotten, places which could so readily be seized by a mutinous force.[1] The reactionary party at length ventured to

---

[1] The main contents of this memorial can be ascertained from Witzleben's Rejoinder of January 25, 1818 (Dorow, Witzleben, p. 93). The personality of its author is manifest from a remark in Witzleben's Diary, May, 1819.

express its heart-felt wishes. Even Knesebeck agreed with the duke, whilst Prince Augustus, who had been one of the first to defend the idea of universal military service, now regarded the undeniable defects of the Landwehr as so serious that he recommended a return to the ancient system of long service with extensive furloughs. Witzleben inveighed with all the anger of his honourable heart against the men " who desired to separate the ruler from the people, the head from the body." Universal military service, he declared in his eloquent rejoinder, is " a bond which unites the entire nation, the ends of this bond being placed in the monarch's own hands." The king was not misled by his brother-in-law's warnings, although in moments of depression he did, indeed, admit that it was a serious matter to make all men soldiers. The responsibility for the difficult experiment, which seemed to him by far the most important task of Prussian statecraft, pressed heavily on his conscience. No other state, he said to Witzleben, is laying such heavy burdens upon its people, and yet it is impossible to proceed with strict justice, and to train all those who are competent to bear arms![1] In the end he agreed that, with all its defects, the new order was a tolerably satisfactory middle course between the old system and the dilettantists' dreams of an armed nation. He never became unfaithful to the ideas of Scharnhorst. But he regarded a closer union between Landwehr and line as indispensable ; and since Boyen obstinately resisted this thoroughly sound plan, there gradually ensued an estrangement between the king and the minister of war which ultimately led to Boyen's fall.

In a few years, and with astonishing rapidity, the nation became fully accustomed to the new military organisation which had at first been so unwillingly accepted. The justice of the principle of universal military service was obvious. The manly view that service in arms is an honour, corresponded to the natural sentiments of a valiant nation ; and however heavy the burden, it did not prove destructive, for in matters of marriage and domicile, in trade and industry, Prussia enjoyed freedoms still almost unknown to the petty states of Germany. With what wonder had the old burghers of Berlin at first shaken their heads when they saw a common soldier driving about in a smart carriage ; soon the *Einjähriger* was an everyday sight, and quite spontaneously it became the rule that the *Einjährige-*

[1] Witzleben's Diary, May 9, 1819.

Freiwilligen did not, as the legislators had expected, enter the yagers and the guards, but whatever detachment of troops were nearest to their homes, so that the cultured youth became distributed throughout the army. Universal military service showed itself the most effective instrument for the amalgamation of the old and the new provinces. Numerous Saxon, Westphalian, French, Polish, and Swedish officers, who flocked especially to the cavalry regiments, rapidly fused with the Old Prussian officers, when all were engaged together in serious work—for since annually almost one-third of the troops were new recruits, the peace service of the officer was no longer, as it had formerly been, a life of busy idleness. In the school of the army, the undisciplined sons of the Polish provinces were trained in order, cleanliness, and good behaviour ; and in this way many of them were first taught to speak German. Although the Rhenish peasant continued as a rule to say commiseratingly of his son serving in the army, " he is in the hands of the Prussians," and although many a soldier of the province of Saxony sorrowfully complained of being " in foreign service," military discipline was extremely good for the young men. Arndt, a man with a keen eye for such matters, soon noticed how remarkably the young men of these provinces began to differ from their fellow tribesmen in the petty states. Among the latter there still prevailed a good-natured and easy-going philistinism, whereas among the former there was seen that stiff " Prussian manner " which was in such ill-repute among the neighbours of Prussia, an abrupt and somewhat arrogant self-assertiveness, which might at times become extremely disagreeable, but which corresponded better with the character of a noble nation than the diffident timidity of the ancient days of undisturbed domestic life. It was through her army that Prussia regained that with which no great nation can permanently dispense, a national style, a proud sense of a secure footing in the world. And the pride of this nation in arms was German through and through ; it was rooted in the consciousness that at long last Germany's destiny was dependent on the black-and-white flag.

The idea of universal military service originated in a political idealism which reminds us of the energy characteristic of the idea of the state in classical days. The same free and broad conception of the state was manifested in the sphere of education. Among all those who had kept their minds alert during the experiences of recent years, the conviction had become firmly established that the reconciliation of the Prussian state with the new culture of the nation, a reconciliation at length realised, must be secured as a permanent acquirement. What was needed was to carry further the work begun with the foundation of the Berlin university, to realise in its completeness the Old Prussian idea of universal compulsory education, to inspire the lower and middle schools with the spirit of the new science, and thus to acquire for the state of Frederick a position in the intellectual life of the nation that would be worthy of Prussia's renown in arms. During the three-and-twenty years of Baron von Altenstein's administration, this task was for the most part solved. The state which, in the hard struggle for existence, had as a rule allowed science to starve, gradually came to utilise its resources more effectively on behalf of popular education than did any other great power of the day, so that the educational institutes of Prussia might be compared with the best in Europe. Thus a practical demonstration was afforded of the futility of that remarkable German prejudice, based upon the unwholesome experiences of domestic history, that the intellectual life can flourish only in the narrows of petty states. Altenstein, Franconian by birth, and inclined from the first towards the liberal views of the officials of Hardenberg's school, understood extremely well how to assimilate the ideas of leading minds, so that even Stein, who had so little in common with Franconian views, gladly employed the talented official to draft his legislative proposals, and was always sure of finding his own ideas faithfully reflected in the work of this skilful pen. When, after Stein's fall, Altenstein had himself become leader of the state, he had indeed suffered a lamentable shipwreck ; his fine intelligence was never deceived regarding the dangers of the situation, but his spirit was timid, so that he lacked the energy of resolution. When for hours in succession he presented his considerations and counter-considerations, without ever coming to an issue, his audience was astonished alike at the clear-sightedness and the barrenness of his mind. Subsequently, at the time of the second peace of Paris, he arranged for the restoration of the books and art treasures which had been stolen by the French, executing this task with expert knowledge, and thus by his distinguished culture he again attracted the attention of the king, who had long borne

a grudge against him for his pusillanimous proposal to cede
Silesia. Consequently, during the changes in the ministry in
1817, he at length entered the sphere best suited to his talents.
A friendly destiny enabled him, by the activities of his later
years, to erase from the minds of his contemporaries the adverse
impressions induced by his disastrous policy in 1809.

He was at home in all branches of science, and never
felt happier than when able to pursue his ideas in a life of
quiet contemplation. To him philosophy seemed the queen of the
sciences, but even in this department, his favourite, he showed
rather a gentle receptivity than the activity of independent
thought; passively he felt the tendencies of the time, and soon
turned from the doctrines of Fichte to the rising star of Hegel.
He took a lofty view of his new office, one to which "the
highest that man can do" was entrusted, and laid before himself
the task of transforming the Prussian state in Hegel's sense,
in order to make of it a realm of the intelligence. Year in
and year out he carried on a good-humoured contest with the
thrifty Ladenberg for the necessary financial resources; if the
board of general control remained inexorable, he availed himself
of his own private means, to provide pensions for the widows
of preachers and travelling allowances for young artists and men
of learning. The freedom of research also found in him a
faithful protector. When the zealots of reaction besieged him
with complaints and denunciations, he quietly endeavoured to
appease them by his favourite saying : " Many of the evils
of the time, time itself will cure."

Altenstein's secular sentiments gave him little understanding
for the newly awakening religious life. The demand for a free
Protestant congregational organisation seemed to him hardly
less dangerous to the state than was the inordinate ambition
of the ultramontanes. Had not Hegel shown so clearly that
the church, the realm of the imagination, must be definitely subordinated to the state, the realm of the intelligence ? Consequently
in ecclesiastical politics he held fast to the moderate territorial
system of the civil code. The supreme head of the state should
directly lead the Protestant church in accordance with Protestant
principles, and the Catholic church in accordance with Catholic
principles, exercising control also in matters relating to the
internal life of these churches, and should endeavour " to adapt "
both to the character of the state. Yet he manipulated his
system warily in the honourable intention of ensuring that the

church should herself feel contented under the benevolent tutelage of the state, and did in fact succeed, in circumstances of exceptional difficulty, in maintaining ecclesiastical peace almost completely undisturbed for two decades. In the council of state, Altenstein presided as representative of the chancellor, and the cautious man was often embarrassed by the violence of party struggles. If a decision was forced upon him, he always took the side of Hardenberg, for whom since Franconian days he had preserved an almost servile devotion. He needed a powerful prop, for Schuckmann could not forgive the subdivision of his department, and soon entered into a conspiracy with the privy-councillors Kamptz and Schultz to fight against the new minister of public worship and education, whom they regarded as inspired by demagogic sympathies.

When Altenstein had shaken down a little in his office, he wrote to the chancellor : " My whole department seems to have become indurated and shrunken, it must be reanimated and set in motion once more."[1] Certainly Schuckmann had troubled himself very little about the problems of higher education, which lay far outside his circle of vision. Among the councillors, however, the spirit of Humboldt had not yet died out. Working in the department of education was Humboldt's friend Süvern, from the Teutoburger Wald, a classically trained philologian, who had once been in regular correspondence with Schiller, and who had remained faithful to the idealism of the great days of Weimar. At the head of the department of public worship was Nicolovius, the pupil and fellow-countryman of Hamann, a strict and pious Protestant. He lived for the idea of the unity of Christendom, and thanks to his friendly intercourse with the circle of Princess Galitzin he had learned to recognise the moral energies of the Catholic church. For many years on intimate terms with Goethe, he followed the literary activities of the time with a happy receptivity. In Königsberg, under Stein's leadership, he had been active in the work of political reform. All the clergy throughout the country remembered the beautiful words in which, at the opening of the War of Liberation, he had exhorted the Christian pastors to the performance of their patriotic duties.

When he took up office, Altenstein found a difficult piece of work nearing its conclusion, the foundation of two universities. The Frederick university in Halle had been twice closed during

---

[1] Altenstein to Hardenberg, December 26, 1817.

the period of foreign dominion, and had been reopened subsequent to the entry of the Prussians. After the desolation of the years of war, it needed a thorough reorganisation, more especially since it was now to provide for the Thuringian regions a substitute for the long abolished university of Erfurt. There had also to be considered the difficult question whether, side by side with the home of Protestant pietism, there could continue to exist in adjacent Wittenberg the ancient enemy, the Frederick university of Electoral Saxony. Nothing lay further from the king's mind than the intention to bring about an atrophy of provincial culture to the advantage of Berlin. It was his hope that, wherever possible, in every province a flourishing university should come into existence, as the intellectual centre of the local life of the territory; least of all could the faithful Protestant desire, without urgent necessity, to interfere with the cradle of the Reformation. But in unhappy Wittenberg there was nothing left to destroy. For two hundred years the university, which had once been the most glorious of all the universities of Germany, had been no more than a caricature of its ancient greatness, the acropolis of a torpid faith in the letter, which fulminated its anathemas *ex cathedra Lutheri*, and where religion was stifled by theology. When at length, towards the close of the eighteenth century, a freer spirit found its way into the reformer's desecrated lecture-hall, it was too late to avert the fall of the university. The siege of 1813 effected its death-blow; the students were scattered, the library was broken up, the university buildings were burned, and the little group of professors, who had fled to Schmiedeberg, themselves proposed to the Saxon court that the university should be united with that of Leipzig.

Was Prussia now to erect a new structure upon these ruins, in a town destined to be a frontier fortress, so close to the three other Saxon universities which already, often enough, stood in one another's light? The living present demanded its rights from the glorious past. Halle, notwithstanding its severe losses, still possessed a tolerably complete teaching faculty, numerous institutions, and a rapidly increasing body of students. It was with a heavy heart that the king, while still in Vienna, in April, 1815, commanded that the two Frederick universities should amalgamate in Halle. Even the Wittenberg professors did not venture to offer any opposition. In the spring of 1817, seven of them joined the new university of Halle-Wittenberg; these seven were all that remained of the brilliant foundation of Frederick the Wise. But the population of the duchy of Saxony complained bitterly that in this jubilee year of the Reformation the university of the old town of Luther should be transferred to Halle. Angrily they declared that Prussia had now torn the heart out of the Saxon land. Only after some years, when the new double university flourished vigorously under the careful guidance of Altenstein, did people begin to see that the king had done what was necessary, and that the province had lost nothing in the way of intellectual energy through the destruction of two decrepit universities. It was only the town of Wittenberg which refused to be conciliated even by the seminary of preachers which was to serve to it as compensation; and as much as a generation later, in the year 1848, it demanded from the Berlin National Assembly the re-establishment of the ancient academic glories.

In taking over the western provinces, the king had promised them a university. Here parity of beliefs was to prevail, for the new institution was to replace at once the completely destroyed Protestant university of Duisburg and the abolished Catholic universities of Cologne, Bonn, and Treves, whilst Münster was to retain its Catholic academy as a theological seminary. A violent quarrel now broke out regarding the seat for the Rhenish university, a quarrel which for the first time brought to light the secret wishes of the clerical party in the west. For centuries Cologne had boasted the greatest university on the Rhine, and the city outshone all the other towns in the country to so great an extent, alike through its historic reputation and through the abundant artistic monuments it could display, that even unprejudiced persons like Niebuhr, Schenkendorff, and Wallraf, the Cologne collector, considered that here alone could the intellectual life of the Rhineland find its proper centre. Friedrich Schlegel, on the other hand, and his ultramontane friends, exploited the romantic charms of the venerable town as a welcome excuse for the achievement of profounder designs. From ancient days the holy city of Cologne had been a bulwark of the Roman Catholic party in the empire, and its population, a full third of whom were still beggars, had borne an evil reputation for dull-witted intolerance. Here the *obscuri viri* of the sixteenth century, and subsequently the papal legates and the Jesuits, had worked after their kind; here, in the shadow of the archiepiscopal chair, a Protestant faculty would be as little able to thrive as would free secular science ; here there was place only for a Rhenish provincial university which would leave undisturbed the profound slumber of the spirit characteristic of the ancient "priest's alley" of the empire ; a university here would have done nothing to further the reconciliation of the western march with the Protestant north. As an intelligent Rhinelander wrote to Hardenberg : " Those who so decisively favour Cologne, do not in intimate conversation conceal their belief that this university might constitute the fulcrum of an opposition. And of what an opposition ! That of the Catholic principle against the Protestant. The more intimately the government becomes acquainted with the regions of the Rhine, the less will it incline to establish the Rhenish university in Cologne."[1] Arndt, too, who had speedily made himself at home by the side of his German stream, and Süvern, who was now engaged in installing the new educational institutions on the Rhine, warned the chancellor against the sacerdotal spirit of the episcopal town, recommending instead, as the site of the university, the charming Bonn, with its beautiful ruined castles.

There in the rich bend of the valley, just before the entrance to the Rhenish wonderland, another Heidelberg might perhaps come into being, a city of free research and cheerful student life, a centre of attraction to the German youth from all quarters. Even the prosy Schuckmann was influenced by the aroma of youth when, on one occasion, from the top of the Coblenz gate, looking across the green river and the luxuriant plain, he contemplated the steep summits of the Siebenge-birge. " This is the place for us ! " he exclaimed in delight. In the little town, the university was mistress, and was sure of undisturbed freedom. During the last days of the electoral regime, there had for ten years existed an active university, representing the freer spirit of the Josephan enlightenment in opposition to the clergy of Cologne. These considerations proved decisive, and on May 26, 1818, on the same day as that on which the new customs-law was signed, the king appointed the town of Bonn as the site of the Rhenish university.

This was the fourth university which had been founded

[1] Memorial regarding the Rhenish university transmitted to the chancellor by Klewitz, February 20, 1817. Other documents concerning the foundation of the university of Bonn will be found in Heinrich von Sybel's *Kleine historische Schriften*, Vol II., p. 433.

or completely reconstituted during this reign, and of all the benefits for which the Rhineland has had to thank the crown of Prussia, it was perhaps the greatest. Here once more was manifested the old truth that the culture of a nation is ultimately determined by the condition of the highest educational institutions. In Rehfues, the talented Swabian, Bonn secured an active and experienced curator, one who was a good judge of men. Hüllmann, Sack, Nöggerath, Harless, and the two Welckers, joined the university at the outset, and Arndt was also summoned by a cordial letter from Hardenberg, " to supply for the youth of the place the keynote of their outlook on life." A few years later, when Niebuhr accepted a chair, the new university was already in a flourishing condition. So strange had been the revolutions of destiny in Germany ; the Prussian state, whose origins, were rooted in the north-eastern region of German colonisation, led back this ancient homeland of German civilisation into the ways of modern culture. In the university of Bonn, and in the other educational institutions which became connected with the university, Protestantism and Catholicism displayed renewed faculty for mutual toleration. It was here that the majority of the Rhinelanders first became acquainted with the works of our classical literature ; and so quickly did the highly gifted population make itself at home in this new world, that the neighbours who had been accustomed to deride the ignorance of the lands of the crosier were speedily silenced.

During the opening years, the Rhenish university involved a higher expenditure than all the other universities combined. Little money was left available for the secondary schools. But the indefatigable Johannes Schulze, whom Altenstein had summoned from the Rhine, always found some way out of the difficulty. His eyes sparkled with delight whenever a thoroughly efficient teacher was gained for Prussia, and anyone who witnessed his zeal on behalf of knowledge was ready to forgive the ardent man his blind preference for the new Hegelian doctrine. Many new gymnasia (higher schools) were founded, especially in Posen and on the Rhine. In the year 1825, 133 were already in existence, and while at first it was necessary to summon pedagogues from elsewhere, Prussian teachers soon gained high repute, and Prussia was able to supply her neighbours from her own superfluity. Nor did Altenstein neglect elementary education. Numerous training-schools for teachers were established, and these soon began to furnish masters whose knowledge was enormously in advance of that possessed by the retired non-commissioned officers of the Frederician age, but who still at times displayed the mischievous conceit of half-culture. Especially characterised by a crude rationalism were the teachers of East Prussia, those who gathered round Dinter, the robust and jovial Upper Saxon—a man with the rough manners of the people. On the Lower Rhine, Diesterweg worked just as vigorously as Dinter, but less one-sidedly. After a few years, Altenstein was able to show that in Prussia a larger proportion of children attended school than in any other great state, although the elementary schools still lagged far behind his desires. In the west, the lower grades of the clergy opposed a stubborn passive resistance, which was almost as difficult to overcome as was the stupidity of parents in the Polish regions of the realm. In the German provinces of the east, the poverty of the numerous little rural communes made improvement extremely difficult.

The abundant activities of the department of education did not satisfy the soaring idealism of Süvern. Like the majority of his contemporaries, the excellent man overestimated the value of that general programme of political reform which Hardenberg had initiated during the years of his chancellorship. He considered it necessary that the leading principles of the educational system should be explained to the nation, and in August, 1817, he arranged for the drafting of an elementary education law which was to serve as an example for the whole of Germany. He undertook this task with intense enthusiasm, inspired with political ideals in which the influence of Platonist thought was unmistakable. The state, he declared in his memorial, is itself a great educational institution, whose children receive a characteristic stamp in respect alike of intelligence and of sentiment ; the motive power of the Prussian state is derived, not from the dead forces of nature, but from the living energies of the human spirit, energies capable of eternal increase and development. Altenstein, too, as a methodic philosopher, demanded above all " a grand general plan," in order that Prussia might be enabled, " through a peculiar combination of earnestness and maturity, to compete for the leading place with the most highly-cultured peoples of Europe." The king did not fail to recognise that the educational problem, conceived in this lofty spirit, touched the very foundations of the entire life of the state, and consequently the committee which was appointed to draft the education law was composed of members of all the ministries—not excepting the ministry of war, which was represented by General Wolzogen.

After twenty months, on June 27, 1819, a carefully considered scheme was brought forward—the first of the numerous education laws at which the Prussian state has vainly laboured down to the present day. When the minister demanded opinions from the lord-lieutenants and the bishops, he was to learn that, in the disputed borderland between state and church, well-intentioned practice attains its goal more easily than does irrefragable doctrine. The general principles of the proposal aroused a storm of contradictory views. On the theoretical plane, no understanding could be secured regarding the participation of the church in the work of education, for the bishops regarded popular education as *causa ecclesiastica*, while the lord-lieutenants complained of the unjust favouring of the church. There was also the thorny question to be considered how the little villages of the east could bear the heavy burden of schooling. Consequently the proposal was shelved, and Altenstein declared to the monarch that, for the time being, he would " effect some kind of provisional organisation of the school regulations." This practical method was really, for the most part, that which best corresponded to the actual needs of the time. The minister dealt with the schools in accordance with the prescriptions of the civil code (T. II, Tit. 12) as institutions which concerned the state alone. He adhered firmly to the three essential ideas of the Frederician educational policy : universal compulsory schooling, parity of creeds, and apportionment of the cost of schooling among all heads of families in the school districts. Now, as before, religious instruction remained the first duty of the elementary school, and it was to be strictly accordant to the creed of the majority in the commune in which the school was situated ; the local clergyman belonged *ex officio* to the school committee, and was entitled to censure defects, but final decisions were retained in the hands of the state. The philosophical minister was not in favour of undenominational schools ; he knew how often they lead to disturbance of religious peace, how they impair the clearness and unity of instruction, and he permitted them only when a mixed commune was not in a position to establish a separate school for those of each creed. The teachers of the higher schools, too, as a rule belonged to one single confession; but Altenstein did not tie his hands in this respect; and in the Catholic gymnasia of Rhineland, he appointed numerous Protestant teachers, so long as a dearth of Catholic teachers continued. Jews were by law excluded from holding office as teachers in Christian educational institutions. Thus the sovereignty of the state was preserved without any interference with the good rights of the church. Friction with the ecclesiastical authorities was rare, for the consequences of the freedom of domicile did not become apparent except by degrees, and the number of mixed communes was still comparatively small.

In the case also of the internal life of the German Protestant church these years of peace were a period of rejuvenescence and renovation, the change being principally due to the initiative of the Prussian crown. Like his Russian friend, the king recognised in the victories of recent years the hand of the living God, to whose will he wished to submit; but whilst the fantastical sentiments of Czar Alexander had inspired him, under the influence of the devout mood resulting from the war, to conceive the pretentious and yet futile design of the Holy Alliance, the sober-minded Frederick William undertook an inconspicuous and yet far more fruitful work. He determined to pluck the ripe fruit of two centuries of peaceful thought, to realise the cherished idea of his pious ancestors, the union of the Protestant churches of Germany. To the new generation, the ancient and unfortunate antagonism betweeen the two sister churches of Protestantism, which long before had so greatly favoured the victories of the counter-reformation and the great desolation of the Thirty Years' War, now seemed strange and hardly conceivable. In bourgeois life, the contrast between the two churches was hardly noticed any longer; even in pastors' families, mixed marriages between members of the Lutheran church and of the Reformed church, which as late as the days of Thomasius had aroused such storms of theological indignation, now seemed matters of trifling importance. The rationalists considered that they had outgrown all disputes about dogma; the offshoots of pietism regarded eternal love as the great central feature of the Christian faith, taking the view formerly expressed by Goethe in his youth, in his touching *Letters of a Rural Pastor*. Even in the circles of the strictly orthodox Protestants, the question was often mooted whether

Protestantism could not return to that unbroken unity which had been its happiness and its pride in the early days of the Reformation. Recently, since the year 1802, Schleiermacher had become the scientific advocate of evangelical union. That which had still remained half concealed from the freest intelligences of the seventeenth century, from Calixt and Puffendorf, from Spener and Leibnitz, was a matter of current belief to the disciple of the new philosophy; he knew that all knowledge of the supersensual world is only an approximate cognition, and that consequently different essays at approximation can exist peacefully side by side as long as they do not abandon the fundamental principle of Protestant freedom. The Reformed church, the branch to which he himself belonged, sought the essence of Christianity in the moral configuration of life, and was therefore from the first more accessible to the idea of " the unity of the evangelical name " than was the sentimentally dogmatic profundity of Lutheranism.

In Prussia, the ecclesiastical policy of the reigning house had long been cautiously preparing for this reunion. Even after the conversion of John Sigismund, the Hohenzollerns continued to regard themselves as attached to the Augsburg confession, and did not abandon their position as rulers of the Lutheran national church; moreover, the *Corpus Evangelicorum* of the Reichstag remained common to both Protestant churches. By severe punishments, and by the example of their own tolerance, they repressed the invectives of the Lutheran pulpit orators; they endeavoured to expel from the dogmatic system of both churches everything which might be mutually offensive, and since they never adopted in their national church the harsh doctrine of predestination, they succeeded after a severe struggle in inducing the Lutherans to abandon the practice of exorcism. Frederick William I was already unwilling to recognise any longer a distinction between Lutherans and members of the Reformed church, saying bluntly that this distinction was "all humbug." By the civil law it was enjoined upon both churches that in case of need they should admit one another's members to the sacrament. In the reorganisation of the administration during the year 1808, the Lutheran consistories and the directorate of the Reformed church were alike abolished, and the ecclesiastical affairs of all three creeds were placed under the supervision of a special section of the district governments. Here economic considerations were decisive. But the king soon recognised that the governance of the church required independent organs, and consequently, by a cabinet order of April 30, 1815, he re-established the provincial consistories, but as common authorities for both Protestant churches. The synods, which were formed on January 2, 1817, also consisted of clergy of both denominations. Thus, step by step, an approximation was made to the formation of a single great Protestant national church.

Through the influence of his tutor Sack, Frederick William had from youth upwards cherished the design of evangelical union. Being inspired with very strong feelings regarding his own relationship to his subjects, he regarded it as a profound misfortune that, notwithstanding the Protestant belief he shared with them, he did not belong to the church of the majority of his people, that the church of Luther, whom he esteemed most highly among all the reformers, was not his own. This sentiment had become even more powerful since in Königsberg he had turned away from rationalism. The prophecy in the Gospels, " that they may all be one; as Thou, Father, art in Me, and I in Thee, that they also may be one in us," [1] moved him to the depths of his soul. " In my humble opinion," he frequently said in conversation with pastors, " the dispute about the eucharist is no more than fruitless theological hair-splitting, when compared with the straightforward biblical faith of primitive Christianity." He regarded the union of the Protestant churches as a return to the spirit of the Gospels, and was delighted to learn that his favourite bishop Borowski, the orthodox Lutheran, was just as favourable to this view as was his own tutor Sack, a member of the Reformed church. The pious old man, whose joyful exclamation, " events come to man in accordance with his faith," had so frequently consoled the prince in his hours of affliction, had been a friend of Kant, and stood near enough to modern science to recognise that the distinctions between the doctrines of the two Protestant churches no longer possessed their ancient significance for the Christian conscience of the present day. The king never doubted that it was his vocation to found the evangelical union. He took a high estimate of the duties imposed upon the sovereign power in respect of church government ; he knew that the Protestant church of Germany was largely indebted to its union with the state authority for many of the virtues by which

---

[1] John xvii. 21.

it was distinguished from the harsh sectarianism of the neighbour lands, that to this it owed its broad spirit of tolerance and its comparatively free attitude in secular matters ; he had little knowledge of, and little liking for, the independent congregational organisation of Calvinism.

Immediately after the first peace of Paris a theological commission was appointed to draw up a common liturgy for the Protestants of Prussia ; the pious prince desired to display his gratitude for the miracles of this war by no lesser service than the healing of the ancient fraternal schism. The tercentenary of the Reformation was now approaching. Marheineke's history of the Reformation, and numerous other works, recalled to the Protestant world, now in a mood of joyful excitement, the deeds of Martin Luther, which had been dear to both churches in their early days ; in Nassau, where the great traditions of the tolerant, heroic race of Orange still persisted, the congregations of both faiths joined to form a single national church. To the king of Prussia also, it now appeared that the decisive hour had come. He wished to issue a personal utterance to his people, to speak to them as the leading member of the church (for he knew that burghers, countrymen, and the army, still attached some importance to their king's word), and he contented himself with the simple, practical proposals which five years earlier Bishop Sack had advanced in his work on the reunion of the Protestant ecclesiastical parties. If in both the evangelical churches the eucharist could be celebrated in a similar way, in accordance with the ancient biblical ritual of all Protestants, and if the pastors of both creeds could be admitted without distinction to all pulpits, this outward union, which would impose no constraint of conscience, might, as the years passed, develop into a living community of spirits.

In the preliminary labours, the monarch was assisted by his court bishop, Eylert, a man possessed of one of those pliable prelate natures, which do not indeed hold up a light with the courage of the confessor, but which are sometimes, as was Thomas Cranmer, indispensable to the church in some work of mediation. At his home in County Mark, where the two confessions were intermingled in motley confusion, the clever courtier had found the soil well prepared for evangelical union, and the idea of a presbyterian organisation was more akin to his mind than to that of the king ; in matters of dogma he was never very far removed from the old rationalism. He now drew up an address from the monarch to the consistories, which was submitted for examination to the leading theologians of Berlin, and was then published, on September 27, 1817. In plain terms the king announced his resolve that at the centenary festival of the Reformation he would receive the eucharist in common with the Lutherans ; he considered that in this way he would be acting in accordance with the spirit of Protestantism, and in conformity with the intentions of his ancestors and of the reformers themselves. He was not contemplating a personal change from one church to the other, but both churches were to combine to constitute a reanimated evangelical Christian church ; reconciliation must proceed from the freedom of individual conviction, and must not result either from over-persuasion or from indifference. His example, he hoped, would exercise a beneficial influence upon all Protestant congregations throughout the land, and would be generally imitated in spirit and in fact. The impression produced by this heartfelt address was profound and enduring. The Brandenburger synod, assembled under the presidency of Schleiermacher, immediately declared its agreement, and the venerable Sack, who died during these agitated days, left the world with the happy presentiment that the seed sown during his life was now springing up.

On October 31st, throughout the country, the Protestant populace flocked to the churches, which had been decorated for the festival. In Berlin, after the joint communion, Schleiermacher grasped hands in front of the altar with Marheineke the Lutheran. In the garrison church at Potsdam, the king and his household, with a number of associates of both confessions, received the sacrament ; on the next day, in Wittenberg, he laid the foundation stone for the monument to the reformer. What a contrast between the two first centenary festivals of the Reformation ! Two hundred years earlier the storms of the great war were threatening ; a hundred years before, the church had been utterly lacking in intellectual energy ; now there was once more displayed a creative act, an act of reconciliation. The awakening of the historic sense had reacted for blessing upon ecclesiastical life. To his nation, Luther no longer appeared, as in the days of the old rationalism, merely the antagonist of Rome ; the new generation began gratefully to recognise the constructive activities of the Reformation. Most of the writings published in honour of the festival were unmistakably characterised by a pious sentiment. The Catholic populace exhibited little ill-will towards the peaceful ceremonial, although dissensions were not altogether lacking, and the polemic writing of the Catholic priest Van Ess evoked a number of angry rejoinders. The thought of union was so inevitable an outcome of the history of German Protestantism, that Frederick William's example was speedily followed by almost all the congregations throughout Prussia and was soon voluntarily imitated by other German states as well. In August, 1818, a formal announcement was made in the collegiate church at Kaiserslautern that, by an agreement on the part of the congregations in the Bavarian Palatinate, evangelical union had been established; but here, certainly, religious indifference played some part in securing this success; many of the enlightened Palatiners merely asked themselves whether the union would increase the church taxes, and at once favoured the project when their minds had been set at rest about this matter.[1] Baden and some of the Hessian provinces followed suit—in a word, all the German territories in which both the Lutheran and the evangelical church had a large following.

The subsequent progress of this great undertaking did not correspond to its auspicious beginnings. The king, in his honourable good-feeling, had scorned to effect a specious adjustment of the quarrel between the creeds, by an artificial formula of unity; the union was founded upon the hope that the spirit of Christian love would look beyond the dogmas which had kept the churches asunder, and would no longer regard them as an obstacle to religious community. But in nearly all places in which the Lutherans were still found almost unmixed, where the name of *die reformierten Sakermenter* was still used as a term of abuse, and where no practical need was felt for the union, this expectation proved illusory; in Saxony, for instance, in Mecklenburg, and in Holstein. To the strict Lutherans, the king's pious undertaking seemed a revolt of reason against revelation; for the religious sentiment, like the artistic, demands always the most definite configuration of its ideals, and is inclined to dread that the truth of salvation will itself be lost if no more than a letter of the writ be regarded as unessential. In the ninety-five new theses that Claus Harms of Holstein despatched to the Reformation festival, this view was put forward with passionate violence. The zealot's

[1] My authority for this statement is afforded by the notes of the Bavarian ecclesiastical councillor von Schmitt.

mind was filled with the image of Luther when, at the Marburg colloquy, he had written on the table in large letters the text, " this is My body," and when to all objections he had answered obstinately, " I cannot depart from the written word." According to Harms, " If at that time Christ's body and blood were contained in the bread and wine, this is still so to-day." He triumphantly recommended the new theses to the Saxon court preacher Ammon, as a bitter medicine for the weak-in-faith of the time. Ammon, the Dresden rationalist, who, guided by the wisdom of this world, merely desired to promote the interests of the great Lutheran national church, was indeed speedily demolished by a vigorous rejoinder from Schleiermacher ; but the profound religious earnestness of Harms, the preacher of Kiel, was not to be conquered by logical superiority. In Wittenberg, too, Superintendent Heubner refused to join the evangelical union, and soon, in this land of Luther, there became manifest a tough passive resistance which, since it sprang from the mysterious depths of the emotional life, ought to have been handled with extreme discretion. Such gentle consideration was not to be expected from the ecclesiastical government of Prussia. It is true that the king would never exercise any pressure upon con- science ; but the more firmly he was convinced of the upright- ness of his own faith, the less was he able to understand the honourable good-feeling of those on the other side. He appears to have said to himself that it was his own personal interven- tion which had alone rendered the union possible, and was now painfully surprised to find that a counter-agitation began, even in the reformed congregations of the Lower Rhine, in the ancient home of the German synodal organisation. Here the union was welcome, but the congregations would not recognise the supreme episcopal authority of the king—to the horror of the officials, who one and all still held firmly to the doctrines of the territorial system. Even the well-meaning Solms-Laubach wrote warningly : " These synodists of Jülich-Cleves-Berg are just as dangerous as the ultramontanes. Both parties are equally attacking the king's prerogative."[1] The unanticipated strength of this twofold opposition was first plainly manifested when the king undertook to provide his national church with a common liturgy. The young union was still to experience

---

[1] Solms-Laubach, Report upon the state of affairs in Jülich-Cleves-Berg, August, 1819.

difficult years, full of fierce struggles and deplorable aberrations, before it could finally prove what its founder had desired it to be, a work of peace.

§ 3. THE PROVINCES.

Thus fruitful activity prevailed in almost all domains of the national life. The far-sighted creative work of the officialdom in Prussia and elsewhere in Germany was largely, perhaps mainly, responsible for the notable increase in the general well-being and for the great advances in culture during this long period of peace, and nothing manifests more plainly the childish political immaturity of the opposition in those days than the reproach of barrenness which the liberal press was accustomed to level against Hardenberg. While the council of state was dealing with the question of fiscal reform, there began in the provinces, always under the immediate supervision of the chancellor, the work of the new administration, a work of reconstruction which was at once more difficult and more varied than had been the tasks which King Frederick had had to undertake after the Seven Years' War.

Nowhere had the dutiful sense of the officialdom to endure such severe tests as in the province of Posen. As long as hopes of gaining Warsaw were entertained, Hardenberg had been willing to allow a certain amount of national independence to the Polish provinces. But when Prussia acquired no more than the narrow territorial area extending to the Prosna, a region in which Germans already numbered nearly two-fifths of the population, more cautious counsels prevailed. Since the treaties of Vienna merely imposed upon the crown in general terms the obligation to deal tenderly with Polish nationality, the territories severed from Warsaw were incorporated in the Prussian state in exactly the same way as were the other acquisitions, and had to render the same oath of allegiance. This new region was not regarded as indivisible. The areas round Thorn were reunited with their old home, the Ordensland ; whilst out of the main constituents of the new territory there was formed, with the addition of certain areas from West Prussia, a new province, which received the name of the grand-duchy of Posen—a name just as unmeaning from the outlook of constitutional law as were the new titles of the grand-duchy of the Lower Rhine and of the duchy of Saxony. Whilst still in

Vienna, the king issued a proclamation to the inhabitants of Posen wherein it was declared : " You have retained a fatherland, and this affords proof of my regard for your devotion. You are being incorporated in my monarchy without having to renounce your nationality." But, as was expressly declared by the chancellor in the preliminary considerations, these words in no way implied a recognition that the province occupied a separate position. In order to do honour to the conquered nation, the king assigned to the grand-duchy as sole distinction from the other provinces, a separate coat of arms, the white eagle of Poland on an inescutcheon charged upon the Prussian eagle, and gave them a statthalter of the blood of the Jagellons, Prince Anton Radziwill. But, just as in the other provinces, the administration was vested exclusively in the lord-lieutenant. The statthalter was merely entitled to demand information regarding the course of affairs, to ascertain the wishes of the inhabitants, and to keep them informed regarding the intentions of the monarch. On August 3, 1815, on the occasion of taking the oath of allegiance, Prince Radziwill expressly warned his countrymen not to entertain dangerous illusions, promising them a full share in the civic liberties which Prussia guaranteed to all her subjects, including respect for their " peculiarities " in language, manners, and customs; but promising them no separate rights whatever.

The new province comprised the nuclear region of the ancient Great Poland. Here, in the celebrated town of Gnesen, the town of the seven hills, the white eagle had once made its eyrie; here were to be found some of the most sacred relics of Polish history, the tomb of Adalbert in Gnesen, and the pilgrimage church of Tremessen ; and the nobility of Great Poland had always been celebrated for ardency of national pride. Among all the vassals of France, the Poles had adhered longest to the side of Napoleon, even down to the time of the battle of Montmartre. During the hundred days, the Germans in the province had flocked to the colours with shouts of joy, but the Polish nobles immediately entered into secret communication with the Tuileries, and the authorities found it necessary to remind them that treason was legally punishable with death.[1] After the Imperator's second fall, discontented spirits turned their hopes towards the neighbouring kingdom of Poland and its new constitution ; the secret envoys of the Warsaw patriots

[1] Zerboni's Report to the chancellor, June 21, 1815.

fanned the flames of national propaganda all the more zealously because they recognised the superiority of the Prussian administration, and seriously feared that the province might become estranged from the motherland through a general increase in prosperity. Again and again for years the rumour recurred that the king was thinking of voluntarily restoring the province to Poland; again and again a propitious aureole shone round the head of the Mother of Poland, the Blessed Virgin in the Carmelite Church of Posen. After the great defection of 1806, the loyalty of the Polish officials seemed everywhere open to suspicion, and Zerboni advised the chancellor in all seriousness that he should demand from the officials a written undertaking in virtue of which they should declare themselves to be traitors to their nation in the event of their breaking their official oath. Hardenberg, however, rejected the proposal, on the ground that men without conscience would not be bound by the redoubled pledge.

After a brief period, the statthalter felt extremely unhappy in his brilliant position, which was, indeed, one carrying little influence. A handsome man, talented, magnanimous, and chivalrous, he combined with the easy social charm characteristic of the Polish nobles, the solidity of German culture; his hospitable house was almost the only one belonging to the high nobility in Berlin where the world of fashion assembled side by side with artists and professors; musicians admired his playing and his romantic compositions. For the past two hundred years the Radziwills had been frequently connected with the Hohenzollerns by marriage; Prince Anton had himself espoused the amiable princess Louise of Prussia, and was in close personal association with the king. But he remained a Pole, and innocently attributed to his compatriots the loyalty with which his own mind was filled. "I am prepared to assure you," he wrote to Hardenberg after taking the oath of allegiance, "that this province will vie in affection with those which have for centuries been subjected to his majesty's rule." In his sermon on this occasion, Canon Kawiecki had spoken in moving terms of the Jagellon blood in the veins of the Hohenzollern, and had ardently assured the nobles: "Bitter experiences have matured our views!" The prince hoped to win over the province for Prussia by "a system of nationality," by an amiable compliance with all the desires of the Poles; but he soon began to waver in his designs when Gneisenau warned him, and when he himself gradually came to recognise, that his own countrymen were regarding him with extreme mistrust and reserve.[1] Nor did Lord-lieutenant Zerboni di Sposetti ever attain to a consistent attitude towards the Poles. In youth a brilliant and excitable hot-head, he had, in common with Hans von Held and Knesebeck, been an enthusiast for the ideals of the Revolution ; he was still an enlightened liberal, devoted to the chancellor, and regarded it as his duty to atone by a considerate mildness for that partition of Poland which by the liberal world had been branded as an iniquity. Since he owned estates in Russian Poland, he was also compelled for personal reasons to be considerate in his actions. At times, indeed, like the statthalter, he was uneasy as to the consequences of his system, for years before, in the administration of Southern Prussia, he had become intimately acquainted with the Polish character.

Unprejudiced persons could have no doubt about the *arrières pensées* of the Polish nobility. The leaders declared, with unexampled arrogance, in the very face of the government, that their country must form a state within the state until its ultimate reunion with Warsaw could be effected. Even one of the most moderate among them, General von Kosinski, who now wore a Prussian uniform and was an intimate associate of the statthalter, demanded from his princely friend the consti-tution of a purely " national " army, officered exclusively by Poles, because the Germans were, after all, regarded by the Poles as nothing more than agents of the secret police. Another moderate, Morawski, sent the chancellor a lengthy memorial concerning the Polish nation. He opened with the assurance : " One who compares the Poles of to-day with those of 1806 is an entire century out of his reckoning." To confirm this claim, he went on to say that Polish civilisation was older than German, although action had of late predominated over speech, and the fertility of Polish literature had somewhat diminished. He also reproached the throne of Prussia for " its system of Germanisation and denationalisation," complaining, in especial, that Polish history was no longer taught in the schools as a special subject. " Since this change was effected, the mothers have begun to teach their infants the national history." In conclusion, he demanded guarantees for the maintenance of Polish nationality, insisting, above all, upon

[1] Radziwill to Hardenberg, August 9, 1815 ; Royer to Gneisenau, May 10, 1817.

the following four points : a statthalter of the royal house or of Polish blood ; a provincial diet, which should defend the rights of the Poles by a standing committee, and which should appoint a committee to carry on public instruction ; all offices, including those in the churches and in the schools, should be filled exclusively by persons of Polish birth, upon the recommendation of the provincial diet ; finally, two Polish councillors, one a civil official and one a Catholic priest, should advise the king, the council of state, and the chancellor regarding Polish affairs. A third Polish nobleman handed to Major von Royer, an intimate friend of the statthalter, a memorial in which it was bluntly declared that this region would not become a Prussian province until it had been formally separated from Poland ; until then it must be dealt with as Polish territory. Consequently no oath must be demanded from the Poles, for " it would be a second crime to keep this criminal oath " ; nor should any of them be decorated in any way, for those who had received decorations had always especially distinguished themselves in the struggle against the foreign dominion.[1]

Insolent words were soon followed by treasonable deeds. In the year 1818, General Dombrowski conceived the design of a secret Polish brotherhood, which came into existence a year later, under the name of the National Freemasons. The authorities looked on inertly at these illegal intrigues, and did not take action until the conspirators, emerging from the obscurity of their lodges, endeavoured to constitute troops of volunteers from among the peasants, giving these bodies the unambiguous name of *Kosiniery* (scythemen).

The design to destroy Germanism, openly manifested in these memorials of the Polish nobility, certainly found no support from the statthalter, but the administration failed to take direct action on behalf of German civilisation. The government fulfilled with meticulous conscientiousness all the promises that had been made to the Poles. After the generous Prussian manner, the ancient memorials and signs of sovereignty were left undisturbed throughout the country ; even to-day in the Ring in Posen, the great Polish coat-of-arms with the heart-shaped escutcheon of the Poniatowskis is displayed immediately above the sentry-box of the Prussian Guard. The Polish

---

[1] Jozéf von Morawski, Memorial concerning the Polish nation, December 29, 1817. Mémoire sur les affaires polonaises, sent by Royer to Gneisenau, April 9, 1817.

officers were pensioned, or enrolled in the Prussian army ; a great number even of the Warsaw officials were taken into Prussian service, although many of them could not write, and most of them had no German, while almost all of them were untrustworthy. The circle government was placed in the hands of chosen administrators, most of whom belonged to the Polish nobility ; but to the great joy of the peasants, the manorial police was not, for the present, reconstituted. The official language of the authorities was German, but in all negotiations with and announcements to the public the tongue was used which was most comprehensible to those concerned ; consequently in the elementary schools of the Polish districts education was carried on exclusively in the Polish language.

Yet even under this administration, long-suffering to the point of weakness, Germanisation advanced unceasingly. As soon as civil order had been re-established, the sluices of the stream of German immigration were spontaneously opened, that immigration which already in the middle ages had fertilised this neglected land. The superiority of German industry and German capital were manifested everywhere, especially in agriculture. At the time of the occupation, the *morgen* of average land was sold at one and a half thalers—about the price attained for areas of primeval forest in the far west of North America. What a change occurred in these barbaric conditions when the government now put into application the agrarian law of the year 1811. Vainly did the nobility, on receipt of " the alarming intelligence of this confiscation of property," send in an address of complaint to the king, displaying in naive words the true character of the renowned Sarmatian junker freedom. " In the unbridled excesses of the sinister and rough countryfolk," so ran the wording of this document, " there will develop the germs of practical Jacobinism." [1] The alleviation of the burdens on the peasantry, though effected very slowly, was really advantageous even to the nobles, who were now forced to abandon their rude natural economy in favour of a monetary economy, and who thereby in the year 1817 secured valuable assistance through the foundation of the new agricultural credit institute.

In this province of the monarchy, richer in towns than any other, there was hardly a trace of a vigorous bourgeoisie. Even

---

[1] Address of the nobles of the grand-duchy of Posen to the king, handed to Minister von Klewitz, September, 1817.

the town of Posen was a desolate place of unplastered houses, a confusion of low shingle-roofed cottages, such as to-day still adorn the suburb of Wallischei, interspersed with ruined churches and dirty palaces. But here also a change began as from year to year the number of German citizens increased and as they found support for their national spirit in the numerous recently founded educational institutions. After a terrible conflagration, the Polish town of Gnesen was rebuilt, for the most part at the cost of the state, and the royal restorer was honoured in a commemorative medal ; still more rapidly did the German town of Bromberg come into existence when trade upon the Netze canal was once more freed. Whereas in relation to other neighbour peoples the Germans were too apt to display a weakly impressionability; here, in the land of the Slavs, they all assumed a proud position as rulers and teachers, as bearers of a superior civilisation ; no German learned Polish unless forced to do so, for what had this miserable literature to offer him ? Moreover, the blindly defiant spirit of the Poles proved a force making for Germanisation. The statthalter had promised that the native-born, when equally competent, should have the first claim to offices in the province. Instead of availing themselves of this rash concession, and instead of studying in Breslau, the provincial university of the new province, in order to prepare themselves for state service, the Polish youths wasted their energies in the evil arts of secret societies. The consequence was that the rising generation of officials consisted almost exclusively of Germans, whilst the incapable Warsaw officials were gradually superseded.

The mass of the people took little part in the intrigues of the nobles. The Polish peasant was well aware that never since there had been a Poland had his class fallen upon happier days ; he did not trust the noble, he had not forgotten the cruel stewards of the old days and the leathern scourge with its knots weighted with lead. The only thing that estranged the good-hearted and guileless common people from the Prussian officials was religious hatred. For from the first the clergy encountered the heretical government with tacit hostility ; the Catholic priests could not forgive the authorities for subjecting the monasteries to the strict prescriptions of the civil code, for instituting everywhere elementary schools, which had hitherto been almost unknown in Catholic villages, and for providing for the education of young priests by new educational institu-

tions. It was owing to the suggestions of the priests that
the peasants felt no gratitude for the benefits of Prussian rule,
and soon in the minds of the common people the terms
" Catholic " and " Polish," " Protestant" and " German," seemed
equivalent. The fires of revolt continued to smoulder beneath
the ashes, but it was not until after repeated acts of treason
on the part of the Poles that the throne at length determined
to adopt the only policy which could secure this threatened
frontierland for the state, determined upon the undisguised
favouring of German civilisation.

In Prussia the situation of affairs was simpler. It was
true that in West Prussia there also existed a nobles' party,
which looked across the border yearningly at the *Restitutor
Poloniæ*. In the regained domains of Michelau and Culmerland
the Polish nobles behaved in a manner so open to suspicion that,
shortly before the oath of allegiance was imposed in Thorn,
President Hippel was moved to write to the chancellor :
" Unfortunately I cannot regard any one of them as worthy
of trust, unless perchance a few strayed sheep may be won
over by special favours." [1] Danzig, too, terribly visited by
the calamities of the war, long remained disaffected towards
the state which had restored peace and well-being. To how
great an extent had this most beautiful of our ancient towns
lost touch, almost as much as Holland, with the community
of the nation to which it belonged. For Danzig, as for Holland,
the Thirty Years' War, which for us had been a period of
profoundest ruin, had been an epoch of blossoming. Nowhere
else on German soil had the spirit of the imperial towns flourished
so defiantly, in continuous conflict with the Polish nobility ; at
the Artushof, and in the high-gabled houses of the patricians,
there were flaunted everywhere the pictures of the republican
heroes, Maccabeus, Camillus, and Scipio. Although few of the
old warrior-patrician families of the northern Venice had survived
the storms of the Napoleonic wars, the alert commercial town
adapted itself with difficulty to the forms of the modern official
state, and even after a generation the Danzigers of the old
stock were unwilling to regard themselves as Prussians. The
greater part of the population of the province, on the other
hand, had for forty years past belonged to the German state,

---

[1] Hippel, Report to the chancellor, July 19, 1915.

and in a difficult time had manifested exemplary loyalty—the Polish country-people not excepted. Consequently in East Prussia, Germans, Lithuanians, and Masurians all thought with equal pride of the diet of Königsberg and of their valiant *Heurichs.*

The two provinces had suffered unspeakable afflictions. The king approved the provision of considerable financial help to the landlords for the re-establishment of their properties ; East Prussia alone received 3,700,000 thalers. The lord-lieutenants were to treat with the provincial diets concerning the apportionment of the money. But what did these sums amount to, seeing that the entire loss of the two provinces since 1806, in damages due to the war and in disbursements for military purposes, was estimated by the diets at 152,000,000 thalers ? Many mistakes were made in the allotment of the funds, especially in West Prussia, where Schön, after his despotic manner, inconsiderately followed his own fancies. The great landlords became divided into two camps : some of them blamed the advanced views of the lord-lieutenant, considering that he was deliberately destroying the old families from hatred of the nobility ; whilst others hailed him no less passionately as the saviour of the nobles, and gave unreserved support to " the great Old Prussian statesman." Since the impoverished state was quite unable to do equal justice to all provinces alike, it was a necessary canon of self-preservation to furnish assistance chiefly to the still insecure new domains, and to leave the old and loyal regions to suffer privation. The result was that, in the case of the disaffected Danzigers, a great portion of the war debt was taken over by the state, whilst Königsberg, which was almost overwhelmed by the burden of its debt, vainly appealed for assistance. In East Prussia, since the beginning of the century, von Auerswald had been at the head of the administration ; this was a warm friend of the peasants, who had abolished serfdom on his own estates before the passing of the law of 1807. He frankly expressed the opinion that the great landlords did not possess the confidence of the nation, and that they were less cultured than the middle classes. During the next few years a settlement between the landlords and the peasants was effected under his leadership. In West Prussia, on the other hand, Schön devoted himself chiefly to furthering educational progress and to the construction of roads, for he regarded these as the two most effective means for promoting Germanisation. During his administration, 400 elementary schools were founded by the communes and by the landlords. He knew how to keep the Polish nobles in order. In his relations with the clergy, he applied with rigidity, and at times with severity, the principles of the civil code, and maintained public order with all the more success because the prince-bishop of Hohenzollern, who is remembered even to-day by the strictly religious inhabitants of Ermeland under the name of the " good prince," was himself ill-disposed towards the nationalist dreams of the Polish priests. Despite the caution of the administration, here in the eastern march the wounds left by the war cicatrised very slowly ; the remote stretches of coast, separated from their hinterland, recovered health with difficulty. In Lithuania, when the German landlord looked down from the heights above the Niemen upon the few miserable rafts of the Polish *Szimken* floating upon the mighty river, he complained that by the officials in Berlin this magnificent country was regarded as a mere source of remounts for the cavalry regiments. The Old Prussians were inspired with bitter feelings towards the privileged westerly provinces, and asked whether they themselves were to be once more, as they had been in the days of King Frederick, the step-children of the Prussian crown.

In Pomerania, Sack, the new lord-lieutenant, soon gained the confidence of the population yet more completely than he had done on the Rhine. Even the discontented New Hither Pomeranians gradually became reconciled with the German state. When the Prussians entered Greifswald, Kosegarten, the local poet, sang plaintively, "aforetime, under the three crowns, we could live at our ease "; and unquestionably the strict justice of monarchical rule had hitherto been quite unknown in this granary of the unhappy Swedish realm, this region which was able to pay no more than 60,296 gold thalers in direct taxes. Whilst in Prussian Pomerania the peasants had been protected by the strong hand of the monarchy, here, the crown, the nobility, the university, and the patriciate of the rich towns, had bought up almost all the lands of the peasants, and had instituted, as in the neighbouring Mecklenburg, a comfortable oligarchical regime. When, in the peace of Westphalia, the mouths of the Weser, the Elbe, and the Oder, were handed over to the throne of Sweden, the Swedish government made Pomerania the principal seat of government for all the German provinces of Sweden. Now, a century and a half later, the fat sinecures of this regime, established for a million subjects as a welcome means of providing for the sons of the aristocracy, persisted unchanged when no more than 100,000 Germans between the Peene and the Baltic were under Swedish rule. The nobles looked down contemptuously upon those of Prussia, for the arms of the Swedish nobles hung in the Ritterhaus in Stockholm, side by side with the escutcheons of the Torstensons and the Oxenstiernas. The university of Greifswald lived cosily upon the revenues of its wide possessions, disturbed only every twenty years or so by a royal visitation ; of all the academical institutions of the wealthiest German university, one only was widely celebrated, the *manège*. The proud Stralsund had faithfully preserved the ancient Hanseatic liberties, in conjunction with the glories of its churches, council-houses, and beguinages, and exercised unrestricted rule over a domain comprising more than one hundred townships. The Prussian authorities approached this vigorously distinctive local life with caution. Notwithstanding the protests of the nobility, most of the old offices were abolished, only the high court of Greifswald remaining as a modest court of appeal ; Stralsund and the other great towns retained their ancient constitutions, but were compelled, after repeated protests, to enter the Prussian circle-organisation. After two years' delay, the authorities at length ventured to introduce the new customs-law. The amalgamation was effected steadily and securely. The majority of the tenant farmers and serfs, especially those on Rügen, had from the first been free from the mistrust felt by the privileged classes, and rejoiced to find in the new authorities a certain amount of protection against the arbitrary exactions of the landlords.[1]

Prussian Pomerania had suffered far more severely from the war than had Swedish Pomerania. The ruins of the harbours of Leba, Stolpmünde, Rügenwalde, and Colberg, still recalled the prosperous days of the peace of Basle. Stettin, which at that time rivalled Hamburg, had now to reconquer its place in the world-market ; but many of the rich old firms were no longer in existence, the harbour of Swinemünde had but recently been reconstructed, and moreover the Sound-dues paralysed the

[1] Memorial concerning the reorganisation of New Hither Pomerania, by Carl Schneider of Bergen, December 3, 1815. Petition of the farmer Arndt and the burgomaster Lüders, representatives of the estate of peasants, to the king, July 20, 1816. Petition from the burgomaster and council of Stralsund to the chancellor, September 12, 1816.

growth of the Pomeranian seaports. In the country districts the immaturity of civilisation and the patriarchal conditions of life aroused the astonishment of the lord-lieutenant. In the circle of Neu-Stettin, there were only 710 inhabitants to the square mile [German], whereas the population in the governmental district of Düsseldorf was 8,537 to the square mile ; and nevertheless the " good Pomeranian still continues to seek his wealth in the ownership of land." Sack importuned the chancellor to grant permission for the settlement of vigorous peasant immigrants, who could set the good Pomeranians an example in the practice of intensive culture, and could make them understand the blessings of the new economic freedom.[1] But where were the resources for colonisation on the Frederician scale ? The province recovered from the sorrows of the years of war with almost as much difficulty as did the other Baltic lands, the only difference being that the quiet Pomeranians bore the troubles of this hard and joyless time with more equanimity than did the passionate Prussians.

Merckel, the lord-lieutenant of Silesia, had already, during the war, become dear to his fellow-countrymen as civil governor. They did not forget that formerly, on a momentous occasion, by his firm confidence in their willingness to make sacrifices, he had prevented the continuation of the retreat ; that subsequently when, during the period of the truce, the monarchs had counselled the evacuation of the exhausted territory, he had pledged his word that Silesia would support the allied armies for an entire year. How happily, after this, had Gneisenau's work, the formation and training of the Silesian Landwehr, been assisted by the powerful aid of the civil governor. The son of a respected merchant of Breslau, at home from childhood upwards in all strata of complex Silesian society, to the people of his native province Merckel seemed the natural leader. The active, serious, and precise manner in which he conducted business, inspired confidence in all ; and anyone who came to see him on pressing affairs, even at a late hour in the night, would find the vigorous little man, who seemed to get on without sleep, seated at his writing-table. From the first he was one of the most zealous supporters of Hardenberg's reforms, was a disciple of the Kantian philosophy,

[1] Sack, brief Report on the administration of Pomerania, Schlawe, July 28, 1818.

richly cultured, almost learned, and profoundly convinced of
the blessings of free investigation. As a strict rationalist, he
was not free from bureaucratic mistrust of the religious life, and
was ever watchful to maintain the sovereignty of the state.
At court he was regarded as, next to Schön, the most revolu-
tionary-minded of the lord-lieutenants,[1] although he despised
the waspish criticism of the East Prussians, and, in truth,
never advanced far beyond the ideas of enlightened absolutism.

At a momentous time, the Silesians had manifested a tenacious loyalty; even the neglected Poles of Upper Silesia displayed a deep devotion to the crown, although they were but
little influenced by the general enthusiasm for the War of Liberation, and they remained completely unaffected by the Polish
nationalist propaganda. Here King Frederick had been truly
loved; few looked back with regret to the " pre-Prussian days ";
even the nobility had ceased to think of their ancient feudal
suzerainty. None the less there still existed in this region
a stubborn particularism, which was zealously fostered in Breslau
by the "Silesian Society for Patriotic Culture." The province
delighted to speak of itself as the jewel in Prussia's crown;
down to the year 1808 it was always governed by its own
provincial minister, independent of the old general directory,
and was greatly mortified that it was now to be placed on
the same footing with all the other provinces. The ancient
capital, whose fortifications had been dismantled, began
to surround the picturesque confusion of its gloomy alleys
with a circle of charming avenues, and constituted the vigorous
centre of a rich and distinctively local life. Breslau was the
head and heart of the province, far more characteristically than
were any of the other provincial capitals, Königsberg not excepted.
Here was the flourishing university, and here the palace of
the one prince-bishop of the monarchy; here was to be seen
the filth of the Jewish quarter side by side with the palaces
of the jovial nobility; here German and Polish nationality,
Protestant and Catholic culture, the officialdom and the bourgeoisie, manufacturing industry and agriculture, jostled one
another indifferently. Rarely as yet did the Silesian look
beyond this motley activity; seldom did he leave his beloved
homeland, where they were all so snugly interconnected by
blood and by marriage. In the army, as in official circles,
the proud Catholic nobility, which as late as the year 1811

[1] Hardenberg's Memoranda, Christmas, 1819.

had continued to establish its younger sons in the benefices of the wealthy cathedral city, was but little represented; the Silesian nobles held aloof from the soldier races of the Pomeranian and Brandenburg knighthoods, and found their associates rather in Vienna than in Berlin. In Silesia, the towns' ordinance, industrial freedom, and the new agrarian laws, had hitherto encountered vigorous resistance, and Merckel had need of all his sagacity and knowledge of the country to carry through the introduction of these reforms step by step, with careful regard for the peculiar circumstances.

How lamentable, now, was the economic condition of the country, which had formerly, after the entry of the Prussians, exhibited so marvellous a progress. What had become of the good fortune of those days when John Quincy Adams had travelled through Silesia to study the marvels of the Frederician administration, when princes and counts led a luxurious life in summer-time in the spas of Warmbrunn and Salzbrunn, when a rich manufacturer dwelt in almost every country-house in the Waldenburger Tal, and when, on the rough Landeshut ridge, among " the Americans," the rich merchants trading with America and Spain, the wine of Hungary flowed in streams? The export trade in linen did not regain its former prosperity; in the weavers' villages of the mountains there prevailed a condition of poverty which at length seemed unbearable even to the cheerful content of this easy-going people; moreover, trade with Poland, upon which Breslau so largely depended for its subsistence, had been greatly damaged by the new Russian customs-barriers. Nevertheless, the manufacture of cotton was increasing, and the wool-market had grown in importance since Thaer had introduced his pedigree sheep into Panten. In the year 1814, the *Fürstentums-Landschaften* which had been founded by Frederick II resumed the payment of interest, and saved the credit of the great landlords, so far as this was possible in view of the depreciation of their properties. The Königshütte smelting works in Silesia soon afterwards resumed operations on a large scale, and gradually in this region, notwithstanding the threatening vicinity of the customs boundaries of Austria and Russia, there came into existence a noble array of new mines and smelting works. But all this was effected with extreme slowness. The Silesian people did not possess the bold and enterprising spirit of aspiring times; here life was passed in deliberate work and quiet renunciation.

It was due, above all, to the personal activities of the lord-lieutenants that the new forms of provincial administration struck root so speedily. Hardenberg had been fortunate in his choice, appointing, almost without exception, to these difficult posts, men of established reputation, and yet men who were still comparatively young. The least adequate, perhaps, of the lord-lieutenants was Heydebreck in Brandenburg. He had gained his experience as an able official of the old school in the collegial deliberations of the war-chambers and domain-chambers, and at first was unwilling to accept " the so-called office of lord-lieutenant," until the chancellor had made him recognise how important and honourable was this office.[1] But he had as subordinate one of the most capable of officials, von Bassewitz, governor of the Potsdam district, a man of marvellous practical knowledge, who carried in his head a map of every parish in Electoral Mark, who knew all about every thaler of the war contributions, and who trained an entire school of efficient administrative officials, so that the Potsdam government maintained the brilliant repute which it had formerly acquired under Sack's regime. Bassewitz held with imperturbable firmness to the principles of the new legislation, and yet understood how to deal with everyone in so circumspect and friendly a spirit that even the feudal nobles were not seriously hostile to the reformer.

In the country-side of this part of the world, the nobility was still as powerful as in Pomerania, although the noble landowners of Electoral Mark possessed property valued at no more than 27,000,000 thalers, and were burdened with mortgages amounting to 21,000,000, whereas the peasantry already possessed land valued at 31,000,000 thalers, which was burdened with debt to the amount of no more than 6,500,000. The prestige of the Landrat was still formidable, especially when he administered his office as efficiently as did the son of old Zieten, the celebrated and exemplary Landrat of County Rüppin. Patriarchally simple were the customs of the countryfolk, even just outside the gates of Berlin, and the primitive triennial rotation of crops was still in vogue. But the activities of Albrecht Thaer now began gradually to bear fruit on all hands. His school at Möglin in Oderbruch, which had just been elevated to the status of a royal agricultural college, attracted a continually increasing number of older and younger agriculturists, who

[1] Hardenberg to Heydebreck, June 29, 1815.

here, beneath the old alder trees beside the pond, received the friendly counsels of the learned and yet thoroughly practical man, whilst out in the fields they were taught how, by a more intelligently regulated rotation of crops, it was possible to dispense with fallows. Since the white fleeces of the Möglin wool-king had driven all other wool out of the field, the prestige of a more careful sheep-breeding had become firmly established, the great landlords gradually began to transform their activities in accordance with the principles of the new "rational agriculture," and Goethe exclaimed encouragingly to the reformer of German agriculture:

> "No clod of earth shall fallow lie,
> And least of all shall man! "

The rapidly developed capital lay like an island amid this agricultural province, completely separated from the interests of the open country. Although Berlin now numbered 188,000 inhabitants, the characters of the life of the city were still principally determined by the court, the garrison, the official classes, and the university. Nowhere in Germany could more refined judgments concerning music and the drama, philosophy and history, be heard than in the simple tea-drinking society of literary circles in Berlin. How many men of talent in after years looked back with fond memories to the hospitable house of the Mendelssohns in the Leipziger Strasse. Here in the quiet park, close to the Potsdam Gate, where for the people of Berlin the world came to an end, were to be found in joyful assembly artists, critics, and men of learning. But society was still stratified in accordance with professional occupation. Even Gneisenau, the new governor, associated almost exclusively with his military colleagues, and all the world wondered at the unprecedented innovation when, in the year 1817, the king allowed subscription balls, open to everyone, to be held in the concert-hall of the opera-house, and when he himself, with the court, made a progress through the motley assembly—though no doubt the price of entry, 1 tlr. 16 gr., was prohibitive to the majority. Outside the circles of the students and the gymnasts, there was little talk of politics. The few political writings which appeared in Berlin after the silencing of the Schmalzian feud, showed only too clearly that neither the enthusiasm for the war, nor the creative activity of the new university, had been able altogether to expel the spirit of Nicolai from the sphere of it origin. Buchholz continued with his customary self-complacency to busy himself with the commonplaces of liberal enlightenment, and J. von Voss aroused the justified indignation of the new provinces by his *A Brandenburger's Letter to the Rhinelanders.* Herein was voiced once again the conceited and presumptuous Berlinism of 1806. Superciliously, " the native of the heart of the country," issued his advice to the Rhinelanders, and announced to them that cultured Berlin would soon dispose of their " extraordinary superstition "— until Rehfues in Bonn took up that pen which he had employed so effectively in the struggle against Bonapartism, and, amid the delighted approval of the Rhinelanders, provided a rough welcome for the wisdom of Berlin.

From the time when, in the year 1818, Giovanoli had opened his refreshment rooms, and other men from the Engadine had followed the example, the cultured world had become accustomed to read the newspapers. There in the dark reading-rooms, political debates sometimes took place, and certainly the lively foreign journals still seemed far more attractive than the gentle tedium of those of Prussia. The bustle of the great town was displayed almost exclusively in the narrow streets of the central regions ; the green-clad gendarmes had ample leisure to arrest without pity every evil-doer who smoked in the street, and when the hot noonday sun blazed down upon the quiet, even lines of houses, it was said that one could hear them snoring —this was the current joke in other parts of the realm, where everyone was willing to make fun of Berlin. After the second peace, a bold speculator placed two-and-thirty genuine Warsaw droschkes on the streets, and the professors von Voss and Spener engaged in a lively dispute upon the question whence were to come all the people who should make use of this park of carriages ; a similar undertaking, a short while before, had ended in a failure, but this venture proved successful. The exchange of letters in the town was effected through the agency of " the worshipful mercantile guild of grocers " ; the town letters were collected in their retail shops, and their messengers took them through the streets, vigorously ringing a hand-bell the while. The mass of the bourgeoisie played little part in the lively intellectual life of high society ; they regarded the legislative innovations with mistrust, and obstinately adhered to their simple petty-town customs. With extreme slowness, and not until after the war, was the difference gradually extinguished between the rough North Germans and the more refinedly cultivated families of the French colony.

In the height of summer, old and young streamed out to the Stralau fish-fair, to regale themselves on the national dishes of eels and pickled gherkins, washed down with the pale ale of Berlin. The matches of the shooting clubs were still greatly patronised, and in the new by-laws of 1813 it was thought necessary to draw express attention to the fact that the champion shot, and his two sub-champions, being well-disposed citizens, would not put in a claim to immunity from taxation. The shop-keepers were subdivided into two sharply distinguished guilds, of grocers and of drapers and mercers. Twice a week the brokers published a list of market quotations, in which there was little mention of foreign paper ; but the petty bourgeois continued to reckon only in pfennige. All heavy goods were sent by water, for there was not as yet an uninterrupted high-road even between Berlin and Hamburg. In winter, business was at a stand-still ; in spring and autumn, boats were numerous on the Spree, but even then one single crane, in the Royal Dock, sufficed to handle the freight of all the carts and shipping. Yet amid these restricted conditions there were already manifest the beginnings of more abundant trade. Near the great warehouses were inns where the wagoners put up and waited for their loads, and the innkeepers began to act as middlemen in the transport service. It was from these carriers' inns that, from 1816 onwards, there sprang the great carrier companies which, favoured by the fortunate situation of the town, soon got control of the best part of the trade of north-eastern Germany. What a sensation was created when, in the first year of the peace, Cockerill built a factory in the new Friedrichsstrasse, to supply all the tools and machinery requisite for woollen manufacture ; here there was at work a steam-engine of nearly 30 horse-power, and it was not long before the workshops were actually lighted with coal-gas. A year later the first Jacquard loom was introduced into the silk-weaving works of Berlin. It is true that the weaving industry, which in the year 1803 had occupied 1,465 looms, had now work for no more than 420 ; the cotton spinners, too, could hardly make a living even after the abolition of the continental system, for the English were well able to keep the secret of their spinning machinery. But cotton-weaving and cotton-printing, fulling, and numerous other industries, made vigorous progress. In this way, by the hard work of a frugal and harassed generation, the foundation was gradually laid for the greatness of the first German manu-facturing town.

In all these new provinces it was merely necessary to unite small portions of newly acquired territory with solid nuclei of Old Prussian land, but complete reconstruction was essential in the extraordinary confusion of two-and-thirty large and innu-merable small domains which now passed by the name of the province of Saxony. Middle and low German areas, Teutonic and Wendish territories, jostled one another here; the old boundary between the dioceses of Mainz and Magdeburg, which had long constituted the line of demarcation between western and eastern Germany, ran across the centre of the new province. There existed also the sharpest contrasts in economic and religious life. In one part were the fertile lowlands of the Golden Aue and of the Magdeburg region; in another part, in the rough plateaus and in the damp valleys of Eichsfeld, were the poor villages of the weavers which had been utterly neglected under the lax rule of the crosier, surrounded by innumerable little fields. In the new governmental district of Merseburg, there was only one Catholic church; the native district of Luther, Paul Gerhardt, and Rinckart, the homeland of the Reformation, was devoted to its Protestant memories. In Eichsfeld, the Jesuits of the elector of Mainz had been completely successful in the work of the counter-reformation, a few villages alone excepted, and it was not until the year 1804 that the Prussians reintroduced Protestant services into Heiligenstadt. Nor was all this complexity compensated by a compact domain. Only for a small portion of the province did the Elbe constitute a common artery of communication, and it did this far less effectively than elsewhere the Rhine or the Oder. The new capital, Magdeburg, had fallen upon evil days as had its half-ruined cathedral; together with its suburbs, the town contained no more than 31,000 inhabitants, and, living entirely by commerce, it could never become the centre of the cultured life of the province, for the days had long passed away in which the free press of the Protestants had found its last refuge in the city.

The loyal inhabitants of Magdeburg and Altmark hardly

troubled to conceal how uncongenial to them was their political association with the Rhenish Confederates of Electoral Saxony, who on their side took the oath of allegiance with heavy hearts, although many zealous police officials reported to the chancellor that the populace was filled with rejoicing. In every castle and every church of the electoral region, the escutcheon with the lozenge-crown recalled the ancient history of a state which had once been the leading power of German Protestantism. Here, from the ease of older civilisation and greater prosperity, people had been accustomed to look down upon the upstarts of Brandenburg ; now it had been necessary to submit to a partition of the kingdom and to the detachment of Lusatia ; the university and the highest governmental authority of the province had been transferred to the Magdeburg region, although the Merseburgers had urgently recommended their own town to the king as the only suitable place for the capital ; [1] moreover, the new royal Prussian religion threatened to oust the old Lutheranism. At first, discontent found such vigorous expression that even in the schools the sons of the Prussian officials had to engage continually in fights with the native-born Saxons. Most incensed of all were the nobles, for although the new regime carefully protected their interests, and left at their disposal the patronage of the wealthy chapters of Naumburg and Merseburg, they felt that in Saxony they had been rulers, and must now descend into the subject class. So great was their hostility to the monarchical regime that, in the council of state, the lord-lieutenant von Bülow urgently recommended that the new tax laws should not be imposed without the approval of the Saxon estates. " In default of this, we shall risk the loss of the little confidence the inhabitants now possess in our rule." The officials, too, complained bitterly of the strictness of the Prussian service, especially the judges, who hitherto in all difficult cases had availed themselves of the convenient back door of the *Aktenversendung*, and who were now forced to give decisions ; many of them, inspired with a sense of wrong, returned to their easy-going old homeland.[2] Even the more intelligent among the Saxons showed on all hands that comfortable preference for the traditional order which, notwithstanding all the noise made by liberal writers, still represented the genuine

---

[1] Petition of the town of Merseburg to the king, October 3, 1815.

[2] Bülow's Opinion regarding the tax proposals, Council of State, May 23, 1817. Bülow to Hardenberg, March 9, 1816. Kircheisen to Hardenberg, June 2, 1816.

sentiments of the Germans. How many fights had Johannes Schulze with the excellent Ilgen, head master at Schulpforta, before he could finally secure the adoption of the Prussian examination regulations at the old princely school, and prevent the town scholarships being allotted any longer according to the favour or caprice of the town councillors.

Friedrich von Bülow had been specially selected as lord-lieutenant for this land of aristocratic sovereignty because in his term of service in Hanover he had already become acquainted with similar conditions, and because years before, in an incisive literary controversy with his compatriot Rehberg, he had shown how rightly he esteemed the superior advantages of monarchical as compared with feudal administration. In his new home he had so thoroughly assimilated the views of Frederician officialdom that at the outset of the movement towards evangelical union he had thought it necessary to take up his pen once again and to warn the throne regarding the dangers of an independent synodal church. But in action he always remained kindly disposed and cautious, and got on tolerably well even with the Saxon nobility. Schönberg, the governor in Merseburg, acted with less discretion; this was a Saxon noble-man who for years had contemplated with profound dissatisfaction the misdeeds of the nepotist regime, and who was now delighted to introduce into this chaos the essentials of modern legal equality. Since he was a man of amiable disposition, brimming over with good humour and jovial spirits, he was a great favourite among the common people; but the members of his own order detested him as a representative of the " democratic official spirit." Among the organisers of the new province, however, by far the most efficient was Vice-president Motz, who administered the governmental district of Erfurt with very little interference on the part of his chief Count Keller, an ex-diplomat. To this district belonged those portions of Thuringia which had at one time been directly governed by Napoleon, and, as an insecure possession, had been bled white and grossly misused. Hence, in this region, all defects were ruthlessly eradicated, for which the routinism of the Saxon authorities and the arbitrariness of the French regime had been responsible; by Hahn, the educational councillor, the work of the higher and of the elementary schools was reorganised; the activity of various societies of general utility, including the athletic grounds, was carefully fostered; and the impoverished population of Eichsfeld was so effectively assisted that the famine years of 1816 and 1817 did not cause extreme distress and Councillor Kunth on his official tour was hardly able to recognise the once so neglected plains of this region.

Everywhere, however, the inchoate condition of Old Prussian legislation proved a hindrance. Since the urgently necessary revision of Stein's town's ordinance had not yet been effected, the authorities got on as best they could with provisional measures, conducting the election of town councillors after the Prussian manner, and introducing a careful audit of municipal accounts. The town of Naumburg was at length induced to arrange for a common police administration for the city and the four suburbs, and as soon as the petty frictions over these laborious negotiations had been successfully overcome, the inhabitants gradually began to feel that better times were in prospect. In a single step, the province effected an advance which had been procrastinated for two centuries during the Electoral Saxon regime. At first the burghers and the peasantry, and at length the nobility as well, became accustomed to the changed conditions, and transferred to their new prince the patriarchal veneration which they had hitherto cherished for King Frederick Augustus. How much simpler, too, and more accessible appeared the new ruler who, at the very outset encountered the discontented Merseburgers with the exhortation : " Do not forget that we are all Germans." The mistrust which the old subjects of Electoral Saxony at first felt towards their fellow citizens of Altmark and Magdeburg, gradually disappeared; but since the Germans could not live happily without hating some of their neighbours, the Saxons of the kingdom of Saxony now began to accuse the contented inhabitants of Torgau and Eilenburg of treason, and to execrate the Prussian Saxons as scum of the " Prussian stock." Within a few years of the greatly deplored partition there might already be seen in numerous frontier villages a Saxon farm and a Prussian farm defiantly flaunting the colours of their respective countries. As well-informed persons had prophesied at the congress of Vienna nowhere did the powerful attractive force of the Prussian state display itself more effectively than in relation to the plastic Upper Saxons.

Just as manifold and yet simpler were the conditions encountered by the new administration in the province of

Westphalia. Notwithstanding the differences in their political destiny, the homelands of the white Saxon steed had always retained a vigorous common tribal pride. The ancient tribal boundary on the heights above Barmen, which had in former days separated the Saxons from the Franks, remained subsequently for many centuries the frontier between County Mark and the duchy of Berg ; the serious-minded and resolute Low Saxon regarded with dislike (which was cordially reciprocated) the easy-going and garrulous Rhinelanders, and spoke with mockery of the " Berg windbags." The Westphalian students always held together beneath the green, white, and black banner of their province, were famed as insatiable topers and brawlers, and, at the close of their university career, never failed to make their way home again to Westphalia. The powerful scions of the Drostes, Spiegels, Galens, and Fürstenbergs held aloof from the foreign military adventures at one time characteristic of the German nobility, and remained for the most part firmly settled at home ; only the collateral branches of the old families, the Kettelers and the Plettenbergs, who had gone with the Teutonic knights to the Dvina, acquired power and fame outside their native country. Now that the whole region of the red earth passed under the sway of the Prussian crown, even in the lands of the crosier, which mistrusted the Protestant monarchy, the reunion of the possessions of Wittekind was hailed with joy, the only complaint being that Osnabrück, the birthplace of Justus Möser, historian of that city, should, with certain portions of Münster, remain in Hanover and Oldenburg.

No one felt this joy more keenly than Lord-lieutenant Ludwig von Vincke, who during the war had been chief of the provisional government, and who was universally regarded as the only possible head of the province. Possessed of an admirable talent for administration, thoroughly well-informed by travel and study concerning political and economic conditions in foreign countries, he had nevertheless remained above all a Westphalian nobleman, blunt, unpolished, and downright, as firmly rooted in his native soil as had been the old painter of Soest who could not conceive even of the Lord's Supper having been eaten without platefuls of juicy Westphalian ham. Wherever the service of the state had led him, in Aurich no less than in Potsdam, he had kept before his eyes the aim which from earliest youth had seemed to him the highest in life : " My fatherland of Westphalia shall henceforward set the example in the matter of perfect institutions."

How great was now his delight when he was entrusted with the administration of the reunited land ; his only trouble, the only thing which his independent spirit found it hard to endure, was " the intolerable official correspondence," and the dependence this involved on the ministers in Berlin. Since early youth he had been on terms of intimate friendship with all the exceptional men who adorned this classic epoch of Prussian officialdom, and had always maintained an intermediate position between the two parties of reform. Since, like Stein, he sought political freedom chiefly in the self-government of a vigorous and independent bourgeoisie and peasantry, he was at one with Stein in resisting the unrestricted divisibility of landed property and the radical abolition of the guilds. But his rigidly monarchical sentiments as an official never failed to exercise a check upon his aristocratic leanings, and he would not hear a word of feudal rights which might endanger the unity of the national will. He rejected patrimonial jurisdiction as " a great nuisance " ; the harassed subjects of the mediatised always secured his loyal support, and that also of his subordinate Kessler, an enlightened liberal ; and although in Berlin he often advised considerate treatment of the Catholics, he nevertheless encountered all encroachments on the part of the hierarchy with relentless severity. The king, when conversing with budding officials, was accustomed to commend to their attention the lord-lieutenant of Westphalia as the model of faithfulness to duty—for Vincke was the most diligent of all the indefatigable members of the officialdom. How often at midday did the people of Münster see him hurrying home to bolt his simple meal, and hastening back to the office to immerse himself in his beloved documents. Yet this dreaded devourer of figures cordially detested the wisdom of the study. All his knowledge had been acquired by travel and experience ; he was at home throughout the country, in the wooded hills and low-lying meadows of the region round Siegen, in the iron-works of County Mark, and in the isolated farms of the Münster heathlands. In blue overall, pipe in mouth, gnarled stick in hand, the impetuous little man with the wise young face would often walk enormous distances across the country to attend to the interests of his beloved peasants. In his early days as lord-lieutenant in Westphalia it happened to him once that a peasant woman whom he found making butter told "the youngster" to turn the churn for her for a time while she went to attend to a job outside ; but in later years every child throughout the country knew the father of Westphalia.

With the one exception of Rhineland, no other German territory was so completely transformed by the industrial revolution of the new century as was Westphalia, which during the first years of the peace was still in evil repute as a desolate and inhospitable land, of great memories and an impoverished present. In mighty Soest, which in former times had despatched its masterful aldermen even as far as Gothland, and whose town laws (*Jus Susatense*) had been adopted by most of the towns of Low Germany, there now lived among the ruins of the magnificent ancient buildings a poor population of town-dwelling farmers. Stadtberge, the venerable Saxon fortress of Eresburg, had almost completely disappeared ; no more than the Roland's column, the whipping-post and two ruined churches, still looked down over the Diemel valley, from the summit of the tall conical hill. In front of the gate of the proud Hansa town of Dortmund, the Freistuhl of the Vehmgericht was so utterly abandoned and so solitary beneath the ancient lime-trees that the Freigraf (vehmic judge) could now have laid the naked sword and the willow-noose in open day upon the stone table. It was only in the Old Prussian regions of the province, in the predominantly Protestant counties Ravensberg and Mark, that trade and industry had already experienced a vigorous revival. In Bielefeld the anciently celebrated linen-weaving industry had not been completely destroyed by the continental system, and immediately after the peace it conquered the American market with its sailcloth. When Stein had made the Ruhr navigable, an important outlet was opened for the produce of the coal-mines and iron-works of Sauerland, and 125,000 tons of coal were already being sent yearly down the valley. In Vincke's view, all this was merely the promising prelude to a new development ; he knew how great were the stores of wealth in the mineral treasuries of his homeland and in the tenacious energy of its inhabitants, and it was a recurring pleasure to him to repeat to his fellow-countrymen the praise of Erasmus, who said that no people in the world had such power of enduring labour as the Westphalians. He regarded himself as Stein's heir, and desired to complete for the whole of Westphalia what Stein had begun in County Mark. When

the lower part of the Ruhr valley was united with the neighbouring Rhenish province, he begged the king to allow him to
retain supervision over the whole length of the river, and did
not rest until he had secured means for the construction of
the riverine harbour of Ruhrort, the gate of exit from the
Westphalian mines. Simultaneously he began the works
necessary to open the Lippe for navigation as far as Lippstadt.

More difficult tasks awaited the indefatigable man in the
new domains. For centuries the duchy of Westphalia had
slumbered under the indolent sway of the archbishops of Cologne;
and subsequently, as a province of Darmstadt, it had been
subjected to the arbitrary rule of five co-ordinate supreme
authorities and innumerable minor officials. Here there was
"an Augean stable to be cleansed." Unaffected by the complaints of County Mark, Vincke arranged that the capital of
the western governmental district should be placed, not in
the busy town of Hamm, but in the rugged hill country of
the upper Ruhr, upon the remote barrier ridge of Arnsberg,
"for you, Markers," he said, "can help yourselves, but here in
the duchy it is we who must give the initial impetus to the
new life." [1] In order to connect the new capital with the
rest of the world, the construction of the network of roads
which Stein had begun in County Mark was pushed vigorously
forward, and as early as 1817 Vincke was able to report to
Berlin that the governmental district of Arnsberg possessed
fifty miles [German] of high roads and coal tramways, whilst
the entire state of Prussia could now boast of no more
than 523 miles of high roads, and the province of Pomerania
did not as yet possess a single metalled road. The roads
of this period took a course which was far from direct;
though running along the convenient valleys, they commonly
climbed up and down the hillsides in wide undulations,
so that the villages on the heights could also play a
part in providing postillions and post-horses. Since the
lord-lieutenant was well acquainted with the needy state
of the national finances, he endeavoured to induce the locality
to provide the funds necessary for road-building, and in one
of the provincial newspapers he informed the Westphalians that
the English, when it seemed to them that a new road, bridge,
or canal, was requisite, invited all those interested in the matter

---

[1] Vincke, General Account of the State of Affairs in the Duchy of Westphalia,
May 9, 1817. Vincke to Hardenberg, July 17, 1815, July 15, and August 14, 1816.

to attend a public meeting, where a committee was elected and money subscribed. But the daring appeal was premature. This harassed generation of impecunious petty bourgeois was not yet to be won over for such bold ventures ; it was regarded as a striking success when a bridge on the road from Arnsberg to Altena was constructed by share capital.

The last bishops of Paderborn had neglected their domain even more atrociously than the electors of Cologne. It was with repugnance that Vincke became acquainted with this Westphalian Ireland, a land in which agriculture was starved and in which the peasants lived in dilapidated hovels, contrasting strangely with the stately farms of the Hellweg region ; the inhabitants, good-humoured but drunken and savage, perpetually at war with the law, so that great bands would often enter the forest with a long train of carts to carry off the trees from a whole area in a single night ; and, to crown all, " the curse of the country," Jewish usurers in every village.[1] Here also, after a period of quiet struggle, the lord-lieutenant gained general confidence, when he had restored civil order with a firm hand, had founded new schools, had provided better salaries for the teachers (who had often received no more than thirty thalers), had imposed obstacles in the way of the settlement of Jews, and had opened new outlets for the produce of home industry. From 1817 onwards, when the great lunatic asylum at Nieder-Marsberg had been acquired for the province, there was constructed the long series of magnificent institutions for the poor, the sick, the deaf and dumb, and the blind, which were the envy of neighbouring countries.

But the nobles of Münster could not forget the proud history of their immediate cathedral chapter, and they retained their ancient grudge against the Prussian dominion. It was admitted that Westphalia was not taxed so heavily as the east ; and that the only oppressive burden, the land tax, which had been very unjustly apportioned by the Napoleonic officials, could not be equitably adjusted until a tedious cadastral survey had been effected ; moreover, there was no longer any reason to complain of the Protestant arrogance of the officers and civil officials, which in the evil days before 1806 had sometimes been offensively displayed. Nevertheless parity of beliefs was as repulsive to the clerical nobility of Münster as it was to the Polish nobles. Among the inhabitants of the Rhenish

[1] Vincke, Survey of the Administration of Westphalia, August, 1817.

and South German regions, lively, fond of sight-seeing, and lovers of beauty, Catholic culture has always preserved the agreeable characteristic of a frank and innocent cheerfulness; among the ponderous and pensive northerners this culture often displayed itself in harsh, morose, and fanatical forms. This was especially the case in Münster, where the iron cages containing the bones of the Anabaptists still hung on the tower of the Lamberti church, to give the converted populace a daily reminder of the horrible sins of heresy. It was resentfully noted that among the ministers of state there was not a single Catholic; among the lord-lieutenants, but one, Zerboni; among the generals, two or three at most—where then was the boasted parity? The disproportion had an obvious explanation, for of the high officials found by the conqueror in the new provinces very few had been willing to enter Prussian service. But subsequently the number of Catholics in the civil service, and still more their number in the officers' corps, remained comparatively small, for the Poles held aloof from official life, and in the manufacturing provinces of the west the members of the cultured bourgeoisie brought up their children for business careers far more commonly than did the members of the same class in the east, while the Catholic nobles of the west seldom entered the service of the state. Most rarely of all did this happen in the case of the old families of Münster, by whom military service under the Austrian crown was still preferred to home service. The nobles lived sulkily at home, associating only with one another and with the clergy; and even when during the winter they visited the city of Münster, the provincial capital, their palaces remained almost inaccessible to the officers and civil officials.

Great difficulties were also imposed by the pretensions of the numerous mediatised princes, who in the governmental district of Münster owned a full half of the land. Many of them, such as the Arnbergs, the Loozes, and the Croys, were Belgians, and exhibited a studied mistrust for the German state; but even those of German blood were frequently hard masters. For years the Arnsberg government was in dispute with the princes of the House of Sayn, endeavouring to secure for the unfortunate inhabitants of Wittgenstein some alleviation of the burdens imposed by their twofold state of subjection; for the governments were delighted to act as protectors of the common people, priding themselves, as Kessler once declared to Beyme, that free collegial deliberation gave them "a sort of popular character.[1] It was thanks to the officials also that certain useful innovations which had been introduced during the period of foreign dominion were partially preserved for the region, although they were not in harmony with the Prussian civil code. The territorial police was reintroduced only in the domains of the mediatised and in those of the immediate nobility, and the landlords did not deplore their loss. Thus completely, in the west, had the feudal order of society already passed away.

Among all the works of the Prussian administration there was none so fruitful for the nation as the quiet laborious activity which the two Rhenish provinces regained for German life. How confidently, at the Vienna congress, had all the enemies of Prussia continued to express the hope that the North German state would dash its head to pieces against the obstacle imposed by this German-French peculiar type of life. The dangerous situation of the remote western march was not concealed from the king, and when he entered into possession of the new provinces he openly declared: "It is by a higher consideration for the German fatherland as a whole that my resolution has been determined; it is for this reason that these primitively German lands must remain united with Germany, they are the bulwarks of the freedom and independence of Germany." For a generation Rhineland was the spoiled darling of the Prussian crown, as had been Silesia in the days of Frederick II. Even the majority of the Old Prussian officials who were sent to the west undertook their duties with profound anxiety, and it was only gradually that they recognised with astonishment how thin was the Gallic varnish which had been superimposed upon these essentially German stocks.

It was in the lower Rhenish territories below Cologne that German characteristics had been most firmly maintained. On the right bank, in the free land of Berg, the Prussians were not regarded as foreigners. For more than a hundred years the Protestant church of Berg had been under the protection of the Prussian crown, and its diet had lived on friendly terms with the diet of its neighbour Mark. The patriotic spirit which

[1] Kessler, Memorial concerning the Introduction of a representative Constitution, Münster, April 12, 1818.

in 1814 was displayed by the men of the Berg Landsturm did not date from yesterday. People still related with pride how Stücker, " the hero of Berg," and his brave peasants had once, on the occasion of the first attack by the sansculottes, carried on a petty war on their own account, in opposition to the will of their Bavarian overlord ; every child in the country was still familiar with the parody of the Lord's Prayer which had come into existence as long ago as the days of Frederick's wars, in reprobation of the French plunderers. The vigorous industry of the people, who had in this region long been accustomed to intercourse with foreign parts, and the rich multiformity of religious contrasts, here gave rise to certain characteristics of free urbanity. The manufacturers of the Wuppertal had already christened their double town of Elberfeld-Barmen by the name of " the German Manchester " ; the men of Solingen referred with self-esteem to the world-wide renown of their cutlery ; all were proud to derive their prosperity solely from their own exertions and all gladly entered into the great relationships of the Prussian state, which opened a wider field of labour for their vigorous energies. No other territory of the north possessed so many popular men engaged in independent work on behalf of the common weal, on behalf of the awakening of the German spirit. There was, for instance, the widely known " hermit of Gauting," Baron von Hallberg, a fierce enemy of the French, who during the war had been commander of the Landsturm on the Seig, and who always took a prominent part when resistance to the French party was in question ; there was Deycks, councillor at Opladen, general legal adviser for the Wupper region, promoter of horticulture and of schools of agriculture ; there was Zuccalmaglio, doctor at Schlebusch, who even during the epoch of foreign dominion had founded the first philharmonic societies, inspired always by the secret hope that they would one day play the French out of the country ; there was pastor Löh of Burscheid, held in equal respect by men of every religious party, who preached tolerance and peace to all ; there was Ascheberg, the preacher, editor of the *Zeitschrift Hermann*, which was widely circulated in Westphalia as well as Berg, and which received the cordial support of Vincke. The activities of the contentious polyhistor Benzenberg extended far beyond the boundaries of Berg. In his industrious homeland this excellent patriot had acquired an economic education which other German publicists still lacked, and subsequently had learned in association with Hardenberg and Gneisenau the aspect of political affairs when seen from above ; he voluntarily devoted his independent pen to the chancellor's service, and indefatigably, with the cheerful frankness characteristic of the men of Berg, he combated the prejudices of the Rhinelanders against the Prussian state.

The Old Prussian territories of Cleves, Mörs, and Guelderland, accepted the new order even more gladly than did Berg. This was true, not only of Wesel and Duisberg, ancient strongholds of militant Calvinism, but also of the rigid Catholic inhabitants of the left bank, who put their trust in the gracious Mother of God of Kevelaer. The inhabitants remembered with pride the long series of brilliant men for whom the state of the Hohenzollerns was indebted to this remote corner of the world ; quite recently the little town of Cleves had provided the Prussian officialdom with four of its best men, namely, Maassen, Beuth, Sack, and Sethe. In loyal Crefeld, Prussian sentiment was so defiantly displayed that the French prisoners returning homeward found their lives in danger on their way through the town. The silk manufacture of the vigorous place at first suffered severely through the separation from France, but such great firms as that of Leyen, and such active merchants as de Greiff, recognised from the first that they would soon be able to make good the inevitable losses of the years of transition.

Higher up the left bank the old opposition between the temporal and the spiritual territories speedily became perceptible to the Prussian officials. The inhabitants of the coalfield of Saarbrücken still preserved their affection for the House of Nassau, which had so long ruled in this region, and whose members had found their last resting-place in the ancient church of St. Arnual ; the Palatiners in Hunsruck and in the Nahe valley had not forgotten the brilliant days when the little town of Simmern had been the tribal seat of the most powerful of the princely races of the Rhine ; all, Catholic and Protestant alike, were familiar with the benefits of German princely rule, and greeted the Prussian dominion with joy since a return to the old dynastics was out of the question. But in the former lands of the crosier, and also in Aix and Jülich, mistrust everywhere prevailed and an intractable spirit of dissatisfaction. Here were completely lacking the monarchical traditions wherein was rooted the German sense of the state; for even Jülich, which the court of Düsseldorf had always treated as a mere apanage, had hardly any sense of dynastic fidelity. These men without a state, already profoundly disaffected by the prolonged period of provisional administration abounding in opportunities for confusion, had now to accept the dominion of an utterly strange ruling house which in these regions had during the regime of the crosier been regarded as the great disturber of the peace of the empire, and whose reputation had of late been further impaired by the mockery of the French. Within a few years so many political storms had blown across the Rhine; why should not this Prussianism, which had so suddenly descended on the country like a snow-storm, vanish in its turn? The people did not yet believe in the permanence of the new regime; they listened greedily to the oft-repeated rumour that the province was to be exchanged for the kingdom of Saxony; and they regarded as a sign of weakness the considerate behaviour of the Prussian government, whose methods differed so strikingly from the dictatorial practices of the Napoleonic prefects.

In so far as any national memories still persisted in this part of the world, these related to the Hapsburgs and to the Holy Empire. What a poor thing to the burghers of Aix seemed the festival of allegiance of the two Rhenish provinces after all the imperial coronations which the proud town had witnessed in former days. In the region of Cologne it was thought that the Prussians could be effectively wounded by the repetition of the old saying, " Hold fast to the empire, peasant of Cologne, hold fast whatever befall "; what a long time was still to elapse before it was understood that Prussia was the heir of the old empire! Although during the unspiritual Bonapartist regime even religious life had become superficial, and although the clergy of Rhineland at the opening of the years of peace were greatly inferior in culture to those of Westphalia or of Bavaria, the church continued to maintain its old prestige. After all, it was not simply the sensual comfort of the rule of the crosier, nor the rich adornments of its court and church festivals, which bound the population of Electoral Cologne and Electoral Treves to the old church. The Catholic faith was firmly rooted in their minds, being here regarded, as it was among the Latin races, to be the only possible form of Christianity; in all the problems of life the priest had been and remained the honoured counsellor of the people. This fact had been impressed upon the Jacobins when, amid the threatening murmurs of the Rhinelanders, they had placed the goddess of Reason upon the altar and had endeavoured to remove the image of the Virgin from the castle of Bonn. Now, when the new Protestant teachers and officials entered the country, when a university in which parity of beliefs prevailed was inaugurated, when in the holy town of Treves, for the first time since the days of the arch-heretic Olevianus, Protestant sermons were preached once again (on the occasion of the tercentenary of the Reformation), the Catholic populace began to complain, not strictly speaking from intolerance, but because the new customs conflicted with traditional usage. The spirit of provincialism indued an ecclesiastical garment. " We are Rhinelanders," said the people, " and that is why we are good Catholics."

The fires of Rhenish particularism were adroitly fanned by the small but quietly growing ultramontane party, whose members had not yet abandoned the hope of once more wresting from the temporal authority these nuclear lands of priestly dominion. When the bishop of Treves made a pastoral journey through his diocese to confirm the junior members of his flock, he was now preceded by mounted peasant lads carrying the colours of Electoral Treves—a practice the bishops had never ventured on under French rule. The Rhinelanders in the episcopal territories complained as loudly as did the Poles of the way in which their homeland was invaded by a swarm of foreign immigrants. The grievance was iterated with so much obstinacy as to find support at length even in the pro-Prussian lower Rhenish territories, and Benzenberg pathetically declared that " indigenacy " was the natural right of every people, that the Great Elector had long before promised the estates of Cleves that the native-born alone should receive appointments in this territory. A thorough purging of Rhenish officialdom had in fact been effected. The prefects, who were all French, had left the country ; so had the sub-prefects, with the exception of three or four of German birth ; communal administration had been utterly neglected because the mayors for the most part understood no French and left the conduct of affairs in the hands of ignorant clerks. Nevertheless the king proceeded very cautiously with the inevitable transformation, declaring it to be his " inalterable determination " that no one on the Rhine was to be deprived of his position except for proved incapacity. For many of the imperial officials their posts were held open for years until they had secured in Bonn the degree of scientific culture which the law demanded from Prussian state servants. In the year 1816, in the six Rhenish governmental areas, there were among the officials 207 Rhinelanders, 23 non-Prussians, and 150 Prussians from other provinces, the latter for the most part in those subordinate positions reserved for soldiers who had served their time. This was certainly a reasonable proportion, especially in view of the fact that the great majority of the Rhenish jurists had devoted themselves to the judicial side of their profession, and the courts in any case were constituted almost exclusively out of the native-born.[1]

Once awakened, however, the hostility towards "cold and rigid Prussianism" took no account of figures. The Rhinelanders, rejoicing in their chosen land, in their civilisation a thousand years older than that of the rest of Germany, still utterly ignorant of the German world (for to them Germany ended at Frankfort), regarded themselves as superior in all things to the Old Prussians. "You are Lithuanians," Görres once exclaimed to his Old Prussian friends; and this represented the view of all the inhabitants of Coblenz. To this thoroughly bourgeois people it seemed especially repulsive that among the Old Prussian officials there were still to be found a certain number of nobles. In a memorial, J. Weitzel, the liberal publicist, assured the chancellor with frank self-satisfaction that justice demanded that every man should be judged by his peers. On the Rhine, he said, this truth is already generally recognised, "because we have here an enlightened public opinion"; consequently in Rhineland there must be none but bourgeois officials. None the less, cases of resistance to authority were incomparably rarer than they had been under the French regime, although by the latter disobedience was punished far more severely than it was by the Prussian law. Over their beer, people might continue to complain of the stiff Prussians, to whom the amiable Rhenish art of "live and let live" was still so utterly unknown; but for all that, nature demanded her rights, and in secret these Germans were in truth heartily pleased that they could once more converse with their officials in the mother tongue. Under the crosier as under the

---

[1] Cabinet Order of November 8, 1816. Survey of the personnel of the Rhenish governmental areas, February 20, 1817.

prefects it had been universally believed that every law could be evaded by cunning or by favour. It was not agreeable to the Rhinelanders to be forced to abandon this belief, and to bend before the majesty of law; but the immaculate justice of the officials, and their perspicacity (indisputable in general, isolated exceptions notwithstanding), ultimately compelled the respect of the people. Already in tête-à-tête one could some-times hear the half-unwilling admission, " The Prussian is severe, but he is just." But public praise of the Prussians was as yet out of the question.

Discontent is regarded as the natural privilege of the genuine Rhinelander, and discontent was continuously nourished by complaints concerning the unprecedented pressure of taxa-tion. This people, firm in the faith, had willingly furnished the church-tithes, since everyone believed that in making these payments he was coming to terms with heaven; the French taxes were regarded as war taxes, and were paid silently upon compulsion. Everything paid to the Protestant king was, however, rendered grudgingly, and to most people it still seemed preposterous that in time of peace the secular arm should levy taxes at all. When vague rumours now reached the Rhine regarding the freedom from land taxation of the Old Prussian landed proprietors, discontent became yet more rife, and for an entire generation almost all the Rhinelanders were firmly convinced that their country was being plundered for the benefit of the east. In reality, Hardenberg was guided by the principle of endeavouring to win over the difficult province by mildness. The king expressly commanded the authorities that in the collection of arrears of taxation great consideration should be displayed, lest for a certain gain in money " the trustful depen-dence " of the people should be shaken.[1] During the first years, the Rhinelanders were plainly favoured in matters of taxation, for even if the land-tax was here somewhat higher than in the east, in compensation, when the *droits réunis* had been abolished, indirect taxation was practically in abeyance. Even when the new customs and tax laws were promulgated, the west was treated so gently that Benzenberg came to the conclusion that except Posen and Westphalia no other province of the monarchy was taxed more lightly. Although the statistics compiled by this eloquent publicist always offered a number of weak points to criticism, it was incontestable that since the days of the Napo-

[1] Cabinet Order to Sack, September 14, 1815.

leonic regime there had occurred a notable diminution in the burden of taxation. In the governmental district of Aix, the taxation imposed in the year 1813 amounted to 5 thalers 2 sgr. 8 pf. per head ; nine years later the figure was no more than 4 thalers 8 sgr. 6 pf., of which 14 sgr. represented local rates. The new government had played its part also in bringing about the low level of local taxation, for it gave assistance to the Rhenish towns in the reorganisation of their complicated debts, and remitted the arrears of taxation down to the year 1815, with the result that the majority of the communes on the Rhine found themselves in a far more favourable financial situation than the towns of the east with their heavy burden of war taxes. These considerations notwithstanding, complaints regarding excessive taxation never ceased ; people spoke as if it had been Prussia's duty to give the Rhinelanders a special reward for freeing them from the foreign yoke.

In the ancient lands of the crosier, the allies at their first entry were by no means received with such unalloyed pleasure as in Berg ; at this time the delegates from the left bank of the Rhine remained one and all in Paris as members of the legislative assembly—in order, as they subsequently maintained, to assist in ensuring the tyrant's overthrow. Now, when everyone was grumbling against the Prussians, the terrible oppression of the Napoleonic regime was speedily forgotten ; its benefits alone were remembered ; enthusiasm was once again displayed for the glorious ideas of '89, French or Belgian newspapers were preferred (for the native press was still in its infancy, and even the *Kölnische Zeitung* was quite a small paper with a circulation of barely two thousand), and everyone swore by the new doctrine that the sun rose over Europe in the west. Yet the reawakening Gallicism of the Rhinelanders served merely to show how essentially German was this people : Rhenish liberalism originated in the same conservative and particularist disposition which in all the other Prussian provinces resisted every change in traditional usage. That which existed was loved simply because it existed, and the government did all that was possible to meet people's wishes in these respects. The economic legislation of the Revolution, which harmonised in essentials with the ideas embodied in the laws of Stein and Hardenberg, was left unchanged ; so also temporarily with the French communal administration. The prefects and sub-prefects were, however, replaced by governmental committees and local councils, and even this valuable innovation was received with nothing but criticism. " We can see," it was bitterly declared, " that the only aim of Prussia is to increase the army of officials unendingly ; the entire new governmental college of Coblenz will never do as much good as did the one man Lezay-Marnesia, the never-to-be-forgotten prefect of the department of Rhine and Moselle." Again and again, stories were related of sinister Prussian designs against Rhenish freedom, and one whose only source of information was the loose talk of the tavern frequenters, might readily despair of the country. When Schwerz, the agriculturist, commissioned by the government for the purpose, was visiting the Rhenish estates, in his native town of Coblenz he had to listen to so many angry remonstrances that he assured the chancellor : " There is not a man here but would give thanks to God on his knees were the country once more to pass under French rule " Other well-disposed observers compared the province to a volcano which might at any moment break out in eruption.[1]

Alarmed by these gloomy reports, Hardenberg for a time seriously believed that a revolt was possible. Yet in actual fact it was only a small minority on the Rhine which wholeheartedly desired reunion with France. The Rhinelanders were well aware of their vigorous return to prosperity, and the bond of economic interests proved stronger than their French sympathies. In any case, there was here no need to dread secret conspiracies ; the best virtue of the Rhenish-Franconians, their candour and good sense, gave a guarantee of this. Yet during the next few years the censure and criticism of " the revolution," as the new change of regime was termed, continually increased. The older generation had had actual experience of the plunderings practised by the undisciplined soldiery of the Republic : but the young men who were now growing up had in their schools listened on the Day of Napoleon and the Day of Austerlitz to ceremonial speeches on the glory of the world-ruling tricolor ; during the years which for most men determine life they had seen the great emperor in person, reviewing his magnificent cuirassiers in the Poppelsdorfer Allee. Since liberalism was now again everywhere beginning to express its admiration of French freedom, this generation,

[1] Governmental Councillor Schwerz to Hardenberg, Coblenz, August, 1816. Report to Klewitz from a landlord of Cologne, January, 1817. Lieutenant-Colonel von Romberg to the Chancellor, August 24, 1817.

which in the twenties and the thirties dominated opinion on the Rhine, was now glad to boast of its French culture ; the French word of command *Dutzwitt* (*tout de suite*) sounded more agreeable to its ears than the German *Rasch* (quick !). The Rhenish students' clubs in the western German universities all sported French colours, and the current stories regarding the atrocities of the sansculottes were now transferred to the credit of the Cossacks.

The mistrust felt by the province towards the government was unceasingly fostered by the separatist activities of the Rhenish nobility. Nowhere else in the empire had the nobles suffered severer losses. A generation earlier they had still ruled the country through its cathedral chapter, and almost two-thirds of the land had belonged to the nobles and the church. Now landed proprietorship on the large scale had been so utterly destroyed that an estate of about fifty acres was considered one of considerable size. In the governmental district of Treves there were only one hundred and two land owners with estates larger than three hundred acres ; in Aix, no more than eighty ; in Düsseldorf, but one. Of the old families competent for representation in the diet there were in Berg no more than twenty-four still extant ; and in Cleves but five, of which two only still possessed landed property. There no longer existed a sharp distinction between town and country, between land-lords and burghers and peasants, and this radical destruction of the ancient feudal classification was an irrevocable fact, for here, in Germany's liveliest route of commerce, even in the middle ages urban life had invaded the rural districts, and the Revolution merely completed with a *coup de main* that for which the way had long been prepared by the intensive economy of the dense population. The few families of knightly birth which had survived the destruction of the Rhenish nobility, the Wylichs, Mirbachs, Spees, and Nesselrodes, were unable to adapt themselves to the changed order ; they expected from the liberators the return of the good old time, and at once demanded in the name of German law and German honour the restoration of tithes, hunting rights, and entail. The officials, on the other hand, whether native-born or immigrant, warned the chancellor against any such step. They knew that the idea of social equality was to the Rhinelanders the dearest of all political principles. Whilst Vincke, on the ground of his Westphalian experiences, defended entail, the Rhenish presidents and councillors declared with one voice that the economic prosperity of Rhineland depended on the free divisibility of the soil.[1] Consequently the demand of the nobles was politely rejected, and from the time of this disappointment they became disaffected towards the Prussian state ; it was only the princely houses of Wied and Solms, which from ancient days had been distinguished by culture and a free spirit, that maintained a worthy relationship towards the crown. Yet the populace could not be persuaded out of its belief that the Prussians were in league with the nobility. Four years after the ceremony of allegiance, Solms-Laubach described the sentiments of the province in the following terms : " A completely satisfactory mood would be attainable only through the instrumentality of the impossible, the nobles must be paid their tithes once more, but the peasantry must retain their exemption from these exactions." [2]

Notwithstanding all such difficulties, this region of variegated and peculiar life, strangely compounded of ancient clerical and neo-French elements, became imperceptibly and securely connected with the new state. Of two lord-lieutenants, one, von Ingersleben in Coblenz, had during the war been at the head of the Pomeranian administration, and had ably supervised the levying and equipment of the Landwehr ; the old man was well received by the Rhinelanders on account of his benevolence and his hospitable geniality. The other, Count Solms-Laubach in Cologne, friend of Stein, and participator in the German central administration, accepted his office from a sense of patriotism, diligently made himself at home in all his administrative duties, and in his work as a monarchical official so completely forgot the mediatised noble that the greedy knighthood of his lord-lieutenancy soon came to regard him as a renegade ; he knew his Rhenish fellow-countrymen, and forbade his subordinates to display the domineering manners of Old Prussia which were intolerable to the self-complacency of the Rhenish Franconians. Neither of these men possessed Vincke's independence of mind, but they were ably supported by the generality of officials, who were almost all men of ability, and who, from Delius, the talented governor of Treves, down to

---

[1] Baron von Wylich to Hardenberg, February 16, to Schuckmann, May 15, 1816. Reports from Governor von Schmitz-Grollenburg, Coblenz, October 9, Governor von Erdmannsdorff, Cleves, October 31, 1817, Councillors Bitter, Hartung, etc.

[2] Solms-Laubach, Report to Prince William, August 18, 1817.

the last gendarme, stood firmly shoulder to shoulder amid the suspicious populace.

No one who looked about him with open eyes could fail to see in every market-place and every street how with the enfranchisement from the foreign yoke there had resulted a return of civic freedom and of the ancient customs of the country. The smugglers and deserters, the curse of the Napoleonic epoch, immediately disappeared, and with them disappeared also the horrible system of police espionage. The towns were once more adorned with their proud escutcheons, which had hitherto been discountenanced as symbols of federalism. Even the old kermises and shooting festivals were revived, although among the flags which adorned the scene there was rarely displayed the eagle banner to which the people really owed the reawakening of Rhenish merry-making. Under the rule of Napoleon, the Cologne carnival had shyly withdrawn itself into the houses : now the cheerful cry *Alaaf Köln! und Geck loss Geck elans!* was once more heard in the streets ; the *Funken* of Cologne once more held their mad parade ; and in order that thanks to the Prussians should not be wholly lacking, on one occasion a great stock-fish tied on the top of a long pole and adorned with a laurel crown was suddenly uplifted above the crowd and greeted with a loud *Heil dir im Siegerkranz!*—for the taciturn king was utterly displeasing to the Rhinelanders, who found the unrestrained liveliness of the facetious crown prince far more to their taste. In the year 1822, an association was formed to undertake the organisation of the beautiful popular festival, which year by year in its brilliant processions of masks displayed more and more plainly the wealth and ease of the once again flourishing Rhenish capital. In order to manifest its good feeling for Rhineland the government also allowed the free passage through the streets of religious processions, which had been prohibited by the Napoleonic law ; in Cologne, from 1818 onward, the festival of Corpus Christi was once more celebrated in the open with its ancient pomp. It was remarkable to note how the romantic ideas which had hitherto prevailed only in the narrow circle of the Boisserées, now all at once permeated the populace, how the Rhinelanders began to remember their great history. When the French had removed the works of art from Cologne and Aix, no one had paid any attention ; but now, when the Prussians brought back the stolen goods, both towns instituted

festivals of rejoicing. Three years later, by a generous bene-
faction, Canon Wallraf laid the foundation of the Cologne art
collections. The government zealously undertook the protection
of the ancient architectural glories of the region ; when the
king and the crown prince visited Treves for the first time
they entered through the Porta Nigra, the fortress gate of the
Cæsars, which had recently been disinterred. Their example
exercised a wholesome influence, and the time at length arrived
in which the Rhenish clergy, whose reputation had hitherto
been so evil, became especially distinguished in Germany for
artistic sense and historical culture.

In the Rhine valley, extensive works for navigation were
immediately begun. Under the French regime the towing path had
been almost completely destroyed and the channel had been
grossly neglected ; it was not until sixteen years later that at
Bingerbrück the mariners of the Rhine erected a monument
to the king, because he had effected a tenfold widening of the
channel through the Bingerloch or narrows at Bingen. The
prefects had paid somewhat more attention to the construction
of roads ; but even the most important high-road of the province,
that from Cologne to Coblenz, was first completed by Prussia.
Year by year a more vigorous activity was displayed upon the
Baienturm jetty in Cologne, where recently the grass had been
growing. Impoverished Cologne seemed already likely to outsoar wealthy Strasburg ; in Coblenz, once so dirty, the mariners
on the Rhine could now see a long row of stately houses showing above the new walls ; all the Prussian towns in Rhineland
increased more rapidly in prosperity than those under French
rule or under the petty princes. On the lower Rhine, the
recovery of industry was so rapid that in Wuppertal as
early as the year 1821 the Rhenish West India Company was
founded, whilst the exploitation of the coal-field of Saarbrücken helped to increase the industrial prosperity of this
region. In the year 1815, the state mines of Saarbrücken,
employing five hundred men, supplied fifty thousand tons of
coal, but within a brief period the yield was doubled—to the
great satisfaction of Bleibtreu, the surveyor of mines, who had
been the first to assure the chancellor that this district rich in
possibilities would prove indispensable to Prussia. Union with
the vine-growing land of France had been unfavourable to the
progress of German viticulture ; but now the North German
market was opened, and as soon as the two great vintage years
of 1818 and 1819, following bad vintage years, had restored

courage to the vine-growers and provided them with fresh means, throughout the vine-growing region, and especially on the Moselle, new vineyards were planted, so that in many communes the vine-growing area was doubled and *Trevir metropolis* could now with better right than formerly enjoy the title *Baccho gratissima,* which had been given to it by its spiritual rulers.

An almost hopeless task was imposed upon the new government in consequence of the horrible devastation of the forests which, among all the sins of the French, the forest-loving Germans found it hardest to forgive. The peasant of Berg clenched his fists when any allusion was made to the ancient glories of the country, the King's Forest and the Franconian Forest. Of the immemorial oaks and beeches, not a single one was left standing. All that the deforestation of the rude hill-tops of Hunsruck and Eifel signified for the climate and for agriculture people were now to learn with horror when, after a storm, the freshets from the mountains poured down into the Moselle valley, washing away in a few seconds the humus which during months of hard work the unfortunate vine-growers had carried up the steep rocky terraces. What quantities of beasts of prey, too, had been allowed to grow up through the French neglect of the chase. In the Kotten Forest, just behind Bonn, wolves were still shot ; and as late as 1817 one hundred and fifty-nine of these animals were destroyed in the governmental district of Treves. Hartig, the leading German forester of those days, was sent to Rhineland from Berlin ; long before, in the days of the great sales of the domains, he had performed an enduring service for the old provinces when he secured that the forests should not also be alienated. Here, in the west, he endeavoured to save all that it was still possible to save ; in many places afforestation was begun, and a strict forest police was instituted, which aroused much discontent among the peasants ; but who could guard against the fierce winds which blew across the bare downs of Eifel ? The terrible desolation could never be completely repaired.

The reorganisation of the system of education proved more fruitful. When the Prussians took over the country, Johannes Schulze found the schools " in a condition of hopeless neglect."[1] Since the French state had never given any support

---

[1] J. Schulze, Memorial concerning Church and Education on the Rhine, December 31, 1816.

to the elementary schools, in more than a third of the communes there were no schools at all. In many hamlets the
peasants considered they did all that was necessary when for
four months in winter they found room in a barn for a
vagrant teacher. Three-fifths of the children grew up without
any instruction at all. Even the lower educational institutions
of the towns were rarely any better than those notorious schools
of the old episcopal days which bore the distinctive name of
Silentium. Here and there only had some vigorous pedagogue
like Weinmann, the schoolmaster of Kreuznach, in arduous
conflict with the French authorities, managed to maintain the
German spirit among his pupils. What labours had to be effected
in this region before the Prussian principle of universal compulsory education could become effective. The change was above
all to the advantage of the Catholics, whose schools had been
especially neglected, but the new teachers from the semimary
at Treves often found their work extremely difficult, for many
of the priests of the Rhenish region had at one time been monks,
and had not outgrown the views of the cloister.

The current of German culture flowed irresistibly across the
liberated frontier land. Till quite recently the entire Rhineland,
the right bank not excepted, had been utterly sterile ground for
the German book trade ; at the beginning of the century even
the rich Wuppertal had not been able to boast a single bookseller's
shop ; but now in Bonn there came into existence a new
centre of literary intercourse, and the energetic Perthes immediately cemented his business relationships. The old patricians
of Cologne, like those of Strasburg to-day, spoke French on
great social occasions, and patois in familiar converse ; but
now the younger generation had to learn an intelligible High
German. Many years of serious struggle and of unfortunate
mutual misunderstanding were still to elapse before the new
province became proud of its union with Prussia. But
Arndt, who was intimately acquainted with the talented,
impressionable, and plastic Rhenish Franconians, ever readily
accessible to all extraneous influences, already felt well
assured that contact with the incisive Old Prussian system
could not fail to redound to the advantage of this people.
It was only the deplorable sloth of the local political system,
only the unnatural conditions of the theocracy and of the
foreign dominion, which had debased the highly gifted stock :
a strong state could alone raise it from this debasement, and

could refertilise the most beautiful and the oldest of all German lands with the vigorous energy of the new national life.

§ 4. BEGINNINGS OF THE CONSTITUTIONAL STRUGGLE.

Thus it came to pass that half or, for practical purposes, the whole of Prussia was in process of transformation. For some years the state required a monarchical dictatorship. Unquestionably the work of administrative reform could be brought to a successful conclusion only in a centralised constitution, whose necessity the king himself had recognised in so many cabinet orders; unquestionably the innumerable conflicting elements in the nation could be aroused to a living sense of cohesion in no other way than by the continuous community of political work and party life; but the essentials of organisation must first be established, before the government was encumbered with parliamentary forms. These millions of Swedish, Polish, Saxon, and French hearts required time in which to weep out their sorrows, in which to accommodate themselves to the new conditions. Who could venture upon the responsibility of allowing particularist prejudices, the thousand injured local interests of a nation which in political matters was still entirely untrained, to jostle one another forthwith in parliamentary struggles? Who could venture to expose at this early date to the attacks of an opposition, universal military service, the tax laws, the subdivision of the provinces—to an opposition which had absolutely no understanding of the vital conditions of a great state, and which to some extent manifestly cherished treasonable designs?

To Prussia's misfortune, the king was no longer in a position to exercise free choice of time for the foundation of the constitution. He had deprived himself of freedom in this respect when he subscribed the unhappy ordinance of May 22, 1815, which promised a representative system based upon delegations from the provincial diets. The charters issued when taking over Swedish Pomerania spoke in the same sense, and the promises made to the Saxons were essentially identical, having been to the following effect:

" You shall retain your representative constitution when it has been adapted to the general constitution which it is our purpose to provide for our entire state." Provincial diets and participation in the national assembly were promised to the other new provinces as well. The royal word had been pledged, and the patriotic press, whose thoughts were directed solely towards the ideal of constitutional government, stormily demanded that this pledge should be fulfilled. To impatient spirits it seemed all the more necessary that speedy action should be taken because the interim territorial representation, which during recent years had served the old provinces as a common representative organ, had finally been abolished in the summer of 1815. This assembly itself, on April 7th, shortly before its close, had determined, upon the motion of the Upper Silesian deputy Elsner von Gronow, to petition the king for the speedy introduction of a definitive representative system and for the revival of the provincial diets.[1]

When Hardenberg, in Vienna, had induced the king to make this momentous concession, it was believed that the fulfilment of the intention would be quite easy ; the first proposal went so far as to suggest that as early as June 1st a committee should assemble, consisting of officials and residents from the provinces under the presidency of the chancellor, and that by September 1st it should bring the Prussian constitution into existence. Since war was imminent, this extremity of frivolousness was happily averted, and the ordinance deferred the summoning of the constitutional committee until September 1st. But it was impossible to arrange matters even at this date, because the king and his counsellors were unable to leave the congress of Paris. When at length they returned, not only was it necessary once again to postpone the constitutional work, on account of the inevitable labours of administrative organisation ; it also speedily became evident that the ordinance which the liberals had so greatly esteemed was nothing less than an irresponsible piece of levity on the part of Hardenberg, the gravest of all his political errors. In the year 1808, indeed, upon Stein's instigation, Vincke, Schön, and Rhediger had drawn up certain resolutions and proposals for the future constitution ; but of all these, little was now of practical utility, since the state domain had been

[1] Minutes of the Interim Territorial Representation . April 7, 1815.

doubled. Nor did the new ordinance itself offer any firm standing ground; and indeed, on close examination, it was manifestly a series of riddles and contradictions. According to this document, the provincial diets were to be re-established, and from them a common Landtag was to be elected. But did there then actually still exist estates which could be considered as providing a representation of the recently constituted provinces? Did they still possess incontestable rights? How were the representative constitutions of the new provinces to be retained, and how were these various constitutions to be assimilated to the common constitution? Did not this mean that the provinces were to be recognised as independent states, and were simultaneously to be incorporated in a new state? And if their constitutions were retained, could they not demand that the common constitution should be created only with the assent of their separate estates? A complex of intricate and insoluble legal questions was here involved; the state itself was favouring the particularism of its territories; the thoughtless promise of the crown gave the signal for a constitutional struggle which threatened the foundations of the national unity established with so much difficulty.

Extremely unfortunate was the form of the ordinance of May 22nd, and extremely comprehensive was the design which underlay that ordinance. Hardenberg revived the far-reaching ideas of reform characteristic of Stein's best days; it was his intention to create a new circle and communal organisation for the entire state; from the circle diets were to proceed the provincial diets, and from these latter was to proceed the central diet. Nothing was further from his mind than a spiritless imitation of the French *Charte* of 1814. Rather it was his endeavour to transform the Old German diets in order to fit them for the purposes of a modern representative system. The royal ordinance made use of the words " representation of the people " and " estates " indifferently, as equivalent expressions; the intention was to constitute a Reichstag divided into three estates; this body was to be based entirely upon the foundation of the constitutional law, and was to represent, not the well-established rights of isolated privileged classes, but the interests of the people as a whole. This plan harmonised with the views of the time; for although the subdivision of the nation into nobles, burghers, and peasants, had long ceased to correspond to the conditions of modern society (above all in the west), public opinion was still familiar with this classification. Moreover, the new South German constitutions started from similar principles; everywhere the upper house was a feudal corporation, in essentials a representation of the nobles, whilst the lower house was, as a rule, a representation of several groups of estates. In Prussia the new circle assemblies, like the national representation of 1811, were constituted by the representation of the three estates; and although the chancellor had no love for social distinctions, he recognised the necessity of adapting innovations to the customary and the traditional.

But even such a constitution as this, intermediating between the old and the new, encountered in Prussia a resistance which had not to be overcome in the states of South Germany. The opposition in Prussia arose from the great and manifold relationships of this state, and from that prudent consideration which, in the long struggle against feudal licence, the Hohenzollerns had ever displayed. In the states of the Confederation of the Rhine, the old diets had long before been abolished by the rough hand of despotic officialdom, and the structure of the new constitution could here be erected upon cleared ground; it was only in Würtemberg that the abolished estates endeavoured to reacquire their rights. But in Prussia certain remnants of the ancient territorial diets had almost everywhere been preserved. Thus in these powerless bodies the king's ambiguous promise suddenly reawakened ancient and long-forgotten claims; the rubbish of the centuries filled the air with dust. The struggle of national unity against particularism, which in the administrative domain had been almost completely fought out, was renewed in the constitutional question. While the mass of the nation remained in a condition of complete inertia, it was only the claims of the old feudal orders which found vigorous defenders; and since nations receive as gifts only what they themselves deserve, the old diets seemed more powerful than they really were, and ultimately gained partial success.

What a difference when the observer turned from the monarchical administration of Prussia to consider its provincial diets! On the one side all was order, unity, and clarity; on the other, hopeless confusion, in which almost every right was contested. The feudal territorial divisions were hardly ever coincident with the administrative areas of the state; their constitution was wholly dependent upon the private law characteristic of the patrimonial state, and was separated by a wide abyss from the legal ideas of the modern state; nowhere did there exist a representation of all classes. The authority of the estates was for the most part limited to the administration of the knightly credit institutes and fire insurance societies, to the assessment of certain taxes, and similar matters. The old order of estates had maintained itself in East Prussia far more vigorously than elsewhere, because here a portion of the peasants, the Köllmers, were represented in the Landtag. Even in the spring of 1813, the Landtag of Königsberg had displayed its efficiency, and the estates of the Mohrung circle cordially assured the chancellor that this ancient constitution, handed down from our forefathers, was the only one well adapted to the German national spirit.[1] In West Prussia, on the other hand, all the powers of the estates were open to dispute. After Frederick the Great had abolished the old Polish estates, his successor, in his year of grace, had issued an ordinance regarding the rights of the estates. It had not been carried into effect. During the years of the war, the government on several occasions summoned assemblies of the estates, whose composition was prescribed from above. No one was able to say what legal rights really existed in this respect, and still less whether Danzig and the Warsaw territories, which had now been added to the province, had any right to claim a share of representation.

In Pomerania there still nominally existed the Further Pomeranian and the Hither Pomeranian Landstuben, a representation of the prelates, the nobility, and the immediate towns, without any participation on the part of the peasantry and the lesser towns. But the once all-powerful Landtag had ceased to assemble after the year 1810; since the estate of peasants had zealously sent its delegates to the new circle assemblies, the old oligarchy had passed into such oblivion that the government of Stargard made enquiry in Berlin whether the Landstuben were still in existence. The reply was to the effect that this would be decided when the question of the re-establishment of the provincial diets was

[1] Memorial from the Mohrung circle diet, September 4, 1816.

settled.[1]   In Silesia, Frederick the Great had abolished the last vestiges of the diets of princes of the imperial days.

All the more loudly vociferated Hardenberg's ancient opponents, the estates of the Electoral Mark.   This Landtag was a peculiar one, representing, as in Pomerania, only the prelates, the nobles, and the immediate towns, an ancient and extremely complicated administration of debts, known as the Landschaft of the Electoral Mark.   In the sixteenth century the estates had taken over extensive territorial debts, and since then, in order to pay the interest on these debts, they administered the yield of certain taxes, which were paid, however, not by themselves, but by the greatly commiserated " taxable estate."   This was the protoytpe of feudal administration, universally distinguished, like the feudal military system, by its incomparable costliness.   An annual income of 300,000 thalers was raised at a cost of 50,000 thalers in emoluments and salaries.[2]   During the first years of Hardenberg's administration, the throne had abolished the *Marsch- und Molestienkasse* together with other feudal rubbish, and now a further step was absolutely necessary.   Since the state was organising its own debts, it was necessary that it should again take this debt of the Mark upon its shoulders ; the days of the Landschaft of Electoral Mark were numbered. Thus the most vigorous prop of the old feudal power began to crumble, and, greatly concerned, deputies of the nobility petitioned the king to restore the ancient constitution and to hear the views of the estates concerning certain necessary changes.   Neumark also possessed its " upper and lower estate " ; Altmark and Kottbus demanded that they should be allowed to rejoin the estates of Brandenburg.   The unfortunate ordinance of May 22nd provided new energy for all these efforts and endowed them with a semblance of right. Moreover, so potent was the charm exercised upon this inexperienced generation by the word " constitution," that Buchholz, the Bonapartist representative of the prudent folk of Berlin, became a zealous advocate of the feudal nobility ; he was the literary spokesman of the feudal party, and in his *Journal für Deutschland* praised the ancient constitution of Electoral Mark, describing it as a genuine example of a constitution.

[1] Memorial from the government of Stargard, April 29, 1814.
[2] Report of the Potsdam Government, December 6, 1809.
[3] Petition of the knightly deputies of Electoral Mark, August 13, 1814.

The system of estates in the old provinces, however, seemed well ordered when compared with the chaotic conditions that prevailed in the newly acquired territories. How proud was Swedish Pomerania of its ancient constitution; the only trouble was that no one had the least idea what this term signified. The old Landschaft of the "circles and towns" of Hither Pomerania had been abolished by King Gustavus Adolphus IV in the year 1806, and in its place there had been introduced the Swedish constitution with its four estates, this change being effected amid the jubilation of the peasants, who now at length secured representation. Four years later, by a further *coup de main* on the part of the crown of Sweden, a new constitution was promulgated, but this never came into actual existence. Consequently the Hither Pomeranian patriot could display his enthusiasm as he pleased for any one of three different constitutions. In actual fact, the "circles and towns" continued to behave as if nothing had happened during these nine years; they regarded themselves as the genuine legal representatives of the country, and besieged the king with grievances. The peasants and tenant farmers, on the other hand, led by the two indefatigables, Ludwig Arndt and Christian Lüders, advocated other views; they had espoused the constitution of 1806, and considered that this was the only one with any legal title to existence.[1]

In Posen there still existed a council of deputies, that is to say, a general council after the Napoleonic style. Since this assembly was nominated by the Warsaw government, since, moreover, it formed only one constituent of the Polish prefectoral system, and since it could not be regarded as a genuine diet, it was with perfect justice abolished by Prussia on August 26, 1818.

An incredible condition of feudal anarchy existed in Saxony—a condition which it is plain Hardenberg had no suspicion of when he promulgated the ordinance of May 22nd. Each one of the seven parts of the duchy of Saxony possessed its own assembly of the estates, and since the quiet life of junkerdom had here never been disturbed by the severe hand of a strong monarchy, the feudal oligarchy distinguished itself from the mob by laborious proofs of noble descent; not long before, King Frederick Augustus had warned

[1] Petition of July 20, 1816.

off a count of the younger nobility from the sacred threshold of the Lusatian estates. In these circles it was regarded as a matter of course that the portion of the Saxon hereditary dominions which had passed to Prussia would continue to retain all the rights which the Landtag of the kingdom of Saxony had possessed, and the demand was even voiced that a separate system of national debt should be retained. When in Lower Lusatia, which now constituted a mere fragment of the new province of Brandenburg, the chancellor would not immediately summon the old Landtag, the estates of the territory declared: "The contents of this ordinance, which with a few momentous words deprives us of all that has hitherto been dearest to us—our well-grounded privileges, our constitutional efficiency, our just hopes, and the beliefs of our childhood—has profoundly disturbed us." They went on to demand, "as representatives of the people, as participators heretofore in administration and legislation," that they should be taken into consultation concerning the new constitution. The estates of the princedom of Querfurt endeavoured on two occasions, on their own initiative, to constitute themselves into a circle diet, although this was forbidden. When the Prussian stamp-laws were introduced into Saxony, the estates of the Thuringian circle issued a passionate statement of grievances to the king, wherein they menacingly declared that this step "had awakened ancient memories." The burghers and peasants, on the other hand, uttered here, as in Hither Pomerania, loud remonstrances concerning the behaviour of the high-born "representatives of the people." Bourgeois landowners of the Görlitz region demanded, while thankfully recognising the just sentiments of the new government, that the provincial diet should be completely transformed, for "the existing condition of affairs is supported solely by the weak foundation of antiquity." The like request was sent in by the town councillors of Naumburg for, they said, "the old estates represented their own interests alone, and the feudal constitution concealed the gravest defects under the semblance of legality." This writing was transmitted to Berlin by President von Schönberg, with the assurance that it voiced the judgment of the cultured people of the province.[1]

[1] Petition of the estates of Lower Lusatia, December 4, 1816. Reports of the Merseburg government, August 8, 1817, October 24, 1819. Petition from bourgeois landowners of Upper Lusatia, March 1, 1818. Petition of the Naumburg town councillors, December 31, 1816.

Since the ordinance of May 22nd decreed the re-establishment of the provincial diets "where they still exist in greater or less efficiency," the former estates of the provinces westward of the Elbe also thought they could derive advantage from the ambiguous royal words. All of them, those of Westphalia, Berg, and Darmstadt, had been abolished by France. Yet some shattered fragments of the ancient feudal institutions had still been preserved almost everywhere; in addition, appeal was made to article 24 of the peace of Tilsit, in virtue of which the new lord paramount had to fulfil all the duties which had hitherto devolved upon the king of Prussia, and the conclusion drawn from these words was, that the representative rights abolished by the governments of the Confederation of the Rhine would now be restored without further parley. The first to move in the matter were the nobles of County Mark, who even during the war had petitioned for the restoration of "the good old constitution." When the oath of allegiance was taken, the estates renewed their demand, saying: "We are Markers and as such are deeply attached to our peculiar fatherland."

Since that time, the same demand had been repeated in countless petitions by the spokesman of the estates, Baron von Bodelschwingh-Plettenberg. "Our constitution exercised its benevolent influence before the Prussian state had a constitution at all. The fact that the scheme for the Prussian constitution is not yet completed can be no obstacle to the leaving of our own constitution at work within its own boundaries." After repeated attempts at conciliation, Hardenberg finally forbade the indefatigable petitioner to use the title of "estates," and subsequently (on May 10, 1820) laid it down as a general principle that where the former estates had been abolished by the foreign authorities recognised by Prussia in the peace of Tilsit, these remained abolished until the introduction of the new provincial diets.[1] The principle was legally incontestable, for the Prussian government was not responsible for the *coup de mains* of the foreign regime, and in the very moment when it was proposed to transform the ancient institutions, it was a matter of political necessity

---

[1] Representation to minister von Reck, from the deputies sent by County Mark to the swearing-in ceremony, dated October 20, 1815. Petition of the estates to the chancellor, March 20, June 2, 1817, etc. Hardenberg's Replies, May 18 1817, May 10, 1820,

to avoid the re-establishment of these same institutions unchanged.

The endeavours of the estates of the Mark constituted no more than one link in the chain of a widely ramified movement of the nobility throughout the entire region of Lower Rhenish Westphalia, which aimed at the re-establishment of the ancient union of the estates of Jülich, Cleves, Berg, and Mark. Unfortunately Stein espoused the cause of these nobles. The great statesman recognised, indeed, that the new constitution could not possibly be harmonised with the former estates; he desired a free hand for the king " with the advice of those whom he chose to summon in counsel," and he warned his fellow-countrymen against the excessive demands of the arrogant nobility of Electoral Mark. But he was filled with passionate hatred against Hardenberg, and was embittered by the hesitating procedure of the government, and he therefore favoured the artificial and illegal attempts to reconstitute the Rhenish Westphalian estates; he regarded this movement as a wholesome stimulus for the government, whereas in reality it was an obstacle to every comprehensive reform. His aristocratic sentiments became harsher and more stubborn with age; his parliament of property-holders was now understood by him to be nothing more than a representation of landed property; and it was not the great landed proprietors as such, but the nobles alone, who were to constitute the first estate. With what strange associates, too, did the baron now enter into relationship. In the Jülich region was Mirbach, who desired proof of noble descent as a title to sit in the diet; in Münster was Baron Merveldt, who demanded a separate assembly of the estates for each one of the ancient territories of Westphalia, and who desired that these bodies should elect the representatives to the provincial diet. " This monarchy," he said, " consists of territories and states possessed of constitutions which, thanks be to God, have not been dissolved by any revolution." Now the estates of the princedom of Paderborn also approached the king, begging for their re-establishment. The Landrats von der Horst and von Borries, as representatives of the estates of Minden, went further still, demanding the re-establishment of the ancient constitution at least to this extent, that the nation of Minden should vote its own taxes, and that the military organisation of the region should be conducted by its own estates.[1] The feudal movement extended more widely day by day. Even in the duchy of Magdeburg, whose estates had ceased to be of any account long before the days of King Jerome, and even in the county of Hohenstein and in Eichsfeld, demands for the reconstitution of the ancient Landtags found expression.

In face of such claims, the unity of the state could be preserved in no other way than by the work of establishing the constitution being left entirely in the hands of the monarchy. The news from Würtemberg, where the king had just before been vainly endeavouring to come to an understanding with a feudal assembly about a new constitution, had produced a profound impression in Berlin. In view of these experiences, who could even dream of harmonising the Prussian constitution with twenty or more feudal Landtags? An entire reconstruction was essential. The new provincial diets must be attached to the modern provinces, not to the old territories; and (in addition to the nobles) the towns, and the small landowners must receive a reasonable degree of representation. At the same time, the reawakening of feudal particularism showed how strong were still the centrifugal forces; for this reason it seemed indispensable that the creation of a Reichstag should speedily follow the establishment of the provincial diets.

All this was clearly recognised by Hardenberg, but among the ministers an utter confusion of views prevailed. They had to face an entirely new problem, and regarded the stubborn resistance of the new provinces and the clamours of the former estates with profound anxiety. Whilst Ancillon, in confidential intercourse, was already espousing the wishes of the feudal party, Klewitz was the first to display open antagonism to these wishes. A straightforward opponent of the feudalists, this excellent man had nevertheless always overestimated the justification for the particularist tendencies of the state, and consequently, in the very memorial in which he recommended the re-establishment of the provincial ministries, he had proposed to the chancellor that, for the present, provincial diets only should be constituted, since the nation would then quietly await the centralised constitution. Six

---

[1] Count Merveldt, Petition to Altenstein, August 20, 1817. Petition of the estates of Paderborn to the king, August 31, 1816. Petition of the estates of the princedom of Minden to Hardenberg, April 10, 1815.

2 P

months later, in the spring of 1817, he took an additional step in the direction of the feudalists. He wrote a new memorial: " What do the Prussian provinces expect from their king, and what can the king agree to give them ? " He answered his own question by saying that these provinces, old as well as new, expected nothing more than what they had customarily enjoyed, what they had always possessed, in so far as this expectation was compatible with present needs.[1] He went on to advocate the establishment of provincial diets and a notable enlargement of their rights, " not so much because the *Zeitgeist* demands it, as because the king desires that the welfare of his state shall advance, and that after its example the welfare of Germany and of Europe shall also advance. By this enlargement of rights, an adjustment or common constitution for the different territories or provinces could be brought into being." Thus the independence of the lord paramount might be secured, whereas this independence might very readily be endangered by a common Landtag. Thus for the first time in an official document did the view find expression that a constitution for the state as a whole was superfluous and even dangerous ; the reactionary party at court and the feudalists in general did not hesitate to turn the timid minister's utterances to their own advantage. Hardenberg, however, offered lively opposition, and the king had not yet been won over.

Klewitz further suggested: " First of all that which has existed from immemorial times must everywhere be ascertained in detail." Delegates from the council of state were to perambulate the individual provinces in order to study feudal conditions, and to ascertain from personal intercourse with the inhabitants the desire of the provinces regarding a constitution ; but the summoning of notables to form constitutional committees, as proposed in the ordinance of May 22nd, seemed an extremely dubious policy in view of experiences in Würtemberg. The counsel was well-intentioned, for unquestionably, in view of the extreme uncertainty of public opinion, an assembly of notables in Berlin might readily be made the arena of social passions and particularist longings But, since the ministry itself had not as yet arrived at any common understanding regarding the principles of the constitution, the proposed visitation of the provinces involved another danger

[1] Klewitz, Memorial of April 28, 1817, handed to the Chancellor on June 1st.

hardly less great. The debates of an assembly of notables must at least lead to the emergence of some sort of average opinion, whereas if some hundred notables were individually to be asked their views in their own homes, it was evident that nothing would result but the ascertaining of a medley of fundamentally subjective opinions which would be likely to confuse and to paralyse the vacillating determination of the crown. This danger was not recognised, and the fear of the confusions likely to result in a constituent assembly prevailed. The king approved the visitation of the provinces.

In such circumstances, on July 7, 1817, the constitutional committee met for the first and only time. As a matter of course it formed a subdivision of the council of state, and consisted of twenty-two members of this body. Hardenberg informed the committee that the king held it to be simpler and safer to send three commissaries into the provinces instead of summoning the notables to Berlin. Altenstein was appointed for the western provinces ; Beyme for Pomerania and Prussia ; Klewitz for Brandenburg, Saxony, Silesia, and Posen ; the committee was not to give its opinion until the reports of the three commissaries had been received. At the same time, in a lengthy address, the chancellor declared that the ancient diets had been unmistakable obstacles to the working of the state machine ; the state owed its improvement and its flourishing condition to the genius of its rulers ; but since the present condition of affairs could not continue without great disadvantage, since the nation was ripe and worthy to receive a permanent constitution and a representative system, since by the valiant defence of the fatherland and by the struggle for its independence the state had given a rare example of civic virtue and loyalty to the king, the latter had voluntarily determined to bestow a representative constitution. There was appended a definite statement of the limits which the monarch imposed upon his concession : "His majesty will gladly consult the future representative assembly regarding the laws that are to be passed, but it is his definite intention to allow only a consultative voice, and all interference in the administration is expressly excluded."

In the late summer and in the autumn, the three ministers completed their circuit. They were commissioned to acquire precise information regarding all the representative institutions which had ever existed in the territories, and as far as the future was concerned they were to propound two questions in especial: whether a representation of the estate of peasants was possible and useful in addition to a representation of the nobles and the towns; and whether a national assembly was desired, or no more than provincial diets. In all, about three hundred persons were asked their opinions (in Silesia fifty-seven notables). More than half of these belonged to the landed gentry, this being a necessary outcome of the nature of previous conditions; but merchants, manufacturers, burgomasters, and the clergy, also gave their opinions in a great many instances, and in the coast provinces Beyme applied for information by preference to the bourgeois classes. Very few opinions, however, were given by the estate of peasants, most of these opinions being from Silesia and Magdeburg, but not one from the regions that had formerly belonged to the kingdom of Saxony, where the peasant was only just beginning to gain relief from the oppressions of the feudal regime.

If an attempt be made to draw a general conclusion from the confusion of opinions, given for the most part in good faith and with German frankness, it becomes apparent that there did not as yet exist a definite and coherent public opinion, or even a passionate popular will, which might have exercised pressure upon the throne; the feudal movement had not yet found its counterpoise among the people; but there was displayed strong support for the naive particularism of the provinces. Almost everywhere a desire was expressed for provincial diets; President von Motz, who for the sake of national unity demanded nothing but a Reichstag, stood quite alone. But many voices declared in favour of provincial diets without any national assembly, some on account of particularism, others animated by a dread of shaking the throne. Most of those who expressed their views recognised that the provincial diets must be attached to the newly formed provinces; yet several advocated Landtags for the governmental districts, and still more numerous were the demands for diets for the territories of ancient delimitation. As regards the form of the national assembly, opinions were also fundamentally diverse. Many thought of a parliament, others of a small corporation containing forty members which should attend the sittings of the council of state. The question whether there should be a unicameral or a bicameral system was rarely propounded. Nor was there any harmony regarding the representation of the estate of peasants. The majority were in favour of this, but many of the nobles and of the burghers expressed doubts whether a sufficient number of "fit subjects" (this was the usual expression) were to be found in the young estate. The gentry were chiefly influenced by the fear of persons who, not being themselves peasants, might advocate the cause of the peasantry, and they invariably demanded that this estate should be represented by peasants alone. A far from inconsiderable minority, consisting of men of all classes, roundly declared that the people was not yet ripe for representative institutions, and that a well-ordered administration was sufficient. Very frequently, with childlike naivety, the sole ground for a constitution was alleged to be that the king had pledged his word and must therefore fulfil it—for the rest, everything could be left to his grace. In this chaos of immature views, the most satisfactory point was the instinctive understanding displayed for the connection between constitution and administration, by which the Prussians were distinguished from the South Germans of those days. Thanks to the old traditions of the state, and above all thanks to the reforms of Stein and Hardenberg, almost everyone here understood the importance of administrative questions. The constitution was regarded, not as the beginning of a new national life, but as the enlargement, the completion, of the reforms which had been begun in communal and circle administration. The influence of French theories of equality was hardly seen at all ; a subdivision of classes was taken as a matter of course.

The notables of Posen had alone attained the altitude of neo-French culture. As if it had been the outcome of a tacit conspiracy, the Polish nobles questioned by Klewitz almost unanimously agreed in demanding an independent provincial diet, which was to supervise education, to appoint the officials, and to administer a separate budget under the control of a provincial treasury. The inevitable general von Kosinski handed in a proposal for a Prussian "federative constitution" based upon a balance of powers : *c'est la Prusse qui doit faire l'époque dans le siècle constitutionnel.* Prussia had hitherto said to her subject peoples, "You are helots, held together by soldiers and by a dominant official caste " ; the state must now recognise its duty "to be a tender mother, must recognise it all the more clearly because it must admit the injustice of Europe towards the nations united under its eagle." In fine, Prussia was to be transformed into a federation of independent provinces, with provincial diets and provincial military forces! Bojanowski demanded "a Declaration of the Rights of Man"; Morawski found that human dignity was fully preserved only where "a superman" ruled, controlled by a *sénat conservateur* and a chamber of deputies. Some of the Germans also showed themselves to have been infected by the French culture dominating this part of the world. Governmental-director von Leipziger brought forward a complete "constitutional proposal," cut on the well-known Parisian pattern. (§ 1. The House of Hohenzollern rules in unbroken line of descent in accordance with the existing local laws. § 16. The Christian religion is the national religion. And so on.) Manifestly such views of the Polish nobles, with their hardly concealed *arrières pensées*, were unlikely to win over the throne for the imitation of French institutions; but they served to teach all the more impressively how dangerous it was to rest content with provincial diets alone. Lord-lieutenant Zerboni laid great stress on this point, asking wonderingly: "Is it our desire to introduce a cantonal constitution like that of Switzerland?" He wrote: "As yet we are not a nation. We exist only *in abstracto*, and become extinct when the idea ceases. Great events lie in the womb of the future. These events will become associated with Prussia. We have no rival, for we seize the role which is allotted to us." Consequently there must be a representative assembly for the state as a whole, with legislative and not merely advisory powers.[1]

In Rhineland extremely divergent views prevailed. On the one hand was the feudal agitation of the Lower Rhenish nobles; these were now joined by Baron von Nagel, who published an unauthorised and detailed work upon the Jülich-Cleves-Berg diet; and also by Hommer, the former syndic of Electoral Treves, who desired the re-establishment of the Landtag of Treves with its spiritual curia. Opposed to these were the democratic views of a thoroughly modern bourgeois society; and in addition, especially among the native-born officials, certain constitutional ideas which suggested the proximity of France. It is true that the town councils of Cologne and Treves, when, during

---

[1] Klewitz, Report concerning the circuit in Posen. Zerboni, Opinion of November 28, 1817.

that summer, the king visited the provinces, merely referred in general terms to the promised constitution ; while Benzenberg, who, with the landowners of the Crefield circle, had audience of the monarch, begged merely for an advisory assembly. President Sethe, on the other hand, submitted a memorial in which it was proposed that the Reichstag should be appointed solely by election, all independent burghers receiving the suffrage, the mediatised alone being excluded because they paid no taxes. Regarding the feudal constitution, he said bluntly : " It is only a shadow and an illusion of representation." In like sense a judge of Düsseldorf suggested representation of the interests of the various social classes with the exception of nobles. Another Rhenish memorial demanded an upper chamber of members appointed for life from among the landowners, the large capitalists, and the men of marked intelligence ; and a lower chamber which was to be appointed, by indirect election, by all independent burghers, and which was to represent the entire people. This, he said, was the necessary complement to the obligation of universal military service. Here were already manifested the ideas which were to ripen in the year 1848. As yet they had little power, for the mass of the Rhinelanders lived solely for industry and commerce, and neither the constitutional movement nor the Teutonising enthusiasm of the younger generation found here any strong support. In Westphalia, Altenstein seems to have conversed chiefly with the nobles. He had an interview with Stein which was equally satisfactory to both parties.[1]

In the eastern provinces the principal dispute concerned the question whether the estate of peasants, which had so recently been enfranchised, was already capable of benefiting by representative institutions. Beyme found the nobles of Hither Pomerania still completely under the influence of feudal views ; very few of them desired reforms, the most notable exception being Prince Putbus, " a true friend of the peasants." Schildener, professor at Greifswald, endeavoured with small success to prove in a pamphlet to the privileged classes that no other estate represented the Pomeranian spirit so faithfully as did that of the despised peasantry. Among the notables of Further Pomerania, the desire for the restoration of the ancient constitution was equally predominant ; but the admission of the peasants to representation was here regarded as unavoidable.

[1] Minutes relating to the circuit in the western provinces.

The minister received an extremely favourable impression regarding " the excellent and vigorous spirit " which the year 1813 had awakened in East Prussia. In this region representation of the estate of peasants was everywhere regarded as essential. In West Prussia, Beyme was astonished by the general political indifference. The towns uttered vigorous complaints regarding the unaccustomed burdens of the town's ordinance, whilst the nobles were especially concerned to advise against the admission to representation of bourgeois landowners.[1]

The majority of the Silesian notables favoured the representation of all three estates in Lower Silesia ; but almost all expressed doubts whether the Upper Silesian peasants were ripe for political activity. So strong had been the impression produced by the royal promise that even the ultra-conservative Field-marshal York declared : " The monarchical constitution and administration such as existed under Frederick the Great, are to me the dearest and best. But a constitution and a representative system have been promised the country, and the pledge must be fulfilled. Moreover, this must be done as speedily as possible, because the continuance of heavy burdens fosters dissatisfaction, and with arms in their hands the people may even become dangerous."[2]

In the Marks there were many complaints because " the ancient constitution has been trodden under foot " ; and there was much anxiety regarding the threatening excessive powers of the burghers and the peasants. The nobles of Altmark were exceptionally broad-minded, for under the Westphalian regime they had learned to lay aside many ancient prejudices, and most of them favoured the representation of the estate of peasants. In Electoral Mark, the peasants, proud of their new circle assemblies, had no doubt that they would send representatives to the provincial diet as well. Minister von Voss-Buch, the leader of the feudalists, still remained cautiously in the background ; in view of the spirit of the age a constitution seemed almost unavoidable, but it might be better to begin at first with a representation of the estates, that is to say, to institute a provincial diet after consulting the estates.

Nowhere did the ancient class hatreds flame so fiercely as in Saxony. Here the " ripeness " of the peasants for repre-

---

[1] Beyme, Report concerning circuit in Pomerania and Prussia.
[2] Opinion of York, Klein-Oels, September 12, 1817.

sentation was doubted by the majority, while all demanded that the province should have the right of voting its own taxes. People referred sorrowfully to the extravagance of the Polish Augustus. Von Berlepsch, an excellent man, declared that this anxiety about money was the only political idea in Saxony. The opinion of Count Wintzingerode-Bodenstein showed how difficult this work of constitution-building seemed even to men of experience. He had at one time collaborated when Frederick of Würtemberg compacted the Swabian territories to form a " realm "; but in a great state such a procedure was not applicable; here the old diets must be established, and for Eichsfeld the diet system of Electoral Mainz must be reconstituted with certain improvements.

One only of the three ministers, Beyme, appended to his report a representation of his own views. These resembled those of Hardenberg, for he condemned the old system as " an offspring of mediæval darkness which could not bear the light of modern days." He saw in America " the ideal of a constitution "; demanded for Prussia a representation of the three estates, temporarily in a single chamber, until a vigorous nobility should have been constituted; he proclaimed the peasantry as the youngest and healthiest of the estates, Rhineland as the most enlightened province. He demanded complete publicity for the proceedings of the Reichstag, the provincial diets, and the circle assemblies. He demanded constitutional rights almost identical with those which exist to-day, and trial by jury for press offences.

All three of the delegates conscientiously endeavoured to fulfil the instruction to enquire into what had existed from immemorial times. Altenstein did not shrink from the labour involved in seeking out the syndics and other office bearers of the old Landtags in the numerous territories of which the new western provinces were composed. Most of these were venerable men, well on in the seventies, " with excellent memories " as the minister assures us; but, after all, they had not been able to retain in their minds every complicated detail of the ancient Franconian furniture of vanished days. Thus with honourable labour was gathered together a long series of historical retrospects. Here were carefully described the *liberum veto* of the Poles and the *precariæ annuæ* of the estates of Electoral Treves, the Silesian diet of princes, and the *Unterherrentag* of Jülich, the *advocatus patriæ* of the duchy of

Westphalia, and the tax chamber of Bleicherode in County Hohenstein, the *Vest Recklingshausen* and the diet of the prince-dom of Corvey, with its five heads and three estates—and, to sum all up, from the whole medley there was one thing only to learn, and this was that there was nothing to learn for the living present.

This perambulation of the provinces gave an extremely scanty result. It provided a fruitless jumble of ancient memories and uncertain wishes. Even the few publicists who concerned themselves with the constitutional question had no advice to give. Grävell, the liberal, in his writing *Does Prussia need a Constitution ?* propounded the innocent demand that the entire legislation since 1806 should be submitted to the national assembly for examination, for he did not even consider how easily this enlightened wish might lead to the destruction of the reforms of Stein and Hardenberg. Benzenberg's book *Upon the Constitution*, to which Frederick William gave friendly recep-tion, unquestionably one of the most mature political works of the epoch, informs us : " At a distance of 90,000,000 miles from the sun, there moves in its orbit around that luminary, a small sphere, whose diameter is 8,000 miles " ; thus beginning at the very beginning, the disquisition proceeds on its way, until, on page 504, the exhausted reader arrives at Germany without learning anything to speak of about Prussia !

The serious question whether this proud, absolute throne, which had so recently manifested its unbroken vital energy in the reconstitution of the army, the administration, and the fiscal system, could without danger share its supreme authority with a representative assembly—this great riddle seemed even more obscure than it had been before the opinions of the people had been taken. Sharply critical liberal writers elsewhere in Germany, who, in view of the one thing which Hardenberg had not done, forgot the great things which he had done, never realised what troubles were besieging the chancellor. For more tragical than all the other proofs of childlike political immaturity which the visitation had brought to light, was the realisation that at least one-half of the Prussian people was still quite unable to look beyond the boundaries of the native province. Count Edmund Kesselstadt, one of the most far-sighted patriots on the Rhine, accurately described the mood of the new provinces in the following terms : " From the great majority of Prussian subjects, the idea of belonging to a great state is altogether remote, for the idea of being German has to them always seemed somewhat strange." [1] If a representative system could be bestowed upon a generation at such a level of culture, it might indeed be hoped that the sense of duty of the conscientious and reasonable population would induce them to accommodate themselves to the new form of the state. But a constitution given at this time would not have been the work of the nation, but, as had formerly been the town's ordinance, would have been a free gift of the royal will, moving on in advance of the nation.

The king, however, disquieted by the news from the south, now began to become estranged from the constitutional plans of his chancellor.

[1] Kesselstadt's Opinion, recorded in the minutes of Altenstein's visitation.

CHAPTER VI.

SOUTH GERMAN CONSTITUTIONAL STRUGGLES.

§ I. THE GOOD OLD LAW IN SWABIA.

THE South German middle-sized states were for the most part spared the laborious work of reconstruction which in Prussia for many years occupied all the energies of her statesmen. During the wars of the last decade, these thrones had in every case adopted the side of the conqueror at a suitable moment, and consequently in the great days of settlement had maintained their possessions with trifling alterations. Their territories had been far less severely visited by the afflictions of the campaigns than had been the north, and there was here no obstacle to the immediate undertaking of the work of constitution-building. Moreover, with the fall of the Protector, there came to an end also the strict dictatorship which for ten years had forcibly maintained the unity of these young state structures. The courts themselves felt that the artificial bonds required renewal. They hoped by the granting of certain harmless representative rights to reconcile discontented subjects with their native land, and to alienate the sentiments of the people from the alarming idea of German unity; at the same time they hoped by the speedy fulfilment of article 13 of the federal act to safeguard their sovereignty against any attack on the part of the Bundestag

Thus it happened that the nuclear lands of the Confederation of the Rhine experienced the first difficult years of constitutional life a generation earlier than did Prussia; and however scanty the political outcome of this time of apprenticeship, none the less the period served to awaken the slumbering forces of the south, and to display to the world for the first time after a long interval what a treasure Germany possessed in the ancient civilisation, in the homely bourgeois culture, and in the warm-hearted public spirit of the highlands. These

High German stocks, which had taken hardly more than a passive part in the political struggles of the eighteenth century, suddenly appeared in the foreground of German history, and anyone who judges German affairs only from information derived from the newspapers, or by the catchwords of party, might readily fall into the error of imagining that the leadership of the nation had now passed from the state of Frederick to Bavaria, Swabia, and Franconia.

Just as formerly the age of our classical poetry had erected its stage outside of Prussia, so now the new political ideals which the spokesmen of public opinion esteemed as the true content of the epoch, could find no root in Prussia ; and the state whose good sword had first, and so recently, opened for the Germans the gates of a new age, seemed, to the liberal world, to be no more than an inert mass, a ponderous load, which hindered the movements of the free limbs of our race. Entangled in the belief that all that is good for the nations is derived from constitutional forms, people had no longer any vision for Prussia's military system and commercial policy, for the quiet work which in Prussia was preparing for the reconstruction of the German state ; and whilst all the proceedings of the Swabian chambers were reported in the press with passionate enthusiasm, in non-Prussian Germany the conditions in Prussia remained so utterly unknown that any ridiculous fable could count upon credulous hearers. In actual fact, the South German constitutions were, as the courts of Munich and Stuttgart had from the first hoped, pillars of particularism. The orators of the petty Landtags had, indeed, the words of German unity on their lips, but the serious side of their political labours remained restricted within the frontiers of their homeland ; and since at the Bundestag the policy of absolutism maintained the upper hand, they soon began to esteem their native provinces as constitutionally exemplary states, each an acropolis of German freedom and enlightenment ; and they ultimately attained to the naive view that their local constitutions stood above the federal laws.

What a misfortune it was for our political culture that in this nation which was so slowly emerging from a condition of dispersed energies, the first constitutional experiences should be effected amid the pseudo-life of powerless and non-independent states. In these narrows, German parliamentarism acquired from the first characteristics of provincial restriction. The momentous problem of continental constitutional life, the problem how parliamentary forms were to be harmonised with the power of an army ever ready for war and with the continuous progress of a great European policy, could not even be mooted in such dependent communities. Every political dispute here became a matter of personalities ; and since the continuance of kingship by Napoleon's grace inspired neither veneration nor forbearance, there resulted from the curse of particularism a morbid ferocity of party struggle which corresponded ill with the good-natured character and the tolerably healthy social conditions of our people. In the end, the behaviour of the petty courts was determined by the will of Austria and Prussia ; so long as these two leading powers refused to adopt the constitutional system, the opposition parties of the new representative assemblies were devoid of all prospect of ever attaining to the guidance of the ship of state. In such a position, without any genuine responsibility, they became accustomed to practise all the sins of political dilettantism ; they considered that their statesman-like duties were adequately fulfilled if they continued obstinately, staunchly, and with passion, to reiterate the essential principles of the constitutional doctrine, and they endeavoured to atone for their lack of power by a boastful self-overvaluation. An almost superstitious honour was paid to the names " constitution," " popular representation," " man chosen of the people " ; anyone who took the side of the monarchy was suspected of being a vile place-hunter. The evil arts of police persecution served to increase at once the bitterness and the arrogance of the opposition, and continued to gain over new adherents for that doctrine of Rotteck which regarded the misfortunes of the blameless populace as solely dependent upon the wickedness of governments. In the bad school of federal anarchy and constitutional petty life, the Germans gradually became the most discontented and also the most docile of all the European peoples.

The very first Landtag of these years of peace, that of Würtemberg, exercised a confusing and embittering influence upon public opinion. Here the long-suppressed and justified discontent with the Rhenish Confederate despotism manifested itself with an impetuous violence which filled all the courts with anxiety ; the democratic ideas of the new century entered into alliance with the defiant spirit of feudal licence ; and on both sides justice and injustice were indistinguishably mingled. Here, also, the struggle for the construction of the new constitutional forms took the form of a legal dispute on behalf of well-grounded liberties established by convention; the questions of power in this matter of constitutional life were judged in accordance with the rules of civil procedure, and the formalist view of the state characteristic of jurists trained in the field of civil law acquired, even during these first constitutional struggles of new Germany, a prestige which became injurious to the free development of German parliamentarism.

Among all the temporal territories of the empire, Würtemberg and Mecklenburg had longest and most faithfully preserved the feudal ordering of the state ; even in the middle of the eighteenth century, in the blossoming time of absolutism, in both these countries the feudal constitution was formally confirmed by a legal settlement. Whilst everywhere else the masses detested the polyarchy of the feudal lords, and revered the growing power of the princes as the protector of the weak, in Würtemberg the good old law was regarded as sacred by the entire populace. Everyone in Old Würtemberg repeated with complacency the saying of Fox : " There are in Europe only two constitutions worthy of the name, that of England and that of Würtemberg." In the defence of the ancient and traditional law, all the political energies of this people were for three centuries monopolised ; here was trained that defiant Swabian legal sentiment which found expression in the saying *parta tueri*. When upon the intercession of Frederick the Great the old J. J. Moser was restored to freedom from Hohentwiel, men, women, and children flocked to meet this martyr of the good old law. Even in the politically well-endowed intelligence of Spittler, the ideas of the constitutional law of his native land were so firmly implanted, that he involuntarily judged all the constitutions of history by the measure of Swabian freedom. The rigidly bourgeois character of Old Würtemberg society was mainly dependent upon this popular affection.

Here, in the land of the town-leagues and of the peasants' wars, upon the most luxuriant soil of the German separatist spirit, the nobles also had from the first been accustomed to go their own way. In the year 1514, when the land of Würtemberg, by agreement with Duke Ulrich, secured its fundamental representative law, the convention of Tübingen, the nobles acquired their liberties as immediates of the empire and scorned to participate; it was only in the court and state service of the house of Würtemberg that the Swabian imperial knight frequently appeared as a privileged guest. The Landtag of the duchy was constituted solely out of the prelates of the Lutheran state church with representatives elected by the town councils. Thus there existed a bourgeois oligarchy which on a small scale was just as powerful as were the States-General of the Dutch Republic, and which, like this body, was in continuous conflict with an inchoate monarchical authority. The duke ruled as absolute master over his great private possessions, whose rich yield was in times of peace entirely adequate to supply the expenses of the court and of the government. But if through extravagance, or through the needs of war, he ran into debt, he then asked the Landtag to vote taxes, and could secure what he desired only when the representative liberties had been once more confirmed and enlarged in a resolution of the Landtag which had the force of a convention. In most of the other feudal territories, the rising monarchical authority utilised the committees of the provincial diets to destroy the power of the Landtag from within outwards. During the eighteenth century, the Würtemberg Landtag was seldom summoned; yet its powers did not pass to the duke, but to the two committees of the estates. The small committee in Stuttgart was the real ruler of the country. It sat continuously, appointed its own new members, levied and made use of the income derived from the provincial taxes at its own discretion, and provided for the children and the relatives of the bourgeois "gentry," the Stockmaiers, Pfaffs, and Commerells, in the official positions at their disposal. If the privy-councillors, who were pledged both to the duke and to the province, should put in an appearance to audit the revenue accounts, the red wine of Eilfing was not spared; in case of need, the hand could be plunged into the renowned secret treasure-chest of the committee. This chest served for all the arts of corruption, those arts with which an oligarchy cannot possibly dispense, for "the friendly removal of a troublesome official, one who censured all malpractices," or for the struggle against the territorial prince. The chartered liberties of the country were firmly maintained by the committee against every encroachment. Help was sought, now from the aulic council of the empire, now from the house of Austria, which would not abandon its hereditary claims upon Würtemberg ; until at length England, Prussia, and Denmark gave formal guarantees for the last great charter of the country, the legal settlement of 1770.

The church also still possessed its church funds, which disposed of the income from numerous estates and forests ; it alone among the Lutheran state churches of Germany had preserved undiminished the entire possessions of the ancient church. It was not for this reason alone that among the Lutheran theologians Würtemberg was spoken of as the apple of God's eye. The little country was the living centre of Protestantism in High Germany. With all the profundity of their temperament, the inhabitants had once voluntarily gone over to the Protestant faith, and had then steadfastly maintained that faith amid severe trials, when the armies of the Hapsburgs on three occasions swept across the country and threatened to annihilate its independence. The church, thus preserved amid struggle and suffering, determined the entire culture of the people. It early gave the country an admirably ordered elementary school system, and maintained among adults a puritan moral discipline by means of the dreaded exhortations " from the pulpit." The three celebrated schools in the quiet forest valleys of Bebenhausen, Blaubeuren, and Maulbronn, where the sons of the gentry received their education, continued to retain all the characteristics of ecclesiastical educational institutions. Even at the university of Tübingen, the theological foundation set the tone : all offices, it was understood, were to be filled from those on the foundation. The clerical families of the Andreäs, Osianders, and Bidenbachs, shared with the burgomaster families the control of the Landtag.

The great days of this bourgeois theocratic oligarchy coincided with the quiet epoch following the peace of Augsburg, when the whole of German life was dominated by theology. At that time, under the good duke Christopher and the pious Louis, who divided his time so peacefully between the beer tankard and his symbolic books, Würtemberg was regarded as the prototype of a Lutheran territory. But as soon as the development of standing armies imposed new tasks upon modern policy, here, as everywhere else, the barrenness of the feudal state became manifest. The artificial structure of this well-secured caste rule was designed for the eternal arrest of human affairs, the power of the sovereign ruler of the country was so unnaturally restricted that Old Würtemberg learned only the sins of monarchy, and never its creative energy. To the people, the duke seemed merely the embodiment of oppression and extortion, since he was continually demanding new taxes and new recruits from the grumbling committee. The excessive sentiment of princely self-esteem, which in the eighteenth century seized this dynasty also, could not here find expression for its activities in the foundation of institutions of general utility, in the care for well-being and culture, but only in courtly extravagance and the occasional exercise of arbitrary force. The grandiose castles of the petty house of Würtemberg rivalled the magnificent buildings of the Polish Augustus, as Hohentwiel and Hohenasperg rivalled the prisons of Königstein; the old capital became impoverished because it had pleased the mistress of Eberhard Louis, the countess Grävenitz, to build, a few miles from the charming gorge of the Nesenbach, a rival residence to Stuttgart, the dreary Ludwigsburg, the most pompous and the most hideous of all the numerous palaces of South Germany. Unworthy favourites, the Jew Süss, Wittleder, and Montmartin, carried on their greedy malpractices at court; the game in the ducal forests laid waste the fields of the thickly populated and fertile country-side, for the duke was the lord only of his own private domain, and what did he care about the weal or woe of the rest of the country, from which the revenues flowed only into the treasure-chest of the permanent committee?

Amid such experiences there came into existence among the Würtemberg people that peculiar political sentiment, strangely compounded of dynastic dependence and angry suspicion, whose traces have not disappeared even to-day. How often under stress of war did the country display its absolute fidelity to its fugitive duke; innumerable songs celebrated the glory of the ancient princely house, of the escutcheon with the stag's antlers, from those folk-songs which had long ago cried to the fierce exile Ulrich, "You are the natural master of the land of Würtemberg," down to the genuinely Swabian poem of the youthful Schiller, which menacingly demanded that "those elsewhere in the world" should humble their pride before the renown of Eberhard the Whimperer.

Yet at the same time the land continually resounded with justified and unjustified complaints against the court, and the view widely prevailed that Swabian liberties could be maintained only if the duke, like a dangerous wild beast, was carefully guarded in a cage. In Prussia the modern German state came into existence upon the secure foundation of universal military service and the duty of paying taxes. In Würtemberg, on the other hand, there still prevailed, in unbroken tradition, the political sentiment of the middle ages; all taxes were regarded as extraordinary burdens for times of special need, and exemption from military service was considered the most valuable of territorial privileges. The unwarlike sense which was everywhere characteristic of the retired life of the feudal German states was manifested more unrestrainedly perhaps than anywhere else among the peaceful prelates and burgomasters of the Stuttgart Landtag. With the utmost obstinacy the estates resisted the formation of a standing army, so that even the patient Duke Christopher complained: "If my country is to be a princedom, it is necessary that I should be able to conduct myself like a prince."

The only member of the house who displayed a certain sense of monarchical greatness, Duke Frederick I, enforced for himself by a breach of the constitution the right of recruiting troops, because with keen prevision he recognised the imminence of the confusions of the Thirty Years' War; but he died before the result had been secured, and the vengeance of the dominant caste was immediately visited upon the head of his able counsellor Enslin. The traitor, who was executed in the market place at Urach, remained henceforward a bugbear, to warn the dukes against military ambition. If the needs of the time enforced the creation of a small army, the estates could never disband it soon enough; they grudged Duke Eberhard III an additional vote of 1,500 florins, wishing to compel him to disband his 170 riders in addition to the infantry; a few years later a terrible robber band of French broke across the unarmed land. It was in this way that Old Würtemberg became defenceless. Whenever a hostile attack was made, the court fled the country, to await reinstatement by foreign aid. Even in the eighteenth century, the military system remained lamentably inefficient; the vigorous sons of the ducal house entered foreign service, and the greatest warrior among them, Frederick Eugene, fought under the banner of Frederick the Great against his Swabian fellow-countrymen. This valiant stock, which in the middle ages had excelled all the other Germans in warlike renown, disappeared from the annals of modern military history; the sole tolerably well-established territorial power which since the fall of the Hohenstaufen had arisen out of the Swabian territorial confusion, remained for two hundred years without influence upon the history of Germany.

The officialdom suffered no less than the military system under the feudal regime. A great part of the administration was in the hands of scriveners (*Schreiber*) of ill repute. These entered as learners, without any academic training, into the office of a town-clerk or of a clerk to a court, and from this position, by nepotist influence, rose to the office of burgomaster or some other high official position. Amid such an ordering of affairs, there was no place for a statesmanlike intelligence, for new political ideas. During many decades the history of Old Würtemberg displays to us only two men of diplomatic talent: the excellent negotiator Burkhardt, and Varnbüler, who, in the peace of Westphalia, effected the re-establishment of the duchy.

In the long run the intellectual life of the country also suffered from the immobility of political affairs. It was with well-grounded satisfaction that the Swabians enumerated the proud series of their poets and thinkers, and asked what other stock, outside that of Upper Saxony, had given the nation so many heroes of the intellect. Fiery imagination and a profound spirit of investigation were happily united in the Swabian nature, and here were manifested the most characteristic lineaments of Teutonic genius: a many-sidedness often transgressing into the realm of the vague and illimitable; and that creative and primitive power of thought, which may, indeed, lose its way in obscurity and subtlety, but can never become dull or meaningless. But the country derived little advantage from this abundance of intellectual energies. Since an educated officialdom was well nigh completely lacking, the prelates and their acolytes remained almost the sole official representatives of higher culture. It sufficed them that the Swabian probationers, next to those of Electoral Saxony, were sought throughout the world as the best private tutors. The time had passed away when the heads of all the Lutheran princely houses had flocked to the illustrious

college at Tübingen; the university now bitterly complained
that it had to languish in a forgotten corner of Germany.
The free spirits of the new century found so little understanding among the priestly leaders of the Würtemberg
educational system, that Duke Charles Eugene at length determined to create a counterpoise to the rigid theology of the
Tübingen foundation, and in his Karlsschule established a
sanctuary for secular science which, during the brief period
of its existence, completely eclipsed the renown of the ancient
university. All the great Swabians who participated in the
labours of the new literature, from Schiller to Schelling and
Hegel, were forced to seek a sphere of activity outside their
own country, in many cases after having first carried on a
severe struggle against the petty prejudices of their homeland. That tragical contrast between intellectual wealth and
political poverty which was the malady of our eighteenth
century, was nowhere more painfully conspicuous than here.

The remoteness of the country, which had long ceased
to be a thoroughfare for world commerce; the manifoldedness
of the physical features of the region, with its jumble of rude
plateaus, richly forested mountain valleys, and smiling vineyards; the misery induced by polyarchy, and the inborn
untamable peculiarities of the population, to whom nothing
seemed more intolerable than political discipline—all these
things in conjunction led in Swabia to a petty dispersal of
energies and to an isolation unparalleled even in Germany.
The lesser towns of the duchy, under the rule of their nepotist
burgomasters, lived a life as completely sequestered as was that
of the neighbouring imperial towns; the unchangeable good
old law left no way open for the ideas of national unity,
or for the consciousness of common political aims, to penetrate
the lands. The whole of Swabia, Würtemberg no less than
the extraordinary state-structures of the imperial towns, the
princely provostships, and the imperial knightly condominions,
was regarded in Germany as the paradise of petty bourgeois
singularity. Indeed, "Gotham" was not far from Hohenstaufen,
and it was in Biberach that Wieland collected the materials for
his *Abderites*. It was not surprising that, in this narrow
world, the rich and busy imagination of the Swabians often took
the form of strange whimsies; nowhere in Germany were
the weak-heads rarer, and nowhere were the queer-heads com-
moner. There was not a single Swabian town, however small,

where there was not to be seen of an evening in the parlour of " The Lion " or " The Ox," some misunderstood genius, spinning his wonderful brain-cobwebs regarding the world and the age, amid his eagerly disputing comrades. Even the unspeakable self-satisfaction of the Swabians exhibited quite peculiar traits. Not here, as among the Bavarians, the Saxons, or the Hanoverians, did particularism display itself in political pride and ambition (for who in Swabia could dream of political power ?), but it manifested itself in social vices. With agreeable self-complacency, all the glories of the homeland, from Frederick Barbarossa and Kepler down to the admirable products of the Swabian kitchen, were unweariedly extolled, whilst everything foreign was decried with gloomy mistrust. In the consciousness of his own wealthy inner life, the gauche and bashful Swabian regarded, half with suspicion and half with contempt, the other Germans, whose eloquence and adroitness could so readily have put him into the shade ; and never did the Old Würtembergers display their refractoriness more intractably than when the duke " just like a foreigner who deprives the children of his country of their bread " had summoned non-Swabian Germans to his court.

As soon as the revolutionary wars broke over this corrupt community, everything was immediately in a ferment. In a country which had so long been wrangling with its prince, the new doctrine of freedom necessarily found a well-prepared soil. For the first time in many decades, the Landtag reassembled. More than one hundred and fifty pamphlets appeared, demanding the abolition of the old malpractices, an extension of the suffrage, and the regular summoning of Landtags. Yet none of these publicists, not even Spittler, knew how to solve the riddle in what manner, out of the dualism of the feudal traditional law, the modern unified state could be brought into existence without a *coup d'état*. Amid these confusions, Duke Frederick II ascended the throne, the most evil and the most talented son of the house of Würtemberg, the refounder of the little state, a man of thoroughly un-Swabian character, one whose merits and whose defects were equally repulsive to the people, hard, brutal, and unconscientious, but at the same time an able politician, a man of quick decision, and free from pettiness. How ridiculous seemed Swabian parochialism to the hereditary prince when, after his extensive travels, after an eventful career in the

Prussian and Russian services, he at length returned to his home as a stranger, rich in experience, equipped with all the brilliancy and all the vices of the great world. The unrestricted authority of an absolute ruler, such as he had formerly admired in Frederick the Great and in Catharine of Russia, remained his ideal, and now that he had brought back with him an English princess, his conceit increased beyond measure. With burning ambition he numbered the hours until his grey-headed uncle, and at length also his father, closed their eyes. At his accession he was already forty-three years of age, so there was no time to lose.

The first thing was to secure for the house of Würtemberg a respectable amount of plunder, as its share of the robber campaign of the German princes against their smaller neighbours. But at every step the duke found himself hindered by his Landtag. Whilst he himself, as a sworn enemy of the Revolution, had taken the side of Austria, the estates demanded neutrality, or adhesion to the side of free France, and sent their own envoys to Rastatt, Vienna, and Paris, in order to counteract the policy of the ruler of the country. Repeated admonitions from the committee, and arbitrary acts on the part of the duke against the leaders of the estates, increased the mutual embitterment. When, during the last days of the Directory, the armies of Moreau streamed over the south-west, and when the agents of France were working to secure the foundation of a South German Republic, secret Jacobin clubs came into existence in Swabia as in Bavaria. A pamphlet propounded the question : *What should we gain if Swabia should become a Republic ?* Meanwhile the duke recognised that he could not secure the desired enlargement of territory without the favour of France. He approached the French, and by the principal resolution of the Diet of Deputation secured his plunder, until at length, overpowered by Napoleon's extraordinary eloquence, he openly adopted the French side, assisted in the destruction of the Holy Empire, acquired a sovereign kingly crown, and with a single blow destroyed the venerable structure of the ancient constitution. The step was so sudden, and exercised so benumbing an influence, that in the entire country only two officials, Georgii and Sartorius, refused to swear allegiance to the new autocrat ; a few others declared that they yielded only to force, and the rest unresistingly recanted their ancient constitutional oath. In the forcible rounding-off of his territorial domain, King Frederick acted with all the violence of a highwayman, and to the commissioners empowered to effect the occupation of the territories of the smaller neighbours, commissioners accompanied by a force of the dreaded black yagers and a body of light horsemen, he gave the blunt instructions: " Whoever among you is most frequently the subject of complaints from foreign governments, will commend himself most to my favour." Like master like man. What a pleasure it was for the rough, uncultured scrivener of Old Würtemberg to make his entry into conquered territory as a " royal Würtemberg sovereign staff-burgomaster," and to tame the " accursed imperial-town arrogance " of the proud burghers of Reutlingen.

Even when thus enlarged almost threefold, the realm of the new king of Swabia still remained an extremely modest middle-sized state, the smallest among the petty kingdoms of the Confederation of the Rhine. Nor did it comprise the entire domain of the East Swabian stock, and northward it extended for no more than a few miles into Franconian terri- tory ; the whole region of the Swabian Alps, the beautiful Algau, went to Bavaria, and so also did Augsburg, the greatest and most renowned of Swabian towns. But in this narrow area were to be encountered the most extreme political, ecclesiastical, and economic contrasts. Side by side with the rigidly ascetic Lutheranism of Old Würtemberg, existed the worldly and cheerful Catholicism of Upper Swabia, with its Josephan enlightenment ; side by side with the petty agriculture of the regions of the Neckar and the Rems, were to be found the great estates of the nobles, and also the enclosed peasant farms of Schussental ; side by side with the bourgeois gentry of the duchy, were numerous princes, counts, and imperial knights—and in Hohenlohe, at least, the inhabi- tants preserved a strong sentiment of dynastic loyalty towards their benevolent old princely race. The Hither Austrians regarded their entrance into this petty state as a humiliation from the first, and the spiritual domains adhered firmly to the imperial house, the old opponent of Würtemberg Protes- tantism. Among the imperial towns, Heilbronn alone possessed a vigorous bourgeois life, for even the wealthy Ulm was impoverished and decayed ; but all these towns, down to Bopfingen and Aalen, were profoundly incensed at the loss of their ancient liberties, and this was above all the case in

democratic Reutlingen, whose inhabitants still preserved upon
the town hall the ancient memorials of victories in feuds
with the counts of Würtemberg.

Intercourse between the old and the new portions of the
country had hardly existed prior to the union ; people in one
region and the other knew one another almost exclusively
through current phrases of mockery. Open resistance was
no longer ventured on after the unhappy inhabitants of
Mergentheim had atoned with their blood for an attempt
at revolt. But, full of animosity, the subjects avoided intercourse with the royal officials, and even at the university
the new fellow-countrymen from Ulm and Hohenlohe lived
in continual disputes with the Old Würtembergers. It was a
manifest political impossibility to adopt this motley little
world into the bourgeois-Protestant constitution of the old
duchy, nor was there any legal warrant for such a proceeding,
for a great part of the new acquisitions was regarded as
compensation for Mömpelgard, which had never been represented in the Stuttgart Landtag. For some years, as a
temporary resource, the new domain, which was everywhere
intermingled with the old, was treated as an independent state ;
the quiet pilgrimage-centre of Ellwangen was constituted the
capital of this extraordinary realm of New Würtemberg,
because the authorities found a convenient place of residence
in the stately palaces of the old provosts. As a permanency,
the unnatural separation between the two halves of the country
could not be maintained, but their union could not be effected
so long as the constitution of Old Würtemberg still existed.

The *coup d'état* of December 30, 1805, by which the
good old law was abolished, was not the outcome simply
of a tyrant's overweening love of power, but also depended
upon an undeniable political necessity. Over the united Old
and New Würtemberg, all the terrors of despotism now raged,
but amid countless acts of an overwhelmingly arbitrary
character, the autocracy also gifted the country with the indispensable institutions of the modern state. The edict of
religions, King Frederick's best work, overthrew the dominion
of the Lutheran church, and gave equal rights to both creeds.
By the secularisation of the goods of the church and the
abolition of the treasury of the estates, unity of the national
economy was established, and the duty of paying regular
taxes was carried into effect, though with such harshness

that the owners of landed property had to pay nearly four-fifths of the net income in taxes. Finally, the defenceless country once again acquired a little army fit for war, an army which, as the king boasted, stood on an equal footing with the troops of other monarchs; and although the old scandal of the scrivener-system was not completely abolished, nevertheless, in the new law courts and administrative institutions there came into existence the first beginnings of a monarchical, academically cultured officialdom, and all the special privileges of the old class of gentry were abolished. Even the educational system, which the king dealt with roughly and disdainfully, at least acquired the possibility of freer development now that the conduct of affairs passed into the hands of temporal authorities.

The entire transformation was effected forcibly, by fits and starts, and therefore imperfectly. Patrimonial jurisdiction was abolished, whilst the oppressive burdens on the land, the corvées, the hunting rights, and the utterly corrupt guild-system, persisted. Nevertheless the reign of terror introduced a certain order into a chaos of outworn territories, and levelled the ground so as to make it possible, perhaps, for a healthier national life to be built up at a later date. With revolutionary impetuosity, the enemy of the Revolution established modern legal equality in his own state; but with the reservation that here, as in Napoleonic France, the first aspect of this equality was the equal slavery of all. It was extraordinary how much energy of life and work the fat, evil king continued to preserve amid all the uncleanness of his excesses. He himself was the soul of his realm, and showed himself indefatigable in new schemes: the port of Freidrichshafen on the Lake of Constance, the iron-works of the Friedrichstal, the steel-works of Friedrichshall, were to hand down to posterity the imperial glories of the first king of Swabia. All his counsellors, whom he summoned by preference from elsewhere in Germany, served him as blind tools, the only one who occasionally exhibited a few ideas of his own being Wintzingerode. Even in his relationships with the Protector, King Frederick, despite all his devotion, knew better how to maintain his princely dignity than did the other kings of the Confederation of the Rhine. He refused to send his troops to Spain, and Napoleon once exclaimed in a rage: " If this man had 100,000 soldiers, I would declare war against him."

It was impossible that the mass of the people should have any understanding of the sound political ideas which co-operated in the overthrow of the old order. All that they could recognise was the destruction of chartered rights, the arbitrariness of the officials, the pressure of taxation, peculation and espionage. In addition, the ancient curse of princely hunting-rights was wantonly increased. There was also the repulsive spectacle of a court endeavouring, through its tasteless extravagance, through the flaunting titles of its royal bannermen, royal marshals, and royal heralds, to rival the glories of the world-ruler. The respectable burghers of Stuttgart blushed to hear of the way in which the father of the country gave expression to his Voltairean mockery of religion, while the effrontery of the depraved royal favourites recalled that of the minions of Henry III of Valois. Just at this time, too, a deplorable family drama in the royal house awakened the indignation of the whole world. The king had forced his daughter Catharine to marry King Jerome, and now, after the fall of the French empire, demanded that she should separate from her husband. The noble woman proudly answered : " I have shared with him his good fortune, and must also share his evil fortune." Thereupon the father had the daughter brought by force from Austria to Würtemberg, and then held husband and wife prisoner for a year in the castle of Ellwangen, in order by threats and maltreatment to force them to hand over their possessions. Poverty and embitterment increased from year to year, and many desperate people were restrained from emigration only by force of law. When, after the despot's death, this prohibition of emigration was annulled, many left the country. The first waves of the great current of American emigration were manifested in Würtemberg as early as 1817 ; the poor people of the Heilbronn region loudly declared on their departure that it was only the severity of the officials and the burden of the taxes which had driven them away from their homeland.

After he had been seventeen years on the throne, the king was still a complete stranger to his own people. How else could he have possibly believed that these loyal and stiffnecked Swabians would speedily get over the loss of their good old law ? He confidently reckoned upon the humble thanks of his people when upon his return from Vienna he determined, by the granting of a constitution, to anticipate the resolutions of the congress. He was soon to learn that the most dangerous moment for a corrupt government comes when it spontaneously undertakes reform. A royal manifesto summoned an undivided Landtag for the new realm. It was to consist of fifty representatives of the nobility, five members of the clergy, and one deputy from each of the sixty-four chief districts and from the seven towns which bore the Napoleonic title of the "good towns." Even before this assembly met, everyone in Stuttgart, and even the diplomatic corps, knew that a great blow against the king was being prepared. Now at length the unhappy people regained the long-suppressed right of free speech, and at once all those who had suffered from the violence of despotism reared their heads : the estates of Old Würtemberg and their powerful family connections, the princes and imperial knights who had suffered injury beyond forgiveness, the imperial towns, and the prelates. Hatred against the king awakened for the first time a feeling of community between the old territories and the new. The Old Würtembergers at once showed themselves resolved to demand the restoration of their beloved constitution, which had, however, never legally existed in the new territories. The New Würtembergers agreed in this proposal, because the involved forms of the good old law offered an entire arsenal of powerful weapons against princely excesses, and because, with such a king as this, the control of the monarchical authority was regarded by all as the most important immediate task. It did not seem that it would be too difficult a matter, by making a few additions regarding the equal rights of the Catholics and the representation of the nobles, to modify this amorphous constitutional structure so as to make it habitable for the New Würtembergers as well.

King Frederick alone had no inkling of these designs. On March 15, 1815, he opened the Landtag in person, and announced that on this day he desired to lay the foundation-stone of the state-structure. Thereupon the new constitution was read, the king solemnly promised to observe it, and declared that herewith it immediately became binding on all his subjects. A Landtag, constituted upon the same principles as the present one, was in future to assemble every three years upon the summons of the crown, to discuss new taxes and new laws ; thus it could neither diminish the existing

intolerable burden of taxation, nor yet subject to its supervision the thousand and one royal rescripts which of late
years had reduced the country to despair. In order to make
matters quite certain, the king had in addition, during the
last few days, promulgated certain new and severe laws
regarding military service and territorial militia. Thus disappeared every prospect of a peaceful improvement of the
condition of the country. The Prussian envoy, von Küster,
an able man who hardly found it possible to endure his
residence at this court, wrote to his king in profound indignation : " Your majesty will readily be able to judge whether
such a constitution corresponds to the wishes of the powers." [1]
The king handed the charter, in a gold casket, to the president
of the Landtag. Hardly, however, had he left the house,
when the hotspur of the mediatised, Count Georg von Waldeck,
rose to his feet, and read an address which had long
previously been prepared, and which in subservient phraseology
rejected the royal gift, bluntly declaring that the people had
elected their representatives solely in the belief that no other
basis could be proposed for the proceedings than the constitution of Würtemberg, which had been inherited from their
ancestors, and which had been sworn to by all the rulers of
the country. The diet, passionately excited, approved the
address by a unanimous vote. The new constitution was
left unregarded upon the table of the house, and in a few
moments it had become a worthless scrap of paper.

The firm attitude of the estates gave the signal for an
outbreak of popular passion. The feudal stubbornness of the
good old time, the revolutionary sentiments of the nineties,
the suppressed fury of the days of the Confederation of the
Rhine, and the new desires for freedom which had been
awakened by the struggle against Napoleon, all jostled one
another. How much nearer than the nebulous questions of
German policy were to this generation the immediate concerns
of their homes ! A petition to the Bundestag for the fulfilment of article 13 secured in Swabia no more than a few
isolated signatures ; but the Landtag of Stuttgart was overwhelmed with petitions, statements of grievances, and resolutions of approval. A number of contentious pamphlets were
published on behalf of the estates, many of them couched in
savage Jacobin phraseology. *An Appeal to the High Liberator*

[1] Küster's Report, Stuttgart, March 16, 1815.

of Germany bore upon the title-page the threatening remark
" imprimatur in virtue of the freedom from the censorship which
prevails in Würtemberg territory," and propounded the question,
" What does this crown cost us ? " The answer ran as follows :
" A perjury that cries to heaven, many thousand enforced
false oaths, numberless acts of arbitrary power, extortion, and
arrogance, and in addition the sale of the blood of from thirty
to forty thousand of the most hopeful youth of the country !
The blood of so many thousand victims is surging, splashing,
and steaming around the throne of the despot ! " A second
Appeal demanded " a sworn brotherhood of right-thinking men
on behalf of the right, and nothing but the right, for the
good old right, with the watch-word ' God and our rights ' !
Those who are free by right will be true by right ! " Thus
the sacred name of right, so irresistible to German hearts, passed
to and fro in a hundred echoes ; and those thus excited required
only a few sophistical fallacies to enable them to ignore the
incontestable fact that in the major half of the country, this
ancient right had never existed at all. The whole German press
enthusiastically took the side of the Landtag because it simultaneously represented the two most sacred sentiments of the
time, faithful affection for domestic customs and an indefinite
yearning for freedom. It was only the *Alemannia* of Munich
which, as always, advocated the cause of Rhenish Confederate
absolutism.

The address of the estates was followed by a strong statement of their rights on the part of the mediatised, and of
the Catholic and the Lutheran prelates. Even the agnates of
the royal house protested against the new and severe military
law, being headed by Duke Paul, a dissolute man of unbridled
ambition, who would gladly have played the part of a Swabian
Philippe Egalité. The king felt unable to cope with the fierce
hatred which manifested itself on all sides, and since the crown
prince represented to him how little reason there was to reckon
on any change of sentiments on the part of the estates he
prudently took a step backwards, and on April 16th declared
himself prepared to treat, through commissioners, with four
plenipotentiaries from the estates, who were to state what portions of the ancient rights the Landtag desired to adopt as
part of the new fundamental law. Thus was abandoned the
ceremoniously announced inviolability of the new constitution.
But it speedily appeared that the Landtag aimed at nothing

less than the re-establishment of the ancient state of affairs with a few unimportant alterations.

The elections in the towns and chief districts had resulted in the return, apart from nine traders, of lawyers, burgomasters, mayors, and scriveners. It is easy to understand that in such an assembly those well versed in historical law maintained the upper hand, such men as Weishaar, Bolley, and Georgii, learned lawyers, full of the ideas of the new liberalism, to whom the oligarchical ancient constitution seemed the securest bulwark of popular rights ; next came the good burgomaster Klüppel of Stuttgart ; and, finally, Zahn and Feuerlein, two virtuosi of the Old Würtemberg scrivener's office, unequalled in all the arts of petty word-splitting. Count Waldeck was the leader of the mediatised, a man of restless intelligence, always on the spot when the South German nobility assembled for the preservation of the rights of caste. He found it possible in the same breath to express enthusiasm for unrestricted popular freedom, and to defend the privileges of his house. The highly noble house of Limburg, he gave people to understand, had hitherto recognised neither the Germanic Federation nor the kingdom of Würtemberg, and could only bring itself to grant them recognition if they would meet him on equal terms. Among the lesser nobility, Baron von Varnbüler was prominent, a typical imperial knight, brave, frank, and extremely obstinate. Subsequently Colonel Massenbach also joined the party of the knighthood, the man to whose name was attached the curse of Jena and Prenzlau. By the publication of unsavoury memoirs, he had already avenged himself for his well-deserved dismissal from the Prussian army ; and now, as a politician, he displayed the same fantastic and superabundant activities which he had formerly displayed as a soldier. In savage, screaming, demagogic writings, he demanded of the nobles that they should undergo a bourgeois baptism, and announced : " All the princes must now conclude new treaties with their peoples ; the change must go so far that every citizen will be able himself to reckon his contribution to the upkeep of the state."

For the time being, the opposition, compounded of such fundamentally diverse elements, held firmly together ; five only of the nobles subsequently withdrew their assent to the address, and a portion of the mediatised also separated themselves from the opposition in order to await the decision of the congress of Vienna concerning the rights of the former estates of the empire. The form of the deliberations still corresponded entirely with traditional custom. For the most part the deputies read lengthy written opinions, and only on rare occasions, when exchanging personal grievances, did they speak extempore. The four plenipotentiaries were supplemented by the Landtag by a committee of twenty-five members, which was to represent the former great committee, and which to every proposal of the government subjoined detailed counter-considerations. Yet not even the tedious formalities of written procedure could prevent frequent stormy outbreaks which voiced intense embitterment with the king. The estates answered the monarch's advances by a statement of grievances. What an impression was produced when this interminable writing was read, and when the incredible arbitrariness of the bailiffs and the monstrous extravagance of the king were brought to light. The court had annually consumed half a million gulden, fully a third of the income of the country. There was a general silence of consternation, and many were in tears; it seemed as if the profoundly injured conscience of the people sat in judgment upon the sins of these nine years. Meanwhile no advance was made in the work of instituting a constitution. In the sharpest terms the estates reminded the king of his broken oath; they continually repeated that all the " nameless misery " of recent years arose solely from the " contempt that had been exhibited for the old and the tried "; and they declared that the most valuable constituents of the ancient constitution were those two institutions which were least compatible with the unity of the modern monarchy, namely, the permanent committee, and the treasury of the provincial diets. Faithful to feudal tradition, they regarded the relationship between prince and people as a natural state of war, and did not hesitate to tell the king to his face that in case of a new dispute the Landtag must possess means of its own for the support of persecuted officials.

After six months of barren dispute, the king at last lost patience. He determined to prorogue the assembly, instructing it to appoint certain plenipotentiaries to continue the negotiations regarding the fundamental law, and promising in the meanwhile to make a strict enquiry into grievances. But the majority of the Landtag would not abandon the formulas of Old Würtemberg constitutional law; they insisted that a great committee must remain sitting as representative of the rights of the country ; and when the monarch refused to accept this accessory government of the estates, the latter defiantly separated without naming plenipotentiaries for the work of formulating a constitution. Before breaking up, the Landtag played its highest trump, applying, on July 26th, to the guarantors of the ancient hereditary settlement, Denmark, England, and Prussia, begging for their mediation, for the acceptance of the royal proposal would be regarded by the people as "treachery." Such was the level of national pride in the south : the greatly celebrated first Landtag of these years of peace came to an end with the endeavour to induce, in the name of popular rights, two foreign powers to intervene in the affairs of Germany.

The country had followed these disputes with increasing excitement. It was with difficulty that during the last decisive sittings the Landtag could restrain the serenades and hurrahs of the populace of Stuttgart. After the prorogation, large masses of the countryfolk flocked to Ludwigsburg, and the king had to order his riders to make sallies from the gates in order to protect the isolated palace from the clamour of the petitioners. When the representatives of the people returned home, they received a storm of extravagant homage which served notably to increase the self-satisfaction of the "advocates of ancient rights." How would it have been possible amid this impetuous popular movement for the noble poet to remain silent, the man who had always found the appropriate word for the heart-secrets of the Swabian people, and whose democratic burgher pride, juristic culture, and family traditions, urged him to take the side of the Old Würtemberg party ? Ludwig Uhland accompanied every phase of the confused struggle with the straightforward popular strains of his patriotic poems, and, availing himself of the right of repetition which the political poet shares with the publicist, he turned over again and again in manifold forms the single idea, writing always in effect :

> " Blest land of wheat and vineyards,
> The finest Heaven e'er saw,
> But one essential lacking :
> The country's good old law ! "

These vigorous poems resounded far beyond the frontiers of Swabia, and served mightily to fan the nebulous excitement of the time. However dignified the form of the verses might be, they invariably expressed the revolutionary doctrine "all or nothing," and voiced the bitter reproach that the wickedness of ruthless rulers had cheated the people of their chartered rights. Restricted within the circle of ideas of his Swabian home, the rancorous feeling, which was not without justification in the dull atmosphere of Würtemberg despotism, was transferred by the poet to the conditions also of the entire fatherland, and as early as the third day of the battle of Leipzig, in the most beautiful and most revolutionary of his political poems, he described the situation of Germany as utterly hopeless. At a moment when the statesmen of Prussia, so recently returned from Paris, had their hands full of work in connection with the organisation of the new administration. Uhland was conjuring up the spirit of Theodor Körner, declaring in the latter's name: "Hopeless is the outlook on every side!" This unjust saying bit into the very marrow of the Teutonising youth, and by the parties of the opposition was repeated in verse and prose, until at length, three years later, the outlook did indeed seem hopeless.

The sole result of the appeal to the three guarantors was, as every unprejudiced person might have foreseen, to rouse the king to fresh efforts. Not one of the three courts considered itself justified in intervening in express terms on behalf of a long-abolished constitution, whose existence was possible only upon the basis of the ancient imperial law. Prussia, in particular, held cautiously aloof, although Hardenberg honestly desired reconciliation between prince and people, for King Frederick, who had recently entered into close relationships with Russia, displayed his ancient rancour against the North German great power in so provocative a manner that Küster was on several occasions on the point of asking for his papers. In such circumstances, an attempted intervention on the part of the cabinet of Berlin could do nothing but harm. Nor did King Frederick himself find any help abroad. His reputation in all the courts was as evil as could be ; and without exception they demanded that the European scandal of Swabian despotism should come to an end. Prince Metternich went so far as openly to espouse the cause of the Landtag, for his own family belonged to the mediatised of Würtemberg, and had in recent years suffered grave injustice.[1]

[1] Küster's Reports, November 1, 1815, and subsequent dates.

The once all-powerful petty ruler was completely isolated : the excitement in the country continued to increase, and from a number of districts protests were now sent in against the new taxes. After his decisive manner, the king quickly adapted himself to the changed situation, and in his necessity summoned to his cabinet Baron K. A. von Wangenheim, a Thuringian, whose name alone sufficed to guarantee an honest change of system. When quite a young man, Wangenheim, then an official in Coburg, had with courageous frankness opposed the maladroit regime of the minister Kretschmann, and in punishment had been banished from the country. He had found an asylum in Franconia, with the chivalrous Baron von Truchsess, who was honoured by the romanticist world as a second Sickingen, and there, at Bettenburg, in the new place of refuge from oppression, had formed a lifelong friendship with the young poet Friedrich Rückert. When, some years later, he came to Stuttgart, commissioned by the small Thuringian court, his brilliant conversation, sparkling with lively sallies, his bright appearance, and his imperturbable staying-power in a carouse, had won the good-will of the king, who immediately took him into his service. Royal favour did not long endure. " My student," as the king termed him, soon aroused offence by the free expression of his German sentiments, and the king was ultimately glad to pack him off to Tübingen, as curator of the university. Here he showed himself to be a judicious favourer of the sciences, associating on friendly terms with all the notable men of learning in the university, but by preference with Eschenmeier the mystic, who initiated the sensitive dilettante into the cabalistic formulas of his nature-philosophical doctrine of the state—for Wangenheim was a man receptive for all the flights of imagination. When the constitutional struggle became embittered, he suddenly came to the front with a writing, *The Idea of a State Constitution*. This remarkable book showed plainly how impossible it was to harmonise the good old law with the modern idea of the state, and went on, with ceremonious emotion, to develop the programme of an inviolable and exemplary constitution which should satisfy all claims of the abstract idea. This was the old doctrine of Montesquieu, in a fantastical dress. The sacred triad of natural philosophy was to manifest itself in the balance of three powers : the popular masses were to display the energy of the idea ; the commune was to supply imaginative force ; whilst the Landtag

was to incorporate the appetitive faculty of the state.
Behind the doctrinaire wrappings there were concealed certain
excellent practical proposals, and since the king could find no
helper anywhere else, he commissioned this literary mediator
to adjust the constitutional quarrel.

With sublime confidence, Wangenheim accepted the call.
He was already affected by that immeasurable self-esteem which
men of talent are apt to display in cramped surroundings, and
believed himself foreordained to offer to Germany a brilliant
example of an incomparable constitution. Although he had a
genuine hatred for the Confederation of the Rhine, he could
not restrain himself from transferring his beloved mystical triad
to the general field of German politics, and long before had
puzzled out the system of a German trias, which unfortunately
resembled very closely the shameful tripartition of Napoleonic days. To him, Austria and Prussia both seemed semi-
foreign powers. Prussia in especial he regarded as the insatiably
covetous enemy of the hereditary princely houses. The totality
of the petty states, "genuine Germany," was to keep these
two powers within bounds, to establish a balance between
them, to lead them ever upwards towards freedom and civilisation : and among the genuinely German stocks, the most genuine
of all was the Swabian. Wangenheim loved his new home to
the point of idolatry, and adhered to the royal house with
a chivalrous loyalty which never failed him even in moments
of well-grounded discontent.[1] He had, however, no more than
a superficial acquaintance with local conditions, and did not
understand how to deal with obstinate persons. Difficulties
enough were imposed upon him from the first by the fact
that he was "a foreigner," and that his pure High German
was offensive to Swabian ears. When he gave vent to free-and-
easy witticisms regarding the "venerable antiquities" of the
ancient constitution, and when, speaking of an Old Würtemberg
scrivener, he said that such persons as this knew nothing in
heaven and earth except how to make calculations which no
one but another scrivener could understand, to the Swabians
he seemed positively sacrilegious. A flood of mockery was
poured forth regarding the "appetitive faculty of the state"
and the other nature-philosophy crotchets of the "Würtemberg
Solon."

[1] I utilise here, among other materials, a collection of letters from Wangenheim to his friend Privy-councillor von Hartmann, communicated to me by
Professor Hartmann of Stuttgart.

The Landtag, resummoned in October, 1815, proceeded once again, in an address running into twenty folios, to demand the ancient constitution for the entire country, adding threateningly : " the people begin to despair of the future." At length, in a ministerial council held on November 11th, Wangenheim won the king over to the proposal to accede their beloved principle to the sticklers for the old law.[1] Two days later, the king astonished the estates by a message, which to the foreign diplomats seemed " almost like a miracle." In this he declared that he did not contest the internal validity of the old agreements, but merely their applicability. He went on, in fourteen articles, to offer the unrestricted right of granting supply, the responsibility of state-servants, and finally, and above all, the general revision of laws passed since 1806. These articles contained, in fact, everything which still seemed viable among the feudal institutions, and granted in addition a long series of new and valuable privileges. The king concluded with the assurance that if these proposals were rejected he would have no option but to re-establish the old law in Old Würtemberg, and to provide the new territories with an independent new constitution.

After these great concessions on the part of the crown, public opinion outside Würtemberg began to undergo modification. Stein, Gagern, and many other well-wishers, who had hitherto been on the side of the estates, now strongly advised that the proffered hand of reconciliation should be accepted. The Landtag, however, had already gone too deep into the struggle ; the dispute had long before become a personal one, and the embittered spirits of the disputants mocked at reason. The estates did indeed agree to treat with the crown once more through a committee ; but the committee immediately proceeded, disregarding the fourteen articles, to elaborate a shapeless constitutional proposal, which, in twenty-five chapters and many hundreds of paragraphs, enumerated all the dusty treasures of the old law, insisting above all upon the permanent committee and the tax-treasury.

Upon these lines the dispute continued for months ; and, to complete the confusion, Wangenheim's doctrinaire zeal led him to attack the one point regarding which hitherto both parties had been agreed, the traditional unicameral system of bourgeois Würtemberg. Without two chambers, the idea of

[1] Küster's Report, November 11, 1815.

the sacred triad could not possibly be realised; the aristocratic element must not fail to constitute the "hypomochlion" which represented the "oscillating counterpoise" between the democracy and the autocracy. The king encouraged these theoretical whimsies (which Wangenheim developed in detail in a new writing) all the more willingly because they harmonised with the calculations of his own sober policy of hard realities. Like most of the princes of the Confederation of the Rhine, he was suspicious of the nobles as the most dangerous enemies of the crown, and regarded it as essential to seclude these distinguished demagogues in an upper chamber, lest they should lead astray the bourgeoisie and the peasants. It was upon such wonderful grounds that the plan originated to constitute a house of peers in a petty state which had manifestly no scope for a vigorous peerage. The advocates of the old law offered vigorous resistance; they had little confidence in their aristocratic associates, and they believed that now, as formerly, they could best make head against the interested activities of the nobles in an undivided assembly of the estates. It was easier to come to an understanding in respect of another German peculiarity, which was to prove yet more injurious to the power of our smaller Landtags, namely, the salaries of the members. It seemed to all to be a matter of course that the representative of the people should be paid for his honourable duties. Regard for the extreme poverty of the cultured classes worked hand in hand with regard for the class views of the officials; the bureaucrat of the old school could not conceive of anyone taking great pains except for a salary. Meanwhile the despotic nature of the king broke forth again and again, now some of those who had signed the address to the Landtag, and now some hot-headed deputy, being haled before the courts. The estates, also, permitted themselves notable excesses. They contended that all the privileges which the future constitution was first to secure for them, were already in their possession, and formally maintained their rights when the king again levied taxes, threatening in case this step was repeated that they would advise the subjects to refuse payment.

This dispute dragged on for an entire year, becoming daily more wearisome and more barren. In August, 1816, Count Waldeck, on his own initiative, made a second appeal to the three guarantors and also to Emperor Francis as the sometime lord paramount of the empire—a document which in classical phraseology expressed the unteachable presumption of the idolators of the old law. " The Old Würtemberg constitution," it ran, " has, in virtue of the decision of the German imperial court and of the high guarantors, in virtue of the unanimous voice of Germany and the blessings of three centuries, maintained itself so conclusively as a work of human perfection, that the annihilation of a single one even of its constituents would, precisely on account of its artificially delicate structure, endanger its entirety, and thus imperil the well-being of the people." [1] The whole country now resounded with the turmoil which since that time has accompanied almost all disputes about German parliamentary life, and this by no means served to increase the respect of the foreign world for the storm in a tea-cup. A savage pamphlet threatened the king with the fate of his ancestor, the refugee duke Ulrich, and when an anonymous writer ventured to advocate the proposals of the crown, his work was nailed to the pillory in Stuttgart.

Everyone was forced to take a side. Even numerous celebrated Swabians outside the country sent letters or printed writings to convey their opinion to the homeland, and the hopeless confusion of the strife was shown in the admiration for the old constitution expressed by the deadly enemies Schelling and Paulus, the former because he regarded the historic law as venerable, and the latter because he thought he could recognise constitutional freedom in the old feudal liberties. Hegel, on the other hand, fought with sophistical skill on behalf of Wangenheim as representative of the modern idea of the state, and proved, altogether in the spirit of the Rhenish Confederate bureaucracy, that it was only through the destruction of the outworn German empire that the " genuine German realm," the new kingdoms, had come into existence. In moving terms the true-hearted Justinus Kerner implored his beloved Uhland to abandon the " money-box system and caste spirit of the scriveners and law-mongers." It was in vain. When Wangenheim's friend Rückert challenged the poet of the sticklers for the old right to a poetic competition, the Swabian occupied the advantageous position of being able to defend the cordial sentiments of emotional politics against the sober considerations of political wisdom, and prepared for the Franconian a poetical

[1] Count Waldeck, Address to the courts of Austria, Prussia, Denmark, and England, August 31, 1816.

defeat which was hailed in Würtemberg as a political triumph. What help was it that the two best political intelligences among the younger men in the country, Friedrich List and Schlayer, eagerly supported the minister ? In the Landtag, Wangenheim had two adherents only, Griesinger, the jurist, and Cotta, the bookseller, the latter becoming an object of suspicion to his parochially minded fellow-townsmen because, as a business man of wide experience, he looked beyond their narrow circle of vision. But the king himself remained the most serious obstacle to an understanding. There could be no doubt that he at length honourably desired peace ; but who was willing to trust him ?

Now, however, a friendly stroke of fortune suddenly removed this obstacle. On October 30, 1816, the king died, lamented by no one. His successor, King William, was received with rejoicing by the entire country. For several years past the loyal populace had been accustomed to compare him with the good duke Christopher because, like Christopher, he had had to pass a joyless youth under the rule of a tyrannical father. Nevertheless the new king, heartless and coldly reasonable by disposition, completely lacked the good-nature of Duke Christopher. Born at Lüben, in the Prussian garrison, the prince had in youth been as strongly Prussian in sentiment as his grandfather, Frederick Eugene ; at that time he still signed himself " Frederick William." When after the battle of Jena he had learned to despise the Prussians, he still remained a proud German officer, and definitely opposed the French policy of his father. The violent dissension in the royal household soon became generally known throughout the country, and secured numerous secret admirers for the crown prince, although the defiant spirit of the unaffectionate son was just as much to blame for these domestic troubles as was the Bonapartist sentiment of the harsh-spirited parent. Upon the king's orders, the prince unwillingly contracted marriage with the Bavarian princess Caroline Augusta, a marriage which was never consummated and which was unhappy for both parties. [1] The laurels of the Napoleonic campaigns offered no attraction to him. It was not until Würtemberg had joined the side of the

[1] A legend widely diffused in Würtemberg, and recorded in the first editions of this book, maintained that Crown Prince William had contracted this marriage in order to avoid marriage with Stephanie Beauharnais. The rumour is false, for Stephanie was already betrothed to the elector Charles of Baden on April 8, 1806, and the marriage of the crown prince William did not take place till June 8, 1808.

allies that he took part in the struggle, and during the winter campaign in France, and especially in the sanguinary affair of Montereau, he displayed himself an efficient commander, so that the Swabian poet Wilhelm Hauff greeted him on his return home as " Prince William, noble knight." These military successes had an unfavourable influence upon his character, increasing the tendency to excessive self-esteem and contempt for others which he shared with his father ; and since his own vision extended far beyond the parochial prejudices of his fellow-countrymen his experiences in the domestic constitutional struggle served merely to strengthen him in the illusion that he knew everything better than anyone else.

His mind was continuously dominated by uncontrollable ambition, and he believed himself to be superior to all other German princes. For a long time Swabia had been too small for his designs. At the congresses of Vienna and of Paris the diplomatic world had several times been astonished by wonderful proposals, suggesting for the hero of Montereau a brilliant position of honour, such as the supreme command in Mainz of the forces of the Germanic Federation, or the sovereignty of Alsace. After the dissolution of his marriage with the Bavarian princess, he espoused the czar's sister, the grand duchess Catharine, a talented, lively, and enterprising woman, who, formerly, during the Russian war, had worked at the equipment of the army as vigorously as any man, and who now found herself ill at ease in the petty relationships of her new home. The prince's dreams now became still more aspiring. " How would it be possible," wrote Küster at this period, " for three so remarkable, energetic, and vigorous individuals as Frederick, William, and Catharine, to get on together ? " A secret correspondence now began between the heir to the Swabian throne and the prince of Orange, to the great alarm of the conversative courts. It was known that both princes cherished revolutionary designs, and that the prince of Würtemberg felt profoundly flattered when here and there a pothouse politician hailed him as the future German emperor. Although both these princes profoundly despised the new liberal ideas, they both hoped, as machiavellian politicians, to secure for themselves some definite good fortune out of a great revolutionary change. Where Prince William's ambition came into play, his sobriety of spirit no longer prevailed, and the most airy structures of his imagination seemed to him attainable possibilities. For many years he brooded over the idea of a South German federation, although he had himself done everything to destroy any possible foundation for these plans for a trias. Arrogant towards the court of Baden, he was profoundly estranged from the court of Bavaria. The hatred of the harsh Frederick for the good-natured Max Joseph was inherited by their sons. The fantastical extravagance of the Bavarian crown prince Louis was intolerable to the dry, self-contained nature of Prince William, nor did the terms between the two men improve when they competed for the hand of Catharine of Russia, and the Bavarian lost the prize.

The simple patriotic enthusiasm of the wars of liberation left this narrow-hearted character cold. His German policy was entirely determined by dynastic pride and love of personal power. Just as he detested Napoleon because the rule of the foreigner over the house of Würtemberg seemed to him a scandal, so was he unwilling to subordinate his sovereign house to any powerful German centralised authority. It seemed to him that the leadership of Germany was his own privilege, and even the good-humoured Küster declared that at heart the crown prince's sentiments were just as particularist as those of his father.[1] From the first he was on bad terms with the two leading powers of the Germanic Federation. The policy of dualism directly conflicted with his plans for a trias, and his petty and irritable characteristics made it impossible for him to repress a sentiment of personal hostility towards the two monarchs. Soon after ascending the throne, he offered the king of Prussia the hand of a princess of Würtemberg for the young crown prince, and received the composed answer that Frederick William would not exercise any constraint over the inclinations of his children.[2] William never forgave this rebuff. At about the same time, Emperor Francis chose the divorced wife of the Würtemberger for his own fourth consort, and henceforward the emperor's old mistrust for the incalculable schemer in Stuttgart continued to increase, and the ill-feeling was cordially reciprocated.

Ever a zealous soldier, an administrator of secure perceptions and great industry, an excellent agriculturist, and an admirable horse-breeder, simple in his manner of life, self-

---

[1] Küster's Reports. October 24, November 11, 1815.
[2] Küster to Hardenberg, Stuttgart, January 18; Instructions by the chancellor, February 24, 1817.

controlled, and, though by no means strictly moral, free from the utter shamelessness of his father, the new king was fully adequate for all those practical affairs of life which could be dealt with by prudence and energy. Whatever lay beyond these fields was a closed book to him. Like his father, he regarded the church with the mockery of the disciple of Voltaire, though to him religion seemed indispensable to keep the stupid masses in order. The "ideology" of free science appeared to him a disagreeable riddle, half ludicrous, half alarming, and thus it was that, as a genuine Rhenish Confederate professional soldier, he never learned to understand the free spirit of the Prussian army. Finally, his love of the arts, like the patronage of many other of the petty princes, never transcended that stage of culture which finds its ideal solely in nude female figures. Such a man, too restless for the quiet life of a petty state, and yet too egotistical to understand the vanity of sovereignty without power, could serve merely to tie a few additional knots in the tangled skein of German federal policy. At heart he was as utterly estranged from the genial profundity of the Swabian folk nature as had been King Frederick himself. The jubilation of the first weeks was speedily dissipated. During a long reign the king, despite his indisputable services to the country, was never really loved by the masses; no one's heart could go out to him, and people soon learned to dread the most detestable trait of his character, his inability to forgive.

The new reign began with valuable reforms. The insane pomp and the hunting scandals of the court were done away with; a number of the taxes were reduced; many prisoners were pardoned; some of the favourites of the deceased prince were quietly banished. During the famine and the subsequent months, the queen devoted her virile energies to womanly occupations. Faithful to her own saying, "a woman's highest function in society is to help," she covered the country with a network of women's societies, savings-banks, useful institutions of all kinds, and in this work of love displayed so great a spirit that, shortly afterwards, her premature death was deplored throughout Swabia as a misfortune to the country. Even Uhland, the despiser of courts, laid a sweet-smelling garland upon the coffin of the mother of the people, and Kerner's lament ran:

> "All too soon by God selected,
> A saint in heaven, lost to earth."

The princess's grave was upon the height where the ancestral castle of the princely house had formerly stood, and the Würtembergers visited the chapel on the Rothenberg with similar sentiments to those which inspired the Prussians in their pilgrimages to the temple at Charlottenburg.

The king met the Landtag in a conciliatory spirit. All the secret designs of his ambition rested in the first instance upon the hope that the nation would regard him as the most liberal-minded of all the German princes. Even though representative forms of government were a nuisance, he felt himself to be strong enough to keep these scriveners in check and in the end to impose his own will, even as a constitutional prince. Consequently he retained Wangenheim at the head of affairs, although these two fundamentally divergent natures had in fact only one point in common, their dreams of the trias policy; and the minister soon observed that the king treated him with concealed hostility, nor always quite honourably.[1] With the aid of the proposal of the estates, a new constitutional plan was immediately worked out—the third, already, in this unending dispute—and submitted to the Landtag on March 3, 1817. The son's offers went a great deal further than the last proposals of the father. Nevertheless the obstinate dispute about the old differences flamed up anew, concerning the unicameral system, the tax-treasury, and the question of permanent committees, and once again the mob of Stuttgart displayed in noisy assemblies its advocacy of the old-established rights.

When these disputes had endured for another three months the king could no longer control his soldier's roughness. Behind the minister's back, he consulted with his friend the baron von Maucler, the leader of the domestic bureaucracy, and laid before the estates an ultimatum which was to be accepted within a week, and one which was, in fact, acceptable. New and fierce anger was displayed at the peremptory measure. On June 2nd the Landtag rejected this last offer, the majority consisting of the Old Würtembergers, the greater part of the nobles, and a small clerical party. Whilst almost all moderate politicians outside the country were now upon the king's side, the embitterment of the majority in the Landtag had increased from day to day. The Old Würtembergers actually claimed the *itio in partes*, that they might be enabled to retain their old

---

[1] Wangenheim to Hartmann, February 3, 1832.

peculiar privileges even against the will of the new portions of the country. When the vote was taken, Baron von Varnbüler bluntly declared that he would rather see the people remain under the present government without a constitution, than renounce, for all time, the claim to the ancient constitution. The court could not get the better of him ; when asked to return the chamberlain's golden key, he sent the precious article through the post, after writing on the cover " sample without value." The Landtag was dissolved amid all the signs of royal disfavour, and the members were even forbidden residence in the capital. An attempt to carry the royal proposal into effect by means of a referendum was a complete failure, and hereupon the monarch declared that he would now await the determinations of the Bundestag regarding the rights of the German provincial diets, and would meanwhile introduce into operation all the other promises contained in his proposal.

For two years longer the king continued to rule as an absolute sovereign, and in rapid succession gave the country a number of beneficial laws which the two " reform ministers," Wangenheim and Kerner (the poet's brother) had long before prepared. Serfdom was at length completely abolished, and a portion (although no more than a portion) of the land taxes was declared to be redeemable, emigration was permitted, the hitherto completely dependent communes received the ancient institution of communal councils in an improved form, and four circle governments replaced the bailiffs. The catholic theological faculty of Ellwangen was removed to Tübingen, so that the rigidly Lutheran ancient university now entered the ranks of the universities in which parity of belief prevailed. In order to educate officials who might usefully fill the administrative positions hitherto monopolised by the scriveners, there now also came into existence the somewhat unsuccessful institution of a special faculty for political science. Since, during the years of the famine, throughout the fruitful land agriculture was almost everywhere in an extremely defective condition, and since the petty peasantry, working almost entirely without capital, largely fell under the dominion of Jewish usurers, the king, with his keen sense of business, undertook vigorous action. He founded a great agricultural union for the instruction and assistance of the landowners, established stud farms and agricultural model farms upon his own private estates, founded an agricultural college in Hohenstein which, under the leadership of the vigorous Rhinelander Schwerz, soon rivalled that of Möglin. It was to the king's personal activities that the reawakening of a new spirit of enterprise among Swabian agriculturists was due ; year by year the peasants thronged to the cheerful agricultural festival which was held in Cannstatt from 1818 onwards, and brought their stallions and bulls to compete for the royal prizes.

Meanwhile the political sentiments of the country continued for a long period to remain so greatly incensed that even Wangenheim, as late as the spring of 1818, issued an urgent warning against the summoning of a new Landtag.[1] Gradually, however, a more peaceful mood was restored. More especially the New Würtembergers began to repent the obstinacy of the estates, and Friedrich List, " the friend of the people," an ardent advocate of the new ideals of popular representation, self-government, and the public administration of justice, found increasing support among the younger men. But, on his side, the king repented his vain offers ; he had learned that the reputation of the most liberal-minded of the German princes was, after all, not to be acquired with so much ease, and now, profoundly disillusioned, he had returned to the thoughts of bureaucratic absolutism which corresponded with his own natural inclinations. Taking action once more behind the backs of his councillors, the monarch summoned to his cabinet Malchus, the finance minister of King Jerome. Wangenheim and Kerner speedily recognised that they could not come to any understanding with this representative of the prefectoral system, and they resigned in November, 1817.

Henceforward the court of Stuttgart began to deceive and confuse public opinion by a detestable double game. Whilst the nomination of Wangenheim as envoy to the Bundestag seemed to guarantee the unalterable liberal sentiments of the king, the Würtemberg diplomats were secretly working for the enactment of a federal law which should especially limit the rights of the German Landtags, and should facilitate for the crowns the rescinding of their promises.[2] Still more disastrous was the effect of the fruitless Swabian constitutional struggle upon the sentiments of the other courts. Loud was the rejoicing of all the reactionaries at the excess of stormy passions displayed in these negotiations. Now, they said, it was proved

---

[1] Wangenheim to Hartmann, April 1, 1818.
[2] See above, page 428 et seq.

that it was impossible to rule in Germany with a Landtag;
a manifesto to the army had on one occasion even been planned
by the advocates of the old rights! For a long time to come
the Swabian estates remained an awful example to every
German prince who was reminded of article 13 of the federal
act, and Metternich wrote to Steigentesch in St. Petersburg:
" Würtemberg, with its imprudent dissensions with the Landtag,
has been of more use to the cause of the revolutionaries than
even the Tugendbund itself."

§ 2. BAVARIA.

More quickly than Würtemberg, but not without serious
struggles, did Bavaria secure its constitution. Just as in
Würtemberg the crown had been hampered by the defiant
spirit of the old estates, so in Bavaria the crown was hampered
by the schemes of the Roman see. Favouring fortune has
decreed that the crassest contrasts of our national life invarably
display themselves in closely allied stocks. It is for this reason
alone that the particularist spirit of the German tribes has been
unable utterly to destroy the bond of national unity, because
centrifugal forces are always counteracted by neighbourly
jealousy. As in the north, Westphalians and Rhinelanders,
Pomeranians and Old Prussians, Markers and Upper Saxons,
sharply distinguished from one another by tribal peculiarities
and by history, lived in close contiguity, so in the south lived
the Bavarians and the Swabians. Whilst Swabia, which had
long lost all political greatness, maintained its place in the
national life solely through its richness in men of distinction,
Bavaria was the oldest of all the German states, the only
one which preserved, not only its ancient territorial inheritance,
but also its ancient power, and its honourable tribal name,
and was consequently the home at once of a political and
of a social particularism whose luxuriant energy manifests, even
to-day, that the dismemberment of the four great tribal duchies
was the salvation of our ancient realm. The Bavarian stock
once gave the nation a Wolfram von Eschenbach and an Aven-
tinus; it was the counter-reformation which thrust the country
back into intellectual dulness. But it had never been rich in
brilliant personalities, owing its historical significance chiefly
to the political power of its tolerably well-rounded domain,
and to the warlike virtue of a vigorous branch of the human

race, whose close relationship with the ancient eastern Teutonic world-conquerors was unmistakable. From Bavaria, Louis the German and his Carlovingian successors ruled the German realm; and under the Saxons, the Salian Franks, and the Hohenstaufen, Bavaria on several occasions maintained a predominant position in the empire, until ultimately Emperor Louis the Bavarian made his country the strongest of all the German territorial powers.

But that disastrous destiny which invariably arrested German state-construction at a stage of half completion, exercised its sinister influence also over Bavarian history. After Tyrol had passed to the Hapsburgs (1363), Bavaria relapsed to the position of an inland power. The Austrian march, which had first been colonised from Bavaria, henceforward championed the struggle against the south-eastern neighbour peoples, a struggle which had previously been led by Bavaria, and outsoared the motherland to such an extent, that the two countries (whose stocks were so closely akin) soon came to occupy a similar relationship each to the other as did Electoral Saxony and Brandenburg—on the one hand the older, more distinguished power, whose development had been arrested, and on the other the ambitious and fortunate upstart. The domestic disputes which were the original sin of the Wittelsbachs, and repeated partitions, weakened the power of the princely race. Cut off from the lands of the Palatine cousins, Bavaria no longer possessed adequate economic forces, inasmuch as the wealth of the lower Bavarian plateau was outweighed by the poverty of the mountain districts and of the stony foothills of the Alps.

Nevertheless the house of Bavaria once again gave a decisive turn to German destiny. The Wittelsbachs were the first to repudiate the common cause of the nation, and, contrary to the decisions of the empire, they expelled the Protestant doctrine from the Bavarian land in those first hopeful years of the epoch of the Reformation, when the peaceful diffusion of the new doctrine throughout Germany still seemed possible ; it was they who in addition to the Hapsburgs, were responsible for the partial defeat of the Reformation in Germany. The Falkenturm in Munich, where the first Protestant martyrs suffered, was the cradle of the German counter-reformation, and as late as the year 1800 the pope spoke with esteem of " the ancient renown " of the country which, unlike any other in the world, had ever remained free from heresy. Subsequently the greatest son of the Bavarian house, the powerful Maximilian I, devoted his rare gifts of statecraft to inflicting upon his fatherland the miseries of a war of religions. He founded the Catholic League; he persecuted, yet more relentlessly than the emperor himself, his Protestant cousins of the Palatinate, and even after the peace of Westphalia, in defiance of the law of the empire, he forcibly restored the Catholic faith in the Upper Palatinate, the fruit of his victory; no heretic was allowed to live in this land of religious unity, and residence in Protestant domains was forbidden to every Bavarian subject. The alliance of the princely house with the Roman see was all the more firmly established because the duchy possessed no bishop of its own, and the rulers of the country required the assistance of the pope to guard themselves against the masterful claims of the seven neighbouring bishops, who were immediates of the empire. This rigidly Catholic policy advantaged the glory of the court, acquiring for it the dignity of an electoral princedom, and provided for the younger sons of the house valuable positions in the great ecclesiastical foundations of the empire, so that Electoral Cologne was for nearly two centuries ruled by Bavarian princes, while three, and at times four, electoral votes were in the hands of the Wittelsbachs. But after the death of the great Maximilian, the dynasty was no longer able to attain to a firm attitude of independent power. Threatened by the lust of conquest of the Austrian neighbour, it again and again formed a sinister alliance with the court of Versailles, so that in Munich, as in Cologne, the French envoy had a decisive voice.

Meanwhile the Old Bavarian people sank into the spiritual slumber of an easy-going particularist life. Whilst Franconians and Alemans everywhere got on well together, the most conservative of all the High German stocks was inwardly more akin to the stolid Lower Saxon populace than to its highland neighbours. It was only the most northerly off-shoots of the Bavarian stock which had mingled to some extent with the Franconians. From the Austrians, to whom they were so closely akin, the Bavarians were separated by ancient political hatred; whilst towards Swabia the Lech had long constituted a strong natural frontier, which almost completely prevented neighbourly intercourse. When compared with the well nigh incredible variety of Swabian life, the life of Old Bavaria seemed that of a circumscribed mass, and only in the Upper Palatinate were trifling differences of dialect noticeable. No doubt the wealthy wheat-barons of Lower Bavaria displayed their peasant pride, their primitive energies, far more unrestrainedly than did the more mobile-minded, song-loving yagers of the Alps, or the straightforward foresters of the poor Bavarian forests ; yet in essentials all Bavarians were chips of the same block. Everywhere were manifest the same lineaments of vigorous courage, inexhaustible joy of life, and good-natured cunning ; everywhere the same naive pride of blood, which in case of need continued to speak of " Germany " as an accessory country ; everywhere there was the same invincible dynastic loyalty. Whilst Swabia sent forth to the world a long series of renowned princely races, the Zähringens, the Hohenstaufens, and the Hohenzollerns, in Bavaria one single race soon came to dominate all the other dynasties. The extremely ancient house of the Schyrens had already in Carlovingian days several times worn the ducal hat, and had now for more than seven hundred years uninterruptedly maintained its territorial suzerainty. Bavarian blood had been poured out in streams for the ancient blue-and-white lozenge escutcheon. On days of festival, the country's flag fluttered even above the dug-outs which, as coarsely constructed still as in the days of the lake-dwellers, continued to navigate the quiet Alpine waters of the Chiem-See and the Walchen-See.

Urban life had never regained vigorous development since Ratisbon, the ancient capital, had been severed from the country. Even Munich, with its magnificent churches and castles, with its seventeen monasteries and seventeen miraculous images, continued to exhibit, in the middle of the eighteenth century, as far as civic culture and industrial life were concerned, very little pre-eminence over the wonder-working town of Deggendorf and the other country towns which served the peasantry for corn markets and places of pilgrimage. The strength of Bavaria lay in the peasants, and in a few renowned noble houses ; but for the countryfolk the church remained the centre of life, and the priests, themselves drawn from the peasantry, were all-powerful advisers in temporal and spiritual needs. The ecclesiastical year, with its endless series of feast-days, dictated all the activities of the peasant household. In the adornment of the churches and in the brilliancy of the processions, it was possible to see how much vigorous sense of colour and form was retained beneath a rough exterior. With breathless attention, the congregation watched at Pentecost until the Holy Ghost should descend through an aperture in the roof of the church ; with iron endurance, on the Friday after Ascension Day they remained at prayer for hours hoping to avert hail-storms from their fields ; the customary unending revels were associated with every feast of the church. Nowhere in the world, so ran the Bavarian proverb, was religion so agreeable, and devotion so joyous.

Under the last of the Bavarian Wittelsbachs, Maximilian III, a ray of light came first to penetrate this dense obscurity. Ickstatt, the Rhinelander, aided by a few other courageous disciples of the new enlightenment, initiated a reform of the educational system, and succeeded in securing that non-Catholic books should be admitted to use in the temporal faculties of the Jesuit university at Ingolstadt. Under the auspices of this freer temporal culture there grew up many of the men who, a generation later, effected the reconstitution of the petrified state. One of these was the talented humorist, Anton Bucher, who, himself a priest, chastised with unpolished popular wit the rude superstitions of his fellow-countrymen. But just as, in the Romance lands, the rule of the Jesuits, by a natural reaction, everywhere favoured frivolous unbelief, so also in Bavaria, as soon as the clerical regime was shaken, there awakened that fanatical hatred of the church which is characteristic of immature free thought. The new secret society of the Illuminati, founded after the example of the Society of Jesus, fought against the " obscurantists " of the Church no less intolerantly and no less unscrupulously than the Jesuits had fought against heresy, and, notwithstanding severe prohibitions, secured numerous adherents from among the upper classes. The reforms of Maximilian III were arrested as soon as Charles Theodore, Elector of the Bavarian Palatinate, ascended the throne. The clergy regained its power, and shameless nepotism prevailed throughout the administration ; the officialdom of the Bavarian Palatinate even included a " Mademoiselle Frontier-Chief-Customhouse-Official " and a " Madame Chief-Forester." When the body of Charles Theodore was carried through the streets, the populace threw stones after the coffin because the Palatiner, whom the Bavarians had continued to regard as a foreigner, had desired to sell the country to Austria. The detestation of this miserable regime and the secret influence of the Illuminati prepared the way for the doctrines of the Revolution. After Moreau's entry, there came into existence in Munich a literature whose Jacobin coarseness exceeded even that characteristic of the contemporary writings of the discontented Swabians ; savage poems announced " war and eternal struggle against all the hypocritical canaille."

In such a situation, whilst the masses were immersed in a dull slumber and a portion of the cultured classes were childishly playing with revolutionary ideas, Max Joseph of Zweibrücken celebrated his entry, and with him entered the new time. The new dynasty at length reunited the long-severed lands of the house of Schyren, and cherished the ambition to resume in its statecraft at once the traditions of the Bavarian and those of the Palatine Wittelsbachs. A sound policy, but one very difficult to carry out, for the Bavarian memories related to Maximilian and the League, whilst the memories of the Palatinate related to Otho Henry, the Reformer, and to Charles Gustavus, king of Sweden.

By means of the territorial donations of Napoleon an entirely new social energy was introduced into the Bavarian state, a brilliant circle of beautiful and celebrated towns became associated with the Old Bavarian peasant lands. It is true that the majority of these proud communes seemed to be nothing more than picturesque ruins of ancient glories. The change in the routes of world commerce had ruined the markets of Lindau and Passau ; nor in the case of the ancient Ratisbon could isolated great businesses, such as the arms factory of Kuchenreuter, restore the lost commerce. The grey turreted walls of Nördlingen now surrounded a quiet country town, to which the peasant from the Ries district came to market ; the urban industry of Bamberg was of little significance when compared with the labours of the market gardeners outside the gates. Rothenburg, with its magnificent churches and council-houses, lay like a town of the dead on the height above the Taubergrund valley. Even Nuremberg was heavily burdened with debt, and in a condition of petrification under the nepotist rule of the nineteen " privileged " families of the small council. In Augsburg alone, thanks to the inexhaustible water-power of the Lech, had an anciently celebrated weaving industry revived to some extent since the middle of the eighteenth century. The Bavarian government could not understand that the way to reanimate this slumbering bourgeoisie was by the liberation of industry. Whilst Munich, overwhelmed with royal favour, continued to grow, almost all the other Bavarian towns remained, as late as the middle of the thirties, in a condition of arrest and debility, so that the more active energies of the North German communes gained an enormous start.

No less slowly did the old hostility between the Bavarians, the Swabians, and the Franconians, disappear. Not one of the three High German stocks was sufficiently numerous in the new kingdom to dominate the others, whilst in the artificially constructed state it was difficult for a sense of political community to come into existence. Since the severance of Salzburg and Tyrol, only half of the population had consisted of Bavarians. Altogether hostile towards the Bavarian masters, with their well-established religious unity, was eastern Swabia, a classical area of German religious dissension. In this region, the caps worn by the girls and the methods of agriculture were already sufficient to acquaint the traveller with the religious belief of the district. Here lived the peasants of the domain of the Fuggers and of the chapter-lands of Kempten and Kaufbeuren, a strictly Catholic population which even as late as the year 1809 was on the verge of making common cause with the Tyrolese in their fight for the religion. Close at hand were Memmingen, a town which had suffered for its Protestantism, and Augsburg, where parity of belief prevailed, and which for centuries past had been visited by ecclesiastical dissensions, where even the position of town-lieutenant and the coffee-house privileges were conscientiously shared between the two faiths. The reputation for tolerance of the house of Zweibrücken was indeed so well established that in Augsburg the Protestants passed under the sceptre of the Wittelsbachs more readily than did the Catholics, yet it was long before the highly-cultured patricians of the proud Swabian towns became accustomed to Bavarian ways.

Yet more vigorous was the resistance in Protestant Franconia, the most valuable acquisition of the young kingdom. Long ago, indeed, the Nurembergers had ceased to hope for the re-establishment of their ancient liberties ; the political vigour of the venerable community had become extinct, and as early as the year 1796, the bourgeoisie had on one occasion, by a great majority, voted to accept subordination to the crown of Prussia. But here from the time of Gustavus Adolphus the Bavarians had been regarded as enemies ; how often, indeed, had the waggish humour of the imperial townsmen, which was now again finding clear expression in the dialect poems of Conrad Grübel, led them to make merry at the expense of these bad neighbours. The town suspiciously maintained its ancient Protestant traditions ; since its university of Altdorf had been closed by the new sovereign, at least the Nuremberger gymnasium should faithfully maintain the spirit of its founder Melanchthon, and, like the neighbouring Brandenburg university of Erlangen, should remain the nursery of Protestant culture in the new state with its parity of religious beliefs. This vigorous little university had continued to keep pace with the literary movement of the north, and even amid the clash of French arms had never renounced its loyal German sentiments. The whole of Brandenburg Franconia continued to look back with longing upon the brief happiness of the Prussian regime. In Ansbach the Bavarian rule could not become firmly established until Bayreuth had also been united with Bavaria ; and even then the loyal populace would not willingly abandon hope of reunion. When Frederick William at length summoned his Prussians to the colours, the Franconians of the Fichtel-gebirge prepared for battle, and it was only the ill-fortune of the war which prevented them from rising.

The Catholic neighbours in the wealthy Franconian episcopal lands had no such cherished memories to overcome ; the Würz-burgers greeted with delight the departure of their grand duke Ferdinand of Tuscany, who had always neglected his German territory as an insecure possession. But even here the Bavarian rule was accepted with disfavour. Delighting in his vineyards, enlightened and witty, the Franconian of the Main, from the jovial grace of his half-Rhenish life, looked down contemptuously upon the rough existence of the Bavarians ; the members of the imperial knighthood felt degraded by the change, for if they had to obey anyone it should have been a Hapsburg. The prudent lenity of General-commissary Lerchenfeld served, however, to allay the disaffection. The court knew that the priceless Tyrol, this Old Bavarian territory, whose whole intercourse was with Bavaria, had been lost solely through the headstrong roughness of its officials, and now therefore acted with extreme caution in the occupation of the new territories.

Most circumspectly of all did Bavaria proceed in the youngest of its provinces, the trans-Rhenish Palatinate, for here it had to encounter a profound hostility which endured even longer than the disinclination of the Rhinelanders towards the Old

Prussians. Since those distant days when the Salian Franks had held court at Limburg, and the Hohenstaufen at Trifels, in this imperilled march no vigorous state authority had ever been re-established. Spires and Worms, Sickingen and Leiningen, Nassau, Baden, Hesse, and Wittelsbach, existed here side by side, all of them animated by that friendly and neighbourly sentiment which found expression in the names of the frontier towers, "Live and let live!" and "Give me my peace!" The sport of two hostile nations, this able and indefatigably industrious people had endured with astonishing vital energy the misfortunes of petty princely despotism, repeated religious persecutions, and horrible devastation, and had only reacquired a secure civic order under the prefects of the empire. Nowhere on German soil did the Revolution plough deeper furrows. Everything which in their history preceded the days of the French regime was regarded by the Palatiners as mediæval, and even those portions of the country which had formerly belonged to the Wittelsbachs hardly gave a thought any longer to their ancient princely house. The nobility had disappeared ; the ancient subdivision of the estates had been completely destroyed ; even the new race of rich men, the wine-barons, who during the sale of the national goods had secured possession of the favoured wine-lands of the Hardt, had to adapt themselves to the bourgeois customs of this thoroughly modern region.

The French principles of social equality and free economic competition had become part of the very flesh and blood of the Palatiners. In the little towns on the Hardt a speculative petty agriculture flourished, utilising every corner of land and finding free divisibility of the soil absolutely indispensable. The shrewd Palatine peasant wore the townsman's doublet, and boasted that for him even the ox must bear calves. All the creeds were intimately intermingled, and all of them were characterised by an aroma of Calvinistic sobriety and tolerant enlightenment ; after so many changes of faith, people had at length learned the art of mutual accommodation. When the storms of the nineties had blown over, the Palatinate had little experience of the terrors of the epoch of war. The industrious inhabitants knew very well how to draw their profit from the great French market ; never again did innkeepers and post-masters see such fat times as these, when all the potentates of the world passed through the country, year after year, on the journey to or from Paris. Well did the court of Munich know how unwillingly the Palatinate underwent detachment from France, and since the ruler of Bavaria continued for a long time to hope to exchange this remote province for the Palatinate on the right bank of the Rhine, the new governor Zwackh left almost all the institutions of the country temporarily undisturbed. Even when this hope had at length to be abandoned, the government was too timid and too poor in creative energy to make any important changes. Not only did the province retain the *code Napoléon*, but also the entire French system of administration ; every notice-board on the high-roads reminded wagoners of the law concerning the *voieries publiques*. What had Old Bavaria to offer this country ? When compared with the purely bureaucratic and yet cumbrous administration of the old provinces, the vigorous order of the prefectoral system could not but seem eminently desirable.

Thus it was that a Franco-German distinctive life continued to flourish undisturbed in a country where every ruined fortress served to remind the beholder of the misdeeds of the French. Particularist enthusiasm for the foreign laws here displayed itself even more vigorously than in Prussian Rhineland. Everything French was regarded as inviolable, because it was Palatine, and it was honoured as a treasure of peculiarly native origin. It was regarded as a visitation of nature that the French fury had not left a single one undestroyed from among the ancient churches and imperial palaces of the country ; no one ventured to remove the red Jacobin cap from the church tower of Landau ; on the walls of the frontier fortress the emblems were still flaunted which the French had once brought there for the humiliation of Germany—over the French gate was the smiling, and over the German gate the frowning, sun of the great Louis. The inhabitants gave little thanks to the Old Bavarians for their lenity. The endowments, the history, and the culture of the two stocks were too widely divergent. The enlightened Palatiner spoke with boundless contempt of the thickness of these Bavarian heads, although his own country took but little part in the literary activity of the nation. Since the severance of Heidelberg and Mannheim, the intellectual life of the trans-Rhenish Palatinate had fallen to an incredibly low level, and the rich talents of the highly-gifted people were shown almost exclusively in business affairs. When two quarrelsome Palatiners exchanged home truths after the frank manner of the country, the colloquy invariably terminated with the most offensive term of abuse known to both, each calling the other an Old Bavarian! With infinitesimal exceptions, all the Palatiners despised state service in the old provinces. It was with profound disaffection that the thoroughly unmilitary people saw their sons " sent to Bavaria to fulfil the obligation of military service." In so unnatural a situation, continually excited by the party struggles in neighbouring France, half independent and yet half chained to an unloved and inefficient German government, the country gradually became dominated by a loquacious, unpatriotic, and revolutionary spirit, whose aim it was to get rid throughout Germany of all historical traditions as "radically" as in the unhappy Palatinate this had been effected by the glorious Revolution.

It was fortunate that not one of these numerous centrifugal tendencies was by itself sufficiently strong to disintegrate the Bavarian state and that not one of them would combine with any of the others. It was fortunate also that the good-natured king so speedily learned how to acquire the personal regard of his subjects. Max Joseph had spent the best days of his youth at Strasburg as an officer in the French service, in a position which was well suited to his capacities, and his fondness for France persisted throughout life, although the Revolution drove him from Alsace. Soon after ascending the Bavarian throne, he begged Alquier the French chargé d'affaires, to regard him as a Frenchman, saying, " Whenever I hear of the successes of the armies of the Republic, I rejoice to know that I am a Frenchman." [1] The Rhenish Confederate policy corresponded not merely to his dynastic interests, but also to his personal inclinations, and it was unwillingly that he abandoned it, although his heart had long been lacerated by all the sacrifices which the Protector demanded from Bavaria. The question whether he did not also possess political duties towards Germany never entered his head ; the uprising of 1813 was a riddle to him, and he lent a willing ear to the accusations levelled against the "Prussian Jacobins." None the less, like many other princes of the Confederation of the Rhine, he remained, after his manner, a German father of his country, honourably desirous of making his people happy and of living at peace

[1] Alquier's Report to Talleyrand, Munich, 6 Ventose, VII communicated to me by Dr. P. Bailleu.

with them. Wherever he appeared his friendly good-nature won the hearts of the masses. Even in Berg, which belonged to him for a few years only, his memory was held in great affection. In Old Bavaria he was immediately received with exuberant delight as the saviour of the country, and this filled him with rejoicing. He found himself at home among the agreeable customs of the country, which harmonised well with his own rough naturalness ; he wore great earrings like a genuine Bavarian, and loved the vigorous men of the high mountains like his own children, not excepting the Tyrolese rebels. It was long before he could forgive the French for having shot his beloved Andreas Hofer. During the later years of his life he usually spent the summer by the Tegernsee, in the old abbey by the quiet waters of the forest lake, where everything beloved of an old Bavarian heart was to be found under a single roof—a royal palace, a church, and a brewery. For miles round, as far as the lonely mountain torrent of Kreuth, there was not a single farm which father Max with his charming daughters had not visited once at least, standing godfather perhaps to the children, or overwhelming the inmates with benefits.

It would have been well if this inexhaustible benevolence had not been associated with so much thoughtless weakness ! The court was never empty of rogues and beggars, and the whole of Munich was familiar with the king's fondness for amiable prodigals ; a swarm of parasites, among whom was even to be found a court jester, received stately allowances. The financial needs of the crown were unending, and the court banker, Seligmann Eichthal, became continually richer, although the king needed for himself little more than he had done many years before when, as a refugee from Strasburg, he conducted his bourgeois household to Rohrbach-on-the-Bergstrasse. When this man of soft and emotional nature became a prey to fear, he repudiated his virile pride and his princely dignity, and was not ashamed to cringe and to lie. All his disgraces of recent years, all the humiliations of the house of Wittelsbach, which contrasted so painfully with the boastful arrogance of the new kingship, were the direct work of the monarch. Bavaria's double-tongued policy on the outbreak of the war of 1805 might be excused on the plea of urgent necessity ; it became contemptible only when King Max pledged his word of honour to Emperor Francis while uttering a deliberate untruth.[1] His lively correspondence with the Protector of the Confederation of the Rhine was dictated by circumstances; it became disgraceful only through the servility of the king who, often without an answer being vouchsafed, besieged the Imperator with servile letters, attended on him personally far more often than was necessary, even asked his orders regarding the marriage of the royal princes, and gave to Napoleon's tools, the dukes of Bassano and Cadore, any gratuities they liked to demand. At a later date, when the dispute concerning the Badanese Palatinate began, the cowardly prince displayed the same unkingly attitude towards Czar Alexander.

He devoted himself to governmental business with praiseworthy zeal; it was believed that he was more often idle than was actually the case, because he was so fond of spending his free hours in the streets. An ordered life was ever burdensome to him, and since he possessed no more than the superficial culture of a French officer of the old school he speedily became dependent upon the superior knowledge of affairs of his ministers and of Ringel, the skilful secretary of the cabinet. He understood very little even of military affairs. In the evening of his life he seldom put in an appearance among his troops, and in times of peace he allowed the warlike efficiency of his army, which under Napoleon's leadership had been so remarkable, to degenerate rapidly. Henceforward this unwarlike attitude remained a heritage of all the Bavarian kings, and was subsequently to be of momentous importance to the state. Easily dependent upon the impressions of the moment, Max Joseph none the less held firmly to two political principles. As a born Palatiner he was so profoundly convinced of the untenability of the Old Bavarian conditions that, in case of need, he did not shrink even from radical reforms; and he greatly detested the greed for power displayed by the priesthood. Here was his strength; when he protected the North German professors in Munich against the bigoted fancies of the mob, he displayed a quite unwonted firmness. He knew what it signified that his house now ruled 1,200,000 Protestant subjects, and he wished these to feel that they belonged to a just state. It was a matter of rejoicing to him to live in a mixed marriage, and it remains his historical glory that he inculcated

---

[1] See Vol. I, p. 6.

this spirit of tolerance upon his children and grandchildren. In three generations since then, the country has known Protestant queens only ; and notwithstanding repeated struggles and relapses, the German idea of religious parity which the good king Max imposed upon his reluctant people, has never been surrendered by the Bavarian state.

Since the treaty of Ried, the position of the all-powerful minister Montgelas had been somewhat shaken. The allied monarchs regarded the leading statesman of the Confederation of the Rhine with natural suspicion, and when he appeared in Frankfort after the battle of Hanau, they received him with such disfavour that subsequently he thought it inadvisable to put in a personal appearance at the congress of Vienna. But he continued to control the three most important offices of the state, foreign affairs, home affairs, and finance, and could securely rely upon his indispensability, for not without reason did he bear a king's crown upon his count's escutcheon. He was the creator of the new Bavarian state. Since the days of the elector Maurice of Saxony, the policy of undisguised and logically pursued particularism had not found so able and successful a representative upon German soil. Although by birth he belonged to Old Bavaria, Montgelas was numbered among those diplomatic mercenaries who so frequently appear in the history of the German middle-sized states, among those men without a home, who, void of all political traditions, seek a sphere of activity wherever ambition may offer them a free field. His friendship for the king, with whom he had already become intimate in the Palatinate, constituted the one emotional tie which chained him to his homeland ; in general he regarded country and people with contempt. It was a matter he could never forgive that in youth, as a member of the order of Illuminati, he had been forced to leave the superstitious land of Bavaria ; and even in old age he judged *cette nation bornée* with the critical detachment of the foreigner. But the caprice of fortune which led him back to this unloved land, had offered to him a rich field of activity. In the consciousness of his own strength, he regarded himself as predestined to raise Bavaria to the position of an independent European power. To him power was an end in itself, and nothing was further from his mind than the question how it might best be used for the advantage of Germany. Anything that reminded him of the confraternity of the great fatherland seemed to him nothing more than a tiresome obstacle to the independence of Bavaria. A cold-blooded gamester, never disturbed by moral considerations, and rarely influenced either by hatred or by love, he freely calculated on the favour of the moment, and selected his friends wherever he could find them. His faithful advocate, Ritter Lang, when, in the year 1814, he defended the minister against the passionate attacks of the friends of Stein, described the most intimate secrets of this materialist cunning in the following terms: "The only true maxim of Bavarian policy is the self-preservation of the state; whichever one of the other powers recognises this principle and supports it with its own authority, is to be regarded as the most genuinely friendly."

For this reason, Montgelas, notwithstanding his semi-French blood and his wholly French culture, took up a firmer attitude against the Protector of the Confederation of the Rhine than did the king. It was not out of any affection for France that in former days he had broken the old alliance with Prussia, but because he recognised that the Bavarian desire for aggrandisement could at the moment expect no help from Prussian weakness, whilst it might expect everything from the vigour of Bonapartism. He zealously participated in Napoleon's wars against Austria and Prussia, because the strength of Bavaria, in his view, was conditioned by the weakness of the German great powers; but he never desired the destruction of these two states, for an all-powerful France might also become a danger to the independence of Bavaria. On two occasions, and this was to him a matter of pride, he hindered the development of the Rhenish Confederate constitution; and again and again he adjured his royal friend not to endanger the liberties of the state by a contemptible servility towards the Protector.

To this cold calculator, the uprising of Germany was unwelcome, since it cut him off from all hope of further enlargements of territory, and it was only with hesitation that he determined to abandon the sinking ship of Bonapartism. For a time he continued to flatter himself with the hope that Bavaria might be able within the great alliance to constitute the nucleus of a South German league, and that Wrede might be able to play the part of another Tilly.[1] When

---

[1] Montgelas to Wrede, October 21, 1813. Heilmann, Fürst Wrede, p. 268.

this hope proved delusive, he next endeavoured to safeguard the sovereignty of the Wittelsbachs against the dualistic schemes of Hardenberg, and secretly fostered the mutual hostility of the two great powers. It was upon this that depended Bavaria's zeal for the restoration of the crown of Saxony. At the time of the second peace congress of Paris, Montgelas even found it difficult to conceal his malicious joy from the Prussian envoy Küster ; what a piece of good luck it would be if the dispute about Alsace and Lorraine were to prove a permanent cause of disunion between Prussia and Austria.[1] But this expectation also proved fallacious, and all that was left open to him was to paralyse the activities of the Germanic Federation, and carefully to protect the Bavarian people from the dangerous doctrines of the North German Jacobins. He speedily noted with satisfaction that there was very little to dread from the powerlessness of the Bundestag, but he relentlessly suppressed the handful of patriots in Bavaria. Even one of the king's favourites, Anselm Feuerbach, was described as an emissary of Prussia, and was banished from the capital because, in his writing *Concerning German Freedom*, he had hailed with delight the overthrow of the foreign dominion, and had declared that the blood of so many heroes must be paid for by the granting of a free representative system. The experienced minister was not deceived as to the instability of the new condition of German affairs. Even in advanced age, it remained his hope that in the next European crisis, perhaps with the help of some foreign power, the smallest German princes might be mediatised, Baden and Würtemberg compensated in Italy, and the whole of the south-west subjected to the house of Wittelsbach. Prussia might continue to grow in the north as much as she pleased, if only one thing could be hindered which to the Bavarian statesman seemed the most terrible, the unity of Germany. Till the great opportunity came all that could be done was to bide his time. It was only for passing moments that his cool intelligence was influenced by fantastic notions about Bavarian superexcellence. Nothing seemed to him more childish than the illusion that a union of the powerless could ever constitute a power, and for this reason he laughingly rejected all proposals for a separate league of the minor German or mid-European states, such as was mooted in Stutt-

[1] Küster's Report, Munich, August 28, 1815.

gart. From the first, moreover, he opposed as hopeless the Palatine plans of the crown prince.

They were a singular pair of friends, the easy-going, slovenly, popular, and homely king, side by side with the courtly figure of the adroit minister. The latter's appearance recalled the old French style, with his powdered hair, his embroidered red court dress, and long silk stockings ; his keen and yet shifty brown eyes, and great overhanging nose, projecting above the large and satyr-like mouth—a countenance expressing in all its lineaments a penetrating understanding. Montgelas and his wife were largely to blame for the frivolous tone which prevailed in the fashionable world of Munich ; his little mansion in Bogenhausen, close to Englischer Garten, offered inexhaustible material to scandalmongers. The old Illuminate could never feel any enthusiasm for the performances of the new German literature and art. Nevertheless he knew that science was indispensable to the reform of the state, nor at his own table could he dispense with the lively conversation of brilliant men of learning. Through his long tenure of power he became autocratically inclined, but was devoid of petty vanity. When contrasted with the false self-praise of Metternich's memoirs, the restrained self-satisfaction which speaks from the memoirs of Montgelas produces an agreeable impression.

In all departments of public life the despotic dispenser of popular happiness had effected a revolutionary transformation, but the new order still displayed everywhere gaps and contradictions, and everywhere were manifest traces of overhasty work. The most successful reform was that of education. The elementary school had been withdrawn from the rule of the Roman church, and universal compulsory education, introduced in 1802, began slowly to make itself at home. The institutions for secondary education were under the control of Niethammer, a worthy advocate of a strictly classical education. At the philological seminary of Munich, Friedrich Thiersch, the Thuringian, in many years of faithful work, educated a number of efficient teachers, so that the influence of the idealistic spirit of this *praeceptor Bavariae* gradually made its way into most of the gymnasia of the country. To the universities of Landshut and Erlangen, was now added that of Würzburg, with the wealthy princely episcopal Juliushospital, an important nursery of the medical sciences. The lethargic slumber of the ancient days of unity of belief had passed away for ever.

Far less complete was the transformation of the legal system and of the administration. The jumble of old territories was, indeed, compacted to form Napoleonic departments, and the officials, for whom reasonable service regulations were drawn up, thus acquired a position as secure as that of the Prussian officials ; but in the lower grades the judiciary and the executive remained combined, and the "worshipful country justices," the terror of the peasantry, continued to exercise unrestricted authority in the country districts Patrimonial jurisdiction still prevailed upon the large landed properties, and it not infrequently happened that the state ceded its own serfs to favoured nobles, in order to enable the latter to constitute independent judicial areas. The evangel of the bureaucracy, the criminal code of 1813, was an honour to the legal perspicacity of its author, Feuerbach, but secrecy of procedure and excessive severity of punishment fostered the spirit of overbearing severity which distinguished this officialdom ; more especially the barbarous means of compulsion which it was authorised to use against accused who obstinately denied their offences, were frequently employed by country justices with revolting roughness. There was also a secret police trained after the Napoleonic model to practise the arts of espionage and to intercept letters. The pressure of the officials was all the more burdensome because Montgelas had destroyed the independence of the communes even more completely than had the First Consul. What a contrast between the towns' ordinance of Stein and the almost simultaneously promulgated Bavarian communes law. In Bavaria, the municipalities were even deprived of the right of administering their own property, and, in a word, they could do nothing without the approval of the royal police officers. Although the new tax laws turned out well, confusion and defalcation prevailed in the financial administration ; the minister himself worked hard, but with the irregularity of the great lord. For the years 1812-17 there was a deficit of 8,800,000 florins, and the real amount of the high total of the state debt was known to no one.

For the masses of the people, however, all these difficulties were more tolerable than were the utterly unfortunate attempts of the minister in the direction of economic reform.

Here it first became manifest how far Montgelas' talents fell behind the statesmanlike energies of Stein and Hardenberg. As far as social liberty was concerned, hardly anything had been gained by all the forcible innovations and pompous promises of these fifteen years. Serfdom had been abolished, but the laws regarding the remission of ground-rents and tithes were full of lacunæ, and were not carried into effect, so that nine-tenths of the peasants still remained serfs tied to the soil and forced to pay ground-rent. The old guild-system, which had nowhere degenerated more hopelessly than in Old Bavaria, was to be done away with by the introduction of a system of police licences for occupation; and, with customary boastfulness, the legislator proclaimed that he would restore to honour the ancient German proverb "skill is not inherited." Now, as formerly, every guild persecuted the work of non-guildsmen; the braidmakers and the lacemakers continued to live in eternal conflict; and anyone who had the good fortune to marry into the strictly closed corporation of the master chimney-sweeps of Munich, was absolved from all earthly cares. The reform remained a patchwork, and served merely to arouse the hostility of the handicraftsmen. In the towns, the right of contracting marriage was subject to the permission to undertake an independent occupation, and since in the country districts the landowners were privileged to forbid marriage at their pleasure, and since the indivisibility of the peasant farms rendered provision for younger sons a matter of difficulty, the result was that this roughly sensual (though by no means immoral) people became tragically distinguished among all the nations of Europe by the rate of illegitimacy. In Lower Bavaria, nearly one-fourth of all the children were born outside the bonds of wedlock. In the Palatinate, on the other hand, the proportion of illegitimate births was barely one-third of this, for here the social liberty of French legislation prevailed, with the severe but wholesome prohibition of affiliation suits.

Montgelas believed himself securely installed in power for the king's lifetime. The great majority of the officialdom was permeated with the spirit of Napoleonic despotism, and in the capital there were only two strong parties, both equally un-German and both equally particularistic: on one side the clericals who during the reign of Max Joseph could never enter into power; and on the other side the adherents of the Illuminate minister. The members of the little colony of North German and Swabian professors who, almost alone in Munich, still held firmly to the political ideals of the War of Liberation, were without influence, and could not venture to resist the minister openly, for at least he offered them a certain support against the anti-foreign hatred of the fanatical Old Bavarians. One of the best men of this circle, Jacobs, the philologian, had already returned home to Thuringia. Being a sensitive man, he could not endure being continually looked down upon as a "northerner," as a beggar growing fat in the Bavarian Canaan. Still greater was the discontent in Franconia. Here the enthusiasm of the years of war persisted for a long time, the communes were furious at the loss of their independent administration, and an emotional writing by Hornthal of Bamberg, which alluded to article 13 of the federal act, secured lively approval. But even here the opposition seemed devoid of danger. In Aretin's *Alemannia*, the unrepentant Rhenish Confederates continued confidently to sing the praises of the great minister, and to utter savage invectives against Germanism, Borussianism, and Anglomania. In Franconia, when the anniversary of the battle of Leipzig was celebrated, these writers in *Alemannia* related in their report that the festival had closed with a cattle show, and that the prize ox had been decorated with the order of the iron cross.

In court circles, where French was still preferred, Bonapartism had secured fresh supporters since Max Joseph's son-in-law, Eugene Beauharnais, had held his court in Munich as prince of the blood and duke of Leuchtenberg, and had collected round him a group of discontented Frenchmen. The most amiable of the Napoleonides soon won the hearts of the bourgeoisie, and worked vigorously in secret for the restoration of the empire. His aide-de-camp, General Bataille, carried on intercourse with the Bonapartists in Milan.[1] The chief superintendent of police winked at what was going on, and many of the postal officials were numbered among the confidants of the Leuchtenberg palace. Subsequently Eugene's sister, Hortense, the former queen of Holland, found asylum with her two sons in Augsburg, playing here with charming grace the role of bourgeoisphile princess, and weaving even more zealously than her brother the threads of Napoleonic

---

[1] Küster's Reports, Munich, May 17, August 20, 1815, and subsequent dates.

conspiracy. Paying no attention to the urgent warnings of the two German great powers, the king let his darling Eugene do as he pleased. For many years Bavaria remained the nidus of German Bonapartism.

Amid such conditions no one suffered more severely than did the high-minded queen Caroline and her stepson, the heir to the throne. In the year 1813 both had ably co-operated in the fortunate turn in Munich policy, and now saw with much anxiety that an honourable relationship to the new Germanic Federation remained impossible so long as the untrustworthy Montgelas held the rudder of state. In the emotional temperament of the crown prince, there was an element of straightforward enthusiasm for Germany's greatness, strangely coupled with fantastical dreams of Bavarian aggrandisement. Born in Strasburg, the prince had subsequently associated in exile with Alsatian *émigrés*, and while still quite a young man had learned to detest the French and their Revolution. The whole of his life since then had been a continuous struggle against the pro-French policy of his father. After the battle of Austerlitz, he had been forced in his native town to participate in the festival of victory of the empress Josephine, and with his customary frank disregard of consequences he had declared : " To me it would be the most agreeable festival of victory if my home were once more to become a German town." A year later, when he was fighting on the Vistula against the Prussians and the Russians, he had already conceived the plan of constructing a magnificent Walhalla for the great men of his fatherland, and in halting verses demanded of the Germans that they should break the chains of the Corsican. Very rarely indeed did he give the lie to his German pride before the powerful Imperator. He regarded Montgelas as merely the satrap of the foreign despot. He made no concealment of his hostility to the minister, publicly treated his brother-in-law Eugene Beauharnais with the extremest contempt, and desired the fall of Montgelas all the more impatiently because his own most cherished plan, his designs upon the Badenese Palatinate, could never succeed without the good wishes of the German great powers.

In these endeavours he found a powerful ally in the much-admired new field-marshal of the Bavarian realm. Wrede detested the North German patriots even more fiercely

than did the minister himself. As he wrote to Montgelas
during the campaign of 1814, what he would like best to do
with this idiot, this devil, of a Stein, would be to load him
into a howitzer and send him as a present to Napoleon. It
was chiefly from wounded vanity that, in the year 1812, the
valiant mercenary, from being a humble servant of Bonaparte
had become an enemy, because the Imperator refused him
the great eagle of the Legion of Honour. But he was able
to boast that sooner than Montgelas he had recognised the
right moment in which to turn his coat, and that he had
brought the treaty of Ried to pass almost against the will
of the hesitating minister. Since then he had plumed himself, not merely as the commander-in-chief, but also as the
diplomatic saviour, of the Bavarian nation. His pretorian
pride scorned all decency, scorned even the laws of the state.
On his own initiative, during the campaign of 1815, he
promised the officers of the four cavalry regiments and
eighteen legions which had been formed for the war only,
that they should not be dismissed when peace came ; when
subsequently Montgelas, moved by the desperate financial
situation, demanded the urgently necessary reduction of the
army, the field-marshal appeared in the ministerial council
as "representative of the army," and carried his masterful
proposal with the monarch. It was not surprising that
Montgelas spoke of him as "the Bavarian Wallenstein," and
looked askance at the new princely title of this favoured
child of fortune. Since the congress of Vienna, Wrede had
been completely won over to the side of Austria, this very
Austria which quite lately, in his thundering proclamations,
he had stigmatised as "our eternal enemy." He, too, as a
born Palatiner, had directed a greedy eye on Heidelberg and
Mannheim, and he knew that his aims in this direction could
be attained only through the favour of the Hofburg.

The mutual hatred of these two powerful opponents was
accentuated by the conduct of the minister in the constitutional question. Although neither the crown prince nor
the field-marshal, who were both men of strongly despotic
predilections, had any love for constitutional methods of
government, they did not fail to recognise that after so many
solemn promises the constitution must at length be granted.
Montgelas, on the other hand, had, as the years passed,
become ever more obstinately confirmed in his bureaucratic

sentiments. He did not carry the unhappy constitution of 1808 into effect, and the man who, by a system of pitiless centralisation, had annihilated all independent life in the provinces, gradually attained to the same view as that which was held by the feudalists of Prussia, considering that a political sense must first be awakened through the provincial diets, since the Germans had no natural understanding of the representative system. The minister could not prevent the king, who desired to anticipate the proposal of the congress of Vienna, from appointing a commission to investigate that paper fundamental law ; but he gave the commission clearly to understand that the Bavarian provincial diets were to have no greater significance than the parliamentary institutions of Napoleon. If from time to time a freer opinion should be voiced in the commission, the blunt answer was to be made that the king and his officials must always be regarded as the proper representatives of the nation ; it was incredible that anyone could even speak of any enlargement of representative rights, since it was merely as an act of grace that the king had renounced certain sovereign prerogatives.

The commission, which, for the most part, consisted of devoted servants of the minister, and contained also a few ultra-conservative Old Bavarian nobles, took this hint to heart, and brought forward a wonderful proposal which gave equal expression to all the desires of the bureaucracy and of the junkerdom. An upper house, adorned with the modest name of " chamber of councillors of the realm," and a chamber of deputies, combined to form the Bavarian " national representation." For the positions of deputies, three candidates were chosen in each constituency by indirect election, out of whom, according to the approved Napoleonic custom, the king nominated one to become a deputy ; the serfs, that is to say, the mass of the peasantry, were completely excluded from representation, on the ground that they were already represented by the lords of the soil. The privileges of this popular chamber corresponded to its composition. In case of urgent need, the crown might even impose direct taxes on its own initiative, and the crown could at any time alienate the public lands without even informing the chamber. Such a situation seemed a mockery. The crown prince felt this ; and when the unhappy proposal reached Vienna in February, 1815, he induced the king to refuse his assent. The commission was dissolved. Montgelas saw the shipwreck of the scheme with quiet malicious joy, and for two years he allowed the vexatious affair to rest untouched. There was no longer any reason to fear that the detested Prussian rival would be before-hand with the granting of a constitution, the Bundestag was not pressing, and in Bavaria there was no trace whatever of a feudal movement. The proud strength of the Old Bavarian Landtag, which long ago, in the stormy days of the Löwler-bund, had so often practised the right of armed resistance, was already broken in the sixteenth century. When Max Joseph ascended the throne, he found in existence nothing more than the lifeless Landtag committee, the *Verordnung*, and had abolished this last vestige almost without a struggle. Vainly did Rudhart, professor at Würzburg, endeavour, by the publication of his erudite history of the Bavarian provincial diets, to reanimate the thought of the ancient representative liberties ; he secured the thanks of the learned, but his book had no influence whatever upon the political sentiments of the country.

Meanwhile, Montgelas directed his attention chiefly to the negotiations with the Roman see, which were destined to be of importance for the whole of Germany, and to have an entirely unexpected reaction upon the work of constructing the Bavarian constitution. Notwithstanding their strictly Catholic sentiments, the old Wittelsbachs, like the Most Christian Kings of France, had always vigorously maintained the supremacy of their state in ecclesiastical matters. For centuries it had been the aim of Wittelsbach religious policy to found a Bavarian national church, in so far as this was possible in conformity with Catholic unity of belief. At the very time when Bavaria was expelling Protestants, there was instituted in Munich a spiritual council, a supreme ecclesiastical authority appointed by the sovereign, a body resembling the consistories of the Lutherans. As soon as the principal resolu-tion of the Diet of Deputation had subjected to Bavarian supremacy the neighbouring bishops, who were immediates of the empire and were ancient opponents of the territorial princely authority over the church, the court of Munich revived this ancient plan of the Wittelsbachs with renewed zeal. The king hoped that it would be possible to conclude with the pope a concordat as advantageous as that which had so recently been concluded by the First Consul, expecting to be able to secure the formation of Bavarian bishoprics whose boundaries should coincide with those of the state domain. He had soon to learn how firmly, even on those days of humiliation, the papacy held to its ancient masterful principles. The papal negotiator, Cardinal della Genga, the ecclesiastic who subsequently became Pope Leo XII, demanded nothing less than the return to the old system of unity of belief. The equal legal rights of Protestants, the recognition of mixed marriages, the supervision of the state over the schools, all the valuable reforms upon which the legal order of the new kingdom reposed in matters of parity of belief, were to disappear. In the year 1809, negotiations were broken off. Nevertheless in Munich hope was not abandoned. How was it possible that the curia should withstand the wishes of a court which was so glad to boast itself as being, after Austria, the first Catholic power in Germany? When the prince-primate Dalberg, in those Rhenish Confederate days, was unweariedly bringing forward airy plans for a German or Rhenish Confederate national church, he found his most determined opponent in Montgelas. At the congress of Vienna, too, Bavaria maintained her proud self-sufficiency, and demanded that ecclesiastical affairs should be withdrawn from the competence of the Germanic Federation.

In view of the weakness of the new federal authority, a change in this decisive resolution was neither attainable nor desirable, for who could wish to entrust to the Bundestag the difficult negotiations with the Roman curia? In this question also, as everywhere else, particularism had won a complete victory. All the German states were now forced to adopt the same course as that which Bavaria and Würtemberg had previously adopted under the Confederation of the Rhine. Individually or in groups, they were forced to treat with the Roman curia, in order to secure the establishment of new territorial bishoprics. All the courts were at one in this well-grounded desire. With the innumerable changes of frontier of recent years, it was simply impossible that the dioceses of the Holy Empire should remain unaltered. Moreover, all except five of the new bishoprics were practically destitute. Since the secularisation of the Catholic church in Germany had deprived them of an annual income of at least 21,000,000 florins, their economic needs were so intense that a remedy was possible only through the help of the state.

Even the Prussian statesmen, who at the congress of Vienna had vigorously favoured the idea of a common German ecclesiastical policy, had now to abandon this idea as untenable, just as they had been forced to abandon their plans for a federal customs system, and many more of the patriotic proposals of those sanguine days. The Prussian federal envoys were instructed not to tolerate any intervention of the Federation in ecclesiastical affairs, if only for the reason that Prussia would never again allow the presence of a nuncio in Frankfort. It was the king's intention to act independently, and by voluntary concessions to set an example to the other German states.[1] Even then, Humboldt proposed that the Prussian state should place formally under the protection of the Federation those rights which it proposed to concede to the Roman church, asking in exchange that the rights of the Protestants in the Catholic states should likewise be placed under federal guarantee. The chancellor, however, rejected this proposal, for he foresaw that neither Austria nor Bavaria would ever agree to accept a plan which would have placed the crown of Prussia in the position of protector of German Protestantism. Since Bavaria now went her own way, and Austria was from the first outside the negotiations, Hardenberg was unable to anticipate any successful issue from joint negotiation with the petty states; the views of the different courts were too widely divergent. The Prussian state also ruled more Catholic subjects than Bavaria and the petty states together; Prussia alone, in the days of the Holy Empire, had possessed territorial bishoprics, and had attained to firm principles of ecclesiastical policy in the school of an extensive experience, principles which, with trifling alterations, could be adapted to the needs of the present day. The minor Protestant dynasties of the west, on the other hand, Baden, Würtemberg, Hesse, and Nassau, had all of a sudden entered into possession of extensive Catholic domains, and were, as yet comparatively ignorant of how to deal with the new tasks which devolved upon them in this situation. They knew, indeed, that the ancient Protestant ecclesiastical authority of the lords paramount could no longer be exercised under the new conditions, and honourably desired to concede

[1] Instructions to the federal envoy, November 30, 1816, Section 31.

to the Roman church somewhat more freedom. But they continued to cherish extremely exaggerated ideas of the rights of the state authority, a self-deception which was not shared by Hardenberg. Consequently, even from Paris instructions were sent to Niebuhr that he was to treat with Rome on behalf of Prussia alone, and that above all he was to effect the re-establishment of the indispensable territorial bishoprics.

It was only Heinrich von Wessenberg who was still unwilling to abandon the idea of a German national church which he had so strongly advocated at the congress of Vienna. By the courts, the much-occupied vicar-general of Constance was regarded as at once a welcome ally and a nuisance, a disturber of the peace ; for, like him, they desired to restrict as much as possible the power of the pope over German prelates, while, on the other hand, the kernel of his plans necessarily appeared an impossible anachronism to sober-minded statesmen. Wessenberg failed to recognise how completely the political character of the Catholic church of Germany had been transformed by secularisation and by the abolition of the noble prebends. He dreamed of a German ecclesiastical state which, under the protection of the Federation, led by a prince-primate, well furnished with noble prelates and national and diocesan synods, could occupy a position equally independent of the papacy and of the territorial suzerains. With naive arrogance he spoke of this aristocratic ecclesiastical constitution as "the German church," although the great majority of the Germans outside Austria were Protestants. He would hear nothing of territorial bishoprics, an indispensable element of the modern national unity ; his distinguished bishops were to exercise their spiritual power simultaneously in several state domains. What a prospect did this open of eternal disputes between the pope, the primate, the Bundestag, the individual states, and these semi-sovereign bishops, who were not to be subjected to any single and specific territorial supremacy !

Whence, moreover, was a German primate now to derive the territorial and princely independence essential to his dignity ? Dalberg himself, prince-primate of the Confederation of the Rhine, had already cut the ground from beneath his friend Wessenberg's patriotic proposals, when, in October, 1813, he had voluntarily renounced the grand duchy of Frankfort in favour of Eugene Beauharnais. This shameful political suicide had served only to increase the hostility of the allies to the Bonapartist prince of the church, nor was their anger diminished when, in the following year, the weathercock enthusiast displayed another sudden change, and paid homage to the revengeful archangel of Europe, Czar Alexander. The discrowned prince then retired to his bishopric of Ratisbon, and there passed the two years before his death (February, 1817) in apostolic simplicity, devoted entirely to the duties of his spiritual office and to works of Christian charity. Many of his political opponents were won over by the serene equanimity of the amiable old man. The peculiar charm of his mind, so strangely compounded of enthusiasm, vanity, and shyness, made him in the evening of his life even more irresistible than he had been many years before when Schiller and Wilhelm Humboldt had taken so much pleasure in his society. But with his territorial suzerainty, his primacy had also been lost beyond rescue. To a Bavarian subject and territorial bishop, no German state would concede the rights of a German supreme shepherd; least of all would Prussia do this, for in Prussia's view, the Rhenish Confederate title to the primacy had no legal validity. For this reason, Wessenberg was coolly received almost everywhere when, in the year 1815, he visited some of the courts, and when he endeavoured to gain over some of the diplomats in Frankfort to his plans for a national church. Not even yet discouraged, in December he proposed to the German governments that before opening negotiations with Rome they should first come to an agreement regarding common principles, and that they should recognise the Bundestag as the supreme judge in all disputes between state and church. To the cousin of Metternich and to the brother of the Austrian privy-councillor Wessenberg, it might seem a trifling matter that the affairs of Prussian bishoprics should be subjected to the co-decision of the emperor of Austria. In Berlin other views prevailed.

It was in Munich, above all, that Wessenberg's reception was unfriendly; Bavaria was self-sufficing, he was bluntly assured, and would not tolerate any further attack upon her sovereignty. In his innovations in matters of ecclesiastical policy, Montgelas encountered but trifling resistance among the bigoted Old Bavarian populace, and, with the arrogance of the infidel man of the world, he inferred from this that the Roman church no longer possessed much vitality. The pride of enlightenment led this able man into an error, which was, indeed, shared by most statesmen of the day, but which was especially ill-placed in the mind of so obstinate an advocate of the absolute power of the state. He hoped, not merely to secure from the pope a bull which should delimit the frontiers of the new Bavarian territorial bishoprics. He also regarded it as a matter of trifling importance to enter into a concordat which should regulate legal relationships between state and church, failing to understand how grossly the sovereignty of the state was endangered by the mere conclusion of a concordat. Every state is empowered to determine the extent of its own sovereign prerogatives, and must not allow this inalienable right to be diminished by treaties with foreign powers, and least of all by a treaty with the curia, which has ever regarded all concessions to the temporal authority as mere indulgences, as revocable favours. The hope, however, of outbidding the Napoleonic concordat, flattered Bavarian pride ; and, in the worst event, the crown of the Wittelsbachs was strong enough to alter the concordat should it choose to do so, disregarding the complaints of the pope. The choice of the negotiator was as utterly mistaken as was the fundamental idea of the whole undertaking. The difficult affair was entrusted to Häffelin the octogenarian bishop. Montgelas was under the illusion that in this gentle ecclesiastic he possessed a thoroughly subservient tool, and overlooked the fact that the weak old man, with his vanity and his fourteen illegitimate children, was equally accessible to the allurements and to the threats of the Vatican.

In such circumstances, the ultramontane party found fresh courage. Since the year 1812, this party had become more firmly knit together throughout South Germany ; and, unaffrighted by the severe prohibitions of Montgelas, had diffused among the credulous populace touching pictures and anecdotes regarding the imprisonment of the pope. The centre of their activities was the see of the bishop of Eichstedt, Count Stubenberg : it was from this place that, during the congress of Vienna, the orators of the Catholic church received their instructions. The literary spokesman of the party, Zirkel, suffragan bishop of Würzburg, entered the field against Wessenberg, and, being an enthusiastic romanticist, demanded the unrestricted suzerainty of the pope over the German church, giving this the high-sounding name of

" ecclesiastical freedom." The clericals still possessed powerful friends at court. They believed that they could even count upon the heir to the throne, for the prince had been educated as a strict Catholic by the court chaplain, Sambuga, and was an enthusiastic disciple of the romanticist school.

The minister's arrogance received swift punishment. Bishop Häffelin played a lamentable part at the Vatican, and at length, in the autumn of 1816, despatched a proposal for a Roman concordat in which there were reserved for the Catholic church "all the rights which attach to it in accordance with the prescripts of canon law." If these words were honourably interpreted, this implied the repeal of the equal rights of the Protestants and the annulling of all the ecclesiastical laws of the last decade. In return for the unprecedented demand, the curia made only one important concession, whose consequences were fortunately not fully recognised in Rome. The papacy was willing to admit that the concordat should be announced as a Bavarian state law. The prudent monsignori manifestly hoped that such an announcement would give the treaty greater stability, and failed to remember that the king could at any time alter the state law as he pleased. In the relentless hands of Montgelas, the rash concession might readily become a dangerous weapon, and as long as he remained at the helm, the humiliation of the throne before the papacy was not to be dreaded.

Suddenly, to the general surprise of the country, there ensued the fall of the minister. In November, 1816, the king had journeyed to Vienna, to visit his daughter Caroline Augusta who had just married Emperor Francis, and also to re-establish the political friendship which had been profoundly disturbed since the Salzburg negotiations. He remained three months in the Austrian capital, and was overwhelmed with honours ; but whenever he touched on political questions, he was met with a calculated reserve, and was finally forced to recognise that the rancour of the Hofburg against Montgelas remained unappeasable. A new cause for this dislike had recently come into operation, for a despatch from the French ambassador Mercy, who made disagreeable disclosures regarding Montgelas' conduct in the autumn of 1813, had fallen into the hands of the court of Vienna. In the presence of the Prussian ambassador, indeed, Metternich assumed the pose of having never troubled himself about these Bavarian affairs. When the king disclosed his designs against Baden, alike from the emperor and from Metternich he received no more than a dry assurance that they would not oppose his plan. Even this promise was not honourably meant, for Metternich simultaneously informed the Prussian chancellor that the undertaking was given solely *par manière d'acquit*, and in the conviction that the Bavarian plans would speedily encounter powerful opposition on all hands.[1] Meanwhile the new empress, a declared friend of the Jesuits, broke out into vigorous accusations against the minister who was hostile to the church, the man who was the sole obstacle to friendship between the two courts ; the diplomats of the curia gave all the assistance in their power, and from Munich there arrived repeated statements of grievances from the crown prince and Field-marshal Wrede.

Disheartened, but as yet by no means determined, the king returned to Munich on February 1, 1817, and announced his intention to visit the minister on the following morning. The carriage had already been ordered, and, as previous experience showed, the interview could be expected to end in no other way than with a fresh reconciliation of the two friends. But at the last moment the crown prince set every possible influence at work. He had had a severe illness, and was still unable to leave his room, and for this reason was able to count upon a friendly hearing from his affectionate father. In a moving letter he reiterated all his complaints against the minister's arrogance and neglect of business, and begged for the dismissal of Montgelas as a proof of royal favour to himself. Wrede took this letter to the monarch in the morning of February 2nd. Trembling, in profound anxiety, the king at length granted his heir's petition. A good-natured weakling, when he desires to display strength, almost invariably errs on the side of harshness. Thus Max Joseph dismissed in the most contumelious way possible this statesman who had won for him his kingly crown, doing it quite after the manner of those capricious Old Würtemberg despots who had been accustomed to get rid of their favourites by theatrically kicking them out of the room. At noon, when the minister was expecting the royal visit, he received instead a blunt letter of dismissal. The blow was

---

[1] Krusemark's Report, Vienna, February 8 ; Hardenberg's Instructions to Küster, March 25, 1817.

so utterly unexpected that at first the inhabitants of Munich believed that the all-powerful minister must have committed some treasonable act. The crown prince exulted, and said to the Prussian ambassador : " After all, my illness has been good for something." The whole country breathed more freely at the fall of the detested bureaucrat. Nor did the two great powers conceal their delight ; on Hardenberg's instructions, Küster had to express the lively satisfaction of his court.[1]

The outcome of the catastrophe cut both ways. It removed the greatest obstacle to the work of constitution-building, but it also removed the only force which was still competent to give a tolerable turn to the unhappy concordat negotiations. The clericals had got rid of a terrible enemy, but none the less they had not attained to power. The new minister of foreign affairs, Count Aloys Rechberg, was their close ally ; but Baron von Lerchenfeld was summoned to take charge of the finances, an open opponent of the Roman claims, and a zealous advocate of the work of constitution-building ; the minister of the interior, Count Thürheim, a converted Illuminate, proved weak and incapable. Moreover, the directors-general of the ministries now received enlarged authority, so that they ranked almost as members of the cabinet ; even Wrede and the secretary-general Kobell continually intervened in public affairs. It is not surprising that old Häffelin was no longer able to hold his own in Rome under this leaderless government. It is true that Thürheim sent him precise instructions, which had been drawn up under Montgelas, expressly insisting upon the right of the state to undertake independent management of the external legal relationships of the church ; but he considered that since the change of wind in Munich he was no longer seriously bound by these instructions. Step by step he allowed himself to be driven into a corner. Count Blacas, the favourite of the Bourbons, who was also negotiating in Rome for a concordat, exhorted the Bavarian to display a yielding disposition. On June 5th, Häffelin, in defiance of his instructions, signed a concordat which satisfied all the hopes of the ultramontanes. In the very preamble, the most arrogant of all the demands of the Vatican was stated, the Roman church was to enjoy

---

[1] Küster's Reports, February 12 and 16 ; Hardenberg's Instructions, March 4, 1817.

all the rights granted by God's ordinance and by the canon law.

When this incredible news reached Munich, the ministers were at first unable to believe it, and the king raged against "the scroundrelly agreement." But the only answer appropriate to a self-respecting crown in such a situation was withheld ; the negotiator who had forgotten his duty was not recalled. Vainly did Lerchenfeld demand that no agreement should be concluded without expressly reserving the rights of the state. Count Rechberg, in the earlier negotiations with Cardinal della Genga, had formed the opposite conviction ; he considered that tacit reserve was sufficient, since the curia did not carry out its conventions in a very precise spirit. Finally, it was resolved that Xaver Rechberg of Eichstadt, the much-loved brother of the minister, should be sent to Rome, and with Blacas' assistance he effected a concordat which agreed with the convention of June 5th except in a few unessential details. The new convention was signed by the king on October 24th. In addition to the recognition of the validity of the canon law, it declared that all ecclesiastical affairs to which no express allusion was made in the concordat were to be dealt with in accordance with the *vigens ecclesiæ disciplina*, and that in doubtful cases there should always be a new agreement between the pope and the king. In article 17 there was even announced the abolition of all laws and ordinances conflicting with the concordat. The bishops were to supervise the purity of belief and morals in the state schools, and had a right to demand from the state authority the suppression of dangerous literature. The right to found new monasteries, and the unrestricted disposal of property acquired by inheritance, were secured to the church. For this price the pope agreed to the foundation of the long-desired Bavarian territorial church, with two archbishoprics and six bishoprics. The proposed formation of one single archbishopric for the entire kingdom was refused in Rome, for how readily could such a metropolitan play the part of a primate ! The king, as a Catholic sovereign, received the right to nominate three of his territorial bishops unconditionally, whilst the five others were to be selected by him from a list of candidates. It was in this matter, and in the tacit recognition of the sovereign's right of patronage over incumbencies, that were to be found the only safeguards of the rights of the state authority. Should

Bavaria desire to adopt a dishonourable course, there did, indeed, still remain a loophole in article 18, which promised in the same breath that the concordat should be kept inviolable— and that it should be promulgated as a state law.

This was the first sample of the European policy of Munich. It was the most disgraceful humiliation which a modern state had ever suffered from the papacy, the well-deserved punishment for the particularist arrogance which had first led to a complete severance from all the other German states, and which now desired to excel them all at any price. Even Küster's successor, the ultra-conservative old general Zastrow, was horrified at the "complete victory of Rome," and wrote to the chancellor, who followed all the ecclesiastical negotiations with close attention, saying : " To this region, in which enlightenment has so recently been introduced, the clergy will once again restore the obscurity and the demoralising influence of superstition." [1] The curia rejoiced, and gave the king " appropriate praise." Max Joseph forgot his kingly dignity so completely that he wrote to beg the pope to bestow a cardinal's hat upon the unfaithful envoy Häffelin. The request was granted, to the disgust of all good Bavarians ; even the cardinals complained that upon such shoulders the purple would be discredited.

It was impossible for the Vatican long to withhold from the world so brilliant a triumph. Already in December the concordat had been published by the curia on its own account, and thereupon the league of Eichstadt immediately induced the highest ecclesiastical authorities to express their gratitude to the crown. The vicariate-general of Bamberg demanded that the authorities should take action against the Franconian newspaper which espoused the cause of Wessenberg. Among the hotspurs of the clerical party the demand was already voiced that all the children of mixed marriages and all foundlings should be baptised and brought up in the Roman church, and that conversion to Catholicism should be permissible to all without distinction of age. These were unprecedented claims which might, none the less, appeal with good reason for justification to the introductory words of the concordat ! The Protestants saw the very existence of their church threatened. What right of the evangelicals could still be regarded as firmly established when the canon law actually took precedence of all

---

[1] Zastrow's Report, December 10, 1817.

the state laws of Bavaria? The consistories of many of the Protestant towns implored the king in moving terms to maintain the principles of the edict of religions of 1809 whereby parity of beliefs was guaranteed. Even Schmitt, the queen's chaplain, raised his powerful voice. But no one fanned the flames of the movement more vigorously than Anselm Feuerbach, who once more did credit to his nickname " Vesuvius." Among the Catholics, Ignaz Rudhart, with customary frankness, espoused the threatened cause of parity ; even many of the clergy did not conceal their anxiety.

The excitement continued to increase, for simultaneously in France a storm broke out against the new concordat concluded by Blacas, and the South Germans were already beginning to follow every wave of public opinion in the neighbouring country. The crown prince also, notwithstanding his romanticist fantasies, began to become anxious, and reminded his father of the example of their ancestor Louis the Bavarian. Max Joseph was ashamed of his own weakness. He could not deny that this concordat had been a falling away, not merely from the principles of his own ecclesiastical policy, but also from all the good traditions of the old Wittelsbachs. But after he had solemnly pledged his royal word there remained open to him only the loophole of article 18, in virtue of which the concordat was to be promulgated as a state law. The government determined (as Rechberg informed the Prussian ambassador in profound confidence) to interpret the convention " in the best way possible." It was their intention to promulgate the concordat as a law for the kingdom, but simultaneously to promulgate a second law which should take the edge off the concessions of the concordat and should appease the Protestants.[1] This was a lamentable way out of a painful situation for which the Bavarian government was itself responsible, and yet, after all that had happened, it was the sole available means of reacquiring the sacrificed rights of the state authority.

The most convenient method of carrying out this design was offered by the redemption of the promise to grant a constitution. On February 11, 1818, on the proposal of Director-general von Zentner, the ministry of state determined to append to the constitution an edict concerning the legal relationships of the Christian confessions. Thus the pliability which had been displayed towards the Roman see had at least one fortunate

[1] Zastrow's Reports, February 15, April 15, 1818.

outcome, namely, that the arrested work of constitution-building
was once again set in motion. The financial needs of the
country also came to the assistance of the friends of the constitution. Under this many-headed regime these needs had
increased so greatly that the crown prince bluntly declared
that nothing but the summoning of the provincial diets could
re-establish the shattered national credit.[1] Dynastic ambition
exercised an influence yet more powerful than all these
considerations. Now, as before, the acquisition of the Badenese
Palatinate remained the leading idea of Bavarian statecraft,
and, since the arbitral decision of the great powers was
not yet forthcoming, in the spring of 1818 the courts of Munich
and Carlsruhe began an extraordinary rivalry for the favour
of public opinion, although this was really of very little
importance. The two opponents carried on their respective
constitutional deliberations with feverish zeal in order to gain
the approval of the daily press for the decision of the territorial
questions. It was chiefly for this reason that the crown prince
and the field-marshal adhered firmly to the side of the constitutional party.

Since February, 1818, the reconsideration of the constitutional
proposals of 1808 and 1814 had been resumed. In the course
of these deliberations the prestige of Zentner increased day by
day. Next to Lerchenfeld, his was the best intelligence of the
Munich cabinet. At one time he had been professor in
Erlangen, but he was free from that doctrinaire egotism
by which, in practical politics, German professors are almost
always conducted to shipwreck. A bureaucrat through and
through, eloquent, prudent, and well-informed, thoroughly
imbued with the idea of the universal authority of the state,
he was brilliant and amiable in personal intercourse, although
his old-bachelor foppishness occasionally aroused a smile. As
director-general in the ministry of the interior, he speedily took
all the burdens of work from the hands of Count Thürheim,
and therewith deprived the latter of any real power. He was
the reorganiser of the Bavarian officialdom, being the first to
introduce a certain amount of discipline and punctuality into
the neglected service, and he gave all who wore the light blue
official uniform expressly to understand that it was from him
alone that favour and honours were to be expected. To such
a man, parliamentary life could offer no allurements, but he

[1] Zastrow's Report, March 15, 1818.

understood that the young crown had need of popular favour, and that the inchoate national unity required new clamps ; and he believed himself to have the power of maintaining the spirit of absolutism even amid constitutional forms. By his influence, the work of constitution-building was carried through with extreme rapidity, so that the Badenese competitors were beaten in the race by several months.

On May 26th the Bavarian herald, clad in blue-and-white, rode through the streets of Munich, to read seven times the royal manifesto announcing the promulgation of the new fundamental law and demanding " from the hearts of all Bavarians their grateful recognition of this fatherly procedure." Thus Bavaria was the first among the greater states of the Germanic Federation to fulfil the promises of the federal act in the spirit of the dominant constitutional doctrine. The country accepted its king's gift with childlike delight ; even the Brandenburg Franconians now manifested for the first time an access of Wittelsbach sentiments. An allegorical picture showed representatives of the military and scholastic professions and of the working classes gracefully dancing round the royal crown, and this gave appropriate expression to the feelings of the people. It would have been well if this reasonable satisfaction had not been intermingled with so much repulsive particularist arrogance ! At every success of the constitutional movement in the south, a flood of scorn was poured out over the backward Prussians, and the old Rhenish Confederate ideas were revived in a liberal dress. After the fall of Montgelas, hardly had the hopes of the Bavarian friends of the constitution been reawakened, when Feuerbach handed to Rechberg a memorial regarding a league of the rulers of all the minor states which, with the support of England, Denmark, and Holland, was to cleave asunder its natural enemy, Prussia, and to the populace of the two great powers was to display " the great and cheerful picture of a free constitution," whilst to the governments of these powers it was to hold up this picture before their eyes as a Gorgon's head.

In truth this "great and cheerful picture " of the Bavarian constitution fulfilled all reasonable expectations. It guaranteed equality before the law, and a not too timorously restricted freedom of the press. In the composition of the two chambers, the customary subdivision of the estates was carefully maintained. The chamber of councillors of the realm was to be composed of the great dignitaries, of hereditarily noble land-lords, and of a minority of members nominated by the crown. One-fourth of the chamber of deputies was to consist of representatives of the lesser landed nobility and the lesser clergy ; one-fourth of the members were to be elected by the towns ; the remaining half of the representatives were to be chosen by the peasants. The deputies were not to represent the rights of their respective estates, but the interests of the country as a whole. The best guarantee for the tolerable success of these constitutional forms was offered by the new communes law, modelled after the towns' ordinance of Stein, and promulgated a few days before the constitution. Beyond question this law was far inferior to its Prussian prototype ; a great part of the affairs of the towns were not as yet to be placed in the hands of the burghers, but were to be managed by salaried communal scriveners. The rural communes remained extremely dependent upon the clerks of the country justices' courts, and for this reason many of the most independent-minded among the peasants refused to accept the office of parish magistrate. But at least the principle of communal self-government was recognised ; the communes acquired the right of disposing of their own property, and could freely elect their own communal authorities. Thus was at length won a foundation for practical popular freedom, a soil in which the new constitution might perhaps take firm root.

As an appendix to the constitution, in addition to other organic laws, there appeared an edict of religions which gave to the concordat the desired "interpretation." In this document the tried principles of the New Bavarian ecclesiastical policy once again found expression : parity of beliefs was recognised in plain terms, in the case of mixed marriages the separate religious education of the children in accordance with their sex was prescribed, and the Old Bavarian right of the *placet* was reserved for the crown. There was not a single sentence in the edict which did not flatly contradict the leading ideas of the concordat. To the curia it seemed simple mockery that the concordat itself should now be promulgated as a state law, of course under reserve of the legal principles of the edict of religions. Rome made vigorous complaints regarding the manifest breach of the convention, and refused to be appeased when the king sent Canon Helfferich, one of the ultramontane orators of the congress of Vienna, with tranquillising assurances. Then old Häffelin, who had now lost all shame in his enjoyment of the cardinal purple, ventured upon a new and gross breach of duty. He gave an assurance, once more upon his own initiative and without previous knowledge on the part of Helfferich, that the edict of religions applied only to non-Catholics, and the pope did not hesitate to announce this disgraceful declaration to the world in a triumphant allocution.

For the second time the Bavarian crown had been publicly humiliated by the unfaithful envoy, and some of the ministers urgently demanded "the punishment of the traitor." But on this occasion also, Max Joseph's good-natured slackness proved incoercible. He contented himself with issuing a rescript to impress upon his circle governments that the edict of religions applied to everyone in the kingdom ; and he had now once more to undertake a disgraceful negotiation with the embittered pope. Such hole-and-corner proceedings were hardly likely to increase the repute of the Bavarian court among the great powers, a repute which in any case had been profoundly depressed since the manifestation of the design for the conquest of the Palatinate. Nevertheless, Bavaria was in an advantageous position in relation to the pope. The curia had been caught in its own nets, having hoped that the promulgation of the concordat as a state law would redound to its own advantage, and now found itself in an almost defenceless position when the import of this state law was restricted by an additional law. The great public remained without any precise knowledge of all the detestable turns of the confused negotiation, and rejoiced unrestrainedly over the victory of the temporal power. For some months Bavaria enjoyed the cheap pleasure of being hailed by the entire German press as the most liberal of all the German states.

§ 3. BADEN.

In Bavaria, the fulfilment of article 13 delivered the secular arm from the burden of the concordat ; in Baden it saved the very existence of the state. For several years the young grand duchy had been in a dangerous condition of intense confusion, and it seemed almost as if this artificial state-structure were destined to disappear as swiftly as it had come into being. The ancient house of Zähringen had at one time exercised a wide dominion on the Upper Rhine, extending as far as the Swiss Üchtland, and had striven with the Hohenstaufen for the Swabian duchy ; its glories were witnessed by the foundation of the town of Berne, of Freiburg-in-Breisgau, and of Fribourg. Its decay began, however, in the thirteenth century, and the Zähringens relapsed into the ranks of the minor dynasties. When towards the middle of the eighteenth century Margrave Charles Frederick of Baden-Durlach became ruler, it was over a little territory of barely thirty square miles [German], dispersed in several fragments from the Swiss frontier to the other side of Carlsruhe, and contributing to the imperial army a total force of ninety-five men. In the year 1811, when his reign of sixty-two years came to a close, the domain had increased almost tenfold. First of all the Catholic Baden-Baden was united with the Lutheran Durlach ; then Napoleon compacted the motley regions on the right back of the Rhine, from Constance to Mannheim, to constitute an extraordinary state extending for sixty miles [German] along the Rhine, consisting almost exclusively of frontier districts, and no more than two miles wide at its narrowest portion. The Hither Austrian territories of Nellenburg, Breisgau, and Ortenau, the Palatinate on the right bank of the Rhine, and fragments of the bishoprics of Constance, Strasburg, and Spires, were thrown together, with numerous similar domains of princes, counts, imperial knights, and imperial towns. Two-thirds of the subjects of the Protestant dynasty were Catholics ; nearly one-third of the country belonged to the discontented mediatised houses of Fürstenberg, Leiningen, and Löwenstein. This confused mass of territories had almost nothing in common in the way of living historical memories ; even in Breisgau, the tribal seat of the princely house, no one thought any longer of the old Zähringen days.

And yet, after all, this entirely modern territorial structure was by no means so unnatural as might appear at first sight. Upon the ridge of the Black Forest, almost upon the very spot where Badenese and Würtemberg land now come into contact, there had stood at one time, in the early years of the Christian era, the boundary stones between the Celts and the Teutons ; and even later, when the Alemans advanced westward as far as the Vosges, the Black Forest still remained a natural frontier. To the east, the Swabian nationality maintained itself in its primitive strength, cut off from the world. The western valleys of the Black Forest and the rich plain beneath the hills were at an early date drawn into the activities of Rhenish life ; through the Upper Rhenish country ran the great military road between south and north, whereas in the direction of Swabia there passed quiet mountain roads only, and even intercourse with Alsace was rendered difficult by the wild and unruly waters of the Rhine. From the days of antiquity, since the Romans had constructed their flourishing spas in the valleys of Baden and upon the height of Baden-weiler, a life of careless enjoyment had been characteristic of this favoured land. Nowhere in Germany did people live more luxuriously ; and the cumbrous Swabian abused as " verbose Frenchmen " these Aleman kin of his on the Upper Rhine, in whose veins there certainly ran much Celtic and Latin blood. The Upper Rhenish people, far more receptive and mobile than their Swabian neighbours, although poorer in creative intelligence, had at all times embraced with noisy enthusiasm the new ideas which were inflaming the world. As long as the church knew how to stimulate the masses by the demagogic means of the crusades and the mendicant orders, there was no German land more devout than the Upper Rhine. Subsequently, with like impetuosity, the people threw themselves into the struggles of the Reformation, and yet only the minority possessed sufficient energy to hold fast to the Protestant faith in the days of trial. Once more, when the fashionable culture of the French made its entry into Germany, nowhere did it find such zealous disciples as upon the Upper Rhine.

The rationalist wisdom of the new enlightenment, which regarded all historical products as utterly arbitrary structures, exercised of necessity an irresistible influence upon this impressionable people, among whom three creeds and a number of powerless, chance-created territorial structures were intermingled within so narrow a space. Here rationalist enlightenment remained supreme, even after elsewhere in Germany classical and romanticist poetry had long before awakened the historical sense ; and now, when through the caprice of the foreigner all these ancient chance-states had been compacted to form a new one, originating as it were out of the void, the region became the natural home of a liberalism without a state and without a history, which speedily modified its political and religious life in accordance with the infallible principles of the so-called "law of reason," and in which the stimulating proximity of France and Switzerland served to encourage the formulation of increasingly bold demands.

It is true that in the large peasant farms of the Black Forest there had still been preserved numerous traditional manners and customs, although less so than in the neighbouring Alsace, where foreign dominion cut the inhabitants off from the new German culture. Moreover, in a few out-of-the-way corners, a strong religious sentiment still prevailed. Here and there, and especially round Pforzheim, there were to be found a few scattered Old Lutheran communities; a portion of the Lake-Swabians still remained clerical; the Franconians from the remote valleys of the further Odenwald continued to make devout pilgrimages to Walldürn, in honour of the Precious Blood, and in their Catholic zealotry they hardly lagged behind the dwellers in Münster—for as in Westphalia had happened with the Anabaptists, so here, in these picturesque and desolate regions, the murderous passions of the Peasants' War had left bloody traces; the peasants' battle-field of Königshofen and the scandalously mutilated church of Creglingen still remained to tell of the saturnalia of the mad Lutherans. But the dominant sentiment of the country was thoroughly modern, urban, and characterised by worldly enlightenment. In Breisgau and the other Hither Austrian domains, the religious and political principles of Joseph II had struck root far more deeply than in the eastern crown-lands of the house of Lorraine; the philosophical emperor was here generally regarded as the ideal prince. On the other hand, after all the horrible wars of religion which had desolated their beautiful homeland, the Palatiners wished now at length to enjoy religious peace, and nowhere was such peace more indispensable than here, where in almost every little town was to be found an undenominational church; they prided themselves upon their Charles Louis, the tolerant elector, who in Mannheim had established the "Peace Church" for all three confessions. Paulus and Voss set the tone in Heidelberg, and Rotteck in Freiburg. The Protestant rationalism of the lowlands joined hands with the Josephan catholicism of the highlands, and the ideas that filled the minds of the cultured classes permeated deeply among the masses of the people, for, owing to the uncontrolled joy of life charcteristic of the Upper Rhine, there did not here exist so sharp a distinction of classes as still prevailed in the north; in the innumerable little towns there was everywhere to be found a comfortable inn, where on market-days the peasants mixed with people of culture.

It was not by chance that precisely in this country of democratic customs the first genuinely popular books of our new literature made their appearance. Since Grimmelshausen, the author of *Simplizissimus*, there had not been any notable poet on the Upper Rhine ; but now high and low alike took delight in the first-rate stories of Hebel's *Schatzkästlein des rheinischen Hausfreundes* and in his poems written in the Alemannic dialect, which spoke of the joys of the charming highlands in the cordial folk-speech, of the dark forests and murmuring brooks, of the chestnut trees and the wines of the country, of the liveliness, the roguishness, the vigorous intelligence, of its tall lads and handsome lasses. In these charming idyls, sun and moon, day and night, the seasons of the year, and the powers of destiny which influence the life of the countryfolk assume the figure and the speech of the Aleman peasants, so that Goethe declared that the upland poet pastoralised in the most frank and charming manner in the world. For this reason, too, Hebel appeared a genuine folk-poet, because he was entirely fulfilled with the spirit of the enlightenment which was here in the very air. A childishly pious rationalist, he regarded the dispute of the creeds with a mildness which seemed almost alarming to the religious zealots, and seldom failed to endow the merry tales of his *Hausfreund* with a home-made moral which, however, never trangressed the limits of true art.

The centre of gravity of the new state lay in the mainly Catholic highlands. It was long before the men of Breisgau could reconcile themselves to the separation from their beloved imperial house. The nobility did not forget the closing of the Freiburg house of estates, and carried on a suspicious intercourse, at first with the French émigrés, and subsequently with the court of Vienna. The burghers complained that the Old Badenese received the preference in the state service, and that the regions which had constituted the old margravate always secured the most efficient officials. Yet at long last the Hither Austrian Alemans could not fail to find their union with their Badenese kin entirely natural.

Far more slowly did the Palatine Franconians of the lowlands accommodate themselves to the new regime. What could Baden's modest history exhibit in comparison with the proud

memories of the oldest of the Rhenish electoral princedoms,
which had so long borne the imperial orb, and which, as a
dreaded disturber of the peace to the surrounding spiritual
neighbours, had constituted a stronghold of the fighting Protestant church on the lower reaches of the Neckar? Notwithstanding all the distresses of recent electoral times, the people
still held fast to the ancient saying : *Fröhlich Pfalz, Gott erhalt's !*
[*Happy Palatinate, God guards it !*] They continued to speak
with delight of the ancient days when there were such grand
times round the great tun at Heidelberg ; and happy mothers said
proudly to their beautiful daughters that they looked just like
Countesses Palatine. Those of free intelligence, when their
beloved old community collapsed before their eyes, turned to
embrace German nationalist ideas. Nowhere else in the south
did so good a German sentiment prevail. The Palatiners of
the right bank had always distinguished themselves from those
on the other side of the river by a more lively intellectual
life, and even when the left bank of the Rhine passed under
foreign dominion they had never lost touch with North German
culture ; how should the Gallicism of the Upper Rhine strike
roots here, where people gave their dogs the names of the
French incendiaries Duras and Melac? But there was not as
yet any trace of Badenese sentiment ; even the old university
still desired to belong to the entire fatherland, notwithstanding
the fact that it owed its new blossoming to the Badenese
princely house. In Mannheim, the residence of the last elector,
there still existed a strong Wittelsbach party, which gladly
lent itself to the covetous designs of the court of Munich. The
former Bavarian officials and the unscrupulous nobles looked back
with longing to the frivolous court of Charles Theodore. In
those merry days even the bourgeoisie had earned much money,
and they complained in addition of the loss of their theatre,
which at one time, under Dalberg and Iffland, had rivalled
the best stages of Germany, and which had been the first
to produce Schiller's *Robbers*. In the Palatinate, no one would
recognise Carlsruhe as the new capital of the country. This
dreary place, founded hundreds of years before by the caprice
of the margrave Charles William, in the ugliest part of the
beautiful country, continued to grow very slowly out of the
alleys of the Hardtwald ; the monotonous rows of houses in
the straight streets looked even more hideous since Weinbrenner
had adorned them with his temple buildings, and had given

proof that of all forms of pedantic style, the worst of all is a debased classic.

No one but a ruler with the personal prestige of the venerable Charles Frederick could hope to succeed in incorporating into a new commonwealth such strongly conflicting forces. The old man had for a long time been regarded as the pattern father of a small country. Enlightened and tolerant, a friend of Charles Augustus of Weimar, he nevertheless adhered firmly to the traditional Christian faith, and among the men of talent of the new literature he favoured those in especial who displayed warm religious sentiments, such as Klopstock, Herder, Lavater, and Jung Stilling. Receptive for the ideas of the new France, an admirer of the economic doctrine of the physiocrats, he yet remained German through and through, always thinking in what way the tottering old empire might be restored to new life by a league of princes, and of how the " universal spirit " of the nation might be awakened by a German academy, and it was in truth an undeserved and cruel destiny by which, in the evening of his life, this true patriot was subjected to the curse of particularism, and was compelled with a heavy heart to endure the fetters of the foreigner. He favoured the culture and the well-being of his country by farsighted legislation which was incomparable in southern Germany, and he was a master also in that speech of the heart which to the patriarchal peoples of our petty states has always seemed more estimable than political service. In every inn of Old Baden was to be seen the " Badenese national picture "—the portrait of the prince beneath which was inscribed his fatherly answer to the expressions of gratitude which his country had sent him on the occasion of the abolition of serfdom. What a chorus of delight arose when Charles Frederick erected a monument to the excellent timber-merchant, Anton Rindeschwender, the benefactor of the Murg valley—when the lord paramount of the country erected a monument to the subject. In Herder's opinion, he was the first prince quite devoid of princely arrogance.

It was for this reason that the propaganda of the French, when from Basle they circulated through the highlands the constitutional charter of the German Republic, found no more than isolated adherents in the contented margravate—far fewer than this propaganda secured in Würtemberg and Bavaria. In the new portions of the country, Privy-councillor Brauer, the organiser of the Badenese administration, worked with a far more considerate hand than did the severe bureaucrats of the neighbour states ; it was only the clergy who complained that even this pious Christian could not overcome the mistrust of the Catholic church characteristic of all Old Badenese officials. Since the nobility in the Palatinate and in Breisgau regarded the new state with suppressed discontent, the officialdom preserved its predominantly bourgeois character. The new order was completed by the introduction of the Badenese civil code, a clever elaboration of the *code Napoléon*. Everything in this state was modern.

It was not until after Charles Frederick's death that the forces of disintegration threatened to overpower the new state. Charles Frederick's grandson, the young grand duke Charles, had been rendered disinclined for serious work by the influence of an ambitious mother. Through early indulgence in excesses he had dissipated his vital energies while still in the prime of life. Gifted and amiable by nature, he lapsed into a mood of dull and gloomy brooding ; whole rooms of his palace were filled with documents, letters, despatches of all kinds, which he would neither deal with himself, nor allow anyone else to handle. Thus the poor sick man passed his life, friendless, secluded, unfathomable, always looking around with his fine but cunning eyes, to see who might be deceiving him. It was only his wife, Stephanie Beauharnais, whom he had unwillingly married upon Napoleon's command, who now drew nearer to him when he was declining towards a premature death, and made him happy with the wealth of her cheerful heart.

Under the rule of such a prince everything became incalculable. With the support of Bignon, the French envoy, the Bonapartist party gained control, and undertook to transform the little state forthwith in accordance with the Parisian example ; by severity and arbitrary measures the new regime now forfeited all the confidence which had so laboriously been acquired. The officials degenerated with astonishing rapidity. Even in the good old time they had been noted for bureaucratic paternalism, and now Baden, with Darmstadt and Nassau, became classic examples of superfluous governmental activities. On many high-roads travellers could wonder at the numbered fruit trees ; and at the entrance to a wide country-road they were greeted sometimes by the inscription " Passage along this road is permitted." At appointed dates the justiciaries would hold the celebrated "courts of unchastity," for the punishment of all girls suspected of being pregnant, and these justiciaries knew well enough how to provide a substitute for the abolished torture, being legally empowered to condemn to a whipping any accused person who told an untruth in the course of the hearing. While practising all these superabundant activities, the petty despots were lax in the performance of their official duties, having no longer to fear the eye of the "master"—for as such did they speak of the duke. The finances soon became seriously embarrassed, owing to the needs of the war and to the debts incurred through careless administration; for the year 1816 there was a deficit of 1,100,000 florins. During the closing years of the Napoleonic epoch an equitable system of taxation was introduced by two able young financiers, Boeckh and Nebenius, a system which subsequently proved extremely valuable, and which for the most part still persists to the present day; but years passed before the inhabitants became accustomed to the new burdens. Discontent increased unceasingly. Everywhere was heard the cry that nothing but a Landtag could impose limits upon the sultanism of this officialdom. The mediatised and the imperial knights had even been deprived of their territorial jurisdiction, in conflict with the promises of the Rhenish Confederate act; they manifested their displeasure with the greatest bitterness, and did not conceal that they no longer believed in the future of this state of yesterday. The work of Charles Frederick was falling to pieces on all sides, and to the internal troubles was now superadded pressure from without, the covetousness of the Wittelsbachs. This was all the more distressing to the grand duke because King Max Joseph had as yet disclosed his Palatine plan to the great powers alone, and did not even vouchsafe an intimation to his brother-in-law in Carlsruhe.

The court of Munich based its pretended claims, not only upon the terms of the treaty of Ried, but also upon the view that the dynasty of the Zähringens was near to extinction. Margrave Charles Frederick had in advanced age contracted a second marriage with the baroness von Geyersberg, whom he raised to the rank of Countess von Hochberg, and at the time of the marriage had expressly reserved the right of succession to the throne for the issue of this marriage, in case his other issue should die out. Since all the agnates had recognised this reservation, and since there were no other claimants, the claim of the counts of Hochberg to the succession was incontestable. Moreover, since the destruction of the empire, the house of Baden had been sovereign, and was therefore empowered to arrange its own domestic laws at its will. But, as is well known, these questions of equality in rank belong to those controversies insoluble beyond all power of human understanding in which the German princely law abounds. In the great German princely houses, the accession to the throne of the son of a mother of inferior rank had always been a rare exception, and although both the Zähringens and the Wittelsbachs had themselves among their ancestry women descended from the lesser nobility, the Bavarian cabinet greedily seized the welcome excuse, and assured all the courts that there could be no question of a Hochberg right of succession. The Hofburg gladly accepted this confidential assurance; all the secret conventions regarding the Palatine succession rested upon the prospect of the dying out of the Zähringens.

Should this ensue, Bavarian royal jurists had a second and no less astonishing legal claim ready. The county of Sponheim, on the Nahe, had formerly, during four centuries, been in possession of the houses of the Palatinate and of Baden, and, in accordance with the Beinheim decision of the year 1425, on the extinction of either of these two houses, the entire county was to accrue to the survivors. Beyond question, the ancient treaty of succession had long ago lapsed, for, in the peace of Lunéville, both the owners had ceded the county to France, receiving fivefold compensation for its loss. Nevertheless, Bavaria now demanded further compensation in case the last issue of the first marriage of Charles Frederick should die. This extinct hereditary claim to Sponheim was to restore to the Bavarian crown prince the desired "cradle" of his fathers, the castle of Heidelberg, together with Mannheim and the beautiful Lobdengau; what a compensation for the impoverished little territory in Hunsruck, for a domain of twenty-three thousand inhabitants! Here was a tissue of legal artifices which showed once more how completely the Rhenish Confederate policy had deprived the petty courts of all shame and of all sentiment of justice.

The situation of the court of Carlsruhe became more sinister day by day. The grand duke had returned from the congress of Vienna still weaker than before. He regarded his nephew, the crown prince of Bavaria, as his sworn enemy, and declared in bitter jest that it was unprecedented that a grown man should long so greatly for his cradle. In a moment of morbid irritability he went so far as to suspect that while he was in Vienna the Bavarians had mixed poison with his food. In the year 1812 his own heir had died, immediately after birth. In May, 1816, another son was born to him, but died suddenly also, a year later. Gloomy reports circulated through the town. Why was it that death had snatched away both the prince's sons, while the princesses all remained alive? Was it not possible that the restless Wittelsbach inheritance-snatcher had his hand here at work? The Bavarian envoy actually encouraged the insane suspicion by referring everywhere, with malicious delight, to the prince's misfortune, significantly adding that in such visitations one could recognise the destiny of a declining state.[1] Of the old Zähringen line there was now only one survivor, the grand duke's unmarried uncle, Margrave Louis; should he also die, the crown would then devolve upon count Leopold von Hochberg, whose claim was disputed by the court of Munich.

Nothing but the protection of the great powers could save the dynasty from destruction, yet the grand duke could not make up his mind to the dismissal of the wretched minister who was chiefly responsible for the desperate situation of the country, and whose reputation in all the courts was of the worst. Baron von Hacke, a rough and frivolous epicure of the school of the old Mannheim court, had been a willing catchpoll to the Imperator, and still continued to practise the Rhenish Confederate policy, in so far as his incurable laziness permitted. Even at the peace congresses of Paris he had endeavoured to found a separate league of the middle-sized states, and towards the Bundestag he displayed himself an obstinate particularist. He treated the Bavarian claims with irresponsible levity, while the cession of the Palatinate in exchange for monetary payment seemed to him not unacceptable, so that the Prussian chargé d'affaires, Varnhagen, wrote to the chancellor : " If the grand duchy of Baden is to continue to exist, it must be actually forced to do so."[2]

No progress was made in the matter of constitution-building. Upon urgent representations from Stein and Czar Alexander,

---

[1] Varnhagen's Report, January 4, 1817.
[2] Varnhagen's Report, Carlsruhe, May 11, 1817.

the grand duke, whilst still in Vienna, had summoned a commission to discuss the new fundamental law ; and in the spring of 1815, this body drafted a constitution, based upon a proposal brought forward by Baron von Marschall, a good patriot of the best days of Charles Frederick. The alarms of war of the following summer brought all this to nothing. Thereupon the lowland nobility took action, demanding in repeated and menacing petitions the fulfilment of article 13, using language as defiant as that which had long before been employed by the Landschadens of Steinach and the other knightly associates of Franz von Sickingen in converse with their neighbour princes. Massenbach and Count Waldeck, the noble demagogues from Würtemberg, gave eager assistance ; and even from bourgeois circles written petitions were sent in. The government, in accordance with Old Rhenish Confederate custom, visited the complaining knights with severe punishment, and Martin, professor of criminal law at Heidelberg, was forced to resign his position. None the less, the work of constitution-building was once more set in motion. In March, 1816, the grand duke formally promised his people to summon a representative assembly on August 1st, and in the course of the summer a third and a fourth proposal were in fact elaborated. Yet on this occasion, too, no decision was attained. Whilst Marschall, an honourable constitutionalist, urgently advised that the dissatisfied knighthood should be conciliated by the constitution of an upper chamber, the Bonapartist officials, secret enemies of the constitution, expressed decisive opinions in favour of the unicameral system being suspicious of the nobles as born enemies of the officialdom, and the doctrinaire hatred of the nobility inspiring the Prussian chargé d'affaires played into their hands. Quite uninvited, and without even consulting Berlin, Varnhagen gave his advice to the court of Carlsruhe, advice which strangely coincided in all respects with the infallible law of reason voiced by his friend Rotteck. " A chamber of nobles might all too readily endanger the throne at the expense of the people. Who were the first in Würtemberg to utter revolutionary language ? " If there must be an upper chamber, let it consist of men distinguished by age or official position. " These propositions," he concluded, with all the self-satisfaction of youthful liberalism, " are truisms, and posterity will never be able to understand why they have not been universally accepted.[1]

[1] Varnhagen to Berstett, May 8, 1816.

Amid these and other disputes, a considerable time now elapsed, until at length the opponents of reform succeeded in persuading the irresolute prince to a fresh procrastination. On July 29th, at the very moment when everyone was expecting the promised summoning of the Landtag, the country was astonished by a rescript postponing the promulgation of the constitution, and declaring that, first of all, the Bundestag must establish the leading principles for the German territorial constitutions. Such were the words that issued from the mouth of the very prince who had concerned himself with constitutional plans solely because he wished to safeguard his sovereignty against the encroachment of the Germanic Federation! The disappointment, the wrath, were general. Here, where there were so many genuine grievances, the folly of inconsiderate promises was punished more severely than in Prussia. A poisonous lampoon entitled *A Picture of the grand duchy of Baden* pilloried the gluttonous minister Hacke, who wished to turn the whole country into sucking-pig and asparagus! The troubles were augmented by the distresses of the year of famine and by the increasing pressure of taxation. In the highlands there was open disaffection when it suddenly became known that, from considerations of economy, the government was thinking of amalgamating the university of Freiburg with that of Heidelberg. All the inhabitants of Breisgau regarded this plan as an attack upon their ancient liberties. Rotteck vigorously espoused the cause of his countrymen, for he was well aware that his Josephan sentiments could not permanently thrive in the Protestant air of the Palatinate. The government did not feel competent to overcome this fierce opposition. The unlucky idea was abandoned, and the venerable Albertina university was preserved, a modest but fruitful centre of culture for the highlands, a continued source of such life as its founder, Archduke Albert, had desired.

Meanwhile the unfortunate country was visited also by religious confusions—by a dispute with the curia, which was to be almost as fruitful for German religious policy as the struggle concerning the Bavarian concordat, for it completed the defeat of the schemes for the foundation of a national church. For years Heinrich von Wessenberg had administered the bishopric of Constance as vicar-general. Esteemed alike by clerics and laymen were his lenity, his conscientious activity, the

apostolic purity of his life ; and from the hands of their beloved
shepherd they willingly accepted innovations which gave expression to the Josephan enlightenment of the highlands, but which
could hardly be reconciled with the strict unity of the Roman
church. Wessenberg introduced German devotional books into
the congregations ; he had the Bible, which he was fond of calling
the book of liberated humanity, circulated among his flock
in German translation ; he reduced the excessive number of
feast-days, and permitted the celebration of mixed marriages,
on condition that the children were brought up in the
respective faiths in accordance with their sex. In the matter
of religious services, he endeavoured to unite the formal beauty
of the Catholic ritual with the impressive doctrines of the
Protestants. Even at the present day, old people on the lake
of Constance love to tell how splendid it was at that time in
church, when the sermon received as full justice as the mass.
His seminary for priests at Meersburg gave a thorough scientific
instruction to aspirants for the priesthood, bringing them up
in the principles of a pacific and broad-minded tolerance which,
indeed, in certain cases led to an unclerical vagueness of mind.
It was not long before the little clerical party of the bishopric
began to complain at Rome about the heretical innovator ; the
curia expressed its disapprobation on several occasions, and the
nuncio at Lucerne was at open feud with the vicar-general.

Wessenberg, however, had no idea that the grandiose consistency of the Roman church leaves to the Christian the sole choice
between subordination and apostacy ; he imagined that he
could resist the pope's orders and yet remain a Catholic prince
of the church. It was not given to this man of pious and
affectionate nature to understand the great contrasts of ecclesiastical life in their pitiless severity. By diligent reading, and
in intercourse with the learned prelates of the old days, he
had acquired an abundance of the most varied knowledge, and
yet had never got beyond the stage of scientific dilettantism.
The numerous poetical, philosophical, and political writings, and
the works dealing with ecclesiastical history, which he published
for the diffusion of "sentiments of Christian philanthropy,"
ultimately effected nothing more than the formulation of well-
meaning moral considerations. They were never utterly trite,
but they were never profound, vigorous, or individual ; not
one of his books acquired any place in literature. From childhood he had grown up to venerate Joseph II, had been an

enthusiast for Sailer's gentle Catholicism, without entering deeply into the brilliant mysticism of the Bavarian prelate, and he now lived in the honourable belief that it was possible to make the wheel of time turn backwards, and to lead the strongly centralised church of the counter-reformation to accept without demur the reforming ideas of the fifteenth century.

Nevertheless he remained a thoroughly sincere Catholic, and despite all his tolerance he rejected the "immeasurable subjectivity" of Protestantism. Whilst to the horror of the clericals he regarded the evangelicals as a party within the church, this served only to show how firmly he believed in the unity of the visible church, in the eventual return of its erring children. The priests under his immediate control, whom he was accustomed to call together frequently in priestly assemblies, honoured him as a saint. As a distinguished man with a knowledge of the world, he felt himself superior to the plebeian clergy who were now growing up around him, whilst to his fellow aristocrats he appeared a miracle of learning. The consequence was that he gradually passed into a mood of excessive self-esteem, although to his gentle spirit arrogance was primitively altogether unknown. He saw the Jesuits engaged "in replacing the religion of the spirit of love and of truth with a compost of formal Judaism and reconstructed Paganism," and he considered himself predestined to avert this danger from the church. When the Society of Jesus was re-established, he at once recognised the serious consequences that would result from this step, and wrote warningly to his cousin Metternich, to the effect that this order had at one time been abolished through pressure from the Catholic courts, but that now the curia was bold enough to re-establish the order without any consultation with the powers, and this offered a gloomy prospect for the future. Metternich returned an indifferent answer to the effect that his emperor had nothing to fear, for that in Austria the Jesuits would never again be allowed to establish themselves.

At about this time, Dalberg, as bishop of Constance, appointed his vicar general as co-bishop, with the right of succession. He immediately received a sharp reprimand from Rome, with an order that he should forthwith deprive this ill-famed Wessenberg of his office as vicar-general (November 2, 1814). The timid primate was careful to keep the bull secret, but did not venture to carry through the nomination. The diocese remained

in this remarkable condition until the death of Dalberg, whereupon the chapter unanimously elected the vicar-general as
administrator. Once more the Vatican declared the election
null and void. In a papal brief, dated May 21, 1817, the pope
now explained to the grand duke why he felt compelled to
reject this man, " one whom all good men look upon with
horror, one who is absolutely without our approval." The
grand duke, who had already sanctioned the election, wished his
prelate well, having been accustomed to ask his advice even in
political affairs, and he felt, moreover, that his princely honour
was affronted, for in accordance with the Josephan doctrine
of the Badenese officialdom, the nomination of the bishops was
one of the inalienable sovereign rights of the lord paramount.
Although the slothful Hacke counselled that a dispute should
be avoided, the prince nevertheless determined, upon Marschall's
advice,[1] to maintain his reputed rights in a strongly worded
answer, and to defend the accused man (June 16th).

To Wessenberg, however, it seemed that the moment for
a great decision had now arrived. Armed with a letter of
recommendation from his court, he went in person to Rome,
hoping, as he openly declared, that he would either by the
force of his personal intervention induce the pope to change his
mind, or else that his failure would lead the nation to take
a more vigorous resolution. His maladroit admirers, of whom
he had but too many, in the public press, did not hesitate
to compare this pilgrimage to Rome with Martin Luther's
journey to Worms, although the new Luther was under the
powerful protection of the Austrian embassy, and could at any
time find a safe asylum in the palace at Venice. In the
Vatican, the German idealist was received with the contemptuous
calm of an old world-power which has long been accustomed
to contemplate occasional disorder in one or other of its numerous
dioceses. He was not admitted to audience with the pope.
Cardinal Consalvi conducted the negotiations, cool and prudent
as ever, submitting to the prelate a recantation which, in the
Roman view, was couched in extremely mild terms. Wessenberg was simply to disavow what his holiness had disavowed.
For some months accusations and letters of defence passed
between the two. Consalvi remained absolutely firm.
Wessenberg had lost the game, for he would neither follow
the example of his beloved Fénelon and sign a recantation

[1] Varnhagen's Report, July 1, 1817.

" which would have enslaved him to the Roman curia," nor yet would apostatise from holy church. On December 16th he informed the cardinal that he was about to return to Baden, and would leave matters in the hands of his territorial sovereign.

At home he was received by numerous signs of warm approval. Almost the whole of the clergy of the diocese remained loyal to him; the officials, to whom the entire ecclesiastical policy of the South German minor states was entrusted, were all on his side; Werkmeister, for instance, in Würtemberg, and Koch in Nassau. He was supported also by Klüber's vigorous pen, and by the majority of the newspapers and pamphlets which discussed the case. But there was no sign of a stormy popular movement, for how could these flabby half-measures arouse strong passion? The Badenese government allowed the offender to administer his diocese unopposed, and the curia was prudent enough to remain silent for the time. Rome could afford to wait; for the grand duke urgently desired the establishment of a Badenese territorial bishopric, and this was impossible without the pope's good-will. One hope still remained, the Bundestag. In a detailed memorial, dated May 17, 1818, the court of Carlsruhe expounded the course of affairs to the Germanic Federation, declaring in conclusion that Baden " now considered the Constance dispute to be a church matter which was the common concern of the German nation." But since ecclesiastical affairs unquestionably did not fall within the competence of the Federation, Baden did not venture to bring forward a proposal in Frankfort, and the Bundestag avoided all discussion of the affair. The memorial was translated into almost all the languages of Europe, and was widely circulated at the courts and among the clergy. For a time Rotteck and his friends continued to write pathetically in the newspapers of the great " German church dispute." Then the movement became extinguished, without ever having deeply permeated the masses of the people. It was only at the little courts of the south-west that Wessenberg continued to retain some influence. At one time these courts had opposed his designs for a national church, on account of their particularist anxieties, but now he appeared to them to be a useful ally against the Roman see. He himself at length began to recognise the impracticability of his earlier dreams, and soon after his return published an anonymous writing,

Considerations upon the Relationships of the Catholic Church of Germany, in which he recommended the institution of territorial bishoprics, but at the same time demanded that the German governments, or as many of them as were inclined to do so, should combine to treat jointly with the curia, and to subordinate their territorial bishoprics to a common archbishop. In this way, the German national church shrank to the dimensions of an ecclesiastico-political Sonderbund of German individual states.

The courts of Carlsruhe and Stuttgart had for some time been occupied with this idea on their own account. After Bavaria had received such a shameful defeat in Rome, they no longer ventured to credit themselves with the possession of the energy which would enable them individually to effect anything with the curia; but if such powers as Baden, Würtemberg, and Nassau were to collaborate, the pope would inevitably be forced to yield. Wangenheim advocated this plan in Frankfort, with fiery zeal. Here at length the opportunity offered of founding the desired federation within a federation, the German trias, and by the humiliation of Rome, to prove to all the world the power of "genuine Germany." Extraordinary contradictions were able to live peacefully side by side in this versatile head. For example, notwithstanding his enthusiasm for natural philosophy, he remained a doctrinaire liberal, and was at the same time an advocate of the Josephan omnipotence of the state. He had a very low opinion of the vital energies of the Roman see, believing that he could already discern in Germany the indications of schism, although the enormous majority of German Catholics remained absolutely faithful to their ancient church, and he confidently hoped that the curia would soon be led by fear to concede all that might be demanded of it. In December, 1817, Wangenheim applied to the federal envoys of Baden, Nassau, the two Hesses, Hanover, Oldenburg, and Luxemburg, and invited these courts, through the instrumentality of their plentipotentiaries in Frankfort, to agree upon the principles of a concordat. The appended proposal was almost identical with the ideas of Wessenberg. It demanded the *placet* as indispensable, the nomination of bishops by the territorial sovereigns, and the training of priests by the state. The imaginative statesman fancied that all this could immediately be secured by an ultimatum to the holy see, although everyone knew that the pope had never yet formally ceded the right of nominating bishops to any non-Catholic prince. Baden, Nassau, and the two Hesses, accepted the invitation, and in March, 1818, the Frankfort "conferences opened under the presidency of Wangenheim. A few of the North German minor states, which were at first parties to the conferences, speedily withdrew. The loudly trumpeted undertaking soon became restricted to the design of instituting a small common archdiocese which should be supreme over the territorial bishoprics of the Upper Rhenish minor states.

Wangenheim had also vouchsafed an invitation to the Prussian federal envoy. If the court of Berlin were willing to accept the ecclesiastico-political leadership of Würtemburg, it might be allowed to participate, but otherwise "genuine Germany" would suffice for itself. Even the good-natured Goltz was repelled by the idea that Prussia should be treated in this casual way, as a mere accessory to the future Upper Rhenish ecclesiastical province, nor could he understand (so he wrote to the chancellor) why Würtemberg should always and everywhere press to the front in this manner.[1] Hardenberg did not vouchsafe an exchange of notes, and contented himself with informing his German envoys that Prussia held aloof from the "conventicles of the minor courts," inasmuch as the peculiar religious interests of the monarchy "could not endure any intermingling," while the masterful tone assumed by the minor states was not likely to secure any results from the Roman see. Metternich also regarded this undertaking of the Frankfort allies as hopeless.[2] Both the great powers knew that it was no longer the pliable curia of the eighteenth century with which they had to deal; they knew, too, that Consalvi regarded the Frankfort conferences as the work of Wessenberg, and therefore from the first looked upon them with suspicion. It was unquestionably a disaster, one whose influence persists to the present day, that even this great opportunity was sacrificed to particularism. But so long as Germany lacked a national state, a German national church remained an irrealisable dream.

Meanwhile a fortunate change had taken place at the court of Carlsruhe. Hacke had received his dismissal, and the barons von Reizenstein and Berstett had entered the ministry. Berstett

---

[1] Wangenheim to Goltz, December 13 ; Goltz's Report, December 18, 1817.
[2] Krusemark's Report, Vienna, April 22 ; Instructions to Krusemark, May 20, 1818.

was a person of little account, no better informed than the
average of his old comrades in the Austrian cavalry, but conscientious and punctual in the fulfilment of his duties, unconditionally devoted to the princely house, and, notwithstanding
his ultra-conservative disposition, not so timid as to be afraid
of a Carlsruhe Landtag. Reizenstein, on the other hand, was
a man of statesmanlike intelligence, worthy of a greater sphere
of activity, and he had been the confidential adviser of Charles
Frederick in the latter's last years. Reizenstein, an object
of suspicion to the French as a German patriot, had co-operated
in all the reforms of that difficult time. It was to him that
was chiefly due the reanimation of the university of Heidelberg ;
not even the caste pride of the professors prevented their admit-
ting that the brilliant, learned, and thoroughly liberal-minded
curator was their equal. He immediately recognised that, after
the death of the heir to the throne, a definite decision upon
the question of the succession was essential, and induced the
grand duke to issue a decree on October 4, 1817, declaring
the indivisibility of the country, and reiterating the right of
the counts of Hochberg to the succession. The Bavarian court
was infuriated, and diplomatic intercourse between Bavaria and
Baden was tacitly broken off. Even Metternich, who was still
encouraging the Bavarians with ambiguous phrases, displayed
himself affronted. So arbitrary a step, he said to Krusemark,
could be explained only by the infatuation which had seized
the minor princes ; this decree reminded people strongly of
the one and indivisible republic of the French.[1]

The imperturbable minister in Carlsruhe did not allow
himself to be diverted from his purpose. Upon Reizenstein's
advice, the grand duke determined to take the bull by the horns,
to make an open attack upon the enemy who for years past
had in obscurity been threatening the little country. In a
letter to King Max Joseph, dated March 12, 1818, the
threatened prince declared that Austria was endeavouring to
pay her debts "with provinces which belong to me." "In
so serious a situation," he continued, "it is impossible for
me to separate the Bavarian government from its monarch,
to continue to see in the monarch my brother-in-law and
friend while the country displays itself as my most deadly
enemy." Should Bavaria employ force, "then I shall call
public opinion to my aid, and your majesty will with difficulty

---

[1] Krusemark's Report, October 18, 1817.

find an ally equally powerful." Manifestly embarrassed, Max Joseph's only way to meet this sharp accusation was his customary one of telling a direct lie. Never, he declared, had the Bavarian government cherished any hostile plans towards Baden ; Bavaria was content " quietly " to await the decision of the great powers, These two letters were communicated to certain friendly courts in the most profound confidence ; shortly afterwards they appeared in print in a Hamburg liberal newspaper, to the delight of all slanderous tongues, the radicals at home and the enemies of Germany abroad.

The traitor was Varnhagen von Ense, the vainest and most untrustworthy of all the diplomats of Prussia. The youthful husband of the celebrated Rahel burned with desire to display himself worthy of his wife's renown by the performance of statesmanlike deeds. During the congress of Vienna, he had devoted his pen to the cause of Prussia, and subsequently the grateful chancellor, who was readily blinded by brilliant conversation and many-sided culture, had appointed him to the difficult post at Carlsruhe. With all the naivety of the literary pedant, he at once began to practise politics on his own account, overwhelming the court of Baden with unsolicited advice, defending revolutionary doctrines which ran utterly counter to Hardenberg's opinions, and entering into confidential intercourse with the liberal party in a way quite inconsistent with his official duty. Yet this bold liberalism by no means prevented him from displaying a byzantine and servile devotion towards the chancellor, continually asking for promotion, and relating with circumstantial self-satisfaction how long the grand duke and grand duchess had remained in conversation with him. Nothing could be more sugary than his letters to Berstett, whom he hated, and whom, at a later date, he calumniated in his memoirs. A well-turned gigantic period of twenty lines hardly served him to express how ardently " I anticipate and hope to see accelerated your return from furlough, how I look forward to renewed intercourse with a man I so cordially venerate, a moment, if I may say so, for which I long with increasing interest." [1] In endless reports he communicated to the chancellor his judgments concerning matters of high policy and communicated also his most confidential intelligence, consisting for the most part of utterly worthless items of gossip, quite in the style of his subsequent diaries. Very rarely did he glean

---

[1] Varnhagen to Berstett, October 8, 1817.

trustworthy information regarding the private proceedings of the court of Carlsruhe, for no one had any real confidence in the feline amiability of this smooth-spoken man. When the constitution at length came into existence, Varnhagen did not even know who was its author, and confidently communicated to the chancellor two wrong names. [1]

His conduct in the Bavario-Badenese negotiations was precisely indicated to him in advance from Berlin. He was to assure the grand duke that Prussia would not tolerate any exercise of force against Baden, but in other respects he was to adopt a reserved attitude, and above all was to prevent the detestable dispute from degenerating into any open scandal. Accordingly he first of all sent a report concerning the grand duke's letter. The letter received his general censure " as an ill-considered and in the best case a superfluous procedure, which can lead only to a rebuff." Shortly afterwards he broke his pledge of official secrecy, and sent this censurable letter to the Hamburg newspaper. It was a telling blow ; almost all the press expressed itself in favour of the good rights of Baden ; even the *Augsburger Allgemeine Zeitung* took side against Bavaria, for the prudent Cotta was unwilling to lose the favour of the king of Würtemberg. Now Varnhagen wrote innocently, saying that the unauthorised publication had attracted great attention, but that the upshot seemed favourable to the court of Baden ; " the appeal to public opinion in the grand duke's letter has powerfully deflected that opinion to the side where it feels itself to be flattered." [2]

To retain the favour of public opinion on the side of Baden, it was necessary to enter decisively into the channel of constitutional politics. Reizenstein was under no illusion upon this point. He also recognised that the promulgation of the constitution was the only means by which the discontented populace could be reinspired with confidence in the future of the state, and by which, at the same time, the favour of Czar Alexander could be regained for the house of Zähringen. The czar displayed a very cool attitude towards the rights of his Badenese cousins. It was he who, at the congress of Vienna, had first mooted the unhappy idea of the restoration of the Palatinate—so at least Wrede assured general Zastrow. [3]

[1] Varnhagen's Report, August 26, 1816.
[2] Varnhagen's Reports, March 18, May 6, 1818.
[3] Zastrow's Report, Munich, November 2, 1818.

As far as Munich was concerned, nothing was spared to keep the Russian well-wisher in a good humour ; the envoy, Count Bray, laid before the czar for his approval all the new constitutional laws designed for Bavaria, and to the Russian autocrat none of the proposals seemed sufficiently liberal.[1] It was in these days that Alexander's Christo-liberal enthusiasm reached its climax. For the anxious letters of Metternich, who to his friend Nesselrode was continually describing " the serious disease that affects Europe," Alexander had merely a contemptuous smile. How much finer did it sound when the emotiona¹ Capodistrias, who was now Alexander's honoured confidant, ardently announced his central principle, " institutions are the great demand of the century ! " On March 27, 1818, the czar opened the first Reichstag of the new kingdom of Poland, in a moving address from the throne which resounded throughout Europe. It demanded from the Poles that they should prove to their contemporaries that liberal institutions, in conjunction with order, constitute the true happiness of the nations, and it promised the Russians that in a short time they should participate in the like happiness.

Two days later, Capodistrias, in a memorial " concerning the act of September 26, 1815," boldly attempted to expound to the courts of Europe that the new constitutional sovereignty was nothing other than the necessary outcome of the ideas of the Holy Alliance. The principles of the Christian moral doctrine recognised by the Holy Alliance, he assured them in unctuous terms, had now found their application in Poland ; it might be hoped that the lofty wisdom of his majesty's allies would do justice to this example. " To the states which already enjoy liberal institutions, the example will show that only the fatherly authority of princes has the power of granting constitutions, and that these institutions, thus applied for the purpose of general welfare, are not merely compatible with order, but even constitute the most powerful guarantee of order. The example of Poland will prove to the nations that the course of civic freedom is henceforward open to all peoples." " Perhaps," he said in conclusion, " even now these considerations may be regarded as belonging to the realm of dreamland . So be it. We ourselves, however, are assured that they are no dreams, and we endeavour to establish the same conviction

---

[1] Blittersdorf's Report, St. Petersburg, August 17, 1818.

among those who exhibit to us their devotion"[1] Thus
Russia formally placed herself at the head of the liberal movement of Europe. The German cabinets, however, had good
reasons for keeping the wonderful programme of Christian
liberalism a dead secret. The czar's address from the throne
had already sufficed to cause a lively excitement among
impatient constitutionalists; the whole liberal press broke out
into comparisons between Polish freedom and German slavery.
Metternich, Wellington, and Richelieu did not conceal their
anxieties. Gentz bitterly complained of the czar's lack of consideration for his neighbours. Even men of more courage asked
in astonishment why anyone should play with fire in this way
among the Poles, who were already once more entering into
secret conspiracies against the Russian yoke.

For the court of Baden no choice was now left. Again
and again Blittersdorf reported how urgently Capodistrias was
reminding him of the promised "institutions." Hardenberg,
too, repeatedly expressed the same warning, simultaneously
recommending that the well-grounded desires of the mediatised
should be satisfied, for in this way " the endeavours of Bavaria
would be completely neutralised."[2] As early as April the
constituent committee reassembled. The financial adviser
Nebenius, the most learned political economist in Germany,
diligently elaborated a fifth proposal, taking as his model the
master work of the Russian well-wisher, the glorious Polish
constitution. Then came the alarming news from Munich that
Bavaria had completed her constitution, that the rival in the
great race had won by a head! To timid spirits the threatening chorus of approval of the liberal world sounded like the
death-knell of the house of Zähringen. Max Joseph, however, did not regard it as inconsistent with his royal dignity
to choose this particular moment for a cure at Baden-Baden,
where, after his cheerful manner, he announced to everyone
what a splendid thing it was that Bavaria had established
its constitution first! As soon as this friendly visit to his
dominion was announced to the grand duke Charles, the latter
immediately left his palace in Baden and went to the quiet
Black Forest spa of Griesbach, and the whole court left Baden
with him. One only remained—of course Varnhagen. He
could not deny himself the opportunity of displaying his political

[1] Capodistrias, *Mémoire sur l'acte du 26 Septembre*, Warsaw, March 29, 1818.
[2] Instructions to Varnhagen, July 11, 1818.

light before the king of Bavaria, to whom he was not accredited. He forced himself into the presence of Max Joseph, and, once more on his own initiative, gave the king such tactless and unveracious declarations concerning the intentions of the Prussian court that a great diplomatic dispute ensued. A sharp reprimand from Berlin at length quieted his mischievous tongue.[1]

Meanwhile, in the evening of his tragical days, the grand duke had found another personal friend, the bold Russian cavalry leader of the War of Liberation, General Tettenborn, a native of Baden. The cheerful mercenary soldier was the daily companion of the sick man, and employed his influence for the good of the country. Though no friend of the liberals, he nevertheless possessed a secure soldierly insight into what was inevitable. It was thanks to him and to the loyal Reizenstein that the prince at length examined Nebenius' proposal, and ultimately adopted it quite unaltered except for one single paragraph.[2] Even during the final weeks, distressing incidents were not lacking. The much-worried Nebenius had to elaborate the new electoral law a second time, because the grand duke had locked up the document, and could not make up his mind to have the box unlocked again.

Enough, on August 22, 1818, the constitution was signed, and the effect of this step was even stronger here than had shortly before been that of the promulgation of the constitution in Bavaria. The discontented spirits in the new territories were momentarily silenced. Round the sick-bed of the dying prince were now heard the joyful acclamations of a grateful people which expected an indefinite and wonderful happiness from the new liberties. The infallible judge, however, public opinion in Germany (that is to say, the liberal press), gave judgment as follows on the competition now concluded : Bavaria has shown itself brisker in the fulfilment of the popular wish, and yet the prize must be allotted to the liberal-minded Baden. Certainly the Badenese fundamental law, as might be expected from the character of the country, exhibited a modern aspect. Whilst the Bavarian Landtag consisted principally of landowners, Nebenius, a true son of a literary generation, started from the standpoint that culture chiefly must be represented ; and since, like all liberals, he sought

[1] Instructions to Varnhagen, July 22, August 22, 1818.
[2] F. von Weech, History of the Badenese Constitution, pp. 93 et seq.

culture in the towns, the Badenese electoral law gave to fourteen towns twenty-two representatives, whilst to the rural electoral districts, whose population was far greater, were allotted only forty-one representatives. Speaking generally, the work did honour to the practical sense of the learned compiler. The fundamental law was not overloaded with particular provisions, so that room was still left to profit by the teachings of constitutional experience, and it was only in outward features, in the formal arrangement, that it resembled the disastrous Polish example. The nobility was satisfied by the constitution of an upper chamber ; the Landtag received an effective power of control, for every two years the entire budget must be submitted to it. Even Haller, " the restorer," had to recognise the German sense of justice which found expression in this constitution, " although," he said, " it has the supreme defect of being a constitution at all."

With all this, however, the Palatinate was not yet safeguarded. The four powers in whose hands the decision lay had made up their minds that the matter should be finally settled in the congress which was to take place in the ensuing autumn. But the impatience of the court of Munich was hardly to be controlled, for the health of the grand duke declined day by day. Both Max Joseph and his minister Rechberg declared to the Prussian envoy that they were ready for a compromise, but that if the grand duke should die before the compromise had been effected then Bavaria would regard the Palatinate as having escheated to her, and would enforce her rights.[1] Soon afterwards reports were current in Carlsruhe that Bavaria was arming, and was moving her troops to the Palatine frontier. The grand duke now recalled all soldiers on furlough. The king of Würtemberg also felt his country seriously threatened ; his cherished plan of a " genuine German " trias was breaking to pieces in his hands. On September 25th his envoy Gremp had to ask the Bavarian minister if it was really true that the king was thinking of carrying out a *coup de main* upon his brother-in-law's death ; such a step " would have as a certain consequence the effectual separation of Bavaria from the Germanic Federation " ; a definite contradiction of the rumour seemed urgently requisite, " above all the present moment, when a straightforward understanding between ' genuine German ' federal states is of such importance." In a disdainful

[1] Zastrow's Reports, August 5 and 30, 1818.

and arrogant reply, Rechberg expressed his amazement, saying :
" His majesty has not hitherto given a moment's thought to
the possibility of ,the event to which allusion is made in your
memorandum, an event whose only effect could be to fill him
with the profoundest sorrow."[1] The gross dishonesty of this
asseveration suffices to show that the suspicions of the court
of Carlsruhe were not unfounded. For the second time within
two years, the ambition of the Wittelsbach ruler threatened
to cause a civil war in Germany. The foreign press was
already aware of the new *querelle allemande.* The rights of
Baden secured dubious aid from the Napoleonic diplomat
Bignon, who henceforward in all German affairs regularly
utilised his skilful pen on behalf of the rights of oppressed
petty princes. Meanwhile the weak vital flame of the grand
duke was not being extinguished with such speed as had been
anticipated ; the four powers had time in which to keep
Bavarian insolence within bounds.

§ 4. NASSAU AND HESSE DARMSTADT.

In Nassau, too, the beginnings of constitutional life were
not unaccompanied by storms. Here, even before the congress of Vienna, on September 1, 1814, a constitution had been
promulgated, and the all-powerful minister Marschall plumed
himself on having led the way for the rest of Germany. But
the liberal world would not allow its darling Charles Augustus
of Weimar to be deprived of the glory of having been the
first constitutional prince, and the liberal world was right. For
although all the officials in Nassau had already taken the
oath of allegiance to the constitution, four and a half years
elapsed before the Landtag was summoned, and Marschall
utilised this interval to provide for the little country
an abundance of organic laws and to introduce a new glory
into German history—the centralised, unified state of Nassau.
Whilst the powerful house of Nassau-Orange in the Netherlands
had filled the world with its warlike renown, the history of
the last centuries had had hardly a word to say about the
German Nassauers beyond recording ever-repeated subdivisions
into new family lines of descent. They indulged this inborn

[1] Memorandum from Gremp, September 25 ; Rechberg's Answer, September
29, 1818.

passion of the German petty princes with a tenacity in which they could give points even to the house of Wettin. For a time in the little town of Siegen here existed two lines of Nassau-Siegen, one Catholic, the other Protestant, each in its own palace, the two halves of the town being separated by a high wall and a fierce national hatred. But fortune was unkind to these diligent endeavours, and the new lines, planted out with such care, continually died out. In the year 1816, succumbed the last of the Usingens, and now the line of Weilburg entered into exclusive possession of that fragment of territory which, as Stein said jestingly, the plastic hand of Gagern had in Paris and Vienna fashioned for the house of Nassau. No other German minister vaunted so loudly as did Marschall the legitimacy of his tribal princely house, and yet this self-praise sounded nowhere more ridiculous than here, in a country whose extent was only eighty-five square miles [German], and in one which had a few years before been distributed among seven-and-twenty different lords paramount.

After the cession of Saarbrücken, Lahr, and Siegen, little was left of the ancient possessions of the house of Nassau, nor had the Old Orange territories much more than the name in common with the German ducal house. What could a petty state offer to this valiant people upon whom the sunshine of world-wide renown had once shed its glories ? In the rough mountains of Westerwald, and in the remote corners of Dilltal, every house had stories to tell of the pilgrimages made by their ancestors to Holland. Here was still standing the lime tree under whose shade William the Silent had received the envoys of the Dutch rebels ; and here was Herborn, at one time the university of Calvinism, ever ready for battle ; but now, instead of contentious theologians, peaceful tillers of the soil passed through the Chaldäergasse of the quiet country town. Still more indifferent to the new princely house were the Rhine valley officials who had formerly worked for the Palatinate, for Treves, or for Hesse. To the bigoted inhabitants of Electoral Treves, it seemed hard that they should come to be lumped together with the Protestants of Katzenellenbogen (*Cattimelibocus*), and that the proud frontier fortresses of the two hostile neighbours, " the Cat " and " the Mouse," should now lie in ruins ; but still harder did it seem that the wonder-working pilgrimage church of Our Lady of Sorrows of Bornhofen should immediately be closed by the bailiff of Nassau. Least of all would the Rheingau of Electoral Mainz come to terms with the new regime. For Rheingau was the Paradise of the Rhenish *joie de vivre*, the delightful land where the poesy of wine filled even poverty with rejoicing. Here, in the busy market-towns and villages, situated so closely together on the banks of the stream as almost to form a single town, revolutionary arrogance was in the very air, and the minister did all he could day by day to provide new material for the mockery of the merry-witted people.

Since a ministry of state, together with a council of state, a military staff, and a treasury, were manifestly insufficient for the happiness of 300,000 souls, the organiser of Nassau added a central governing board, which worked under the same roof with the ministry, but which was allowed to communicate only in writing with the supreme authority; there were also twenty-five local authorities, among which were the communes, whose mayors nominated the government. Besides the lower courts, there were two primary courts of appeal, and a supreme court of appeal. This enormous army of uniformed officials was freed for itself and for its children from the duty of military service, enjoyed a privileged legal position, and rivalled the minister in rudely despotic manners. The good President Ibell, a strict but well-meaning and able official, did his best with the new legislation, but could not make headway against Marschall's evil example. The Prussian authorities had often occasion to complain of the pugnacious arrogance of these neighbours; an agreement had already been arrived at with Prussia concerning a military road, but Marschall wished subsequently to make changes in this, and only gave way when General Wolzogen in effect put a pistol to his head. Bureaucratic red-tape remained undisturbed. When, after half a century, the new duchy disappeared, the road through the thickly populated Rhine valley had not even then been completed; anyone wishing to drive along the Rhine had to cross over to the Prussian high-road on the left bank.

Thus the organisation of the boards and of the communes was established without the help of the Landtag, although the constitution promised the provincial diets that they should co-operate in new legislation. There followed the separation of the domain treasury from the tax treasury, an apparently harmless measure, which was intended to pave the way for a serious *coup de main*. This separation of the treasuries had hardly been completed when Marschall astonished the country by announcing that all the domains were the private property of the territorial sovereign, and thereby opened the endless series of struggles concerning the royal domains which remained for many ensuing decades a hateful peculiarity of German particularism, and which helped to destroy the monarchical sentiment of this primarily well-disposed population. The question whether the royal domains belonged to the state or to the princely house was certainly one difficult to decide, and one which could not everywhere be answered in the same manner, for most of the minor territories had as late as the beginning of the new century been ruled in accordance with the principles of the patrimonial state, and had therefore known hardly anything of the distinction between constitutional law and civil law. The political kingdom of the Hohenzollerns had, a hundred years before, declared the domains to be national property ; Bavaria and some of the other great princely houses now followed this example. On the other hand, the minor princes were inclined to regard their countries as private estates, and to consider their sovereignty simply as a right useful to themselves ; they felt that their power reposed principally upon their wealth, and hastened to secure their houses against the vicissitudes of the future, for the fate of the mediatised was before their eyes. Thus, in Nebenius' proposals for a constitution, there was only one point which aroused anxiety in the mind of the grand duke of Baden, and he insisted that the domains should be assigned to his house, as patrimonial property. In Nassau, at least a portion of the claims of the lord paramount were utterly without justification, for the domains of Electoral Mainz, that glorious vineyard of Rheingau, whose wines were stored in the renowned monastery cellars of Eberbach, had unquestionably belonged to the archiepiscopal foundation, that is, to the state.

A fresh and still more astounding demand of Duke William's at length threw the whole country into a 'fury. In the year 1818, the revenues derived from hereditary servitude were abolished, the lords of the soil receiving compensation for their losses. A medal had been struck to commemorate this act of enfranchisement effected by the house of Nassau. But now the duke, who inertly followed the lead of his masterful minister, suddenly came forward with the demand that the national treasury should pay him 140,000 florins yearly for the long-before abolished dues of hereditary servitude on the royal domains, which he himself had just annexed as his own property by an arbitrary exercise of power! Baron von Stein, who from his castle at Nassau on the Lahn could watch what was going on close at hand, could hardly find words sufficiently strong for the expression of his contempt. "The time will come," he said, "when this crime will be punished, and when Providence will execute a severe judgment upon the criminal; of this I have no doubt whatever."

In March, 1818, the Landtag was at length summoned, and it entered upon its work with a step which displayed all the mental poverty of this officialdom—the exclusion of Stein. As a Prussian subject, the baron could not take without reservation the oath which was demanded from the members of the upper chamber. The government did not raise a finger in order to secure some trifling concession in this purely formal matter, and allowed the first man of the country to be excluded from the chamber. What valuable work he could have done here in the deplorable quarrel about the domains, and in dealing with the insatiable monetary demands of the father of the country! The estates soon followed the example of those of Old Würtemberg, and rushed into a barren dispute about rights, opposing injustice with injustice by desiring to declare all the domains national property. This dispute continued for nearly twenty years, until the Landtag paid the duke a portion of his claims; but the legal questions involved were never completely settled as long as the duchy existed. Meanwhile, Marschall continued to rule light-heartedly in his customary manner, deciding all things as he pleased by arbitrary edicts. Down to the year 1848, only six laws of any importance were laid before the Landtag. Nevertheless the Nassauers, priding themselves upon their constitutional liberties, looked down compassionately upon Prussian slavery.

Hesse-Darmstadt secured its constitution, the most artificial among the state structures of the Confederation of the Rhine, later than the other South German territories. The strangely compounded land of Nassau at least constituted a connected area; but the territories which now received the names of the grand duchy of Hesse and By-Rhine were dispersed in two larger fragments, and in a number of smaller pieces whose situation was known only to initiates, stretching from the

Neckar valley of Würtemberg into the Westphalian mountains. Especially in the Frankfort region, where the grand duchy came into contact with four other states, there was to be found an extraordinary variety of haphazard frontier-lands which procured for the federal city the favour of all the vagrants of Mid-Germany. Anyone who was expelled from Darmstadt took a short walk through Homburg or Nassau, and cheerfully found his way back again by another route. In Odenwald there was even to be found a Badenese-Hessian condominion, whose frontiers were altered ever and again when a peasant sold a small area of land. To crown all, these ornaments, of the map of Germany, were not, as were the equally dispersed territorial fragments of Thuringia, an inheritance from the Holy Empire, but were the work of up-to-date German policy.

In the two centuries since its separation from the main stem, the younger line of the Hessian house had frequently changed its possessions. The landgraves of Darmstadt had first ruled over no more than the upper county of Katzenellenbogen in Odenwald and a few strips of Wetterau. In accordance with German princely custom, they manifested their independence by continual quarrels with their cousins, and as strict Lutherans always took the side of Austria, whilst Cassel inclined to the reformed church, and was allied first with Sweden and subsequently with Prussia ; the reformed university of Marburg was counterpoised by the Lutheran Giessen. Subsequently County Hanau-Lichtenberg was acquired, and now the centre of gravity of the territory began to move towards the left bank of the Rhine. The court resided by preference in the beautiful castle of Buchsweiler, and in Pirmasens created for itself a South German Potsdam for its world-renowned giant guards. Even Caroline Henrietta, the friend of Frederick the Great, known as "the great landgravine," was unable to disperse the spiritless tedium of this land where people played at soldiers. The minister, Carl Friedrich von Moser, had also to learn from his humiliating dismissal that there was no place here for a fiery spirit who wished "to disaccustom the Germans from a dog-like submissiveness." It was only through the presence of Merck and his circle of friends that the quiet town of Darmstadt was able to remain to some extent in touch with the new German culture. During the wars of the Revolution, the trans-Rhenish possessions were lost, and the dynasty received in compensation, among other regions, the remote duchy of Westphalia. After the fall of Napoleon, this unnatural acquisition was also abandoned, in exchange for the narrow strip of land on the left bank of the Rhine between Worms and Bingen. It was thus that the new grand duchy first received its political character through the treaties of Vienna at a later date than the other High German states. Henceforward its history consisted of the struggles between the left and the right bank of the river.

Except for certain Westphalian territories, the whole country was South German, Franconian. Since ancient days, the frontier between North German and South German civilisation had passed straight across the upper valley of the Lahn, between Giessen and Marburg. But what contrasts existed among these fragments of the Franconian stock. Of the two provinces on the right bank of the Rhine, Upper Hesse was entirely restricted to intercourse with the north, whilst Starkenburg associated rather with the south. In both regions, urban life was but little developed. Neither the imperial cities of Friedberg and Wimpfen, nor yet the charming little towns dispersed among the vineyards of Bergstrasse, possessed a well-developed bourgeoisie, one which would have been able to encounter the grand duke's army of officials in an independent spirit. In the lonely forest valleys of Odenwald, on the barren heights of Vogelsberg, and even in the rich plain of Wetterau, the peasants continued to practise many time-honoured customs. The subjects of the numerous mediatised, of the Erbachs, the Isenburgs, the Solms, and the Leiningens, still continued loyal to their tribal dynasties. More especially County Erbach remained a little world by itself. When the inhabitants of Odenwald flocked annually to the favourite popular festival, the Eulbach fair, they spoke only of the founder of the festival, the artistic-minded count Francis, whose collections in the castle of Erbach greatly excelled those in the Darmstadt museum; whilst everyone was disaffected towards the Hessian regime, because its first effect had merely been to double the burden of taxation.

How was the newly-acquired trans-Rhenish strip of territory, which now received the tasteless name of Rhenish Hessia, to accommodate itself to these patriarchal conditions? In this region the peasants were almost more urbanised than in the Bavarian Palatinate, and were perhaps even more eagerly devoted to " profiteering (*das Profitieren*)," while the townsmen were accustomed to wider relationships through the world intercourse of the great river. Contemptuously did the citizens of Mainz look down upon the miserable new capital city in the sand plain on the river Darm, mocking at its servile-minded inhabitants, and at the one and only referendary who at noon " swarmed " into the Rheinstrasse. In golden Mainz there was now, indeed, hardly to be heard a word of the great days of old, of the power of the former imperial archchancellor, of the civic greatness of the Walpodens and of the Gensfleisches. The episcopal city of St. Boniface, which had at one time been so glad to term itself a true daughter of the Roman church, remained for a generation the most revolutionary town in Rhineland, and the one animated by the most ardent French sentiment. The spirit of the Illuminates and the immorality of the later electoral times had here encouraged the growth of a frivolous and loquacious arrogance, which came to a climax in the arid activities of the republican clubs, and which was not silenced until the days of the strict Napoleonic regime. But now, under a government which was at once weak and detested, this movement again appeared in all its audacity. A short time before, the bourgeoisie had greeted the German conqueror as a liberator, and had wished ill to the retiring French who had left traces of their barbarism in the desecrated cathedral and in almost every street. But soon all this was forgotten. Now people thought only of the services of the excellent prefect, Jean Bon Saint-André, of the numerous advantages which the Imperator had vouchsafed to his favourite German town, and the *code Napoléon* was regarded as the bulwark of Rhenish Hessian liberties. The new ruler had in fact guaranteed the province the undisturbed enjoyment of its French institutions, but the Mainzers knew very well with what dislike the Old Hessian officialdom viewed this concession, and at every change of ministry they trembled at the possibility of an attack upon their territorial liberties. The deplorable quarrels among the troops of the federal garrison, could hardly serve to strengthen the prestige of the German regime ; and the Bundestag was made a mock of, if only for the reason that it sat in Frankfort, for every child of Mainz drank in hatred of the neighbour city with his mother's milk. Nor did Hessian Rhineland secure any extensive share of the blessings of peace. In earlier days, as long as the valley traffic predominated, Mainz had remained the chief town among the cities of the Rhine. But since colonial trade had increased, and mountain roads had been constructed, the centre of gravity of Rhenish trade necessarily moved towards the mouth of the river. The illiberal legislation of electoral and of Napoleonic days continued for a time to exercise a restrictive influence whereby the ports of Holland were favoured at the expense of Cologne. It was only in the nature of things that under the protection of the Prussian laws Cologne should become the first commercial city of the Rhine, but the men of Mainz ascribed this natural growth of their ancient rival chiefly to the sins of omission of the Darmstadt government.

To Hesse, the French particularism of the Rhinelanders was far more dangerous than it was to Prussia or Bavaria, for Rhenish Hessia comprised nearly one-third of the population of the grand duchy, and in its economic development was greatly in advance of the regions on the right bank of the Rhine. In view of these difficulties, the grand duke Louis I adopted in the first instance as his only resource a strict bureaucratic regime, a policy which in any case harmonised with his inclinations and customs. He was the refounder of the state, remaining on the throne for forty years from 1790, and by servile Darmstadters was gladly compared with Charles Frederick of Baden. In intelligence and magnanimity he was unquestionably inferior to the Zähringen rulers. He had displayed his honourable intentions at the very outset of his reign when he gave due satisfaction to the ill-used Carl Friedrich von Moser. Towards the Imperator he did now show himself any more servile than the majority of the Rhenish Confederate princes. Prince Emil displayed greater zeal for the French cause, thus acquiring the special favour of Napoleon, and after the peace he long kept alive Bonapartist sentiment in the vigorous little army. The difficult days of the Confederation of the Rhine brought the country a Napoleonic prefectoral system, the annihilation of all freedom of the communes, and the inevitable abolition of feudal representative institutions ; but it brought also many valuable reforms, such as the abolition of serfdom, and the beginnings of that excellent agrarian legislation which was henceforward the pride of the Darmstadt officialdom. To the prince's love of the arts, the capital owed the theatre, the library, the museum, and the awakening of a more vigorous intellectual life. Every year the principal families of

Darmstadt spent their summer holidays in the charming pleasure palace of their patriarchal ruler at Fürstenlager in Odenwald.

Like the other South German princes, the grand duke had recognised at the congress of Vienna that a representative constitution was inevitable. But on his return home, finding plenty of work in the difficult task of incorporating Rhenish Hessia, he postponed the decisive step from year to year. Meanwhile the country, which was severely visited by the distresses of the years of famine, began to grow restless. The burden of taxation and the arbitrariness of the officialdom were no longer to be borne. Disrespectful and threatening petitions exhorted the grand duke to keep his word ; revolutionary pamphlets consoled the countryfolk with references to the approaching revolution. At the university of Giessen, party spirit ran high. F. G. Welcker, the talented philologian, had to resign his professorship, because he was unable to get on with the celebrated Bonapartist, Crome. Finally, the people ventured to hold great public meetings, begging the prince to establish the longed-for constitution, the certain remedy for all earthly ills. But all was still in vain.

Such was the situation of the south in the autumn of 1818. In Würtemberg and Hesse there was a notable condition of ferment ; in Bavaria and Baden there were loud rejoicings over the happily acquired new constitutions, with childish dreams of the wonderful ilberties which were to ensue. At the same time among the students at the universities there was in progress a turbulent movement which seemed to warn the perturbed governments of the approach of a general revolution.

APPENDIXES

TO

VOL. II.

I.—E. M. ARNDT AND WREDE.

(APPENDIX TO P. 19, VOL. II.)

In his well-known book *Meine Wanderungen und Wandelungen mit dem Freiherrn vom Stein* (p. 218), E. M. Arndt relates the following incident : " Stein's anger against Wrede had very special causes. Among all the German troops under French command, the Bavarians and the Darmstadters had in North Germany earned the most evil reputation for roughness, lack of discipline, and inclination to plunder. Wrede was certainly blamed with justice, not merely for having looked on while his men misbehaved themselves, but even for having set them the worst possible example. Stein had now caught him in the act. Wrede was stationed at Oels in Silesia, in the castle of the duke of Brunswick. Here he had thoroughly imitated the greedy and unashamed methods of the French plunderers, the methods of Soult, Masséna, and men of that ilk, who made it their custom to pack up the silver (spoons and plates) with which they were served by their hosts, and to carry it off with their baggage. Thus Wrede, in Oels, quite after the manner of a French marshal, had on his departure added all the ducal plate to his baggage. The unfortunate steward of the castle had been able to do nothing to prevent this, but lest he should himself be regarded as responsible for the robbery of the ducal treasure, he asked the marshal for a document to the effect that the silver had been handed over

697

under stress of war. With German simplicity, and quite taken by surprise, the field-marshal on his departure had actually given the desired written assurance. Now, in the year 1813, this paper fell into the hands of Stein, and in the following year Wrede was forced to compensate for the robbery by the payment of a handsome sum of money."

The form of this report produces the impression that it was based upon Stein's own communications, that is to say, that it was direct evidence ; it contains nothing antecedently improbable, and is penned by a man whose strict love of truth is well-known, whilst no less well-known is the astonishing vigour of his memory, which was preserved into advanced age. In Silesia the deplorable story was frequently repeated among the circles of the older men who had had personal experience of the French invasion, was repeated by them, as I know on the best evidence, long before Arndt's book was published. Consequently there was no reason to doubt its truth.

Arndt's book appeared in that blossoming time of arrogance of the middle-sized states which a few years later was to find its punishment upon the battle-fields during the Main campaign to 1866. The Bavarian government was not sufficiently dignified to leave the events of a chapter of history which had been closed for fifty years to the decision of historical science, but had the author prosecuted for slandering the Bavarian army. Many of my readers will still remember what a painful attention this trial aroused throughout Germany. In the initiation of this criminal procedure Arndt could see nothing more than deliberate spite ; he refused to appear before the Bavarian court, and in December, 1858, was sentenced *in contumaciam* by the assizes of Zweibrücken to two months' imprisonment. The decision of the court was inevitable, for anyone who, in a matter where questions of honour are concerned, fails to bring before the court evidence of the truth, must necessarily be declared guilty of slander. But for the historian, who is not bound by the forms of criminal procedure, this judgment was worthless.

Arndt himself considered the truth of his relation to be absolutely inviolable, and in the course of the long newspaper controversy which followed the trial he made the suggestion on one occasion that Wrede's misdeed might perhaps have taken place towards the end of February, 1807, for at this time, according to recent information from Silesia, Bavarian troops had been domiciled in Oels. This suggestion was now utilised by a Bavarian officer (presumably Major Ehrhard) to prove the innocence of his hero (anonymous pamphlet, *The Accusation of Wrede by E. M. Arndt*, Munich, 1860). He showed that while it was quite true that Wrede's division had, on February 23, 1807, visited Oels, on the way through to Poland, at this time Wrede himself was still in Bavaria, on a sick-bed. Still, this was plainly not enough to refute Arndt's relation, for, regarding the precise date of the robbery, nothing more had been put forward than unsupported suggestions, and the possibility remained open that Wrede might have committed the offence somewhat later in the year 1807. It was a proved fact that in this year Wrede had twice been in Silesia. The first occasion was in the end of March, when, having recovered from his illness, he was journeying to join the army ; according to the memoranda of a contemporary, which are to be found in the town library of Breslau, he was at Breslau on March 26th. Then, after the peace of Tilsit, and down to December 2nd, he was for several months in Silesia with his troops ; and since the French and their allies, during this peaceful occupation, are known to have behaved almost as arrogantly as previously during the war, it was quite possible that the robbery might have been effected at this period. Consequently Arndt did not allow himself to be misled by the fallacious arguments of Ehrhard's pamphlet ; he considered that he could trust his own excellent memory, and reprinted his account unchanged in subsequent editions of his book. Knowing my beloved old teacher as well as I did, I considered it indubitable that he must have had excellent reasons to hold so firmly to so strongly contested a report, and therefore had no hesitation, in a casual reference in the present work, to speak of this report of Arndt's as unquestionably accurate.

Since then, however, a Bavarian, Major-General Heilmann, has published a biography of Wrede, a valuable and instructive work, which would certainly produce a more pleasing impression if the author had not endeavoured to place an excellent mercenary soldier, a man without a country, in the same rank with our national heroes, with Scharnhorst, Blucher, and Gneisenau. General Heilmann gives a detailed account of this episode in the life of his hero, but advances no new data, merely repeating Ehrhard's contentions. Without giving any reasons, he simply assumes that the act of robbery must have taken place (if at all) between February 23rd and March 8th, and, on this assumption, has no difficulty in establishing an alibi for Wrede. The gaps in this remarkable demonstration are then concealed by the author by showering over old Arndt an abundance of elegant epithets, which have very little in common with the customary forms of scientific polemic. When Arndt is described as being, in questions where historical truth is concerned, "a careless old man," "credulous in his prejudices," "obstinate," one "whose political associates had completely turned his head," I have nothing more to say in answer than that I also have been honoured with epithets more vigorous than graceful.

When I was recently preparing a new edition of the first volume, I naturally subjected to a fresh examination all those passages which had been specially exposed to criticism, and among them my remark about Wrede. Heilmann's book did not give me sufficient information, and I therefore determined to do myself that which Wrede's biographer had unfortunately omitted to do, and made enquiries in Silesia. After I had knocked vainly at various doors, I received at length from Breslau (through the kindness of Herr Grünhagen, director of the archives), and simultaneously from Oels, various reports, which, all agreeing in essential points, completely contradicted Arndt's assertion. Every unprejudiced person will understand that the old man cannot have created simply out of his own imagination the story that he relates with such confidence. If we may believe in any man's good faith, we can unquestionably believe in that of Arndt. It suffices to read in Heilmann's own work the incredibly brutal letters in which Wrede expresses his fury against "this devil, this fool of a Stein"; so measureless a hatred as this is hardly explicable solely out of the political hostility between the two men. But how was it that Arndt fell into this error? Had Wrede carried out elsewhere some forcible acts of robbery which secured for him in Silesia the nickname, at one time widely diffused, of the "stealer of spoons"? Or was this evil reputation entirely undeserved, and had Arndt confused two quite distinct persons? I cannot decide here. I learn from Munich that at this time there was also serving in the Bavarian army a lieutenant-colonel Wrede, of whom nothing more is known. However this may be, this particular accusation against Wrede must definitely be dismissed as false.

Appendixes

I have before me the memoranda of a deceased ducal official of Brunswick who, during the years from 1806 onwards, when quite a young man, lived in the castle of Oels, memoranda which were placed on official record in July, 1858, owing to the newspaper controversy which followed the publication of Arndt's book. According to this report, which is entirely confirmed by the utterances of other officials whose evidence was taken at the same time, Prince Jerome Napoleon and General Lefebvre made their headquarters at the castle of Oels for some days in December, 1806, at the time when the siege of Breslau was begun ; they had with them French and Bavarian troops. In these days (that is to say, *not* in February, 1807) part of the duke's plate and his team of greys were stolen. The perpetrators of the robbery remained unknown. All the reports voiced unanimous complaints regarding the roughness of the Bavarian troops, but no one is able to say whether French or Bavarian soldiers were the robbers. This much, at least, is certain, that Wrede was then still in Bavaria. The same memorial goes on to give the most specific assurances possible that after that date, no Bavarian general was ever quartered in the castle. Consequently Arndt's relation falls to the ground.

However much I may regret that these facts have only come to light when it is too late for Arndt to disclose to us the sources of his error, it is none the less a great pleasure to me to be able to afford Wrede's biographer a small contribution for a new edition of his book. Perhaps he will now recognise that we Prussian savages are, after all, better men than he imagined. After his gentle manner, he says that Arndt's "infamous lies will continue to be repeated in defiance of all historical truth, and in mockery of all morality." He must excuse me for contradicting him ; the accusation will be repeated no longer, since it has been proved groundless. But as long as there was nothing stronger to set against Arndt's relation than the arbitrary and false assertion that the robbery must have been effected in February, 1807, 'so long was' every historian justified in regarding as truthful the account given in a book which is numbered amongst the best and most trustworthy memoirs of our day. The crimes of that Napoleonic epoch have long ago been atoned by a faithful brotherhood in arms, and we need no longer dread the return of the old fratricidal struggles. It is time that we should contemplate

with a certain equanimity these days that have passed away
for ever. Even the Bavarians should at length learn to speak
of the sins of that Rhenish Confederate age just as frankly
as every reasonable Prussian has long ago learned to speak
of the year 1806. But in this respect, unfortunately, the
Bavarians still fall far short of what might be wished. When,
not long ago, Gustav Freytag, in the last volume of his *Ahnen*,
described the conduct of the Bavarians in Silesia in terms
of strict historical truth, he was grossly abused on this account
by the Bavarian press. Thus, also, the gentle Heilmann, by
his excessive zeal for Bavaria, has secured a success which I
cannot grudge to so diligent an investigator. If, in the elucidation of this Silesian episode, he had displayed somewhat less
indignation, and a somewhat more diligent investigatory spirit,
he might himself have established the proof, which I have had
to establish in his place, that Wrede took no part in the
robbery at Oels.

II.—BLUCHER UPON THE MUTINY AT LIÈGE.

(APPENDIX TO P. 167, VOL. II.)

FIELD-MARSHAL Prince Blucher to King Frederick Augustus of
Saxony.

YOUR MAJESTY,

By your earlier proceedings your majesty has brought
the profoundest disaster upon your subjects, a respected branch
of the German nation.

It may result from your subsequent conduct that this
branch will be overwhelmed with shame.

The rebellion in the army, which has been organised from
Friedrichsfelde and Pressburg, has broken out, has broken out
at a time when the whole of Germany is rising against the
common enemy. The criminal offenders have openly proclaimed
Bonaparte as their protector, and have forced me, who during
five-and-fifty years of active service have been in the fortunate
position of never shedding any blood but that of my enemies,
for the first time to carry out executions in my army.

By the enclosure,[1] your majesty will see what I have hitherto done in the hope of saving the honour of the Saxon name, but it is the last attempt.

If my voice is not heard, I shall be compelled, not without pain, but with the repose of my own good conscience and sense of duty fulfilled, to restore order by force, and, if it should be necessary, to have the entire Saxon army shot down.

The blood that has been spilled will one day at God's judgment-seat be visited upon him who is responsible : and before the throne of the Almighty to have given commands, and to have allowed commands to be given, will be regarded as identical.

Your majesty is well aware that an old man of seventy-three can no longer have any other earthly desire than to make the voice of truth audible and to make the right prevail.

For this reason your majesty will have to receive this letter.

BLUCHER.

Headquarters at Liège,
May 6, 1815.

III.—TREITSCHKE'S PREFACE TO THE SECOND VOLUME OF THE GERMAN EDITION.

[In the English edition, the matter corresponding to this volume begins with the chapter entitled " Mental Currents of the First Years of Peace " and ends with the close of the chapter (in Vol. III of the English edition) entitled " The Change of Mood at the Prussian Court."]

To my historical colleagues this volume will display more evidence of new historical research than did the first. Lay readers, I fear, will require to make an effort before they will be able to read these dry materials.

In an epoch of world-moving events such as the first volume had to describe, the complex variety of German history was still capable of being to some extent compressed into a single view. But when it becomes necessary to demonstrate

---

[1] Enclosed was the well-known proclamation ot Blucher ro the soldiers of the Saxon army-corps dated May 6, 1815.

the almost imperceptible germs of new developments during a quiet period of peace, the historian experiences in his own flesh and blood the curse of a disintegrated national life. It is simply impossible to recount strictly in chronological order events which took place on twenty or more petty stages simultaneously. I have therefore placed general German and Prussian affairs in the lime-light, touching upon the history of the minor federal states wherever this was significant in relation to the destiny of the fatherland as a whole. Consequently, in this volume the South German constitutional struggles and the literary and political movement in Thuringia are discussed in detail. The right place for the consideration of the minor North German states will be in the third volume, when the question comes to be answered why it was that the South entered the Prussian customs-union earlier than the North. I need offer no excuse for giving a detailed description of the opening proceedings of the Bundestag, notwithstanding the futility of these proceedings. The subsequent course of events would be incomprehensible without a vivid picture of the character of the new federal authority.

The references in the notes are for the most part to unprinted documents, for a complete reference to authorities would have swelled the book to too great a size. As it is, the work has become more comprehensive than I desired. So confused a history, and one so much distorted by party fables, can be mastered only by a very thorough treatment, and I was forced to decide to distribute the events down to the year 1830 through two volumes.

These pages contain the record of many painful experiences. If I wished to yield to the mood of the moment, and to write history as a partisan, I would gladly draw a veil over many of the old sins of Austria and of the German thrones, for in the present ordering of German affairs our high nobility manifests itself more perspicacious and readier for sacrifices than a great proportion of the bourgeoisie, and no one but a fool would wish to disturb the friendship which unites our state with Austria. My task was to give a faithful account of what has actually happened. The position of the monarchy in our fatherland can only be advantaged if Germany's princes should not forget the gloomy days when their forefathers were on the point of becoming completely estranged from the national life ; on the other hand, our free alliance with Austria will stand all the more firmly, the more frankly it is recognised by both parties that Germany was justified in refusing to accept any longer the dominion of the court of Vienna.

Despite all its errors and disillusionments, the greatly maligned epoch which the present volume describes was not only rich in scientific renown, but was also fruitful for our political life. Unless I have struck an entirely false note, my readers will receive the impression that they have under their eyes the history of a rising nation.

HEINRICH VON TREITSCHKE.

Rome,
  October 20, 1882.

PREFACE TO FOURTH EDITION.

FEW changes have been made, in this new edition. The two concluding chapters, however, contain some supplementary data, based upon materials derived from the State Archives in Weimar.

T.

Berlin,
  May 30, 1892.

IV.—SCHMALZ AND THE ORDER OF THE RED EAGLE.

(APPENDIX TO PP. 367 AND 368, VOL. II.)

A LAMPOON which Professor H. Baumgarten has published in Strasburg, under the title of *Treitschke's German History*, contains, amid a desert of vulgarly expressed abuse and suspicion, which I will leave others to deal with, a few isolated attempts at refutation in matters of fact. Among these there is not a single one which need induce me to change a word in my book, although I am quite willing to learn even from an abusive opponent.

Baumgarten blames me for servile flattery of King Frederick William III—this is the sum of meaning in all his lengthy writing—because, concerning the world-famed order of the red eagle which was presented to Professor Schmalz in the year 1815, I found nothing stronger to say than the following words : " The turmoil now subsided, but everyone felt that the bad seed sown by the accuser (who, at this juncture was distinguished by a Prussian order and by one from Würtemberg) had not fallen upon perfectly sterile soil." I find it difficult to retain my gravity in face of an accusation which shows so plainly that Baumgarten has occupied himself with this epoch in so cursory a manner. Every historian well informed regarding Prussian affairs must recognise immediately that my words on this matter are based upon a prolonged and arduous investigation. I expressed myself intentionally with a certain reserve, not only because I am of opinion that a historian who is unwilling to decline to the level of such a scandal-monger as Vehse need not devote much time to an order of the red eagle of the third class, but also because, on this occasion, I was influenced by a critical consideration which has completely escaped Baumgarten's perspicuity.

This order of the red eagle could have historical significance only if Schmalz had in truth received it as a reward for his denunciations. Has this been proved ? Baumgarten assumes it without full investigation, for nature has gifted him with the fortunate talent of recognising historical truth *a priori*. Since I myself lack this endowment, I looked for proofs, and found as established this fact alone, that Schmalz had received a Prussian order and a Würtemberg order at the time when the literary disputes concerning his pamphlet were still in progress. Anything beyond this is gossip, collected from letters and newspapers. Now it may be maintained without undue levity that the Würtemberg order was a reward to the denunciator for the writing which he had sent to the Swabian king, for, as far as is known, Schmalz had never previously done any service to the court of Stuttgart, and the Bonapartist sentiments of King Frederick could not fail to be rejoiced by a work which entered the lists against the reputed secret societies of the Borussomaniacs. It was but natural that in the excited state of public opinion people should assume without further enquiry that the Prussian order also was a reward for the denunciation. But is it legitimate for the historian of to-day to accept without enquiry all the hateful rumours of a profoundly disordered time ?

A dispassionate examination will readily show that as far as the Prussian order is concerned, matters are not so simple as might appear at first sight. Unfortunately the denunciator was not a man of no account, but a useful official who had done good service in connection with the foundation of the university of Berlin, a professor of established reputation, of whom his brother-in-law Scharnhorst never failed to speak with respect, a tried patriot who during the French occupation had suffered for the Prussian cause, who during the wars of liberation had made great pecuniary sacrifices, had given lectures of general utility, and so on. Moreover, he was far from being a man to hide his light under a bushel. Even in those days, so efficient and vigorous an official could hardly escape the distinction of the red eagle, although this order was at that time not scattered with so free a hand as to-day. Little as this petty commerce interests me, I have none the less instituted a search into all the corners of the literature of the subject, in order to ascertain the reasons for which the order may have been bestowed. Recently, I have had enquiries made in the national archives, and finally also in the personal records of the general orders committee. The enquiry was fruitless, for the records of this epoch have already been destroyed. Hitherto, only one document has been discoverable throwing a certain light upon the personal relationships between the king and Privy-councillor Schmalz, this being a cabinet order addressed to Schmalz under date August 6, 1814, running as follows : " The intention you have communicated to me, to devote the sums gained by public lectures to providing comforts for those invalided from military service who have received the iron cross, is one which I treasure at its full value."

This document affords a characteristic indication of Schmalz's activities, and anyone who knows in how thorough and deliberate a manner preparations were made in the Prussian officialdom before bestowing orders, can hardly fail to recognise it as probable that the order given to Schmalz in October, 1815, may have been the reward for the before-mentioned patriotic lectures. But it is also possible that the order may have been given in recognition of other official services. A few weeks later than Schmalz, two of his colleagues in the academy of sciences, Bode and Hermbstädt, two men with no inclination to political activities, received the same order. Thereupon the opinion was at once bruited abroad that this had been done only in order to conceal the true ground for giving Professor Schmalz the distinction—and so on *ad infinitum*. Need I plunge any deeper into this sea of gossip? No, everything has an end, and there must therefore be an end also to my researches concerning this worthless red bird. May it continue in Baumgarten's philosophy of history to play the same part as the momentous fork in the fate-tragedy: as far as I am concerned enough time has already been wasted on the matter. I take my formal leave of it, and modestly declare that I really do not know why Schmalz received the order of the red eagle of the third class, and because I do not know, I have expressed myself with extreme caution regarding this nauseating affair.

In any case it was unfortunate that the distinction should have been granted at this precise moment; but I have certain reason to know that it was not the king's intention, when bestowing the order, to humiliate Schmalz's opponents in any way. For in the very days in which Schmalz was decorated, the most notable of these opponents, Niebuhr, was officially informed that the king had decided to appoint him to the post of confidence in Rome; and very shortly afterwards, E. M. Arndt, the very man whom Schmalz had calumniated most fiercely, was nominated professor in Bonn. Still more clearly is the king's lack of partisanship manifested by the ordinance which brought the dispute to a close. I stated in the text, that this ordinance was "worthily conceived and amiably worded." Since Baumgarten cavils at this judgment also, I am compelled to feel serious doubt whether he knows the whole wording of the ordinance. It is buried in the Prussian legislation of the year 1816, which is now but rarely disinterred, and runs as follows:

"Ordinance concerning the alleged secret societies, January 6, 1816.

"We, Frederick William, etc., have noted with just displeasure the party spirit which displays itself concerning the conflict of opinions regarding the existence of secret societies in our state. When the fatherland, seriously visited by misfortune, was in great danger, we ourselves at first approved the foundation of the Society for the Promotion of Moral and Scientific Progress, because we recognised therein a means for advancing patriotism, and recognised therein also the possession of those qualities which are competent to raise the spirits of those in misfortune, and to give them courage to overcome misfortune. But in the proposals for the charter of this society, which were submitted to us for approval, and in the then existing political situation of the state, we found reasons for the suppression of the society and for the prohibition of the printing of all discussions about the matter. Since that time, the same principles and sentiments which induced the first formation of the society have come to animate, not merely a number of the former members of the same, but also the majority of our people, in consequence of which, with the help of the Most High, there have resulted the salvation of the fatherland and all the numerous great and beautiful deeds by which that salvation has been effected. Now, when peace has everywhere been restored, when every burgher of the state can have but one spirit, but one aim, namely, by strict attention to duty to maintain so gloriously preserved a national sentiment, and to live according to the laws so that the benefits of the peace may be secured for all, and so that the wellbeing of all, which it is our steadfast purpose to maintain, may be brought to the greatest possible perfection—now secret societies can have none other but a deleterious influence and one which will counter-operate these aims."

Hereupon, the well-known prescriptions of the civil code (T. 2, Tit. 20) and of the edict of October 20, 1798, regarding secret societies, are recalled. The ordinance closes with the words : " In view of the existence of these legal powers, the dispute now carried on in the public press regarding the existence of secret societies and their aims, is useless, disquiets our loyal subjects, and nourishes a deleterious partisan spirit We therefore will and decree :

" That henceforward, subject to the aforesaid fines and terms of imprisonment, no one in our states shall print or publish anything relating to the matter."

Now I ask whether that is the language of a monarch who takes sides with the denunciators. Anyone who imagines himself back amid the patriarchal views of absolute monarchy must admit that the king could not have acted otherwise. He was forced to put an end to a dispute which was disturbing the public peace ; which on the one side was evoking poisonous calumnies, and on the other the equally false opinion which the Prussians had formed for themselves of the future constitution. No prosecution or investigation occurred as a sequel to this royal ordinance, down to the year 1819. The king's policy was not reactionary for those days; in all the great matters in which he was then concerned, he regularly decided for the cause of reform, and in taking over the new provinces he formally declared on several occasions that, exclusively concerned with the future of the state, he regarded the past as past. In his secret heart he cherished suspicions, which were fostered by Metternich and Wittgenstein on the one hand, and by members of the Burschenschaft and by the press on the other; but the change of policy did not begin until after the murder of Kotzebue.

I have recently discovered certain documents which confirm what has been said above. In August, 1815, the representatives of the town of Berlin put forward the quite unprecedented claim that the companies of civil guards and riflemen which during the absence of the army had undertaken the protection of the capital should no longer, as was prescribed by the ordinance of July 17, 1813, be commanded solely by their own military chief and by the police president, but should be placed under the supervision of the municipal authorities. The police president, von Le Coq, reported on the subject from Paris (police report of August 12th to 18th) expressing himself in very severe terms regarding the spirit of the opposition, as increased by arrogant writings. Thereupon the king drew the chancellor's attention to the fierceness of partisan spirit (cabinet order of September 1, 1815), adding: "I trust that you, being acquainted with the nature of influences disadvantageous to the well-being of our subjects, will refuse to allow such influences access to a people whose character has hitherto maintained itself so conspicuously free from the acceptance of foreign principles, and which for this very reason has elevated itself to such a height in the struggle against foreign oppression." For the time being, this cabinet order remained without result, for the necessary measures, as is expressed in a marginal note of Hardenberg's, "must be specially designed to meet each part'.cular case." But it served to show that the king was in an uneasy mood, which had manifestly been rendered more uneasy by the contemplation of the party struggles in Paris.

On the other hand, a confidential writing of the king, dating from the same period, shows how thankfully he recognised the patriotic attitude of his loyal people. When the two friends had separated, Czar Alexander (under date January 15/27, 1816) sent the king a letter containing exuberant assurances of "sacred friendship." The task now before them, he said, was to secure the fruit of their labours, to maintain peace. Consequently he thanked the king cordially for the energetic measures he had taken against the secret societies. (These measures, however, consisted solely in the reinforcement of a prohibition which had long existed in Prussia as in all the other states.) In March, Frederick William sent an answer which contained the following reference to the Schmalzian affair : " Il ne faut aujourd'hui que calmer l'effervescence des esprits, suite naturelle des agitations politiques. Je me félicite de l'approbation que V. M. veut bien accorder aux mesures que j'ai cru devoir prendre dans cette occasion. Mon unique ambition est comme la Vôtre, Sire, d'assurer le bonheur de mes peuples. C'est une dette sacrée que notre cœur se plaira d'acquitter après . tant de preuves de leur amour et de leur dévouement. Vous voyez, Sire, que le désir de m'épancher avec V. M. est devenu un besoin pour moi."

Is it likely that a prince who expressed himself in such confident terms regarding his people, would have rewarded the calumniator of the War of Liberation for his calumnies ? It remains conceivable that the current rumours were well founded, and that it was not until subsequently that the king regained his ease of mind ; but it is just as probable that the granting of the decoration was no more than accidentally coincident with the denunciation.

To sum up, I consider that regarding the king's conduct I said in the text precisely what a conscientious historian was entitled to say.

INDEX.

Index

Index

Index

Index

Index

Index

Index

Mendelssohn, Fanny, 268
Mengs, 275, 288
Merck, 692
Merckel, 447, 471, 485, 535, 537
Mercy, 652
Merian, 35
Merveldt, 576, 577
Mesmer, 320
Metternich, 10, 11, 12, 13, 14, 15, 24,
    29, 30, 35, 37, 39, 40, 41, 42, 43,
    44, 47, 48, 49, 51, 59, 60, 61, 62,
    63, 64, 65, 66, 67, 68, 69, 71, 74,
    75, 76, 78, 79, 81, 89, 95, 100, 103,
    104, 105, 107, 110, 113, 116, 117,
    120, 121, 123, 124, 125, 129, 130,
    131, 145, 161, 204, 205, 206, 211,
    214, 219, 220, 224, 225, 337, 340,
    372, 373, 374, 375, 376, 377, 378,
    379, 380, 381, 385, 387, 388, 389,
    390, 399, 401, 404, 406, 409, 412,
    414, 415, 418, 423, 427, 428, 429,
    432, 443, 444, 452, 456, 458, 610,
    623, 639, 650, 652, 653, 675, 679,
    680, 683, 684, 710
Meusebach, 457
Michelangelo, 292
Mignet, 236
Milhaud, 174
Milosch, 376
Miltitz, 33, 54
Milton, 268
Minerve, 371
Mirbach, 458, 576
Molière, 248
Moltke, 305, 359
Moniteur, 61
Montesquieu, 245, 357, 360
Montgelas, 19, 31, 55, 57, 88, 106, 385,
    439, 636, 637, 638, 639, 640, 641,
    643, 644, 646, 647, 650, 651, 652,
    653, 654
Montmartin, 594
Morawski, 527, 528, 582
Moreau, 599, 627
Moreto, 254
Morocco, Sultan of, 438
Moser, Carl Friedrich von, 692, 695
Moser, J. J., 591
Möser, Justus, 297, 546
Motz, 383, 418, 419, 472, 473, 544, 580
Mozart, 291, 292
Müffling, 201, 202, 206, 233, 320
Müller, Adam, 55, 145, 204, 341, 343,
    362, 363, 364
Müller, Carl, 34
Müller, Johannes, 397
Müllner, 251, 254
Münchener Alemannia, 55
Münster, 18, 19, 20, 21, 22, 41, 43, 66,
    70, 82, 83, 84, 98, 105, 107, 108,
    109, 110, 112, 113, 119, 123, 149,
    155, 215, 217
Murat, 26, 27, 78, 147, 148

N.

NAGEL, 582
Nägeli, 294
Nagell, 72
Napoleon, 6, 8, 10, 14, 17, 25, 28, 56,
    71, 78, 84, 90, 91, 99, 118, 119, 135,
    137, 138, 139, 140, 141, 142, 143,
    144, 146, 147, 148, 149, 150, 153,
    155, 156, 157, 159, 160, 167, 171,
    172, 173, 179, 180, 181, 182, 183,
    184, 185, 188, 189, 190, 191, 197,
    202, 213, 235, 270, 292, 337, 344,
    350, 351, 369, 370, 381, 525, 544,
    564, 588, 605, 618, 628, 633, 635,
    637, 640, 643, 644, 645, 647, 662,
    671, 693, 694
Napoleon II (see King of Rome)
Nassau, Duke of (see William)
Nebenius, 437, 669, 684, 685, 690
Nemesis, 95, 494
Nesselrode, 14, 206, 218, 219, 455, 683
Netherlands, King of (see William I)
Newton, 319
Ney, 171, 176, 177, 180, 186, 189, 190,
    209
Nicholas, Grand Duke, 383, 449
Nicolai, 274, 540
Nicolovius, 510
Niebuhr, 56, 58, 59, 96, 235, 237, 257,
    269, 276, 288, 297, 300, 302, 306,
    307, 314, 321, 334, 346, 354, 360,
    367, 368, 447, 468, 512, 514, 649,
    708
Niebuhr, Carsten, 305
Niethammer, 639
Nöggerath, 514
Nostitz, 55, 174, 179
Novalis, 307, 314

O.

OBERLIN, 336
Oesterreichischer Beobachter, 142, 229,
    341
Oken, 95, 319, 432
Olevianus, 556
Oppell, 33
Oppositionsblatt, 469
Orange, Prince of (see William I, Wil-
    liam III, William Prince of Orange)
Orleans, Duke of (see Louis Philippe of
    Orleans)
Otho Henry, The Reformer (Electoral
    and Rhenish Palatinate), 628
Overbeck, 288, 290
Overberg, 339

P.

PALM, 403
Pappenheim, Countess, 452
Paul, Duke of Würtemberg, 606
Paulus, 330, 343, 344, 615, 664
Pericles, 282

Index

Index

Index

Index

Printed by Jarrold & Sons, Ltd., Norwich, England.